ELIZABETH AND MARY
COUSINS, RIVALS, QUEENS

JANE DUNN is the biographer of the relationship between Virginia Woolf and Vanessa Bell, of Mary Shelley, and most recently a groundbreaking biography of Antonia White. She is a Fellow of the Royal Society of Literature and lives in Bath.

ELIZABETH

AND

MARY

Cousins, Rivals, Queens

JANE DUNN

HARPER PERENNIAL

Harper Perennial
An Imprint of HarperCollins*Publishers*
77–85 Fulham Palace Road,
Hammersmith, London w6 8jb

Harper Perennial is an imprint of HarperCollins Publishers

www.harpercollins.co.uk/harperperennial

This edition published by Harper Perennial 2004

9 8 7 6 5 4 3 2

First published in 2003

A catalogue record for this book
is available in the British Library

ISBN 0 00 653192 X

Calligraphic genealogy by David Williams

Set in Postscript Linotype Minion with
Spectrum and Janson display by
Rowland Phototypesetting Ltd,
Bury St Edmunds, Suffolk

Printed and bound in Great Britain by
Clays Ltd, St Ives plc

In memory of a much loved father
DAVID ROLF THESEN
1923–2002

'out of the strong came forth sweetness'

CONTENTS

LIST OF ILLUSTRATIONS ix

CHRONOLOGY xiii

THE TUDOR AND STUART DYNASTIES xxii

ACKNOWLEDGEMENTS xxv

AUTHOR'S NOTE xxvii

PREFACE xxix

1 The Fateful Step 1

2 The Disappointment of Kings 43

3 The Education of Princes 81

4 Apprenticeship for a Queen 126

5 Wilfulness and God's Will 170

6 Complicity and Competition 214

7 Raison de Coeur: Raison d'État 254

8 Seeking a Future King 296

9 Outrageous Fortune 337

10 Double Jeopardy 381

11 Singular Foes 428

12 The Consequence of the Offence 475

NOTES 507

SELECT BIBLIOGRAPHY 519

INDEX 525

LIST OF ILLUSTRATIONS

Mary and François II, from the Book of Hours, artist unknown. © *Bibliothèque Nationale de France, Paris.*

Mary, *c.* 1555, aged about twelve, attributed to François Clouet. © *The Ossolinski National Institute – The Lubomirski Museum in Wroclaw, Photo Andzej Niedzwiecki.*

Elizabeth, in her coronation robes, 1559, artist unknown. © *National Portrait Gallery, London.*

Elizabeth's mother, Anne Boleyn, by Frans Porbus the Younger. © *The Art Archive/Civiche Racc d'Arte Pavia Italy/Dagli Orti.*

Elizabeth, aged about thirteen, attributed to William Scrots. *Reproduced courtesy of The Royal Collection.* © *HM Queen Elizabeth II.*

Mary's mother, Mary of Guise, attributed to Corneille de Lyon. © *The Scottish National Portrait Gallery.*

Mary in White Mourning, after François Clouet, *c.* 1559–61. © *The Scottish National Portrait Gallery.*

The Family of Henry VIII, *c.* 1545, artist unknown. *Reproduced courtesy of The Royal Collection.* © *HM Queen Elizabeth II.*

Mary I, *c.* 1544 by Master John. © *National Portrait Gallery, London.*

Henry VIII, *c.* 1536, about the time when Elizabeth was a child, after Hans Holbein the Younger. © *National Portrait Gallery, London.*

Edward VI, *c.* 1547, Elizabeth's only brother, artist unknown. © *National Portrait Gallery, London.*

Painted genealogy showing Mary's, and therefore her son's, Tudor ancestry, *c.* 1603. © *Parham Park, West Sussex/The Bridgeman Art Library.*

James V of Scotland and Mary of Guise, Scottish School, nineteenth century. © *Falkland Palace, Fife, Scotland/The Bridgeman Art Library.*

Catherine de Medici, by François Clouet. © *Victoria and Albert Museum, London/The Bridgeman Art Library.*

François, 2nd Duc de Guise, by François Clouet. © *Photo RMN: Gérard Blot.*

Mary, *c.* 1560–65, artist unknown. © *National Portrait Gallery, London.*

Elizabeth, *c.* 1560, artist unknown. © *National Portrait Gallery, London.*

Elizabeth, the 'Sieve Portrait', *c.* 1570, by Quentin Massys the Younger. © *Sotheby's Picture Library.*

Mary, after the Nicholas Hilliard miniature of 1578. © *National Portrait Gallery, London.*

Robert Dudley, Earl of Leicester, *c.* 1560–65, attributed to Steven van der Meulen. © *Wallace Collection, London/The Bridgeman Art Library.*

William Cecil, Lord Burghley, *c.* 1560–70, by or after Arnold von Bronckorst. © *National Portrait Gallery, London.*

Sir Francis Walsingham, *c.* 1587, possibly after John de Critz the Elder. © *National Portrait Gallery, London.*

Henry Lord Darnley, with his brother Charles, *c.* 1562–3, by Hans Eworth. *Reproduced courtesy of The Royal Collection.* © *HM Queen Elizabeth II.*

James I and VI, *c.* 1580, Mary and Darnley's son as a child, by Arnold von Bronckorst. © *The Scottish National Portrait Gallery.*

James Hepburn, 4th Earl of Bothwell, artist unknown. © *The Scottish National Portrait Gallery*

David Riccio, artist unknown. © *The British Museum.*

Mary, *c.* 1578, by Elizabeth's miniaturist Nicholas Hilliard. © *Victoria and Albert Museum, London/The Bridgeman Art Library.*

Mary, *c.* 1580s, electrotype after Jacopo Primavera. © *National Portrait Gallery, London.*

Elizabeth, *c.* 1588, Armada medallion, after a design by Nicholas Hilliard. © *British Museum, London/The Bridgeman Art Library.*

Mary, *c.* 1558, miniature by a follower of François Clouet. © *Victoria and Albert Museum, London/The Bridgeman Art Library.*

Elizabeth, *c.* 1575, artist unknown. © *National Portrait Gallery, London.*

Mary, artist unknown. © *Blairs Museum Trust.*

Elizabeth, 'Rainbow Portrait', attributed to Isaac Oliver. *Reproduced courtesy of The Marquess of Salisbury.*

From The Marian Hanging, *c.* 1500, embroidery designed and worked by Mary while imprisoned in England. © *Victoria and Albert Museum, London.*

Cruciform embroidery panel of a ginger tabby cat with a mouse, said to represent Elizabeth and Mary. *Reproduced courtesy of The Royal Collection.* © *HM Queen Elizabeth II.*

The Octagon Monogram from The Marian Hanging, Elizabeth and Mary monograms under a crown. © *Victoria and Albert Museum, London.*

Sixteenth-century painting traditionally believed to show Elizabeth dancing with Lord Robert Dudley. It could alternatively be of a French court scene. *Reproduced courtesy of Penshurst Place.*

Elizabeth on a royal progress, surrounded by her court, attributed to George Vertue. © *Sotheby's Picture Library.*

Execution of Mary at Fotheringhay Castle, 1587, artist unknown. © *The Scottish National Portrait Gallery.*

Elizabeth, the 'Armada Portrait', *c.* 1588, attributed to George Gower. © *Woburn Abbey/The Bridgeman Art Library/Christie's Images.*

CHRONOLOGY

1457	28 JAN	Henry VII born
1485	15 DEC	Catherine of Aragon born
1486	19 SEPT	Arthur, Prince of Wales, born
1489	29 NOV	Margaret Tudor born (grandmother of Mary Queen of Scots)
1491	28 JUNE	Henry VIII born
1501	14 NOV	Catherine of Aragon marries Arthur, Prince of Wales
1501		Possible year of Anne Boleyn's birth
1502	2 APRIL	Arthur, Prince of Wales, dies (aged 15)
1509	22 APRIL	Henry VII dies (aged 52); Henry VIII ascends to the throne (aged 17)
	11 JUNE	Catherine of Aragon marries Henry VIII
1512	10 APRIL	James V of Scotland born
1515	20 NOV	Mary of Guise born
1516	18 FEB	Mary I born
1520	13 SEPT	William Cecil, Lord Burghley, born
1532	1 SEPT	Anne Boleyn becomes Countess of Pembroke
1533	25 JAN	Anne Boleyn marries Henry VIII
	23 MAY	Thomas Cranmer, Archbishop of Canterbury, pronounces marriage between Catherine of Aragon and Henry VIII invalid
	28 MAY	Cranmer pronounces Henry VIII and Anne Boleyn married

	1 JUNE	Anne Boleyn crowned
	11 JULY	Henry VIII excommunicated
	7 SEPT	Elizabeth I born; possible date of birth of Robert Dudley
	10 SEPT	Elizabeth baptized at Greenwich
1534	20 APR	Elizabeth Barton, 'Maid of Kent', executed
1535	22 JUNE	Bishop John Fisher executed
	6 JULY	Sir Thomas More executed
1536	7 JAN	Catherine of Aragon dies (aged 50)
	29 JAN	Anne Boleyn miscarries a son
	17 MAY	George Boleyn, Anne's brother, executed
	19 MAY	Anne Boleyn executed (Elizabeth aged 2 years 8 months)
	20 MAY	Henry VIII betrothed to Jane Seymour
	30 MAY	Henry VIII marries Jane Seymour
	1 JULY	Mary Tudor and Elizabeth declared illegitimate
1537	5 JULY	Queen Madeleine, wife of James V of Scotland, dies
	12 OCT	Edward VI born
	24 OCT	Jane Seymour dies (aged 28)
1538	9 MAY	James V of Scotland marries Mary of Guise
1540	22 MAY	James, Prince of Scotland, born
	28 JULY	Thomas Cromwell executed
1541	APR	Robert, Duke of Albany, James V and Mary of Guise's second son, born
	29 APR–MAY	Both Scottish princes, Robert and James, die within days of each other
1542	24 NOV	Scottish forces routed by English at Solway Moss
	8 DEC	Mary Queen of Scots born
	13 DEC	James V dies (aged 30) and Mary becomes Queen of Scotland (aged 5 days)
1543	JUNE	Mary Tudor and Elizabeth reinstated in the succession

	JULY	Treaties of Greenwich; allowing for marriage of Mary to Prince Edward, Henry VIII's heir
	12 JULY	Catherine Parr marries Henry VIII
	9 SEPT	Mary Queen of Scots crowned at Stirling Castle
1544	19 JAN	François II of France born
	14 SEPT	Henry VIII's forces capture Boulogne
1545	7 DEC	Henry Stuart, Lord Darnley, born
1547	28 JAN	Henry VIII dies (aged 55); Edward VI ascends to throne (aged 9)
	20 FEB	Edward VI crowned, Edward Seymour, Duke of Somerset, Lord Protector
	3 MAR	François I dies (aged 52); Henri II succeeds to French throne; Thomas Seymour and Catherine Parr betrothed
	10 SEPT	English rout of the Scots at Pinkie Cleugh
1548	7 JULY	Marriage contract between Mary Queen of Scots and the Dauphin François
	29 JULY	Mary Queen of Scots sails to France
	5 SEPT	Catherine Parr dies (aged 36)
1549	16 JAN	Arrest ordered of Sir Thomas Seymour, Lord Sudeley
	20 MAR	Sir Thomas Seymour executed
1550		Mary of Guise visits her daughter Mary Queen of Scots
	4 JUNE	Lord Robert Dudley marries Amy Robsart
1551	2 MAY	William Camden born (died 1623)
1552	22 JAN	Edward Seymour, Duke of Somerset, executed; John Dudley, Duke of Northumberland, new Protector
1553	21 MAY	Lady Jane Grey marries Guildford Dudley
	6 JULY	Edward VI dies (aged 15), succeeded by Mary I
	10 JULY	Lady Jane Grey proclaimed Queen of England
	20 JULY	Mary Tudor proclaimed Queen of England

	3 AUG	Mary I and Elizabeth enter London
	21 AUG	John Dudley, Earl of Northumberland, beheaded
	30 OCT	Mary I crowned
1554	FEB	Wyatt Rebellion
	12 FEB	Lady Jane Grey executed (aged 16)
	18 MAR	Elizabeth in Tower
	11 APR	Sir Thomas Wyatt executed
	19 MAY	Elizabeth released from Tower and goes to Woodstock
	25 JULY	Mary I marries Philip II of Spain
	16 OCT	Bishops Ridley and Latimer burnt at stake at Oxford
	30 NOV	Philip Sidney born
1555	18 OCT	Elizabeth goes to Hatfield
	25 OCT	Holy Roman Emperor Charles V hands on his imperial position to brother Ferdinand, and sovereignty of the Low Countries to son Philip II
1556	21 MAR	Archbishop Thomas Cranmer burnt at stake
1557	7 JULY	Mary I declares war on France to support Philip II
1558	5 JAN	Calais lost to the French
	24 APR	Mary Queen of Scots marries François, Dauphin of France
	21 SEPT	Charles V dies
	17 NOV	Mary I dies (aged 42); Elizabeth I succeeds to the throne
		Henri II declares Mary Queen of Scots Queen of England and Ireland
1559	15 JAN	Elizabeth I crowned Queen of England and Ireland
	2 APRIL	Treaty of Cateau-Cambresis between England and France
	2 MAY	John Knox returns to Scotland

	8 MAY	Elizabeth's Acts of Supremacy and Uniformity passed, implementing the Elizabethan religious settlement
	10 MAY	Scottish Lords of Congregation rebel against Mary of Guise's regency
	20 JUNE	Henri II seriously injured in jousting tournament
	22 JUNE	Elizabeth's prayer book issued
	10 JULY	Henri II dies; François II becomes King of France and Mary his queen,
	18 SEPT	François II crowned; he and Mary claim they are King and Queen of England and Ireland too
	21 OCT	Mary of Guise deposed for allowing French to fortify Leith
	18 DEC	Elizabeth sends aid to Scottish rebel lords
1560	27 FEB	Treaty of Berwick
	MAR	Tumult of Amboise, failed coup d'état against Guise domination and French persecution of Protestants
	11 JUN	Mary of Guise dies (aged 44)
	6 JUL	Treaty of Edinburgh between Scotland and England, Mary's claims on English throne nullified, but Mary refuses to sign treaty
	11 AUG	Scottish Parliament establishes the reformed Protestant religion in Scotland
	8 SEPT	Lady Dudley (Amy Robsart), Lord Robert's wife, found dead
	5 DEC	François II dies (aged 15) Mary becomes dowager queen of France; Charles IX King of France, Catherine de Medici as regent
1561	22 JAN	Francis Bacon born
	14 AUG	Mary leaves France
	19 AUG	Mary Queen of Scots returns to Scotland (aged 18)
1562	1 MAR	Massacre of Protestants at Vassy, instigated by Duc de Guise, beginning of French wars of religion

	26 MAY	Shane O'Neill leads a rebellion in Ireland
	OCT	Elizabeth seriously ill with smallpox
	28 OCT	Mary victorious over Earl of Huntly and his men at Corrichie
1563	22 FEB	Pierre de Chastelard executed
	24 FEB	François, Duc de Guise, assassinated (aged 44)
	JUNE	Mary's first Parliament
	27 JUL	Havre surrendered to French
1564	6 FEB	Christopher Marlowe born
	23 APRIL	Reputed birthday of William Shakespeare
	25 JULY	Maximilian I succeeds as Holy Roman Emperor, as King of Austria, Bohemia and Hungary on death of Ferdinand I. Rest of Hapsburg dominions to Archduke Charles
	29 SEPT	Lord Robert Dudley created Earl of Leicester
1565	FEB	Henry Stuart, Lord Darnley, enters Scotland
	29 JULY	Mary Queen of Scots marries Henry Stuart, Lord Darnley (she is 22, he 19)
	AUG–OCT	The Chaseabout Raid when Mary suppresses Moray's rebellion
1566	1 JAN	Mary's pregnancy announced
	9 MAR	David Rizzio murdered
	19 JUN	James, Mary's son, born (James VI and I 1566–1625)
	NOV	Mary at Craigmillar Castle where she discusses the Darnley problem
	10 NOV	Robert Devereux, Earl of Essex, born
	17 DEC	Prince James of Scotland baptized at Stirling Castle
1567	10 FEB	Darnley murdered at Kirk o' Field, just outside Edinburgh (aged 21)
	19 APRIL	Ainslie Bond signed by Scottish nobles accepting Bothwell's suit of Mary
	24 APR	Mary 'abducted' by James Hepburn, Earl of Bothwell
	7 MAY	Lord and Lady Bothwell granted a divorce

	15 MAY	Mary marries Bothwell as her third husband
	15 JUNE	Mary surrenders to Confederate Lords at Carberry; Bothwell escapes
	17 JUNE	Mary imprisoned in Loch Leven Castle
	24 JULY	Mary forced to abdicate, James is declared King of Scotland (aged 13 months)
	29 JULY	James VI crowned at Stirling, James Stewart, Earl of Moray, becomes regent
1568	17 JAN	Lady Catherine Grey (Lady Catherine Seymour), Countess of Hertford, dies (aged 29)
	2 MAY	Mary escapes from Loch Leven
	13 MAY	Mary and supporters defeated at Langside
	18 MAY	Mary lands in Cumbria and conducted to Sheffield Castle
	23 MAY	Prince William of Orange defeats Spanish at the start of revolt in Low Countries
	15 JULY	Mary moved to Bolton Castle
	OCT	York conference to investigate Mary's part in Darnley's murder
	25 NOV	Enquiry moves to Westminster
1569	26 JAN	Mary moved into custody of Earl of Shrewsbury at Tutbury Castle
	APRIL	Elizabeth decides Mary must be returned to Scotland
	JULY	Moray declines to have Mary back
	10 OCT	Duke of Norfolk arrested
	14 NOV	Northern earls take possession of Durham Cathedral in Northern Rebellion
	22 NOV	Mary moved south to Coventry
	16 DEC	Northern earls flee to Scotland
1570	21 JAN	James Stewart, Earl of Moray and regent, assassinated
	25 FEB	Elizabeth excommunicated by Pope Pius V
	AUG	Norfolk released from Tower
1571	FEB	William Cecil created Baron Burghley

	APRIL	Ridolphi Plot revealed
	SEPT	Darnley's father, Earl of Lennox and Regent of Scotland, assassinated
1572	JAN	Duke of Norfolk's trial
	2 JUNE	Duke of Norfolk executed
	24 AUG	St Bartholomew's Massacre
1574	30 MAY	Charles IX dies, succeeded by Henri III
1577	13 DEC	Francis Drake leaves Plymouth to attempt circumnavigation of the globe
1578	14 APRIL	Earl of Bothwell dies in Danish prison
1579	JAN	Jehan de Simier arrives in London to conduct courtship between Elizabeth and his master, François, Duc d'Alençon
1580	26 SEPT	Francis Drake enters Plymouth having completed his circumnavigation
1581	4 APRIL	Sir Francis Drake knighted
	6 JUNE	Execution of Regent Morton
	1 DEC	English Jesuit Edmund Campion executed
1582	5 OCT	Gregorian calendar adopted by Catholic countries when 5 Oct becomes 15
1583	NOV	Throckmorton Plot revealed
1584	10 JULY	William, Prince of Orange, assassinated
	OCT	Bond of Association
	NOV	Act of Association
1585	APRIL	Sir Amyas Paulet becomes Mary's jailer
	8 DEC	Leicester sails for Low Countries as Elizabeth's Lieutenant General
1586	24 JAN	Leicester accepts title of Governor of the Provinces
	JULY	Babington Plot
	1 JULY	Treaty of Berwick between Elizabeth I and James VI of Scotland
	14 AUG	Sir Antony Babington arrested

	20 SEPT	Babington executed
	25 SEPT	Mary brought to Fotheringhay Castle
	15–16 OCT	Trial of Mary Queen of Scots
	25 OCT	Mary pronounced guilty of conspiring to murder Elizabeth I in Star Chamber at Westminster
1587	1 FEB	Elizabeth signs Mary's death warrant
	8 FEB	Mary executed at Fotheringhay Castle (aged 44)
1588	end JUL– 8 AUG	Defeat of Spanish Armada
1603	24 MAR	Death of Elizabeth I

The Tudors and Stuarts

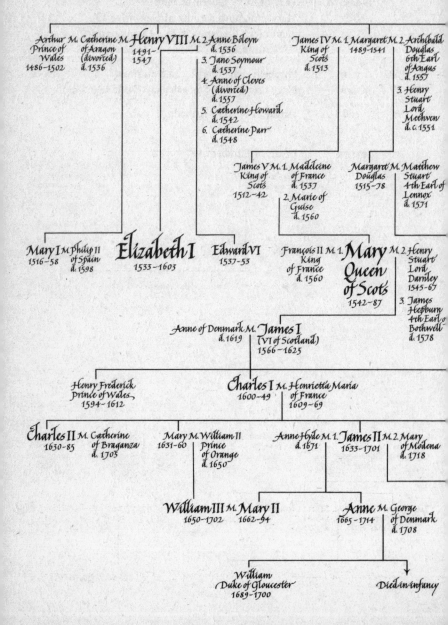

Arthur M. Catherine M. **Henry VIII** M. 2. Anne Boleyn
Prince of | of Aragon | 1491– | d. 1536
Wales | (divorced) | 1547 | 3. Jane Seymour
1486–1502 | d. 1536 | | d. 1537
| | | 4. Anne of Cleves
| | | (divorced)
| | | d. 1557
| | | 5. Catherine Howard
| | | d. 1542
| | | 6. Catherine Parr
| | | d. 1548

James IV M. 1. Margaret M. 2. Archibald
King of | 1489–1541 | Douglas
Scots | | 6th Earl
d. 1513 | | of Angus
| | d. 1557
| | 3. Henry
| | Stuart
| | Lord
| | Methven
| | d. c. 1551

James V M. 1. Madeleine
King of | of France
Scots | d. 1537
1512–42 | 2. Marie of
| Guise
| d. 1560

Margaret M. Matthew
Douglas | Stuart
1515–78 | 4th Earl
| of
| Lennox
| d. 1571

Mary I M. Philip II   **Elizabeth I**   **Edward VI**
1516–58 | of Spain
| d. 1598   1533–1603   1537–53

François II M. 1.   **Mary Queen of Scots** M. 2. Henry
King of | | Stuart
France | | Lord
d. 1560 | 1542–87 | Darnley
| | 1545–67
| | 3. James
| | Hepburn
| | 4th Earl of
| | Bothwell
| | d. 1578

Anne of Denmark M. **James I**
d. 1619 | (VI of Scotland)
| 1566–1625

Henry Frederick   **Charles I** M. Henrietta Maria
Prince of Wales | 1600–49 | of France
1594–1612 | | 1609–69

Charles II M. Catherine   Mary M. William II   Anne Hyde M. 1. **James II** M. 2. Mary
1630–85 | of Braganza   1631–60 | Prince   d. 1671 | 1633–1701 | of Modena
| d. 1703 | | of Orange | | | d. 1718
| | | d. 1650

William III M. **Mary II**   **Anne** M. George
1650–1702 | 1662–94   1665–1714 | of Denmark
| | d. 1708

William   Died in infancy
Duke of Gloucester
1689–1700

Henry VII M. *Elizabeth of York*
1455–1509   d. 1503

Louis XII M. 1. Mary M. 2. Charles Brandon
King   1498–1533   Duke of Suffolk
of France   d. 1545
d. 1515

Henry Brandon   Henry Grey M. 1. Frances M. 2. Adrian   Eleanor M. Henry Clifford
Earl of Lincoln   Marquis of Dorset   Brandon   Stokes   d. 1547   Earl of
1516–34   Duke of Suffolk   1517–79   d.c. 1581   Cumberland
                     d. 1554   d. 1570

Charles Stuart M. Elizabeth Cavendish
6th Earl of
Lennox
                          Jane Grey M. Guildford   Catherine   Mary Grey
                          d. 1554   Dudley   Grey   d. 1578
                                      d. 1554   d. 1568

Arbella Stuart M. William Seymour
d. 1615   Duke of Somerset

                                              Elizabeth M. Frederick V
                                              1596–1662   Elector Palatine
                                                          of the Rhine d. 1632

Elizabeth   Henry   Henrietta M. Philip   Sophia M. Ernest Augustus   Rupert
1635–80   Duke of   1644–70   Duke of   1630–1714 Elector of Hanover of the
            Gloucester   Orleans   Duke of Brunswick- Rhine
            1640–60   d. 1701   Luneborg   1619–82
                                                           d. 1698

James Francis Edward M. Maria Clementina   Louisa   George I M. Sophia Dorothea
'The Old Pretender'   Sobieska   d. 1712   1660–1727   of Celle
1688–1766   d. 1735   1666–1726

    Charles Edward M. Louisa of   Henry Benedict
    'The Young Pretender' Stolberg-Gedern Cardinal York   House of Hanover
    1720–88   d. 1824   1725–1807

ACKNOWLEDGEMENTS

Words cannot praise the London Library highly enough. It is a private institution where a member has access not only to an extensive library but can carry off great numbers of books, even reference books, for loans that can extend crucially into years. My only dread was the call of another member in need of one of 'my' volumes. Heartfelt thanks go to this great, individualistic institution and its unfailingly helpful staff. There are many individuals who have helped me write this book. Thanks first to Sheila Murphy who fifteen years ago or so first suggested the queens as a marvellous subject for a book. The idea lurked in my subconscious during my next two writing marathons. Only then was I able to begin. Sheila has been the first critical eye to read every one of my books, and her suggestions and generous editorial comments on *Elizabeth and Mary* were invaluable. Others I should like to thank include Lola Bubbosh; the late Sheila Dickinson; Sue Greenhill; Beryl Hislop; Rosalind Oxenford; Dr Peter Shephard; the late David Thesen; and Elizabeth Walston. Particular thanks to Robin Bell for permission to quote from his elegant translations of Mary Queen of Scots' poems, previously published as *Bittersweet Within My Heart*.

On a professional front, I could not have a better agent than Derek Johns and his great team at A.P. Watt. Derek has transformed my working life. Warm thanks to him and his assistant Anjali Pratap. Derek's greatest gifts to me as his author are my editors, Carol Janeway at Knopf in the United States and Arabella Pike at HarperCollins. Arabella has brought an incisive intelligence to everything, applied with such warmth and humour that it has been a delight to work with her. Around her are a team whose extraordinary quality was epitomized by a magical candle-lit banquet and firework display at Hampton Court Palace. Tilly Ware organised it, and nobody lucky enough to be there will ever forget it.

The last year of writing this book was inextricably linked for me with the final illness of my father. A great family enterprise brought our whole band of brothers and sisters together to care for him: so Karen,

Mark, Isabel, Brigid, Tricia, Andy and Sue, with their own generous families, have all become a part of it, and none more than our mother Ellinor, with her zest for life and instinctive understanding of death.

The writer's life is inevitably isolated and hard for those closest to her. My own family, Lily, Ben, Jess and Nick's daughter Sophia, have brought patience, insight and support to me during difficult times. And Ellie and Theo have arrived to gladden our hearts. Closest of all to the rock face is Nick, my partner in most things, my linguist, lightning conductor and love.

AUTHOR'S NOTE

I have retained early modern English in quotations where they occur thus in the source. On occasion I have clarified words or phrases and put them in square brackets. Otherwise, most quotations are in modern English, which is how they occur in the source.

Catholic countries changed from the Julian calendar to the Gregorian in October 1582, when they lost ten days. This meant the English calendar continued ten days behind. The period of history that this book encompasses is mostly pre-1582 and consequently all dates correspond with the Julian calendar.

Four hundred years ago, on 24 March 1603, Elizabeth I died. She was in her seventieth year. Having been propped for days on cushions on the floor in her chamber, she had been persuaded to take to her bed at last. To her Archbishop of Canterbury, silencing his praise, she said, 'My lord, the crown which I have borne so long has given enough of vanity in my time.' These words struck to the heart of the tragedy that had befallen Elizabeth and Mary Queen of Scots. This same crown had been the focus of Mary's ambition too; her claim to Elizabeth's throne was the obsession of her adult life from which so many disasters flowed.

Elizabeth realized that her crown and all the powerful interests that surrounded it were what drew her and Mary together, and yet fatally divided them. Despite possessing the throne of England, with all the pride of a daughter of King Henry, she was haunted by a deep-rooted insecurity as to her own legitimacy. When pressed by Parliament to sign Mary's death warrant, Elizabeth railed in anguish against the crown that had made this unnatural decision hers alone. Instead she wished that Mary and she 'were but as two milkmaids with pails upon our arms', and she regretted, 'that there were no more dependency upon us but mine own life were only in danger and not the whole estate of [her people's] religion and well-doings'. It was their royal rather than their human status that had brought these queens to such straits that one had to die.

Sixteen years before Elizabeth's own natural death in old age, Mary was beheaded at the age of forty-four. From that one act of regicide, a queen killing a fellow queen, a mythology of justification, romance, accusation and blame has been spun that retains its force to the present day. Of all the monarchs of these islands it is Elizabeth I and Mary Queen of Scots who most stir the imagination. They divided powerful opinion in their lifetimes and were the focus of passionate debate in the centuries that followed their deaths. Murderess, 'whore', daughter of the devil were epithets flung at both queens by their detractors, while their supporters claimed Elizabeth as hero and saviour, Mary as martyr and saint. It was the relationship between them that heightened these extremes of partisan feeling. Even in death, through history and myth, they continued locked together in complex rivalry, somehow embodying the ancestral character and mutual suspicion of their respective kingdoms.

In this new millennium, people identify with each queen still, arguing their merits and failures, and thinking they see some likeness in themselves. Elizabeth, the Virgin Queen, arguably the greatest monarch we have ever had, is certainly the one who most attracts superlatives. Unfashionable in her belief in self-discipline and sacrifice, she is irresistible as a reminder of England's past glory and pre-eminence in the world: a phenomenon of her own making, without precedent or successor. And Mary, a queen celebrity, *femme fatale* and flawed heroine, valuing pleasure over duty and adventure most of all. She even cast her kingdom away for illicit love – what more modern sacrifice could there be? Finally, the brilliant *coup de théâtre* of her death opened a path back to redemption.

And I myself am far from immune from this fascination. When I opened the volumes of *State Papers* covering their reigns I was amazed by the vivid immediacy of the voices. Both queens, their ambassadors and ministers, all speak to us through the centuries with more forthright, revealing and affecting language than one would ever expect from official documents today. From letters, speeches, prayers, poems, diplomatic dispatches and ministers' reports, the queens' voices would explain themselves. By placing them centre stage and writing of their relationship with each other and the world, there was more space to explore their characters through their own words and those of their contemporaries.

Consequently, this is not a dual biography of these queens. Instead it is a kind of hybrid, about historical figures but not a history charting every aspect and incident of their lives. Chronological, but not strictly so, it follows the dynamic interaction which shifted as each queen took the initiative by turns, one never entirely dominant, each highly aware of the other. The balance of power was never clear cut: Elizabeth appeared to hold all the best cards, but Mary played those she had to disconcerting effect.

There are many fine biographies already of these most written-about queens: for Elizabeth, the classic J.E. Neale, and more recently Anne Somerset's elegant, authoritative work, Alison Weir's popular trilogy, and David Starkey's vivid portrayal of the princess's youth; for Mary, nothing has superseded in more than thirty years Lady Antonia Fraser's impressive and sympathetic Life, although Jenny Wormald's study of Mary as a monarch is marvellous. But the wealth of primary sources is so great that the scope for bringing new illumination to the story is almost boundless.

Elizabeth and Mary is about the relationship between the queens, one that seemed, during their lifetimes, to evolve a life of its own, and in the end hold both captive to it and each other. It was the most compelling relationship of their lives, affecting their political policy and personal attitudes. Unlike Elizabeth with Burghley and Leicester, or Mary with Moray, Darnley and Bothwell, this was a relationship neither had chosen, nor could escape, even in death. Elizabeth realized with some despair how their fates were inter-twined: when she was ostensibly Mary's jailer she declared, 'I am not free, but a captive.'

The indissoluble bond between them was forged by two opposing forces; their shared inheritance and rivalry for Elizabeth's crown set against their natural solidarity as regnant queens in an over-whelmingly masculine world. They had a fascination and sympathy for each other; they were cousins in an age when family mattered and when, for much of their lives, both lacked closer kin. Mary chose to emphasize her familial relationship with Elizabeth, her letters often supplicating, daughterly, even lover-like. 'How much better', she wrote to Elizabeth, 'were it that we being two Queens so near of kin, neighbours and living in one isle, should be friends and live together like sisters, than by strange means divide ourselves to the hurt of both.' And Elizabeth responded to these emotional pleas with a tone that was bossy, condescending and, for a while, elder-sisterly in her exasperated care. And yet they never met.

This is the great dramatic centre of their story. In the absence of reality a rival grows in stature in the imagination, becoming something superhuman, but also less than human and therefore easier to kill. Their failure to meet also became an expression of frustrated desire and control. Mary never gave up pleading for personal contact, certain that her charm would alter her case with her cousin. Initially willing, Elizabeth then grew increasingly distant and aloof, fearful of what she believed was Mary's almost magical power to enchant, already exaggerated in her imagination and fuelled with the stories of others. Elizabeth was perplexed: 'There is something sublime in the words and bearing of the Queen of Scots that constrains even her enemies to speak well of her.'

Part of the drama of their lives is this great opposition between their natures, their earliest experiences and the kinds of rulers they wished to be. All her life, Elizabeth had steeled herself to prove to the world she had the heart and mind of a man, so aware was she of the accepted inferiority of being merely female. She often boasted that in this masculinity her strength resided, yet she had all the passions of a woman, and expressed these most notably in her love for her favourites and her tenderness for her people. Mary was seen as recklessly emotional and liable to nervous collapse, and yet she showed a more ruthless resolve to see her sister queen murdered than Elizabeth could summon up for the judicial execution of Mary herself. So unlike in temperament, these queens nevertheless were well matched in the vigour of their ambitions and their obstinacy of purpose. The weapons they used were different, but each had just as great a capacity for harm.

In considering Elizabeth's and Mary's lives in relation to each other, illuminating symmetries occur. They both had remarkable mothers who, for different reasons, were lost to them. Anne Boleyn was a clever woman, radical in her Protestant sympathies, courageous and spirited, but a stranger to her daughter through death, and erased through the dangers inherent even in her memory. Mary of Guise, redoubtable queen and role model for Mary, but largely absent and unknown, due to the dynastic ambitions that made both mother and daughter exiles in each other's land.

Each queen was involved in scandal over a favourite possibly implicated in murder, but they dealt with the crises they faced in completely different ways: Elizabeth's action safeguarded her throne and gave her the moral foundation from which to impose her future authority; Mary's decision lost her not only the throne but her freedom, and eventually her life. In the early years of Elizabeth's reign it was the English queen who was consistently compared by foreign ambassadors, to her detriment, with her cousin, the Queen of Scotland. Elizabeth was the intractable monarch, the wanton queen, while Mary lived a model life as dauphine, then queen, then dowager queen of the great kingdom of France. Her return to Scotland marked the beginning of the adventures that would reverse these comparisons in epic fashion.

From that moment the tension in their relationship mounted. There was a struggle for supremacy and a desire in each to claim the moral high ground. Mary's marriage and the birth of her son confirmed her conformity with expectations of what it was to be a good queen, while Elizabeth continued to prevaricate and evade her duty to provide for the succession. Then with Mary's rumoured involvement in the murder of her husband and marriage to the likely murderer, heedless of Elizabeth's trenchant advice, she set the English and Continental courts agog. There followed civil war in Scotland and humiliation for Mary, then imprisonment, fear for her life, miscarriage, forced abdication, night-time escape and precipitate flight to England. A plaintive existence as a genteel prisoner for seventeen years was enlivened with various plots to attain her freedom, and even her eventual elevation to the throne of England.

Even in death Mary sought to wrong-foot Elizabeth. Found guilty of incitement to kill her cousin, she went to her execution nobly insisting she was sacrificed for her faith alone. By dying heroically as a Catholic martyr, she rescued her reputation from the wreckage of her life. Elizabeth, as an old queen dying after more than four decades of transforming rule, was aware instead of the galloping hooves of the messenger's horse riding north. The next incumbent of her jealously guarded throne would be Mary's son, James, King of Scotland and now King of England too. This would mark Mary's final triumph, the succession of the Tudors by the Stuarts. But there was triumph for Elizabeth too, for Mary's son ruled their newly united kingdoms as a Protestant state.

The story of Elizabeth's and Mary's relationship is punctuated with reversals of fortune: murder mysteries, sexual intrigue, reckless behaviour, avowals of affection, heated battles and cold war. Fear, heartbreak and tragedy were its underlying strain. Yet surging through natural barriers of prejudice, masculine perspective and vested interest, these two queens emerge evergreen in their importance and fascination: Elizabeth, regardless of her weaknesses, confounding every prejudice against women in power; and Mary, despite her strengths, fulfilling in the end every foreboding, but with astounding boldness and abandon. They are welcome exceptions in the vast congregation of men who jostle for space in their domination of history.

That these two remarkable queens should have been contemporaries, neighbours in one small island, is gift enough for any writer. That they should be united by blood but inextricably enmeshed in a deadly rivalry for the same kingdom, the same throne, gives the story of their relationship the brooding force of Greek tragedy.

I came to this book as a biographer not a historian, believing that character largely drives events, explains motivation, and connects us to each other through the centuries. These queens lived lives vastly different from our own, but they behaved and felt in a way fundamentally familiar to us now. The outbursts of defiance, the flagging spirit, the pride in achievement and longing for love, all this is expressed in their own clear voices, as are the less familiar qualities of kingly pride, autocratic power and bloody revenge.

As a biographer one lives for years exploring the world and the mind of a stranger. For me in this case it was two strangers. Yet in those years these strangers gain a certain sense of intimacy and their lives a foothold in one's own. In living so closely with these queens, inevitably my ideas and prejudices have changed. I became more aware of the profound loneliness of their role; the fear, the danger and responsibility were daunting, yet they accepted this and even revelled in it. The physical suffering and discomfort of their everyday lives was overlaid with such magnificent show and animated with an enormous zest and appetite for life itself. Above all, it is their characters that have gripped me, with their different energies and ambitions, their distinctive voices and the complexity of their human responses and feelings.

Mary was clearly a passionate and impetuous woman, but with a personal charm so disconcerting that even Elizabeth feared to meet her. She emerges a more intelligent and subtle thinker than I had initially thought her to be, and with a courage and energy in action that was breathtaking; her ruthlessness and desire for revenge more Medicean than Stuart in its lack of compromise or pity. Elizabeth, so obviously crafty, clever, and in imperial command of herself and others, also surprised with how tentative she could be, how affectionate, tender, and full of humour and charm. I hope that in these pages will be found some sense of that vitality; that through their own words, and the exploration of their relationship, we can look anew at these remarkable women and redoubtable queens.

CHAPTER ONE

The Fateful Step

'I am already bound unto an husband, which is the
kingdom of England' . . .
Stretching out her hand she showed them the ring.

Queen Elizabeth's first speech before Parliament, 10 February 1559

THESE WERE DANGEROUS TIMES. The second quarter of the sixteenth century had made Elizabeth Tudor and her generation of coming men watchful, insecure, fearful for their lives. Nothing could be taken for granted. Health and happiness were fleeting, reversals of fortune came with devastating speed. This was the generation raised in the last days of King Henry and come of age in a time of religious and political flux. The religious radicalism of Edward VI's reign had been quickly followed by reactionary extremism and bloodshed in Queen Mary's. During the political tumult of these years there was no better time for ambitious men to seize position, wealth and honours. No longer was power the exclusive prerogative of old aristocratic blood. When a Thomas Wolsey, son of a butcher, or a Thomas Cromwell, son of a blacksmith, could rise in Henry's reign to be the mightiest subject in the land, then what bar to ambition during the minority of Edward, the turmoil of Mary, and the unpromising advent of Elizabeth? But vaulting ambition and exorbitant rewards brought their own peril. The natural hierarchy of things mattered to the sixteenth-century mind. Men elevated beyond their due estate, women raised as rulers over men were unnatural events

1

and boded ill. Those with the greatest aspirations could not expect to die peaceful in their beds.

God remained at the centre of this febrile and unpredictable world. His will was discerned in every random act. Death was everywhere. It came as sudden sweating sickness and struck down communities of healthy adults. It came as fire to purify heretic beliefs. It came through poison or the deadly thrust of steel to dispose of inconvenient obstacles in the machinery of power. The supernatural had a physical presence, and spirits and magic were natural companions to everyday life. They were part of the grand cosmic scheme which constituted God's hierarchical universe. Analogy, interconnectedness, fixity were deeply impressive to the Elizabethan mind, mutability and disorder a sign of man out of harmony with God's plan. Superstition and religion were ways to make sense of suffering, attempts at warding off the apparently random blows of fate. Yet the insecurity of life itself made the living intense, the wits sharper, the senses more acute. For sixteenth-century men and women there was a life after death, for the godly well-mapped and glorious, but life on earth was a precious and precarious thing to be seized and drained to the dregs.

At a time of augury and superstition, there was nothing to foretell the events of 1558: no sightings of whales in the Channel; no preternaturally high tide, nor monstrous births nor the mysterious, lingering trajectory of a comet across the northern sky. Even Nostradamus, whose prophecies were consulted by those in a fever of uncertainty, appeared unaware of its significance. The year opened without cosmic fanfare. Yet this was to become one of the momentous dates in every British schoolchild's history rote. Along with the Battle of Hastings of 1066 and the Great Fire of London in 1666, 1558 was one of the markers of a seismic shift in English experience, to be chanted in schoolrooms through subsequent centuries. It was a year of grand transfers of power, as one reign came to an end and a new era began. It was a time of inexorable religious schism, when universal monopolistic Catholicism was permanently supplanted by the state religion, Protestantism.

Scotland's most recent history had been less convulsive. By the beginning of 1558 it was balanced in a certain equilibrium. A significant number of lords had proceeded informally down the road of religious reformation and the opposing factions had forged an uneasy coexistence. Clan loyalties and rivalries would always be the defining identity which cut across ideology, matters of faith or political allegiance. Rather than a religious cause, any growing unrest and sense of danger came more from Scottish resentment against the increasing presence of the French, garrisoned in various towns and awarded lucrative offices over the heads of the native Scots. As a child ten years previously, Mary Queen of Scots had escaped the clutches of the English and sailed for France. Her French mother Mary of Guise was courageous and just as regent but inevitably favoured her own country with which Scotland was in alliance. This cosy relationship was about to be challenged when, in 1559, the Reformation turned militant and anti-French, and John Knox, the inspired Calvinist preacher, returned home after twelve years' exile to become its hectoring mouthpiece.

At the beginning of 1558, however, both Elizabeth and Mary were poised on the margin between apprenticeship and their public lives as female monarchs. By the end of that year both had embraced their fate. The defining moment for Mary came with a kiss – in effect a marriage. For Elizabeth it came with a death – and an exclusive contract with her people.

It was apparent that a woman in possession of a throne must marry, and do so without delay. All biblical and classical texts, with which the educated sixteenth-century mind was imbued, stressed the natural order of the male's dominion over the female. A female monarch was a rare and unnatural phenomenon which could only be regularized by speedy union with a prince who would rule over her in private and guide her in her public, God-given, role as queen. Only by restoring man's necessary dominion could the proper balance of the world be maintained.

Although her cousin Elizabeth was revolutionary in her lifelong resistance to this obligation, Mary Stuart was more conformable and fulfilled this expectation of her status and sex – not once but three times. In early 1558 she was fifteen and had been a queen since she was six days old. She had never known any other state. First as a queen of Scotland, the land of her birth and a country she did not know: secondly as Queen of France, the country of her heart. Having lived from the age of five at the centre of the powerful French court, Mary had grown into a charming and accomplished French princess, destined to become the wife of the Dauphin of France. Her spectacular dynastic marriage, reinforcing the 'auld alliance' between Scotland and France, was set for the spring. Mary would marry her prince on 24 April 1558. François, the beloved companion of her childhood and King Henri II's eldest son, was just fourteen years old.

In England, Elizabeth Tudor was twenty-four years old and living quietly in the country at Hatfield some thirty miles north of London. Expectant, and fearful of losing the one thing she desired, she was fearful too of its fulfilment. She had already been bastardized, disinherited, often in danger and always waiting, never certain of the prize. Elizabeth had seen her two siblings (and a cousin, fleetingly) succeed to the throne before her. If any had had children then her position on the sidelines of power would have become permanent. But Edward VI died in 1553, unmarried and childless, aged sixteen. He was followed not by either of his elder half-sisters but by their hapless teenage cousin, Lady Jane Grey. Sacrificed to further the ambitions of her father-in-law, the Duke of Northumberland, she was queen in name only and then barely for nine days. Immediately imprisoned she was executed seven months later. Now in 1558, Henry VIII's eldest child, Mary I, herself appeared to be ailing.

Elizabeth had survived much danger. She knew well how closely scrutinized her actions were and how much she was the focus of others' desire for power. The previous two decades had seen so many ambitions crumble to dust, so many noblemen and women imprisoned and beheaded, accused of heresy or treason, tortured, tried and burnt, or if a traitor, hung, drawn and quartered, in the terrific ways of judicial death.

At the beginning of 1558, Elizabeth and her supporters knew that some great change was in motion. But change brought disruption too and increased danger. Her half-sister Mary Tudor had been queen for nearly five years. Suspicious, suffering, devoutly Catholic and zealous to maintain the supremacy of the old faith, her reign had grown increasingly unhappy. Mary's worst mistake had been her insistence on marrying Philip II of Spain, for the English hated foreigners meddling in their affairs, and they hated the Spanish most of all.

The fanatical purges of heresy by her decree, and the torture and burnings of hundreds of martyrs, would earn Mary the epithet 'Bloody Mary' from generations to come. The country grew ever more tired and repelled by the bloodshed. The dreadful spectacles had become counter-productive, alienating her subjects' affections for their queen and strengthening the reformers' support. In reaction to the mood of the country, the burnings in Smithfield were halted in June 1558. But nature seemed to be against Mary too, for the harvests also failed two years in succession. In 1556 people were scrabbling like pigs for acorns and dying of starvation. The following year they were ravaged by disease as various epidemics swept through the land. Famine and pestilence – people wondered, was this God's retribution for the sins of Mary's reign?

By the beginning of 1558, Mary was herself sick and in despair. Still longing for a child and heir, once more in desperation she had made herself believe she was pregnant again. But Philip had not bothered to hide his antipathy to his queen and anyway had been absent from her for too long. Her delusion and humiliation were evident even to her courtiers. Elizabeth, who had waited so long in an uneasy limbo, under constant suspicion, her sister refusing to name her as her heir, would have lost everything if this miraculous pregnancy turned out to bear fruit. No one could know, however, that the symptoms which Mary interpreted as the beginning of new life and hope were instead harbingers of death.

The queen's spirit that cold January had already been broken over the loss of Calais. The last trophy left to the English from their ancient wars with France, this two-century-old possession had been lost in the very first days of the year. Since the previous June,

Mary had supported her husband by embroiling her country in an expensive, unpopular and now ultimately humiliating war with France. The loss to their old enemy of Calais, remnant of Plantagenet prowess, was more a symbolic than strategic catastrophe, and it cut her to the heart.

This latest humiliation of English pride had been inflicted by François, Duc de Guise, nicknamed 'le Balafré', 'scarface', after a wound inflicted by the English at the siege of Boulogne fourteen years earlier. A lance had smashed through his face from cheek to cheek but he had overcome all odds and recovered his life, his sight, and even the desire to fight again. He was a brilliant soldier, and the eldest and most powerful of Mary Queen of Scots' six overweening Guise uncles. The ambition of these brothers knew no bounds. They claimed direct descendency from Charlemagne. Catholic conviction and imperial ambitions commingled in their blood. Their brotherhood made them daunting: they thought and hunted as a pack, their watchwords being 'one for all' and 'family before everything'.

Taking advantage of their monarch's gratitude for the success of the Calais campaign and riding on a wave of popular euphoria, the Duc de Guise and his brother the Cardinal of Lorraine agitated for the marriage of their niece to the youthful heir to the French throne. The fortunes of the girl queen and the triumphant family of her mother, Mary of Guise, were fatally intertwined. At this time, the Guises seemed to be so much in the ascendant that many of their fellow nobles resented and envied their power, fearing that it was they who in effect ruled France.

Elizabeth and Mary Queen of Scots had always been aware of each other, of their kinship and relations to the English crown. As cousins, they were both descended from Henry VII, Elizabeth as his granddaughter, Mary as his great-granddaughter. European royalty was a small, elite and intermarried band. As the subject of the English succession loomed again, Elizabeth was acutely conscious of the strength of the Queen of Scots' claim to the English throne. Certainly she knew that if her sister Mary I's repeal of Henry VIII's Act of Supremacy was allowed to stand then her own parents' marriage would remain invalid and she could be marginalized and disinherited as a bastard. To most Catholics Henry's marriage to Anne Boleyn had always been invalid and Mary Queen of Scots was legally and morally next in line to the English throne. If Mary united the thrones of Scotland, France and England then this would ensure that England remained a part of Catholic Christendom.

However, if the Acts of Mary Tudor's reign should be reversed then Elizabeth's legitimacy was confirmed and she, as Henry VIII's legitimate daughter, had not only the natural but the more direct claim. She also had popular, emotional appeal. Her tall, regal figure and her reddish gold colouring reminded the people, grown nostalgic and selective in their memory of 'Good King Harry', of her father when young. Her surprisingly dark eyes, an inheritance of the best feature of her mother Anne Boleyn, were not enough to blur the bold impression that the best of her father lived on in her.

In fact, despite the stain on her mother's name, it was to Elizabeth's credit that she was not the daughter of a foreign princess, that unadulterated English blood ran in her veins and that she had been born in Greenwich Palace, at the centre of English royal power. In early peace negotiations with France, Elizabeth had Cecil point out she was 'descended by father and mother of mere English blood, and not of Spain, as her sister was'. This meant she was 'a free prince and owner of her crown and people'.[1] She was an Englishwoman, and she knew this counted for much in this island nation of hers. 'Was I not born in the realm? Were my parents born in any foreign country? Is there any cause I should alienate myself from being careful over this country? Is not my kingdom here?'[2]

At the beginning of the sixteenth century, a Venetian ambassador noted the insularity and self-satisfaction of the English even then:

> the English are great lovers of themselves, and of everything belonging to them; they think that there are no other men than themselves, and no other world but England; and whenever they see a handsome foreigner, they say that 'he looks like an Englishman', and that 'it is a great pity that he should not be an Englishman'.[3]

In early 1558 this pride seemed rather misplaced. As the French celebrated their victory over the English at Calais, it was clear that the greater power was with them, and Mary Stuart, Queen of Scots, and soon to become Dauphine and eventually Queen of France, basked in this radiance. Meanwhile England was impoverished and demoralized by unpopular government and wasteful war, and the Lady Elizabeth, hopeful successor to the throne, remained sequestered in the country. Both she and the English people seemed overcast by a cloud of stasis and failure, fearful of the past and uncertain of the future. A historian and near contemporary expressed it thus:

> For every man's mind was then travailed with a strange confusion of conceits, all things being immoderately either dreaded or desired. Every report was greedily both inquired and received, all truths suspected, diverse tales believed, many improbable conjectures hatched and nourished. Invasion of strangers, civil dissension, the doubtful disposition of the succeeding Prince, were cast in every man's conceit as present perils.[4]

The triumphalism of France and the pre-eminence of the Guises were publicly enacted in the spectacular wedding celebrations of the youthful Mary Stuart and François de Valois. Both Catherine de Medici, the dauphin's mother, and Diane de Poitiers, Henri II's omnipotent mistress, argued that the marriage need not be hastened, that these children should be given more time. There may have been some concern at their youth and the dauphin's sickliness, but both women were more exercised by the growing influence of the Guises whose power as a result of this union threatened to become insurmountable.

Objections were put aside, however, and the day was set for Sunday 24 April 1558. It had been two centuries since a dauphin had been married in Paris, and the streets around the cathedral of Notre Dame were thronged with an excited and expectant crowd. A large stage had been erected so that as many of the public would see the proceedings as possible. Blue silk embroidered with the arms of the Queen of Scotland and gold fleur-de-lis arched above the

scaffolded platform to suggest a star-studded sky. The magnificent
Gothic cathedral dwarfed the fluttering silk and national flags, its
magisterial presence adding spiritual gravitas to the carnival spectacle. The people's hero, the Duc de Guise, was master of ceremonies. He played to the crowds and waved the bejewelled
noblemen aside so that the common people might better see. It
was Guise policy always to court the Paris mob even at the expense
of their popularity with their fellow noblemen.

And what the mob craned to see was the arrival of the wedding
procession with Mary Stuart as its cynosure. Leading the assembly
was the ubiquitous Duc de Guise closely followed by a band of
Scottish musicians dressed in red and yellow, the colours of their
queen. Then came a vast body of gentlemen of the household
of the French king followed by the royal princes, the bishops,
archbishops and cardinals, as brilliantly plumed as parrots. The
sumptuous clothes and jewels were a spectacle in themselves. The
diminutive figure of the dauphin then arrived, looking younger
than his fourteen years, stunted in growth and with the frailty and
pallor of a lifelong invalid.

Of greatest interest was his young bride, a queen in her own
right. The French had taken her to their hearts ever since she had
been sent as a child to their shores for safekeeping from the English.
She arrived that Sunday morning escorted by the king himself and
another of her uncles, the Cardinal of Lorraine. Mary had grown
up with an unwavering sense of destiny and a natural flair for the
theatrical: she knew what was expected of her and to what she had
been born. But she had not learnt from her uncle a respect for the
power of the people. As a prospective queen of France, she did not
need to. The French monarchy was so rich and self-confident that
it sought to remove itself still further from its subjects and advertise
to all, particularly its competitor monarchs abroad, the extent of
unassailable wealth and the power of the crown.

Although only fifteen, the young Queen of Scots was already tall
and graceful; she and her uncles towered over the young dauphin
and were all taller and more impressive than even the king and
queen themselves. Mary's much vaunted beauty was not just a

construct of the conventional hyperbole of court poets and commentators, but a beauty that had as much to do with her vitality and vivacity as the symmetry of her features. She had a fine complexion, chestnut brown hair and intelligent, lively eyes beneath prominent lids and fine arched brows. She had a strong active body and was good at sports, loving to ride hard and to hunt the wild animals with which the royal forests surrounding the châteaux of her youth were stocked.

Dressed in white for her wedding, Mary confounded the usual tradition of cloth of gold; white was more usually the colour of mourning. She trailed a pearl-encrusted cloak and a train of grey velvet. Neither did her jewels disappoint for on her head was a specially commissioned crown studded with gemstones (the canny Scots had refused to let their crown jewels leave Scotland) and round her throat was a grand diamond necklace. This diamond was most probably the 'Great Harry' which she had inherited from her grandmother, Margaret Tudor, to whom it had been given by her own father, Henry VII of England. The importance of her Tudor inheritance was embodied in this priceless jewel.

Magnificence was the order of the day. Sublimely present, but far removed, Mary made her marriage vows elevated in front of the crowds pressing towards the great doors of Notre Dame. As a symbol of imperial munificence, inviting too perhaps a reciprocal generosity from heaven, the heralds took handfuls of gold and silver coins and threw them amongst the people crying, 'Largesse! . . . largesse!' So desperate was the rush that many were trampled, some fainted and others scrabbled and fought savagely for a salvaged ducat or sou. Fearing a riot, the largesse was prematurely dammed and the heralds' moneybags stowed away. The young Queen Mary of Scotland and her even younger husband, now known as the King of Scotland, were shown again to the surging crowd.

It was the first time Mary was to experience the hysteria of a crowd whose energies were focused wholly on herself. Although this time they were benign and wished her well, there was always something potentially terrifying in the sheer force and power of the mob, crying out, shoving each other, sweating, straining to touch her hand or grasp a passing fragment of her robe, to catch her eye and elicit some recognition or blessing.

But the grandeur of French ceremony was aimed at distancing royalty, projecting them to god-like proportions, not just to their subjects but to themselves. It was an inflation that could only make the young dauphin and dauphine think of themselves as close to divine. The populace was excluded from the archbishop's palace where the extravagant wedding banquet was held. On a day fraught with symbolism, and exhausting in its demands, Mary's fifteen-year-old head was beginning to ache under the weight of her crown and she was permitted to relinquish it to the king's gentleman of the bedchamber. Then once the feast was cleared away the ball began, with the king leading out his new daughter-in-law, taller than he was, altogether more regal in her mien and a notably graceful dancer.

However, the highlight of the celebrations was yet to come with the removal of the wedding party and guests to the Palais de Justice for a series of fantastical pageants. Twenty-five wicker horses arrayed in cloth of gold, with the young Guise sons and Valois princes on their backs, entered pulling coaches filled with people dressed as pilgrims, singing in praise of God and the young bride and groom. A dozen bejewelled unicorns, the heraldic and mythical symbol of Scotland, more carriages filled with beautiful young women dressed as the Muses, and more celestial music all captured the imaginations of the glittering wedding guests.

The *pièce de résistance* was kept for last as six gauzy ships, their sails filling with an artificial breeze, appeared to float across a painted, billowing sea. In each was a prince, brilliantly attired in gold and wearing a mask, with an empty throne beside him. As the ingenious fleet approached the great marble table at which the wedding party sat each masked prince disembarked to choose his princess and place her on his throne, to the evident pleasure of both the participants and the spectators. The smallest of them all approached one of the tallest of the young women, as the Dauphin François claimed his young dauphine. He and the young Queen of Scots sailed away in a make-believe ship to a fantasy land.

These were purposefully extravagant fun and games, full of

symbolism and self-indulgent conceit, and executed with peculiarly French stylishness and wit. The country had been brought close to bankruptcy by wars with England and Spain, and riven with religious and political factions. Such pomp was a necessary reassurance to themselves and assertion to their neighbours that the imperial greatness of France remained undimmed. But at heart it was a fairytale confection, an entertaining froth for the diversion of a complacent, self-regarding court. The focus of all this fuss was the fairytale princess herself, undeniably beautiful, intelligent and robust but disabled by the fantasy, and burdened with vain pride.

There were many epithalamia written in France and Scotland in praise of the marriage of Mary and François, of Scotland with France. The French, not surprisingly, stressed the supremacy of France in the union, some getting carried way with the vision of empire extending into Britain and throughout Europe. More modestly, Michel l'Hôpital, in his famous wedding poem of 1558, described proud Scotland as, 'a kingly crown, a subject land./Light in its weight, in truth, with ours compared'.[5] Another song, published by one of the Pléiade* group of poets, Jean de Baïf, celebrated Mary's legitimate claim on the English throne: 'without murder and war, France and Scotland will with England be united'.[6]

Back in Scotland, the local poets saw the marriage as a union of equals. Sir Richard Maitland characterized the relationship as fraternal, 'Scots and French now live in unity/As you were brothers born in one country . . . Defending other both by land and sea'.[7] The celebrations too were inevitably a more muted and frugal affair. Mary's mother, Mary of Guise, regent since 1554, ordered the great cannon, nicknamed 'Mons Meg', to be fired from the ramparts of Edinburgh Castle. But then, with suitable economy, she dispatched a body of men to retrieve the monster shot so that it could be

---

* La Pléiade was a group of seven French writers, led by Pierre de Ronsard and including Joachim du Bellay, Jean Dorat and Remy Belleau, who aimed to elevate the French language to the level of classical Greek and Latin as a medium for literary expression. They were named after the constellation and are considered the first representatives of French Renaissance poetry.

dusted down and used again. When France exacted a tax on the Scottish people to finance the nuptials of the queen who had left their shores as a small child, more than ten years before, there was some muttering. When France then came back for an even larger contribution, resentment became more entrenched. The independent-minded nobles and lairds had largely put up with the influx of French courtiers and advisers around Mary of Guise, particularly if a strong French presence threatened their old enemy England, but no true Scotsman could stomach any sense of their country being annexed in some unequal alliance.

Monarchies when women or children inherited were notoriously susceptible to powerful factions and self-seeking ambitions amongst their subjects, and Scotland had had more than its fair share of premature royal deaths and restive noblemen. During Mary Stuart's minority and absence in France, the reformed religion had flourished with little real curb under the eleven-year governorship of the indecisive Earl of Arran, followed by that of her own mother. Although Mary of Guise was not a natural persecutor of heretics, her family was the pre-eminent force in France and hardline in its Catholicism and antipathy to dissent. The court became thick with Frenchmen, some of whom held lucrative posts, most of whom seemed to the more impoverished and frugal Scots to be arrogant in their manner and wantonly extravagant in their tastes. French interests were seen by the Scots to be increasingly paramount in their increasingly partisan government.

In France, the wedding celebrations lasted for days, in part aimed at bolstering the people's support for their monarchy and in the process uniting some of the alarming and bitter rifts caused by the fiery advance of the reformed religion fuelled from Geneva. But the really important political union was transacted privately in the weeks before the public celebration. Nine Scottish commissioners braved the February storms to sail to France. They survived seasickness and shipwreck in order to be there in person to act on behalf of Scotland and her queen in the negotiations of the marriage treaty. Everything seemed to be generous and convivial enough. Scotland's independence was assured; Francis would become King of Scotland alongside his queen; if they should have a son he would inherit both realms; if they only had a daughter she would inherit the crown of Scotland alone, being prohibited from claiming the French throne.

Henri II also apportioned money and land for Mary's own use, and if she should be widowed then her rights to that property at least remained. If she and François did not produce an heir then the Scottish throne would revert to the ancient line of Scottish succession,* not be absorbed into the French inheritance. The Scottish commissioners could find nothing objectionable in this.

However, in an act of gross duplicity by the king and his advisers, Mary was asked that same day, 4 April 1558, to sign further secret documents, without the knowledge of her commissioners, which so compromised Scotland politically and financially that in effect it would have made her country a satellite of France. One signature allowed that if Mary should have no heirs, then Scotland, and also her claim to the English throne, would be inherited by Henri II's successors. Another document promised virtually a limitless mortgage on the Scottish treasury to repay France's expenditure in the defence of Scotland against England, even the costs to the French royal house of the hospitality extended to Mary during the time she had lived with them at court. In a final act of perfidy, the French king had this young woman, to whom he had acted as guardian and father figure, sign a further document invalidating any subsequent attempt she might make to modify or nullify these larcenous orders.

On the face of it these secret documents, signed by Mary behind the backs of her own commissioners, constituted a betrayal of her country. It is hard to believe that she knew the full meaning of

---

* The Hamiltons became nearest family to the throne when Lord Hamilton married James II's daughter, Princess Mary, in *c.* 1474. Their grandson James Hamilton, 2nd Earl of Arran, born about 1516, engineered his position as regent and heir presumptive on the death of James V. But Matthew Stewart, 4th Earl of Lennox, was also descended from Princess Mary and so believed he too had a claim to be heir presumptive, possibly even more indubitably legitimate than Arran who was born of a marriage which had followed a divorce. The Hamilton–Lennox rivalry was one of the dynamic power struggles of the reign of Mary Queen of Scots.

what she was signing. The plea that she was but a young woman of fifteen, keen to please and in awe of her powerful uncles and the fond King Henri, is just enough. Although it excuses her the worst motives, however, it does not do her much credit. Fifteen was not considered as youthful then as it is to modern minds. Fifteen-year-olds were leading men into battle, having children and dying for their beliefs. The Queen of Scots' political naivety and lack of judgement, even if merely following the advice of these apparently trustworthy men, did not bode well for her political deftness in the future. Her lack of respect for the independence of her own ancient and sovereign kingdom was a failure of education and imagination. In fact the comparison with her cousin Elizabeth at the same age could not have been more marked.

When Elizabeth Tudor herself was merely fifteen, she was involved in early 1549 in a political crisis revolving around the ambitions of the Lord Admiral Seymour, the husband of her favourite stepmother, Catherine Parr. Elizabeth was cross-examined about the extent of his relationship with her when she had lived under their roof. As a possible successor to the crown, all Elizabeth's relationships were considered political. It was dangerous to encourage any overtures not previously sanctioned by the monarch and his advisers.

At this time her young brother Edward was king and Seymour's elder brother, the Duke of Somerset, was Lord Protector. The Seymour brothers were ambitious men. Scurrilous rumours were abroad that Elizabeth and Seymour had been secretly married, were at least sexually involved with each other, even that she was already pregnant. All this was dangerously discreditable to her and potentially fatal for him. Seymour was thrown into the Tower of London and her own closest servants taken into custody. Elizabeth was isolated and at real risk. Yet she conducted herself with remarkable intelligence and self-control and could not be wrong-footed by her experienced interrogator: 'She hath a very good wit, and nothing is gotten of her but by great policy,'[8] the exasperated man wrote to the Lord Protector. Elizabeth steadfastly maintained her innocence, prevaricated when things became difficult, and in the end prevailed.

Mary had been just as youthful at this test of her judgement but, at fifteen, she thought of herself as a French rather than a Scottish queen. Scotland and the interests of her people were a long way from where her heart lay. Although her wits were sharp enough, her ambitions dynastic and her will strong, her characteristic motivation was in action and desire. Decisions would spring always more readily from impetuous feeling. This was to make her attractive as a woman, compelling as a romantic heroine and impressive in command when things went her way. But it made her tragically fallible as a queen.

However, there were certain more sinister aspects of political life to disturb Mary's apparent ingenuousness. News reached her of the tragic return journey of her Scottish commissioners that September. All were stricken with violent sickness and four of them died within hours of each other. Mary's illegitimate half-brother Lord James Stewart was young enough and strong enough to survive but was left with a constitutional weakness for the rest of his life. Rumours abounded that they had been deliberately poisoned. Subsequent commentators thought the Guises quite capable of such an act if they had thought their private treaty with Mary and the betrayal of Scottish interests had been discovered. Certainly tradition had it that the French and Italians vied with each other for the reputation as Europe's most artful poisoners. And even though, at the time, any case of sudden death was quickly supposed to be due to the poisoner's art, for so many adult men to die in such quick succession appeared suspicious indeed. Surprisingly, nothing subsequently was seriously investigated, let alone proved, but back in Scotland it was used by Knox and others as powerful propaganda for anti-French feeling.

Mary seemed to be little moved by the tragedy but was generally uneasy. Her husband was away from her in Picardy, with his own father the king, at a camp where sickness was rife: everyone was ready for peace with Spain and England, yet progress seemed to be slow. She expressed her disquiet in a letter to her mother in Scotland. Fearing the factions in the court at that time she was resigned, 'unless God provides otherwise . . . because we have so few people of good faith it is no wonder if we have trouble'.[9]

So 1558 was significant for Mary as the year she married the person she was to love most in her life, albeit with a sister's affection rather than a sexual love. With that marriage she had fulfilled the ambitions of her mother, her mother's family and the King of France himself. Her previous ten years in France had prepared her solely for this, to be a princess and eventually queen consort of France. To her family in France, Scotland was of little value or interest except as England's Achilles' heel, the gateway for a future French invasion. As she married the heir to the French throne it was clear to her that her greatest duty was to promote the Valois dynasty and to produce the male heir that would continue their dominance of royal power begun in 1328.

The lessons of her past were with Elizabeth always. Born an heir to the throne she nevertheless had endured disinheritance, reinstatement, exclusion, humiliation, imprisonment and real fear for her life. 'Taught by Experience and Adversity, (two most effectual and powerfull Masters)'[10] was how William Camden,* Elizabeth's first chronicler, characterized her cast of mind at this time. She had been alone and without powerful protectors and had learnt patience, circumspection, discipline and the absolute necessity of command. She had also discovered the extent of her own courage and the coolness of her intellect under fire. This gave her a special confidence, proof against any challenge to come. The whole purpose of her life was to inherit what was rightfully hers; the daughter most like her father who most deserved his crown. And she meant to rule like a king. Everything else was secondary to that desire. Yet the question of her own legitimacy, denied by the Catholic powers, upheld by her own people, was an ever-present liability.

Although ambitious men would seek her all her life for dynastic

---

* William Camden (1551–1623) was an antiquary and historian, one time headmaster of Westminster School where Ben Jonson was his pupil and claimed that he owed him 'all that I am in arts, all that I know'. In 1615 Camden published his ground-breaking and authoritative *Annales Rerum Anglicarum et Hibernicarum Regnante Elizabetha* which marked a new departure in the writing of history with its use of state papers and lively, often first-hand, description, combined with academic detachment and lack of bias.

alliances, Elizabeth, from a very young age, had rejected the orthodoxy that a woman must marry, that a princess, particularly, had a duty to marry. Given all the human and political circumstances of tradition, expectation, security, and dynastic and familial duty which pressed in upon her, Elizabeth's insistence that she would not marry was a remarkable instance of revolutionary action and independence of mind. In May 1558, she reminded Sir Thomas Pope that even when Edward VI was king she had asked permission 'to remayne in that estate I was, which of all others best lyked me or pleased me ... I am even at this present of the same mind ... I so well like this estate, as I perswade myselfe ther is not anie kynde of liffe comparable unto it ... no, though I were offered the greatest Prince in all Europe.'[11] To remain unwed was also a masterly diplomatic ploy for the unfulfilled prospect of her marriage to various foreign princes kept the equilibrium between the great European powers in constant suspension.

Part of this determination had to be as a result of experience and contemplation. She was twenty-five and had been through a rigorous training for something much greater than submission to a husband in marriage and sharing her monarchic power with a prince. She had her sister Mary's sad example in near memory; her father's ruinous effect on the women he married as a more distant example. Yet to remain unmarried flew in the face of the pleas of her increasingly desperate councillors. Almost every parliament included a petition that she should marry. For a monarch so insistent on her primary concern for her people it seemed perverse to persist in celibacy and risk at her death the eclipse of the Tudors and the possibility of civil war.

But to remain unmarried also flouted the hierarchical order of life which kept the nation safe, the universe in harmony. If Elizabeth continued to ignore the immutable laws of interconnectedness and the due place of everything, including herself and her rights and responsibilities as a monarch, then she risked the catastrophe of chaos. In the first years of her reign, her bishops of Canterbury, London and Ely expressed a similar fear 'that this continued sterility in your Highness' person to be a token of God's displeasure towards us'.[12] In this decision Elizabeth confounded every shade of opinion. She stood alone and unsupported. How could she not sometimes have faltered?

As the year drew to its wintry close, the opportunity Elizabeth had barely hoped for all her life was hers at last. By the beginning of November it became clear that her sister Mary was mortally ill. The swelling in her belly which she had prayed so desperately was a growing child was most probably ovarian or uterine cancer. As Mary slipped in and out of consciousness the courtiers who had danced attendance at her door melted away. They joined the hasty ride from London towards Hatfield, ready to ally themselves to the new source of power and patronage. All her life Elizabeth was to remember her unease at this precipitate turning from the dying monarch to court the coming one.

And she was the coming queen. She was Henry's legal heir, after the deaths of Edward and Mary, as declared by the succession statute of 1544. There was, however, the small matter of an earlier statute when her father had declared her and Mary 'preclosed, excluded, and barred to the claim'.[13] This remained unrepealed, although Mary had taken steps to legitimize herself. Elizabeth chose to rely on the 1544 statute for her legitimacy, but the insecurity she felt when faced with the claim of her cousin Mary Stuart remained. She was however the popular choice, the only choice as far as the people were concerned. The dying Mary had even given her blessing, urged on by Philip of Spain, who feared Protestantism less than the imperial ambitions of France. She had sent two members of her council to Elizabeth to let her know 'it was her intention to bequeath to her the royal crown, together with all the dignity that she was then in possession of by right of inheritance'. Elizabeth's reply illustrated partly why the long-suffering Mary found her younger sister so exasperating to deal with: 'I am very sorry to hear of the Queen's illness; but there is no reason why I should thank her for her intention to give me the crown of this kingdom. For she has neither the power of bestowing it upon me, nor can I lawfully be deprived of it, since it is my peculiar and hereditary right.'[14]

So it was that on the 17 November 1558, a Thursday, Elizabeth learned the waiting was over and her father's crown was finally hers. She sank to her knees, apparently momentarily overcome, breathing deeply with emotion. But with the breadth of her learning and her cool self-possession she was not long lost for words: '*A domino factum est illud, et est mirabile in oculis meis!*' was her first utterance as queen. Quoting part of Psalm 118 she had declared, 'This is the doing of the Lord and it is marvellous in my eyes.'[15]

Fortuitously Parliament happened to be sitting that day, and when the Lords were brought the news of Mary's death, in measured tones 'with joint consent of the whole assembly' they declared 'the Lady Elizabeth might forthwith be proclaimed Queen'.[16] This was broadcast by the herald-at-arms at the front door of the Palace of Westminster, at the cross in Cheapside and at other prominent places in the city. Weary of bloodshed, fearful of foreign wars, weakened by bad harvests and disease, the people welcomed the new queen. But there was foreboding too as to what the future would bring. Another female monarch, after the last disastrous experiment, seemed to be too risky when England was in need of inspired and powerful leadership. There was a profound cultural and religious acceptance that it was unnatural, indeed impossible, for women to be successfully in command. But the prospect of marriage for Elizabeth also brought the real fear, acted out in Mary's reign, of alliance with a dominant foreign power. It was not surprising there were mixed emotions beyond the general feeling of relief. Sir John Hayward,* an early historian, wrote: 'Generally, the rich were fearful, the wise careful, the honestly-disposed doubtful, the discontented and the desperate, and all such whose desires were both immoderate and evil, joyful, as wishing trouble, the gate of spoil.'[17]

And trouble was what everyone expected. The transition from old monarch to new was inherently uncertain. Diplomatically too, it upset the status quo between nations. The death of a stalwart Catholic during a period of fomenting religious debate changed the

---

* Sir John Hayward (?1564–1627) a historian who was imprisoned by Elizabeth for offending her with his dedication to the Earl of Essex in his history of Henry IV (1599), suggesting Essex was likewise capable of usurping the crown. Hayward subsequently wrote a lively account of the early part of Elizabeth's reign.

tensions between the ancient neighbours and rivals, France, Spain, Scotland and England.

The fiery Scottish Protestant John Knox was also to remember 1558 as a year of particular significance. His tract *The First Blast of the Trumpet Against the Monstrous Regiment of Women* was published, with unfortunate timing, just as Elizabeth came to the throne. By monstrous regiment he meant unnatural government and his blast was directed against the women rulers in Europe at the time of his writing whom he saw as implacable enemies of the reformed religion: Mary I of England and the Scottish regent Mary of Guise.* Unfortunately, the new Queen of England who could have been his most powerful ally was instead greatly offended. She did not find it amusing to be hectored in his main argument: 'to promote a Woman to bear rule, superiority, dominion, or empire above any Realm is repugnant to Nature; contrary to God, a thing most contrarious to his revealed will and approved ordinance, and finally, it is the subversion of all good Order, of all equity and justice'.[18]

An intemperate and gifted preacher, Knox was barred from returning from Geneva to England to resume his preaching career. He wrote to Elizabeth trying to ingratiate himself into her favour but even that letter turned into a rant on this most sensitive of subjects, and he never recanted his anti-woman stand, accepting the consequences of his inflexible principles: 'My First Blast has blown from me all my friends in England.'[19] Instead he returned to Scotland in 1559, the most powerful and vociferous opponent of Catholic and French influence, and the mouthpiece of Scottish Calvinist conscience. He remains to this day a brooding, implacable and self-righteous symbol of the Scottish Reformation.

Knox's view of the natural and divine order of things, with woman subservient to man, was a commonly accepted one. His stance was uncompromising and his language colourful, but he was not saying anything new. The lower orders knew of woman's inferiority through the traditions of their lives and the discrepancy between the sexes in simple brute force. The educated aristocracy

---

* The French queen, Catherine de Medici, was yet to assume full regency and exercise her considerable authority and guile in the religious wars which convulsed France.

was imbued with the necessity for this human hierarchy from their readings of classical authors, like Plato and Aristotle, and the thundering metaphors of the Bible. Did not God say to Eve, 'I will greatly multiply thy sorrow and thy conception; in sorrow thou shalt bring forth children; and thy desire shall be to thy husband, and he shall rule over thee'?[20] In fact the mortality rate of women in childbirth made it clear that they were the more expendable half of the species, that God and nature put a lower value on womankind.

The male was the norm and the female a deviation, the mysterious, less adequate 'other'. For Elizabeth Tudor and Mary Stuart these were accepted philosophical, theological, legal and medical truths that permeated the way the world was interpreted and relationships between people understood. Everything these young women read and were taught informed them of their intellectual and moral limitations and the narrowness of their vision. Classical and biblical texts were ever-present in the Renaissance mind; the myths a ready source of reference. The scientific humanism of Aristotle was highly influential. He had no doubt of the right order of things: 'Man is active, full of movement, creative in politics, business and culture. The male shapes and moulds society and the world. Woman, on the other hand, is passive. She is matter waiting to be formed by the active male principle. Of course the active elements are always higher on any scale, and more divine.' Not only endowed with more of the best qualities, man was also closer to God.

In classical Greece, women were seen as perpetual minors: worse off even than the disregarded Victorian child, they were exhorted to be neither seen nor heard. A woman's name was not given in public unless she was dead or of ill repute. In Pericles's famous funeral speech, Thucydides set out the aspirations of womankind: 'Your great glory is not to be inferior to what God has made you, and the greatest glory of a woman is to be less talked about by men, whether they are praising you or criticising you.'[21] Silence best became her.

This was the philosophical inheritance that informed both Elizabeth and Mary's view of what it was to be a sixteenth-century woman. Mary's often quoted saying was, 'The best woman was only the best of women.' Elizabeth, while cleverly using her perceived incapacity as a woman to dramatic effect in grand speeches and diplomatic letters, nevertheless in her irony reflected a profound and universally held truth when she spoke in these terms to her Commons: 'The weight and greatness of this matter [their request that she should marry] might cause in me, being a woman wanting both wit and memory, some fear to speak and bashfulness besides, a thing appropriate to my sex.'[22] These were the prejudices they had to overcome.

In the most commonly held myth of the birth of Athena, the goddess of war and wisdom springs from the head of her father, Zeus, fully formed, without any contribution from her mother. In this way, the necessarily male source of all that is active and intellectually pre-eminent is not diluted by the female. By stressing all her life her relation to her father, Elizabeth claimed not only some of the lustre of this Tudor Zeus but perhaps also tried to distance herself from the perceived weaknesses of her mother's (and all women's) femininity: duplicity, moral deficiency and treachery.

Both Elizabeth I and Mary Queen of Scots were of course regnant queens, monarchs in their own right, ordained by God. A female monarch was in a different relationship with the world: she had a public, political and spiritual contract as ruler of her people, while her personal and private relationship as a woman made her naturally dependent on the male. Elizabeth at least was able to counteract the perceived weaknesses of her sex with the certainty that as a queen she was divinely chosen above all men, 'by His permission a body politic, to govern'.[23] This confidence and certainty she could bolster with the knowledge that she had more intellectual and executive competence than almost anyone of her acquaintance.

Mary's sense of herself as queen had been with her from the dawning of her consciousness. It was never disputed or tested, as was Elizabeth's. This awareness of her pre-eminence was her companion through life, something taken for granted, the responsibilities to which she did not apply much profound thought nor, in the end, much value. However, philosophers as various as Knox and Aristotle considered even the God-ordained female ruler to be an aberration of the natural order, a phenomenon that could only bring inevitable disorder and strife to the realm. It was a measure perhaps of Elizabeth's sensitivity to this pervasive point of view that made her react so uncompromisingly against the author of *The First Blast of the Trumpet Against the Monstrous Regiment of Women.*

But she was assailed too by a potentially more serious discredit than merely being the wrong sex. Just as the death of her sister Mary I transformed Elizabeth's destiny, so too it altered the course of the life and aspirations of the youthful Queen of Scots. Catholic Europe could not accept Henry VIII's Act of Supremacy and considered his only legal wife to have been Catherine of Aragon. Given this fundamentalist approach, Elizabeth was undoubtedly a bastard born to a royal mistress not to a wife. Consequently much of Europe considered the more direct legitimate heir to be Mary Queen of Scotland and Dauphine of France.

This fact caused excitement and consternation abroad. Philip II of Spain, acting from pragmatic and political, rather than religious, principles feared his loss of influence in England especially since France seemed to be establishing an increasing presence in Scotland. Even before the death of his wife he had manoeuvred himself into position as a possible husband for her sister. While Mary I had lived, Spain had been an influential ally, but Elizabeth had not the slightest intention of continuing this relationship by accepting him as a husband for herself.

However, within the triangular tension that maintained a certain balance between England, Spain and France, an outright rejection of Philip would be impolitic. By evading his offer for as long as possible, therefore, Elizabeth could ingeniously sidestep an unequivocal rejection. Then she invoked precedence and the law by pointing out that for her to marry her widowed brother-in-law was no different in fundamentals from the marriage her father had made with his widowed sister-in-law, Catherine of Aragon. As had been so crucially argued at the time as the basis of her father's split with Rome, this was a relationship contrary to biblical law. To accept Philip would in effect be to deny her own legitimacy.

But it was in the French court, within the grandiose schemes of King Henri II and the Guise family, that the death of the Queen of England raised the greatest ambitions. With Mary as their tool, her uncles and Henri decided to claim the title Queen of England and Ireland for the house of Valois, and quarter Mary's arms with those of France, Scotland and England. At this time France was seen as distinctly the more powerful country, England as the weakened neighbour under threat. This was particularly marked with the recent loss of Calais and the accession of another woman to a throne already undermined by disastrous female rule. This act of acquisitiveness was not initiated by Mary, but her acceptance and over-riding pursuit of it altered her destiny for ever. It gave her a compelling idea of herself as rightful heir to the English crown, an aspiration she maintained throughout her life. In the end it was a presumption which cost her that life, and this aggressive early claim on Elizabeth's throne flung down the gauntlet.

Traditionally English monarchs claimed nominal dominion over France. Mary, however, as Dauphine of France and Queen of Scotland, both England's old enemies, was in dangerous territory. To claim England and Ireland as her realms too was considered an insult to Elizabeth, not least because it publicly rehearsed all the hurtful insecurities of her cousin's anxious youth. All those whispered calumnies she had endured during the wilderness years were given a kind of legitimacy of their own. Mary's claim implied that Elizabeth's mother was a whore not a wife; that Elizabeth herself was a bastard child and not the legitimate daughter of the King of England; that she had no claim on a divine right to rule but instead had usurped another's.

Little over a year later, in the proclamation of her peace treaty with France and Scotland, Elizabeth diplomatically accepted, 'that the title to this kingdom injuriously pretended in so many ways by the Queen of Scotland has not proceeded otherwise than from the ambitious desire of the principal members of the House of Guise'. And she went on to patronize Mary and her husband François for their youthful folly: 'the King, who by reason of his youth ... the Queen of Scots, who is likewise very young ... have [not] of themselves imagined and deliberated an enterprise so unjust, unreasonable and perilous'.[24] But these judicious, diplomatic words masked a more troubling recognition that the tacit had been made explicit; the challenge once made could not now be undone.

The earliest authoritative history, written by Camden, recognized the train of events set off by such over-reaching ambition: 'in very deed from this Title and Arms, which, through the perswasion of the Guises, Henry King of France had imposed upon the Queen of Scots being now in her tender age, flowed as from a Fountain all the Calamities wherein she was afterwards wrapped'. The protagonists were henceforth acutely aware of each other. There were such networks of vested interests surrounding both queens that gossip and intrigue and misrepresentation found their way into every discussion where direct dealing would have been less divisive: 'For hereupon Queen Elizabeth bare both Enmity to the Guises, and secret Grudge against [Mary]; where the subtile Malice of men on both sides cherished . . .'[25]

The crowning of the new Queen of England needed to be quickly done, but at an auspicious time too. The country was impoverished by injudicious wars, humiliated by the loss of Calais, vulnerable on the Scottish border and confused and suspicious after the reversals of religious dogma during the previous two reigns. Elizabeth's potential as a queen was unknown but her popularity among her people was certainly growing. Since her accession she had been the centre of intense activity at Hatfield with the selection of advisers and discussions of policy, but within the week, she began her progress to London. People travelled many miles out of the city to greet her. Her reign began as it so distinctively would continue, with a lively interest in and concern for her people exhibited in an exceptional common touch:

> All her faculties were in motion, and every motion seemed a
> well guided action; her eye was set upon one, her ear listened
> to another, her judgement ran upon a third, to a fourth she

addressed her speech; her spirit seemed to be everywhere, and yet so entire in herself, as it seemed to be nowhere else. Some she pitied, some she commended, some she thanked, at others she pleasantly and wittily jested, condemning no person, neglecting no office; and distributing her smiles, looks, and graces so [artfully], that thereupon the people again redoubled the testimonies of their joys.[26]

A few days later, on 28 November, Elizabeth took possession of the city in style. Alone in her carriage, surrounded by horsemen and the trappings of monarchy, she entered through Cripplegate, to be greeted by fluttering banners of the guilds and excited Londoners hanging from the windows and pushing through the narrow lanes. At the gate to the city she mounted her own horse, on this occasion a striking grey. Elizabeth, dressed in purple velvet, was skilled as a horsewoman and graceful in the saddle. This majestic spectacle of their new queen on horseback was glamorized further by the first sight of her Master of the Queen's Horse, riding just behind her on a magnificent black charger.

An excellent judge of horseflesh, Lord Robert Dudley always made sure he had a mount that equalled his own physical splendour. Elizabeth's friend from her youth, and a lifetime favourite, was a tall, powerful, handsome man, probably the best horseman in England and one of the most ambitious of an ambitious line. Elizabeth's first biographer pointed out that her 'rare and Royal Clemency' meant she had 'heaped Honours upon him, saving his life, whose Father would have Her destroyed'.[27] In fact the consummate ability and ambition of the Dudleys was akin to that of the Guises but, unlike the French, the English peers were strong enough to chop them down. And when the hated Lord Robert was too well loved by the queen for them to harm him, Elizabeth was clever enough to keep him ultimately in check herself.

To all who hailed her from the crowd, Elizabeth exhibited the authority and gift of attention that had so distinguished her in her dealings with her subjects so far. A salty humour and an air of God-given majesty seemed to her eager people to be united in

Elizabeth Tudor in irresistible combination. She indulged in the kind of direct dialogue and repartee which the French court never encouraged in their monarchs. The Tower was her final destination and as she entered the dark stone portal, she recalled the memories of the last time she had been there as a prisoner, frightened for her life. With genuine emotion and a natural appreciation for dramatic peripeteia she addressed the people around her: 'Some have fallen from being Princes of this land, to be prisoners in this place; I am raised from being prisoner in this place, to be Prince of this land', and she thanked God for her elevation.[28]

Even a devout Catholic observer, like the Italian Schifanoya,* with a natural bias against her, was in no doubt about Elizabeth's appeal: '. . . the Queen, by frequently showing herself in public, giving audience to all who would wish for it, and using every mark of great graciousness towards every one, daily gains favour and affection from all her people'.[29] Her ability to unite magisterial grandeur with informality was at the heart of her unique attraction to even her humblest subjects. It also discomfited her enemies. The Spanish ambassador related with disapproval how, on her return from the Tower, Elizabeth caught sight of Catherine Parr's brother, the Marquis of Northampton, watching from a window. He was suffering from one of the periodic malarial fevers which afflicted most of the populace then. The queen pulled her horse out of the procession and rode up to his window and spent a good time commiserating with him about his health, 'in the most cordial way in the world'.[30]

But there was still a general uneasiness as to what sort of monarch she would make. When she succeeded to the throne no one was certain even quite what form her religious policy would take. There was a national longing for a strong wholly English king. Despite her many good personal qualities and the great swell of popular support with which she began her rule, Mary I's reign had been disastrous. Now people wondered if Knox and Calvin, the Classical philosophers and the Bible were all correct in deploring a woman

---

* Schifanoya, resident in London at the time, was the author of some descriptive and lively dispatches to the Spanish court in Brussels.

raised beyond her natural estate to be a ruler over men. What if Elizabeth, with all her well-known virtues, was to fail as calamitously as her sister? There was a natural optimism at the prospect of this new reign after the miseries of the last, but everyone from her greatest ministers of state to her lowliest subjects agreed Queen Elizabeth had to marry, and marry quickly. A king was desperately needed, first as her consort, the steadying hand on the tiller of this vast ship of state, and then as the progenitor of a male heir to secure the succession.

Whom she would marry was one of the major topics of gossip and at times it seemed that any man of noble enough birth was mooted as the chosen one. Apart from Philip II of Spain and Crown Prince Eric of Sweden, there was the Earl of Arundel, although court chatter suggested also younger, more romantic possibilities: 'a very handsome youth, 18 or 20 years of age* . . . because at dances and other public places she prefers him more than any one else'.[31] But then, it was said, there was also that fine looking young nobleman, Sir William Pickering, still in exile in France because of his religion: the general speculation and excitement was palpable. No one seemed to take seriously Elizabeth's own often expressed contentment with the spinster state. In fact, in her first speech before Parliament she could not have made it plainer. She was married to her kingdom with all the advantages that conferred on her people. 'In the end this shall be for me sufficient: that a marble stone shall declare that a queen, having reigned such a time, lived and died a virgin.'[32]

Equally serious and compelling to Elizabeth-watchers during the first months of her reign was the subject of religion. She was known to have been brought up in the reformed religion alongside her brother Edward, but her exact beliefs and her intentions so far as the nation's spiritual leadership were concerned were far from clear. Protestant exiles were beginning to stream back into the country, expecting a return to the pre-Marian state of radical reform. Her Catholic subjects and the Catholic states watched anxiously. When

---

* Possibly Charles Howard, a handsome courtier born in 1536 who became Lord Chamberlain and Lord Admiral and eventually was rewarded with the earldom of Nottingham in 1597.

necessary Elizabeth was a master of equivocation. Never was this more evident than in her stance on religion. As Francis Bacon famously said of her, she did not choose to make windows into men's souls and her soul was conveniently adaptable, and naturally more conservative than any of her closest advisers.

Court life had revived within the month. Having been secluded for so long, careful to be seen as modest, scholarly and not overly ambitious, Elizabeth now joined her courtiers, feasting and dancing into the early morning. Her physical vitality reminded the older ones present of her father when a young man; but unlike him, her energy and physical fitness lasted well into late middle age when she still could hunt and dance her noblemen to a standstill. Elizabeth began that Christmas to exhibit something of her capacity for epic enjoyment. In another dispatch, Schifanoya was rather disapproving: 'The Court is held at Westminster, and they are intent on amusing themselves and on dancing till after midnight,'[33] he sniffily reported to the Mantuan ambassador at the court of Philip II in Brussels. A month later he was deploring 'the levities and unusual licentiousness' at Elizabeth's court, refusing to detail the profanities acted out on the feast of the Epiphany, traditionally Twelfth Night, when mummers dressed up as crows wearing the habits of cardinals, or as asses in bishops' regalia and wolves in abbots' clothing. While the court and the young queen greeted this ribaldry with wild laughter, our devout Italian observer was not amused at the wider implications as to Elizabeth's intentions towards the true religion: 'I will consign it to silence.'[34]

The timing of the coronation was of crucial moment. With the implicit threat from the French with Mary Queen of Scots' claim to the English throne in their pocket, and the obdurate insistence of two popes that Elizabeth was illegitimate, it seemed politic to claim her crown as soon as possible. By then it was well-established law, 'that the crown once worn quite taketh away all Defects whatsoever'.[35] But these new Elizabethans had a complicated relationship with the supernatural. A teeming spirit world coexisted with the material, and divination, astrology, alchemy and other esoteric beliefs flourished as part of the natural sciences. Nostradamus was closely consulted for his prophecies (Catherine de Medici, the mother-in-law of Mary Queen of Scots, was a particularly fervent devotee). According to this seer, 1559 was an inauspicious year: to anyone who could read or was susceptible to tavern gossip there was not much better to be hoped for than 'divers calamities, weepings and mournings' and 'civil sedition'[36] which would sweep the land. It was not the best omen for the beginning of the reign of another woman and it added to the atmosphere of anxious uncertainty.

Lord Robert Dudley was entrusted with a mission to seek out Dr John Dee, a remarkable and learned man, who was to become Elizabeth's own consultant philosopher and who numbered astrology amongst his many accomplishments. Unlike Nostradamus with his mysticism, Dr Dee was known for his more scientific approach to divination by mapping the positions of the planets. His task was to draw up a horoscope of the most auspicious day and time for Elizabeth's coronation, the formal birth of her reign. Apparently the best astrological augury pointed to 15 January 1559, with Jupiter, the chief god of the planetary system, positioned satisfactorily in Aquarius, to signify a universality to this Jovian power and Mars, the planet of war and assertive action, placed in indomitable Scorpio. That date of greatest promise was what the queen accepted.

The Christmas of 1558 was even more busy than usual as everyone prepared for the coronation, working 'day and night both on holidays and week days'.[37] There was such a run on crimson silk and cloth of gold and of silver that any sale of it was embargoed until Elizabeth had made her choice for herself and her household. Her noblemen and women were determined to cut a dash and make their mark. With a new reign there was much insecurity and jostling for position and preferment. This was the greatest opportunity for dressing up and showing off, parading one's wealth or influence, or the wealth and influence to which one aspired. It was a chance to catch the royal eye.

Across the English Channel cloth of gold was in similarly short supply. Mary was caught up in the flurry of preparations for another grand celebration at court. Only nine months after her own magnificent wedding, she was to be one of the leading guests at the wedding of the king's second daughter Princess Claude, with whom she had grown up. This girl was not yet twelve years old and was marrying the nominal head of the Guise family, Charles, the young Duc de Lorraine. This was yet another triumph for his uncle the Duc de Guise, 'le Balafré', whose family consolidated further its position at the heart of the French royal family.

Again no expense was to be spared. In a country still struggling under the levies of war, the young duke spent nearly 200,000 crowns, raised in taxes from his people, on the wedding and the week-long jousting and masquerades which were traditional accompaniments to such regal nuptials. Part of his expenditure was on the livery of cloth of gold and silver for his team of twelve jousters and the matching eight or nine dresses of extravagant construction for the main female guests. Mary was presented with one of these creations, richly embroidered in gold and silver and lined with lynx fur against the January weather. There were countless other beautiful gowns offered as gifts to the ladies of the court.

This display of ostentatious wealth and munificence was commented on even by the worldly-wise Venetian ambassador. Mary herself could not have been oblivious to the grandeur and self-confidence of her family inheritance exhibited at every possible occasion. United in her youthful person was the pride and valour of the Guises with the God-given pre-eminence as both a Stuart queen and – she hoped – a queen of the house of Tudor. This powerful dynastic mix was further enhanced through marriage with the mighty Valois, royal family of France. Born to all this, it was understandable if such a young queen had a share of the hubris of those she had grown up amongst. It made it difficult for her to recognize that even such certainty as her right to be the Queen of Scotland, the kingdom she valued least of all, was not immutable.

Perhaps the same astrological phenomena Dr Dee used were pored over by French diviners looking for auspicious signs, for this marriage was solemnized on 22 January just a week after the coronation of Elizabeth as the new Queen of England.

Elizabeth's coronation managed to be both a grand spectacle and yet intimately involving of her subjects. This ability to combine 'a superb show'[38] with a certain informality at great state occasions seems to have been a characteristic peculiar to the English at the time, differentiating them from the Italians and the French. A perceptive Italian observer in his eyewitness account commented on this, not entirely favourably: 'the English having no Masters of the Ceremonies ... and still less caring about formalities'[39] seemed to rely less on pomp and ceremonial. He thought the cheery way Elizabeth answered back to the jocular crowds who clamoured for her after her coronation was equally deplorable. This informality and sensitivity to the popular mood was to appear to her Catholic observers to extend even into her attitude to religious worship and allow a fatal backsliding, they feared, to her brother's radicalism.

This ability to unite grandeur with a genuine common touch was memorably displayed in Elizabeth's state entry into London on the Saturday afternoon, the day before her coronation. The sky was dull with heavy snow clouds, in fact some snow even fell on the waiting crowds, some of whom had been out all night 'their untired patience never spent, eyther with long expecting (some of them from a good part of the night before) or with unsatiable beholding of the Ceremonies of that day'.[40] There was thick mud everywhere, brought on by the rain and churned up by the increased traffic of carts and horses, and each householder had taken it upon himself to strew sand and gravel in front of his house to make the going less difficult. The whole court was present and so brilliantly arrayed the weather hardly mattered. They 'so sparkled with jewels and gold collars that they cleared the air'.[41]

Her court preceeded her on horseback, numbering about a thousand, one eyewitness estimated. Then Elizabeth herself finally arrived in an open carriage entirely upholstered in gold. She was dressed in cloth of gold and on her head over her unembellished hair she wore the simple gold crown of a princess studded with precious stones. Her hands held nothing but her gloves. Around her were her footmen in their crimson velvet jerkins with the white rose of York on their chests and the red Lancastrian rose on their backs. They wore too the letters E R in bold silver gilt relief, the first time the crowd had seen their new queen's insignia.

Behind her carriage rode Lord Robert Dudley, resplendent on his fine horse, followed by the Lord Chamberlain and the lords of her Privy Chamber. At the Tower Elizabeth stopped the cavalcade. So deeply impressed had she been by the terror of her two months imprisonment there, and so struck by the subsequent transfiguration of her life, that once more she felt moved to make a heartfelt speech thanking God for delivering her from that place: as 'he had delivered Daniell from the lyones denne' so he had 'preserved her from those dangers wherwith shee was both invironed and overwhelmed, to bring her to the joye and honour of that daye'.[42] On her first formal entry into London as queen at the end of November, Elizabeth had expressed a similar gratitude to God for her deliverance from that place. Her tenacity of mind and loyalty of feeling meant that she revisited many times in her speeches the trials of her past as well as the triumphs. In this way she involved her people in an act of sympathetic imagination and in her lifetime created her own biography for them to share.

What struck the commentators who watched her stately progress through the city was the attentiveness and light-heartedness of her manner to everyone who called out or approached her. She was quick-witted and could be alternately funny and moving in her ripostes to the crowd. Her progress was leisurely; she kept on stopping to receive blessings, appeals and posies of flowers from even the poorest and humblest of her subjects. Her carriage became filled with modest bunches of rosemary and anything remotely flower-like that might have struggled to life through the January frosts. Being short-sighted, Elizabeth had to draw especially close to see those who spoke to her or to accept the gifts she was offered and this added to the sense of attentiveness and intimacy which so charmed the crowds. An eyewitness recalled: 'her grace, by holding up her hands and merry countenance to such as stood far off, and most tender and gentle language to those that stood nigh to her grace, did declare herself no less thankfully to receive her people's goodwill than they lovingly offered it to her'.[43]

A number of tableaux were acted out for her on her progress, each of which symbolized an aspect of England's history and the people's hopes for Elizabeth's reign. At each was hung a painting of specially composed verses explaining the meaning of the pageant in both Latin and English and, as the queen approached, a child stood forward to recite in English. So excitable were the crowds and noisy the bands of musicians that accompanied each set piece that the queen asked for quiet so that the child could be heard.

Elizabeth's face was closely watched as she listened, nodding and smiling, before thanking the child graciously and turning to the crowd with encouraging words. No one was inclined to call her a great beauty. Elizabeth's colouring was much admired; the pale skin and reddish gold hair were considered closer to perfection than dark hair and olive skin, but her face was thought rather too long, as was her nose with its 'rising in the middest',[44] for classical beauty. Her eyes though were strikingly dark like her mother's, and full of intelligence and humour. They had the largeness and the sweetness of expression of the very short-sighted. But what set her apart from all others was the vitality and force of her character and mind. 'Her vertues were such as might suffice to make an Aethiopian beautifull',[45] where an 'Aetheopian' was seen by one of her earliest chroniclers as an example of someone as exotic and rebarbative as it was possible for a late sixteenth-century mind to imagine.

As the queen approached Gracechurch Street she came upon a tableau set within a triumphal arch, complete with battlements, and a three-tiered stage. Meant to evoke the union of the houses of York and Lancaster, the first tier supported two children representing Henry VII sitting with his wife Elizabeth, their hands joined in matrimony, the king clothed in the red rose of Lancaster and his wife in the white rose of York. Above them the two rose stems twined into one which flowered round the figure of Henry VIII, with his queen Anne Boleyn beside him. Both of these were represented also by children richly dressed and crowned, with a pomegranate between them, symbol of their blessed fertility in producing the precious Elizabeth, and each carrying sceptres, in an obvious reference to Elizabeth's mother's legitimacy as Queen of England. The rose stem wound on up to the top tier where sat another child representing 'the Queen's most excellent Majesty,

Elizabeth, now our most dread Sovereign Lady'.[46] The whole edifice was festooned with red and white roses, the royal arms of England and various trophies and symbols. The child orator interpreted it to the queen as a longing in the people for unity and concord: just as Henry Tudor's marriage with Elizabeth of York had healed the wounds of the War of the Roses, so this new Elizabeth would heal the divisions over the succession and religion of the previous reigns, for now 'she is the only heir of Henry VIII, which came of both Houses as the knitting up of concord'.[47]

Another tableau had characterized Elizabeth as Deborah, 'The Judge and Restorer of Israel'.[48] Deborah was the prophetess and judge of the Old Testament who was used as a convenient example of God confounding his own dictates in sending a woman successfully to rule over men. But by this exemplar, Elizabeth was also reminded, 'that it behoveth both men and women so ruling, to use advice of good counsel'.[49]

As the day drew to its triumphant close, a final symbolic act from the last of the tableaux involved a Bible, translated into English, let down to her on a silken cord by a child representing Truth. Elizabeth, ever mindful of the visually dramatic, kissed both her hands as she reached out to receive it and then kissed the Bible itself and clasped it to her breast. She promised the expectant crowd she would study and learn from it, but her enthusiastic embrace of a Protestant Bible promised more.

And so Elizabeth left the city with cheers and blessings in her ears. The extraordinary emotion of the day was like a common exhalation of the anxiety and fear of the last years replaced with an inspiration of hope for what was to come: 'some with plausible acclamations, some with sober prayers, and many with silent and true-hearted teares, which were then seen to melt from their eyes'.[50]

The ancient ritual and solemnity of the coronation on the following day, a Sunday, was charged with even greater moment by the question everyone at home and abroad wanted answered: how would Elizabeth's preferences on religion be revealed?

Nowhere was this more keenly monitored than in France where Henri II, with his eye firmly on his daughter-in-law, Mary Queen of Scots, and the opportunity she presented of further advancing his empire, was attempting to enlist the pope as a powerful ally in his plan to outlaw Elizabeth and annex England. The grandest of Spanish ambassadors was Count de Feria who, in his report to Philip II, saw nothing but doom to Spanish hopes, to the world, if France got its way. 'Whenever the King of France finds means in Rome to get this woman declared a heretic, together with her bastardy, and advances his own claim',[51] Feria believed, France would be able to walk into England, so debilitated was its exchequer and so disabled by having yet another woman ruler, this time of dubious legitimacy. All the French needed was the pope's authority assuring the support of the English Catholics and the seductive substitute queen, Mary Stuart, as the rightful heir: already he had the one and was working on providing the other.

Elizabeth and all her court made the journey from Westminster Hall to Westminster Abbey on foot. The great church, rebuilt by Henry III as a soaring monument to faith three centuries before, dominated the skyline and drew thousands of the new queen's subjects from the grandest to the lowliest to witness and participate in this ancient rite. Elizabeth walked in procession to her coronation along a carpet of purple cloth which seemed to melt like snow and disappear the moment her feet had passed, as the crowd grabbed what they could, tearing and cutting it away, for any scrap as a memento of this auspicious day.

Tall and slim, Elizabeth followed the procession of lords and ladies of the court and her bishops, her face pale, her hair worn loose and unadorned over her shoulders as a symbol of virginity. As she arrived at the abbey all the church bells in the city were ringing out in a clamour of celebration. Then Elizabeth mounted the high platform raised in front of the altar that exhibited her clearly to everyone and the question was asked of the people whether they wished to have her as their queen. The roared 'YES' was followed by a cacophony of 'organs, fifes, trumpets, and drums playing, the bells also ringing, it seemed as if the world were come to an end'.[52]

The coronation Mass proceeded to its centuries-old pattern of prayer and elaborate ritual lasting several hours, with Bishop Ogle-thorpe of Carlisle officiating. Resplendent on her throne, Elizabeth retained all aspects of the ceremony and Mass, except for the crucial elevation of the Host. This was a rite which she had already made clear was distasteful to her; she had ordered once before the same bishop to desist from elevating the Host at his Christmas Day mass and when he had refused she had withdrawn from the service.[53] Now at her coronation, when the Host was elevated, with all the concomitant meanings of transubstantiation, a doctrine considered clearly idolatrous by the Protestant reformers, the queen once more withdrew. She only returned to her throne once the offending ritual was over.

There was one other modification that would have given her bishops and their Catholic supporters pause for thought. At the end of the coronation ceremony itself, just prior to the Mass, the monarch accepted a ritual homage from her bishops and peers. Traditionally the archbishops headed the queue in order of senior-ity, followed by the bishops and then the lords. This was the order followed by Elizabeth's father and the founder of the dynasty, her grandfather Henry VII. It was also followed closely by her sister Mary. Her brother Edward, however, accepted homage first from the Protector, the Duke of Somerset, followed by the Archbishop of Canterbury and then all the bishops and peers together with no distinction between his lords temporal or spiritual. Elizabeth instituted a significant change in accepting homage first from her officiating bishop but 'then the Lordes went up to her Grace kneel-ing upon their knees and kissed her Grace. And after the Lordes had done, the Bishops came one after another kneeling and kissing her Grace.'[54] This was a clear message to her bishops, and the church they represented, not to take their pre-eminence for granted.

The news travelled fast to her Continental neighbours. The Count de Feria, always full of foreboding and implacable in his dislike and suspicion of the English and 'that woman' wrote to Philip of Spain in outrage and a sense of doom: 'I had been told that the Queen [the following continued in cipher] took the holy sacrament *sub utraque specie* [both wine and bread] on the day of the coronation, but it was all nonsense. She did not take it.'[55] His spirits were lowered further when Elizabeth told him she resented the amount of money that flowed out of the country yearly for the pope's use and that she considered her bishops to be 'lazy poltroons'.[56] It did not need a Dr Dee to divine that change was going to come.

Mary, along with her father-in-law Henri and her own Guise family, was increasingly concerned about the growing strength of the reformed religion in France and the inevitable factions and unrest. A desultory peace process between Spain, France and England had already begun before Elizabeth's accession to the throne and this progressed slowly throughout the early months of her reign. Mary wrote to her mother with some of her anxieties: 'We were hoping for a peace but that is still so uncertain . . . God grant it all turns out well.'[57]

The greatest stumbling block in the peace negotiations between France and England was the emotive question of Calais. This was not helped by the insolence of the French negotiators who had stated initially: 'that they knew not how to conclude a peace with the Queen's majesty, nor to whom they should deliver Calais, but to the dolphin's wife, [Mary Queen of Scots] whom they took for Queen of England'.[58] Elizabeth's Minister of State William Cecil, who had noted this insult in a report written in his own hand, *On the Weighty Matter of Scotland,* was also concerned by Mary's manner towards Elizabeth, revealed 'by her own disdainful speech to diverse persons'.[59] The young Scottish queen's disparagement of her older cousin was not confined to her acolytes at court but rashly had been expressed to some of Elizabeth's own gentlewomen in France. Mary's impetuous nature and political naivety had already begun to store up trouble for her in the fast evolving dynamic between the two queens.

As Elizabeth left the abbey on her coronation day as Queen of England, wearing her heavy robe of cloth of gold and carrying her orb and sceptre in each hand, she was greeted by the clamour of the crowds, their voices and their musical instruments sounding, and all the city's church bells ringing. Young, alone, and with her ministers and court processing behind her, she seemed in no way overwhelmed by the solemnity and significance of the occasion. On the contrary, she was beaming so broadly, greeting everyone who greeted her, shouting witticisms back to the crowd, sharing her delight with her exuberant subjects to such an extent that at least one of her foreign, Catholic observers looked on with disapproval: 'in my opinion she exceeded the grounds of gravity and decorum'.[60]

It was remarkable indeed that Elizabeth, still young and quite inexperienced, should exhibit such confidence and revel so obviously in the acquisition of power. Her animal high spirits naturally reciprocated her own subjects' ebullience, and they loved her for it. In fact her ability to be affectionate and informal with the crowd was all the more surprising given that this was a queen who was a natural autocrat of the most self-conscious kind, in all ways the daughter of a ruthlessly autocratic father to whose burnished memory she aspired. With a penetrating intelligence and lively sympathy, Elizabeth was never to be as brutal or warlike as Henry, nor as self-serving, but she was capable of being as princely as Machiavelli could ever have prescribed in her pragmatic ability to do what was necessary.

The Spanish ambassador was surprised at how superstitious he found the English to be: 'so full of prophecies ... that nothing happens but they immediately come out with some prophecy that foretold it ... serious people and good Catholics even take notice of these things.'[61] And so as Elizabeth walked amongst them on that cold January day, what were the prognostications for her reign? Some Catholics hoped she would only rule for a short time before Philip II of Spain was once more back in power, presumably as her consort; others thought her growing popularity and the promise of change would pacify the discontented; others looked to a French Catholic alliance with Mary Queen of Scots as queen. But most rejoiced in the fact that Elizabeth was a monarch in whose veins ran unadulterated English blood. The Venetian ambassador also noted, 'She prides herself on her father and glories in him; everybody saying that she also resembles him more than [Mary I did]; and he therefore always liked her.'[62] If this imperious and clever daughter could prove herself even half the man her father was they would be happy.

Her sex was a problem, but they consoled themselves with thoughts of Deborah, and God's trust in her, of Mathilda, Boudicca, even of Cleopatra VII whose courage in holding off the Romans was well known to the educated through their reading of Horace and Plutarch. They had claimed Cleopatra's conversation rather than her beauty was the secret of her fascination. But even if there were a few precedents for successful female rulers, no one considered that a woman could effectively rule alone. One thing everyone agreed on, from her first minister, William Cecil, to the lowliest beggar in the stocks: the queen must marry, and marry soon. No one seemed to take seriously Elizabeth's professed contentment with the ring of state she had worn on her marriage finger since pledging herself to the nation at her coronation: 'bound unto an husband, which is the kingdom of England'.[63]

And so with Mary Stuart's marriage and Elizabeth Tudor's coronation the two most important celebrations of their lives marked the increasingly divergent yet interdependent paths of the Queen of Scotland and the Queen of England. The one had married her prince to pursue her destiny as a woman. The other had married her people in recognition of her destiny as a queen. Mary's status as queen also mattered greatly to her but she considered it an immutable right, somehow divorced from any real sense of self-sacrifice and responsibility. Whereas Elizabeth never doubted the awesome responsibilities of her task, 'the burden that is fallen upon me maketh me amazed'[64] were amongst the first words she spoke as queen to her Lords. The struggles, triumphs and tragedies that followed were a direct result of each woman's individual decision: the one to put the personal increasingly before the political; the other to sacrifice the personal and place her responsibilities as queen at the centre of her life.

A fatal complication ensued when Mary turned her sights on the greater crown of England, believing it her rightful inheritance and a prize worth pursuing. Elizabeth's fundamental insecurity in her own legitimacy, where the whole of Catholic Europe was ranged against her, the 'bastard child of a whore', increased the tension and emotional volatility of the issue. The complex rivalry, the feinting and parrying of their personal relationship, sprang from the challenge Mary had made for Elizabeth's throne and the unassailable legitimacy of her claim. The powerful passions this relationship engendered in each was a result of their strikingly different natures. The fact they never met allowed their rivalry to inflate in each queen's imagination, their qualities elaborated upon by ambassadors and courtiers intent on their own ambitions.

In a tradition instituted by William the Conqueror, the Champion of England on coronation day would ride up through Westminster Hall and challenge anyone who disputed the right of succession. In front of the newly crowned queen and her peers, the clatter of hooves announced the arrival of the queen's champion. Sir Edward Dymoke, the latest member of the family who for centuries had enacted this role, rode into the hall in full armour, and flung down his gauntlet, challenging anyone who questioned Elizabeth's right to the English throne. An uneasy silence fell on the assembly. No voice was raised on this day. But Elizabeth and Mary knew that the question had already been asked, that the contest was engaged, and in a more public arena, with wider repercussions for everyone.

A rivalry had been instituted that 'could not be extinguished but by Death'.[65]

CHAPTER TWO

The Disappointment of Kings

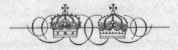

The primogenity and due of birth,
Prerogative of age, crowns, sceptres, laurels,
But by degree, stand in authentic place?
Take but degree away, untune that string,
And, hark, what discord follows!

Troilus and Cressida, act 1, scene 3

IF THE RIVALRY BETWEEN these two queens would only be resolved through death, the individual significance of their births had a certain symmetry too. Both entered the world as bitter disappointments to their fathers, and the birth of each princess was a contributory factor in the untimely death of a parent. It was all a matter of sex. Both fathers were kings without legitimate male heirs. Had Elizabeth not been a girl but the longed-for, expected prince it is most unlikely that her mother would ever have been executed. It is even possible that Henry's popular reputation might have rested more on his Reformation, encouraged by his independent-minded reformist Queen Anne, than on his grotesque failures as a husband and father.

In the case of Mary Queen of Scots, her birth in 1542 was followed almost immediately by her father's death. Already sick and humiliated, James V, on hearing his heir was a girl, literally turned his face to the wall like a wounded animal, and waited to die. His valedictory words showed him defeated as much by fate as by life: looking back two centuries to Marjorie Bruce, founder of the

43

Stewart dynasty, he reputedly said to the messenger bringing the news of Mary's birth: 'It cam' wi' a lass, it will gang wi' a lass.'[1] In fact, James was as poor a prophet as he was survivor. He died aged only thirty and without seeing his daughter and heir. The Stuart* dynasty, however, managed to teeter on for a further century, despite revolution and republicanism, although Scotland's absolute independence did not survive the reign of his daughter Mary.

Nine years separated these two princesses, born in neighbouring kingdoms in an outlying island of Europe. England and Scotland were small and relatively unimportant, impoverished lands, mostly under threat from the many times larger and richer Continental powers of France and Spain, and spasmodically at war with them, and with each other. The newly established and insecure Tudor dynasty was in urgent need of a male heir; the Stewarts, although an ancient race of kings, were ill-fated, desperate for a monarch who could survive to middle age and produce a strong male heir. The last five Scottish kings had been children at their accession, most of them still in the cradle. (Mary Queen of Scots and her son, James VI, were also to succeed to the Scottish throne as infants.)

The Stewarts were plagued by their history of monarchs dying violently and dying young (James I and James III were murdered and James II, a murderer himself, was blown up while watching his own cannon being fired) and they were undermined by the subsequent power of factious regents and murderous clan rivalry. When they eventually succeeded at the start of the seventeenth century to the English throne and moved south, their life expectancy improved. The dynasty's star, however, continued as mismanaged and bloody as ever it was in earlier centuries, with both Mary and her grandson, Charles I, tried and beheaded for treason.

Elizabeth was born on 7 September 1533 to a father who was already forty-one and who had longed for a healthy son during the twenty-three years of his marriage to the unimpeachable Catherine of Aragon. In despair at producing only one surviving child, Mary, born in 1516 (his other three sons and two daughters were either

---

* There is some confusion over the spelling of the dynasty. I have opted for Stewart prior to Mary's accession, and for Mary and her descendants Stuart thereafter.

stillborn or died soon after birth), Henry began to wonder if somehow his lack of male heirs was not a personal punishment by God.
He looked across to France at his main rival, François I, a chivalrous
and extravagant Renaissance king whose reign of thirty-two years
corresponded with Henry's so closely that they even died within
two months of each other, in 1547. Henry identified with this
athletic, popular, resplendent monarch whose procreative vitality
seemed gallingly superior to his own. François's fragile Queen
Claude had managed to produce seven live children, three of them
sons, before herself dying of exhaustion at twenty-four.

In an age of superstition and magic, where God's agency and
the spirit world controlled the elements and directed daily lives,
barrenness, and the lack of a son as heir, was never just a matter
of chance. There was an uneasiness in kingdoms without male heirs
that somehow the natural order of things had been disrupted and
disappointment, rupture and discord would ensue. To continue the
quote at the head of the chapter of the speech which Shakespeare
gave Ulysses on the essential patterning of the universe:

> The heavens themselves, the planets, and this centre,
> Observe degree, priority, and place,
> Insisture, course, proportion, season, form,
> Office, and custom, in all line of order:
> And therefore is the glorious planet Sol
> In noble eminence enthron'd and spher'd
> Amidst the other; whose med'cinable eye
> Corrects the ill aspects of planets evil,
> And posts, like the commandment of a king,
> Sans check, to good and bad.

In such a closely ordered world where everything had a reason, and
that usually a supernatural one, Henry feared that his virtually
barren marriage indicated he had transgressed some article of holy
writ. The words of Leviticus particularly troubled him: 'If a man
shall take his brother's wife, it is an impurity: he hath uncovered
his brother's nakedness; they shall be childless.'[2] Had he not done
precisely that in marrying Catherine, the widow of his elder brother

Arthur? But Henry was also an opportunist. Although conservative and orthodox in his own religious beliefs he cannot have failed to give thought to the Continental reformers whose disdain for the pope and evangelical zeal for an individual faith drawn directly from the Gospels gave him a different approach to his own immutable church. His troubled conscience, however, his questioning of a possibly invalid marriage, were made all the more insistent by the fact that Henry had long ago tired of his wife and found a determined replacement in an attractive, nubile, lady-in-waiting, Anne Boleyn. It was significant that this clever woman was part of the radical religious faction at court and her own conversation was as tantalising to the king as her physical charms.

Emotionally, Henry was a crass and simple man. He could be handled by any adept and resolute woman who managed to withhold from him something he desired. For more than six years Anne drew him close and reeled him out. At times he was driven almost to distraction by her seductive manner combined with her steadfast refusal to become his mistress. Henry had already produced a bastard son by Elizabeth Blount, a boy he was fond of and ennobled as Duke of Richmond and Somerset. But the prize Anne held out to the king was a legitimate son and heir. The longing to secure the succession with a male heir propelled him to marry again. So Henry put in train the momentous events which led him to sweep aside the Catholic Church and proclaim himself supreme head of the newly established Church of England. Spurred on by fear and desire, Henry drove this pragmatic revolution through Parliament. He had the support of the Protestant apologist Thomas Cranmer and his tireless executor Thomas Cromwell. His immovable Lord Chancellor Thomas More, however, paid with his life.

By the beginning of 1533, however, Anne Boleyn's long game seemed to have paid off triumphantly. Showing remarkable self-confidence and independence of mind, she had refused the considerable honour of becoming the king's mistress (having first been married off for propriety's sake to a compliant nobleman). She had the presence of mind and the boldness to play for the much higher stakes of becoming his queen. This really was a remarkable ambition given that there was already a genuinely popular possessor of that title in Queen Catherine, and divorce was not an obvious or easy option. It suggested a woman of will and vision who, through force of character, could impart that vision to others. Certainly she did not appear overawed by her evident destiny, believing that God had elevated her to this high estate in a divine intervention of a personal kind: she told the Venetian ambassador that God 'had inspired his Majesty to marry her'.[3] The poet Thomas Wyatt, probably half in love with Anne, certainly arrested in the debacle of her downfall, left a compelling image of her mysterious and self-possessed attraction. His poem envisaged her as a magical deer whom only the king could hunt, her tameness an illusion:

> Whoso list to hunt? I know where there is a hind,
> . . . .
> Who list her hunt, I put him out of doubt,
> As well as I may spend his time in vain!
> And graven with diamonds in letters plain
> There is written her fair neck round about:
> '*Noli me tangere*' [do not touch] for Caesar's I am
> And wild for to hold, though I seem tame.[4]

Anne Boleyn's trump card was the promise of fecundity. The point of a queen was to produce the male heir, ideally a number of possible heirs to ensure against disease, misfortune and sudden death. In fact, Anne's resistance to Henry's sexual desire had been overcome sometime prior to their secret marriage at the end of January 1533. By then, already a month pregnant, she had proved her fertility. Perhaps her strategic surrender was Henry's reward for ennobling her as Lady Marquess of Pembroke on the first day of September the previous year. With this honour came considerable estates and authority. Or perhaps Anne's capitulation came little over a month later, after the triumphant diplomatic meetings with the French king King François I in Calais and Boulogne which she attended as Henry's consort and where she gained gratifying recognition from this influential potentate. Whatever the timing, Anne quickly conceived and that boded well for her. Queen Catherine was much more widely loved but by 1533 she was beyond childbearing: for the people to be prepared to accept their new queen, Anne had to provide the hoped-for prince.

At her coronation the pageants stressed this contract with the people. One had Clio, muse of history, chant 'Anna comes, bright image of chastity, she whom Henry has chosen to his partner. Worthy husband, worthy wife! May heaven bless these nuptuals, and make her a fruitful mother of men-children.'[5] It was the first day of June and Anne was already almost six months pregnant. The whole of Christendom had been defied for the sake of this baby; no one seemed to doubt that it would be a boy. But childbirth was dangerous for both mother and baby. It was customary for a woman who had any property to leave, to make her will before entering the dark wood of labour for there was real uncertainty as to whether she would return. But the omens were fair: the late summer weather had been warm and sunny, the harvest was expected to be a good one, there were no epidemics or plagues to disturb the surface calm. Good order was all around: the spirits seemed appeased.

There was an underlying uneasiness and dissension, however, in all segments of society. People did not like to see their good queen Catherine, who had behaved with nobility and utmost probity throughout, so humiliated and ill-treated. Henry's subjects were largely conservative and did not care for the extreme measures he had pursued in order to satisfy his desire to marry again and produce an heir. Happy as they may have been at the thought that the excesses and corruption of the established church in England would be redressed, there was less support for so radical a reform of religion that papal authority was abandoned and spiritual power vested in the king. Certainly the pope's* excommunication of Henry in July, and the declaration that his marriage to Anne was invalid, was serious and unwelcome to a conservative and still Catholic people.

* * *

* Pope Clement VII (1523–34), a Medici prince, nephew of Lorenzo the Magnificent.

During the summer of 1533, augury and prognostication were more prolific than ever. Most significant perhaps were those of a visionary, Elizabeth Barton, known as 'the Maid of Kent', who was well known and respected for her power of prophecy. However when she began prophesying that Henry would cease to be king one month after marrying Anne Boleyn, and that in God's eyes his status as divinely ordained monarch would be immediately forfeit, there was real consternation. Many eminent churchmen and politicians, amongst them Sir Thomas More himself, considered her to have genuine spiritual authority. But such reckless courage and moral fervour was dangerous. A month after the coronation this young nun was arrested, tortured and imprisoned in the Tower. She and her associates were eventually convicted of high treason and hanged the following spring.

So with more weighty anticipation perhaps than accompanied any other royal birth either before or since, Queen Anne settled in to Greenwich, the favoured royal palace and birthplace of Henry himself, to await the event which would seal the fates of many. The expectant father had already chosen the baby's names, Edward or Henry, and had ordered the elaborate celebrations expected to honour a male heir. Anne seemed to be as certain as Henry was of the desired outcome of her pregnancy. In dismissing a book which claimed that marrying the king would literally be the death of her, she reputedly said: 'I think the book a bauble; yet for the hope I have that the realm may be happy by my issue, I am resolved to have him [the king] whatsoever might become of me.'[6]

Elizabeth's birth was not easy. She was her mother's first child and the labour, according to Anne's earliest biographer, was particularly painful: the sight of the red-faced infant lacking the prerequisite male genitalia would not immediately have replaced pain with triumphant euphoria. The same biographer mentions that the baby looked more like her father than her mother, which was less surprising given that many newborn babies seem to bear a passing resemblance to Henry VIII, whose features by that time were beginning to sink into his surrounding cheeks and multiple chins.[7]

'The King's mistress was delivered of a girl, to the great disappointment and sorrow of the King, of the Lady herself, and of others of her party, and to the great shame and confusion of physicians, astrologers, wizards, and witches, all of whom affirmed that it would be a boy,'[8] reported Chapuys, ambassador to Charles V. As a stalwart Catholic representing the Holy Roman Empire whose emperor, Charles, was the nephew of the divorced Catherine, any *schadenfreude* at the unexpected confounding of Henry's schemes was only to be expected.

The sixteenth-century mind sought significance in everything, made connections between apparently random events and attempted to bring order and understanding to chaos. Anne, confronted with her fundamental failure in bringing forth a daughter, pointed out the fortuitous circumstances of this baby's birth in an attempt to salvage some divine justification for her life from the critical flaw of her sex. She was born on the eve of the Virgin Mary's own feast day, and in a room hung with tapestries depicting the histories of the holy virgins, a room which had therefore become known as the chamber of virgins. Anne too would have grown up knowing that Saint Anne, after whom she was named, was the mother of the Virgin herself. So the symbolism of the pre-eminent Virgin, the woman elevated above all others, was associated with Elizabeth from the moment of her birth.

None of the mother's frantic reasonings, however, mitigated the outraged disappointment of the baby's father. Surely he had done all he could, endured enough penance, prayed night and morning, changed his wife for someone younger and untainted by scriptural ambiguity, even altered the tenets of Christianity. Such a blatant blighting of his hopes had to have some deeper message, and it could not be a comforting one.

Eustace Chapuys, admittedly a hostile witness, gave a verdict on Henry's disappointment which most of Catholic Europe and many of his own English subjects would have shared: 'God has entirely abandoned this King, and left him prey to his own misfortune, and to his obstinate blindness that he may be punished and completely ruined.'[9] The pageant and jousting which had been organized to celebrate the birth of a son was cancelled, although the elaborate christening and confirmation went ahead as planned three days later in the friars' church at Greenwich. But there was no disguising the general sense of disappointment underlying the ancient rituals and the lack of spontaneous enthusiasm on the streets. There were even many who were as hostile to this new princess as they were to her mother. They could not accept the sophistry which had transformed Queen Catherine from faithful wife of twenty-four years to Henry's unwitting concubine, and reduced her daughter from Princess Mary, her father's heir, to Lady Mary, her father's bastard. To these sceptics, Anne Boleyn was the impostor queen and Elizabeth her cuckoo in the nest, although the epithets used then were more frequently 'whore' and 'bastard'.

Oblivious to all these adult judgements, the baby Elizabeth was carried back from her christening to the palace and to her mother who was traditionally in seclusion until 'churched' about a month after childbirth. Certainly Henry was not expected to be present at the christening but there was no mention that he was even at Greenwich that day. As was the custom, a wet nurse was immediately found for Elizabeth, for queens of England and noblewomen generally did not feed their babies themselves. Royal and aristocratic women were mostly of value as brood mares and binding up the breasts of a new mother to staunch her milk would make her sooner able to conceive again, thereby continuing her procreative duty.

In fact by the beginning of 1534, just four months or so after Elizabeth's birth, Anne was thought to be pregnant again. But strain and anxiety were an inevitable part of the pressure to produce, a pressure which the baby Elizabeth's sex had intensified. By the late summer a miscarriage, or possibly the realization that her symptoms were due to a hysterical pregnancy, had robbed Anne and Henry again of their longed-for prince. Anne had failed twice and her hold on Henry and the throne was beginning to feel precarious.

Elizabeth spent only three months in Greenwich Palace with her mother and the court before being sent to the old palace at Hatfield, some thirty miles from London, to establish her own household under her governess Margaret, Lady Bryan. Elizabeth's day-to-day care was already the responsibility of her women attendants, with the queen's role more as visitor to the nursery, but this banishment from her mother at such a young age would not have been a conscious wrench. Elizabeth was never to live with her again.

At the same time, by orders of their father, Elizabeth's half-sister Mary was deprived of her own household and sent to become a lady-in-waiting to the new heir presumptive. The manor she had been ordered to leave had been granted to Queen Anne's brother, George Rochford, and the new governess to whom she was subject, Lady Anne Shelton, was the new queen's aunt. In this way the influence of the Boleyns extended even into Mary's most private life and could only seem to her to be all-pervasive and utterly malign. Together with the insults to her much-loved mother, whom since 1531 she had been forbidden to see, these new strictures were particularly cruel humiliations for an unhappy young woman of seventeen. She was to take these hurts, unforgiven, to her grave. Despite her loneliness and misery, however, Mary seems to have been as taken with her baby sister as anyone, commending her to their father when she was three: 'My sister Elizabeth is in good health (thanks to our Lord), and such a child toward [a forward child], as I doubt not, but your Highness shall have cause to rejoice of in time coming.'[10]

If a girl child was unwelcome as heir to a king, she did have her uses as a future bride in the strategic game of dynastic alliances. When Elizabeth was barely six months old, Henry opened negotiations with François I to see if they could reach an agreement to marry his new daughter, and currently still his heir, to Francis's third son, Charles, Duc d'Angoulême. The French and Spanish ambassadors were introduced to the baby princess who was presented in full regal apparel: '[she] was brought out to them splendidly accoutred and dressed, and in princely state, with all the ceremonial her governess could think of, after which they saw her quite undressed'.[11] The undressing of high-born infants, whose health and survival – and sex – were of strategic importance in their families' marital bartering, was a common enough procedure at the time. Nine years later, the baby Mary Queen of Scots was to be undressed in the coldest of Scottish winters to show her health to Henry VIII's envoy. Elizabeth, however, was pronounced a healthy and anatomically perfect girl but her father's demands were excessive and the marriage negotiations eventually came to nought.

As the baby Elizabeth thrived in the care of her attendants in the country, a terrible momentum was building which would catch her mother helplessly in its tide. Anne Boleyn had never been a popular queen. And she was too clever and forthright, too vivacious and sexually bold to overcome these natural prejudices against her. A French diplomat reported back from a mission to visit Henry and Anne's court in the early autumn of 1535: 'the lower people are greatly exasperated with the Queen, saying a thousand ill and improper things against her'.[12] For many years before their marriage and for a short while after, the king had been blatantly obsessed with her. A contemporary Scottish theologian, Alexander Alesius,* known for his eyewitness accounts, described the king's emotional avidity: 'so ardent was he when he had begun to form an attachment, that he could give himself no rest; so much so that when he was raving about Queen Anne and some of his friends were dissuading him from the divorce, he said he preferred the love of the Queen to half his realm'.[13]

In a society used to dynastic marriages, brokered by diplomats, and public displays of affection bounded by the etiquette of courtly love, the love-struck middle-aged man was an unsettling sight. When that ageing man was a king, ordained by God, the uneasiness grew, for here was an all-powerful being in thrall to a woman, an omniscient monarch behaving like a fool. In Henry's case, however, the obvious way to absolve that feeling of unseemliness in the spectator was to blame Anne. The harlot had somehow made him succumb to her wishes through the exercise of her powers, and those were most probably unnatural. Rumour abounded as to the nature of Anne's hold over him.

---

* Alexander Alesius (1500–65) writer and theologian. Born Alexander Alane, he became a canon of St Andrew's Cathedral but adopted the Greek name 'Alesius' (meaning 'wandering') to signify his exile from Scotland after the trauma of witnessing his Lutheran mentor, Patrick Hamilton, burned at the stake in 1528. From 1535 he was in England at the heart of the English Reformation and is valued for his lively accounts and reminiscences.

Gossip, rumour and innuendo are a powerful triad in any royal court when too much power, patronage and money circulates in a closed society of ambitious people with too little to do. In Henry's court, life was made more treacherous by the sense of the nearness of death – through sudden illness, injury or an inexplicable eclipse from royal favour. At this point in his life, Henry was a sun king turned tyrant, and his whims could be fearsome. This ever-present threat of random violence was made more unnerving by the widespread belief in the supernatural, the practice of necromancy and the ready presence in everyday life of the devil. Rumour and speculation energized idle chatter, but too easily gained a life of its own: whispered puffballs had a habit of turning into stone-shod facts. When those rumours were of bewitchment and sexual depravity then the sixteenth-century victim of these accusations had little chance of restoring any reputation for virtue and probity. She had not much better odds of escaping with her life.

The court was full also of the stories of Henry's new mistresses, one even a cousin of Anne's. There was talk of the king no longer in thrall to his wife, resentful of her temper, intelligence and assertiveness. The Venetian ambassador reported home that Henry 'was already tired to satiety of this new Queen'.[14] But the bitter accusations and estrangements were followed still by reconciliations with much merriment. Anne continued to view Catherine of Aragon's existence as a threat and her daughter Mary, whose obstinacy and flagrant rudeness to her new stepmother – whose status she refused to acknowledge – was a constant thorn. Both were a continuing barrier to her own daughter's inheritance and the further advancement of her ambitious family.

A story, aimed at revealing Anne's ruthlessness and malice, did the rounds of the court and diplomatic reports in the early summer of 1535. Anne was supposed to have paid a man to proclaim – to Thomas Cromwell and even to Henry himself – that he had had a revelation that the queen would not conceive again as long as Catherine and her daughter lived. Lives could hang on threads of trumped-up prophecy, divination and manipulative lies. And rumours could kill.

But it was not just Anne's appearance of sexual boldness which exercised her detractors; her strong evangelical leanings and active promotion of the reformed religion gained her some important enemies who were working always to find a way of diminishing, if not effacing, her influence on the king. Certainly her library was known for its inclusion of radical reform literature from the Continent and she was credited with introducing to Henry the polemical *Obedience of a Christen Man* by William Tyndale, a copy of whose English translation of the New Testament she owned soon after publication in 1534. All the chaplains she promoted to her service were evangelicals. According to Alesius, however, the interference in religious policy that focused the hostile forces against her was her instigation through Henry of the delegation sent to the German Lutheran princes in 1536. Before they had returned the trumped-up charges against her had been contrived.

In fact, Henry's ruthlessness towards the moral leaders of the opposition to his Reformation, specifically Sir Thomas More, his Lord Chancellor, and John Fisher, Bishop of Rochester, was to shock the whole of Catholic Europe. Fisher, whom the pope provocatively had made a cardinal while he was imprisoned in the Tower, was the most bold and implacable of opponents and his downfall came when he refused to take the oath of succession, which placed Elizabeth as her father's heir over Mary. Incarcerated in the Tower, both men were eventually executed in 1535, along with a number of other Catholic martyrs, as a result of a new treason act, which made 'malicious' denial of the king's title punishable by death. The bluff and hearty Good King Hal had completed his metamorphosis into the paranoid tyrant of his later years. And Anne was blamed by many for the executions. It was even possible that Henry's uneasiness at having destroyed More, once so close and admired a friend, meant he exorcised some of his guilt by blaming his wife for this too.

In this atmosphere of alarm and fear, there was a short respite for Anne, for by the end of 1535 she was pregnant again. Despite the rumour, there was no indication that harm had been done to Catherine or her daughter to ensure this pregnancy. Quite soon, however, the divorced queen was mortally ill. Although her health had been failing for a long time, when Catherine finally died in January 1536 at the age of fifty, there were the inevitable rumours that Anne had succeeded at last in having her poisoned. This story was given some credence at the time by the news that when Catherine's body was opened up they found her heart was 'black and hideous to look at' with a dark growth attached. Subsequent medical experts have stated this was much more likely to be a signature of the cancer which probably killed her.[15] The royal lack of sympathy for Catherine was evident up to and beyond death. Right to the end, she and her daughter Mary had been forbidden to see each other, in an act of petty malice. And the news of her death after much suffering was greeted by the king without any show of guilt or sorrow.

Anne and Henry celebrated in unseemly delight, with Anne – and possibly the king too – clothed from head to foot in yellow, more the symbolic colour of jealousy and betrayal than of mourning. Elizabeth, just over two years old, was taken to church in grand ceremonial 'to the sound of trumpets' and then, in her father's embrace, shown off to his courtiers.[16] Here was his legitimate heir, his actions proclaimed, although Henry still hoped to displace her with a son.

This celebration of Elizabeth's place in the succession, however, was to be short-lived. Rather than consolidating Anne's position, Catherine's death left the queen horribly exposed. While Catherine lived Henry would have found it very difficult to cast Anne off in order to marry for a third time. Now that protection was gone. There was a powerful argument, maintained by the conservative Catholic faction and which many in the general populace found sympathetic, that Henry's marriage to Anne had never been legal and now, with his only true wife dead, he was an unencumbered widower who was free to marry again. But although the momentum was building inexorably against her, Anne still felt a certain optimism and relief: her new pregnancy brought hope. Her personal wheel of fortune she believed must have revolved by now. This time her body had to be nurturing a healthy boy. On this her fate, even her life, depended.

What happened next was a catastrophe for Anne. In late January 1536, the precious prince was born, but so premature at just over three months that Henry and Anne's son was more a miscarriage than a stillbirth. Anne blamed this untimely birth on the shock to her nervous system caused by news that Henry had fallen heavily while jousting and, it was rumoured, lain unconscious for two hours. She also said that her husband's blatant flirtations, particularly with one of her own ladies in waiting, Jane Seymour, had added to her upset and strain during this precarious time. Anne was desperate to absolve herself from some of the blame for the failure of this last pregnancy. But the tragedy was possibly even graver than the loss of a prince, for Henry articulated the chilling accusation that Anne's powers sprang from a sinister and supernatural source, and this miscarriage of the longed-for son was her punishment alone, relieving him from responsibility. Chapuys, the busy and hostile Spanish ambassador, reported something the king had said in confidence to one of his courtiers in a serious and confessional tone: 'that he [the king] had made this marriage seduced by witchcraft, and for that reason he considered it null; and that this was evident, because God did not permit them to have male issue'.[17] The fact that it was assumed that Anne was now incapable of producing a healthy male heir could be an expression of the fear that Anne was somehow tainted by her involvement with unnatural practices, like sorcery.* Her many detractors now had a powerful weapon to use against her.

Accusations of witchcraft were easily made and impossible to disprove. The existence of witches was accepted even by the learned and rational. It was self-evident that their powers were malignant and destructive, the result of a supposed secret pact with the devil. They often bore the brunt of the everyday struggle to manage and understand the natural world. It was generally believed that with a few incantations and a sacrifice or two a witch could blight the harvest, turn milk sour, make bonny children sicken and die. She

---

* One of Anne's recent biographers, Retha M. Warnicke, has suggested that this miscarried son was in some way deformed; this in a time when monstrous births were considered another fingerpost of witchcraft. But that thesis has to remain speculation.

could create a flash flood out of nothing, dry up the wells, invoke a freak storm, kill lambs with a glance and strike land, animals and women barren.

It was in the area of sex that the activities of witches were most feared and decried. A witch was represented as the embodiment of the inverted qualities of womankind: where natural women were weaker than men and submissive, witches were harsh, with access to forbidden power; where women had kindness and charm, witches were full of vengeance and the will to harm; where women were sexually passive, witches were voracious in their appetites and depraved. Witches were privy to recipes for aphrodisiacs and could make men fall helplessly in love with the most unlikely of women – even with their own benighted selves.

Lust was the domain of witchcraft. Incest and sodomy were intercourse with the devil and witches invariably gave birth to deformed children as a result of these deviant practices. Certainly it was believed that just as a man could be bewitched into illicit sex so he could also be rendered impotent. It was rumoured witches would even sacrifice babies in the pursuit of their terrible power.

The fact that proof of witchcraft was spurious was no obstacle to the accusation. It was a powerful and ancient belief which gave a meaning to misfortune in a world of suffering, and a cathartic focus for blame and revenge. Any woman who was somehow eccentric to her immediate society, difficult, lonely, odd in her behaviour, unbridled in her speech – even just the possessor of a cat – was at risk of becoming the scapegoat for her community, her perceived malevolence responsible for all the ills that befell it. Witchcraft was established as a crime in the parliamentary acts of 1542 and 1563 and evidence was a congeries of hearsay, superstition, malice and fear. There were periods when witch-hunts were instigated as a manifestation of the spiritual war between God and the devil. Likely women were sought out and prosecuted, their confessions often extracted under torture. Many were executed as witches, often on the vaguest anecdotes of a neighbour's ill fortune and a run of unlucky coincidences.

Accusations of witchcraft were largely made against poor rural women. But it was a charge that could be levelled against any woman (men were rarely charged) and there were cases of aristocratic women accused of weaving malevolent spells, with mysterious powers to do harm, the crime being *maleficium*. Anne Boleyn's confidence and sense of power had been noted as unbecoming in a woman. Now, in her failure for a third time to present the king and his people with the necessary male heir, Anne's downfall was inevitable. This was all the more brutally so if the failure of her last pregnancy could be used to intimate her gross malevolence and unnatural appetites.

The speed and ruthlessness of Queen Anne's destruction suggest fear of her power amongst the king's closest advisers, most notably Cromwell, and a growing animus towards her, disgust even, on Henry's part. Henry was susceptible to his own propaganda, and it was only a small matter to transform convenient surmise into cold reality. There was a widespread belief that a witch bore a mark on her face or body which revealed her true nature: either hidden peculiarities like a third nipple, a hairy birthmark, an odd lump, indentation or discoloration, or outright deformities. In the attempt to defame Anne as a witch, stories gained momentum after her death of an extra finger or some grotesque mole-like growth on her neck.

The main published source for details of her disfigurement came from a Catholic priest who never knew or even saw her. Nicholas Sander's tract *De origine et progressu schismatis Anglicani*, posthumously published in 1585, described her fantastically libidinous life, labelled her marriage with the king as incestuous (claiming Anne was Henry's daughter) and listed her physical imperfections thus: 'Anne Boleyn was rather tall of stature, with black hair and an oval face of a sallowish complexion, as if troubled with jaundice. She had a projecting tooth under the top lip, and on her right hand six fingers. There was a large wen under her chin, and therefore to hide its ugliness she wore a high dress covering her throat.'[18] Despite being under the closest scrutiny during her life as consort and queen, none of the contemporary chroniclers of the time mentioned any abnormalities in Anne's appearance. In fact, the Venetian ambassador who, like his fellow hostile ambassadors, was avid for any disparaging detail to report home, thought her 'of middling stature, swarthy complexion, long neck, wide mouth, bosom not much raised . . . and eyes, which are black and beautiful'.[19]

Unable initially to find any legal reason to invalidate Anne and Henry's marriage, her accusers sought another way to destroy her. Anne was a natural flirt and an accomplished social creature. Emotionally expressive and thin-skinned, her education in the French court had added to her manner a gloss of worldliness and wit that her more stolid compatriots regarded with some suspicion. To charge her with adultery of the most depraved kind seemed an obvious and usefully double-barrelled weapon: if it could be suggested that this last abortive pregnancy was the result of Anne's moral turpitude with another man (or the devil) then Henry was absolved of any responsibility. The baby was then a punishment of Anne's behaviour, not of his.

The Tudor state could act with expedient ruthlessness. Within only three months of Anne's miscarriage she and seven men were arrested and sent to the Tower. Of the two who were released one was the poet Thomas Wyatt, an admirer of Anne's from before her marriage. The remaining five, however, including her own brother George Rochford, were accused of fornication with the queen. Only one, Mark Smeaton, a court musician and a gentle and artistic man, confessed, probably under torture, to this dangerous adultery: 'The saying is he confessed, but he was first grievously racked,' it was reported to Cromwell.[20]

The charges worked up to ensnare the queen and destroy the power of her family, by implicating her brother, involved Anne's incitement of these men to commit adultery with her. A second charge of conspiring the king's death was also brought. Again it was Anne's malignancy, her powers of bewitchment, which were implied in the wording: 'The said Queen and these other traitors . . . conspired the King's death and destruction . . . And the King having a short time since become aware of the said abominable crimes and treasons against him took such inward displeasure and heaviness, especially from the said Queen's malice and adultery, that certain harms and perils have befallen the royal body.'[21] The evidence brought against the defendants was so tenuous as to be merely a gesture, an incoherent ragbag of gossip, innuendo and misinterpreted courtliness. She did dance with the king's chamberlains, but then so did all the ladies of the bedchamber; she did kiss her brother and write to him of her pregnancy but then, as Alesius pointed out, 'it is a usual custom throughout the whole of Britain that ladies married and unmarried, even the most coy, kiss not only a brother, but any honourable person, even in public'.[22]

However one piece of evidence was of terrific moment and had also the ring of authenticity. Anne was accused of making an unguarded comment to her sister-in-law, Lady Rochford, who had subsequently become a hostile witness against her husband and queen. The rash female confidence was: 'que le Roy n'estait habile en cas de soy copuler avec femme, et qu'il n'avait ni vertu ni puissance' [that the king has not the ability to make love to a woman, for he has neither the vigour nor the potency].

This was so sensitive an area of discussion that when Lord Rochford at his trial was asked to comment on this statement he was handed a piece of paper with the words written down rather than have them broadcast to the packed court. (He inadvertently – or otherwise – read them out loud.) To cast aspersions on Henry's virility was bad enough. To say such things about a king so wilful in his drive for a son and heir, and so ruthless in his actions to achieve that, was dangerous in the extreme. And the danger was doubly reflexive against Anne, for a powerful man's impotence was readily blamed on the woman. Perhaps the words of the indictment against Anne, that due to her activities 'certain harms and perils have befallen the royal body', referred implicitly to that dreaded loss of virility which may well have periodically affected the king.

So the net closed in around the queen. She was almost certainly innocent of the gross charges brought against her, as were the men chosen as luckless tools in her downfall. The evidence produced against them was barely plausible let alone proof of anything more than acquaintanceship and, in Lord Rochford's case, fraternal affection. Pride, reckless indiscretion and ill luck were Anne's undoing at the hands of a king with absolute power, his fickle heart and tyrannical nature in harness to a fanatic pursuit of a male heir.

There was one poignant glimpse of the baby Elizabeth, only two and a half years old, being held up to her father by a distraught Anne for the last time. In his letter to Elizabeth on her accession, Alesius wrote: 'Never shall I forget the sorrow which I felt when I saw the most serene Queen, your most religious mother, carrying you, still a little baby, in her arms and entreating the most serene King, your father, in Greenwich Palace, from the open window of which he was looking into the courtyard . . . the faces and gestures of the speakers plainly showed that the King was angry.'[23] Anne must have been dispatched immediately to the Tower for just as Alesius arrived in London from Greenwich the cannon thundered out, heralding the imprisonment of a person of the nobility or higher.

Having collapsed in hysterical terror when first imprisoned, Anne recovered her composure to impress even her enemies at her trial. On 19 May 1536 she was beheaded. As a special dispensation a swordsman was imported from France so that her execution was effected not by an axe on the block but by a sword. His dexterity was so great that Anne appeared unaware of the moment of death and those present thought the whole process looked more like sleight of hand than the gruesome butchery it so often became. Her arrest, trial and execution had all taken place within seventeen days. Three days before she died, the final humiliation was delivered by Archbishop Cranmer, her fair-weather friend. He had managed to elicit from Anne some statement that could be used to nullify her marriage to the king, possibly concerning the contractual status of her previous engagement to Lord Henry Percy. So Anne went to her death, still a young woman but technically no longer a queen.

The baby princess's future also was in the balance. Although she too was to be threatened with a traitor's death eighteen years later, at this time she was not in peril. Elizabeth's own status, however, was inextricably bound up with her mother's and just as the legality of Anne's marriage was denied, so too was her daughter's legitimacy. Two months after her mother's execution, an act removing her from the succession stated she was 'illegitimate . . . excluded and banned to claim, challenge or demand any inheritance as lawful heir

... to [the king] by lineal descent'. From being the much-vaunted Princess Elizabeth, for a time sole heir to her father's crown, she now became just Lady Elizabeth, with no clear place in the Tudor succession. Significantly, given the sexual charges against her mother, there was never any occasion when Henry chose to doubt the fact that Elizabeth was his true daughter.

Although largely oblivious at the time, for she was not yet three years old and living in a separate household, Elizabeth's subsequent demeanour and expectations were affected fundamentally by the legacy of Anne's spectacular fall from favour, her execution for treason and subsequent vilification for obscene acts and rumours of evil. Of all Henry's wives, her own mother, Anne Boleyn, was to attract the most attention and opprobrium during her lifetime and the most scandalous stories in the centuries which followed. Lurid tales of incest and witchcraft grew with the telling. And witchery was strongly believed to be passed to subsequent generations as a hereditary taint: people born of 'bad and wicked parents' were deemed likely to be witches themselves.[24] This was a damnation that would fuel her daughter's enemies and echo in unexpected ways down the years.

But even more damaging to Elizabeth's confidence was her disputed legitimacy and shifting status as one of her father's heirs – or not – as his own dynastic struggles continued. Even as a small child she appeared to be conscious of her demotion. When the new queen, Jane Seymour, recalled the Princess Mary to court in the spring of 1537, the three-and-a-half-year-old Elizabeth was reputed to have said to the governor of her household: 'How haps it, Governor, yesterday my Lady Princess, and today but my Lady Elizabeth?' This insecurity would become a lasting strain in her life, played upon and exacerbated by the indubitable claims on the English throne of her cousin and rival Mary Queen of Scots.

Prior to Mary's birth and the beginning of her own lifelong competition for the English throne, her father, James V of Scotland, was already locked into a futile arm-wrestling with his uncle and neighbour Henry VIII, both conducting raids and counter-raids of the border lands between their two kingdoms. Although James had managed to wrong-foot his uncle in the marriage stakes by winning the hand of Mary's mother, Mary of Guise, from under Henry's nose (Henry had her in mind as his fourth wife), he was having less luck with his frontier skirmishes against the English king. Henry had launched spasmodic raids across the border and James, increasingly demoralized by the lack of solidarity from his lords (many of whom were accepting money from the English exchequer), had attempted a counterattack. In 1542, in the bitter end of November, James presided over an ill-judged retaliatory invasion of the Debatable Land, the unruly and ungovernable strip of wild country to the west of Liddesdale. In this godforsaken heath he suffered a humiliating rout of his men by the English troops at Solway Moss. His uncommitted nobles had deserted him and over a thousand Scots were taken prisoner.

James was left to ride north, broken in spirit and submerged in deepest melancholy. He was an intelligent, sensual man, a creative builder of beautiful palaces, personally attractive to his people but temperamentally more suited perhaps to the life of an enlightened landowner than to the crown of thorns of the Scottish monarchy. He had a complex character, combining opposing qualities of rapacity and a certain identification with his people. He tried to break the domination of his lords and establish a rule of law but earned the suspicion of both church and nobility with his attempts at raising money from their assets in order to build grand palaces such as Falkland and Linlithgow. Striving to secure a male heir for his dynasty he, nevertheless, was known for his licentiousness and fathered seven or more illegitimate children, at least five of whom were sons. John Knox managed succinctly to sum up his double-sided nature, a polarity that fatally weakened him as a man and a king: 'Hie was called of some a good poore mans king; of otheris hie was termed murtherare of the nobilitie, and one that had decreed thair hole destruction. Some praised him for the repressing of thyft and oppressioun; otheris dispraised him for the defoulling of menis wiffis and virgines. And thus men spake evin as affectionis led thame. And yitt none spack all together besydis the treuth: for a parte of all these foresaidis war so manifest that as the verteuis could nott be denyed, so could nott the vices by any craft be clocked [cloaked].'[25] After a long night's ride James arrived at Linlithgow, where Mary of Guise was awaiting the birth of their baby, the much-needed son and heir.

Part of the king's melancholy lay in the recent deaths of his two baby sons and heirs, cared for in separate establishments but dying within days of each other in a tragic synchrony. The timing was so inexplicable and shocking that poison was suggested, as it always was in cases of sudden death. But these deaths mingled natural grief in James's mind with a supernatural warning. They seemed to give ominous meaning to a nightmare that had haunted him. In his dreams a dead man, possibly his old friend Sir James Hamilton (whose property James V had appropriated after he had been executed on trumped-up charges), approached, brandishing a sword. The animated corpse then cut off both the king's arms and swore he would return to cut off his head.

When, in the late April of 1541, King James's eleven-month-old heir, James, and the week-old infant, Robert, died it seemed to James as if he had in fact symbolically lost both his arms, as the dream had foretold. All that remained now was for him to lose his head and thereby his life. With the betrayals of Solway Moss followed so closely by the birth of Mary, not the replacement prince who would bring hope for the future but a weak and premature girl, James's own death seemed to him to be an awful certainty.

As the King of Scotland rode further north and collapsed into bed in Falkland Palace, the following day Mary of Guise went into labour at Linlithgow. She cannot have been in a peaceful and optimistic frame of mind. Contemporary reports suggest that the labour was not full term and so the subsequent risk to the child was increased, especially as she was born in the heart of a storm in the deepest of bitter winter. Her husband too had just left her in a state so utterly distraught that she could not be sure when or if she would ever see him again. The country was in dire peril without an effective king and with a ruthless neighbour in Henry threatening invasion and war. Religious divisions were sweeping Europe, the Reformation had a dynamic all its own which James V had resisted, but which focused factions within Scotland and inflamed dissent.

And all the while the Scottish nobles were in disarray, captured, bribed by the English, unwilling to serve the crown before their own interests. Scotland that December was especially cold, dark and dangerous. On the 8th of that month a small frail baby entered the world. Unwelcome as she may have been to her father, she was her mother's fifth child* and her first daughter. Mary of Guise was a redoubtable woman and a fond mother, with a close relationship with her own mother, and there is every reason to believe that, despite the dynastic disappointment of her child's sex, she was happy to have given birth to a girl.

Both Elizabeth Tudor and Mary Stuart were to become queens regnant in their own right but aware always of the pitfalls and inveterate expectations of their roles. Just as for less exalted women, marriage was their unequivocal duty and procreation the necessary thing. But the marriage contract for princesses and queens traditionally had little to do with personal choice and everything to do with political expedience. Just as the three-month-old Elizabeth had been offered in marriage by her father to a French prince, in order to build an alliance between historic enemies, so the infant Mary, now Queen of Scots, became the focus of a fierce struggle between these same old adversaries.

Mary, as a female heir, may have been equally as disappointing as was her cousin, but her marital prospects in 1543 were much more dazzling. For Mary was already a regnant queen while Elizabeth's chances of inheriting the crown, having been bastardized and disinherited by her father, seemed very remote. It was traditional that the kingdom with the misfortune to be ruled by a queen was considered part of her dowry in the marriage negotiations. The

---

* Mary of Guise had been married to the Duc de Longueville in 1534 and had two sons, François born in 1535 and Louis in 1537, a few months after his father's death. Louis died and François, as the new duke, was left with her Guise relations when she travelled to Scotland to marry James V.

future dispensation of Scotland, therefore, made Mary's tiny, oblivious form the immediate focus of her ambitious neighbour. Elizabeth's father, the ageing bully Henry, was determined to annex Scotland and prevent for ever his old enemy France from getting a base from which to invade England. He meant to claim the infant Mary as a wife for his five-year-old son, Edward.

On 12 October 1537 Henry had at last been awarded his prince and heir after marrying his third wife, Jane Seymour, within eleven days of the execution of the second. The eruption of happiness in court and country was crowned with the baby's magnificent christening later that October. Elizabeth, just four years old, was carried to the ceremony by Edward Seymour, uncle to the new prince. The elder of the ambitious brothers of the queen, Edward Seymour was to become Lord Protector on Henry's death, the most powerful nobleman in the land.

But the birth of a male heir came at a high cost. After a gruelling three-day labour, Queen Jane was dead in less than a fortnight of a postpartum sepsis. She died in the midst of her triumph aged only twenty-eight. Henry seemed to be genuinely grief-stricken, writing to François I of France, 'Divine Providence has mingled my joy with the bitterness of death of her who brought me this happiness.'[26]

However, the monarch's round of marriages, alliances and wars continued with barely a pause. And so, five years later, when his old Scottish adversary, James V, died in the winter of 1542 with a sole female heir, just five years younger than the English male heir, it appeared to Henry to be a God-sent opportunity. The Spanish ambassador considered it a possible double boon for Henry, for the ageing king was in need of a wife himself, caught in an unusual marital lacuna between Catherine Howard, whom he had just executed for adultery, and Catherine Parr, whom he had yet to woo. Certainly, for those with any memory, there was a certain justice in the possibility of Henry finally winning the admirable, and fertile, Mary of Guise, having lost her the first time to his nephew James of Scotland. Such a marriage would have brought the baby Queen of Scots into closest sisterhood with Elizabeth, most probably sharing a similar education and upbringing in England. How different her future would have been. But the idea of marrying the dowager queen did not appear to fire Henry's imagination as it had five years before.

The marriage of his heir to Scotland's heir was a much more rewarding enterprise. Henry wanted to get his hands on this intractable kingdom and there was no easier way, it would seem, than through such a marriage alliance. The fact that the English provided the male side of the bargain ensured England's natural superiority in any union with Scotland, just as a husband had dominion over his wife. From the English point of view there was something right and natural about uniting these two sea-bound kingdoms, with England as the senior partner. Such a marriage of neighbours would annex Scotland in an expansion of Henry's own house and territory and thereby reduce the attrition on the border and, more seriously, close the back door to France.

Needless to say, Scotland, with a real pride in her own ancient history and fiercely protected independence, saw the situation rather differently. There was also the small matter of how revenues were raised and where they were spent: 'if both the realms were under one, all should go to the King of England out of the country of Scotland not to be spent there, whereby Scotland now being poor already should be utterly beggared and undone'.[27] But Henry had a fistful of Scottish noblemen captured at Solway Moss, whom he would treat well, bribe with money and promises of patronage, and return to Scotland to work on his behalf to facilitate the marriage contract. Ten of these signed a secret pact recognizing Henry as King of Scotland should Mary Queen of Scots die without an heir.[28] This was a shameful precursor of the secret treaty Mary herself, when a young woman, was to sign with the Guises and the French King Henri II, ceding Scotland to France in the event of her death without issue.

Initially there were fears for the baby queen's survival: 'a very weak child and not like to live'.[29] Even two weeks after her birth, Chapuys, the Spanish ambassador, was writing that not only the child but the mother too was expected to die. However, the frail baby did thrive and by March the following year, Henry's ambassador, Sir Ralph Sadler, had travelled north to oversee the marital negotiations and examine the prize himself.

Sadler, a loyal but literal-minded man, was shown into the presence of the dowager queen, Mary of Guise. After discussing the marriage proposals, Mary led Sadler to the nursery to see the new queen. The baby Queen of Scots was not yet four months old. Her mother asked the nurse to unwrap her and show her quite naked for Sadler's approval. Sadler, a fond husband and father himself, seemed touched and impressed by the sight: 'I assure your majesty, it is as goodly a child as I have seen of her age, and as like to live, with the grace of God,' he reported back to Henry.[30]

Sadler's conversations with Mary of Guise and with Arran, the regent, were doggedly relayed back to his master in meticulous letters of epic length which make them an invaluable source of information, conveyed with an immediacy which transcends more than four and a half centuries of intervening history. Sadler was ever puzzled as to whom he should trust. Mary of Guise was charming, intelligent and a skilful stateswoman. She was quite capable of dissembling when need be. Mary gave the impression that the King of England's plans for her daughter were exactly what she would have hoped, and Sadler was naturally credulous. But Arran had warned him, 'that I should find her in the end (whatsoever she pretendeth) a right French woman', with her main motive to keep England at bay and the ancient Scottish alliance with her own country strong.

No one could fail to appreciate the incongruous weight of responsibility which had fallen to this unwitting infant. She was already queen in name. One day she would have to become queen in deed of a kingdom of proud, disputatious clans centred on ancient tribal strongholds spread out across a sparsely populated, mostly mountainous, beautiful but inhospitable land. And as Mary lay in her cradle the factions were already entrenched in their rivalries, working for their own advancement and against their foes.

The immediate struggle for influence was between Cardinal Beaton, a powerful, worldly, pro-French ally of Mary of Guise, and the Earl of Arran, a vacillating opportunist and the leader of the pro-English tendency. Arran won the first round by wresting the regency from the churchman and declaring himself, as a Hamilton, next in line to the throne after Mary. But even these allegiances were not as they seemed, for Arran was rumoured to be intending to marry his own son to the new queen, and thereby doubly ensure his family's hold on the crown. This meant that, despite being in the pay of Henry, he was unlikely to be working to promote the English king's ambitions. On hearing this, Henry decided to offer his daughter Elizabeth to Arran for his son: in return Arran was expected to support the marriage proposal that really mattered to Henry, that between his heir Edward and the baby Queen of Scots.

Elizabeth was nine years old at the time, serious, highly intelligent and so well educated that those who met her inevitably remarked on her evident abilities. When she was only six years old her father's courtier, soon to be secretary, Wriothsley was struck by the small girl's grace and presence of mind: having been offered the king's blessing, Elizabeth gave her humble thanks and then '[asked] after His Majesty's welfare, and that with as great a gravity as she had been forty years old'.[31] Yet at the age of nine, Elizabeth was unlikely to have been informed of her father's offer of herself in marriage to Arran's son, a mere compensation in the hopes that the real prize, Elizabeth's new cousin, Mary, would be saved for Henry's grander scheme. But her impromptu place in this scheme showed that in Henry's mind his illegitimate daughter, by the woman he had hoped to erase forever, was valued rather lowly on the scale of marital barter.

Just as in his first abortive negotiations over his daughter Elizabeth's prospective betrothal, Henry's conditions for the marriage of Mary Queen of Scots to his son were self-defeatingly excessive and heavy-handed. One of the main areas of disagreement was over the immediate possession of the baby queen. Henry, hoping to be supported by his recently released Scottish lords, had demanded that she be put into his hands, to be brought up in England until she was old enough to marry. The Scottish Parliament had met in March 1543 and passed a set of articles agreeing in principle to the marriage, but insisting that Mary should remain in Scotland until she was ten years old, 'that hir personne be kepit and nurist principallie be hir moder'.[32] The same Parliament gave a nod in the direction of the reformed religion by authorizing the reading of the Bible in the vernacular, an activity which previously had been widespread but discreetly done.

On 1 July the Treaty of Greenwich allowing for the marriage of Prince Edward and Queen Mary of Scotland was drawn up. But Henry's influence in Scotland was already on the wane. With a Guise as queen mother and dowager queen, France's importance, on the other hand, had never been in much doubt. Towards the end of June a fleet of French ships was tracked making their way to the offshore waters of Scotland, lying off Aberdeen and then Arbroath. Rumours abounded; there were 4000 men of war on board, 1000 of them at least were hackbuteers, armed with the fearsome firearm, the harquebus: 'they come to convoy away the young Queen, and also the old'.[33] Sadler was much concerned by this threat as he reported back to the Privy Council, but his fears were partly allayed by Arran who assured him that the Palace of Linlithgow was properly guarded, and anyway the young queen could not be moved 'because she is a little troubled with the breeding of teeth'. This seemed to be accepted at face value by Sadler who added, 'by my truth I cannot but see that [governor Arran] tendreth as much her health, preservation, and surety, as if she were his own natural child'.[34] As the tenuous thread of the infant Mary's life was all that stood between Arran and his ambitions as next heir to the kingdom, this observation may have been more an expression of Sadler's honourable credulity and his own paternal affections than Arran's careful concern.

Under armed escort of more than three thousand men, the seven-month-old queen was moved to safer ground that summer. But she went not to Edinburgh as Henry had demanded but to Stirling Castle, the great medieval stronghold much beautified and domesticated by Mary's father James. This castle, with its lovely new French-inspired palace building, belonged to Mary's mother through her marriage contract. Now ensconced there with her daughter, Mary of Guise's own power was greatly increased. She was keen to appear conciliatory to their powerful neighbour and requested Sadler's presence at Stirling where she asked him to assure his king 'that as nothing could be more honourable for her and her daughter than this marriage, so she desired the perfection thereof with all her heart'.[35] Again, she wished to show off her daughter, this time with evident maternal pride at how tall she was growing and how advanced she seemed, declaring, 'that her daughter did grow apace; and soon,' she said, 'she would be a woman, if she took of her mother'.[36] This, as Sadler reminded Henry, was a reference to the queen mother's own unusual height, a general characteristic of the physically splendid Guises which was shared too by Mary Queen of Scots.

By the beginning of September, Sadler's much exercised credulity was finally worn thin when the irresolute Arran relinquished his support of the English and reformed religion and joined forces with Cardinal Beaton. The volte-face was further underlined by the Earl of Lennox, home after many years in France fortified with French cash and promises of support, who later that month joined the pro-English party solely to continue in opposition to his arch rival Arran. No imperative was more important to a Scotsman than maintaining the tribal status quo and the Lennox–Hamilton hostility was one of the dynamos of Scottish history at the time. In the midst of all this duplicity, the baby at the eye of the storm was crowned Mary Queen of Scots on 9 September 1543, aged nine months. It was an ancient but modest ceremony, 'with such solemnity as they do use in this country, which is not very costly'.[37] The pro-English noblemen refused to attend.

Sadler realised that he could trust no-one when the factions were so opportunistic and shifting, and the noblemen within them motivated by frustrating old enemies rather than consolidating new friends. Nonplussed by the dour Celtic passions which could keep alive ancestral feuds over centuries he expostulated: 'There never was so noble a prince's servant as I am so evil intreated as I am among these unreasonable people; nor do I think never man had to do with so rude, so inconsistent, and beastly a nation as this is.'[38]

As the baby Mary peacefully continued her life circumscribed by sleep, food and play, the tensions in her kingdom intensified. Although the Treaty of Greenwich, promising her in marriage to Prince Edward of England, had been ratified, albeit belatedly, her mother, desperate to try and lure Lennox back to her pro-French cause, offered the greatest prize of her daughter and the kingdom to him.[39]

Marriage to the infant Queen of Scots, a marriage that would make him king, thereby obliterating Arran's power and his rival claim as next in line to the throne, was on the face of it an irresistible offer. There was the small matter of the age gap of twenty-six years but, although Lennox entered into negotiations with the queen mother for a while, he knew the offer was merely a ruse to defuse his capacity for trouble. Already his gaze had alighted on another royal bride, Lady Margaret Douglas, daughter of Margaret Tudor, and niece of Henry VIII, rather closer in age to himself, whose advantages of birth would become immediately available to him. The dream of kingship, however, would be worked out in the subsequent generation. The marriage of Lennox in 1545 with this strong-willed, red-headed Tudor, full of pride in her royal blood, produced an ill-fated son, Henry Stewart, Lord Darnley.

Henry VIII was increasingly impatient with the Scottish lords' refusal to submit to his demands. He misunderstood the complex loyalties and shifting alliances of interest, which only included him and the English cause to the extent that they could extract more English gold through unsubstantiated promises of support. However his intimidation and threats of reprisals did not force the mettlesome Scots into compliance. In fact it had the contrary effect. In December 1543, their Parliament solemnly annulled the Treaty of Greenwich: the marriage, the peace and the small concessions to the reformed religion were all duly cancelled. It was obvious that the 'auld alliance' with France was again pre-eminent and Henry and the English were clothed in their ancient habit of the 'auld enemie'. Perhaps, in reality, it had ever been thus.

Henry's revenge was to be bloodthirsty and terrible. The first raid he launched was in May 1544. The directions to his executor

Hertford were as merciless as they were exact: 'put all to fire and sword, burn Edinburgh town, so razed and defaced when you have sacked and gotten what you can of it as there may remain forever a perpetual memory of the vengeance of God lightened upon [them] for their falsehood and disobedience'.[40] The series of invasions, burnings, massacres and lootings that followed were to become known as 'the Rough Wooing'. But in love as in war, Henry's judgement had become skewed with illness and age. He would never manage now to unite the two kingdoms in his lifetime, although that possibility tantalizingly remained throughout the lifetime of his children and came to haunt his daughter Elizabeth.

At the beginning of 1543, the young Lady Elizabeth was as far away from the English throne as she had ever been. Still illegitimate, still barred from the succession, she and her half-sister Mary, nevertheless, were on warmer terms with their father and now included in court ceremonial. But they remained marginal to the future of the monarchy. However, that spring Henry's mind turned to the fundamental issue of securing the Tudor dynasty. Perhaps he was beginning to realize that his god-like being was mortal after all. Hugely obese and in failing health, he suffered excruciating pain from a chronically ulcerated leg. In June, Parliament formally restored Mary and then Elizabeth to the succession, to follow their half-brother Edward. However, Henry did not choose at the same time to reinstate the legitimacy of both his daughters, leaving them with a fundamental insecurity and vulnerability to counterclaims on their throne.

At this point it seemed unlikely that Elizabeth would ever become Queen of England, but her restoration to the succession made the dream at least possible. Aged nearly ten, this clever, watchful, ambitious girl was no longer a child and was beginning instead to think about her own destiny. She was uncritically adoring of her distant father and grateful for the warmth and authority of her new stepmother, Catherine Parr, a mature and intelligent woman who was herself avid for education and self-improvement. That summer

Elizabeth and her half-sister Mary had been summoned to court to meet the young widow and then attended as special guests the sixth and last wedding of their father. Closer to him than she had ever been previously, Elizabeth's most vivid memories of Henry as a father and king would date from these last three years of his life when the turmoil of his private life was over and he turned once more to engage in self-aggrandisement abroad. Ill-judged and costly as these grandiose schemes may have been, they energized the ageing king with something of the charismatic vitality and splendour of his youth.

It is impossible to know what Elizabeth knew of her father's military campaigns against both their Scottish neighbours and the French in the summer of 1544. But he was in her thoughts when, on the last day of July, she wrote her first extant letter, to her stepmother Catherine Parr, and ended this exercise in courtly Italian with the sentiments: 'I humbly entreat your most excellent highness that in writing to his majesty you will deign to recommend me to him, entreating ever his sweet benediction and likewise entreating the Lord God to send him best success in gaining victory over his enemies, so that your highness, and I together with you, may rejoice the sooner at his happy return.'[41] Elizabeth was living at St James's Palace, immersed in her books and study, reading and translating from Latin and Greek the stories of classical battles and mythic heroes. While she laboured at home, her own flesh and blood hero Henry was so revivified by war that he led the siege of Boulogne himself in a last gesture of defiance against the French, his doctors and the approach of death. Eventually he entered the city in triumph in the middle of September. For that moment, perhaps, he felt he had turned back the years.

Elizabeth was at Leeds Castle in Kent to welcome him home, an awe-inspiring father and, it would seem to her then, a Hercules among men. Although when she was queen she was to choose equivocation and peace rather than confrontation and war, all her life Elizabeth was to consider it as the highest compliment to be likened to him, the man she loved and admired more than anyone; 'my own matchless and most kind father'.[42] The king she saw in the last years was an ageing old lion but in his young daughter Elizabeth's opinion, he was 'a king, whom philosophers regard as god on earth'.[43]

As queen she was to invoke the glorious reputation of her father whenever she felt at all defensive as a woman with her all-male government ranged against her, or facing military aggression from abroad: 'though I be a woman, yet I have as good a courage answerable to my place as ever my father had',[44] she was to tell her Lords in November 1566, when she was thirty-three and still angrily resisting their pressure to marry or otherwise settle the succession. And writing to her father at the time of his 'Rough Wooing' when she herself was only twelve years old, Elizabeth claimed not only kinship with her 'illustrious and most mighty' father but also an intimate intellectual and personal bond with him: 'May I, by this means [the trilingual translation of her stepmother Catherine Parr's book of prayers], be indebted to you not as an imitator of your virtues but indeed as an inheritor of them.'[45] It took courage and confidence in this girl to place herself on a par with her father, a distant figure of gigantic proportions and terrifying reputation, a tyrant and a divinely ordained king.

Her public identification was always with her heroic father, but in private it seems Elizabeth honoured the memory of her mother too. At some point in her life she began to wear a diamond, ruby and mother of pearl ring with a secret compartment which revealed a portrait of Anne, face to face with a companion miniature of her daughter. They folded together when the ring was closed. The vilification of Anne's reputation and the disputed legality of her marriage, together with the dangerous imputations of witchcraft, incest and depravity attached to her name, meant Elizabeth's attempt at some identification and intimacy with her mother was necessarily secretive. She did show, however, interest and sympathy for her Boleyn relations, promoting her cousin, Henry Carey, Mary Boleyn's son, to the baronetcy of Hunsdon. Anne may not have been publicly celebrated by her daughter but she was not forgotten.

Although Boulogne was a short-lived victory for Henry and virtually bankrupted his country, it did a great deal for the old king's morale and his people's insular pride. Knowing once more the thrill of conquest he could forget the years of domestic frustration and impotence. Scotland and the baby queen were to be casualties of his new energy and belligerence, for he was determined to force the marriage of his heir with Mary, Scotland's queen. By the autumn of 1545, Henry was furious at the Scots' continued recalcitrance and once again unleashed his warlord, the Earl of Hertford, Edward Seymour. While the almost three-year-old Mary was kept in close confinement by her mother at Stirling Castle, the marauding English rode over the border to burn and destroy crops and towns and particularly the abbeys and religious establishments. Kelso Abbey, Melrose Abbey, and the abbeys of Dryburgh and Jedburgh were all put to the torch, and their inhabitants and the surrounding populace dispersed or killed. As great a destruction as possible was wreaked on the fair and fertile valleys between these towns as Hertford and his troops swept through on their vengeance raids. It was harvest time and Henry wanted the Scots to reap their bitterest for spurning the English alliance.

Henry's counterproductive 'Rough Wooing' was to be continued even more ruthlessly after his death in 1547 by Edward Seymour, now the Lord Protector of Edward's reign. The baby Scottish queen had grown into a bonny child, intelligent and charming who, having outlived the extreme perils of infancy and risks of neonatal disease, now had to face the dangers of her predatory neighbour. So important was it for England to secure Scotland as insurance against her Continental enemies that Somerset remained intent on prising Mary away from her mother and her country to ensure her alliance with the young English king, himself not yet ten years old. On 10 September 1547, a day that became known in Scottish annals as 'Black Saturday', Somerset's troops routed the Scots under Arran's ineffectual command at Pinkie Cleugh near Inveresk. Once more the flower of Scottish nobility was slain or taken prisoner. Once again the Earl of Arran managed to escape unscathed from the bloody destruction of the best of Scotland's fighting men.

This latest defeat was so devastating that Mary of Guise feared that even Stirling Castle, that great bulwark against attack, might not be able to protect her daughter from the English. Lord Erskine, one of the queen's guardians, and a man already grieving the loss of his son at Pinkie, suggested he take the precious child into safekeeping and install her on the nearby island of Inchmahome, where the secluded Augustinian priory there was surrounded by the deep waters of the Lake of Menteith. Although Mary was not yet five years old and was only to stay for two to three weeks, the stealth and urgency of her departure from Stirling and the mysterious atmosphere and beauty of the place may well have impressed her with a visceral memory of excitement and tension.

Perhaps at this impressionable age Mary's natural polarity of impetuous courage and nervous sensibility thus was etched deeper in her developing psyche. The atmosphere of isolation and meditation on the mysterious island was far removed from the world from which she had been plucked, of aggressive self-interest, anxious politicking and the alarms of war. The sixteenth century was not a time troubled by modern ideas of child rearing and the fragility of the emergent self, and Mary's retainers would have talked freely in front of her. Even at so young an age this child not only would have sensed the fear and the excitement of the adults around her but she would have understood intellectually some of the facts of the situation.

Within weeks she was back with her mother at Stirling but, at the next invasion of the English, the queen mother dispatched her precious daughter to Dumbarton where the French, for whose help she had petitioned in increasing desperation, could easily arrive by sea and collect her. The new King of France had an infant son and heir, named François after Henri's own illustrious father. This firstborn but sickly boy seemed to unloose a surge of fertility in his mother Catherine de Medici who, after eleven anguished years of childless marriage, suddenly produced ten children in the following twelve years.

Mary of Guise had never lost her primary allegiance to her home country and cajoled her lords into allowing her to negotiate a marriage contract between her young daughter and the even younger Dauphin of France. On 7 July 1548 the treaty was signed and Mary's fate was sealed. Neither England nor Scotland now was to be her home. Instead she was to be brought up as a French princess and would learn to rate her adopted crown of France higher than that of Scotland, and covet for most of her adult life the crown of England. The child queen was made ready for the next poignant journey of her life, as a fugitive from the marauding English and an emotional and political captive of the French.

Just as the five-year-old Mary Stuart was beginning to attain consciousness of herself as a queen while imbibing the adrenaline of flight and concealment, adventure and romance, her older cousin Elizabeth Tudor was deep in her studies at various royal manors in the country outside London. Just fourteen, she was polishing her French and Italian, and reading and translating from Latin and Greek. Pindar's poetry and Homer's *Iliad* were among the specific works in her mind when she wrote to her brother Edward in the autumn of 1547: 'Nothing is so uncertain or less enduring than the life of a man, who truly, by the testimony of Pindar, is nothing else than a dream of shadows.'*[46] Her father had died the previous January and this letter was in elegiac mood. What more telling example could there be of the essential transience of all things than the fact that someone as superhuman and magnificent in life as this omnipotent king had to succumb to death as inevitably as the commonest thief or beggar?

In fact Henry's death was the beginning for Elizabeth of a decade of uncertainty and at times extreme danger. These painful years were the furnace that would temper her nature for good and ill. While Elizabeth learnt her lessons the hard way, Mary was to have the danger of her birthright as Queen of the Scots deferred. Instead she entered her defining decade in the French court, pampered, admired, groomed for the mostly decorative role as Dauphine, then fleetingly Queen of France. John Knox, austerely Calvinist in his sympathies, recognized the decadence of this French courtly inherit-ance from his experiences at the time as a prisoner and galley slave

---

* Elizabeth was refering to the Pythian Ode: 'Creatures of a day, what is a man? What is he not? Mankind is a dream of a shadow. But when a god given brightness comes, a radiant light rests on men, and a gentle life'.

of the French. His warning of the effect on the young Queen of Scots, growing up away from her country and her people in this artificial and alien air, had a terrible truth: 'to the end that in her youth she should drink of that liquor, that should remain with her all her lifetime, for a plague to this realm and for her final destruction'.

CHAPTER THREE

The Education of Princes

> I was one day present when she replied at the same time
> to three ambassadors, the Imperial, French, and Swedish,
> in three languages: Italian to one, French to the other,
> Latin to the third; easily, without hesitation, clearly, and
> without being confused, to the various subjects thrown
> out, as is usual in their discourse.
>
> *Elizabeth's tutor Roger Ascham to his friend John Sturm in 1562*

> She has grown so much, and grows daily in height,
> goodness, beauty and virtue, that she has become the
> most perfect and accomplished person in all honest and
> virtuous things that it is possible to imagine . . . I can
> assure you that the King is so delighted with her . . . she
> amuses him with wise and witty conversation, as if she
> was a woman of twenty-five.
>
> *Cardinal of Lorraine to Mary's mother in 1553 when
> the Queen of Scots was ten*

IF EXILE IS NOT JUST A PHYSICAL ABSENCE from home but an emotional and spiritual disconnection from one's earlier self then in the late 1540s both these young queens entered a simultaneous period of exile which would mark them more deeply than anything else in their lives. The reasons, experiences and effects for Elizabeth and Mary individually, however, could not have been more different, or more significant in their differences.

For Elizabeth, the exile was gradual, a journey towards singularity. At first it was the loosening of familial ties which came with orphanhood, then the spiritual estrangement during her sister's reign, culminating in the physical constraint on her movements, place of residence and then the denial of her rights to safety, even to life. Her contemporary, John Foxe, expressed his outrage: 'Into what fear, what trouble of mind, and what danger of death was she brought?'[1] The transient nature of her security, prospects and hopes, the unpredictable perils she encountered, toughened Elizabeth's character, sharpened her wits and gave her a powerful sense of her own autonomy. This exile from certainty and ease made a precocious girl endure the most testing initiation in her journey to become a great queen. Camden realized the value of these unhappiest of years: 'taught by Experience and Adversity, (two most effectual and powerfull Masters,) she had gathered Wisedom above her age'.[2]

For Mary her exile was more clear cut. She was removed to France before she was six years old in what was to be a physical and spiritual severance from her homeland. Already betrothed to the dauphin, her future now was mapped out by foreign interests. She was to be a French princess and then a French queen, with Scotland as her dowry. John Knox considered in retrospect this French exile to be a poisonous inheritance for his young Scottish queen. Hayward, an early chronicler, mourned the loss to her personally: 'our young Quene is married into France, where she nowe lyveth as a stranger both to them and us . . .'[3] In fact this dislocation and re-education was to prove so complete that Mary, the Queen of Scotland, would come to consider her French years as the happiest time of her life.

For Elizabeth it was a painful decade which began with the death of her father on 28 January 1547. Her brother Edward was brought to see her at the manor of Enfield and they were told the news together. In a spasm of grief, so the story went, Henry's two younger children clung together and wept bitterly, then Edward continued on his way to London and the thirteen-year-old princess returned, for the time being, to the studious patterns of her life.

The new young king, himself only nine years old, wrote to this favourite sister: 'There is very little need of my consoling you, most dear sister, because from your learning you know what you ought to do, and from your prudence and pity you perform what your learning causes you to know.' His letter was in answer to one from her seeking to console him and place their loss in the context of her classical and religious studies. She had obviously shown herself to be in control of her emotions for Edward added, 'I perceive you think of our father's death with a calm mind.'[4]

Elizabeth had never lived intimately with either her mother or her father and essentially both were unknown to her. However, in her governess Catherine Ashley she had the most loyal, if limited, of mother figures who had been with her all her life and was to remain, until her death, the woman Elizabeth cared for most. The death of Henry and her subsequent status as an orphan was not a personal wrench so much as a loss of the idealized father as hero. Practically too, Elizabeth could no longer rely on that powerful umbrella of protection and instead was exposed to the untrammelled ambitions of others. Henry's death marked the end of a certain status quo.

Elizabeth's stepmother, Catherine Parr, Henry's last wife, was an affectionate woman with a talent for nurturing and inspiring the young. Her previous stepdaughter, Margaret Neville, left a glowing affidavit in her will: 'I was never able to render her grace [Catherine] sufficient thanks for the godly education and tender love and bountiful goodness which I have ever more found in her.'[5] On marrying Henry in 1543 Catherine had embarked on her new life as his queen with a sense of vocation and had fulfilled her duties admirably. She was thirty-one, already had been twice married and twice widowed and was a mature woman of considerable character and independent means. Catherine was the first of Henry's wives to make any real attempt to take responsibility for the royal children and was to be a particularly important influence on the clever, watchful and spirited Princess Elizabeth. Only ten years old at the time, the young princess was already emotionally self-protective, yet avid for experience and knowledge.

Henry had at least settled the succession before he died. His immediate heir was his son Edward, for whose precious existence he had prayed, plotted and laid waste so many lives, even the foundations of his country's faith. Edward's children were to be next in line, followed by Princess Mary – and her heirs – and only then by his second daughter, Elizabeth.* At this time there was every reason to hope that Edward, an intellectually gifted, brave and independent-minded boy, would survive to manhood and have children of his own. For much of her girlhood there was little expectation that Elizabeth would ever be more than a royal princess.

The death of such a long-reigning despot as Henry VIII inevitably released a ferment of long-suppressed ambitions, for power, wealth and the propagation of the reformed religion in England which Henry's equivocation had stalled. The powerful men around the new young king, specifically in his Privy Council in whose hands his father had left the governance of the kingdom, were predominantly reformist. The most notable among them were Thomas Cranmer, Archbishop of Canterbury and architect of the enduring Edwardian prayer book, John Dudley, and the boy-king's uncle, Edward Seymour, who became Lord Protector, awarding himself the dukedom of Somerset.

There was a second powerful and ambitious Seymour brother, who was to teach the teenage Elizabeth some malign lessons on the delusions of sexual desire and the snares of ruthless men who would be king. Thomas Lord Seymour of Sudeley, at nearly forty years old, still cut a dashing soldierly figure having distinguished himself in diplomatic, naval and military campaigns under Henry. He became Lord Admiral early in the reign of Edward VI under the protectorship of his own elder brother, Somerset. Thomas Seymour had not only been admired by Henry, he had been loved by his queen. In marrying the King rather than this love, Catherine Parr had sacrificed her heart for the sake of duty. However, on Henry's death her sense of obligation was fulfilled and after only four months of widowhood, Catherine married Seymour. This was considered

---

* It is interesting that in what he hoped was the unlikely event of none of his three children producing children themselves, Henry chose to ignore the better claims of Mary Queen of Scots, granddaughter of his elder sister Margaret, and instead vested the succession in the children of his younger sister Mary, who had married the Duke of Suffolk. Her grandchildren were the ill-fated sisters, Jane, Catherine and Mary Grey.

indecorous haste, especially for a queen – and for a couple well into Tudor middle age. But even more surprisingly the thirty-five-year-old queen, who had remained childless throughout her first three marriages, now belatedly conceived. This could only enhance the self-confidence and reputation of an already proudly virile man. It seemed inevitable that such a man would have sired a son.

Elizabeth was still only thirteen when her stepmother, of whom she was most fond, married for love. The young princess remained in her care, living principally with her at her dower houses at Chelsea and Hanworth. Ever curious and watchful, Elizabeth could not fail to have noted the effects of the sudden transformation in Catherine Parr's life. From patient, pious consort of an ailing elderly king she had been transmuted into a lover, desired and desiring. Although not legally her stepfather, Thomas Seymour assumed his role as head of the household and with his manly demeanour and exuberant animal spirits he became for the young princess a charismatic figure of attraction and respect. Some twenty-five years her senior, Seymour in fact was old enough to be her father and the glamour of his varied heroic exploits in war and diplomatic dealings brought a welcome worldly masculinity into Elizabeth's cloistered female-dominated life.

Up until now, Elizabeth had never lived in daily proximity with a man other than her tutors and servants. Her father had been a distant, revered, almost superhuman figure to her, someone she strove to impress with something of her own talents and individuality, but it is unlikely that Henry offered her more than the scantest recognition. From the start, there was evidence that Seymour paid Elizabeth most gratifying attention.

From a purely political point of view, Elizabeth was worthy of this attention for Seymour always had an eye for the main chance and this receptive young woman was a royal princess, third in the line of succession. But Elizabeth was also attractive in her own right, tall with fair reddish-gold hair, fine pale skin and the incongruously dark eyes of her mother, alive with unmistakable intelligence and spirit. She was young, emotionally inexperienced and understandably hungry for recognition and love. She easily became a willing if uneasy partner in the verbal and then physical high jinks in the newly sexualized Parr–Seymour household.

There can be little doubt too that this perceptive girl noticed a marked change in the energy and manner of her much-admired stepmother. Catherine was scholarly, dutiful, religious, yet courageous and radical in a way that was similar to Elizabeth's own mother in her promotion of the evangelical reformed religion. She maintained the heretical belief that everyone should have access to a Bible and be able to read the great book for him- or herself, a belief that had brought lesser personages than her to the stake.

She was also a woman of active feelings and, in following her passion at last and marrying the love of her younger self, both she and Seymour were aware that the prime of their lives was past and there was little time now to lose. This can only have heightened the emotional temperature and in an age when prudery had little place in personal lives it must have been clear to the curious girl that sex and love were powerful, transformative things. They could also prove to be most dangerous if you were a young woman and a princess, without wise counsel or family elders to protect you.

Events started to become unsettling, and in the end alarming, for Elizabeth when the good-natured horseplay, which in the beginning gratifyingly had included her, turned more serious. Seymour began to focus his boisterous sexual energies on his wife's young stepdaughter sometime during Catherine's pregnancy. Elizabeth's loyal governess Mrs Ashley had always been very taken by Seymour's charm and even maintained that before Henry's death he had all but obtained the old king's approval for a marriage between himself and Princess Elizabeth: 'that if the King's Majesty, that Dead is, had lived a little longer, she should have been his wife'.[6] This was rather unlikely and, although Seymour surely considered the advantages of his marrying either one of the royal sisters, he knew that once his astute elder brother had become Lord Protector any such political advancement for himself would be strongly resisted.

The idea persisted, however, not least with Catherine Ashley who, in her limited way, felt such a marriage would be a good one for her much-loved charge. She lost no opportunity to talk of Seymour to Elizabeth, who blushed, with a 'Countenance of Gladness, when he was well spoken of'.[7] But Elizabeth's governess was also foolishly fuelling romantic fancies and the natural rivalry which any girl might feel for an older woman who had prior claim on a man they both desired: 'Kat. Ashley told me', Elizabeth admitted under later cross-examination, 'after that my Lord Admiral was married to the Queen, that if my Lord might have his own Will, he would have had me, afore the Queen.'[8] Even if the young princess at that time had not considered Seymour in a romantic light, given such a provocative piece of information by her trusted governess, it is unlikely that Elizabeth could continue to view Seymour neutrally.

But it was a respectable marriage for Elizabeth for which Catherine Ashley hoped, and the Lord Admiral seemed to her the most eligible suitor: 'I would wish her his Wife of all Men living,'[9] she had declared. However, when Seymour, as a married man, began behaving over-familiarly with the girl, risking her reputation, Mrs Ashley exhibited all the fierce protectiveness of a mother. On one occasion Seymour had attempted to kiss Elizabeth while she was still in bed and been roundly told off by Mrs Ashley, who 'bade him go away for shame'.[10]

The relationship between the Lord Admiral and the young princess was a gradual progression from playful affection to something intrusive and oppressive, denying her a necessary privacy and sense of safety in her home. In all there was an element of sexual attraction that Elizabeth felt for this flashy man of action, the first of a particular type who, throughout her life, would capture her romantic imagination. But for a young and inexperienced girl, this emotional complicity merely added confusion and guilt to the already potent combination of fear and desire his attentions aroused in her.

At first, Seymour would appear in Elizabeth's bedchamber, before she was up and dressed, and tickle her in bed, sometimes slapping her 'upon the Back or on the Buttocks familiarly'. Other times he would open the curtains of her bed and wish her good morning, 'and make as though he would come at her. And she would go further in the Bed, so that he could not come at her.' It is not clear whether Elizabeth's shrinking from his threatened embrace was through excitement or alarm, or whether a confusing mixture of both. Certainly Catherine Ashley told of occasions when Elizabeth, wishing to avoid these early-morning incursions, rose earlier from her bed, so that Seymour then found her dressed and at her books rather than vulnerably half-dressed. On another occasion, Elizabeth, caught out and hearing the lock on her door open, rushed from her bed to hide with her women of the bedchamber until Seymour, having tarried a while, gave up and left the room. Mrs Ashley remonstrated with him on this occasion and on another when he came to bid Elizabeth good morning in a state of semi-undress himself, 'in his Night-Gown, barelegged in his Slippers'.[11] He answered the governess's warnings with anger and self-justification; he meant no harm and to suggest otherwise was to slander him.

The whole confused business was further clouded by the unexpec-ted involvement of the Dowager Queen Catherine herself in some of her husband's excesses. There was an episode in the garden at Hanworth when Seymour remonstrated with Elizabeth over some-thing and then cut to ribbons the black gown she was wearing, revealing her undergarments. Elizabeth explained later to her horri-fied governess that she could do nothing to protect herself because the queen had been holding her down during the whole process. A possible explanation of Catherine's implication could be that newly married, just pregnant and very much in love with her hus-band, she was careful to indulge him, afraid of reproving him. Perhaps she harboured some anger at Elizabeth for the continued flirtation between her stepdaughter and him. It was a historic and religious tradition that sexual attraction between a man and woman was invariably seen as the woman's responsibility, even if she be just a girl and he a much more experienced man, old enough indeed to be her father.

There came a point, however, when Queen Catherine recovered her confidence and good sense and brought this difficult situation to an end. She had come upon Elizabeth and her own husband in an embrace. This was a traumatic debacle for the young prin-cess and was vividly related by her treasurer, Thomas Parry: 'I do remember also, [Mrs Ashley] told me, that the Admiral loved

[Elizabeth] but too well, and had so done a good while; and that the Queen was jealous of her and him, in so much that, one Time the Queen, suspecting the often Access of the Admiral to the Lady Elizabeth's Grace, came suddenly upon them, where they were all alone, (*he having her in his Arms:*) wherefore the Queen fell out, both with the Lord Admiral, and with her Grace also.'[12]

In fact, although the queen did not fall out with either husband or stepdaughter for long, this episode propelled Elizabeth and her retainers out of her stepmother's house. As Parry continued in his confession: 'as I remember, this was the Cause why she was sent from the Queen; or else that her Grace parted from the Queen: I do not perfectly remember whether . . . she went of herself, or was sent away.'[13] It was sometime in the summer of 1548 and late in Catherine's pregnancy and the queen's tolerance and patience had run out. She certainly lectured Mrs Ashley on her responsibilities in keeping Elizabeth's behaviour within bounds and her reputation free from scandal. It is evident that she also pointed out to Elizabeth the necessity of guarding her good name and the dangers of indiscreet behaviour giving rise to unwelcome talk.

It was a humiliating and unhappy situation for the fourteen-year-old princess. She had betrayed her stepmother's kindness and trust and her pride was wounded. Her own feelings for Seymour were distressing and confusing, with elements of fear and desire, of longing and recoil. The chastened girl replied in a letter to Catherine: 'truly I was replete with sorrow to depart from your highness, especially leaving you undoubtful of health. And albeit I answered little, I weighed it more deeper when you said you would warn me of all evils that you should hear of me; for if your grace had not a good opinion of me, you would not have offered friendship to me that way.'[14]

Thus in exile from her stepmother's house for her own unseemly behaviour, Elizabeth was denied any further exposure to this lively intellectual household, where her cousin Lady Jane Grey had also spent some time. Instead she was sent to Cheshunt in Hertfordshire to stay with Sir Anthony Denny and his wife. It was not a particularly lively household for Sir Anthony was a scholar and had been a loyal chief gentleman to her father but now was very near the end of his life. Elizabeth turned increasingly to the consolation of study.

At the beginning of 1548 her tutor Grindal had died of the plague. This young man had been an inspirational tutor to the princess since she was just eleven years old. The excellence of her grounding in Greek, Latin and foreign languages was so outstanding that his mentor Roger Ascham admitted he did not know 'whether to admire more the wit of her who learned, or the diligence of him who taught'.[15] The commonplace but tragic death of someone so young and close to Elizabeth stripped more security from her life. Both Ascham and Elizabeth's step-parents had other suggestions for a successor for the talented Grindal, but she insisted, against some resistance, on replacing him with his friend and teacher, Roger Ascham himself. This was the first example of another interesting pattern in Elizabeth's life. Lacking parents, lacking close family, unmarried as she would remain, and childless too, Elizabeth when queen surrounded herself with brilliant men, loyal advisers and favourites whom she made as close as family to her. When they became too old, as did William Cecil, Lord Burghley, or died, like Robert Dudley, the Earl of Leicester, she took on their sons. Although for the old queen, Leicester's stepson the Earl of Essex was a less happy replacement as favourite, the young princess's insistence on replacing Grindal with his own mentor and tutor was inspired. This was to prove a most successful marriage of teacher with pupil, with the princess impressing the scholar from the start with her native intelligence, diligence and remarkable aptitude for learning.

During those difficult months after her banishment Elizabeth's health suffered 'an affliction of my head and eyes'[16] and she did not like either her governess or her tutor to leave her side. This suggested a kind of nervous collapse; perhaps these familiars provided the only security and family feeling left to her in an increasingly menacing world. On the last day of August, Catherine Parr's difficult pregnancy came to an end with the birth, not of the expected son, but of a daughter, Mary. However the relief and happiness at a safe delivery were short-lived. Instead a commonplace tragedy was set in motion. Almost immediately the queen started to sicken with a fever. She became delirious as the infection took hold and within six days was dead of puerperal fever.

Apart from Catherine Ashley's passing mention that she was sick in the period immediately after the queen's death, we have no further record of how Elizabeth took this latest loss. She had left her stepmother's company only a few months before, when she was healthy, hopeful of the birth of her first baby, the 'little Knave'[17] as she called it, full of life and love. But Catherine's death showed just how dangerous love could be to life. To a clear-sighted logical young woman like Elizabeth there was no denying the evidence that if a woman's destiny involved sex it was fraught with pain and danger. Her own mother had survived Elizabeth's difficult birth only to die because the baby was the wrong sex; her brother's mother, Queen Jane, had died in giving birth to him; now Catherine, the closest the young princess had come to having a mother and a female intellectual mentor, was dead herself, in the process of giving life.

Given the general sacrifice of young women to their reproductive functions it was understandable that the gods, and even God Himself, was seen to value women less highly than men. Men died prematurely in war as a result of man's will but the risks to women's lives through childbirth seemed inextricably bound up with some divine plan. It was not surprising if any clever, perceptive girl came to the conclusion that women were more expendable than men, but only if they succumbed to sexual desire and the usual consequence, childbirth, with its handmaidens of pain and possible death.

But sexual desire was dangerous for a woman too if it compromised her reputation. Catherine Howard, one of the more racy and fleeting of Elizabeth's stepmothers, had lost her life for her sexual incontinence and Anne Boleyn, Elizabeth's own mother, had been vilified with terrible accusations of immorality and incest. Trumped up as they almost certainly were, such charges were enough to merit her death. Princes could be murderous, mad, licentious, fathering bastards at any opportunity, and still continue to rule. Princesses had to be very careful.

We cannot know what factors contributed to Elizabeth's decision to remain celibate, despite the stirrings of her own heart and the most telling pressure from her advisers throughout her life. We only know that by the time she ascended to the throne at the age of twenty-five this revolutionary decision had already been made. It is not too fanciful to think that in her mid-teens, steeped in her classical and religious texts, drawing conclusions from sharp observations of society around her, this thoughtful girl was pondering her fate and deciding what she wanted to make of her life.

There was danger too for Elizabeth in Catherine's death. Almost immediately Seymour reprised his ambitions to marry her, thereby dragging the young princess into a scandal which rapidly evolved into treason, with all the peril that entailed. Seymour's jealous politicking against his brother, the Lord Protector Somerset, had alerted the Privy Council to his reckless schemes: 'the World beginneth to talk very evil favourable of him, both for his Slothfulness to serve, and for his Greediness to get, noting him to be one of the most covetous Men living'.[18] It transpired that Seymour had tried to undermine King Edward's confidence in his elder uncle. He had bribed the boy, who resented how short he was kept of funds, with gifts of money. He corrupted an official at the Bristol Mint fraudulently to raise thousands of pounds in readiness for any possible uprising. He put into action his ambitious wooing of the Princess Elizabeth.

To be so indiscreet in his rapacity was suicidally risky, for all these activities could be interpreted as treason. Nicholas Throckmorton, in conversation with one of Seymour's servants, spelt out the danger. 'My Lord is thought to be a very ambitious Man of Honour; and it may so happen that, now the Queen is gone, he will be desirous for his Advancement to match with one of the King's Sisters.' Then in confirmation of the servant's response that seeking to marry Elizabeth without the consents of the King and his Council would bring upon his master 'his utter Ruin and

Destruction', Throckmorton replied: 'it is most true, for the Desire of a Kingdom knoweth no Kindred'.[19]

When Thomas Seymour was arrested and sent to the Tower of London in January 1549, Elizabeth's natural feelings of guilt, fear and shame were intensified: the whole business of the Lord Admiral's intentions towards her were extracted under oath and spread before the Privy Council. The first she knew of how serious the situation had become for her was when her governess Catherine Ashley and her treasurer Parry were arrested at Hatfield. Elizabeth was left alone to be interrogated by Sir Robert Tyrwhit, an agent appointed for this purpose by the Privy Council. On learning that her two loyal servants had been incarcerated in the Tower too, Elizabeth was momentarily very afraid. 'She was marvellous abashed, and did weep very tenderly a long Time, demanding of my Lady *Browne*, whether they had confessed any Thing or not.'[20]

Elizabeth was not just frightened for her life, at this point her reputation was almost as precious to her. If she wished to safeguard her place in the succession, or even continue to be considered eligible for a good marriage, she had to remain virtuous and be seen to be virtuous. This was of particular sensitivity in her case because of the traumatic history of her mother's downfall. These rumours of lascivious relations with a stepfather were too close an echo of the accusations of incest brought against Anne Boleyn and her own brother.

Elizabeth had been caught unawares. The Lord Protector and the council had their suspicions that Elizabeth herself, aided and abetted by her servants, had been complicit in some of Seymour's plans, not least the one secretly to marry. Elizabeth needed time to collect herself and edit the story that would best protect her from these serious allegations. At this first interview she was unprepared and alarmed and could not hide her agitation. Tyrwhit reported back to the Lord Protector: 'in no Way she will not confess any Practice by Mistress *Ashley* or the Cofferer [treasurer], concerning my Lord Admiral; and yet I do see it in her Face that she is guilty'.[21]

Catherine Ashley and treasurer Parry were even more afraid. On facing arrest, Parry had rushed into his wife's room and said to her in great distress that he wished he had never been born 'for I am undone, and wrung his Hands, and cast away his Chain from his Neck, and his Rings from his Fingers',[22] as if he expected then and there to be beheaded.

The following day, Tyrwhit interrogated Elizabeth again, but by now she had composed herself. She appeared to be wholly cooperative but gave only careful, anodyne answers: she could not be certain what Parry or Catherine Ashley had been induced to reveal but she kept her own hand as close as possible to her chest. Tyrwhit thought her calmness and reason meant he was getting round her with his subtle questioning but he did have the intelligence to realize that he was up against a fifteen-year-old girl who was already a formidable advocate: 'I do assure your Grace', he wrote to Somerset, 'she hath a very good Wit, and nothing is gotten off her, but by great policy.'[23]

Although Elizabeth's servants talked more fully as Tyrwhit's tactics frightened or tricked them, they never revealed anything that could be construed as a conspiracy between their mistress and Seymour. Any marriage involving the princess, they declared, was always dependent on the knowledge and approval of the king, the Lord Protector and the Council. Tyrwhit was suspicious that there was much more to be confessed, but he was frustrated in his investigations by the consistency of their blameless story: 'They all sing one Song, and so I think they would not do, unless they had set the Note before.'[24]

The fear of torture and the discomfort of the conditions in which Elizabeth's servants were held cannot be underestimated. It was winter and Mrs Ashley had been moved into a windowless dungeon to induce her further to talk. Here during freezing February she could neither sleep at night, the cold was so intense, nor see by day where no light could penetrate. Always too was the ever present threat of death. In fact it was remarkable that everyone managed to keep that one song in tune, despite the threats, cajolery, forged letters and invented confessions which were flung at them during that chilling start to 1549. Eventually Tyrwhit gave up disgruntled. As far as he was concerned Elizabeth was the architect of this resistance: 'I do believe that there hath been some secret Promise, between my Lady, Mistress *Ashley*, and the Cofferer, never to confess to Death; and if it be so, it will never be gotten out of her.'[25]

After her initial discomposure, Elizabeth's confidence had grown as the interrogations proceeded. Indeed, she was able to summon a tone of remarkable self-righteousness, an attitude which was to become one of her favourite and most effective stances in negotiations throughout her life when she felt she was on dubious ground. In a letter to the all-powerful Lord Protector Somerset she alternated her tone between imperiousness and submission to achieve her effect: 'Master *Tyrwit* and others have told me that there goeth rumours Abroad, which be greatly both against my Honour, and Honesty, (which above all things I esteem) which be these; that I am in the Tower; and with Child by my Lord Admiral. My Lord these are shameful Slanders.' She then requested urgent permission to come to court and show herself 'as I am', distinctly signing herself with the poignant reminder of her youth, her vulnerability and his responsibility, as protector of the realm, towards her, 'Your assured Friend to my little Power, Elizabeth'.[26]

Here was a girl, just turned fifteen, without any powerful guardian to protect her interests, or even her life, reminded in her interrogation that 'she was but a subject',[27] and how perilous her situation had become. She was bullied, threatened and lied to but had managed to keep her wits about her to such an extent that she was able to get the better of her inquisitor and make demands of him and his master, the Lord Protector. When the council decided they would replace Catherine Ashley with Robert Tyrwhit's wife, who would keep a closer eye on the young princess, Elizabeth threw a fit: 'She took the Matter so heavily, that she wept all that Night, and loured all the next Day.'[28] Tyrwhit was no match for such a dramatic display of grief. He did allow her to write to Somerset and argue her case (although he grumbled that she would take none of his advice). Through sheer force of will, emotion and logic, Elizabeth got her way. Eventually Tyrwhit's wife was withdrawn and Mrs Ashley reinstated. Tyrwhit was nonplussed by many things about Elizabeth, not least her devotion to her governess. 'The Love yet she beareth her is to be wondered at,' he wrote.[29] His own job as interrogator was done and he himself withdrew from the fray, relieved no doubt and uneasy at the thought that somehow he had been forestalled by a mere girl.

It is impossible to know just how far Elizabeth compromised herself with Seymour, although there is plenty of evidence that she found him attractive, as well as how troubling she found that attraction. But Tyrwit may well have been right that her servants' loyalty and courage and her own intelligence and coolness under fire prevented something more damaging to Elizabeth's prospects, even her life, from emerging. Elizabeth was distressed by the fact that even by March, Catherine Ashley was still imprisoned in the Tower and, despite her fears that this might implicate her in any of her governess's perceived guilt, she wrote another impassioned letter to the Lord Protector:

> My lord:
> I have a request to make unto your grace which fear has made me omit till this time . . . I will speak for . . . Katherine Ashley, that it would please your grace and the rest of the Council to be good unto her . . . First, because she hath been with me a long time and many years, and hath taken great labour and pain in bringing of me up in learning and honesty. And therefore I ought of very duty speak for her, for Saint Gregory sayeth that we are more bound to them that bringeth us up well than to our parents, for our parents do that which is natural for them – that is, bringeth us into this world – but our bringers-up are a cause to make us live well in it.[30]

Elizabeth never forgot the sacrifices of these partners in her first ordeal. On her accession and throughout their lives she treated both with great favour, knighting Parry and making him treasurer of the household and visiting Catherine Ashley on her deathbed in July 1565, mourning her deeply.

Elizabeth and her servants escaped further punishment but the Lord Admiral Seymour was tried for treason, found guilty and beheaded on 20 March 1549. The whole lethal business had taken just three months. Through this treacherous time Elizabeth had learned some lessons as to the value of circumspection over spontaneity, the necessity of will and intellect ruling the heart. She also learnt about loyalty, the depths of her own, and how her very life could depend on the loyalty and love of her servants, her people. Nothing would make her join in the vilification of Seymour even when she was still under some suspicion herself. 'She beginneth now a little to droop,' the disliked Mrs Tyrwhit noted when Elizabeth heard that Seymour's lands were being divided up and dispersed, but she then added, 'She can not hear him discommended.'[31] However, at fifteen, Elizabeth already had absorbed a wisdom that at forty had eluded the ambitious, swaggering Seymour. On the day of his execution she is reputed to have made the possibly apocryphal comment, 'This day died a man with much wit and very little judgement.'[32] From that day on, Elizabeth would ensure that no one could ever say that of her.

While Elizabeth, exiled from safety, protection and power, endured her baptism of fire, her cousin Mary was embarking on her own more literal exile with a cheerful heart. Her mother, Mary of Guise, had got her way at last: her daughter was to be taken to safety, contracted to marry the dauphin to become eventually Queen of France. The marriage treaty was signed on July 7 1548 and with it the alliance with France was strengthened. Mary hoped that now the French would give her much-needed aid in her struggles to protect her daughter's kingdom from the English.

These marauding English had seized the town of Haddington, John Knox's birthplace, in the eastern Borders. The Scottish troops, reinforced with some five thousand or more Frenchmen, were attempting to wrest it back again when Mary, intrepid as ever, just two days after signing the marriage treaty for her daughter, rode to the town to exhort the troops to greater resistance. Accompanied by her entourage of lords and ladies she headed for the nunnery on the edge of town, from there to gain a better vantage point. But unfortunately her party arrived just as the English gunners were perfecting their range. In an immense explosion of dust and smoke sixteen of her accompanying gentlemen and others of her party were mown down, along with their horses, in a scene of terrible carnage. Even for a woman of her fortitude and experience this horror was too much to bear; the dowager queen fainted with shock. Nothing could have convinced her more graphically of the wisdom of the imminent dispatch of her daughter.

The French fleet sent to spirit the young Queen of Scots away had sailed around the north coast of Scotland to elude the English and finally came to moorage at Dumbarton. To accompany her to her new life in France she had a bevy of Scottish children, among them the subsequently celebrated 'Four Maries' – Mary Fleming, Mary Livingston, Mary Seton and Mary Beaton – all daughters of noble Scottish families. Her adult court included the lords Erskine and Livingston and Lady Fleming, her stepaunt and governess. Also accompanying the young queen was her eldest illegitimate half-brother James Stewart and two younger, Lord Robert and Lord John. Seventeen years old, educated and adventurous, Lord James was to spend some time at the French court in the entourage of his young sister, and it is quite probable that during this time Mary forged her strong affection for this brother, a trust she found hard to relinquish even when he, as Earl of Moray, was made regent in her place years later. Mary's mother was grief-stricken at sending her only daughter from her, on a journey which was inherently hazardous, and made all the more so by the threat of intervention from the aggressive English fleet.

By the beginning of August the French galleys bearing their important cargo eventually sailed down the Clyde and out to sea. There was every evidence that the Queen of Scots was blessed with an adventurous spirit which was to be one of the main motivating characteristics of her life. While others faded with homesickness or seasickness, Mary thrived. The journey around the west coast of England was plagued with storms and fears of an English attempt at ambush and kidnap, but nothing seemed to sap her robust health and merry temperament. Her mother meanwhile was overcome with sadness: 'The old Queen doth lament the young

Queen's departure, and marvels that she heareth nothing from her.'[33]

The French commander de Brézé had in fact sent a series of letters to console the grieving queen mother and in them consistently asserted that Mary, alone of all the party, remained cheery of temper and free of seasickness, despite the terrible storms that almost overwhelmed them off the coast of Cornwall. 'Madam,' he wrote on 18 August 1548, 'in the belief that it will be a comfort to you to have news of the Queen, your daughter . . . she prospers, and is as well as ever you saw her. She has been less ill upon the sea than any one of her company, so that she made fun of those that were . . .'[34] In these leviathan seas they had broken their rudder but Providence, he claimed, came to their aid and the essential steerage was mended without loss of life. After almost a week at the mercy of the sea, the royal entourage arrived at Roscoff on the dramatic coastline of Finistère. There were members of that party whose suffering would have made them think it well named as 'the end of the world'.

Mary's charm, high spirits and adventurousness had already impressed the whole company who had shared her eventful voyage. The kind de Brézé wrote again on 1 November, 'I believe, madame, that [the king] will find her as pleasing and as much to his fancy as all those who have seen her and found her pretty and of clever wit.'[35]

In the middle of the sixteenth century, the French court was the most magnificent and sophisticated in Europe. When Mary arrived in 1548 it was dominated by two women, Catherine de Medici, the wife of Henri II, and Diane de Poitiers, his mistress. These women were indeed powerful but it was power exercised covertly, through influence and manipulation, through persuasion and pillow talk, bribery and possibly even poison. While Henri lived, Catherine appeared to be eclipsed by the phenomenon of Diane de Poitiers. Preternaturally beautiful, seductive and socially skilled, she was nearly twenty years his senior, a woman whom age could not diminish. But it was Catherine who was the more remarkable. Patiently willing to bide her time, wily, pragmatic, treacherous, she was to prove herself the ultimate stateswoman in utter control of herself and the dynasty through control of her children.

Diane had been the king's mistress since he was about nineteen. The story went that François I, in despair at the death of his eldest son, had been complaining to Diane, widow of the Grand Sénéchal of Normandy, of the melancholic nature and uncouth manners of his second son, who had so tragically become dauphin and heir to his throne. Diane had laughingly replied 'he must be made to fall in love, and that she would make him her gallant'.[36] Her plan worked so well that not only did she civilize him but, in introducing him young to the charms of her company, she ensured he was incapable of ever replacing her as the most influential woman in his life. For the following twenty-one years until his death Henri spent up to a third of each day in Diane's company.

Catherine had none of her advantages of beauty or facile personality. She was a neglected scion of the Florentine merchant family of Medici, and had never been popular in France. Married at fourteen, she had to countenance very early her husband's evident preference for his mistress and faithfulness to her until death. After ten miserable years of barren marriage, Catherine became sullen in her unhappiness and sinister in her superstitions and suspected occult powers. It had seemed to Catherine only supernatural intervention could save her from humiliation, and the threatened repudiation by her husband. The fact that she then managed to produce ten children, four of them sons, in a twelve-year flurry of miraculous fecundity explained some of her preoccupations with the occult and her subsequent absolute control over her family. Once Henri II died in 1559, however, the true power of the Medici sprang forth from its long incubation.

Catherine's motto could well have been that genius is a long patience. With the successive reigns of her sons came her chance to show the world how they had underestimated this disregarded queen. What Catherine lacked in beauty she made up for in intelligence, cunning and family ambition. After years of silence and antipathy her time at last had come. But it was not vengeance so much as power which she desired. From that point on, the interests and fortunes of her children were her main concern. Through the youth and inadequacy of her sons as kings she became the real power driving the French monarchy for the last thirty years of her life, as omnipotent queen mother throughout three reigns.

The France that Mary first encountered in 1548 was a country increasingly riven by religious dissent. Calvinism and evangelicalism were well established among the lower clergy and the urban bourgeoisie and were already infiltrating into the higher strata of society. François I's intellectual sister, Marguerite, Queen of Navarre, was strongly evangelical in her faith, although she never broke definitively with the Catholic Church. Everywhere, heresy was enthusiastically rooted out with threats of torture, banishments and public burnings. Banned books were placed on an index and booksellers who defied these proscriptions risked being burnt along with their heretical volumes.

The court, however, seethed with its own factions and intrigues and increasingly was drawn into the religious wars. In the sixteenth century it was a lavish self-contained community, of king and queen and their families, the nobles from the provinces and their entourages, the foreign ambassadors and the *princes étrangers*, who, although with territories outside the kingdom, nevertheless attended the French court. This huge superstructure, centred on the glorification of the king, needed an even more vast army of workers, with priests, soldiers, officials, tradesmen, domestic servants, huntsmen, grooms, entertainers, poets, teachers and musicians. It was a largely peripatetic court, just as it had been in the Middle Ages, on the move between a series of châteaux, driven as much by the royal passion for hunting and the desire for new forests and new animals to kill, as by the more pragmatic need to clean the residences every few months or so, find new sources of food having exhausted the immediate hinterland, and display the king to his people.

To give an example of the logistics involved during François I's reign, stabling was required for somewhere in the region of 24,000 horses and mules needed for transportation and recreation alone. His son's court was no less prodigal. Wagons carried the plate, tapestries and furniture and when the roads became too difficult the court and all its entourage and equipment took to the water. Most of the favourite royal châteaux sat beside the mighty River

Loire basking in its pleasant, hospitable climate, bordered by lush forests filled with animals, often artificially stocked for the king's pleasure, sometimes even with imported exotics. Mary was a fine horsewoman all her life, as was her mother, and Diane de Poitiers looked particularly picturesque acting out one of her many roles as Diana the huntress. But it was Catherine de Medici who was the most fearless of all the court women. She rode as fast and recklessly as any man, and in order to facilitate her speed and manoeuvrability, had invented a way of riding side-saddle that was much closer to the modern technique, and much more effective than the old-fashioned box-like affair in which women were meant sedately to sit.

Everywhere was evidence of François I's passion not only for hunting but for building, and the appreciation of art. This he had expressed actively, acquisitively, by collecting masterpieces for his royal palaces, particularly for Fontainebleau. Excellence in all things was the mark of an extrovert Renaissance king. Naturally, it was to the Italian masters that he turned. The king's greatest coup was to persuade Leonardo da Vinci at the end of his life to come and live at court. He arrived in 1516 with *La Gioconda* (the Mona Lisa), *The Virgin with Saint Anne*, and *Saint Jean Baptiste* in his luggage, and settled at Amboise.

The great sculptor Benvenuto Cellini also spent some time at court and sculpted for François in 1544 his *Nymph of Fontainebleau*. On the walls of the bathhouse, situated immediately under the library, François hung his da Vincis and Raphaels and a magnificent portrait of himself by Titian, portraitist of the age to popes and kings. Although by the time Mary arrived in France, the first François was dead, the visual richness and cultural diversity of his legacy lived on in every royal palace. She would grow up amongst these treasures and then, as queen to the second François, a pygmy shadow of his grandfather, she would fleetingly inherit it all.

However, aged not yet six and newly arrived in her adopted country, Mary first had to meet the royal children, among them the dauphin, and her own Guise relations. She had been placed by her mother under the guardianship of her maternal grandmother, the remarkable Antoinette de Bourbon, Duchesse de Guise. Antoinette and her husband Claude de Lorraine had founded the Guise dynasty with their brood of ten, tall, strong and mettlesome children. Antoinette had proved a wise and rigorous mother and adviser to her impressive daughter: she would endeavour to pass on the same family pride and courage to her granddaughter.

The little Scottish queen was welcomed into this rich and glamorous court with sentimental excitement: had she not just been rescued from their mutual enemy, the brutal English? Had not French courage and nobility of purpose snatched this innocent child from the ravening beast? But there was real fascination too. She was their future queen, a pretty and spirited girl with the novelty of her Scottish tongue and the mystique of her distant mist-wreathed land to charm them. Although there was a long historic relationship between Scotland and France, and some intermixing of the countries' nationals, Scotland was still considered by the French to be barbaric in climate, terrain and the character of its people. Mary's beauty and charm of manner was celebrated all the more because of this piquant contrast.

Most important for the development of Mary's character was the fact that her future father-in-law, Henri II, decreed pre-eminent status for the Queen of Scots. She was to grow up with his own sons and daughters but on any official occasion she was to precede the French princesses, a visual reminder to her companions and to the child herself of her unique importance even among the elite of the French court.

Two months after her arrival on the smugglers' coast of Brittany, Mary was introduced to the grandeur of the French monarchy, which was now to become her own. By easy stages her party proceeded via Morlais and Nantes to St Germain-en-Laye, once a medieval fort but subsequently domesticated and decorated by François I to befit a great renaissance king. King Henri was away on progress through his kingdom and so at the palace she was greeted by his children, the family amongst whom she was to live until she was an adult. They were all younger than she was, and with her Guise inheritance she would remain taller and handsomer, even as they grew.

Her own betrothed, the Dauphin François, was not yet five and having been rather sickly since birth was much smaller and frailer than the Queen of Scots, but their friendship seemed to be forged immediately. Montmorency, the Constable of France, writing to Mary's mother reported, 'I will assure you that the Dauphin pays her little attentions, and is enamoured of her, from which it is easy to judge that *God gave them birth the one for the other*.'[37] François's sister Elizabeth, just three and a half years old, was to become a real friend and as close as a sister to Mary. Claude, another sister, was just a baby, while Catherine de Medici was pregnant again with her fourth child, due the following February. Mary was entering a nursery full of much-doted-on children, to whom Catherine was to add another seven, her last pregnancy in 1556 producing twin girls, who died almost immediately.

Given Catherine's unhappy decade of childlessness and the rigours she had gone through in attempting to conceive, these children were not just precious, semi-miraculous creatures, they were immutable proof to her enemies of her own fitness to be queen. No minutia of their health and wellbeing was too trivial for her concern. They were fussed over and indulged, the darlings of their parents and the court. Due to this odd conjugation of circumstance, Mary was introduced into, what was for the time, an unusually child-centred world, in which she was the star. Even the king, the most important personage in the land, was interested in meeting this five-year-old. He congratulated the Duc de Guise on his niece and said how much he was looking forward to seeing her: 'no one comes from her who does not praise her as a marvel'.[38]

Despite her later antipathy, there is no evidence that Catherine de Medici was anything other than kind to Mary when she was a child. But there was no doubt that she and the factions around her, who opposed the rapidly ascendant power of the Guises, were unhappy with the proposed alliance of the Valois monarchy with Mary Queen of Scots. Seen as merely a Guise in Scottish disguise, Mary, in marrying the dauphin, would be delivering the most terrific coup for the family. To complicate these political antagonisms further, Catherine's arch rival, Diane de Poitiers, was an influential supporter of the Guises (her elder daughter was married to the third Guise brother, Mary's uncle Claude) and Madame, as Diane was known, exercised the most influence of all with the king.

Diane de Poitiers's charm and her interest in the young queen attracted Mary's confidence and affection. Writing to Mary's mother in Scotland, Diane recognized the young girl's pre-eminent status and promised to extend to her a motherly care: 'As to what concerns the Queen, your daughter, I will exert myself to do her service more than to my own daughter, for she deserves it more.'[39] This seductive and cultivated courtesan was to become one of the poles of female influence on the growing girl.

The other was Mary's austerely devout and authoritative grandmother, Antoinette, Duchesse de Guise. A few of her letters to her daughter, Mary's mother, remain and in their psychological insights and human responsiveness they speak across four and a half centuries of timeless affections and concerns:

'I was more glad than I can say to learn of the arrival of our little Queen in as good a health as you could wish her to have.' The duchess wrote to Mary of Guise on 3 September 1548, just before introducing her granddaughter to her new family.

I pity the sorrow that I think you must have felt during her voyage, and I hope you had news of her safe arrival, and also the pain that her departure must have caused you. You have had so little joy in the world, and pain and trouble have been so often your lot, that methinks you hardly know now what pleasure means. But still you must hope that at least this absence and loss of your child will at least mean rest and repose for the little creature, with honour and greater welfare than ever before, please God. I hope to see you yet sometimes before I die ... But believe me, in the meanwhile I will take care that our little Queen shall be treated as well as you can desire for her. I am starting this week, God willing, to meet her and conduct her to St Germain, with the Dauphin. I shall stay with her there for a few days to arrange her little affairs, and until she grows somewhat used to the Dauphin and his sisters. Lady Fleming will, if the King allows it, remain with the child, as she knows her ways; and Mademoiselle Curel will take charge of her French education. Two gentlemen and other attendants are to be appointed to wait upon the little Queen, and her dress and appointments shall be fitting for her rank.[40]

To her son, the Cardinal of Lorraine, Antoinette conveyed her first impressions of her little granddaughter, 'I assure you, my son, she is the prettiest and best at her age you ever saw.'[41] And when Henri II eventually met his prospective daughter-in-law in early December, he was as charmed as everyone else: 'I have no doubt that if the Dauphin and she were of age, or nearly so, the King would soon carry the project [of their marriage] to completion. They are already as friendly as if they were married. Meanwhile he has determined to bring them up together and to make one establishment of their household, so as to accustom them to one another from the beginning. He has found her the prettiest and most graceful Princess he ever saw, as have also the Queen and all the court.'[42]

The conversion of this charming Scottish girl into a French princess was considered the overriding purpose of her education from this point on. Apparently she had arrived speaking Scots and not much else – although very soon was speaking French with great facility and learning Latin. As French culture was universally judged to be far superior to Scottish, and her Scottish entourage already had attracted some unfavourable comment for their roughness and lack of personal hygiene, it would be unlikely that there was much attempt by her new family and tutors to keep the young Queen of Scots' own culture alive. Her sovereignty over Scotland was always considered to be secondary to her potential as consort to the King of France. Although Mary retained some of the original household who had accompanied her from Scotland, within two years all but Lady Fleming were superseded by French men and women.

The 'Four Maries' remained part of the young Queen of Scots' circle of acquaintances in France and were to return with her to Scotland in 1561, where their association with her continued more intimately. There is not much evidence, however, that they were included in her immediate life at the French court. It was possible that for a time they were educated in nearby convents or visited occasionally other French noble families, in the peripatetic way of aristocratic life then. All of them, apart from Mary Fleming, had mothers or stepmothers who were French, and therefore some connections already of their own in France. Mary's mother, Lady Fleming, added French zest to her thoroughly Scottish blood by becoming a mistress of Henri II and, rather scandalously, bearing his child. The four Maries, although of Scottish noble families, were not of high enough social status to be considered ideal companions for Mary now that she was being groomed as a princess of France.

Almost immediately, Mary was sharing the bedchamber of the dauphin's young sister, Elizabeth de Valois. Such was the importance of precedence and hierarchy these girls invariably were given the best room on the strength of Mary's pre-eminent status. They were both prizes in the European marriage stakes. England was to continue to press both the Scots and the French for the return of Mary to fulfil the marriage treaty with Edward VI. The last formal offer of marriage was made in the presence of Henri II and Mary herself in June 1551, when Mary was not yet nine but already happy with the idea of marrying her French prince instead. Failing Mary, it was suggested that her newly adopted sister, Elizabeth de Valois, would make a substitute bride for the English king. But this young woman was to end up married at fourteen to an even greater potentate, Philip II of Spain, only to die at twenty-three giving birth to her third child.

In years to come, both she and Mary were to exhibit individually to their supporters a kind of tragic glamour that was to fuel rumours and fantasies which confused and inflated the posthumous reputation of each. Physical beauty helped, but prerequisite were extreme circumstances and strange congruities in life or death. For the young Queen of Spain, to die so young in childbirth was a common enough occurrence in the sixteenth century, but her tender (and almost certainly chaste) affection for her stepson – exactly her age – the physically deformed and psychologically tormented Don Carlos, inspired through the centuries a profusion of rumours and tragic romances.*

* Most significantly Schiller, the great German poet and dramatist, took the stories of both these ill-fated queens and wrote separate blank verse dramas, *Don Carlos* and *Maria Stuart*, charting their denouements and violent ends. Verdi, too, moved by Schiller's dramatization (and historical distortion) wrote his opera *Don Carlos*, where Elizabeth de Valois is immortalized as its tragic heroine.

Despite Catherine de Medici's reliance on the prognostications of astrologers and fortune tellers, these two girls as yet knew nothing of the lives they were to live as women. There were, however, the immutable facts that one was already a queen and the other might well, through marriage, become one. At the end of 1548, Mary was six and Elizabeth de Valois was nearly four. Their interest in each other had been cemented in a court and at a time when royal children were most pampered and lavishly entertained. Mary's Guise grandmother, writing to her daughter in Scotland, gave a lively picture of a happy and attractive young girl, revelling in the attention and affection that surrounded her: 'It is impossible for her to be more honoured than she is. She and the King's eldest daughter, Elizabeth, live together, and I think that this is a great good thing, for they are thus brought up to love each other as sisters. It is not enough to say that they do not trouble each other in the least, for she [Mary] never works at night or sleeps in the daytime, and is very playful and pretty, and the two children are as fond as they can be of each other's company.'[43]

Not just a doting grandmother but even her prospective father-in-law, Henri, King of France, set apart by pomp and the *amour-propre* of one chosen by God, indulged the little Scottish queen as readily as everyone else. He declared he had never seen a more perfect child, a remark reported back to Mary's anxious mother in Scotland, and he and his courtiers smiled on benignly as the diminutive dauphin danced with his intended bride at the wedding in December 1548 of Mary's eldest uncle, François, Duc de Guise.

Surrounded by doting adults, Mary had her own instant family of brothers and sisters. Apart from the Dauphin François and his sister Elizabeth, there was the baby sister Claude and then three infant brothers were added in quick succession before Mary had reached nine years old. But it was the eldest three children to whom she was closest. When Elizabeth de Valois left France, while still just a girl, to live with her husband Philip II, Mary felt the loss so keenly she claimed in a letter to the Spanish king to be 'the person who loves her the most in the world'.[44] This childhood intimacy with her sister-in-law was most influential in shaping Mary's per-

ABOVE LEFT Mary and François II, her first husband, from the Book of Hours belonging to her mother-in-law, Catherine de Medici. Artist unknown.

LEFT Mary, *c.* 1555, aged about twelve, attributed to François Clouet.

ABOVE Elizabeth, in her coronation robes, 1559. Artist unknown.

OVERLEAF LEFT Elizabeth's mother, Anne Boleyn, by Frans Porbus the Younger.

RIGHT Elizabeth, aged about thirteen, attributed to William Scrots.

ABOVE LEFT The Family of Henry VIII, *c*. 1545. Artist unknown. On his right hand is his heir Edward VI, beside him Edward's mother, Jane Seymour, although she died soon after the birth and Catherine Parr was his queen at the time. Further to his right is Mary I. To his left, showing how far down the succession, is Elizabeth, and in the archway, his fool.

ABOVE Mary I, *c*. 1544 by Master John.

FAR LEFT Henry VIII, *c*. 1536, about the time when Elizabeth was a child. Artist unknown.

LEFT Edward VI, *c*. 1547, Elizabeth's only brother. Artist unknown.

Painted genealogy showing Mary's, and therefore her son's, Tudor ancestry, *c.*1603. Mary is shown (centre of second row) holding hands to signify marriage first with François II and secondly with Lord Darnley, father to James VI and I. Beneath Mary (to her right) are her parents, James V of Scotland and Mary of Guise; beneath Darnley are his parents, Lady Margaret Douglas and Matthew Stewart, Earl of Lennox. Mary and Darnley share a grandmother, Margaret Tudor (centre of fourth row), Henry VII's elder daughter, who first married James IV of Scotland (on her right) and was the mother of James V, and then married Archibald Douglas, Earl of Angus. On the bottom row are the founders of the Tudor dynasty, Henry VII of the House of Lancaster, and Elizabeth of York.

sonal female relationships and, as this letter showed, her spontaneous warmth of feeling was already well in evidence.

Mary, throughout her life, sought her friendships with women. She was attracted to sisterly relationships where she, a queen since birth, was naturally deferred to, and elicited much devotion from the women who knew her. But this made her ill-equipped to deal with a woman like Elizabeth Tudor, a woman who looked to men, not her own sex, for the great friendships of her life. Although proud of family and naturally loyal, Elizabeth refused to be seduced by intimations of female solidarity and any play on the natural bonds of sex and blood. In the early years of their direct relationship, this was Mary's main method of approach to her, and on the whole it gained her very little. She was to be most frustrated, however, by Elizabeth's obstinate evasion of any projected meeting, for this forced Mary into an unnatural role as supplicant for another's favour, and disarmed her potent weapon of charm.

Mary was surrounded in her childhood by powerful women: the French queen, Catherine de Medici; the king's lover, adviser and friend, Diane de Poitiers; Mary's grandmother, Antoinette de Guise, and finally her own mother, the dowager queen of Scotland. In direct contrast, Elizabeth's earliest experiences were of the transience and impotence of women. Her mother had no real existence for her, her life snuffed out when she was no longer useful to the king. Stepmothers came and went, powerless in the grip of fate or the terrifying whim of her autocratic father. Even Catherine Parr, who inspired in the young Elizabeth a certain affection and admiration, was prematurely erased from life by the scourge of puerperal fever. The only constant image of power in Elizabeth's growing years was the once magnificent, but increasingly mangy and irascible old lion of England, her father, the king.

In the childhood of Mary Queen of Scots the opposite was true. Her father through death was absent and unknown to her. Her father-in-law, Henri II, a shade of the magnificent François I, was an unimpressive figure, lacking in confidence and ruled by women. Mary's husband, loved as he was by her, was weaker both physically and intellectually than she, and dominated during his short reign by her Guise uncles and his mother, Catherine de Medici, the dowager queen. Apart from the Duc de Guise and Cardinal of Lorraine, whose ambitions and guile powered the family's rise, in Mary's immediate experience, those who controlled events were women. These women got what they wanted through force of will and character, disguised by charm, beauty and artfulness. No woman in her acquaintance exhibited the undisguised authority of her own mother in her role as dowager queen and regent of Scotland. It was to Mary's eternal detriment as a queen herself that her mother's true work and effortful sacrifice were unknown to her daughter, hundreds of miles away in her adopted kingdom.

Rather than return to a pampered life with her children and extensive family in France, Mary of Guise had bravely battled on in an inhospitable land to try and gain some peace and prosperity for the kingdom of Scotland on behalf of her daughter. But despite the hardships and loneliness of her task, she obviously relished the challenge for herself too. A devout woman, she believed she was fulfilling God's purpose by remaining in Scotland. A Guise, she was also being true to her proud genetic inheritance of seeking and wielding power to the advantage of one's family. Scotland represented the only chance she would ever have to exercise real power so she determined to take the regency for herself. But her daughter never experienced firsthand the daily grind of the dutiful ruler, the astute strategic reasoning of the political mind. The fact that her mother was such an excellent example for her was largely lost to Mary, cocooned in her royal fantasy in the court of the Valois kings.

In order to effect the transference of the regency from the Earl of Arran, who had been rewarded with the French dukedom of Châtelherault, Mary of Guise needed some support from France. A visit to her homeland was mooted in the summer of 1550, for Mary also longed to see her daughter again, and the son she had left behind when she had set sail for Scotland and marriage to James V, twelve years before. The young Queen Mary was overjoyed at the thought of a reunion with her mother. Writing to her grandmother she passed on 'les joyeuses nouvelles': to see her again Mary claimed 'will be to me the greatest happiness that I could wish for in this world'. In her enthusiasm, she promised her grandmother she would work particularly hard at her studies and 'become very wise, in order to satisfy her [mother's] understandable desire to find me as satisfactory as you and she could wish'.[45]

In fact this was to be a significant period in Mary's development. She was nearly eight years old by the time her mother arrived in France in September 1550 and nearly nine by the time she left. Mother and daughter were never to see each other again, and so this year together would gain a certain lustre in memory.

The sixteenth century was still a world bounded by order. Hierarchies were essential in every area of the spiritual and temporal worlds, the animate and inanimate; and these intricate relationships were created and maintained by an overarching power. The monarch in his court and country was like the sun in its solar system, there by the grace of God, pre-eminent among his satellites, but responsible too for sustaining the universe. This sun, the king, was inevitably male. So, to have before you the example of your mother as a successful ruler over men might inspire any young queen looking to understand her role.

But during this time together in France, Mary was not to see her mother in any executive role. Instead the full extravagance of court life was amplified. The spectacle of grand ceremonial whirled on. The young Queen of Scots accompanied her mother on her journeys and listened and watched. Mary of Guise remained in her homeland for more than a year, much of the time with her daughter and the court in its magnificent progresses from royal palaces to hunting châteaux. She was welcomed with the full honours of this most lavish state. In a financial crisis caused by its European wars, and France's support of Scotland in its resistance to the English, the king's spending seemed to become more extravagant as the exchequer teetered towards bankruptcy. Pageants, masques, balls, hunting expeditions, were organized at every opportunity. The pageant which welcomed the dowager queen and her young daughter, at Rouen, involved elaborate constructions of unicorns, to signify Scotland, pulling a chariot, followed by elephants transporting various nymphs and goddesses, along with representations of monarchy and the Virgin and Child. The French monarchy were aiming to ally themselves with the divine, while aggrandizing their secular kingdom.

There was a reason and a grandiose purpose behind such display. Henri II and the Guises had imperial ambitions that extended far beyond Scotland and her borders. Now that the young Scottish queen was safely in their hands, and the English had been repulsed from their 'Rough Wooing', these ambitions could begin to be worked out. In an extraordinarily revealing letter to Suleiman the Magnificent, the grand sultan at Constantinople, the French king in September 1549 outlined his vision of empire: 'I have pacified the Kingdom of Scotland which I hold and possess with such command and obedience as I have in France. To which two kingdoms I have joined and united another which is England of which by a perpetual union, alliance and confederation I can dispose of as King . . . so that the said three kingdoms together can now be accounted one and the same monarchy.'[46]

This whole bold scheme centred on Mary and her invaluable claim on the throne of England. The English were uneasily aware of these ambitions. John Dudley, Earl of Warwick, and Lord Robert's father, had asked the French ambassador to Edward VI's court, whether Henri II referred to the little Queen of Scots as his daughter. When told that he did, Dudley caustically replied: 'After his Majesty has eaten the cabbage I fancy he wants to have the garden also.'[47] The full extent of the French king's intent was exposed to the light of day on the accession of Elizabeth I when he made clear Mary's implicit rights, and so instigated the deadly rivalry between the two cousins.

The continued alliance between France and Scotland was the first piece of this ambitious plan and Henri's enthusiastic appreciation of Mary's mother's efforts to maintain order and repulse the English was expressed in extravagant hyperbole and spectacular celebrations: as the English emissary sourly reported, 'in this court she is made a goddess'.[48] The eight-year-old Queen of Scots could only enjoy the pageantry and wonder at the magnificence of her family's celebrations, but she would never know the daily struggles, danger and frustrations that were companions to her mother's duties in Scotland. She was never to see at first hand the extent of the strategic planning, responsibility and diplomacy of government. Indulged within the hothouse of the royal nursery, flattered and celebrated more than was good for her outside it, Mary was given little chance to see any of the day-to-day workings of the French monarchy. In fact her Guise uncles encouraged the dauphin and their niece in their pursuit of pleasure, mostly in the form of the daily chase, rather than acquiring the arts of kingship. This was partly due to the fact that François was a physically weak and wilful child who showed little aptitude for study, but it also suited the Duc de Guise and the cardinal to maintain the dauphin's fecklessness and indifference to matters of state. Thereby they assured the reins of power could be grasped by their ready hands when fate made François king.

Mary was naturally more intelligent and competent than the dauphin and she was fortunate in being a central figure in a cultured court where education mattered. But she was educated to be an accomplished consort to a great nation's king, rather than to be a ruler in her own right. She seemed naturally to excel at dancing and music making, playing the zither, the harp and the harpsicord, and able to accompany her own singing voice in songs. In the early part of 1553 when Mary was ten and staying with the royal children at the Château of Amboise, the cardinal found her a credit to his proud line and reported such to her mother:

> She has grown so much, and grows daily in height, goodness, beauty and virtue, that she has become the most perfect and accomplished person in all honest and virtuous things that it is possible to imagine ... I can assure you that the King is so delighted with her that he passes much time talking with her, and for an hour together she amuses him with wise and witty conversation, as if she was a woman of twenty-five.[49]

It was not just her family members, however, who sang the young queen's praises. Capello, the Venetian ambassador to France, described Mary when she was just into her teens: 'she is most beautiful (*bellissima*), and so accomplished that she inspires with astonishment every one who witnesses her acquirements. The Dauphin, too, is very fond of her, and finds great pleasure in her company and conversation.'[50]

Mary was also a horsewoman of style and energy, and was as enthusiastic in the chase as even the most fanatical of the French court. She had arrived in France as a very young child, capable from the start of handling her own hunting hawk, much to the admiration of the French courtiers. She would continue to display her love of hunting and outdoor pursuits all her life, her energetic nature suffering keen frustration when she was constrained or thwarted in any way.

Even if her courtly accomplishments were practised daily, Mary's intellect was hardly neglected. Her French was fluent and graceful and it would remain her language of choice all her life. She learnt some Italian and completed her Latin exercises diligently. A collection of these have survived in an exercise book into which Mary copied her Latin translations of French essays given to her as themes, their content meant both to exercise her Latin but also to enlarge her philosophical mind. Predominantly completed in 1555, when Mary was in her thirteenth year, they are not competent enough to claim her as an exceptional scholar, and she was never as diligent in her studies as her cousin Elizabeth Tudor. They are of interest, however, in understanding some of the meditations thought edifying for a royal daughter of France.

Mary took her lessons with Elizabeth de Valois, and most of these exercises in translation were addressed to her. Fifteen are filled with references to learned women as an encouragement to the royal girls themselves. It is interesting that there was little of the prudery of later centuries in sixteenth-century France when Sappho, author of passionately affective homoerotic poetry, is offered to this young queen and princess as an example of an inspirational woman, 'admirable in all kinds of poems'.[51] Hypatia, the first-century academic, is also lauded for the fact she 'wrote books on astronomy and taught in Alexandria various disciplines with such dexterity of mind that scholars came to her from all sides'.[52] Queen Zenobia of Palmyra was celebrated in another essay for her linguistic ability. The priestess Diotima and Pericles's mistress Aspasia were also members of this female elite, paraded to inspire Mary and Elizabeth de Valois in their studies: '[both Diotima and Aspasia were] so proficient in philosophy that ... Socrates, Prince of Philosophers, was not ashamed to call [Diotima] his teacher, nor was he ashamed to go to the lectures of [Aspasia], as Plato has related'.[53]

These Latin exercises also suggest the girls had possibly read the great humanist and scholar Erasmus, or at least his *Colloquies*, published some twenty-five years earlier and an excellent example of the revived and revitalized Latin style of the Renaissance. Although at this stage in Mary's education he may have been studied more for his style than his substance, she cannot have been unaware of Erasmus's undogmatic humanism and questioning of all religious certainties. This and his witty and open-minded scholarship endeared him at first to the religious reformers, but he frustrated them too by sitting on the fence, remaining temperamentally conservative, sceptical all his life of any ideology whatsoever, and as fearful of the new orthodoxies as he was scathing of the old.

In *Colloquies* Erasmus used satire to attack various human institutions and beliefs, especially those to do with the Church and popular superstitions. Again, this was enlightened material for the receptive minds of the young females of a devout Catholic monarchy. Although Mary was to be personally devout and uncompromising in her beliefs all her life, despite the close influence of her militantly Catholic Guise relations, she was not dogmatic about the beliefs of others and never became an avenging scourge of heretics.

The editor of the published version of Mary's translation exercises suggested that they were preparation for an important speech in Latin which she made on New Year's Day 1555 before the king and court assembled at the Louvre, its subject the merits of female education. Although the speech was largely written by others, Mary obviously acquitted herself well in her recitation. One of her tutors, Antoine Fouquelin, with courtly hyperbole explained: 'at which point I would say with what admiration from everyone you would have been heard and what hopes would have been formed for you by all that noble company, if I could say it without a suspicion of flattery. Which sentiment I prefer to find expressed exactly by this verse of Ovid where he speaks of Germanicus Caesar, grandson of Augustus:

> When your celestial mouth had broached your concern
> They say that the gods were wont to speak in that way
> And that of a prince was worthy such excellence
> So much sweetness was in your divine eloquence.'[54]

Mary had been brought up to believe she was a precocious prodigy, irresistible as a beauty and beyond gainsaying as a queen. With such unremitting adulation, it was very hard for her to know the true nature of her abilities and limitations. Her uncle, the cardinal, gave a revealing insight to Mary's already well-developed sense of her own importance, her clear appreciation of what was due to her in her status as queen, asserted even at the age of ten: 'She came hither the other day', he wrote to her mother, 'with my said lords and ladies (the children of the French king) and brought her train, all that she has been accustomed to have . . . In regard to this estate, my advice to you is, that there should be neither superfluity or meanness, which is the thing in this world she dislikes the most; and believe me, Madam, her spirit is already so high and noble that she would make great demonstration of displeasure at seeing herself degradingly treated.'[55] Tractable and eager to please when her charm worked to her advantage, Mary tended to be wilful and hysterical in the rare event that she was crossed.

There was a revealing episode of clashing wills with Madame de Parois, the French governess who replaced Lady Fleming, Mary's sexy and spirited Scottish governess who had borne the king a son. (In trespassing so blatantly on the territories that belonged to his powerful mistress and wife, she was precipitately banished, and eventually deported to Scotland.) The series of letters Mary wrote to her mother complaining about the first person to appear immune to her charm have a febrile emotionalism: 'For, Madame, to tell the truth I have as little occasion to content myself with my lady de Parois as of the world's opinion, for . . . she has done what she could to put me in the bad grace of Madame my grandmother and in that of the Queen . . . she has nearly been cause of my death for the fear which I had of being out of your good grace.'[56] She begged her mother to get rid of the governess for her.

While Mary's energies were being expended on these domestic quarrels, in the process threatening her mother with the death of her only daughter if the offending servant was not replaced, Elizabeth Tudor, at the same age, had been negotiating for her life and the lives of her servants during the investigations of treason involving them and Thomas Seymour.

In the years immediately following this ordeal, Elizabeth retired even further from court life, careful to dress in sombre clothing, conduct herself blamelessly, her only ostentation being the studiousness and piety of her life. Her tutor Ascham wrote approvingly of her self-effacement, even though as history would prove such restraint in her costume was to be short-lived: 'she greatly prefers a simple elegance to show and splendour, so despising "the outward adorning of plaiting of the hair and of wearing gold", that in the whole manner of her life she rather resembles Hippolyta than Phaedra'.*[57] In exile at Hatfield, Elizabeth intended to safeguard herself from any more scandals or taints of treason by association. It was no great hardship for her to bury herself in her books. Born with a penetrating intellect, brought up largely away from court, natural ability had combined with circumstances to make the young princess a prodigy of learning. Like her father she was also blessed with remarkable energy and a love of horses and hunting. Country life away from court had its consolations.

But Elizabeth was lucky too to be living during the sixteenth century when the education of princes and women was a central concern to Renaissance England. Despite the extent of her abilities

* Where Hippolyta, Queen of the Amazons, embodied a virginal resistance to marriage and Phaedra was seen as passionate, flashy and unscrupulous.

and learning, Elizabeth's only disadvantage was that even the most enlightened philosophers considered that the terms 'woman' and 'ruler' were mutually exclusive. One of the most influential educationalists of the age was the Spanish humanist Juan Luis Vives, whose writings influenced Roger Ascham himself.

Vives was a friend and compatriot of Henry's first wife Catherine of Aragon who, concerned herself about the education of her own daughter, Princess Mary, had commissioned him to write a treatise on the education of women. He was a prolific author and the resultant *De Institutione Feminae Christianae* was one of his most successful works. Published first in 1523 it ran later to forty editions. Accepting the received wisdom of woman's subservience to man and the inferiority of the female mind, Vives, nevertheless, was radical in his concern that all women be educated and not in isolation but with fellow students. Piety, chastity and proficiency in the useful arts 'applicable to the purposes of ordinary life' were the main objectives, as he saw it, of education. And like the educationalists who followed him he believed that the study of classical literature, chosen for its moral as well as intellectual content, was the basis for a liberal education which, for a woman, should shape her conscience and develop virtue.

Ascham no doubt learnt much from this great philosopher who preceded him by almost a quarter of a century in the procession of Renaissance educators. His dealings with the Princess Elizabeth, however, completely dispelled any lingering prejudices he may have had about the inferiority of the female mind. Another great influence on Ascham's approach to educating Elizabeth came from a contemporary, the Strasbourg educationalist Johannes Sturm. He discussed in a series of letters to Sturm his agreement on the value of logic and rhetoric in education, and the primary importance of eloquence. In bringing these masculine disciplines to his education of Elizabeth, he was flying in the face of Vives whose influence on the education of her sister Mary Tudor, and on aristocratic daughters generally, had been so marked. Vives was adamant that rhetoric and speech-making were quite contrary to the central purpose of female education, which was to promote chastity, dutifulness and virtue. Women's silence was desirable and any spoken or written word should be solely to promote that personal virtue.

The first known impact of Roger Ascham on Elizabeth's education came in a letter to her governess Catherine Ashley, whose husband was a friend of his from his student days at Cambridge. In this he propounded his advanced theory of the importance of gentleness and responsiveness towards the pupil: 'The younger, the more tender; the quicker, the easier to break. Blunt edges be dull, and dure much pain to little profit ... If you pour much drink at once into a goblet, the most part will dash out and run over; if you pour it softly you may fill it even to the top, and so her grace, I doubt not, by little and little, may be increased in learning, that at length greater cannot be required.'[58] When he officially became the princess's tutor in 1548, Elizabeth was still only fourteen and Ascham found her proficiency with languages remarkable enough and her appetite for study delightful. Together they read Greek in the morning and Latin in the afternoon. Apart from studying the Greek New Testament, Ascham presented his eager pupil with the best classical authors, chosen for their skills at oratory and literary expression. He, like other educators of the time, wanted his pupil not only proficient in linguistic skills but also able to absorb the style and moral content of these classical authorities.

Isocrates and Demosthenes, the great Attic orators, were favourite sources of instruction and inspiration. Elizabeth was expected to translate them out of Greek into English and then back into Greek again. By the time she had completed these tasks she was becoming deeply imbued with the arguments, cadences and modes of expression of the masters. Of the two, Isocrates represented the most elaborate and seamless style, concerned with expression above all, sometimes even to the detriment of meaning. Believing as he did in the importance of prose rhythm, on occasion he could sacrifice lucidity to form – a criticism levelled at some of the later Elizabethan speeches.

However, Demosthenes provided her with a complete contrast in style for this was the orator known *par excellence* for the simplicity and sincerity of his language. A convincing and lucid interpreter of arguments, he was a master of metaphor, but with the dramatic sense to use it sparingly. Demosthenes would call upon a wide variety of styles, alternating complexity with plainness in a speech, projecting a sense of spontaneity in even the most carefully prepared oration. His language and style was at its most simple when he expressed something of greatest moment: this was certainly true of the most compelling sections of Elizabeth's speeches. Addressing the heads of Oxford university, for instance, just after her fifty-ninth birthday, with an oration in Latin which appeared to be quite spontaneous, she thanked them for their unwavering love to her: 'It is such that neither persuasions nor threats nor curses can destroy. On the contrary, time has no power over it – time that eats away iron, that wears away rocks, cannot disjoin it.'[59]

After Greek in the morning, Ascham then took Elizabeth through her Latin studies in the afternoon. Here he used the same exercises of double translation as he had with her Greek, out of Latin into English and then back into Latin again. The works of Cicero made up almost the full surviving corpus of Latin oratory, as well as providing the basis for Roman philosophy, and Elizabeth studied his texts closely. Ascham's favourite work was *De Officiis*, Cicero's last work on moral philosophy. In this he aimed to give advice, ostensibly to his son, on the way to conduct himself in the world, based on Stoic principles, where virtue is happiness and the highest good is a community of reason. Ascham pressed copies on at least two of his friends and Elizabeth read it too, quoting from it in a letter to her equally well-read brother Edward when she was fourteen.

Two years later, Ascham summed up her accomplishments to Sturm with pride, aware too how they must reflect on his own ability as a teacher:

> The Lady Elizabeth has accomplished her sixteenth year; and so much solidity of understanding, such courtesy united with dignity, have never been observed at so early an age. She has the most ardent love of true religion and of the best kind of

literature. The constitution of her mind is exempt from female weakness, and she is endued with a masculine power of application. No apprehension can be quicker than hers, no memory more retentive. French and Italian she speaks like English; Latin, with fluency, propriety, and judgement; she also spoke Greek with me, fluently, willingly, and moderately well. Nothing can be more elegant than her handwriting, whether in the Greek or Roman character. In music she is very skilful, but does not greatly delight.[60]

A slightly more jaundiced view of the same linguistic power was provided by the Venetian ambassador, writing some seven years later: '[She] speaks Italian more than [Mary I] does, taking so much pleasure in it that from vanity she will not speak any other language with Italians'.[61]

If Cicero was Elizabeth's brilliant companion then it was Plutarch who helped teach her how to govern. In his masterpiece, *Parallel Lives*, read by Elizabeth and quoted often, she read of the lives of great men, written not so much as strictly factual biographies but more to explore character and exemplify individual virtue. Shakespeare was to use them as source material for *Julius Caesar, Antony and Cleopatra, Timon of Athens* and *Coriolanus*, and Elizabeth quoted from them on various occasions, most significantly a conversation she had early on in her reign about her reluctance to name Mary Queen of Scots as her successor. '*Plures adorant solem orientem quam occidentem*/ [More do adore the rising than the setting sun],'[62] she explained to the Scottish ambassador Maitland of Lethington, adding that it was natural for people to think the successor preferable to the incumbent, the dream better than any awakening.

Plutarch's *Lives* dealt exclusively with men. In the biographies of Julius Caesar and Mark Antony, however, there emerged an incandescent portrait of a woman and a great queen. Cleopatra dominated the page wherever she appeared and the Princess Elizabeth reading this could not ignore the lessons of ultimate female power. As her sister Mary ascended the English throne in 1553, when Elizabeth herself was not yet twenty, her own chances of becoming queen seemed suddenly less remote. Would Plutarch's description of this brilliant Egyptian daughter, who ascended her father Ptolemy's throne when she was eighteen, appear to have some parallels with Elizabeth and her believed destiny, as the rightful heir of her own revered father?

> Her own beauty, so we are told, was not of that incomparable kind which instantly captivates the beholder. But the charm of her presence was irresistible, and there was an attraction in her person and her talk, together with a peculiar force of character which pervaded her every thought and action, and laid all who associated with her under its spell. It was a delight merely to hear the sound of her voice, with which, like an instrument of many strings, she could pass from one language to another, so that in her interviews with barbarians she seldom required an interpreter, but conversed with them quite unaided, whether they were Ethiopians, Troglodytes, Hebrews, Arabians, Syrians, Medes, or Parthians.[63]

Ascham rated Elizabeth's written Greek so highly he doubted there were four men in England who could better her, and marvelled that in all these languages, and Spanish too, 'within the walls of her privy chamber, she hath obtained that excellency of learning to understand, speak, and write both wittily with head, and fair with hand, as scarce one or two rare wits in both the universities have in many years reached into'.[64]

Livy, the great historian of the Roman Republic, was also extensively studied by the young princess. Again, not particularly troubled by dry fact, his patriotic narrative of the formative age of Rome sought to inspire in his reader a greater understanding and moral force through learning the lessons of history. Machiavelli studied him for examples of political cause and effect, and Elizabeth read most of his output in her two years with Ascham. He had the imagination and language to convey atmosphere and emotion and his history was full of direct and indirect speech, his heroes making rousing set pieces about the battles to come.

Elizabeth's own rallying cry to her troops at Tilbury on 9 August 1588, readying themselves to meet the regrouped Armada, owed much, perhaps, to the heroic style of speech she read in Livy, for instance: 'Let tyrants fear . . . being resolved in the midst and heat of the battle to live and die amongst you all, to lay down for my God and for my kingdom and for my people mine honour and my blood even in the dust. I know I have the body but of a weak and feeble woman, but I have the heart and stomach of a king and a king of England too.'[65] She was also attentive to the vision of herself as a warrior queen, again with more classical allusion: 'The Queen rode through all the squadrons of her army as armed Pallas attended by noble footmen'[66] was how an eyewitness described her dramatic progress on that portentous day. In another account Elizabeth was said to be wearing a symbolic breastplate of gold.

It is not fanciful to consider Elizabeth's mind and expression deeply affected by her scholarly reading and study, a discipline and an enjoyment which she continued throughout her life. The solitariness of her youth; her natural aptitude; her attempts at gaining her father's approval through the exercise of her intellectual skills; her subsequent loss of family and isolation from court; the consequent danger and fears for her life: all conspired to make her books and her studies gain an emotional force far beyond the merely scholastic. As her life as an insecure princess meant increasingly there were fewer living people she could trust, the company of these sublime dead became for Elizabeth a refuge and a consolation. They were the family circle of friends who expected nothing of her, could not betray her and yet taught her some of the most valuable lessons of her life.

Ascham, who had studied her as devotedly as she had her books, noted with admiration that his pupil was not just technically brilliant but deeply steeped in the culture and philosophy of her authors which meant she could inhabit those larger horizons. 'When she is reading Demosthenes or Aeschines, I am very often astonished at seeing her so ably understand . . . the feeling and spirit of the speaker, the struggle of the whole debate, the decrees and inclinations of the people, the manners and institutions of every state, and all other matters of this kind . . .'[67] In short, her intimacy with the classical authors had given Elizabeth a more complex grasp of human psychology and motivation, and an awareness that there was more variety in human experience than any one philosophy could encompass.

While Elizabeth pored over her books, often excluded from court, hoping perhaps, but not yet expecting, that one day she would be queen, her cousin Mary was growing up at the very heart of the most glamorous and decadent court in Europe, reminded every waking minute of her destiny as queen. Although there was nothing to suggest that Mary, while a girl, had any direct exposure to the worst excesses of Europe's most flamboyant court, there was some evidence that her uncle the Cardinal of Lorraine was concerned to remove her from the immediate environment of court life. He wanted to extricate her from the immediate influence of Catherine de Medici and Diane de Poitiers, and establish her in her own household. He wrote to his sister, Mary's mother: 'I do not forget to keep in mind some care as to what she [Mary] says, but to tell you the truth they [the court] are so immoral that I have a great desire to see her mistress [of her own household] and her fate separated from them.'[68]

There is no doubt that a clever inquisitive girl would have been aware of some of the irregularities of behaviour at court given the all-pervasive gossip and the evidence of her own eyes. Even one of her closest adult guardians, the lively and attractive Lady Fleming, her governess from the days she first came to France, had been indiscreet enough to become pregnant by the king and then boast about it around court: 'God be thanked! . . . I am with child by the King, and I feel very honoured and happy about it,'[69] adding for good measure that the royal blood must have some special ingredients because she found herself in such excellent health. The scandal of her pregnancy and the unhappy business surrounding her dismissal cannot have passed Mary by. There was personal loss too.

Given the cardinal's family ambitions and his own opportunism it could be argued that in pushing for the establishment of Mary's independent household and removing her from the immediate influence of Catherine de Medici, he was keen to maintain his unequalled influence on this valuable political commodity, the royal niece who was to unite the French royal family with the ascendant house of Guise. This he accomplished in January 1554, adding considerable expense to the Scottish exchequer, but drawing the eleven-year-old queen closer into Guise control.

Being a queen from birth inevitably meant Mary was surrounded by excessive flattery and tainted praise. As a diplomatic pawn of inestimable worth, she was also manipulated by the ambitions and fears of others. Lacking challenges she grew up unaware of her own capabilities and strength of character, cocooned instead in a false security and a fatal detachment from her subjects.

On the other hand, her cousin Elizabeth, disregarded and in danger for much of her youth, learned that her fate largely lay in her own hands. She had survived through vigilance and quick-wittedness, and a lifelong capacity to connect with her people. In middle age, she herself recognized something of this truth: 'for those rare and special benefits which many years have followed and accompanied my happy reign, I attribute to God alone, the Prince of rule, and count myself no better than His handmaid, rather brought up in a school to bide the ferula [rod] than traded [trained] in a kingdom to support the sceptre'.[70]

The educationalist Vives's stern admonition to parents and educators of women and princesses, 'the daughter should be handled without any cherishing [pampering]. For cherishing marreth sons, but it utterly destroyeth daughters',[71] would prove to have poignant echoes in the lives of these two queens.

CHAPTER FOUR

Apprenticeship for a Queen

Some have fallen from being Princes of this land to be
prisoners in this place; I am raised from being a prisoner
in this place to be Prince of this land.

*Elizabeth's speech at the Tower of London the day before
her coronation*

PRINCES ARE BORN; HEROES MAKE THEMSELVES. The hero
figure in myth and legend, archetype and fairytale, grows in stature
and glory through a series of tests and temperings of character and
will. And the prince who would be a hero is in no less need of
transformation. Pre-eminent by birth, she has to know the human
self within the pomp, and overcome fear, pain, humiliation and
loss of faith in the process. A challenge is essential for every hero,
to attain superhuman strength and renown; but the heroic prince
needs to face her own vulnerability, and in the process grow
wise. Early in her life circumstances gave Elizabeth a descent into
terror and powerlessness which steeled her character and prepared
her for the crown. For Mary the trials came too late and were too
extreme for a nature bred on adulation and ease. Their different
responses to flattery and menace show the two sides of a harsh
Greek truth familiar to them both: παθει μαθος, pathei mathos –
through suffering learning.* Elizabeth's triumph was her painful

* Agamemnon, 177. The first printed edition of Aeschylus was published by the celebrated
Venetian Aldus Press in 1518.

transformation from prisoner to prince: Mary's tragedy was her headlong reversal of that journey.

But before Elizabeth could become the great queen of collective imagination, she confronted the fundamental problem that she was a woman. Even the enlightened thinkers of the Renaissance found it contrary to natural law that a woman alone, without the alliance and natural reinforcement of a husband, a brother, a father or son, could be a leader of men. And in her public utterances at least Elizabeth appeared to accept this orthodoxy that women generally lacked the capacity to rule. In speeches and letters she referred often to her innate weakness as a woman before claiming, with the power of antithesis, her unique gifts of courage, of care for her subjects, of genetic inheritance from her father. Her apparent acceptance of female inferiority was certainly in part a rhetorical flourish. It was also a clever political ploy to feign incompetence and thereby lull the opposition. It was an integral part of the greatest diplomatic game she was to play, the virgin open to bids for a dynastic marriage. But this reiteration of female inferiority was an expression too of a not quite unshaken confidence in herself, an inability to discount completely the venerable opinions of her intellectual masters.

For Elizabeth, however remarkable, was still a woman of her time, brought up in accordance with the prevailing expectations for aristocratic young women of the early sixteenth century and personally deeply influenced by her religious and classical education. Despite her sense of destiny, she cannot have escaped the unanimous message of her education that it was an aberration for a woman to govern – 'monstriferous'[1] was John Knox's blunt verdict. Worse still, female governance disturbed the natural and sacred order of the universe. Aristotle was cited, as was St Paul, and contemporary statesmen like Sir Thomas Elyot who could call on his depth of scholarship of Renaissance humanism to declare: 'in the partes of wisdome and civile policy, [women] be founded unapt, and to have litell capacitie'.[2] Even reformist theologians like Calvin, adopting as conciliatory a tone as possible in writing to William Cecil, Elizabeth's principal secretary once she was queen, could only see female rule as unnatural, a punishment from God for sin:

'a deviation from the primitive and established order of nature, it ought to be held as a judgement on man for his dereliction of his rights, just like slavery'.[3]

The way Elizabeth philosophically explained the anomaly of female rule was through the medieval theory of the king's two bodies. This proposed that there was a natural body and a body politic. In Elizabeth's case the natural body, the corporeal self with all the weaknesses and vitiation that implied, was where her feminine frailty resided. But as queen, she could claim also a body politic, with all the 'masculine' virtues of judgement, decisiveness, courage and probity, which her female self was deemed to lack. Three days after she acceded to the throne, in her first speech to her assembled lords, the young queen sought to minimize her disadvantages of youth and sex by invoking this mystical duality:

> considering I am God's creature, ordained to obey His appoint-
> ment, I will thereto yield, desiring from the bottom of my heart
> that I may have assistance of His grace to be the minister of
> His heavenly will in this office now committed to me. And as
> I am but one body naturally considered, though by His per-
> mission a body politic to govern, so I shall desire you all, my
> lords . . . to be assistant to me.[4]

Elizabeth learned how to use this ambivalence to her advantage, creating for herself during her long reign an androgynous identity which gave her a unique protean power. She could offer her unbroached female body to invoke the iconic power of the Virgin herself, chosen by God, beyond reproach and distinguished by the characteristic of mercy. She could as readily become the mother of her people when she wished to convey love and careful nurture. She played the lover, outrageous, flirtatious and vain. She played the housekeeper, excusing her legendary parsimony and mean-ness on the grounds that she was merely doing what any good woman would do. In her political negotiations she could shamelessly trade on the accepted feminine trait of indecisiveness, confounding the schemes of her advisers and enemies with a self-proclaimed female incapacity, while summoning political shrewdness and will.

However, when it suited her purposes, Elizabeth would claim the maleness inherent in her 'body politic'. Invoking her kingly majesty, she assumed all the qualities traditionally ascribed to the masculine; the heart of a lion, the mind of a scholar, steadfastness in the face of her enemies, jealousy of her honour and the courage to act militarily in defence of her country and her people.

Elizabeth was both a virgin and a prince, when virginity was a positive virtue which elevated a woman above her carnal and inferior destiny and a prince was ordained by God and pre-eminent amongst mortals. By maintaining her supremacy in both masculine and feminine roles, Elizabeth made it difficult for her detractors. More often than not they resorted to personal attacks, accusing her of illegitimacy or elaborating rumours of her sexual abnormality and her freakishness as a woman. Mary Queen of Scots, herself, joined in the demeaning innuendo with the so-called 'scandal letter' she wrote Elizabeth from her imprisonment in the winter of 1584. In this she catalogued the sexually charged rumours about the queen, suggesting that the consummation of marriage to any man was made impossible because 'indubitably you were not like other women'.[5]

It was difficult for Elizabeth to overcome the established, deep-seated prejudices against female rule. And given the scarcity of examples of women of authority in previous centuries, there was bound to be a certain prejudice and lack of confidence to overcome within herself. Writing a century earlier, a prolific French intellectual and writer, Christine de Pisan, expressed something of the effect on thoughtful women of the accumulation of negative opinion about their own sex. In the introduction to her refutation of misogynist texts, *The Book of the City of Ladies*, she wrote, '[It] made me wonder how it happened that so many different men – and learned men among them – are so inclined to express both in speaking and in their treatises and writings so many wicked insults about women and their behaviour.' So demoralized did she become by this unremitting prejudice from fine scholars and godly men whose opinion she revered that she ended up 'detest[ing] myself and the entire feminine sex, as though we were monstrosities in nature'.[6]

Although Elizabeth was living a century later and, as a royal princess, could claim a certain distance from the general run of womankind, she was reading the same classical and biblical texts as de Pisan, in which were promulgated the same orthodoxies of women's unfitness for responsibility outside family life. In England's long history there had been no regnant queens apart from the twelfth-century Queen Matilda, whose indecisiveness and lack of judgement indirectly caused civil war. And Matilda was never crowned as queen. Now four centuries later there would be four regnant queens in one isle; the first to inherit a throne in her own right in 1542 had been Mary Queen of Scots, but she was not to return to Scotland and her throne until 1561. By then Mary Tudor in 1553 had brushed aside Lady Jane Grey (whose uncrowned nine-day reign barely counted) and succeeded to the English throne. On her death in 1558 she was followed by Elizabeth herself.

The prejudice against sovereign queens was not so personally troublesome to the two Marys, or indeed to Jane, who mitigated the abnormality of their status by marrying. By following the prescribed pattern of alliance, female rulers were expected to find in their husbands, who on marriage became kings, the statesmanlike qualities and powers denied to them as women. This had its own inherent political problems, but the queens' advisers and subjects were at least spared the worrying aberration of a woman as sole monarch.

By refusing all her life to marry, despite the weight of history and consistent, at times almost hysterical, pressure from her advisers, Elizabeth was refusing to accept publicly this view of her implied inadequacies in being a mere queen. This also made her more exposed than her sister and cousin to the perceived unnaturalness of her position. She recognized this vulnerability and invoked revered biblical women in an attempt to appear less alone. In a prayer written in Spanish in the early part of her reign she addressed God, 'Thou hast done me so special and so rare a mercy that, being a woman by my nature weak, timid, and delicate, as are all women, Thou hast caused me to be vigorous, brave, and strong ... persist, in giving me strength so that I, like another Deborah, like another Judith, like another Esther, may free Thy people.'[7]

Her prayers are her conversations with God and her people, and in publishing them in volume form she broadcast an affective voice to her subjects. They were not only tracts for private meditation, but also powerful propaganda for herself as her people's God-ordained queen. In a book of the queen's prayers, published in 1563, some of Elizabeth's Latin compositions, although addressed to God, are more clearly promotional literature addressed to the world: 'I am unimpaired in body, with a good form, a healthy and substantial wit, prudence even beyond other women, and beyond this, distinguished and superior in the knowledge and use of literature and languages, which is highly esteemed because unusual in my sex. Finally I have been endowed with all the royal qualities and with gifts worthy of a kingdom.'[8] Her persistence in rehearsing her kingly qualities of mind and character in her prayers, her conversations and her speeches, revealed Elizabeth's sensitivity to the fundamental prejudices against her sex.

By refusing to marry, yet holding out the possibility that one day she might, Elizabeth also turned the accepted male orthodoxies on their head and used her self as the main bargaining bait in the wiliest of diplomatic games. In this way she kept the great European powers at bay by playing each off against the other until she was strong enough to dominate her neighbours through intelligence, superior naval power and nearly half a century's peace and prosperity at home.

But this strategy was far from formed as Elizabeth stood on the threshold of power, watching her half-sister Mary Tudor seize the initiative and claim her rightful place as queen. It was during her reign that Elizabeth was to suffer the greatest ordeal of her life, the memory of which would never leave her.

Elizabeth's half-sister Mary was seventeen years her senior and had endured a different series of ordeals in her progress to the crown. She, like Elizabeth, had been stripped of legitimacy and denied her place in the accession. But it had been Elizabeth's birth that had blighted Mary's youth. She was demoted, humiliated and ostracized by her father for her devotion to her mother, Catherine of Aragon. Then as Edward VI faced death, in his desire to maintain the reformed religion he had promoted so strongly in his short reign, he diverted the accession from his sisters Mary and Elizabeth to his cousin, the Protestant Lady Jane Grey. This plan was encouraged, if not instigated, by the newly elevated John Dudley, Duke of Northumberland, who then married Jane to his son, Guildford. On Edward's death on 6 July 1553, the plan seemed to have succeeded, but then Mary courageously gathered her forces and, buoyed on a wave of popular support for Henry's rightful heir, faced down Northumberland and was proclaimed queen. Dudley was beheaded for treason the following month, and Guildford and Jane were executed six months later.

Mary shouldered her responsibilities with appropriate seriousness of purpose. The maintenance of her principles, although lacking in pragmatism and political expediency, had an element of the heroic. But her reign was undermined by two fatal passions. Mary was pathetically devoted to her husband Philip II of Spain, who was unmoved by her and much hated and mistrusted by her people. She was also absolutely committed to her faith and the need to avenge the wounds and humiliations inflicted on her mother, the faithful, and herself in the establishment of the new church. This zealotry resulted in her immediate and forcible restitution of Catholicism, in a country that was beginning to embrace the reformed religion, and value autonomy from the dictates of Rome. In restoring the old heresy laws in 1555, Mary unleashed the persecutions that resulted in an orgy of burnings. These autos-da-fé, some three hundred or so, inspired one of the great emotive tracts of the sixteenth century, *Foxe's Book of Martyrs*,* in which in lines of

* John Foxe (1516–87) was a writer and evangelical cleric, unusual at the time in his abhorrence of burning heretics of any religion. While in exile during Mary I's reign he started to compile the histories of anti-papal martyrs that he published in 1554 and 1559. His first English edition, called *Actes and Monuments*, but popularly known as *Foxe's Book of Martyrs*, was published in 1563 and became a huge publishing success. The affecting verses of the lives and deaths of ordinary people were much enlivened by grisly woodcuts, an unusual addition at the time. In 1571, every cathedral and most churches were ordered to have a copy for their congregations to consult.

poignant verse John Foxe recorded the names and circumstances of the deaths of ordinary, yet extraordinary, people:

> June 16 1557
> When JOAN BRADBRIDGE, and a blind maid,
> APPELBY, ALLEN, and both their wives;
> When MANNING's wife was not afraid,
> But all these Seven did lose their lives.
> When these, at Maidstone, were put to death,
> We wished for our ELIZABETH[9]

These pitiful deaths earned the queen the posthumous nickname 'Bloody Mary'. Not a personally cruel woman, but a passionate and fanatic one, she believed that this purge of heretics would save the souls of the benighted. But she had completely misjudged her people and the spirit of the times. They had welcomed her reign with much rejoicing; many still were sympathetic to and nostalgic for the old faith. But fanatical persecution did not suit the English temperament, and Mary's personal unhappiness, and her people's growing misery and fear combined to make her reign a dark one. Its failure was compounded in the last months of her life with the loss of Calais to the French. Of great symbolic moment, both Mary and her people recognized this as a damning verdict on her reign.

Mary Tudor did little to commend female rule to a suspicious populace, one of its major detriments being her marriage to a foreign prince, and a Spanish prince at that. No foreigner had been King of England since William the Conqueror and there was a visceral fear of 'strangers'. Queen Mary's alliance with a Hapsburg prince seemed to its opponents no less than the enemy's conquest of England by marriage.

Politically, too, it was feared that such an alliance would make England even more vulnerable to the French who already had assured their passage into the realm via Scotland. For the rest, all the ills of the reign could be blamed on this most unpopular of consorts: 'Queen Marye's match with King Phillip, was so farre from enrichinge England, that never prince left it more indebted, both at home and beyond the sea,'[10] was the verdict of most of her people.

In January and February 1554 confirmation of this projected marriage fuelled an uprising of disgruntled gentlemen, several of whom were members of the House of Commons, intent on denying any Spanish influence in England, but concerned too to save the new evangelical religion from suppression by the old. In an extensive conspiracy aimed at involving most of the central and southern counties, Mary was to be bundled from the throne, even assassinated it was whispered, and Elizabeth raised in her stead. Whether Elizabeth knew of this or not it was extremely perilous for her to be implicated, or even mentioned in the same breath, as such deadly treason.

This dangerous episode became known as the Wyatt Rebellion, after Sir Thomas Wyatt the younger, the son of the poet Sir Thomas Wyatt who had loved Anne Boleyn and lost her to the king, yet managed to survive her fall. Sir Thomas the younger was a brave military commander but a reckless and impetuous man. Asked to join the rebellion by Edward Courtenay, Earl of Devonshire, who was hoping to marry Elizabeth on the successful outcome of this coup, Wyatt had cheerfully agreed. However, as it transpired, he was the only competent one among them. When all the other conspirators were arrested it was left to him to carry through his part of the insurrection alone. This he did with some success, marching the rump of his four thousand men right into the heart of London, and into a trap.

Imprisoned in the Tower and examined under torture he refused to implicate Elizabeth in the conspiracy, insisting that he had only 'sent hir a letter that she shoulde gett hir asfar from the cyty as she coulde, the rather for hir saftye from strangers'.[11] For his part, he swore that he had not desired the queen's death but had been motivated by his patriotism: 'myne hole intent and styrre [stir] was agaynst the comyng in of strandgers and Spanyerds, and to abolyshe theym out of this realme'.[12] But even Wyatt's stalwart denials could not save Elizabeth. Her sister Mary was heavily reliant on the advice of Renard, the Spanish ambassador, who was implacably opposed to Elizabeth and, like Mary's Lord Chancellor, Bishop Gardiner, deeply suspicious of the religious and dynastic interests that focused around her. Renard's purpose was unequivocal. He pressed the queen to charge her sister with treason and execute her, even suggesting that Philip's arrival in the country to take up his marriage vows should be dependent on the dispatch of Elizabeth.

Elizabeth's true attitude to religion was a matter of much debate for Mary and her advisers. She had learned young the necessity of expedience, and the value of compromise. At this time of religious and political ferment Elizabeth needed to keep her wits about her and attract as little attention as possible. Fearing her sister's disfavour for her lack of enthusiasm for Catholicism, Elizabeth requested an audience, and in the presence of the queen threw herself on her knees, weeping. She explained that her religion 'was excusable, because she had been educated in it, and had never even heard the doctrines of the old faith'.[13] To Mary's gratitude and relief, her sister then asked for books and suitable instruction that might show her the error of her beliefs.

However, there were more cynical courtiers who thought this but a ploy by Elizabeth and they watched her closely as she attended, or found excuses not to attend, Mass. An atmosphere of suspicion and menace surrounded her. The French ambassador, writing to the King of France, offered his interpretation: 'Madame Elizabeth, after much solicitation, has been compelled to hear the Mass with the Queen, her sister. Nevertheless, everyone believes that she is acting rather from fear of danger and peril from those around her than from real devotion.'[14]

By the end of 1553 she had left court, in part to get away from the spies, malicious gossip and talk of plots and conspiracies that dogged her every movement. Elizabeth had been periodically indisposed since her unhappy removal from her stepmother Catherine Parr's household some five years before. By the beginning of the new year she was more acutely ill with a debilitating disease, possibly some kind of kidney inflammation, which had weakened her considerably and made her face and body swell with fluid. On the outbreak of the Wyatt Rebellion in February 1554, Mary had summoned her from Ashridge, where she was living in Hertfordshire, to London, but Elizabeth had a genuine excuse for not complying immediately. Once Wyatt was arrested, however, the summons came more forcefully. On 11 February three lords arrived at her gates, with orders to convey her immediately to London, one of whom was William Howard, a kinsman of the Boleyns. Their request was made more compelling by the presence in their retinue of two hundred and fifty men on horseback.

The queen had also sent two doctors and they confirmed that the journey was not life threatening. Elizabeth was in no position to demur. She was so unwell, however, that she came close to fainting 'three or four times' as they got her ready to depart, her household shocked at 'the careful fear and captivity of their innocent Lady and mistress'.[15] Her progress was painful and slow. It took nine days before she arrived in London where she was met by sympathetic members of the court on horseback and a spontaneous crowd of ordinary Londoners, 'who then flocking about her litter, lamented and greatly bewailed her estate'.[16] There were rumours, as there always were with unexplained illnesses, that Elizabeth had been poisoned, 'because she is so distended and exhausted that she is a sad sight to see'.[17]

Ill as she was, Elizabeth was not too weak to notice what was perhaps her first experience of the force of a collective emotion focused on herself. The rough goodwill and human sympathy, faces peering to see, hands outstretched, voices shouting, as the mass of humanity surged towards her: she was their princess, they were her people. Always sensitive to the emotive power of image, she 'caused her litter to be uncovered, that she might show herself to the people'. Elizabeth knew the effect that the sight of her in such a plight had on them. She was young. She had dressed herself entirely in white, the colour of purity, and her natural paleness had become almost transparent with illness, fatigue and fear. But her expression was, according to the hawkish ambassador to Spain, 'proud, lofty, and superbly disdainful; an expression which she assumed to disguise her mortification'.[18]

Mary was under pressure to send her sister to the Tower, to

share her fate with all the other rebels and heretics. Feelings were running high. On 12 February, the day after Elizabeth was sent for, Lady Jane Grey, 'the nine days' queen', had been executed in the Tower, out of sight of the general populace. Stories had circulated as to her piety and dignity on the scaffold, the pathos of this sixteen-year-old girl, blindfolded and in a fright feeling for the block on which to lay her head. Rather than saving her, her royal blood had been her undoing. Innocent herself, she was executed for her father's implication in the rebellion. There was every reason to believe that Elizabeth's life might as easily be tossed away.

There was general alarm and confusion. Rebel soldiers were being rounded up and hanged in market places throughout the south. At every gate to the city of London gallows were erected. Body parts of rebels who had been hung, drawn and quartered were strung up along the city walls. The prisons were so full that prisoners 'of the poorest sort'[19] were locked up in churches and taken from there to be hanged. The main conspirators were brought to the Tower to be 'straitly examined'[20] and if found guilty then taken to the scaffold on Tower Hill. The French ambassador, who also opposed the Spanish marriage, described Mary's severe justice. The gibbets hung, he wrote, with 'some of the bravest and most gallant men that she had in her kingdom',[21] the prisons bursting with the best of English nobility.

As Elizabeth's pallid form passed through the emotionally stirred crowd she appeared a powerless innocent in the grip of an avenging government, a daughter of King Harry brought low and vulnerable to suffering as they were. Yet her status made her a ready candidate for heroism, or martyrdom. It was possible, however, that she knew more about the uprising than anyone was telling.

Elizabeth was closely confined at Whitehall while those implicated in the rebellion were interrogated. The queen, Bishop Gardiner, her Lord Chancellor and Renard, the Spanish ambassador, were keen to extract information that pointed to Elizabeth's guilt. There is no record of Elizabeth's feelings during her three-week isolation, but there is no doubt that she was acutely aware of the danger she was in and fearful of what case might be constructed in her absence: 'I pray God [that] evil persuasions persuade not one sister against the other'[22] was one of her anxious pleas to the queen.

But Queen Mary's persuasions were already set resolutely against her. Michiel, the Venetian ambassador, gave a shrewd and plausible analysis. However much Mary tried to hide it, her 'hatred . . . scorn and ill-will' manifest towards her sister in all kinds of ways, was a direct result of the misery and humiliation she and her mother suffered from Henry's behaviour during the divorce. 'But what disquiets [Mary] most of all is to see the eyes and the hearts of the nation already fixed on this lady as successor to the Crown from despair of descent from the Queen.' Not only was this an embittering reminder of Mary's own infertility but, Michiel implied, a denial of everything she held most dear – her religion, her mother's memory, her own legitimacy. 'It would be most grievous', he agreed, 'not only to her but to any one to see the illegitimate child of a criminal who was punished as a public strumpet, on the point of inheriting the throne with better fortune than herself, whose descent is rightful, legitimate, and regal.'

Elizabeth's own behaviour at this point did not help matters. For, insecure in the knowledge of the debatable circumstances of her legitimacy, she armed herself with a fragile but galling confidence. 'She is proud and haughty, as although she knows that she was born of such a mother, she nevertheless does not consider herself of inferior degree to the Queen, whom she equals in self-esteem; nor does she believe herself less legitimate than Her Majesty.'[23]

Regardless of her innocence or guilt in the Wyatt Rebellion, the real danger to Elizabeth lay in the fact that she was a popular focus for every kind of dissent and discontent with her sister's government. Michiel declared, 'never is a conspiracy discovered in which either justly or unjustly she or some of her servants are not mentioned'.[24] Any hothead or madman might implicate her in his own private fantasy or place her as a figurehead for a full-scale conspiracy against the crown. In a later speech to Parliament she recalled this sinister time: 'I stood in danger of my life, my sister was so incensed against me. I did differ from her in religion and I was sought for divers ways.'[25]

While she was confined Elizabeth was told of one of the more bizarre manifestations of her value to the opposition. A wildfire rumour had swept through London of the miraculous talking wall that appeared to add supernatural approval for the new religion and Elizabeth as queen. So febrile were everyone's emotions that by eleven o'clock in the morning 'more than seventeen thousand people', according to Renard, had mobbed the house in order to hear what they believed was the voice of an angel. 'When they said to it, "God save Queen Mary!" it answered nothing. When they said "God save the Lady Elizabeth!" it replied "So be it." If they asked it "What is the Mass?" it replied "Idolatry." '26 Elizabeth was quick to dismiss this as a trick, as was the government. It was generally recognized, however, that the people were unhappy about the prosecutions of so many rebels and the increasing intolerance towards adherents of the new religion, now damned as heretics. While she lived, Elizabeth made an obvious and attractive focus for their disparate grievances.

The arrests and interrogations continued. Despite the lack of hard evidence, Mary's suspicions remained. Elizabeth's character 'was just what she had always believed it to be',27 she had remarked with some bitterness to Renard. On Bishop Gardiner's urging the council agreed Elizabeth had to be imprisoned while the investigations continued. On 16 March, Elizabeth was told what she dreaded most, that she was to be incarcerated in the Tower. There could be no more baleful proposition: it was, as she pointed out, 'a place more wonted for a false traitor than a true subject'.28 Elizabeth's own mother, Lord Admiral Seymour and, most recently, Jane Grey, had entered the Tower as a prelude to their grisly deaths. And those who did not die quickly languished there for years suffering the slow death of disease, fear and loss of hope.

When they came for Elizabeth the following morning she begged to be allowed to see her sister face to face, to protest her innocence for herself. There would be a tragic symmetry when nearly two decades later Mary Queen of Scots would beg to be allowed to present herself before her cousin Elizabeth to plead her innocence. She was to be refused by Elizabeth, just as Elizabeth was now refused by her own sister. Elizabeth then asked for permission to write a letter to the queen instead, as indeed Mary would also do to her.

Elizabeth's famous letter, written on the eve of her imprisonment, was perhaps the greatest letter of her life. Composed while she was at her most agitated, the language was straightforward and unadorned. Her life in the balance, Elizabeth's careful script and measured tone argued for her innocence: 'I protest afore God (who shall judge my truth, whatsoever malice shall devise) that I never practiced, counseled, nor consented to anything that might be prejudicial to your person any way or dangerous to the state of any mean.'[29] She had stripped her style of all hyperbole. Instead of her usual stately metaphors and classical allusions, Elizabeth mentions only – and revealingly – the example of the Seymour brothers, whose enforced separation when the Lord Admiral was arrested, increased the misunderstandings between them, with fatal consequences. 'I heard in my time of many cast away for want of coming to the presence of their prince, and in late days I heard my lord of Somerset [the Lord Protector] say that if his brother had been suffered to speak with him, he had never suffered. But the persuasions were made to him so great that he was brought in belief that he could not live safely if the admiral lived, and that made him give his consent to his death.' At this moment of personal strain and danger it was understandable that she should recall the last time she feared for her life, again with accusations of treason hanging over her. But perhaps being so ready to use the example of the Lord Admiral and his fate in a letter pleading for a fair hearing for herself, and possibly for her life, showed too how vividly he remained in her memory.

The appearance of this letter is eloquent of Elizabeth's fear. Her anguished plea for an audience and protestations of innocence ended only a quarter of the way down the reverse page. The remaining empty space Elizabeth filled with heavily scored diagonal lines, fearful as she must have been of any unauthorized inclusions. At the bottom left hand corner, she added 'I humbly crave but only one word of answer from yourself' and then signed herself at the opposite corner 'Your highness' most faithful subject that hath been from the beginning and will be to my end, *Elizabeth*'.[30] This careful letter had taken Elizabeth so long to write, perhaps intentionally so, that she and her escort missed the tide 'which tarrieth for nobody'.[31] Now they could only travel the following day as the queen had insisted the prisoner be conveyed to the Tower by river. To travel through the city's narrow streets risked demonstrations and even possible rescue.

On the morning of Palm Sunday they came for her. Londoners had been told by the council to go to church as usual. So hasty were Elizabeth's custodians to depart that the barge carrying the princess into captivity had to wait on the river for an hour or so, in the bitter cold and in some danger, before the bargemen were willing to risk the fast flowing water through the narrow races of the old London Bridge. As they approached the forbidding fortress itself, Elizabeth asked her accompanying lords Winchester and Sussex if she could be spared entering by Traitor's Gate. This was against their orders, they told her. It was raining as she stepped off the barge and one of the lords offered her his cloak, which she turned briskly away.

Looking up to heaven, Elizabeth addressed the warders and soldiers who lined the entrance, 'Ohe Lorde! I never thought to have come in here as prysoner; and I praie you all, goode frendes and fellowes, bere me wytnes, that I come yn no traytour, but as true a woman to the quenes majesty as eny is nowe lyving; and theron will I take my deathe.'[32] Told by the lords who accompanied her that this was no time to argue her case, she replied smartly: 'You have said well, my Lords! ... I am sorry that I troubled you!'[33] The contemporary chronicles of this central drama in Elizabeth's life convey an immediacy in the reported conversation and singularity of detail which is compelling in their portrait of the princess and her ordeal.

As she proceeded further into the Tower, Elizabeth asked why there were so many men in full armour, adding, 'yt needed not for me, being, alas! But a weak woman'. She asked that they be dismissed from duty and the chronicle related that the men knelt down before her 'and with one voice, desired GOD to preserve Her Grace'.[34] At this point her strength and bravado gave out and she sank down on the cold wet step. Chided to stand up and come out of the rain, Elizabeth replied, 'Better sitting here, than in a worse place! For, GOD knoweth! I know not whither you will bring me!'[35]

The Tower was a terrifying leveller. Everyone who entered as a prisoner knew it was the antechamber to death which few escaped. Elizabeth was as aware as anyone what efforts were being made to find enough evidence to incriminate her. Within those walls men were being tortured; who could blame them for what they said to save their racked bodies from further pain? A contemporary wrote: 'It would make a pitiful and strange story . . . to touch and recite what examinations and rackings of poor men there were, to find out the knife that should cut her throat!'[36] But Elizabeth was not entirely alone in her troubles. Many of the council were uneasy at her treatment; she was popular with the government and increasingly loved by the people. The remarkable William Cecil, an able administrator in her brother's government, was already a friend with good connections, working clandestinely on her behalf, eager that she should live to inherit the throne.

As Elizabeth was ushered into her quarters in the Tower, in 'an insignificant but wide turret'[37] from which she would not emerge for more than a month, her spirit again failed her. She asked one of her gentlewomen for her Bible and prayed that God might help her build her foundation upon the rocks 'whereby all blasts of blustering weather should have no power against her'.[38] As the great bolts were shot on the door to her prison, it all became too much for the Earl of Sussex who, with tears in his eyes, remonstrated with his fellow lords: 'She was a kinges daughter, and is the quenes syster . . . therefore go no further than your comyssyon, which I knowe what yt is.'[39]

Just as Elizabeth had been initially taken aback when first cross-examined during the Seymour incident, only to recover her composure and acquit herself admirably, so too when some of the council arrived to question her over a conversation she was alleged to have had, prior to the Wyatt Rebellion, about moving from Ashridge to Donnington Castle, she at first denied knowledge of such a place. This gained her time to marshall her defence in her own mind. Suddenly her memory improved, she did in fact remember Donnington, not surprisingly, as it was actually one of her own properties. But she added quickly that she had never stayed there.

They then confronted her with Sir James Croft, the man with whom she was said to have had this conversation. He had been tortured, 'marvellously tossed and examined', but apparently had revealed nothing incriminating. Restored to confidence, Elizabeth rolled out her debating skills and the ever ready righteous indignation which seldom failed to shame her interlocutors: 'But my Lords! ... you do examine every mean prisoner of me! Wherein, methinks, you do me great injury! If they have done evil, and offended the Queen's Majesty, let them answer to it accordingly. I beseech you, my Lords! Join not me in this sort with any of these offenders! And as concerning my going unto Donnington Castle, I do remember Master HOBY and mine Officers, and you Sir JAMES A CROFT! Had such talk: but what is that to the purpose, my Lords! But that I may go to my own houses at all times?'

So abashed were some of the council members present that Lord Arundel fell to his knees and expressed his sorrow at troubling her so. With magisterial grace Elizabeth replied, 'My Lords, you did sift me very narrowly! But well I am assured, you shall do no more to me, than God hath appointed: and so, GOD forgive you all!'[40]

The court was electric with every piece of news and rumour in this dangerous and rapidly changing situation. From reported conversations like these, the Venetian ambassador made this judgement on Elizabeth's abilities, which he dispatched to the senate: 'Her intellect and understanding are wonderful, as she showed very plainly by her conduct when in danger and under suspicion.'[41]

She may have appeared to be calmly in control of the situation but neither the danger surrounding her nor her fearfulness diminished. Her servants were bringing in her food daily, desperate to protect her from any attempt at poisoning. But they had to fight for the chance to deliver the food to her directly and not leave it with 'the common rascal soldiers'[42] at the outer gate of the Tower. The Tower was filled to the roof with prisoners and during March and April 1554, while Elizabeth was incarcerated, there were frequent executions and new arrivals. Suffering was everywhere. Fear and rumour were rampant and as the examinations of prisoners continued Elizabeth's life remained in the balance.

Behind the scenes, the Spanish ambassador was discussing with the queen a further strategy to get rid of Elizabeth. If they were unable to collect enough evidence to 'bring her to death' then they had better marry her to a stranger and in that way banish her from the kingdom for good. The gallant young Emmanuel Philibert, Prince of Piedmont and Duke of Savoy, was a cousin to Philip of Spain. Marriage to him would not only remove Elizabeth to his impoverished and French-occupied lands, it would also put her firmly in the control of the Holy Roman Emperor Charles V.

Eventually on 11 April the prime rebel, Sir Thomas Wyatt the younger, was taken to Tower Hill. There, in his speech from the scaffold, he clearly exonerated 'my lady Elizabeth' of any foreknowledge of his uprising; 'And this is most true.'[43] The gruesome punishment of the traitor was then enacted on his body. Beheaded, his body was immediately quartered and each part hung from different landmarks of the city. His head was put upon a spike on the gallows beyond Saint James's.*

After a month of close confinement, Elizabeth requested permission to walk outside her quarters in order to try and improve her failing health. She was allowed to walk in a corridor as long

---

* This head mysteriously disappeared on the day that the staunch Protestant, Sir Nicholas Throckmorton, was acquitted to general rejoicing. He had argued his case so passionately and effectively the jury refused to convict him, although he was obviously guilty. The council were so incensed at the jury's independence that they were imprisoned in the Tower and the Fleet prison as punishment, and stayed there for the rest of the year. Having lost at least half of his nine lives on this occasion, Sir Nicholas lived to become a successful ambassador to France under Elizabeth and a friend to Mary Queen of Scots, only to lose another life or two in his supposed complicity in the rebellion of the northern Catholics in favour of Mary. He managed to die, however, in his bed (although rumour had it poisoned by the Earl of Leicester).

as she did not look out of any windows. When she was later allowed a turn around the gardens all the prisoners whose windows overlooked the garden were commanded neither to talk to Elizabeth, nor even to glance at her. So anxious were the council to keep Elizabeth isolated that guards were positioned in the adjacent cells to prevent these other prisoners having any contact or communication with her.

In this atmosphere of menace and almost daily executions of prisoners, any unexpected change in routine unnerved Elizabeth. When in May the new Constable of the Tower was appointed, Elizabeth was suddenly afraid. Sir Henry Bedingfield, a bluff knight from Norfolk, arrived with one hundred soldiers and she grew very agitated, asking of anyone she could, '"Whether the Lady JANE's scaffold were taken away or not?" fearing, by reason of [the soldiers] coming, lest she should have played her part'.[44] Even when told she was to be moved at last from the Tower and taken by Bedingfield and his blue-coated soldiers to another destination she was so dismayed at being in the charge of a stranger, whose orders were unknown to her, and guarded by his 'company of rakehells', that she argued to be allowed to stay in the Tower.

Elizabeth was taken from the Tower by river. The people had grown increasingly resentful of her long imprisonment and despite the government's careful plans word was soon spreading through the streets, and she was greeted with spontaneous expressions of support and celebration. As her barge passed the steelyard, she was given an impromptu salute of three rounds of artillery fire, which displeased the queen and her council. On her progress west the bells in parish churches rang out. Bedingfield attempted to suppress such effusions by having the bellringers put in the stocks, but to little avail.

If Foxe, that famous contemporary, is to be believed, Elizabeth still feared greatly for her life. The first night on her journey to Oxford was spent in Richmond and the months of fear and uncertainty suddenly overwhelmed her with a terrible foreboding. She was certain that there was some secret and malevolent plan afoot. Elizabeth called her gentleman usher and asked him and all her retainers to pray for her '"for this night" quoth she, "I think to die"'.[45]

Not that she could have known it, but at this point she was in less danger of dying than she had been in the previous two or three months. The idea of marriage as a way of securing her freedom was to be put to her at Richmond and if she refused the suggested suitor, the Duke of Savoy, then she would be conveyed to her palace of Woodstock to continue her imprisonment there. Philip of Spain was due to arrive to fulfil his marriage contract with the queen and the country was being made ready. The gallows in and around London were removed, and any focus of public disquiet was neutralized or obscured as best as possible. Philip's father, Charles V, wanted both Mary and Elizabeth in his power, in the event that Philip's coming marriage did not produce any heirs. His main fear was the accession to the throne of Mary Queen of Scots and the inevitable ascendancy of his implacable enemy, France.

Although Elizabeth was near to prostration with nervous exhaustion at the months of imprisonment and intimidation, she still had the strength and conviction to maintain her stand on marriage. In the first year of her reign she recalled this fearful period of her life: 'There certainly was a time when a very honourable and worthy marriage would have liberated us from certain great distress and tribulation . . . but neither the peril of the moment, nor the desire for liberty could induce us to take this matter into consideration.'[46]

Having refused the marriage alternative as a more subtle form of imprisonment and exile, she travelled on by water from Richmond to Windsor on the next leg of her rustication. On the banks of the Thames she saw a group of her servants hoping to catch a glimpse of her as she passed. Elizabeth was obviously still full of anxiety about what fate awaited her for she turned to one of her men standing within earshot and said, 'Yonder, I see certain of my men; go to them! And say these words from me, *Tanquam ovis*! (like a sheep to slaughter!)'[47] She may not have been led to slaughter 'but when she arrived at Woodstock she was certainly closely penned, confined to four rooms, guarded day and night by armed men. Her visitors and letters were restricted, her movement limited, her horizons deliberately closed in and obscured.

For a young woman with a vigorous mind and body, to have her energies so blocked and frustrated was inevitably debilitating. Elizabeth still half expected to be hurried to her death. That summer she was unwell again and had to be bled by the doctors sent to tend her. Powerlessness, uncertainty and fear took their toll on her nervous system and she suffered physically and psychologically. During her imprisonment, and in the dark days of isolation and uncertainty that followed, she was reduced to sharing more closely the hopes and the fears of an ordinary Tudor citizen.

From this terrifying experience came understanding. Out of this humbling came something of the real affection, loyalty and respect she expressed for her servants, and her genuine concern for the common men and women who flocked to laud her – but also to banter with her – as if she was one of their own. When she was finally queen, Elizabeth was to be criticized by some of her foreign ambassadors for treating her common subjects with more respect than she offered august members of her court, like them. The fiery Count de Feria writing to Philip II of Spain in the immediate aftermath of 'that woman's' accession complained, 'She is very much wedded to the people and thinks as they do, and therefore treats foreigners slightingly.'[48]

A large measure of this was pragmatic. Tudor monarchs did not keep large standing armies and so were much more dependent for their continuing rule on their people's good will. But what was so rare and explained some of Elizabeth's extraordinary popularity was the fact that her relationship with her people was a two-way affair. They loved and admired her but equally she made them believe she felt the same way about them. Her imagery in speeches was full of this reciprocity. She was promised to her people, they were the only spouse she needed or desired. To a virgin and solitary queen, without close relations, they were her family. In her first speech to Parliament, Elizabeth could not have made the nature of this relationship more plain: 'I am already bound unto a husband, which is the kingdom of England . . . everyone of you, and as many as are English, are my children and kinsfolks.'[49]

For nearly a year, Elizabeth was closely confined at Woodstock under the authority of the worthy Bedingfield. He would allow her no concessions without permission from the council, even where she walked and what books she read came under his punctilious rule. Paper and pens were banned, and in the event of her being allowed to write to someone then the necessary materials were doled out and reclaimed afterwards. No-one was allowed to visit without express permission and constant chaperoning. The loyal Parry, her treasurer, lodging in an inn nearby in the village of Woodstock, was suspected of being a go-between but managed to continue to see the princess despite threatened banishment.

There was no doubt a great deal of gossip and intrigue amongst her servants to which Elizabeth must have been privy. She bridled under the restrictions on her movements, friendships and study and was particularly bereft when one of her waiting women was dismissed, on orders of the queen who felt this was 'a person of evil opinion, and not fit to remain about our said sister's person'.[50] That 'said sister' refused to speak to Bedingfield for quite some while afterwards, which might have been a relief for the man was harrassed by Elizabeth's forceful requests that he write to the council for various concessions in her treatment. When she herself was given permission to write to the queen, the insistence of her protestations of innocence and her circumlocutory style further alienated her sister who banned any further direct communication in future. 'We shall not be hereafter molested any more with her disguised and colourable letters.'[51]

Thus, as the queen's plans for marriage to Philip of Spain proceeded in the summer of 1554 amid growing opposition, Elizabeth was effectively isolated, silenced and disabled. Two poems composed by her during her captivity at Woodstock show both her despondency and defiance. Denied pen and paper, she scrawled in charcoal on a wall (some say a shutter). These lines were found and copied by subsequent visitors to the house:

> O Fortune, thy wrestling, wavering state
> Hath fraught with cares my troubled wit,
> Whose witness this present prison late
> Could bear, where once was joy flown quite.
> Thou causedst the guilty to be loosed
> From lands where innocents were enclosed,
> And caused the guiltless to be reserved,
> And freed those that death had well deserved.
> But all herein can be naught wrought,
> So God grant to my foes as they have thought.
> *Finis.* Elizabetha a prisoner, 1555
> Much suspected by me, but nothing proved can be.[52]

The famous last line also was found inscribed into a glass window pane, most probably etched by Elizabeth using one of her diamonds:

> Much suspected by me,
> Nothing proved can be.
> *Quod* Elizabeth the prisoner.[53]

With the description 'prisoner' appended to her name, both verses revealed a sense of outrage at the loss of freedom, even some self-pity for a life frustratingly stalled by the interests of others.

But more fiercely engraved into her spirit was the protracted fear that at any hour on any day she might be summoned and duly executed, 'condemned without answer and due truth'.[54] This fear did not diminish on her release from house arrest at Woodstock. At the end of April 1555, Elizabeth was summoned to Hampton Court to arrive by the back entrance and live in seclusion, seeing no one apart from a modest retinue of servants. The profound anxiety of these days was graphically illustrated (perhaps with some poetic licence) by John Foxe who related how when Elizabeth was summoned unexpectedly to her sister's presence at ten o'clock at night she truly believed her hour had come. She called her servants and asked them to pray for her 'for that she could not tell whether ever she should see them again'.[55]

Her previous defiance of Bishop Gardiner, the promoter of the burning of heretics and an implacable enemy of Elizabeth's, when she had refused to admit her fault and beg forgiveness from the queen, dissolved in the face of her terror. Shown by torchlight into the presence of her sister, Elizabeth fell on her knees and in tears protested 'her truth and loyalty to her sovereign Majesty'. The queen remained unmoved, certain of Elizabeth's duplicity but afraid that to act against her would antagonize her council. The ensuing interview was apparently witnessed by King Philip, lurking behind a curtain in the chamber, and from this time Foxe believed 'he showed himself a very friend in the matter'.[56]

Elizabeth remained the unwitting focus for any half-baked rebellion and when another was uncovered in the summer of 1556, during her retirement at Hatfield, she wrote in alarm to Queen Mary, her quickened anxiety inflating her style into convoluted hyperbole. She wished 'that there were as good surgeons for making anatomies of hearts that might show my thoughts to your majesty as there are expert physicians of the bodies, able to express the inward griefs of their maladies to their patient. For then I doubt not but know well that what other should suggest by malice, yet your majesty should be sure by knowledge, so that the more such misty clouds obfuscates the clear light of my truth, the more my tried thoughts should glister to the dimming of their hidden malice.'[57] This can only have added substance to her sister's bitter disbelief.

Elizabeth's experience of imprisonment in the Tower and the grim aftermath was the most strenuous kind of apprenticeship for a queen. Powerless, afraid, treated no better than a criminal and in real danger of dying a traitor's death, it was the ordeal of her life. With her unerring sense of the theatrical and her training in classical rhetoric, she was to use the experience to great dramatic effect throughout her reign, summoning it frequently thereafter in speeches, prayers and letters. The horror of her incarceration in the Tower was a defining event Elizabeth could never forget. It made a passionate heart more circumspect, a complex nature more contradictory, and a fine intelligence sharp as a blade.

These difficult, secluded years allowed her to focus her thoughts and energies so completely that when at last the call came for her to be queen she could spring, fully armed, to her throne. She saw her life as an apprenticeship and in a prayer she wrote early in her reign, she listed the experiences which brought her to this place:

> Thou hast willed me to be not some wretched girl from the meanest rank of the common people, who would pass her life miserably in poverty and squalor, but to a Kingdom thou hast destined me, born of royal parents and nurtured and educated at court. When I was surrounded and thrown about by various snares of enemies, Thou hast preserved me with Thy constant protection from prison and the most extreme danger; and though I was freed only at the very last moment, Thou hast entrusted me on earth with royal sovereignty and majesty.[58]

Although memory of the fear would never leave her, Elizabeth was proud of what she had endured. It had given her a greater confidence in her strength and self-reliance in the process.

It was extraordinary that Mary Queen of Scots was to suffer a very similar ordeal, imprisoned under suspicion of being a focus for treason, if not a traitor herself, kept isolated in the country, continually watched and physically constrained. Unfortunately, for Mary this period of introspection came too late to teach her lessons about her role as queen and the government of her people. By then her youth was fraying and her time for ruling had passed. It did, however, give her the means to become if not a heroic prince then a heroic martyr. If Mary was to be denied the chance to rule with nobility the least she could do was to die with majesty. With every bit as much of the great actress about her as her cousin, she managed to turn her death into a bravura performance. The judicial execution for treason, which Elizabeth escaped for herself, made Mary a martyr for her country and her faith, far more famous through the ensuing centuries for her dazzling recklessness, executive failures and the manner of her death than if she had been merely a moderately competent monarch who died in her bed.

Mary's real apprenticeship for her role as Queen of Scotland was conducted while she was still in France. Henri II's Queen Catherine de Medici and his mistress Diane de Poitiers were examples to Mary of women wielding power. Although entirely unalike in their natures and their way of dealing with the world, these were women of intrigue and faction. They had no real jurisdiction of their own but exercised great covert power. Seduction and control for the mistress; motherhood and endurance for the wife. These were the obvious female routes of influence, but the intelligence and ambition of both Diane and Catherine had to be hidden, expressed only through their relationships with kings.

During her time in France, Mary's Guise uncles were in the ascendancy. It was a period when there was widespread fear that they, not the king, were the effective rulers of France. It served their purposes to encourage their niece and her young husband François to spend their days in courtly amusements: hunting by day (hawking was a particular enthusiasm), and dancing by night. It was true François showed little of the inspiration and drive of the grandfather after whom he was named, but his wife was an intelligent, energetic and curious young woman who would have responded well, perhaps, to serious lessons in statecraft. If not taught formally the business of effective monarchy, Mary cannot have failed to recognize that in the only court she knew moral and sexual laxity did not appear incompatible with religious devotion. Her adoptive father, the king, lived openly with both his wife and mistress. His mistress, as long as the king lived, was treated as a lady of the highest social standing, her daughters' hands sought in marriage for the scions of aristocratic families.

As she grew older and more aware of the behaviour of those adults around her, Mary also could not ignore the fact that her uncle, the Cardinal of Lorraine, although by rank a great churchman and by repute a skilful and impassioned preacher was also by far the richest cleric and by nature one of the most rapacious of men. Court life everywhere was rife with gossip, rivalries, passionate liaisons, bitter rifts and rampant opportunism. The French court which Mary inhabited just happened at the time to be more extravagant and more extreme than any of the other European courts of the day. The young queen was to learn that scheming, duplicity and opportunism were the everyday tools of a successful courtier, and the ability to anticipate and out-scheme was the response of a successful queen. While her cousin Elizabeth's youth was largely spent outside court life with her books and plans, and the occasional visitor to engage her thoughts, Mary's life from the age of six was lived at the very centre of the most glamorous court in Christendom.

For a while yet, her star could only grow brighter as everything for which her family had hoped and schemed came to fruition. Mary was still only fifteen, her destiny inexorably in the hands of others more powerful and ambitious than she. She seemed, however, more than happy with the future mapped out for her and in the spring of 1558 made a glorious dynastic marriage by marrying her fourteen-year-old prince.

Mary's marriage indicated to herself and the world that she was assuming the role that the expectations of her position and sex had made hers from birth. Her increased status as dauphine brought her closer to becoming the pre-eminent woman in one of the richest and most powerful monarchies in Europe and, superficially at least, this amplified the pleasures of her life at court. George Buchanan,* the great Scottish scholar who knew her well, described some of her future joys in the poem he wrote for her wedding:

> But let not fond regrets disturb your mind,
> Your country, and your mother left behind!
> This is your country too; what wealth of friends,
> What kindred on your nuptial pomp attends!

---

* George Buchanan (1506–82) was a brilliant scholar and writer, tutor to Mary's eldest illegitimate brother James Stewart, later Earl of Moray, and to Mary herself, both in France and when she returned to Scotland, when they would read Latin together. He also tutored her son James VI. He turned venomously against Mary during the Darnley period and testified that the 'casket letters' were indeed written by her. He became a Protestant and anti-monarchist and his *Detectio Mariae Reginae* (1571) was a devastating and distorted attack on Mary, both personally and politically, implicating her in Darnley's murder and worse. In *De jure regni apud Scotos* (1579) he argued for the possibility of a just rebellion against a tyrannous monarch. His great history *Rerum Scoticarum Historia* was published in 1582.

All are alike to you where'er you tread,
The mighty living and the mighty dead;
And one awaits you, dear beyond the rest,
Smiles on his lips and rapture in his breast,
The eldest, gentlest of the royal line,
Linked in fraternal fellowship with thine.

Fellowship and rapture may indeed have awaited her, but with such elevation came added responsibility and danger too. Mary was yet to appreciate how her triumph and her complicity in the attendant schemes of her family would open the way to irresolvable conflict with her cousin.

That autumn Elizabeth's accession as Queen of England focused in the mind of Mary's new father-in-law, Henri II, his long-term ambition of constructing a French empire that included Scotland along with the kingdom of England and Ireland. Central to this expansion was Mary's claim to the English crown. Almost immediately he approached the pope* for clarification as to Elizabeth's illegitimacy and Mary's entitlement, as closest legitimate heir, to her kingdom. Camden characterized Henri's determination with a vivid phrase: 'the French King did now labour tooth and nail at Rome, that Mary Queen of Scots might be pronounced lawfull Queen of England'. In a letter to Lord Fleming in the January of the following year, Mary and her husband already styled themselves 'King and Queen Dauphins of Scotland, England and Ireland'.[59] This development was watched with as keen interest by Spain, just as determined as Elizabeth that England should not be included in a French empire. As an English agent based in Flanders noted at the time: 'To make a hard comparison England may be likened to a bone thrown between two dogs.'[60]

To transform that bone into a new beast, with flesh and blood and teeth, Elizabeth had to begin work immediately. On 17 November 1558, she ascended to one of the weakest thrones in Europe, but she had arrived there with all her faculties sharpened, her senses acute, ready for the challenge of the only role in life she had ever

* Pope Paul IV 1556–9.

wanted. At her side as her new Secretary of State was William Cecil who, in covert contact during her perilous years in waiting, had already prepared for this moment. Any death of the old monarch and accession of the new was fraught with danger. Such a momentous transfer of power opened up possibilities of counterclaims and rebellion. It also involved struggles for patronage and influence from the highest nobility and ministers of state through to the lowliest official. Ambitions were unleashed in aspiring courtiers who strove to be the coming men of the new regime.

Elizabeth and the contemporaries who would make up her executive were used to the crisis of change. They had lived through the audacious coup that placed Lady Jane Grey on the throne instead of Mary Tudor and could not take for granted that this time the throne would automatically be delivered to Elizabeth. There were various cousins descended from Henry VII waiting in the wings: two Grey sisters remained, Catherine and Mary; the Countess of Lennox's son, Henry Stuart, Lord Darnley, who although only thirteen was nevertheless a rare Tudor male; and there was Mary Queen of Scots herself, in direct descent from Henry VII's elder daughter, Margaret, and therefore armed with the most clear-cut claim of them all. Apart from the internal dissatisfactions and domestic ambitions, this transfer of power excited intense interest abroad where the European powers were anxious to augment their advantages and frustrate their enemies.

Cecil was prepared for any eventuality. He was a man who liked making lists. On Elizabeth's day of accession he was ready with his 'Memorial' of twelve essential tasks, written in his own orderly hand. His first directive was clear: 'To consider the proclamation; to proclaim it; to send the same to all manner of places and sheriffs with speed; and to put it in print.' Then he turned to matters of security. The Tower was put in the hands of 'trusty persons' and made ready to receive Elizabeth should she need the safety of its defences while she settled her officers and council. He intended to write in Elizabeth's name to the keepers of all the castles and forts. The ports were temporarily closed, with particular care taken with those places closest to France and Scotland, and money could not be taken out of the country without the queen's express permission. New justices of the peace and sheriffs would be appointed in each county and all preachers were to be dissuaded, in the short term, from touching on anything doctrinally controversial in their sermons. Cecil's twelfth and last directive was 'To consider the condition [disposition] of the preacher at Paul's cross, that no occasion be given to him, to stir any dispute touching the governance of the realm',[61] where Paul's Cross was notorious as a platform for rabble-rousing sermons against the establishment. Security at home and abroad was the overriding concern. Faced with an impoverished and demoralized country, Elizabeth quickly moved to conclude peace with France.

The retrieval of Calais loomed large for the English as a matter of sentiment and principle, but it was clear that England was not in a strong bargaining position, and France had no intention of yielding this prize so easily. Peace mattered to Elizabeth more than anything at this time but she was determined to show that she would lead her country herself, impoverished and disadvantaged as it might be, without the support of foreign interests. 'Queen Elizabeth, being a Virgin of manly Courage, professed that she was an absolute free Princess to manage her actions by her self or her Ministers'[62] was how Camden expressed her resolve. The Spanish ambassador, succinctly characterizing the instability of her inheritance, thought this independence foolhardy: 'Really this country is more fit to be dealt with sword in hand than by cajolery, for there are neither funds, nor soldiers, nor heads, nor forces, and yet it is overflowing with every other necessary of life.'[63] Camden was even more stark:

the State of England lay now most afflicted, imbroiled on the one side with the Scottish, on the other side with the French War; overcharged with Debt incurred by Henry the Eighth and Edward the Sixth; the Treasure exhausted; Calice [Calais] and the Country of Oye [the area round Calais], with great Provision for the Wars, lost, to the great Dishonour of the English Nation; the people distracted with different Opinions in

Religion; the Queen bare of potent Friends, and strengthened with no Alliance of foreign Princes.[64]

In the first set of suggestions from the French was that Calais would be returned to England as the dowry in a marriage contract between the putative offspring of Elizabeth and of Mary Queen of Scots and her husband the dauphin, soon to become king. Whom the new English queen would marry was the subject of the most pressing importance. William Cecil, writing from Edinburgh the following year where he was negotiating the Treaty of Edinburgh with the Scots, showed his own ever-present anxiety on the matter (and a revealing frankness): 'And we beseach Almighty God bless your Majesty "with fruites of peace, and as we may be bold to wryte, with the fruit of your womb"'.[65]

Elizabeth, knowing her opinion already on the possibilities of motherhood, did not find credible the idea of this fantasy marriage contract uniting the children of England and a Scotland subsumed by France. Instead, with urgent pragmatism she agreed that Calais would be restored after a period of eight years, or that financial compensation would be paid to England. The Treaty of Cateau-Cambresis was signed on 2 April 1559. Although Elizabeth's subjects did not trust the French to honour any future promises over Calais there was widespread relief that the pointless debilitation of war had ceased.

Her advisers however were increasingly alarmed and incensed by the pretensions of the French towards the English crown. During the peace negotiations they had claimed insolently that they could not conclude a treaty with Elizabeth, whom they implied was an illegitimate usurper on the throne. They amplified their insult by proclaiming they knew not to whom they should return Calais as they considered the Queen of England to be their own dauphine. The 'deceits and trumperies of the French' were dangerous enough in their control over Scotland for, in Cecil's warning to Elizabeth, they used that country as 'an instrument to exercise thereby their malice upon England, and to make a footstool thereof to look over

England as they may'.[66] But this persistent claim by Mary of the title of Queen of England and Ireland was not just humiliating, it was intimidating too. No one was more aware than Elizabeth of the vulnerability of her legitimacy, due in part to her own father's mendacity when she was declared illegitimate at not yet three years old, prior to her mother's execution.

Although agreeing in the peace treaty no longer to style themselves Queen and King of England, Mary and her husband continued to use the English arms at all official occasions. Perhaps the most seriously unsettling for Elizabeth was their making of the Great Seal with the arms of all four countries quartered and the legend '*Franciscus et Maria, Dei Gratia Franciae, Scotiae, Angliae et Hiberniae Rex et Regina*'. This was sent to Scotland, and a matching heraldic device was engraved on all Mary's silverware, in continuing defiance.

Elizabeth was not persuaded by the French ambassador's assurances that this presumption had nothing to do with Mary's own wishes but was imposed on her by the ambitions of her father-in-law. Cecil delivered the verdict: 'Her Majesty thinks this excuse very strange or very imperfect.'[67] For although Mary was young and could be said to be acting under the authority of her husband, it was pointed out that both continued to use the English title and arms even after the death of Henri II.

At the ratification of the peace treaty conducted in London that May, Elizabeth set out to dazzle the proud French entourage with the splendour of her hospitality. This was the first occasion of her reign when she could play the grand monarch upon an international stage. It was important to set down her mark. She intended to shake the complacency of the haughty French and the watching European powers with the realization that England was no inferior kingdom, that she was no inconsiderable queen. The French may have chosen to insult her personally and patronize her country but she would have none of them say she did not know how to put on a show. The ambassadors were brought to Whitehall Palace to meet the queen 'who received them very joyfully and graciously', before they and their accompanying entourage of courtiers went off to the surrounding royal park to see two deer killed, one by dogs, the other with arrows from a company of archers.

They all returned to a 'sumptuous feast' in the garden under the gallery, decorated with gold and silver brocade and 'wreaths of flowers and leaves of most beautiful designs, which gave a very sweet odour and were marvellous to behold, having been prepared in less than two evenings so as to keep them fresh'. Although the table at which the French and English courtiers were to dine was fifty-four paces long, the farthingales worn by the fashionable Frenchwomen were so wide that there was not enough room for everyone at table, so members of Elizabeth's privy chamber 'ate on the ground on the rushes'. The 'precious and costly drinking cups of gold and of rock crystal and other jewels' were passed around filled with wine. And what of the food? Our Italian eyewitness reported that the joints of meat were large and of excellent quality, 'but the delicacies and cleanliness customary in Italy were wanting'.

But it was the newly anointed Elizabeth who drew all eyes. Gone were the days of the circumspect princess, sober in dress, despising – as she told Ascham – all outward adornment and wearing of gold. Instead the twenty-five-year-old queen appeared before them, 'dressed entirely in purple velvet, with so much gold and so many pearls and jewels that it added much to her beauty'. How well this illustrated her notorious mercurial ability to be all things to all men. Then Elizabeth as resplendent queen contrived to show her mind was just as richly endowed as her person: 'She took M. de Montmorenci [Constable of France] with her right hand and M. de Vielleville [ambassador] with the left, and they walked in the private orchard for more than a full hour, her Majesty speaking with them most sweetly and familiarly in French, as readily as she does Italian, Latin, and Greek, all which tongues she uses at pleasure, and in so loud a tone as to be heard by everybody.'[68] Elizabeth intended her neighbours and rivals to know her full measure, and beware.

For Mary, the practical preparation for her main role as the Queen of Scotland (with pretensions to becoming the Queen of England too) could well have begun with her husband's accession to the throne of France. The fact that their short seventeen-month reign occurred at all was due to a freak jousting accident, the futility of which seems symbolic of the ill-fatedness of Henri II and his run of unimpressive sons who followed François I to the throne. Despite the disappointing quality of these later Valois kings, the strength and the unifying central spine of the French monarchy was Catherine de Medici, the true centre of power as queen mother to three kings of France, her influence only ceasing with her death.

Opposed to the power of the Guises, less fanatically Catholic in her sympathies, Catherine was likely to view with suspicion any attempt by Mary to get involved in politics. From a personal point of view, she endured rather than embraced the presence of this young, attractive princess to whom everyone declared their love, from her husband to her eldest son through to the court and their effusive poets, Ronsard, du Bellay, Chastelard and other members of the Pléiade. Temperamentally these two women were unalike and Catherine had for too long suffered unfavourable comparisons with the irresistible attractions of Diane de Poitiers, forced to bite her tongue and bide her time. Understandably the queen mother was unwilling to have her young daughter-in-law step into Diane's charming shoes. It was hardly surprising that she was motivated by duty rather than love in her dealings with her.

Just over a year after Mary's marriage to the Dauphin François tragedy struck when least expected, in the middle of triumph and celebration. During the summer of 1559 the court could speak of nothing but the costumes and the plans for the celebrations for the forthcoming double wedding. Philip II of Spain, who had half-heartedly wooed Elizabeth I and been politely rebuffed, was affianced to Elizabeth de Valois, Mary's favourite sister-in-law. Marguerite, the king's youngest sister, was to marry Emmanuel Philibert, Duke of Savoy, another former suitor to Queen Elizabeth of England when she was but a princess in disgrace. With these marriages, the alliance between Spain and England was further weakened as Philip looked to France for his wider peace.

During the days of extravagant tournaments, pageants and festivities Mary, as dauphine and Queen of Scots, and François, as dauphin and now provokingly King of Scotland, were at the centre of the elaborate ceremonies. One of the high points was the three-day jousting tournament that celebrated the signing of the marriage contract between Madame Marguerite and Savoy. This was also an occasion for broadcasting to the people, and to France's enemies abroad, the full power and pretensions of the state. The heralds accompanying the dauphin's party were magnificently arrayed with the arms of France and Scotland but also 'with an [e]scutcheon of England set forth to the show, as all the world might easily perceive'. Just to impress further on the watching crowd, and on every eagle-eyed ambassador and foreign dignitary, the young dauphine and Queen of Scots' right to the throne of her cousin, England's arms also were embroidered on the front, back and sleeves of the heralds' tunics. All these details were duly noted by the English, deepening their growing distrust of the imperialist ambitions of the Guises, with Mary Queen of Scots as their irrefutable prize.

On the third day, the king entered the lists accompanied by the Duc de Guise and two other noblemen, and they challenged all comers. Henri was dressed in black and white, the colours of Diane de Poitiers, and successfully ran several courses, watched by the ladies and gentlemen of the court. The king was urged by all to retire in triumph. Against the strongest advice he insisted on being given a fresh lance and running one more course. So determined was he to test his luck to the limit he commanded a reluctant young captain of the Scottish guard to oppose him. During this final joust the king was struck by a blow which smashed the magnificent plume of feathers from his helmet: a splinter from his opponent's shattered lance was driven up under the visor, through his eye and into his brain. Henri was carried from the field, his head covered, his limbs motionless, it seemed 'as one amazed'. The watching courtiers were overcome with grief and fear, men and women openly weeping, uneasy at the evident workings of a divine will. 'Thus God makes Himself known' ambassador Throckmorton reported back to the English lords of the council, 'that in the very midst of these triumphs suffers this heaviness to happen.'[69]

Catherine de Medici had received from her soothsayers various warnings of the unexpected nature of Henri II's death. She had apparently also dreamt the exact details of his demise. To the super-stitious queen there was suddenly an awful certainty that even as the surgeons laboured and Henri lingered there could in fact be no hope of recovery. The ill-starred king died ten days later in the night of 10 July at forty-one years old: his unprepared, inadequate, fifteen-year-old son, François, succeeded to the throne. Aged six-teen, Mary had achieved everything her family had desired; she was now queen of the grandest monarchy in Europe. But real power resided elsewhere.

Catherine de Medici quickly dispatched Diane de Poitiers to the country, divesting her of the jewels given her by the dead king and the lovely château of Chenonceaux. With their own kin now as Queen of France, the Guises were suddenly elevated to the right hand of monarchy. Having laid their plans and exhibited their patience and cunning, the Duc de Guise and Cardinal of Lorraine seemed to have the prize of ultimate power in their grasp. The young king and queen were well schooled to look to them for guidance. They were inexperienced and keen to delegate the mighty authority of state. On that transitional eve it appeared likely that François II's reign would be the cloak for extreme Catholic and Guise-centred policies to prevail. Throckmorton, writing to his new queen, Elizabeth, expressed his unease, 'the house of Guise is like to govern all about the King, who is much affected towards them'.[70] But the Guises could not control fate, nor the irresistible force for religious reformation, nor in fact the ambitions and patient guile of the queen mother, Catherine de Medici.

This could have been Mary's chance to translate her influence over her devoted young husband into a wider responsibility for the course of his government. She had all the natural intelligence, strength of mind, energy and purpose to make her a worthy gov-ernor like her mother. But she was too much in thrall to her uncles' influence, bred in her from childhood, and too pampered and inexperienced at this stage to choose such a path of authority and responsibility. There was, however, one authority she would come to seek above all others, to her own tragic end, and the seed of this desire was planted here by her uncles and her father-in-law. The pursuit of her claim on the crown of England, in preference to her cousin Elizabeth or, failing that, as Elizabeth's named successor, became the overriding ambition of her life. Camden recognized her persistence in this claim as the factor from which 'flowed as from a Fountain all the Calamities wherein she was afterwards wrapped'.[71]

Given that the Queen of Scots' legitimate claim on the English throne made for an inherent threat to Elizabeth, it was particularly tragic that Mary was not equipped with natural good judgement or the wise counsel of others with more experience and diplomacy than herself. Elizabeth had her brilliant, self-sacrificing William Cecil at the centre of a group of loyal men, while Mary had but the cunning, self-serving Guises during her ascendancy in France, and a shifting band of unreliable supporters in Scotland (an untrustworthy half-brother and two ruinous husbands among them) fuelled with their own ingrained tribal feuds and alliances.

In fact it was growing unease amongst the French nobility about the power of the Guise brothers that brought Mary Queen of Scots closest to danger in her short reign as Queen of France. The religious reformers were gaining voice and ground. Huguenots were increasingly vocal and in the aftermath of the peace of Cateau-Cambresis the Guises stiffened the heresy laws. Anyone holding or even attending illicit meetings risked the death penalty. The denunciation of such meetings also was made obligatory on pain of death, which encouraged and rewarded informers and further deepened the rifts in French society.

The rebels looked to the King of Navarre, the next prince in line to the throne after Henri II's sons, and to his brother the Prince of Condé as figureheads for their campaign. A minor nobleman from Périgord, la Renaudie, was charged with command of the rebel troops. A secret assembly of malcontents met in February 1560 in Nantes to restate their loyalty to their young king François but at the same time confirmed their determination to bring the Guises to account. Their coup was planned to take place on 10 March but was postponed for six days. However, news of this conspiracy leaked out and the whole court, including the new young king and Mary, was quickly moved to the Château of Amboise, set high above the Loire and considered impregnable enough to withstand any attack or siege.

The religious reformers were offered the Edict of Amboise by the king, most probably at the urging of his mother Catherine de Medici. It was an apparently generous recognition of their griev-ances: an amnesty for all peaceful dissenters; release of all religious prisoners; the possibility of petitioning the king. However, this tolerance was not extended to the conspirators. As they gathered in the woods surrounding the château, some still unarmed, they were set upon by a force of the royal cavalry. Many were killed on the spot, including la Renaudie, whose body was carried back to Amboise and hung on a gibbet, 'before the Court gate', as an awful warning. Around his neck hung the inscription: 'La Renaudie, chief of the rebels'.[72]

Others were hunted down and dragged back into the town, tied in groups to the tails of the cavalry horses. Summary trials and executions were enacted in their hundreds. A great deal of reckless courage was shown by the rebels during the 'Tumult of Amboise' but the revenge of the Guise brothers was ferocious. According to the sixteenth-century chronicler, Louis Regnier de la Planche, the brothers strove to convince the king that this uprising had little to do with disaffection towards the Guises and was aimed primarily at murdering François and possibly Mary too. Mary, no doubt trusting her uncles' judgement, was instrumental in persuading her husband he was in mortal danger. The terrified boy-king then nominated the Duc de Guise as his lieutenant-general of the king-dom, thereby giving him unlimited powers and unleashing his bitter revenge.

No one in the castle or town was immune to the horror of what then followed. There were not sufficient gibbets for the slaughter, and so ordinary rebels were hung in groups from any convenient structure; even the château and its walls were shadowed with these pathetic bundles: '*les créneaux et les portes du chateau furent chargés de grappes humaines*'.[73] Others were drowned in the Loire, attached six or eight at a time to poles, and more were thrown into the great river tied in sacks. On 17 March, twenty-two rebels died in this way, followed by another twenty-five the following night. Some unfortunates were 'appointed to die on the wheel'. Throckmorton, Elizabeth's ambassador with the court at Amboise, added to his catalogue of death, 'among these that are taken there are eighteen of the bravest captains in France'.[74] The captains and nobles were saved for more theatrical executions, their deaths being enacted in front of the whole court after dinner. Louis Regnier de la Planche described the depraved entertainment:

> Those of Guise reserved the chiefs until after dinner, in order to afford some pastime to the ladies, and they and the ladies placed themselves at the windows, just as though it had been a question of enjoying the sight of some mummery; and, what is worse, the King and his young brothers appeared at these spectacles, as though one had wished to embitter them, and the victims were pointed out to them by the cardinal [de Lorraine], with the gestures of a man greatly rejoiced; and when they died with noble constancy, he observed: 'Look, Sire, at those shameless and desperate men. See how the fear of death is powerless to abate their pride and wickedness! What would they do, then, if they held you in their power?[75]

These were men, often of the nobility, who were tortured with ingenious ferocity (the Guises suspected that the Bourbon Prince of Condé was behind the rebellion and needed cast-iron evidence before convicting a prince of the blood). Their death sentence was carried out in front of the court: they were beheaded, or hung, drawn and quartered. The Venetian ambassador noted that on 17 March, for instance, six or seven were hanged, 'towards nightfall ... all dying with the greatest constancy as the others did this morning, saying that for every one of them who died, twenty would come in their stead'.[76] They sang psalms as they died; the last sounds on their lips were in celebration of their 'true God'. It was the duty of each member of the watching royal family and courtiers to show no squeamishness or pity. Faced with the punishment of their enemies, they could not flinch or turn away. One of Catherine's young daughters, Claude, could not maintain the aristocratic code of dispassion and went in tears to her mother, distressed by the '*cruautés et inhumanités*'[77] of what she was forced to see. Mary, although not much older herself, was expected to be an impassive witness. There is no record of the effect such a spectacle had on her.

In a period of history when terrible cruelties were routinely enacted man on man and by ruling powers on the weak, when heretics were burnt alive, often having had their tongues torn out to stop them praying aloud or singing hymns at the stake, and when extremes of torture were an accepted part of interrogation, the excessive bloodthirstiness and cruelty of the reprisals at Amboise horrified many of the spectators and participants. According to contemporary records, some of those present never regained their health or peace of mind. Catherine de Medici apparently prostrated herself in front of the Guises in an attempt to save an old family friend, the Baron de Castlenau. Chancellor Olivier, a mild-mannered and tolerant man, friend to many of the rebel noblemen, was so mortified that he had not had the strength of character to oppose the Guises, took to his bed a broken man. With his friends' reproaches, as they went to their deaths, echoing in his ears he died before the month was out. The convulsion of horror at the events still haunted the town centuries later.

As queen, Mary was at the very centre of the tragedy. When even great heroic generals like her uncle were rattled and for political reasons warning, in apocalyptic terms, what destruction would be wreaked on the Valois monarchy if the rebels had their way, when the whole court was gripped by fear, there must have been moments when Mary herself feared for her life. Over a period of about a week the king's troops rode out every day to engage with any rebels, round up the survivors and bring them back to Amboise for interrogation and execution. The women, Mary and Catherine de Medici among them, remained closely confined for most of the month of March in a much fortified castle and town, full of alarms and rumours of incursions.

Mary had a naturally adventurous and courageous spirit and, although a committed Catholic, was not a natural fanatic, not a persecutor of those whose beliefs were not her own. We have no evidence as to what she thought of the relentless pursuit and punishment of the rebels, but there was every reason to believe that she had accepted her uncles' assurances that these men were murderous traitors. It had been impressed on the young royal couple that they had been intent on murdering François and herself; that it was a personal rebellion rather than one fuelled by religious conviction and real political grievances against her uncles' greed for power and heavy-handed persecution of dissenters.

Perhaps her relaxed attitude to the reformed religion in her own kingdom, when she eventually returned the following year to become the reigning and resident Queen of Scotland, could be dated in part from this lacerating experience. Even the fanatic persecutor, the Duc de Guise, came to realize that Protestantism had become too deeply rooted in France for it ever to be satisfactorily eradicated through violence and suppression.

If Mary had been better schooled in governance and less dependent on her uncles it is possible to believe that she might have been a moderating hand in the treatment of the French heretics. But even if she had managed to throw off the mantle of the Guises she had to contend with Catherine de Medici, older, wiser, more determined, more wily, and intent this time on maintaining her grip on power. Mary's apprenticeship was limited by her natural respect for her family elders and her acceptance of the prevailing view that women should not presume they had as great a capacity for government as men.

In fact, her chance to rule in her own right would come more quickly than she could ever have imagined, but she had to endure the deaths of the two people closest to her before she could stand on world stage as a monarch alone. Mary was to arrive heavily encumbered with the ambitions of others and the folly of her youth, her claim on the English throne blighting her relationship with her cousin Elizabeth before it had had a chance to blossom. As a contemporary saw it: 'For hereupon Queen Elizabeth bare both Enmity to the Guises, and secret Grudge against her; which the subtile Malice of men on both sides cherished, Emulation growing betwixt them, and new occasions daily arising, in such sort that it could not be extinguished but by Death.'[78]

The Tumult of Amboise brought to the fore the real suspicions throughout Europe that Elizabeth I had been fomenting rebellion, on grounds of religion, in France and Scotland, in an attempt at destabilizing both the nations which were most threatening to her. The Venetian ambassador reporting back from the bloodbath of Amboise declared: 'So this has been the greatest conspiracy of which there is any record, for there was knowledge of it in England, Scotland, Germany, and almost all over Christendom.'[79] And the Guise brothers themselves, writing to their sister the dowager queen Mary of Guise, made it clear they considered Elizabeth had 'been stirring the coals . . . to draw fruit of her evil disposition'.[80]

Certainly this kind of internal uproar within the country which most threatened England's security was greeted with opportunistic delight by the new Elizabethan government. The English ambassador Throckmorton, writing to Cecil from Amboise, underlined the obvious: 'present affairs [of the French] are great and many. They will accord with [Elizabeth's] demands, but redeem the time till these garboils [tumults] are overblown and their affairs in better readiness . . . Now is the opportunity; now may she do what she will. Whereunto this stir will grow God knows . . . for they begin to stir in a great many more places.'[81]

Elizabeth's Privy Council wanted her to make full use of this opportunity to support the Scottish rebels and attempt to expel the French from Scotland. But Elizabeth was not to be bullied or hurried. 'The joy of the Queen was very great'[82] at the news of the French king's death, as the Spanish ambassador reported back to Philip. There was no doubt she was delighted with the news, for it meant increased dissension and internal rifts within France itself. But she was not a natural warmonger. She had seen how her father's military exploits, her sister's ill-judged alliance with Spain against

France, had exhausted the exchequer and wasted so many English lives for no lasting good: she argued with her councillors, 'it is a dangerous matter to enter in war'.[83]

The men around her considered that such feminine equivocation, such 'womanish tolerations',[84] would quickly be overridden when she had taken a husband. They could then deal with the familiar kind of mannish intolerance and, with a masculine hand on the reins of government, wars could be prosecuted without these inconvenient ambivalences. To find a king for this new queen was their ever-present anxiety. But Elizabeth had always had other ideas and she had conducted her life from her earliest days in preparation for this time when she would rule in her own right. As she told her Members of Parliament some quarter of a century later, she had consciously made the hard lessons of her youth her apprenticeship for the greatest job on earth:

'I did put myself to the school of experience, where I sought to learn what things were most fit for a king to have, and I found them to be four: namely, justice, temper[ance], magnanimity, and judgement . . . as Solomon, so I above all things have desired wisdom at the hands of God. And I thank Him He hath given me so much judgement and wit as that I perceive mine own imperfections many ways and mine ignorance in most things.'[85] At that point in her reign there were few in Europe who would not consider her a match for any king.

CHAPTER FIVE

Wilfulness and God's Will

> If she had ever had the will or had found pleasure in
> such a dishonourable life, from which may God preserve
> her, *she did not know of anyone who could forbid her*, but
> she trusted in God that nobody would ever live to see
> her so commit herself.
>
> *Elizabeth's answer to concern about scandalous rumours of her*
> *relations with Robert Dudley, as reported by Baron Breuner to the*
> *Emperor Ferdinand, 1559.*

AFTER THE URGENT MATTER OF PEACE with France had been
concluded, there were two outstanding problems created by Elizabeth's accession. Whom would she marry and what form would
her version of religion take? Both questions were made even more
urgent by the spectre of Mary Queen of Scots whose undoubted
claim to Elizabeth's throne was backed by the ambitions and military might of the French. Religion also was inseparable from this
rival claim, for Mary represented an inveterate Catholicism, tainted
with something of her uncles' reputation for fanatic enforcement.
Elizabeth, of course, was the child of the English Reformation, her
conception the impetus for the breach with Rome, and although it
was not yet clear how radical her own position might be, she was
certainly considered by the whole of Catholic Europe to be of
heretical upbringing and cast of mind.

If Elizabeth's councillors could persuade the English queen to
marry and produce an heir then not only would the direct Tudor

succession be more secure, but Mary's claim would be downgraded, for her lifetime at least. With this security, the new religion could be properly established against the ever-present claims of the old.

The answer to these problems seemed obvious to everyone: the English queen must marry, and marry soon. The Speaker of the House of Commons made it the central point of his speech, a matter 'of great importance for the general state of all the realme', for by her marriage, 'as well for her owne comfort and contentment, as for assurance to the realme by her royal issue ... the feares of her faythfull subjects and frendes, as the ambitious hopes of her enimyes, should cleane be cutt offe'.[1] While the whole country expected that Elizabeth would conform to this human and constitutional imperative, the European powers schemed, jockeyed for advantage, watching and waiting.

But the steps of an extraordinarily compelling courtship dance of advance and retreat, of flirtation and feint, frustration and desire, were already being rehearsed by this most self-possessed and enigmatic of queens. These were to be repeated through the decades of her rule, to the exasperation of everyone involved, and the unique but lonely triumph of Elizabeth herself. The result was the evolution of an image of almost mythological power, etched into the passionate heart of a nation and an age; the Virgin Queen presiding over nearly half a century of unprecedented calm and prosperity for her people. But at the beginning no one, except perhaps Elizabeth herself, could have suspected the exceptional nature of the queen and the singularity of her reign.

Soon after her accession, the Venetian ambassador recognized something of Elizabeth's ability to control and disconcert: 'The Queen is by nature high spirited, and has become yet more so owing to her good fortune and to the many physical and moral endowments which she possesses; so she has lofty designs, and promises herself success in all of them. She has many suitors for her hand, and by protracting any decisions keeps them all in hope. Persuading herself that in her need they will do what they can from rivalry to gain her love and matrimonial alliance.'[2]

Just as she would attempt to keep all the possibilities in play as far as her suitors, and thereby her foreign policy, were concerned, so too Elizabeth did not hurry to show her hand in matters of religion. She was the mistress of equivocation. This way she neither panicked the Catholics nor disaffected the reformers, even while they muttered at the slowness of her processes of change. So important were both these issues for the lives of her people and the security of the realm that she was watched like a hawk, her every action interpreted by a hundred busy tongues. The English were considered by their European neighbours to be peculiar in their general lack of religious fervour. The Spanish ambassador broadcast his bafflement: 'These people are so curious that they think the question of religion is of the least importance.'³ In fact the coolness came directly from Elizabeth's dislike of proscription in spiritual matters, her aversion to opening 'windows into men's souls'.

She was a new and unpredictable force in European politics, and her marital and religious proclivities were of consuming interest in her rivals' courts. There was even greater interest at home with constant gossip and excitement at court, her nobles vying for attention and favour, the foreign ambassadors seeking preferment over their rivals, everyone wagering the odds on a rotating field of possible contenders. The ambassadors were particularly sharp-eyed in their surveillance and their dispatches to their masters were lurid with surmise and foreboding.

The Spanish ambassador Feria, bitter at losing the pre-eminence he enjoyed during Mary Tudor's reign, was the most lively and opinionated: 'what can be expected from a country governed by a Queen', he wrote gloomily to Philip II, 'and she a young lass, who, though sharp, is without prudence, and is every day standing up against religion more openly? The kingdom is entirely in the hands of young folks, heretics and traitors . . . the old people and Catholics are dissatisfied, but dare not open their lips . . . Everybody thinks that she will not marry a foreigner and they cannot make out whom she favours, so that nearly every day some new cry is raised about a husband.'⁴

Certainly her people hated the idea of Elizabeth marrying a

foreign prince. They had seen more than enough of the disadvantages of such an alliance during her sister's reign. In their eyes England had been impoverished and diminished by becoming a satellite of Spain, embroiled in Spanish wars for Spanish interests. 'Never prince left [England] more indebted, both at home and beyond sea', was the common verdict on the unhappy reign of Mary I who had made Philip her king. London had been overrun by wily and over-confident Dons, and the English, notoriously proud, insular and xenophobic even then, could not wait to see the back of them.

However, the more measured response from Cecil and the other councillors was that marriage with a powerful prince did bring some important benefits. The arguments were rehearsed in a contemporary treatise: 'Marienge a stranger, she uniteth hir husband's power unto her, and is thereby backed and strengthened'. But foreigners unfortunately were an untrustworthy lot, 'more prone to temptation of the flesh, both Italians, French, Spaniards, and Germans, which shadow that fault with their dronkennes'. And there was always the problem of diffused loyalties: 'In marieng a stranger, and unityng regions, the more trouble, more danger, more charge.' The emotive examples of queens closely related to Elizabeth were called on to illustrate the undesirable consequences of a foreign match: her sister Mary was the obvious and most painfully recalled, but also Mary Queen of Scots, who had 'empoverished hir realme by hir match in France, through the oppression of the French'.[5] It was implied that both Queen Marys, through marriage, had sacrificed the wealth, pre-eminence and security of their own kingdoms.

Although marriage to an Englishman kept that precious royal blood undiluted and the affections focused wholeheartedly at home, the argument went that there would be jealousy amongst the noblemen not chosen for this honour. There was also a fear of the perceived diminution of the queen's own status in allying herself to someone of inferior rank: 'In marienge an Englishman, she maneth her subject, disparageth hirself.'[6] These were the bare bones of the debate which exercised her ambassadors and councillors in all their foreign policy, and periodically gripped the people with alternating bouts of anxiety and hope.

In the first years of Elizabeth's reign, the gamblers in her court were putting money on her marrying Lord Robert Dudley, the ambitious, confident and physically magnificent Master of the Queen's Horse. A contemporary of Elizabeth's (some said an exact contemporary, claiming they shared the same birthday), Dudley had known her when young and suffered a similarly disrupted, demoted and fearful youth. His brother, father and grandfather were beheaded for treason; he himself spent some years in the Tower and was tried for treason in Mary I's reign, living like Elizabeth, under an unpredictable threat of death.

Not only did they share the painful bond of a precarious youth, Elizabeth had strong reason to be grateful to Lord Robert at a time when friends were hard to find. Soon after her accession, however, she felt she had to explain her affection and lavishness towards him: 'I only show him favour because of his goodness to me when I was in trouble during the reign of my sister. At that time he never ceased his former kindness and service, but even sold his possessions to provide me with funds; and on this account it seems to me but just that now I should give him some reward for his fidelity and constancy.'[7] Elizabeth was known for her natural loyalty to the small band of friends and advisers who constituted her inner circle and remained with her for most of her life, but from the start Dudley was the most obviously favoured.

Certainly, on her accession his career took off like a meteor across the Elizabethan sky. Fuelled by the queen's love for him and a loyalty forged in a time of youthful suffering, his trajectory barely faltered. Surviving storms, scandals and betrayals, theirs was a life-long love affair, almost certainly unconsummated but all the more compelling for that.

Their attraction, mysterious and passionate, fascinated their contemporaries. It was rumoured there was even something supernatural in the enduring bond between such wilful natures. Camden, Elizabeth's first biographer, was as bemused as the rest. Perhaps it was due to some hidden virtue in Dudley he thought; or their 'common conditions of Imprisonment under Queen Mary'; or indeed 'a most strait conjunction of their Minds', due to the position of the stars at the hour of their births; what that magic ingredient was 'a man cannot easily say'.[8] Perhaps it was just that the male mind could not understand the attraction. All Elizabeth's chroniclers, councillors and ambassadors were men. The detail and emphasis that comes down through history is filtered through male eyes and interpreted by masculine sensibilities. Robert Dudley's main appeal to the queen may have been simpler, more visceral. He was a virile figure of a man, as impressive in the saddle, be he in the chase or on the battlefield, as in a courtly dance. 'A man of flourishing age, and comely Feature of body and lims',[9] he was a man of charismatic sexuality and she, a woman of strong appetites, responded to this magnetism.

The conduct in public between Elizabeth and Dudley gave cause for much salacious comment and outraged disapproval. Even in an age of general laxity in the behaviour between men and women, Elizabeth's overt attraction to her handsome Master of the Horse made tongues wag and the wildest rumours fly. It was said, 'her Majesty visits him in his chamber day and night';[10] or that they were already secretly married, that indeed, she was pregnant by him, in fact already had had children by him. The outgoing Spanish ambassador, Feria, although not liking or trusting Elizabeth, recognized her sexual nature and the behaviour that added a certain plausibility to some of these rumours. Writing to his master Philip II he pointed out that Elizabeth was far more likely to have children than her sister Mary I, due to 'age and temperament, in both of which respects she is much better than the Queen now in heaven, although in every other way she compares most unfavourably'.[11]

As a woman there were times in her youth when she appeared to want nothing better than to marry Lord Robert, her 'sweet Robin', but as queen, Elizabeth quickly realized that to do so could risk everything. Arrogant, magnificent, duplicitous, ambitious, he epitomized the soul of Elizabethan adventurism, and was as cordially loathed by the people as she was passionately loved. Perhaps he was too closely a mirror of the brazenness of the Elizabethan age and the exorbitant rewards and perils of his kind of high aspiration. He disconcerted those who found in his reflection something uneasily like themselves. Certainly his fellow noblemen resented his influence, and the high-minded William Cecil suspected his motives. Rumours of his capacity for opportunistic assassination circulated freely, never more so than after the tragic death of his young wife. Yet in an age of treachery and with a queen who made inconsistency high art, Robert Dudley maintained his pre-eminence in Elizabeth's heart.

Although he was to remain her favourite, he was by no means the only suitor for her hand, neither was he the only one to believe he had every chance of success. In the early summer of 1559, while Lord Robert was away for a day's hunting, a handsome nobleman, Sir William Pickering, was brought to the queen's chambers. An exile since the Wyatt Rebellion, he had returned with the idea that he stood a chance of becoming Elizabeth's consort, and the next King of England. The Venetian ambassador to Philip II described him: 'about 36 years old, of tall stature, and handsome, and very successful with women. For he is said to have enjoyed the intimacy of many and great ones.'[12]

For a while he held extravagant court amongst the nobles keen to support his suit and thereby scupper Dudley's, and his dashing manner and smooth Continental ways seemed to flatter the lively affections of Elizabeth. He favoured hosting lavish banquets but, in keeping with his pretensions, insisted on dining apart 'with music playing'.[13] The cunning ambassador Feria reported: 'In London they are giving 25 to 100 that he will be King. They tell me Lord Robert is not so friendly with him as he was, and I believe that on the first day that the Queen saw him secretly Lord Robert did not know of it, as he had gone hunting at Windsor.' Superior as ever he added, 'If these things were not of such great importance, and so lamentable, some of them would be very ridiculous.'[14]

Uncompromisingly Catholic, Feria found Elizabeth and her youthful and brash court hard to stomach. He thought the country having 'fallen into the hands of a woman who is a daughter of the devil and the greatest scoundrels and heretics in the land' was fast on the road to hell.[15] Everyone was watching Elizabeth intently, and speculating as to her nature and the character of her government. 'She seems to me incomparably more feared than her sister and gives her orders and has her way as absolutely as her father did ... she is a woman who is very fond of argument', was one of Feria's early verdicts. He still wanted his master to pursue the courtship of this difficult queen and, perhaps with a nudge, reminded him how much Elizabeth loved attention, jewels and presents, 'and her one theme is how poor she is'.[16] Capricious, vain, a maddening tease, she also had a mind like a gin trap and was entirely in control of herself. No wonder Feria's successor, the urbane Bishop Quadra, after a particularly gruelling discussion with the queen about marriage, had to admit defeat: 'I am not sure about her, for I do not understand her.'[17]

The marriage dance continued with other suitors taking the floor. The Austrian Archduke Ferdinand, a narrow Catholic bigot, was one; his younger brother Charles, distinguished by an abnormally large head, was another. Despite first appearances, either prince seemed, to influential men like William Cecil, Sussex and all Dudley's many enemies at court, to offer a potentially valuable alliance. It was thought that such a match, supported by the Emperor and Spanish interests, would keep the French at a respectful distance.

Elizabeth appeared to be collaborative. She allowed the Spanish ambassador to propose his suit. She tolerated her advisers' hopeful speculations. She played along with the general optimism that a husband had been found for her at last. She said she could not trust portrait painters and wished to see him in person. When that seemed about to be arranged, she protested 'he had better not give his master so much trouble in order to see so ugly a lady as she'.[18] And so it went on. Elizabeth dancing light on her feet to keep the suits alive but twirling out of reach when anyone came too close. As a final escape she could always return to the old mantra, 'back again to her nonsense', as the Spanish ambassador in exasperation called it, and claim 'she would rather be a nun than marry without knowing with whom'; she 'did not mean to marry'; 'she meant to die a maid'.[19]

Certainly requesting a suitor to turn up in person went against convention, for the humiliation of rejection to his face was too great a risk to his dignity. But Elizabeth did not wish that either; it was just part of her delaying game. So the archduke was not to be sent for, but then neither was he to wait. In a flash of the facetious manner which so discomforted her officials, she told the ambassador that amongst the other princely qualities expected of her future husband 'he should not sit at home all day amongst the cinders, but should in time of peace keep himself employed in warlike exercises'.[20] No wonder nobody but her closest and oldest friends and advisers knew how to deal with her, and even they could suddenly find themselves unexpectedly capsized.

Though certainly no Cinderella, and not quite her Prince Charming, Lord Robert Dudley was gaining in the queen's affections daily as she imposed increasingly impossible conditions on her suitors. Elizabeth publicly made up to Lord Robert, favouring him so overtly that the gossips could not contain themselves. He was 'a very handsome young man (*giovane bellissimo*)' the Venetian ambassador reported, 'towards whom in various ways the Queen evinces such affection and inclination that many persons believe that if his wife, who has been ailing for some time, were perchance to die, the Queen might easily take him for her husband'.[21]

Throughout all these marital manoeuvrings was the ever-present concern with Mary's claim to the English throne. This was no dormant or academic threat, but a real and present danger given her alliance as Queen of France with one of the great European powers. Elizabeth's marriage with someone who could summon Spanish might and influence would balance this rival queen politically, but there was the significant problem of religion to be overcome, and the real risk of rousing the antagonism of her people. A compromise position, which appealed to the religious reformers in England, was to try and secure Scotland in the absence of its queen by marrying Elizabeth to their premier nobleman.

The Earl of Arran, son of the Duke of Châtelherault and next in line of succession after Mary, returned secretly to England in July 1559. Driven into exile in Switzerland by a French directive to capture him dead or alive, in order to prevent just such an alliance, he came trailing good political and Protestant credentials. Elizabeth had been offered to him by her father when they were both young children and now that the boy was a man he nursed the hope not only of sharing Elizabeth's throne but possibly even of deposing Mary and uniting both kingdoms under the reformed religion. His inflated hopes and zealous energies may have been exacerbated by an incipient mania for, sadly, he would go insane within three years.

But just as Cecil favoured this marriage prospect so Dudley opposed it, encouraging the Austrian archduke's suit, and then transferring his allegiance when the chance to confuse matters further arrived in the form of the Swedish embassy. The Swedes arrived with boatloads of presents, in pursuit once again of a marriage with their prince and heir Eric, who was the same age as Elizabeth, reputed to be one of the best looking men in Europe and soon to become King Eric XIV of Sweden. Dudley's switching of horses was no more opportunistic than that of anyone else at the time but his flashy ambitions and intimacy with the queen were fuelling ugly rumours to which a tragic event would shortly give the imprimatur of truth. The new Spanish ambassador Bishop Quadra was happy to pass on to Philip II all the latest gossip:

> I had heard from a certain person who is accustomed to give me veracious news that Lord Robert has sent to poison his wife. Certainly all the Queen has done with us and with the Swede, and will do with the rest in the matter of her marriage, is only keeping Lord Robert's enemies and the country engaged with words until this wicked deed of killing his wife is consummated. The same person told me some extraordinary things about this intimacy [with the Queen], which I would never have believed, only that now I find Lord Robert's enemies in the Council making no secret of their evil opinions of it.[22]

Elizabeth was concerned about these rumours and the effect on her reputation. She had learnt a painful lesson during her girlhood flirtation with Thomas Seymour when it was clear how readily salacious stories gathered a momentum of their own. She had been powerless and vulnerable then. Now she was all-powerful. That meant, however, she was even more closely watched and her reputation all the more eagerly sullied by those who wished merely to entertain themselves, and by others who more seriously intended to do her harm. During one of her fencing conversations with the Spanish ambassador about the possibility of her accepting the Austrian Archduke Charles, she said, only half in jest, that 'if the Archduke heard any of the idle tales they tell about her', ('and they tell many' the ambassador added), 'he might take advantage of them to the detriment of her honour'.[23]

Bishop Quadra diplomatically reassured her. But in fact these rumours were so lurid and persistent that even her own ambassador Sir Thomas Chaloner, then resident at Philip II's court in the Low Countries, thought it necessary to warn Cecil of what was being scurrilously said abroad: 'I count the slander most false, so a young Princess cannot be too wary what countenance or familiar demonstration she maketh, more to one than another . . . This delay of ripe time for marriage, besides the loss of the realm (for without posterity of her highness what hope is left unto us?) ministereth matter to these leud tongues to descant upon, and breedeth contempt.'[24]

If these scandals were rife in Philip's austere court then they were enjoyed all the more by the French. Mary Queen of Scots, at this time a devout young woman, a wife most probably still only in name, was privy there to all the discreditable stories of her rival's unseemly behaviour, much coloured in the telling by 'the malicious French'.[25]

In 1559 these cousins were virgin queens aged almost seventeen and twenty-six. With one, her reputation for chastity and probity was at its height, while the other was embroiled in rumour and vicious innuendo. Many years later, bitter in captivity, having lived a life characterized by even more vivid scandals than those attached to her cousin's name, Mary was to write an extraordinary letter to Elizabeth. Possibly deflected by Cecil and never seen by his queen, it alluded offensively to continued rumours and accusations about Elizabeth's lascivious behaviour, as passed on to her by her jailer's wife, the Countess of Shrewsbury: 'that one [Robert Dudley] to whom she said that you had made promise of marriage before a lady of your chamber had lain infinite times with you, with all the licence and intimacy which can be used between husband and wife'.[26]

Then Mary mentioned the slander that seemed to cancel out this first rumour, that Elizabeth was 'not like other women' and somehow physically incapable of consummating a marriage. This was the arena where Elizabeth was most personally vulnerable. Having held out for her revolutionary vision of herself as the Virgin Queen, ruling successfully and alone, without the need of a husband for emotional, intellectual and moral support, she opened herself to accusations that she was more a freak of nature than a true woman. It was not her avowed virginity which appeared so perverse. The choice of the celibate life was an honourable, even admirable, course of action in a Christian society then. 'Virginitie above matrimonie, because followed by Christ ... Virginitie, because it is so hard to be kept, is more laudable in princes.'[27] The more anarchic and disturbing aspect of Elizabeth's choice was her freedom from convention, expectation and the supremacy of the male. In a society and a religion that accepted as indisputable fact the innate superiority of men and the foolishness and intellectual weakness of women, their queen's insistence that she could accept the most powerful position in the land and yet govern alone without a king beside her, flouted this fundamental law of nature.

In this matter, her cousin Mary Queen of Scots claimed a distinct advantage over her. There was no disputing her credentials as a woman. Having lived chastely and free from scandal as an unmarried queen she fulfilled her destiny as a female and as a monarch by marrying young, and continuing to marry. Accepting responsibility for securing the dynasty, she managed to produce a son and heir in the process. All her husbands predeceased her, the last two in tragic and dubious circumstances, and scandal hung round her name. Ultimately she may have failed catastrophically as a sovereign but, unlike Elizabeth, Mary had proved her womanliness and fertility. In accepting the necessity of having a king beside her, she had reinforced the natural order of things and reassured her kingdom. In producing a son and heir she had discharged her constitutional duty and secured the succession.

Failing on all these counts, Elizabeth forged on without precedent to support her. The scurrilous rumours detailed in Mary's 'scandal' letter began their vigorous life during these first few years of Elizabeth's reign when her passion for Dudley was at its most febrile, and her conduct was at its most flirtatious and abandoned. That it was too dangerous for her to follow her heart was a lesson begun with her experiences with Thomas Seymour. It was to be hammered home by the scandal that engulfed Robert Dudley, and threatened to dishonour her as queen. In all the speculation about Elizabeth's marrying her Master of the Horse, there was a salient fact that was largely overlooked; Lord Robert Dudley already had a wife. Married in the summer of his seventeenth year to Amy Robsart, the daughter of a Norfolk landowner, Dudley had lived his increasingly glittering life at Elizabeth's court mostly separated from his wife. The court followed the centuries-old pattern organized on a masculine foundation. The only women present were invited there as attendants on the queen.

It was the inconvenience of his marital status that fuelled the rumours of poison, plotting or divorce. But courtship stratagems and speculative gossip were only two of the major preoccupations of the early years of Elizabeth's reign. The eternal problem of her relations with Scotland was made more acute with the accession of Mary to the French throne in 1559 and the concomitant elevation of the Guises to ultimate power.

In his judicious memorandum, 'Discussion of the weighty Matter of Scotland', written in the summer of 1559, Cecil punctiliously pointed out that through historical precedence the crown of England was superior to that of Scotland and 'By this title and dignity doth the French Queen, as Queen of Scots, owe homage to the crown of England'. To his considerable disquiet, however, it was obvious that Mary, encouraged by her French family, had not only rejected such reasoning but shown by her assumption of the Queen of England's arms and by her 'disdainful speech' how little respect she had for Elizabeth. It had been reported too that as Mary entered her chapel ushers preceded her with the cry, 'make way for the Queen of England'. With gloomy prescience, Cecil noted how the malice of Mary and the French towards the English queen had been 'augmented and taken root, by their false pretended title'. Even in this first year of Elizabeth's reign Cecil realized that as long as Mary Queen of Scots lived, 'this quarrel now begun, is undoubtedly like to be a perpetual incumbrance of this kingdom'.[28]

There was an ancient and deep hostility between England and Scotland, the latter historically providing a valuable bridgehead for England's enemies into the otherwise seabound kingdom. Mary of Guise was tiring of her efforts as regent to rule the factious, intractable Scots. Her health was failing, the Protestant reformers were becoming more offensive, with mobs rampaging through churches, smashing effigies. Protests had been particularly violent in Perth where monks were hounded from their monasteries. The regent was outraged and alarmed.

The tide of reformation which had rolled with such force through mainland Europe had reached this island outpost, its momentum now irreversible. Confirmation came from across the border where Elizabeth's careful equivocation over the practice of faith had given way to a more wholehearted endorsement of the reformed religion with legislation authorizing use of the 1552 English prayer book, inaugurated in her brother's reign. Although the Protestant rebels were careful to proclaim their loyalty to her daughter Mary Queen of Scots and to François, her husband, their king, Mary of Guise believed that religion was just a cloak for her schismatic nobles to undermine the authority of the crown and eject the French from Scottish soil.

Certainly the native Scots had grown increasingly resentful and intolerant of the growing numbers of French in their midst, dominating the best-paid positions, lording it over the locals, insisting on an extravagant standard of living far beyond what this impoverished country could afford. There was no doubt too that these representatives of a powerful and sophisticated court could be arrogant and dismissive of their more modest hosts. Racial prejudice and resentment, similar to that expressed by the English towards the ubiquitous Spanish during the last years of Mary I's reign, were stirred into the subversive brew. To add to her problems, the ill and weary regent suspected that the new young English queen, bastard-born and raised a heretic as she was, intended to supply secret aid to the Scottish rebels.

In Scotland the summer of 1559 was riotous. The rebel forces gained in confidence and boldness while the troops loyal to the regent quarrelled amongst themselves, the Scots against the French, rival clans against each other, one Scottish interest against another. More monasteries and churches were sacked, the ancient and sacred palace of Scone was looted and burned. Mary of Guise retreated to Dunbar to await fresh French reinforcements. While she waited she heard that Henri II had died on 10 July and her own daughter was now Queen of France. Her long sacrifice was rewarded at last.

The death of the French king and accession of his unpromising fifteen-year-old son was greeted with delight by Elizabeth and deep gloom by the expatriate French who 'confess that the Scotch affair is lost'.[29] Young or weak monarchs made for stronger internal factions. The political and religious divisions in France were gathering force. This meant French eyes and energies were turned inwards again. Not surprisingly the Protestants in Scotland were greatly encouraged in their ambitions to drive out the foreigners and establish a reformed church.

An influential section of the nobility, banded together as the Lords of the Congregation, were prime movers whose cause was given a blast of fire and brimstone by the return to Scotland of the great reforming preacher John Knox. Twelve years of exile, some of them as a galley slave of the French, had diminished neither his vigour nor his rhetoric. Within little more than a week of Henri II's death, the Congregation, led by Knox, had written simultaneously to Cecil and to Elizabeth, declaring their desire for union with England and requesting help in resisting the French. Knox declared this new amity with England was based on a shared spiritual foundation rather than any 'temporall commoditie', unlike the alliance of Scotland with France which had been 'maid by worldlie men for worldlie proffett'.[30]

John Knox was a master of militant self-righteousness and the lofty moral stance. Nevertheless, it was precisely that disdained temporal commodity – cash – which he and his fellow reformers required from Elizabeth. She saw this as an opportunity covertly to weaken French influence across the border and, initially without the knowledge or consent of her full council, she and Cecil authorized £3000 to be smuggled through to the reformers' cause. Her facility in continuing to deny to foreign ambassadors any involvement with the Scottish rebels was doubly exasperating. The Spanish ambassador Bishop Quadra, writing to Philip II of Spain, could not contain his irritation: 'I have lost all hope in the affairs of this woman. She is convinced of the soundness of her unstable power, and will only see her error when she is irretrievably lost . . . her language is so shifty that it is the most difficult thing in the world to negotiate with her. With her all is falsehood and vanity.'[31]

Elizabeth was learning her craft as a diplomat, practising her protean roles as elusive friend to all, ally to none. While the Earl of Arran travelled north, spurred with the queen's blessing and financial support, to take his part in the Protestant uprising and offer himself as a titular head with a hereditary claim on the Scottish throne, she was assuring the French ambassador of her best intentions towards Mary of Guise. Elizabeth blamed any rumours of her duplicity on others. 'She well knew that there were men who spread wicked lies in order to cause trouble', she protested. Then, rather than undermine her own spurious innocence, she even implicated members of her council in a remarkable echo of modern democratic government. 'It was quite likely [she said] that some of her ministers had been foolish enough to meddle with the evil practices among the Scots, but that she had ordered an enquiry to be made, and had sent a man expressly to set matters in order.'[32]

As the Scottish situation deteriorated, however, it became clear that she could not maintain for long her fiction of non-involvement in the rebels' cause. In October 1559, having requested that Mary of Guise desist from fortifying Leith, and having her and her French allies 'obstinatlie procead in thare wicked enterprise',[33] Knox and the Congregation formally declared at the market cross in Edinburgh that the regent was deposed. They were careful to insist that the authority of Mary Queen of Scots and France and François II, now King of France and of Scotland, remained unimpaired. 'The battell is begun scharpe yneuht [enough]', Knox attempted to cheer himself, 'God geve the issew to his glory and our confort.'[34] However, the reformers lacked the men, munitions and resources to enforce their rebellion against Mary of Guise and her French garrisons in the field. They looked to Elizabeth and England.

This was Elizabeth's first real trial as queen. The country was in a parlous state. The whole of Europe knew that she had assumed the crown of a weakened kingdom: the war chest emptied by her sister's fruitless war with France; her army and navy depleted; her munitions meagre; her fortifications neglected. There was little hope that England at this time could have repulsed even a half-hearted invasion. The presence of Mary Queen of Scots, with her unimpeachable claim on Elizabeth's throne and the might of France at hand to enforce it, made the threat of neighbourly acquisitiveness all the more real. Her ambassador Throckmorton, writing from France, was unnerved at Mary's bold pretensions, 'the young French Queen, since the death of the French King [Henri II], has written into Scotland that as God has so provided, as notwithstanding the malice of her enemies she is Queen of France and of Scotland, so she trusts to be Queen of England also'.[35]

Mary's rebel Scottish lords were uneasy as to what allegiance their queen might truly show. Addressing Elizabeth in their plea for help they pointed out: 'our young Quene is married into France, where she nowe lyveth as a stranger both to them and us, unable to use the liberty of her crowne'.[36] Her powerlessness they believed was due to the irresistible influence of her mother-in-law Catherine de Medici and her uncle, the focus of whose interest lay in 'this invasion of Scotland . . . to open an entraunce thereby into England'. The lords tried to stiffen Elizabeth's resolve by appealing to her sense of *amour-propre*: 'Let others sit downe and lament their losses;

it is the part of wise men to sit downe, and foresee, and to prevent them.'[37]

Cecil too was warning Elizabeth that summer that these threats were real: '[France] seeketh always to make Scotland an instrument to exercise thereby their malice upon England, and to make a footstool thereof to look over England as they may.'[38] But Elizabeth was afraid of committing herself to any unequivocal alliance with the Scottish Protestants to rid their homeland of this colonizing power. She feared opening England to humiliation by the French on Scottish soil, and inviting retaliatory aggression towards her own realm at home. She was never keen to encourage any kind of insurrection against sovereign power, realizing how fast sedition could spread across borders, and was ever mindful that the success of her monarchy relied absolutely on the support of her people, and an ancient reverence for their monarch. But without Elizabeth's overt help the Scottish Reformation appeared to be faltering while France increased in stature on the footstool at her borders.

Surprisingly perhaps, the cerebral and pragmatic Cecil was the most hawkish of Elizabeth's advisers at this time. He had to work hard to persuade the council of the necessity of intervention in Scotland, as allies of the rebellious Protestants, as the only way to halt the expansion of the French: 'good corrage in a good quarrell, as this is, to delyver a realme from conquest, and consequently to save our owne, will much furder ye matter'.[39] Elizabeth, not surprisingly, was the most reluctant of them all. She was naturally averse to war, particularly when her own country seemed so unprepared, understocked in every kind of ordnance and weak in human and financial resources. Due to her own nature, and the early experiences of threat and danger, Elizabeth felt more secure with a policy of illusion and sleight of hand. Her own history had taught her she was vulnerable if she admitted to anything, and that to stand up and be counted could cost her her life. Conversely, by maintaining her favourite position, the Janus face at the entrance to her kingdom, she could dissemble and deny everything. She could sue for peace while she prepared for war.

Cecil wanted her to sue for war and this, her first great test, she could not bring herself to do. By the end of 1559, he had won over the council but still had to persuade his mistress that the time had come to send an army openly into Scotland. Sir William Paget, an ageing politician who had known Elizabeth from the Seymour years, had written to Cecil earlier in the year about the threat of France's invasion through Scotland. He showed an appreciation of the young Queen's qualities of mind as well as her diffidence over initiating hostilities: 'For Godd's Sake move that good Quene to put her Sword in to her Hand ... to use that goodly Wytt, that goodly Knowledge, and that gret and special Grace of Understanding and Judgement of Things that God hath gyven her, and so I beleve she shall *quaerere regnum Dei*, and maynten her own *Regnum* also [and so I believe she shall seek the kingdom of God, and maintain her own reign also].'

The council still could not persuade Elizabeth to take up her sword but Cecil's exasperated resignation letter, written 'with a sorrowful heart and watery eyes',[40] forced Elizabeth's hand. By the end of February 1560 she agreed to a treaty with the Scottish lords, the Treaty of Berwick, whereby England pledged to help protect Scotland from any attempts by the French to 'conquere the Realme of *Scotland*, suppresse the Libertie thereof, and unite the same to the Crowne of *France* perpetually'. This protection would extend as far as sending 'with all speed ... into *Scotlande* a convenient Ayde of Men of Warr on Horse and Foot'. Elizabeth could maintain something of her Janus face by insisting in the treaty that the Scottish 'Nobilitie and Subjects' continue to acknowledge 'theyr Soverain Lady and Queene', her own cousin and counterclaimant to her throne, Mary Queen of Scots.[41]

Still she demurred, however, at the idea of translating this offer of paper protection into incontrovertible force on the ground. To her council, pressing for action, she would only say despondently: 'It is a dangerous matter to enter into war.'[42] This was a sentiment well supported by the run-down state of her nation. All of Europe knew what the Spanish Count de Feria bluntly told Throckmorton, who passed it on to Elizabeth: 'Will she take upon herself to meddle with other Princes' rebels? And the French being driven out, will she maintain the Scots in their religion? . . . What doth she think? We know well enough what her forces are: . . . no friends, no Council, no finances, no noblemen of conduct, no captains, no soldiers. And no reputation in the world.'[43]

However, Elizabeth seemed personally to be putting on a brave face as far as her Spanish ambassadors were concerned: 'The Queen rides out every day into the country on a neapolitan courser or a jennet to exercise for this war, seated on one of the saddles they use here. She makes a brave show and bears herself gallantly. In short the people here are full of warfare and armaments.'[44] Her bold behaviour was encouraged by the presence of her dashing Master of the Horse, Lord Robert, riding high in the saddle, in her heart and her esteem. Her diffidence about waging war, however, was overcome finally, and by the end of March nearly eight thousand men under Lord Grey's command crossed the border to join the Scottish forces and together put Leith and its French defenders under siege.

While Elizabeth was struggling with this first crisis of her reign, Mary, only six months into her reign as queen consort of France, was facing the first incursion of fear and violence into her courtly upbringing. The anti-Guise passions of the French Protestants were running so high that the lives of the young king and queen themselves appeared to be at risk, the threat culminating in the conspiracy at Amboise in March. In an age when sudden and untimely death was commonplace, these periods of upheaval and revolution added an extra dimension of anarchy and danger to which even queens were not immune. Both of Mary's uncles, the Cardinal of Lorraine and the Duc de Guise, had taken to riding with a bodyguard of 'ten brave and faithful men . . . each man with a loaded pistol under his cloak',[45] every time they left the relative safety of the court.

Although the focus of antipathy was the overweening power of the Guises, the brothers themselves sought to obscure the personal animosity directed against them, and make it appear more a generalized rebellion against Catholicism and the monarchy. Convincing the young king and his queen of their own personal danger meant the Guises were given a free rein in their avowed protection of the crown. In sowing real fear in the court they were then able to advocate swingeing reprisals and thus escalate the violence in a malign circle which drew the whole of France into a bloody religious war. 'By giving the King guards upon guards, [the Guises] ende-voured nothing, they sayd, but to enterteine him in distrust of his subjects, and his subjects in fear and hatred of him.'[46]

The French Protestants may have been a threat to Mary but her Catholic uncles, and by association she herself, were seen as a real threat to her cousin, the English queen. Elizabeth received from her French ambassador dire warnings of an assassin already dis-patched by the brothers: '[there exists] a pestilent and horrible device of the Guises to poison her by means of an Italian named Stephano, a burly man with a black beard, about forty-five years of age [who will] offer his services to the Queen as an engineer'.[47]

Such rumours of murder and mayhem were rife; rebellious citi-zens and foreigners with sinister intent were everywhere. And mur-ders were common in every social stratum, assassinations were a part of state policy and death was as likely to arrive prematurely with violence as timely in a bed. Even the seemingly invincible Duc de Guise was destroyed by an assassin's bullet on his forty-fourth birthday in 1563, and his much reviled brother the Cardinal, although escaping the violence of others, died eleven years later as a result of inflicting violence on himself.*

The spring of 1560 marked a crisis point for both queens. While decisive and difficult action was required from Elizabeth, who was naturally constrained by an analytical and wary mind, Mary, by nature headstrong and drawn to impetuous action, was powerless in the grip of her overweening family. Ideologically too their ener-gies were opposed. Elizabeth was being asked to act in order to protect the rights of the Scottish reformers while Mary was the passive focus for the French reformers' rebellion, and spectator of her family's bloody retaliation.

---

* Having become a flagellant, he caught a chill while wearing inadequate clothing during a session of self-mortification, and never recovered.

As discussed earlier, there is no evidence as to how Mary reacted to the sights and sounds of torture, and wholesale carnage, which assailed every inhabitant of Amboise during the days of Guise revenge. But it cannot have passed her by without effect. Mary was a robust, impulsive and physically active young woman with passionate and volatile emotions. Her life had been characterized by accesses of energy expended largely on hunting, hawking and dancing, followed by short-lived collapses in health. Her periodic ill-health was due in part to the three to four days' fever (tertian and quartan ague) commonly associated with endemic chronic malaria, suffered by the majority of the population of the time.

Emotional crises would also affect Mary dramatically. One such was reported by Throckmorton to Elizabeth. News of her mother's seriously declining health and the escalating hostilities in Scotland elicited an outpouring of anger and grief: 'On 25 of this present [April 1560] the French Queen made very great lamentation, and wept bitterly, and, as it is reported, said that her uncles had undone her, and caused her to lose her realm.'[48] Her fears in the spring of 1560 for both her mother and her inheritance were justified by the facts, but also amplified perhaps by the extreme violence and suffering of the Protestant rebels which she had just witnessed in bloody and claustrophobic detail at Amboise. A letter she sent to Mary of Guise in Scotland, probably at the end of March and from this blood-stained town, was almost incoherent with anxiety for her mother's safety and health, *'la poine que j'é entendu que vous vous donnés, me fait tant craindre que n'aiés mal'* ['The trouble that I have heard you are in makes me fear so much you will be ill'].[49]

Mary promised to ensure that her husband, now king, would keep his word and send more men to help her mother resist the English and the rebel Scottish forces. But her letter also revealed just how much the new queen deferred to the power of the old, Catherine de Medici, relying on her advice and trusting in her apparent affection. Try as Mary might to alleviate some of the suffering of her valiant mother, she was powerless to act. France, with its own troubles at home, did not send Mary of Guise her hoped-for salvation, and this neglect can only have added to Mary's grief and consternation when her mother finally died in June 1560, her doughty heart failing her at last.

Elizabeth's first war did not begin well. In the spring of 1560, the English forces failed disastrously in their first attempt at capturing Leith. Elizabeth's worst fears seemed to be confirmed. It was mooted that between 1000 and 1500 men of the alliance were killed (although later reports put it at a tenth of that number, most of them Scots). She hated the loss of life, but above all she hated to be beaten. Cecil once more bore the brunt of her rage and grief. 'I have had such a torment herein with the Queen's Majesty as an ague hath not in five fits so much abated,'[50] he confided to Throckmorton. However, Elizabeth was determined now to avenge this defeat and finish with glory an enterprise so reluctantly begun. She exhorted everyone to be of good cheer, backed up her words with more men, money and munitions, and directed the Duke of Norfolk to 'use all Meanes possible to comfort the Lords of *Scotland*, and to assure them that the Quene's Majesty will never give over this Enterprise, untill she have this revenged, and that Land sett at Liberty'.[51] The English queen was showing already her natural ear for the ringing phrase and her gift for personalizing the relationship of monarch to her people.

This belated resolution combined with fortunate timing meant Elizabeth triumphed without any further bloodshed. The French, pragmatically realizing their limitations while they struggled with religious rebellion at home, were aware also that the besieged forces in Leith were running out of provisions and needed reinforcements urgently. Mary of Guise too was near to death. All these considerations meant they were forced to accept a negotiated settlement.

The eventual outcome was the Treaty of Edinburgh, signed on 6 July, in which the French agreed to withdraw all but a handful of men, agreed too that Elizabeth was the rightful heir to the throne of England and Ireland, and Mary Queen of Scots and François II would no longer assume the style or arms thereof. Elizabeth's confidence and reputation were greatly enhanced. The Earl of Arran had written to Cecil of his admiration and gratitude for 'the exceeding pity it has pleased her Grace to take upon our miserable afflicted country . . . hazard[ing] also the displeasure and enmity of divers mighty estates and princes . . . God has framed her in the shape of a woman, to excel any of her progenitors, and that he of his infinite wisdom will show what he is able to work to the manifestation of his glory in such a vessel and kind.'[52]

Already the incongruity of Elizabeth's slight body, her femaleness, her youth, combined with an ability to govern and an appetite for robust action equal to the best of men, was beginning to exercise a certain fascination. Even the lusty Lord Robert Dudley had recognized this quality of courage and will. He gave an insight into the queen's nature in a letter to the Lord Deputy of Ireland about her desire for some more spirited horses: 'especially for strong, good gallopers, which are better than her geldings, which she spareth not to try as fast as they can go. And I fear them much', he wrote, 'but she will prove them.'[53]

This adventure to support the Scottish Protestants and expel the French was Elizabeth's first piece of risky foreign policy. She had invaded another sovereign country and made herself vulnerable to the ire, or worse, of two much greater powers, France and Spain. She had gambled and won, her success having far greater ramifications than might have been evident at first. The terms of the treaty had effectively ended French supremacy in Scotland and helped establish the reformed religion. But this also marked the end of the first stand-off between the two young queens. As Elizabeth was triumphant, so Mary was humiliated and incensed. She was most upset by the clause that renounced her claim to the English throne, and most troubled by the new Scottish Parliament's abolition of the Mass and papal jurisdiction. All she and François, as Queen and King of France and Scotland, could do was threaten to refuse to ratify the treaty.

1560 was a year of deaths which would change for ever the destinies of both Elizabeth and Mary. The first death was that of Mary of Guise who died on 11 June, worn out at the age of 44. Despite chronic heart failure, her force of will had kept her in active government and still prosecuting the war right up to the last few days.

This death hastened Elizabeth's first victory and personally robbed Mary of a passionately loved though little-known mother. It robbed her also of a spirited protector of her interests in her own kingdom of Scotland, and France of its convenient satellite. Mary was still only seventeen when her mother died, and so violent were her feelings that the Venetian ambassador had declared '[she] loved her mother incredibly, and much more than daughters usually love their mothers'.[54] In fact, so concerned were her family about her reaction, Mary was not told of her mother's death for at least a week. The belated news was brought by her uncle, the Cardinal of Lorraine, and her reaction was as extreme as they all feared. 'Her majesty showed and still shows such signs of grief that during the greater part of yesterday she passed from one agony to another.'[55]

Back in Scotland, her subjects sensing their near success at throwing off the yoke of France, fired ordnance into the air in celebration. 'They say they wish the young Queen were in the same state as her mother.'[56] For a while Elizabeth was more popular with the Scots than their own distant queen. In fact there was an influential movement from the Scottish lords to encourage the talk of a marriage between Elizabeth and the Earl of Arran, next in line after Mary Stuart to the Scottish throne, with an eye eventually to unite the two kingdoms. The Spanish ambassador certainly believed this was more than a possibility for he risked Elizabeth's displeasure by declaring to her face 'that her real object was to make herself monarch of all Britain by marrying the Earl of Arran'.[57] This anxiety Elizabeth did not attempt to dispel, for a month later in conversation with the same ambassador she casually mentioned that she had heard that the Queen of Scots was very ill, 'and if she died without an heir the Duke of Châtelherault would be glad for his son the Earl of Arran to succeed to the throne [of Scotland]'.[58]

From the stresses of making war, Elizabeth had turned with abandon to the pleasures of love. It was summer and Lord Robert was an attentive and seductive companion in all her vigorous pursuits, hunting recklessly by day and dancing most of the night. Cecil, who had laboured long and hard in the prosecution of the war, and then in negotiating the peace, returned to London. It proved indeed to be 'daungerous Servis and unthankfull'[59] for he was welcomed by Elizabeth not with praise and gratitude, and some material reward, but with majestic froideur and the galling sight of his queen gallivanting with her Master of the Horse. Robert Dudley was Cecil's *bête noire*, and he feared the ruin of Elizabeth and the country should Dudley ever achieve his grand ambitions.

The queen's fond old governess and most intimate lady of the bedchamber, Catherine Ashley, the nearest she had to a mother, did not mince her words of warning and reproof. On her knees, she 'implored her to marry and put an end to all these disreputable rumours'. If Elizabeth did not marry soon, she said, she feared her reputation would be ruined and her subjects discontented. If she was to die without issue there would be 'much bloodshed in the realm'. Warming to her admonitory role, Mrs Ashley continued, 'Rather than this should happen she would have strangled her Majesty in the cradle.'[60]

Elizabeth was conciliatory and reassuring, but she had no wish, she said, to marry. Then, turning disingenuous and appealing to her old nurse's sympathetic nature and their shared memories, she continued: 'in this world she had had so much sorrow and tribulation and so little joy' and so the 'graciousness' she showed towards Lord Robert was nothing more than a reward for his generosity on her behalf and a little light relief for herself. Catherine Ashley would have recognized everything to which Elizabeth alluded, for she knew more than anyone what her young charge had endured. She knew how abandoned and afraid Elizabeth had been. She also knew everything that went on in Elizabeth's bedchamber, a fact the queen was not slow to point out as she declared that she had never given anyone just cause to doubt her honour. Elizabeth could not resist, however, a flare of imperious defiance: 'If she had ever had the will or had found pleasure in such a dishonourable life, from which may God preserve her, *she did not know of anyone who could forbid her.*'[61] That one autocratic phrase (the emphasis mine) so crackles with Elizabethan reality, her character is propelled into the present.

Cecil had written to Elizabeth after his triumphant negotiations were completed with a frankness which would be considered unseemly today, urging her to proceed with her side of the bargain: 'my continual prayer that God would direct your heart to procure a father for your children, and so shall the children of all your realm bless your seed. Neither peace nor war without this will profit us long.'[62] However, Cecil could not believe that Elizabeth would be so rash and wrong-headed as to choose such an opportunist as Lord Robert to provide the fertilization of that precious seed. At this point in her life Elizabeth was behaving as if her reputation and the diplomatic marital manoeuvres counted as nothing against her desire for lovemaking with the glamorous companion of her youth.

The Spanish ambassador described Cecil's reservations. 'He clearly foresaw the ruin of the realm through Robert's intimacy with the Queen, who surrendered all affairs to him and meant to marry him.' He related a strikingly prescient, and indiscreet, comment allegedly made by Cecil: 'He ended by saying that Robert was thinking of killing his wife, who was publicly announced to be ill, although she was quite well, and would take very good care they did not poison her.' Elizabeth too, apparently indulged in some premature prognostication, telling the same ambassador, as she returned from hunting, 'that Robert's wife was dead or nearly so',[63] and this all, he implied, occurred before the news of Amy Dudley's death reached London.

Bishop Quadra was a clever politician with his own agenda. He loathed Elizabeth and her heretic court. He had scant regard even for the worthy and redoubtable Cecil of whom he declared there was nobody worse to command such authority in the kingdom. But damning as these rumours were they were just part of a wider, and wilder, set of conspiracies the rest of the country was busy embroidering. Elizabeth seemed quite unashamedly to be besotted with Dudley, a young man, obviously opportunistic with aspirations of the highest kind. His father and grandfather had been executed by their monarchs for excessive ambition, and the whole country and the gossips abroad expected this scion to follow family tradition in lurid style.

These heady summer days for Elizabeth, and the uneasiness of

Cecil, were abruptly terminated by the tragic death so many times foretold. It occurred on 8 September, the day after Elizabeth's twenty-seventh birthday. The electrifying news that Dudley's wife was found dead at the bottom of a staircase at Cumnor Hall in Oxfordshire, the country house where she had been staying, reached London the next day. It was particularly shocking news because it had been long expected, and carried the most heinous implications. Gossip over Elizabeth and Dudley had centred on the fact that he would have to get rid of one wife before he could claim the greatest prize of all, the Queen of England – in the process becoming king himself. In a society rife with superstition and ulterior motives this sudden and tragic event could only be invested with the most sinister meaning. Rumours of Dudley's long-planned infamy now became as good as fact. Even though he had been at Windsor on that day, he was popularly thought to have instigated the death of his inconvenient wife, through poison, hired assassin or some black art.

Amy Dudley's death brought an abrupt end to any pretensions Elizabeth may have had that she could marry the man she loved. She had learned young the dangers of serious scandal being attached to her name. Her position as a monarch ordained by God and sustained by the love and loyalty of her people was something she valued above everything. She had endured fear and suffering to reach this place, and now, just two years into her reign, she had no intention of risking any loss of power or popular affection. Suddenly fate, it seemed, had given her what she had wanted, but the gift had been poisoned in the giving. Thomas Lever, a friend of Roger Ascham and the evangelical Archdeacon of Coventry, wrote to Cecil of his congregation's unease and urged an enquiry: 'here in these Parts, semeth unto me, to be a grevous, and dangerous suspition, and muttering of the Death of her, wich was the Wife of my lord *Robert Dudlei* . . . if no search, nor inquire be made, and known, the displeasure of God, the dishonor of the Quene, and the Danger of the whole Realme is to be feared.'[64]

It was not just in the provinces that people were shocked and uneasy. In London too, according to the Spanish ambassador, 'The cry is that they do not want any more women rulers, and this woman [Elizabeth] may find herself and her favourite in prison any morning.'[65] There was even talk of what male heir could be found to succeed her. So desperate were some for the security of a male ruler that Henry Hastings,* Earl of Huntingdon, another more distant cousin, was hurriedly put in the frame. Elizabeth recognized immediately how compromised she appeared to be. She acted quickly. Dudley was rusticated to Kew, banished from court and from her presence until the results of an enquiry were known.

Bishop Quadra's comment implying the rank inferiority of female rule revealed that Elizabeth was still on probation. She had a long way to go before she lived down the bitter memory of her sister's reign and disproved the religious, intellectual and popular prejudices against women in positions of power. The expectation remained that she would exhibit the moral weakness, intellectual limitation and emotional untrustworthiness thought endemic in her sex. Elizabeth was clear-sighted about the need to earn her people's loyalty and trust. 'Her owne state was not well established', she had told the Scottish lords, 'as neither herself beinge settled in authoritie nor her subjects in obedience.'[66]

Impassioned as she was, Elizabeth above all was a tough-minded young woman whose long and hard apprenticeship had prepared in her the self-control necessary for government. Her heart was to be sacrificed for her kingdom. This was the moment when she demonstrated to the world that she was queen first; that her people's loyalty and trust mattered. Within the month she had told her long-suffering, and relieved, Secretary Cecil that she did not intend to marry Lord Robert. It remained obvious that her feelings for him had not changed but the circumstances and their implications had. Elizabeth knew as queen that in any conflict between private desire and public good it was desire that had to be overruled.

---

* Henry Hastings, Earl of Huntingdon (1535–95), was a companion to Edward VI in their youth, and later brother-in-law to Robert Dudley. His claim to the English throne came through descent on his mother's side from Edward IV's brother George, Duke of Clarence. Puritan in his sympathies and, more importantly, male, he was the favoured candidate as a successor to Elizabeth for the majority of the Protestant lords at various crisis points in her reign. Mild-mannered and unremarkable, he died without heirs.

With radical insight she told Cecil '[her people] have the right of controlling the public actions of their sovereigns'.[67]

Her cousin Mary never accepted this hard rule of self-control and personal sacrifice. When faced with a similar scandal six and a half years later she showed a watching world she was a woman first – and a reckless one at that – before she was queen. With her too, as with Elizabeth, the drama included an inconvenient spouse and an opportune death, a suspect ambitious lover and a clear need for judicial enquiry. But the responses of both queens could not have been more different, and the resolutions of the crises transformed each reign.

Elizabeth coolly distanced herself from the man who was the cause of the contaminating scandal, and favoured a legal investigation. In the process she strengthened the monarchy and the perception of her ability to rule, while maintaining her relationship with her favourite for the rest of his life. But Mary, compromised, even complicit, in more baleful circumstances, refused all such careful counsel, even from Elizabeth herself. Instead she embraced anarchy and rushed headlong into a union with the prime suspect, casting princely duty to the winds. Humiliation, alienation, danger, immediately engulfed her: the loss of her kingdom and liberty, and finally her life, inexorably followed.

In fact, Mary did have a chance to learn from her cousin's painful example, although she chose to ignore it. She was at the heart of the French court where details of the Dudley affair offered endless hours of amusement to Elizabeth's detractors and enemies. The English ambassador Throckmorton, naturally of a pessimistic cast of mind, was beside himself with embarrassment and foreboding: with 'weeping eyes' he wrote to the Marquis of Northampton of the 'dishonourable and naughty reports that are made here of the Queen . . . which every hair of my head stareth at and my ears glow to hear'.[68] The outpouring of *schadenfreude* from the 'malicious French'[69] sought to discredit the new queen, the new religion and the probity of the English generally. 'One laugheth at us, another threateneth, another revileth the Queen. Some let not to say, What religion is this that a subject shall kill his wife, and the Prince not only bear withal but marry with him?'[70] Mary herself was not averse to pouring her own particular scorn on her cousin for she, a Queen of Scotland, was married to no lesser personage than the King of France and yet here the Queen of England, Mary reportedly sneered, was intent on marrying her horsekeeper, 'who has killed his wife to make room for her'.[71] Not only a servant but a criminally murderous one too.

The facts that led to Amy Dudley's death remained as elusive as the full story of the scandal which seven years later would lose Mary her kingdom. But an enquiry into the Dudley affair was soon under way. For many months before her death there had been rumours that Amy was ill, that she had 'a malady in one of her breasts'.[72] She had many reasons to be unhappy and could well have been in pain. There was a good deal of contemporary speculation as to her state of mind. On the day of her death Lady Robert Dudley had insisted that all her servants leave her to spend the afternoon at a fair in Abingdon. There were those who were unwilling to comply, but she was adamant, they all had to go. Just two women remained with her in the house.

The evidence of her lady's maid's was significant. 'Divers times', she said in an unguarded moment, she had heard her mistress 'pray to God to deliver her from desperation.'[73] Then, realizing this implied her lady might have committed the irredeemable sin of self-destruction, she was keen to stress what a godly person her mistress was and how her death was most likely a terrible accident. Modern medical opinion also indicates that if Amy Dudley had had a cancer in the breast which had migrated into her bones then theoretically it was possible that she could have broken her neck as a result of even a trivial fall.

She had died in the residence of a man, Anthony Forster, from whom she and Lord Robert rented their apartments. He was universally respected as an honest and honourable man, which soothed some of the wildest speculations of conspiracy. 'His great honesty doth much curb the evil thoughts of the people.'[74] Robert Dudley's reputation, however, was of a man capable of doing anything to achieve his ends.

In fact, Lord Robert appeared to be genuinely bewildered by the sequence of events, and as keen as anyone to discover the truth. He did seem, however, to be less grieved by the sudden death of his wife than shocked by this abrupt reversal of his fortunes. As the main suspect, he did not feign a widower's grief, as a guilty man might be expected to do, but rather revealed to Cecil the opportunist's heartfelt concern over his fall from royal favour and exile from the court. 'I am sorry so sudden a Chance shall breede me so great a Change', he wrote after Cecil had visited him at Kew, 'for methinks I am hear all this while, as it were in a Dreame, and so farr, so farre, from the Place I am bound to be . . . Forgett me not, though you se me not, and I will remember you, and fayll ye not.'[75]

The enquiry returned a verdict of accidental death. But the evidence was too sketchy and the popular suspicion of Dudley's motives too entrenched for the young favourite to cast off the slur that he was somehow implicated in the tragedy. In the Elizabethan mind where the occult and the material world were closely intermingled, wishing for something could be interpreted as actually willing it to happen. After a lavish funeral for his wife, Lord Robert returned to court in mourning, but was soon restored to the queen's side as if nothing had interrupted the momentum of their relationship. She protected him from his detractors and loyally sprang to his defence when people disdained him, for he was everything to her, long-established brother, lover, friend. But she knew his reputation would not enhance her own. Much as her heart was touched by him, her watchful intelligence did not sleep.

Robert Jones, ambassador Throckmorton's secretary, was sent from Paris in November to warn the queen exactly what scandals were being spread abroad, just how much the Queen of Scots and the rest of the court enjoyed her discomfiture. Elizabeth tossed aside the accusations, declaring that Lord Robert's honesty and her own honour had been vindicated by the enquiry. But Jones thought the whole business 'doth much perplex her'. He remarked that the first time the document creating Dudley an earl, drawn up on the queen's instructions, was proffered for her signature, she took not a quill but a blade to it, cutting it to shreds, declaring that he came from a long line of traitors.

Despite these temporary setbacks Dudley's ambitions were as grand as ever, his attractiveness to Elizabeth was undiminished, but her perspective on the conflicting demands of being a great prince and a woman had changed. Inadvertently and inevitably, he had tainted her with his own crisis. But she had never underestimated the power of public feeling nor the speed with which allegiances could turn. Her position was still precarious, the contenders for her throne were in waiting, the prejudices against female rule were ready to be confirmed. Somehow Elizabeth had to transcend the disadvantages of being a woman, unequal, carnal, fallible, as she was reckoned to be. Somehow she had to become extra human in her relationship with her people but superhuman in her role as queen.

The Virgin Mother was a potent symbol for Elizabeth and for every contemporary in Christendom. Ideologically downgraded by the new reformed church, she nevertheless maintained an enduring place in people's hearts, in their traditions, stories and spiritual life. The Virgin was thoroughly human and could sympathize with the suffering of others, but was herself chosen by God above the rest of her sex, and through His intervention elevated to the divine. With a decreasing role for the Catholic Virgin Mary, mother of God, any vacuum in people's imaginations could affectively be filled by the new secular Virgin Queen, Elizabeth, the consort of her people. Adoration for the Virgin Mary could be transmuted without much ado to a personal love and loyalty for Elizabeth, their singular queen who, in remaining unmarried remained theirs alone.

There is no way of knowing whether this was a conscious thought in her own mind. The experiences of Elizabeth's life, however, increasingly indicated that, even ignoring a natural antipathy to marriage, the political ramifications of any marital choice she might make as queen were complex and troublesome. To remain unmarried, but available to all, proved to be a most successful piece of foreign policy, for to continue a potential ally to every European monarch was to be an enemy of none. This way, equivocation prevailed and Elizabeth's councillors, ambassadors and suitors drifted in a fog of confusion and doubt. They jumped at shadows, pursued chimeras and constructed fantastic castles of cause and effect around their red-haired maiden queen. There was wild hope too: in imagination anyone stood a chance of claiming the virgin and becoming king. Even her people could believe that in belonging to no one their queen was somehow uniquely theirs.

Mary Queen of Scots shared the Catholic Virgin's name but not her public sexual status. As a married woman, albeit of a probably unconsummated union, it would be considered that she had relinquished that singularity. Unlike her cousin, she had chosen to accept the conventions and fulfil her duty as a marriageable and valuable diplomatic pawn, to begin with at least. In the late autumn of 1560, while her cousin Elizabeth was enduring the malicious gossip about her own moral turpitude and Lord Robert's uxoricidal vice, Mary was enjoying the reputation of an irreproachably married young queen, innocent of any sexual irregularity, probably innocent even of the briefest conjugal relations. The French court was still enjoying themselves at the expense of the English queen, her ambassador humiliated on her behalf by the gossip 'accompanied with much spite, and set so full of horror . . . he never heard or read of sorer or more slanderous discourse'.[76]

Mary had busied herself on her accession to the French throne that summer by examining the crown jewels. They were one of the significant accoutrements of monarchy, and whoever held them had symbolic power. Despite stressing to Elizabeth that being her blood cousin made her a congenial neighbour, she also consistently refused to ratify the Treaty of Edinburgh, telling the English ambassador Throckmorton with some asperity, that 'My subjects in Scotland' had sent an inferior representative to see her while 'they have sent great personages to your mistress. I am their Sovereign, but they take me not so; they must be taught to know their duties.'[77] She had felt that no one sympathetic to her interests had been present at the negotiations and so felt justified in her refusal.

Her resistance in fact was not merely passive, she continued to bear the English and Irish arms quartered with her own, generally accepted as a considered insult, and showed scant respect for Elizabeth behind her representatives' backs.

But Mary's high hopes as queen of the powerful French empire were to be cut to the ground, the fine future for which she had been bred was about to be erased. By mid-October, her young husband had moved with the court to Orléans, partly in fear of assassination but also to further the Guise offensive against the heretics. Most importantly for François, it allowed him to devote himself to the chase, the only activity he engaged in wholeheartedly and with enjoyment. As the religious conflicts deepened, the king was happy enough to leave government to his wife's uncles while he planned an extended hunting trip. By the middle of November 1560, as the weather turned from unseasonably mild to a bitter chill, the teenage king was struck down with a terrible earache, possibly a precursor to meningitis.

Court gossip was always avid and contradictory. Some said this latest illness to strike their weakling king was trifling, the fact that he was kept in his bedchamber was simply due to his mother's over-protectiveness. Others insisted the situation was far more serious than anyone admitted, and the astrologer's baleful prediction at François's birth that he would not see his eighteenth birthday was grimly rehearsed in the speculations of ambassadors and courtiers. There was a sense of awful inevitability. His wife Mary and mother Catherine de Medici kept their vigil by his bed. Alternating between hope and despair, Mary suffered from nervous strain as she followed the agonizing vicissitudes of his illness.

Only six months previously she had endured the loss of her much-loved mother; now she was facing the death of the companion of her earliest childhood, the only other person in the world who really loved her. In terrific pain, enduring draconian treatments from anxious doctors, forced to be over-zealous by the Guises' desperation to hold on to power, François appears to have borne his torments with unexpected fortitude. The infection migrated into his brain and Mary, refusing to leave his side, watched delirium and then death overcome him. François finally died on 5 December aged only sixteen. Mary herself was three days short of her eighteenth birthday.

It was a notable feature of Mary's constitution that her active emotional nature gave rise to great eruptions of feeling and, in times of crisis, physical and nervous collapse. 'I hear she is troubled with such sudden passions after any great unkindness or grief of mind,'[78] one of the ambassadors in Scotland wrote to Cecil having seen the young queen collapse with nervous exhaustion. No one else seemed to mourn the dead king much but Mary was catapulted into a period of deepest grieving, made all the more poignant because she seemed so alone in her despair. The Venetian ambassador, prone to romantic hyperbole when writing about Mary, was nevertheless perceptive about her plight:

> by degrees every one will forget the death of the late King except the young Queen, his widow, who being no less noble minded than beautiful and graceful in appearance, the thoughts of widowhood at so early an age, and of the loss of a consort who was so great a King and who so dearly loved her, and also that she is dispossessed of the crown of France with little hope of recovering that of Scotland, which is her sole patrimony and dower, so afflict her that she will not receive any consolation, but, brooding over her disasters with constant tears and passionate and doleful lamentations, she universally inspires great pity.[79]

Writing to Elizabeth the day after the French king's death, Throckmorton was less romantically inclined, although even his lugubrious heart was touched by the sight of the beautiful, grieving widow: 'he departed to God, leaving as heavy and dolorous a wife, as of right she had good cause to be, who, by long watching with him during his sickness and painful diligence about him, and specially by the issue thereof, is not in best tune of her body, but without danger'.[80]

Notwithstanding the personal pathos of the situation, the political consequences were what really exercised the monarchs of neighbouring kingdoms and their ambassadors laboured to interpret the signs. François was succeeded by his ten-year-old brother Charles IX. On the face of it the Guise hold on power had evaporated with François's last breath and Catherine de Medici's patient wait was over. During her husband's lifetime her power had been covert and largely domestic while Henri listened more to his mistress; in François II's reign, the Guises grasped the initiative through their family connections with the new queen: only now, with another even younger son as king, could she come into her own. Catherine's reign as queen mother and regent with unchallenged authority had begun.

But for Mary, François's death was the shipwreck of all her hopes. Not only had she lost the brotherly companion of her childhood and youth, in one vagary of fate she had lost the whole world and her status in that world for which she had been bred. Since she was six, Mary had been trained to consider herself a French fairytale princess who would eventually be transformed into a French queen. The most illustrious throne was fleetingly hers. Suddenly, her king was dead and her glittering future had been relegated to the past. As a childless dowager queen, Mary had no role and little status. The loss of everything she had taken for granted was painful and disorientating. Her own need to uphold her status, and her family's political concern to maintain through her their hold on power, meant the question of her next marriage was already being discussed in courts across Europe.

The ever-anxious Throckmorton urged Elizabeth to consolidate her position in relation to France and the new reformed religion as fast as possible, 'to make a sure and larger seat for herself and her posterity for ever, to God's glory and her own unspeakable fame'.[81] One anxiety remained, however. He feared that the Duc de Guise and his brother the cardinal might engage in a last-ditch attempt to maintain their family's grip on power by marrying their niece to the new young king. He surmised in a letter to the council that Mary herself might welcome this remarriage for she rated being Queen of France highly indeed and would be reluctant to suffer relegation to the second division. This was to prove an astute assessment of Mary's motivation at the time.

The Protestants across Europe had no such apprehensions that this marriage would take place. They celebrated the death of François and the dethroning of the Guises, seeing in the successive destruction of Henri and his son some pattern of divine deliverance from persecution. Knox was savagely triumphant, but Calvin took a longer, more measured view. 'Have you ever heard or read anything more seasonable than the death of the King? There was no remedy for the extreme evils, when suddenly God appeared from Heaven, and He, who had pierced the eye of the father, smote the ear of the son. I only fear lest the joy of some by expressing itself too much may overturn the hope of a better state of things. For you could scarcely believe how inconsiderately many exult and even wax wanton over it.'[82] The unexpected transition of power to a minor inevitably added to the ferment of uncertainty and fear: 'by which change the state of France did fall from a fever to a frenzie'.[83] Different factions struggled to grasp advantage, a struggle that would become complex and bloody, precipitating the wars of religion which convulsed and debilitated the nation for nearly four decades.

While half of France rejoiced at the death of her husband, and her companions at court busied themselves seeking preferment from the new regime of the boy king and his mother, Mary alone grieved. And the grief was for the loss of François but also for the loss of herself. She wrote to Philip II: 'You have comforted by your letters the most afflicted poor woman under heaven; God having bereft me of all that I loved and held dear on earth ... without his aid I shall find so great a calamity too insupportable for my strength and my little virtue.'[84] To Elizabeth, who had sent letters of condolence, she responded through Elizabeth's ambassador, 'with a very sorrowful look and speech that she thanked the Queen for her gentleness in comforting her woe when she had most need of it'.[85]

In private she expressed her grief in poetry:

En mon triste et doux chant	In my sad, quiet song,
D'un ton fort lamentable,	A melancholy air,
Je jette un oeil tranchant,	I shall look deep and long
De perte incomparable,	At loss beyond compare,
Et en soupirs cuisants	And with bitter tears,
Passe mes meilleurs ans.	I'll pass my best years.

Fut-il un tel malheur	Have the harsh fates ere now
De dure destinée	Let such a grief be felt,
Ni si triste douleur	Has a more cruel blow
De Dame Fortunée	Been by dame Fortune dealt
Qui, mon coeur et mon oeil,	Than, O my heart and eyes!
Vois en bière et cercueil?	I see where his bier lies?
Qui en mon doux printemps	In my springtime's gladness
Et fleur de ma jeaunss	And flower of my young heart,
Toutes les peines sens	I feel the deepest sadness
D'une extrême tristesse,	Of the most grievous hurt.
Et en rien n'ai plaisir	Nothing now my heart can fire
Qu'en regret et désire.	But regret and desire.[86]

In her fifth verse Mary explained that the world would see her grief in the paleness of her face, 'mon pâle visage/De violettes teint/Qui est l'amoureux teint', a paleness which the court chronicler Brantôme said she did not lose: 'Never after she was a widow, during all the time that I had the honour to see her in France and in Scotland, was her complexion restored.'[87] Although self-centred poetry was a convention of the age, it was nevertheless surprising perhaps that this poem, affecting as it is, was entirely to do with what Mary had lost. But there was every reason to think she was for a while in a state of shock as well as grief at the full extent of the dereliction of her world.

Just eighteen years old, Mary had been deprived of more than her status and power at the centre of the monarchy. Suddenly she was bereft too of close family connections. Her mother was recently dead, also her father-in-law, who had been like a father to her. Her brotherly husband now, in traumatic circumstances, was unexpectedly taken from her; so too Elizabeth de Valois, her intimate sister-in-law had recently been dispatched to be Queen of Spain, never to be seen again. Now Catherine de Medici was turning from friend into foe and, apart from her uncles and her grandmother, Mary was alone. Catherine, as her mother-in-law and close companion at court, had been the nearest to a mother figure that Mary had known. Writing to her Scottish administration shortly after François's death, she described her as 'the most worthy and virtuous princess in the world ... in whom since we have been here, we have found so much goodness, love and humanity and so amiable affection ... that we can expect from [her] what a daughter can hope from her own mother'.[88] From the age of five and a half, absent from her own mother, brought up among the Valois children, Mary had naturally looked to Catherine and her husband as parental figures. Henri II's affection for her had been real enough but Catherine was a much more considerable and complex personality. She had suffered great anguish and humiliation during her years of childlessness, and when her babies finally arrived she then invested every pent-up emotion, frustrated ambition and zest for power in her children and their dynastic futures. She had proved how steadfastly she could bide her time, how ruthlessly she would secure her own power through her family, how Machiavellian she was in her ability to do what had to be done.

During the years of Diane de Poitiers and Guise ascendancy, Catherine had dissembled and appeared complaisant. Mary belonged to that old and painful axis of power. While she was married to Catherine's son and he was king then Catherine played the game of feigned affection and support. But once the power of Mary and her uncles had expired then Catherine's energies turned from her old allegiances to focus on the new. The order she signed requesting Mary to return the crown jewels, and dated just one day after François's death, appeared symbolic of the cavalcade passing on, leaving the now disregarded young queen in its wake. Catherine's implacable opposition to the Guise suggestion that the newly-widowed queen should marry the new king, her brother-in-law and Catherine's next son, was indicative of the waning of Mary's star and the ascendancy of her own.

This turning aside by the queen mother, intent on her own regency and her succeeding son, exacerbated Mary's sense of loss. Sir James Melville, an insider in the service of the Scottish queen, believed Catherine became a deadly enemy to anyone who had had influence over either her husband or her eldest son. Because of Mary's complete identification with the Guises, Catherine had 'a greet mis-lyking of our Quen'[89] and also nursed a long grievance against her for a misjudged comment. Apparently Mary had been heard to say dismissively that Catherine was, after all, just a merchant's daughter. This kind of indiscreet haughtiness had caused her trouble already with her cousin, Queen Elizabeth. It would cause her trouble again.

The courtiers too, once so attentive, were falling away. They now moved to a different beat. No longer in thrall to the Guise faction they ingratiated themselves with the new regime. Even her beloved Guise uncles when their paths diverged were capable of putting their own interests before hers. The Spanish ambassador to Elizabeth related how Catherine de Medici feared Mary's alliance through marriage with Spain, 'having regard to the Scotch Queen's claims to this [England's] crown', and so put pressure on the Duc de Guise to oppose it. He chose self-interest over Mary's wishes and 'promised as the Queen-Mother desired', adding, as he waved his niece off from France for ever, that 'he could not give her the counsel that was best for her, but that she herself should look where her best interests were'.[90] Within six turbulent months the emotional and political landscape of Mary's life had changed radically. There was some reason to fear that even the kingdom to which she had been born and had given scant regard might reject their absent monarch now that she no longer brought to her subjects any guarantee of French wealth and protection. Writing to her Scottish lords she expressed her '*incroyable regret*' if the misfortune of François's death would weaken the '*alliance que Dieu avoit mise entre nous* [the alliance that God had placed between us]'.[91]

This now was the time for Mary to act with authority and return to Scotland to claim the throne her mother had kept warm for her with such unwavering loyalty and self-sacrifice. This sudden reversal and the suffering and loss it brought could have been the impetus for transformation from a pampered princess to an effective queen. It should have propelled Mary away from the past as passive consort and into the present, to become what she was born to be, a ruling Queen of Scotland. Already she was beginning to exhibit the qualities that suggested she had the makings of a considerable queen. Throckmorton was pleasantly surprised: 'During her husband's life there was no great account made of her, for that, being under band of marriage and subjection of her husband . . . there was offered no great occasion to know what was in her . . . now [those who once discounted her] seeing her wisdom both honour and pity her.'[92]

But at this critical time her will appeared to falter. Instead Mary looked to a second marriage alliance to restore her previous status and return her to the life of a richly endowed consort of a powerful king. The English ambassador recognized the overriding importance to Mary at this time of maintaining prestige. The day after François's death he wrote, 'As far as I can learn, she more esteemeth the continuation of her honour, and to marry one that may uphold her to be great, than she passeth to please her fancy by taking one who is accompanied with such small benefit or alliance as thereby her estimation and fame is not increased.'[93] And while Scotland wondered and waited their queen spent the next eight months meandering through France, visiting Guise relations and hoping her next prince would come.

In imagination Scotland had become an alien and inhospitable place to its young widowed queen. The reformed religion had been established without her agreement, and Elizabeth had supported the Protestant rebels in their intent to expel the French and overtake Catholicism. In effect this was akin to outlawing Mary herself, for she was above all French and Catholic. She was to return to the country of her birth as queen only with some reluctance when she had exhausted other possibilities. The preoccupation with another foreign marriage, the reluctant return, did not suggest a deep-rooted and reciprocal bond between the Queen of Scots and her distant people.

Elizabeth and her ministers were initially delighted with the unexpected turn of events over the Channel. The end of Guise domination could only be interpreted as favourable to England and the new religion. The fading of Mary's star as Queen of France was also good news; no longer was there such imminent threat of French reinforcement of her claim on the English throne. As always, every silver lining was accompanied by a darker cloud. If Mary was to return to Scotland to take up her birthright she would establish her power base in the same island, in territory where only a strip of lawless border land separated England from its independent monarchs and unpredictable and factious people.

In fact Mary had expressed her wish to be friends, with a sweet reason which charmed Throckmorton. She pointed out that she and Elizabeth were 'both in one isle, both of one language, the nearest kinswoman that each other had, and both Queens'.[94] But like much of Mary's sweetness it was possible to discern a bitter aftertaste. Given her ambitions, there was an inevitable threat in all that professed intimacy. She would prove herself a formidable adversary for Elizabeth. It would be a mistake to think because she fought with different weapons she was any the less capable of harm.

Mary was also now, like Elizabeth, a queen without a husband, and the question of whom she might marry was as important and vexing as it was for Elizabeth and her advisers. In fact, there was only a limited number of candidates for either, and this would prove a further area for rivalry and discontent. The shifting foreign alliances and internal policies of each country affected the power balance with the other. Throckmorton was quick to see the difficulties of this newly unattached rival and was himself not immune to her charm. He offered his own solution in a letter to Lord Robert Dudley, and by association to Elizabeth too. He began, however, with a veiled comparison and reproof of his own queen's indiscreet behaviour: 'The Queen of Scotland, her Majesty's cousin, doth carry herself so honourably, advisedly, and discreetly, as I cannot but fear her progress. Methinketh it were to be wished of all wise men and her Majesty's good subjects, that the one of these two queens of the Isle of Britain were transformed into the shape of a man, to make so happy a marriage as thereby there might be an unity of the whole isle and their appendants.'[95]

If 1558 had been the year when both queens accepted their larger fates then 1560 was the year of reckoning. Two years earlier, Elizabeth had survived the ordeals to succeed to her throne. She had pledged herself to her people and claimed she would not marry. Her subjects represented all the family she would ever need. But her love for Lord Robert Dudley was the lasting test of her commitment to her kingdom. Although tempted to break her vow of celibacy and marry her greatest love, against all opposition, she chose instead the loneliness of princely duty. She promised Cecil she would not marry Dudley, and no one at court was unaware of that sacrifice. Even six years later the Venetian ambassador to France was relating the still commonly-held belief 'that the love her Majesty bears Lord Robert is such that she will either finally take him for husband, or will never take anyone else'.[96] And yet no one wanted either possibility to come about. Elizabeth's settled intent was to show that the latter was her only true option. It was to define her as the Virgin Queen.

Mary too held to the path she had chosen in 1558, the year she accepted her dynastic marriage to François II. Less than two years later when this glittering alliance suddenly fell away she set herself to replicate it. She would seek immediately to ally herself to a stronger power, for herself and for her lineage. Strength of character, energy, the capacity to govern, all these she had. But it was wilfulness, within a larger pattern of emotional dependence and conformity, which was to seal the destiny of the Scottish queen.

CHAPTER SIX

Complicity and Competition

Of this Queen's [Mary] affection to the Queen's Majesty,
either it is so great that never was greater to any, or it is the
deepest dissembled, and the best covered that ever was.

*Randolph to Cecil, about Mary's affection, or otherwise, for
Elizabeth, 30 January 1562*

MARY QUEEN OF SCOTS securely fixed in France, first as
dauphine and then queen, had represented one kind of challenge
to Elizabeth and her throne. But Mary, cut loose, single again,
in search of a husband and a dynastic alliance, represented a completely new and unknown danger. And that danger was coming
home.

To have a rival living next door presents its own particular problems. To have a rival in such proximity, but one you never meet,
inflates the imagination. Character lours into caricature, conversations relayed through third parties inevitably grow distorted and
facts become sullied with the interests of others. When that rival
claims not only one's God-given vocation, the very purpose of one's
life, but also one's identity and birthright, threatens even life itself,
the rivalry becomes a mortal combat.

At first Elizabeth and her advisers felt that Mary's return to
Scotland would be favourable to England. There she would be easier
to keep an eye on and perhaps even better to control. Certainly it
was a relief that her interests were no longer shared by the French

royal family and backed by their diplomatic and military might. It was a relief too to see Guise ambition so unexpectedly capsized. After the English support of the Scottish Protestant lords' rebellion against the French and their regent – and in effect therefore against their queen – Elizabeth expected to maintain her position with the influential lords as a neighbourly *persona grata*. With the establishment also of the reformed religion in Scotland, she could believe for a while that she rather than their own queen, a stranger to them and a resolute Catholic, might seem the more sympathetic.

However Throckmorton's increasingly admiring asides from France about the personal qualities of the young Scottish queen may well have alerted Elizabeth to what was to become the most troubling characteristic of her rival. Mary, now just eighteen, was to prove disconcertingly attractive and affecting to most of the men who crossed her path. It is gratifying for historians in search of motive to recognize retrospectively her fatal attraction, but it appears from contemporary responses that Mary's appeal was every bit as powerful then. In an age that believed in witches, angels, divination and the supernatural it appeared that she was possessed of 'some enchantment, whereby men are bewitched'.[1] It was certainly a charismatic charm that never deserted her, even when she was middle-aged and had lost her health, her beauty and temporal power.

On the last day of 1560, Throckmorton wrote two letters that contrast his view of the Scottish monarch with that of his own difficult queen. His warm approval of the intelligent and modest conduct of Mary contrasted forcefully with the exasperation and despair he felt at Elizabeth's continued indiscretions with Robert Dudley. Writing to Elizabeth's council he declared of Mary:

> Since her husband's death, she hath showed (and so continueth) that she is both of great wisdom for her years, modesty, and also of great judgement in the wise handling of herself and her matters, which, increasing with her years, cannot but turn greatly to her commendation, reputation, honour, and great benefit of her and her country.[2]

As English ambassador to France, Throckmorton felt justified in writing the following caution to Cecil about their own queen's conduct and her ministers' reluctance to curb her:

> if Her Majesty do so foully forget herself in her marriage [with Robert Dudley] as the bruit runneth here [in France], never think to bring anything to pass, either here or elsewhere. I would you did hear the lamentation, the declamation, and sundry affections which have course here for that matter . . . remember your mistress is young, and subject to affections; you are her sworn counsellor, and in great credit with her.

He then urged Cecil to do his best to dissuade Elizabeth from what appeared to be her disastrous course, 'so as Her Majesty's affection doth find rather wind and sail to set it forward than any advice to quench it, my duty to her, my good will to you, doth move me to speak plainly'.[3]

Quite contrary to the posthumous reputations of these two queens, at this point in their relationship there is no doubt that it was Elizabeth who was considered the wanton and flighty one whereas Mary was seen to exhibit every feminine and queenly virtue. Within six years this dynamic would be completely reversed as Mary relinquished her reputation, good sense and sovereignty in a moment of emotional and sexual abandon. But interestingly, Mary was considered an exemplary queen during the time she remained innocent of the power of sexual desire. Elizabeth had discovered already the dangerous attractions of erotic love, albeit deferred, in her flirtations with Seymour and more unambiguously with Robert Dudley. This irrepressible side of her nature, together with her sharp tongue and intent to rule, meant that for a time she was considered less favourably in all comparisons with her cousin Mary.

Throckmorton had taken personally the French court's ribaldry over his queen's conduct with Dudley, and chose to rub salt in the wounds of Elizabeth's own council by pointing out how tractable was the young Scottish queen. 'Her wisdom and kingly modesty so great, in that she thinketh herself not too wise, but is content to be ruled by good counsel and wise men (which is a great virtue in a Prince or Princess, and which argueth a great judgement and wisdom in her).'[4]

Mary, however, was not as compliant as she appeared. In the months following widowhood, once she began to emerge from the shadow of the powerful family around her and act on her own behalf, the foreign ambassadors were given '[more] occasion to know what was in her'.[5] As direct negotiations with her proceeded it became evident just how intelligent and self-willed she could be. If she had not in fact been born wily she made it clear she had learnt a certain craft at the knees of those great masters of guile, Catherine de Medici, Diane de Poitiers and the Cardinal of Lorraine. One of Throckmorton's more thankless tasks every time he saw the Queen of Scots was to press her to ratify the Treaty of Edinburgh, which withdrew her claim on Elizabeth's throne. Initially she replied that she could give no authoritative answer until she had consulted with her Scottish Estates. Elizabeth, however, was tenacious and quick to anger. When, in the summer of 1561, Mary requested a safe conduct through English waters for her journey to Scotland, while continuing to resist ratification of the treaty, Elizabeth lost her temper, and in great dudgeon refused the passport.

Mary had as unerring a sense of the theatrical as did her cousin, and in a situation where Elizabeth was thought, even by her own ambassadors, to have behaved in a rash and unstatesmanlike way, Mary, inexperienced though she was, effortlessly assumed the higher ground. Her response was a sophisticated mixture of courteous reasoning spiced with a veiled threat that went to the heart of Elizabeth's fears. Turning aside the studied insult of her assumption of the English arms and the title of Queen of England and Ireland, she explained that it was simply an expression of her husband and father-in-law's will and that since their deaths she had used neither arms nor title. With Elizabeth's invasion of Scotland in support of the rebel lords raw in her memory, Mary then revealed her ability to disconcert her rival by pricking her insecurity and intimating her own power to raise dissent. Declaring that she, as Queen of Scots, had never tried to harm Elizabeth in any way, Mary pointed out that neither did she plot with Elizabeth's subjects against her, though there were those 'inclined enough to hear offers', claiming that she represented more nearly those of Elizabeth's disaffected subjects who 'be not of the mind she is of, neither in religion, nor other things'.[6] This was the threat that was to echo through the years in their battle of wills.

Not only intelligent, wilful and defiant, the young Queen of Scotland proved she had a striking facility also for self-dramatization: 'I am determined to adventure the matter, whatsoever come of it; I trust the wind will be so favourable that I shall not need to come on the coast of England; for if I do, then, Monsieur l'Ambassadeur, the Queen your mistress shall have me in her hands to do her will of me; and if she be so hard-hearted as to desire my end, she may then do her pleasure, and make sacrifice of me.' For good measure she then added a dollop of self-pity, 'Peradventure that casualty might be better for me than to live.'[7]

By this time, Elizabeth had realized that Mary's proximity in the neighbouring realm was a less than happy proposition. Her charm was already well advertised, her self-possession was becoming more evident, and the last thing Elizabeth needed in the early days of her reign and establishment of the new religion was an attractive focus for Catholic and every other disgruntled opinion in her own kingdom. Despite the success of the Protestant Parliament in Scotland, already it was clear that enthusiasm for the return of their queen was growing daily amongst the populace at large. The Spanish ambassador to Elizabeth's court was watching affairs over the border with particular interest: 'the Catholic party and those who desire the coming of the Queen are so numerous that, if she were present, they would restore religion in spite of the others; and, as they understand this well here [in London], they do all they can to prevent it'.[8]

Elizabeth, frustrated by the obstinacy of the Queen of Scots' refusal to ratify the treaty, wrote instead to the Estates of Scotland to remind them of their duty, and to include her own more overt threat. 'We must plainly let you all understand that this manner of answer without fruit, cannot long content us . . . We think it strange she has no better advice, and require you all the Estates of the realm, to consider the matter deeply, and make answer whereto we may trust. If you support her breach of solemn promise, we shall accept your answer, and doubt not by the grace of God, you shall repent it. If you will have it kept, we promise you the like, and all shall go well with your Queen, yourselves and posterities.'[9]

The withdrawal of the safe conduct might have delayed the departure of a more timorous young woman, but Mary was temperamentally drawn to adventure, and was not used to being thwarted. In fact Elizabeth quickly relented and sent her cousin the passport, but it arrived too late. Bravely and in a turmoil of emotion at leaving her beloved adopted country and the people who had been all the friends and family she had ever really known, Mary took to the water on 14 August 1561. With her was a small entourage, in just two boats: three Guise uncles escorted her and the Four Maries, the girl companions, now women, who had accompanied her to France nearly thirteen years before. In her party also were two men, the young courtier and poet Chastelard and Patrick Hepburn, Earl of Bothwell, whose support of her mother against the Lords of the Congregation's revolt had recommended him to Mary. Their presence seemed unremarkable at the time but these men were to play differing roles in the bloodstained tragedy of Mary's life, and because of her attractions were to die themselves in pitiable circumstances, long before her own violent end.

With more speed and less danger than on her first voyage, which as a five-year-old she had weathered so robustly, Mary and her companions arrived at Leith sooner than expected, after a mere five days' journey. There were many commentators ready to read significance into the fact that the Scottish queen's historic return to her kingdom was shrouded in a dense sea mist. It was either an omen for the sorrow that lay ahead for the young queen and her people or it was symbolic of the spiritual obfuscation and oppression of the old religion which Mary, as a devout Catholic and half a Guise, was expected to reintroduce. Knox, who could always be relied on for thundering sentiment and a rousing phrase, was full of doom:

The verray face of heavin, the time of hir arryvall, did manifestlie speak what confort was brought into this cuntrey with hir, to wit, sorow, dolour, darkness, and all impietie . . . The sun was not seyn to schyne two dayis befoir, nor two dayis after. That foirwarning gave God unto us; but allace, the most pairt war blind [but alas, the most part were blind].[10]

There were those who were not only blind to Knox's prognostication but instead saw the fog as something positive, a celestial swaddling of the boats' precious cargo which allowed Mary to pass unseen and unmolested by either pirates or Elizabeth's navy. None of these speculations seemed to cloud the reception with which the Scottish people welcomed their returning queen. The cannons broadcasting her arrival brought them into the streets, the nobles hastening from Edinburgh to greet her, partly in curiosity, partly in delight to have a Stuart monarch back on Scottish soil again. Mostly they came, however, to introduce themselves, gloss their actions during her absence and sue for position in the new court.

Lord James Stewart, Mary's eldest illegitimate brother, was a main influence on policy, which, since he was an admirer of Knox and a prime mover of the Reformation, meant that initially 'all matters touching religion should stand as she found them'.[11] William Maitland of Lethington, her mother's subtle and astute secretary, was now Mary's chief minister and most influential in her foreign policy. Together he and Lord James guided her first years of government. Although the celebration of Mass had been banned by Parliament the previous August, Mary was allowed to attend her own private Mass conducted at her chapel at Holyrood House. The Protestant lords were vocal in their disapproval and a dissenting rabble initially caused a commotion by trampling candles underfoot and threatening the priests. A plea for mutual religious toleration, however, and an insistence that Mass would not be reinstated, but remain a private affair for the queen and her immediate circle, calmed the situation.

Mary's youth, beauty and gracious demeanour did not fail to touch everyone. She had come with a small entourage and without arms, and her vulnerability and trust in her people encouraged their protectiveness. There was a fascination about her personal history too. The pathos of her story together with her physical attraction was enough to make even battle-scarred chieftains weaken. She appealed also to the patriotism in all Scottish breasts for she was a Stuart monarch returning to the land of her birth. There was an undeniable glamour around Mary's person that drew men in and enhanced Scotland's pride, for a little while at least.

Knox alone seemed immune to Mary's charm, reducing her to tears at their first meeting with his ferocity against the Mass and his threats of 'the greveus plagues of God that had fawlen upon all estates for commyttinge of idolatrye'. Informing Cecil of the clash, Randolph, Elizabeth's agent, was not sure if Mary's tears were of grief or anger, but she had had the temerity to urge the hellfire preacher to 'use more meeknes in his sermons'.[12] Many in his audiences might have agreed with her. Maitland sent a knowing aside in a letter to his opposite number Cecil: 'Yow know the vehemency of Mr Knox spreit, which cannot be brydled, and yet doth sometymes uter soche sentences as can not easely be dygested by a weake stomach.' He nevertheless thought Mary's willingness to enter the debate with Knox 'declare[d] a wisdome far exceeding her age!', that exclamation mark expressing admiration for the young queen's courage in issuing a countercharge.[13]

In fact, unlike that of Elizabeth, Mary's attitude to her religion was more a matter of the heart than of the head. During a discussion with Throckmorton before she left France she had explained 'the religion that I profess I take to be most acceptable to God, and indeed neither do I know, or desire to know, any other. Constancy doth become all folks well, but none better than Princes and such as have rule over realms, and especially in the matter of religion. I have been brought up in this religion, and who might credit me in anything if I should show myself light in this case? And though I am young and not greatly learned, yet I have heard this matter disputed of by my uncle, my Lord Cardinal.'[14] About the Mass she admitted to Knox a similar unquestioning and conventional faith, 'she coulde not reason, but she knewe what she ought to beleve'.[15] He considered this a sure sign of how corrupted her heart had been by her uncle. He was also certain of something that few at the time would even speculate; that beneath Mary's mild, conciliatory manner was a fanatic intent to restore the true religion not only to Scotland but to her neighbouring and, she believed, rightful English kingdom too. From the beginning Knox had considered 'maynie men are dysceaved in thys woman; he fearethe yet that *posteriora erunt pejora primis* [many men are deceived in this woman; he feared that the later things will be worse than the first]'.[16]

However, welcomed by her people with 'good entertainment, great cheer, and fair words',[17] Mary's homecoming included many rude shocks and some danger, not least the fact that only a month after her arrival her bed and its hangings caught fire, and she was almost suffocated as she slept. This seemed to fulfil some old prophecy 'that a Quene sholde be burnte at Sterlinge',[18] which held a certain menace. The atmosphere was edgy. Her priests still risked being attacked when they attempted to celebrate Mass. Mary had been exposed to the brutality and danger of rebellion and its aftermath at Amboise, but there she had been cloistered in a protected citadel, her brilliant soldier uncle in charge, a loyal army of horsemen at his disposal, a ruthless policy of punishment and suppression already in place.

In Scotland she was much less distanced from the people. Their affection and displeasure was immediately apparent and directly expressed. One of her early historians had characterized her arriving in Scotland 'suddenly . . . as if she had flown through the air',[19] and what a rare, brightly plumaged bird she must have appeared. But also, who could have prepared Mary herself for the radical change in every aspect of her life as a result of this homing flight north?

She had left the rich soil and balmy climate of the Loire valley. She would never see again its royal châteaux built in honeyed stone and sumptuously furnished as ostentatious monuments to the power and plenitude of the Valois dynasty. The court which had fashioned her manners, accomplishments and expectations was luxurious, rich and profligate. Crowded with sumptuously dressed, bejewelled princes and their courtiers, serviced by armies of retainers, it was a showplace of culture and decadence where she as their princess and then their queen had been the brightest star. It was as if she had flown direct from high summer into autumn, from feast to frugality. Scotland was much poorer, the landscape harsher, the climate colder. The court was small and the Scots were not known for their facile tongues, studied flattery or unwarranted admiration. The castles and palaces had their own beauty but they loured, the toughness of their granite walls as resistant to embellishment as to battery. The light was cold and grey, and the people as hardy, obdurate and resistant to authority as the stone.

A scattered population who were independent and contentious, with deep-held clan loyalties but often scant respect for the law, were a difficult people to govern, 'hard to be held in bridle even by the arme and authoritie of men'.[20] Piracy at sea and plundering, or reiving, of their neighbours' livestock were widespread. A teenage queen was unlikely to persuade such subjects to abandon a centuries-old way of life. The more remote of her people, like those in the Highlands of Argyll, were called 'wylde men'[21] even by their fellow Scots.

In leaving France for Scotland, Mary had not just crossed a stretch of sea. She had left behind a world where she had been a precious princess, protected from reality, asked to perform nothing more onerous than to appear beautifully dressed, pursue courtly pleasures, and accept the admiration of that inward, narcissistic world. Instead, in Scotland, she was brought face to face with a rough and red-blooded reality that she could not easily evade by collapsing into tears or retreating to the virginal or her needlework. But Mary was robust and loved outdoor pursuits, particularly hunting and hawking. She was young enough and adventurous enough to rise to the challenge. Mary spent the years immediately after her return to the country on lengthy and at times arduous progresses, extending as far north as Inverness and as far south as her borderlands, inspecting her country and showing herself to the people. She was a good horsewoman and, like her father, she enjoyed disguise, on occasion dressing as a man – she was taller than most men – and riding with a pistol in her belt.

Mary did make an early attempt to catch and punish some of

the 'theeves and revers' in these borders, and in conversation with Randolph, Elizabeth's agent, asked him what he thought of her country. When he said it was good enough but could be better she replied, 'Th'absence of a prince hathe cawṣed yt to be worce.'. Then her curiosity got the better of her: 'But yet is yt not lyke unto Englande?' she enquired artfully, to which Randolph replied that there were many countries in the world worse than Scotland but few better than England, which he trusted 'som tyme her grace sholde wytnes'.[22] This Mary said she would like as long as it pleased Elizabeth. Always her eye was on her cousin and never far from mind was her own claim to the English throne. She was impatient to visit this neighbouring land and test whether her charm would work as gratifyingly on Elizabeth's subjects too.

Signs may not have been propitious for co-operation between Elizabeth and Mary, but their relationship as neighbouring queens began with at least a show of amity. In her letters and messages through her ambassadors, Mary employed a tone of sisterly affection, stressing their blood ties and natural bonds as women: 'Yt is fetter for none to lyve in peace then for women: and for my parte, I praye you thynke that I desyer yt with all my harte.'[23] She liked to foster intimacy between them and requested that Elizabeth's letters to her should be in her own hand. Mary's main advisers, Lord James and Lethington, both favoured close ties with England, thereby weakening the French connection and reinforcing the Protestant cause. Cecil and Lord Robert Dudley, Elizabeth's main counsellors, were also amenable to this policy of friendship.

Both sets of advisers sought to persuade their respective queens that there was a satisfactory resolution to the stalemate of the Treaty of Edinburgh. If Mary would ratify the treaty and thereby withdraw her claim on the English throne then Elizabeth would name her as her successor, in the event that she had no children to succeed her. But persuading each queen of the necessity to fulfil the other's requests was an exhausting and in the end fruitless obstacle course where their ambassadors always seemed to return on a loop to the beginning. A transcript of a remarkable conversation between Elizabeth and Mary's secretary Lethington showed something of the vividness and intellectual tenacity of Elizabeth's debating style. It also makes clear how difficult to deal with she was:

To begin with Elizabeth was exasperated by Mary: 'When the Queen has done to me that thing she is obliged anent [concerning] the ratification, then were it time to require me to do her any pleasure; but before that time I cannot with honour gratify her in anything.' To which Lethington replied that although Elizabeth considered her inheritance of the throne to be entirely lawful there were many abroad, not least all Catholics, who did not. Mary's claim, on the other hand, was 'without all controversy'. The Scottish queen herself, he warned, had the idea of the validity of her claim 'deeper rooted in her head' and it was unlikely she could 'be easily persuaded to forgo it'.[24]

Elizabeth could be as frank and revealing of her own feelings and fears: 'I have always abhorred to draw in question the title of the crown, so many disputes have been already touching it in the mouths of men. Some that this marriage was unlawfuly, some that someone was a bastard, some other, to and fro, as they favoured or misliked.' The conversation flowed seamlessly into a defence of her resistance to marriage for herself: 'So many doubts of marriage in all hands that I stand awe myself to enter in marriage, fearing the controversy. Once I am married already to the realm of England when I was crowned with this ring, which I bear continually in token thereof.' She then returned again to Mary's aspiration to be named as heir, 'Howsoever it be, so long as I live, I shall be Queen of England; when I am dead, they shall succeed that has most right.'[25]

Elizabeth was adamant that she would do nothing to impair Mary's claim, but insisted it was quite unreasonable, in fact actually dangerous to her own security, to name a successor, 'to require me in my own life to set my winding-sheet before my eye! The like was never required of no prince.' It was a subject she came back to time and again, the impossibility of a prince resting secure when there was an heir in waiting. She explained how she had experienced personally in her sister's reign the fickleness of popular feeling: 'I know the inconstancy of the people of England, how they ever mislike the present government and has their eyes fixed upon that person that is next to succeed; and naturally men be so disposed: "*Plures adorant solem orientem quam occidentum.** [More do adore the rising than the setting sun.]" And what danger it were, she [Mary] being a puissant princess and so near neighbor, ye may judge; so that in assuring her of the succession we might put our present estate in doubt. I deal plainly with you, albeit my subjects, I think, love me as becomes them; yet where is so great perfection that all are content!'[26]

In the ebb and flow of their conversation over a number of meetings Elizabeth, so often criticized for the obscurity, equivocation and duplicity of her diplomatic exchanges, was remarkably frank and comprehensive in her responses. She explained her opinions and motivations without evasion or pretence, and in fact during the forty-one years that remained of her reign was to change nothing of the substance of what she said to Lethington during that autumn of 1561, having just turned twenty-eight. She never married, she kept and built upon that conjugal bond with her people, and she resisted naming an heir until she was nearing death when the winding sheet was inescapable.

From these earliest exchanges between the two queens, with the dispute over the accession to Elizabeth's throne as the central stumbling block, it was clear that each woman was as uncompromising as the other, each determined to maintain every advantage possible over her cousin. Mary's sense of *amour-propre* had been developed during her years as princess and then Queen of France. To maintain that image of herself, she required a kingdom larger and more important than Scotland alone. Elizabeth, on the other hand, had an overdeveloped sense of insecurity due to the ambivalent circumstances of her birth, together with the experiences of fear and powerlessness she suffered during the last years of her sister's reign.

This insecurity made Elizabeth intensely suspicious of any clear

---

* *Life of Pompey*, Plutarch.

successors to her throne. During Lethington's visit, while resisting Mary Queen of Scots' blandishments, her mind was preoccupied with the problem of the succession as represented by the remaining Grey sisters, particularly the elder, Catherine. Like the Queen of Scots, Lady Catherine and Lady Mary Grey were great-granddaughters of Henry VII and therefore cousins of Elizabeth, once removed. Their sister Jane, having been propelled by Dudley's ambition to the throne in 1553, in place of Mary Tudor, was eventually executed in 1554. Just as the Queen of Scots claimed an irreproachable legitimacy in her direct line to the founder of the dynasty, so too could Jane's sisters.

Elizabeth and Catherine Grey did not like each other. Elizabeth thought Catherine stupid and self-important. Catherine, proud of her bloodline, was foolish and arrogant enough to disdain Elizabeth's parentage, in her hearing. However, her proximity to the throne only began really to trouble Elizabeth when she heard that the Spanish were keen to secure a possible heir to the English crown, (at the time the French had Mary and were pursuing the Stuart claim) and intended to inveigle her into marriage with a Spanish nobleman. Having treated her with scant regard and ignored her expectations of the highest courtesies at court, Elizabeth realized it was better not to push Catherine too far. She made an effort to include her more in court ceremonial and even talked of adopting her. Such a move, however, was more to spread consternation in the Queen of Scots' camp, by stressing that there were other claimants for the English throne and Mary could not take her supremacy for granted.

Lady Catherine, however, sidestepped Spanish ambitions and confounded Elizabeth by marrying for love. She was rash enough not only to do this behind her sovereign's back but to choose as her husband a scion of another traitorous family, Edward Seymour, nephew of Thomas Seymour, the man who had first stirred Elizabeth's heart. It was forbidden for anyone in the line of succession to marry without the sovereign's approval, but in Catherine's case there was an added threat. There was a generalized fear that Elizabeth was about to plunge into marriage with Robert Dudley, a match made all the more divisive by rumours that his suit was supported by the Spanish, with the understanding that once he was king he would persuade Elizabeth to re-establish the Catholic religion. So many nobles were opposed to Dudley and his pretensions to be king that it was suspected that some encouraged Catherine's marriage in order to make her a suitable successor to Elizabeth in any attempt to depose her.

Catherine had courted disaster with her duplicity and the suspicion that it was part of a larger, more sinister conspiracy directed at Elizabeth's throne. This disaster was compounded, however, by Catherine becoming pregnant and producing a son. At the time of Elizabeth's conversation with Lethington, Lady Catherine had been imprisoned by the queen in the Tower and had just given birth there. As long as Elizabeth remained childless, these other claims on her throne gained momentum. Most in Catholic Europe considered her legitimacy dubious and so sons, particularly, born to any of her rivals inspired a certain hope, embodying a renewed threat.

To Lethington, Elizabeth confided that she preferred Mary to any of her other putative successors, and then added: 'You know them all, alas; what power or force has any of them, poor souls? It is true that some of them has made declaration to the world that they are more worthy of it [the crown] than either she or I, by experience that they are not barren but able to have children.'[27] Cecil was not as sanguine. His queen's intransigent opposition to marriage burdened him with a frustration and foreboding that no amount of scheming on his part could ease. To Throckmorton he confided: 'I am most sorry of all that her Majesty is not disposed seriously to marriage, for I see likelihood of great evil both to this State, and to the most of the good particular persons, if she shall not shortly marry.' He went on plaintively, hopefully, 'Well, God send our Mistress a husband, and in time a son, that we may hope our posterity shall have a masculine succession.' He had explained this forcefully to Elizabeth. There was no doubt she was subject to unrelenting pressure to agree to marriage, a matter that Cecil characterized as 'too big for weak folks, and too deep for simple'.[28]

In fact it seemed so simple to the men who surrounded her, a matter of diplomacy and pragmatic duty. If only Elizabeth could be induced to marry and bear a son then all these problematic female claimants on her throne would be disarmed in one decisive blow. Cecil was specifically concerned with Mary. He considered there was everything to gain by agreeing to her request to be named as successor but then disabling her with the *coup de grâce* – Elizabeth's marriage and then a son for England! But in this Cecil was left with just his dreams.

Elizabeth did not choose Cecil's obvious solution. Her only recourse against this latest cousin determined on being named her heir was to try and prove Catherine's own illegitimacy. Failing that, proof of the invalidity of her marriage to Seymour, on the grounds of there being no witnesses, therefore would illegitimize her son. The following year, Catherine's marriage was declared void and yet she remained in prison, separated from Edward Seymour, although they still managed during one visit to conceive another son. Still under house arrest, Catherine Grey died of tuberculosis in 1568 aged twenty-nine. Her younger sister Mary also married for love without Elizabeth's approval. She was abnormally short and a hunchback and her husband, Thomas Keyes, a royal serjeant-porter, was abnormally tall. Lady Mary Grey had never been seriously considered as an heir to Elizabeth but this defiance combined with her royal blood nevertheless ruined her life. Both she and her husband were imprisoned and although she was eventually released she died prematurely in 1578, aged thirty-eight.

Elizabeth's harshness in her treatment of the Grey sisters might not have been entirely due to her fear of possible claimants to her throne. These young women of royal blood had defied duty and dynastic expectation to marry the men they loved. Elizabeth had just emerged from the lonely struggle between passion for Lord Robert and her duty as queen. Contemporary reports recognized that there was an emotional component to Elizabeth's reaction. It had been suggested that she had sought to have it 'decided by law that the Lady Catherine was [Seymour's] wife, whom he had married for his pleasure, and therefore that she [the queen] might legally marry the Lord Robert for hers'.[29] Having decided on duty, however, her feelings for Dudley could not be expected to subside. In fact, such is human nature that the unattainable becomes all the more desirable. For Elizabeth the pleasures of the beloved's company and his continued exertions to woo her can only have brought home the painful extent of her sacrifice.

In the Grey sisters, she was faced by two younger cousins who expected to be awarded the prize of succession without being prepared to practise any of the self-discipline that such authority required. Some years later, Mary Queen of Scots was to shock Elizabeth with her reluctance to favour responsibility and duty over the impetuous fulfilment of desire. If self-sacrifice makes a stone of the heart, when faced by these self-indulgent women who aspired to be queen of her kingdom without any costs to themselves, then Elizabeth's heart was stony indeed.

Elizabeth's fear of successors was an overriding consideration in all her dealings with Mary. Mary's assumption of the arms and title to Elizabeth's kingdom and its continual rehearsal had dealt a fatal wound to the relationship. It bred suspicion, resentment and insecurity on Elizabeth's side, and unrealistic ambition and inflated self-importance on Mary's. Camden recognized it as straightforward rivalry of queens: 'Emulation growing betwixt them, and new occasions daily arising . . . For a Kingdom brooketh no Companion, and Majesty more heavily taketh Injuries to heart.'[30] The wily Spanish ambassador writing to Philip II was more matter-of-fact: 'This Queen . . . bases her security on there being no certain successor to whom the people could turn if they were to tire of her rule', as he went on to explain just why Elizabeth was fearful of Mary's choice of husband.[31] For the marriage question just added yeast to the already active ferment between the two women.

For two years since her accession to the throne Elizabeth had been at the centre of a flurry of marriage speculation and proposals. As the most eligible woman in Europe, she had been courted by any man with a grand ambition and half a chance of becoming her consort and king. Picking his way through the marriage bazaar was the most ambitious and physically attractive of them all, Lord Robert Dudley, companion of Elizabeth's youth and Master of her

Horse. But not even his ambition and her love were large enough to persuade her to risk a kingdom in pursuit of heart's desire. So the charades continued with the embassies of foreign princes trudging to Elizabeth's door, Cecil and her council tearing at their hair, and foreign policy inadvertently held in convenient suspension.

Elizabeth's disdain towards her suitors, however, began to have an undesired effect. After the unexpected death of François II of France and the return to market of his nubile widow, the contrary Queen of England lost her lustre. Nowhere was the abrupt switching of suit more blatant than with the Swedish prince who had now become King Eric XIV. Eric had doggedly pursued Elizabeth's hand in marriage, so much so that he had become a laughing stock of her court, as they relieved him of his sumptuous presents. But only a month after Mary's return to Scotland it appeared he had instructed his ambassador to transfer his courtship to the Queen of Scots instead: 'and though this King had entertained great love for the Queen of England, yet her delays, and the diligence which the Guises used to induce him to espouse their niece, had made him change his mind'.[32] The full extent of English concern at any powerful foreign alliance that Mary might make was evident in March 1662. When news that the King of Sweden's envoy had offered King Eric's hand to the Queen of Scots, a panicky response saw English warships prepared and troops assembled on the border ready for action.

In returning to Scotland to take up the reins of power, Mary had cut herself adrift from the powerful triumvirate of advisers, the Duc de Guise, Cardinal of Lorraine and Catherine de Medici, who had steered policy when she was their queen consort. In Scotland, she had no loyal minister, no Cecil, whom she could trust to put her interests and the interests of their country before all else. She trusted her bastard half-brother Lord James more than she should, and William Maitland of Lethington, although described by a contemporary as 'a Scotch Cecil' was calm and judicious but never acquired the authority and stability of his English counterpart. It became painfully clear to Mary that she was in need of powerful friends both at home and abroad. The old national alliances and enmities on which she had been brought up had been swept aside by her change in status and kingdom, and a new order was in the process of evolving.

Not only would Mary never see France again, but the powerful protection that country had afforded her from the moment she was born to her Guise mother was also at an end. During the rest of Mary's life, the two kingdoms most important to her would be ruled by women: France by the queen mother, Catherine de Medici, and England by Elizabeth. Both grew to seem indomitable and died in their seventieth year, Catherine mythologized as the omnipotent mother of impotent kings and Elizabeth as Gloriana, the Virgin Queen. Both were monarchs of craft and intellect who shared a dislike and mistrust of Mary. Consummate pragmatists, they were untroubled by religious conviction and fluid of policy. Having waited so long for power, neither intended relinquishing any advantage to another, and Mary's histrionics and insinuating charms availed her nothing against their unwavering purpose.

Marriage was the obvious way for Mary to increase her influence, make new alliances and develop new friendships. However, for different reasons, as a prospective bride she was to prove as difficult to please as Elizabeth. Mary very quickly had made it clear that she would not marry a Protestant 'even if he were lord of half the world'; nor would she accept 'a husband less great and powerful than the one she has lost'; certainly she could not contemplate anyone approved by Elizabeth; and 'would rather die than accept'[33] one of her own subjects, for that would lower her status and impair her claim to Elizabeth's crown.

The one suitor who seemed to fulfil Mary's exacting criteria was Philip II's son and heir Don Carlos who offered her an alliance with the staunchest Catholic power. Mary had been favourable to this match from well before she left France. It was her best chance of keeping the upper hand diplomatically in her negotiations with Elizabeth. On a personal level too, it would unite her with her favourite sister-in-law, Elizabeth de Valois, who was married to Philip II, Carlos's father. Inevitably Elizabeth and Catherine were more alarmed by the prospect than by any of the other possibilities mooted. Spain, with one foot firmly planted in Scotland and the other poised over England and Ireland, boded nothing but ill for both Catherine and Elizabeth. The weak link in Mary's plan, however, was the nature of Don Carlos himself.

Mary was described by the Spanish ambassador, Bishop Quadra, in a letter to Don Carlos's father as a queen who would make 'a wife of such excellent qualities . . . in prudence, chastity and beauty, equalled by few in the world',[34] but there was nothing positive to be said of the personal qualities of the young Spanish prince they wanted her to marry. Already opinions like this were being voiced publicly: 'he is usually so mad and furious that everyone here pities the lot of the woman who will live with him'.[35]

Three years younger than the Queen of Scots, Don Carlos was congenitally deformed, a desperate creature increasingly prone to terrifying episodes of violent insanity, with a reputation for torturing women and small animals. None of the marriage brokers, or the prospective bride herself, seemed to be in the least concerned by what could be interpreted in other circumstances as a major stumbling block. There was every indication that Don Carlos's mental condition would deteriorate further and a chance too that it was hereditary (due to incestuous marriages, Juana the Mad was his great-grandmother twice). In what might be considered a further disqualification in the marriage stakes, there were rumours that the Spanish prince was impotent and unlikely to sire a future king.

Despite these personal foibles, however, Don Carlos's dynastic credentials were so attractive to Mary and her Catholic sympathizers that he remained the prize suitor. Interestingly, Elizabeth was not too dazzled by his political advantages to realize there was something personally ominous about him. Although the Spanish ambassadors tried to keep the full story of the prince's mental state from the world it was impossible to suppress it in the gossip maelstrom of court life. Certainly one of Elizabeth's ambassadors was writing to her in the summer of 1562: 'the appearance of the Prince's manners and disposition seemed to denote him to be of a Saturny [sullen], cruel mode, much misliked and feared'.[36] When Elizabeth spoke to the Spanish ambassador that summer about

Mary's ambitions to marry their prince she had been rudely dismissive about the boy. To Philip II the ambassador wrote in cipher: 'This was at the time when we had bad news of the health of His Highness, and she used a great many impertinent expressions, which I refrain from repeating, but answered as they deserved.'[37] Mary only gave up on Don Carlos as a prospective husband when Philip withdrew his son from the negotiations in 1564: in 1567 the frenzied prince was incarcerated and in 1568, aged only twenty-two, he was dead, poisoned it was rumoured by his despairing father.

While Elizabeth worried about possible Spanish alliances with her cousin across the border, she was also suspicious of the ambitions of certain of her own nobility at home. Lady Catherine Grey had been dealt with summarily but there was consistent talk too about the machinations of the formidable Margaret, Countess of Lennox. As Elizabeth's cousin and a favourite of her sister Mary Tudor, she had for a while taken precedence over the Princess Elizabeth in Mary I's court. Subsequently, when Elizabeth had inherited the throne, the countess had not bothered to hide her contempt for the reformed religion and her doubts about Elizabeth's legitimacy.

Most worrying to the queen, however, was the scheme of this most ambitious of women to promote her elder son Henry Stuart, Lord Darnley. He too was a cousin once removed to Elizabeth and shared a grandmother with Mary. They were both great-grandchildren of the founder of the Tudor dynasty, Henry VII. Soon after the death of François II in December 1560, with an eye ever alert to the main chance, the countess had dispatched her favoured son to France to re-introduce himself to the newly widowed queen. Darnley was fifteen and Mary just eighteen. Despite her recent bereavement she was already aware of the necessity of her next marriage, although at that point she had wished to marry someone of the highest estate.

As the Countess of Lennox's dynastic ambitions became clear she and her husband were placed under surveillance by Elizabeth and eventually imprisoned, separately, for well over a year. Darnley, however, managed to evade the fate of his parents and slipped away to France. Mary's claim on the English throne was strong enough on its own to worry Cecil and Elizabeth; they did not relish seeing her united with Darnley who had been born within the kingdom and whose royal blood had the added advantage of being English. Elizabeth's nervousness was evident to everyone, 'the prison will soon be full of "the nearest relations of the Crown"',[38] an ambassador reported with some irony. And certainly, as with the Grey sisters, the Countess of Lennox's legitimacy was investigated in an attempt to pronounce her mother Margaret Tudor's second marriage invalid. But the legitimacy or otherwise of second marriages was dangerous territory for Elizabeth, and the investigation was dropped after an indignant outburst from the countess.

By the beginning of 1562 Mary's conciliatory policies, driven by the Protestant Lord James and Maitland of Lethington had resulted in a generally peaceful and successful beginning to her government. Her one failure had been to persuade Elizabeth to agree to name her as her successor. This, together with a natural curiosity and desire to forge a closer friendship, meant she was delighted with the suggestion that the two queens should meet.

Mary had grown up relying on her personal charm to achieve what she wanted. How could Elizabeth, a kinswoman and a neighbour, fail to grow friendlier when faced with the flesh and blood woman rather than the construct of court rumour and ambassadors' reports? Lethington writing to Cecil at the beginning of the year expressed Mary's wishes thus: 'The Thing in the World she most ernestly desyreth, is to see her good suster, so that by occasion theroff they myght speake and frankly conferre together without Mediatours, and that for no Respect, but only for naturall Affection.'[39] In fact it appeared that Mary's spontaneously warm feelings were suddenly focused on her cousin, and she spoke emotionally about her love for Elizabeth and looked forward to receiving a portrait of her: '"Yt wyll", saythe she, "do my good to have yt, but yt wyll not contente my harte untyll I have bothe seen her and spoken with her."'[40]

This was the one occasion in the power struggle at the heart of their relationship when Elizabeth seemed to desire a meeting as keenly as Mary. Her council, however, had strong reservations about the wisdom of letting Mary travel into the north of England where the Catholic sympathies were strongest. Lethington was anxious himself about the meeting of the queens. He feared Mary might not manage to hold her own in any debate with Elizabeth, for there was 'no such maturity of judgement and ripeness of experience in high matters in his mistress, as in the Queen's Majesty [Elizabeth], in whom both nature and time have wrought much more than in many of greater years'.[41] Despite the protestations of their advisers, a tentative date was set in August for Mary and Elizabeth to meet in Nottingham, or failing that York, and a safe passage assured for Mary and her train, 'to the Nombre of one thowsand Persons'.[42]

However, all these plans depended on the extent of religious unrest in France where Catherine de Medici was attempting to contain the violence and prevent it escalating into civil war. Elizabeth, like Catherine, feared the return to power of the Guises and she was tempted to send support to the French Huguenots. In fact Bishop Jewel of Salisbury believed that Mary's warm embrace of Elizabeth was suggested by her uncle, the Duc de Guise, who hoped that the diplomatic manoeuvrings and plans for celebrating their historic meeting would distract Elizabeth from what was happening over the Channel.

The effusiveness of Mary's affections and her continued fascination with the minutiae of Elizabeth's character and mode of life, however, made it more likely that she was genuinely excited by this chance of meeting her at last, hopeful no doubt that face to face she might get her way on the succession. Much to the surprise of the English agent Randolph, Mary slipped a letter she had received from Elizabeth 'into her boosame nexte unto her schyne [skin]' and when she read it again and replaced it against her breast with as much intimacy she told him, 'Yf I could put it nerrer my hart, I wolde.' During the interview, Mary handed to him a special present for Elizabeth, a ring with a heart-shaped diamond to remind 'my good syster' of her love.[43] A conversation three weeks later with Randolph conveyed something of her expressiveness. Having just received Elizabeth's portrait Mary asked 'How lyke this was unto her lyvelye face', to which Randolph replied that he hoped she would soon 'be judge thereof her self, and fynde myche more perfection then coulde be sette forthe with the arte of man'. This was greeted warmly: 'That is the thynge that I have moste desyered ever since I was in hope therof . . . and I truste that by the tyme that we have spoken togyther, our hartes wylbe so eased that the greateste greef that ever after shalbe bewene us, wylbe when we shall tayke leave thone of thother; and let God be my wytnes, I honor her in my harte, and love her as my dere and naturall syster.' In transcribing this conversation verbatim in his letter to Cecil, Randolph obviously thought the Scottish Queen's professed affection might sound to an English ear a little exaggerated and so added, 'Believe me I do not feign.'[44]

In France the religious conflict went from bad to worse. The Duc de Guise's responsibility for a massacre of Huguenots at Vassy in March 1562 was the spark that set civil war aflame. Initially Elizabeth tried mediation but the stories of the atrocities committed against the Protestants in other parts of France too, their cries to her for help, and her own desire to get her hands on Calais again persuaded her that she should intervene. Her implacable hatred of the Guises made her fear the threat they posed if they ever regained power to pursue their aggrandizing schemes. Their niece, should they wish to reinforce her claim, was now established at England's back door.

By July it was obvious that Catherine de Medici had an uncontrollable fire on her hands as the first French war of religion was ravaging the land. Elizabeth vividly expressed her shock to Mary: 'For what hope can be in strangers when cruelty so abounds in a family? I pass over in silence the murders on land, the burials in water, and say nothing of men cut in pieces; pregnant women strangled, with the sighs of infants at their mothers' breasts, strike me through', and used this as eloquent reason for her committing men and money to the Huguenots' cause. But more immediately, the projected meeting of the two queens had to be postponed. Elizabeth could not now turn her mind to social events, and the danger to Protestants abroad meant she dare not risk leaving London, her centre of operations and power, at a time of general unrest. 'We must guard our houses from spoil when our neighbours' are burning.'[45]

When the message of postponement arrived in Edinburgh, Mary

freely expressed her disappointment with a downcast face and floods of tears. Having already revealed her propensity for emotional collapse when faced with stress, frustration or failure, Mary once again took to her bed in an overwrought state. She soon recovered her equilibrium with the promise that a new meeting would be arranged in the spring. Mary's tears may not have seemed so disproportionate, however, if she had known that this first postponed meeting was the closest the two cousins would ever get to a direct encounter.

The fact that they were never to meet is the black hole at the heart of their relationship, the dramatic axis of their story. It fuelled a tragedy that ended in bitterness, fear and death. The lack of human connection allowed each to make what she would of the other. The idea of the rival could grow out of all proportion to become a shadow more threatening than any flesh and blood, something superhuman but also less than human and therefore easier to kill. This lack of intimacy and absence of knowledge also meant the opinions and interests of others held powerful sway. Mary, always more avid for personal contact, became the supplicant to her cousin, pleading, increasingly desperate, for an audience, for intimacy. Elizabeth, increasingly suspicious, withheld her presence, backed off, fearing her rival's reputation for enchantment, then disdainful of her undoing.

Within a month of her disappointment Mary embarked on her first progress to the north. It was August 1562, she was not yet twenty, and this kind of outdoor adventure appealed to her energetic and passionate nature. Randolph accompanied her, his plaintive reports to Cecil indicating just how little he cared for the discomforts and privations that seemed to so inspirit the Scottish queen. It was 'a terrible journey both for horse and men, the country is so poor and victuals so scarce'.[46] They travelled up through Stirling to Aberdeen, Randolph still complaining, this time of the foul weather and the scarcity of corn, so green this late in the year it had no chance of ripening. Mary's high spirits seemed undiminished, she regretted nothing other than 'that she was not a man, to know what life it was to lie all night in the fields, or to walk on the causeway with a jack and a knapschalle [a kind of helmet], a Glasgow buckler, and a broadsword'.[47] This dream of being a man of action, a man of war, free to pursue his own destiny, illustrated her own appetite for life and pleasure in her physical energies, a gift from her Guise inheritance explored to the full in dangerous and physically demanding circumstances. Mary was always less able to deal with emotional strains, and became hysterical at any attempt to curb or thwart her ambitions, but on the open road nothing seemed to disconcert her.

However, a strange and unsettling incident occurred, which became known as the Huntly Rebellion, and ended with two of her staunch northern allies and many of their supporters dead. At the beginning of the year, Mary had awarded her half-brother Lord James Stewart the Earldoms of Mar and Moray, extensive areas of land and influence in the northern territories. For more than a hundred years, under an informal agreement with the crown, these had been administered (and the revenues collected) by the Earl of Huntly, a powerful Catholic magnate and a natural and potentially valuable ally to Mary, whose Gordon family were to claim the proud epithet 'Cock of the North'. This impulsive gift of Mary's aimed at pleasing her half-brother was ill-judged and badly handled, and could only foment trouble. As befitted a northern earl not much used to anyone's authority but his own, Huntly had unruly sons, the wildest and handsomest being his second, Sir John Gordon. He had already been imprisoned in Edinburgh for an attack on another lord but had escaped and fled north. Known to the queen for his dashing manner and the fact that he professed to have fallen in love with and was determined to marry her, John Gordon was an extreme example of his independent-minded lineage.

Possibly Huntly was already nurturing a grudge against Lord James, although the full extent of his depredations on the Huntly fiefdom was not made public knowledge until September. Perhaps he was committed to protecting his errant son. As Mary and her party, including Lord James, soon to be Earl of Moray, approached Gordon territory, Huntly rode out to meet them at Aberdeen. Defying her request that he limit his entourage to a hundred clansmen, he arrived surrounded by fifteen hundred, all armed and implicitly threatening. Mary had already been provoked by Sir John's refusal to surrender himself at Stirling. When she reached Inverness Castle to find that the captain there refused her entry on the orders of Lord Gordon, Huntly's eldest surviving son and heir, her hackles were up and she was ready for anything. With the growing support of the local people, drawn to see for themselves the vision of their lovely young queen on horseback among them, the castle eventually was surrendered. The captain, another Gordon, was summarily hanged from the ramparts.

Randolph was amazed at the way Mary thrived in what was a turbulent, violent and dangerous enterprise. While the unpredictable and predatory Sir John Gordon was still at large, riding with his loyal clansmen among his own hills, he remained a marauding threat to her. But Mary had never seemed happier. To Cecil, and by extension Elizabeth, Randolph exclaimed in admiration: 'In all these garboils I assure you I never saw her merrier, never dismayed, nor never thought that so much to be in her that I find.'[48]

In fact, until this point sex and marriage had been for Mary a matter of diplomatic and political concern. Proposals were forwarded and alliances made with little thought of any personal attraction between the two dynastic candidates. Status and power had been the overriding consideration for herself and her ambassadors. But here, in the rough and beautiful land of her birth, amongst its robustly masculine and independent lords, it was not surprising if this, probably still virginal, nineteen-year-old's appreciation of sexual desire should begin to stir. It was not surprising that men were drawn to her. It was entirely likely that Mary's youthful delight in exercising her power of attraction over them should surround her with a certain sexual energy. Certainly the strict Protestants in her court had already complained that she was too light-hearted and fond of pleasure. Knox railed from the pulpit 'sore agaynste the Quenes dansynge and lyttle exercise of her self in vertue or godlines'.[49] Her foreign, flirtatious, courtly manners may well have been misinterpreted at times by the rougher, bluffer Scots. Her impetuosity and warmth of feeling were seductive qualities in themselves. Her youth and beauty were irresistible enough to quicken even elderly, more fireproof hearts.

Undoubtedly John Gordon thought he had a chance as an exciting if totally unsuitable suitor. The contemporary historian Buchanan described him as 'a handsome young man in the very flower of youth, more worthy of a royal bed than to be cheated by the offer of it'.[50] He and his clansmen continued to harry their young queen until father and son were soundly beaten at the Battle of Corrichie at the end of October. At only nineteen, Mary may have been a charming and seductive figure but she was also intelligent, masterful and ambitious. Unsentimental, her desire to please her half-brother disposed her to be ruthless. She believed she could not afford to be merciful in victory for both father and son had proved themselves contemptuous of her authority, and Randolph was convinced that she was 'utterlye determined to brynge hym [Huntly] to utter confusion'.[51]

She was as good as her word. After a strenuous battle, the overweight and overwrought earl dropped dead, probably of a heart attack, at the moment of surrender and his unruly son was tried quickly at Aberdeen and found guilty of treason. His execution was conducted in front of the queen in order to quell any rumour that she had somehow encouraged his advances. For Mary this was even more of an ordeal than she had expected. 'He was a handsome young man in the very flower of youth', Buchanan wrote. 'What roused much indignation as well as pity was the fact that he was mangled by an unsuccessful executioner.'[52] The gruesome butchery of this youth, known to her, probably attractive to her, shocked her so much she was in a tearful state of collapse.

Mary's unnecessary ferocity towards a potentially loyal Catholic earl and his family can be understood best as her attempt to bond her closest surviving relation to her, by pursuing his interests to the end. Having been brought up among her adopted and blood family in France, she was more like a queen in exile now that she was transplanted back to Scotland, isolated from everything she had known and loved. Lord James Stewart was the half-brother who had accompanied her into both exiles, as a child to France and as a woman back to the kingdom of her birth. He appeared to be the one person who could provide some of the warmth of family connection and support which she now so sorely missed. Earldoms, revenue, power and the diminishment of Catholic might suited the ambitious and fervently Protestant Lord James.

As Mary prepared for the successful rout of the Gordons, her first military enterprise, Elizabeth's own enterprise in France was doing less well. Elizabeth had determined to hold Havre* (which the English called Newhaven) against the future return of Calais. In fact, in early October, Mary received news of her uncles' victories over the Protestants: 'many thousands were slain'. Almost more welcome news to Mary and her French court seemed to be the fact that Elizabeth's three thousand soldiers were expected to be driven back within the month. 'These have made our Court so merry, for 3 whole days we had almost no other talk.'[53] The eclipse of the Guises appeared to be temporary, as the duke's military genius and ruthless prosecution of war once more was in the ascendancy.

This news had depressed Randolph, not a natural optimist at the best of times. It also concerned him that the Duc de Guise apparently had taken Throckmorton prisoner and destroyed his house in Paris, injuring his servants. Mary herself seemed to be in the highest spirits, complaining that the messenger had diminished the extent of Guise victory and 'made the English so few'.[54] While she was celebrating this and mustering her forces for the big push against Huntly, she received Elizabeth's letter explaining her reasons for sending succour to the French Protestants. It was the last letter she would write for some weeks for the queen ended it with the ominous words, 'My hot fever prevents me writing more.'[55]

Elizabeth had taken a bath to try and ease the fever but had caught a chill and suddenly was very ill indeed. Quickly she was diagnosed as having succumbed to the dreaded smallpox. Cecil was immediately sent for and told to expect the worst. In the extremity of the illness Elizabeth was unconscious and incapable of speech. She recalled later how close to death she had come: 'death possessed

---

* Now called Le Havre as France's second port, situated at the mouth of the River Seine.

almost every joint of me, so as I wished then that the feeble thread of life, which lasted (methought) all too long, might by Clotho's* hand have quietly been cut off'.[56]

After a week of violent fever all hope for her seemed gone. The queen was not expected to live and the court was in turmoil. In the midst of all the anxieties over English intervention in a French war of religion, there was this very real fear that Elizabeth would die. And die without having named her heir. Hurried meetings of the council were convened at which some members favoured Catherine Grey, wishing to honour the spirit of Henry VIII's will as well as ensure the continuance of the Protestant religion; others, including Lord Robert Dudley, favoured the Earl of Huntingdon, staunch Protestant and another cousin to Elizabeth. Most auspiciously of all, he was male, the natural sex of monarchy. The more moderate argued for less haste, fearful that 'they would divide and ruin' the country if each candidate's claim was not weighed judiciously.

Luckily, civil unrest was averted and the queen's fever began to subside. Revealingly, the first words she uttered, believing herself to be dying, were to promote her beloved Lord Robert. More physically weakened than she would be for the next forty years, she uncharacteristically 'begged' her council to make Dudley protector of the kingdom with a title and an income of £20,000. The council were keen to concur with anything she said, but the wily Spanish ambassador noted, 'Everything she asked was promised but will not be fulfilled.' Perhaps the most remarkable words Elizabeth spoke as she returned from the grave were a declaration as to her immutable chastity, despite the depth and longevity of her feelings for her favourite, and the behaviour that might have suggested otherwise. 'The Queen protested at the time that although she loved and had always loved Lord Robert dearly, as God was her witness, nothing improper had ever passed between them.'[57] The timing of this confession and the simplicity and directness of her words had the definitive ring of truth.

News travelled fast over the border to Mary that Elizabeth was

* One of the three Fates, although Clotho spins the thread of life and it is Atropos who severs it.

mortally ill. In fact it was Mary who had received her last letter with the ominous valedictory line. But the news most troubling to the Queen of Scots was just how unwavering the English council were in their antagonism to the idea of her as their future queen. She was not once considered a possible candidate in the urgent discussions as to whom they preferred as the inheritor of Elizabeth's throne. According to the Spanish ambassador, however, a powerful and silent Catholic minority favoured the Queen of Scots and were particularly fervent in the matter of her marriage to Don Carlos and the consequent alliance with Spain.

Despite mixed private emotions, Mary's official concern for Elizabeth centred on the terrible depredations the disease could exact on the complexion. Writing in early November: 'I thank God with all my heart, especially since I knew the danger you were in, and how you have escaped so well, that your beautiful face will lose none of its perfections.'[58] At the request from Randolph for the recipe of a potion to prevent a relapse of the disease, Mary mentioned Fernel, the French king's chief physician, by then dead, who refused to divulge the recipe for the special water with which he used to swab her face and body as a preventative. Elizabeth's complexion may have been saved but Lord Robert's sister, Lady Mary Sidney, who devotedly nursed her through the disease, not only fell victim to it but was disfigured for life.

Elizabeth's attack of smallpox may not have had any lasting effect on her face but it frightened Cecil and her council almost to death. Civil war was the spectre they feared most. There was an increased urgency in their desire to clarify the succession, ideally by persuading her to marry and produce an heir but failing that, and in the short term, to line up a suitable candidate. Elizabeth resisted the added pressure that was brought to bear on her. She was emotional about it. Any talk of the succession stirred all the old insecurities and she wished it to be left aside until the time was right to make her choice known.

Just a month after her recovery Elizabeth heard about a meeting of her noblemen at the Earl of Arundel's house, called expressly to discuss this inexhaustible subject. It lasted until two in the morning and the general view was that in an unexceptional field Lady Catherine Grey's claim was the most favoured. This news upset Elizabeth greatly. She 'wept with rage' and sent for the earl to rail further at him. Arundel's response was stern and paternalistic. 'He told her that if she wanted to govern the country by passion he could assure her that the nobles would not allow her to do so.'[59]

Modest characters valuing an unmolested life were filled with foreboding as the searchlight of succession ranged over their family trees. The Earl of Huntingdon wrote in panic to his friend Lord Robert after he was promoted as a possible claimant. 'How far I have been always from conceiting any greatness of myself, nay how ready I have been always to shun applause, both by my continual low sail, and my carriage . . . What grief [this consanguinity to the crown] hath concealed within my poor heart (but ever true).'[60] But Arundel pointed out that the lords were opposed to the claim of the Earl of Huntingdon because Lord Robert approved of him, although that was not likely to have been the reason stressed to the queen. Elizabeth agreed with Arundel.

The council decided to release from the Tower the unfortunate Earl of Lennox, Lord Darnley's father and the husband of Lady Margaret, whose own claim, along with her son, could appease the Catholic interest in the country. It would also provide a claimant less alarming to Elizabeth's government than Mary Queen of Scots.

Her council were full of foreboding at Elizabeth's continued resistance to any attempt to secure the succession. It was a fundamental necessity of a peaceful interregnum, and they were growing desperate. The Commons' petition to their queen in the Parliament of January 1563 showed how much they feared a disputed crown. 'the unspeakable miseries of civil wars: the perilous intermedlings of foreign princes with seditions, ambitions, and factious subjects at home; the waste of noble houses; the slaughter of people'.[61] No doubt the passion in their address to their monarch was in response to the terror that the civil war currently raging in France had visited upon its people, and the consternation felt by all Protestant neighbours. Elizabeth's reply advised procrastination, reminding her Parliament of the papal jurisdiction from which she had saved them, while soothing them with parental omniscience and care. 'Do not forget that by me you were delivered whilst you were hanging on the bough ready to fall into the mud – yea, to be drowned in the dung ... I assure you all that though after my death you may have many stepdames, yet shall you never have any a more [natural]* mother than I mean to be to you all.'[62]

In the same petition the Commons made clear how vivid were their memories of the heresy trials and burnings conducted under Mary I's fanatic decree, and they allied it with their antipathy to the idea of Mary, tainted with the Catholic fanaticism of her Guise family, ever having dominion over them. After reminding their sovereign of 'the great malice of your foreign enemies, which even in your lifetime have sought to transfer the right and dignity of your crown to a stranger', they explained they feared those traitorous subjects who, 'not only hope of the woeful day of your death, but lay in wait to advance some title under which they may renew their late unspeakable cruelty to the destruction of the goods, possessions, and bodies, and thralldom of the souls and consciences of your faithful and Christian subjects. We see nothing to withstand their desire but your life. Their unkindness and cruelty we have tasted.'[63] As if to reinforce the council's wish and underline her own fitness to be the next heir to the throne, Lady Catherine Grey, still imprisoned in the Tower, gave birth to her second son just ten days later.

Elizabeth felt beleaguered on all sides. When the Lords also weighed in with their demand for a named successor she lost her temper and told them that the marks on her face were healing pox scars not wrinkles, and 'although she might be old [she was 29] God could send her children as He did to Saint Elizabeth'.†[64] One of the strains in Elizabeth's life was to be eased a month later. As her hated enemy, the Duc de Guise, was about to overrun the Huguenot resistance at Orléans, he was assassinated in February 1563 by a young Calvinist who had witnessed and never forgotten the Guise vengeance at Amboise.

---

* This is added in another good manuscript of the speech, see *Collected Works*, 72, note 6.
† Luke recounts how Elizabeth, a kinswoman of the Virgin Mary, was 'in advanced years' when sent a son by God. This son became John the Baptist.

Although this first religious war would be concluded with the Peace of Amboise the following month, it was a peace detrimental to England's hopes for Calais and the long-term prospects for the Huguenots in France. This was to prove a harsh lesson to Elizabeth on the risks and cost of an active foreign policy. But the duke's death had the greatest effect on Mary. It was first of all a political loss to her cause. For as long as the duke lived there was always the possibility that he could mobilize French military might to assert any rights or ambitions of his niece. From the day of Elizabeth's accession he had been the one French individual most feared by the English. Randolph, Elizabeth's agent in Scotland, hoped the duke's demise might mark an even better stage in the relationships between the English and Scottish queens: 'As [the Guise family] have occasioned in times past great misliking between our sovereign and this Queen, so nowe seinge God hathe taken awaye the cheiffeste autour [chief author] of that dyscorde, I hope well that he wyll so yoyne their hartes togyther, that the kyndnes betwene them by no meanes shalbe dysseverde [dissevered].'[65]

Bishop Quadra, the Spanish ambassador to Elizabeth's court, was not so keen to see greater accord between the two queens and recognized drily that Mary's 'chance in the matter [of the English succession] has been quite spoiled by the death of the Duc de Guise',[66] so much so that he believed Lethington would try to restore Mary's standing in the balance of power by renegotiating a marriage for her with her young brother-in-law, Charles IX of France. This was a match with political ramifications as unfriendly to Elizabeth as the much-discussed match of Mary with Don Carlos of Spain.

Less easy to quantify was the extent of Mary's personal grief for the man who had been at the centre of her life. She had first met him when she arrived in France as a fatherless – and virtually motherless – child-queen of not quite six years of age. Heralded as Monsieur de Guise *le grand* by his contemporaries, he was Mary's favourite uncle, the leading figure in a band of charismatic brothers who, for the whole of Mary's youth in France, had represented the real authority in the kingdom. This opportunity for power was due to their own natural ability exalted by their relationship with Mary. This mutual enhancement meant that the Guise family treated their charming and valuable little niece with precious devotion. A brilliant soldier, cunning, courageous, ruthless in the pursuit of his ambitions and legendary for his prowess in the field of battle, he was the heroic male on a grand scale in Mary's pantheon of influences.

The English ambassador Sir Thomas Smith recognized the fanatic in him. 'He was so earnest in his religion that he thought nothing evil done that maintained that sect', and yet Sir Thomas could not hide his admiration in his dispatch to his queen. 'He was the best general in France, some will say in all Christendom, for he had all the properties which are to be wished in a general: a ready wit, a body to endure pain, great courage, experience to conduct an army, courtesy in entertaining men, eloquence to utter his mind, and liberal in money and honour.'[67]

These soldierly qualities were a large part of Mary's inheritance, the source of much of her pride. The physical robustness and courage she displayed in her quelling of the Huntly Rebellion she would display again in her struggle with other seditionary lords. This appetite for battle was remarkable and as clearly a gift from her Guise ancestry as were her height and good looks. But the news of the death of the Duc de Guise was received very differently on either side of the English–Scottish border. Elizabeth and her council felt it was somehow providential, that the massacre of the innocents had been averted, while Mary looked to God to 'not leave me destitute'.[68]

When she heard the new of his death, Mary was 'mervileus sadde, her ladies shedinge of teares lyke showres of rayne'.[69] Elizabeth's condolences were received by the Queen of Scots with a great show of affection and gratitude. Randolph was struck by the tenderness with which Mary treated the letter, requesting that he convey her feelings to Elizabeth with the words 'though I can neither speak nor read but with tears, yet think you not but that I have received more comfort of this letter than I have of all that hath been said unto me since I heard first word of my uncle's death ... I will show myself as loving as kind unto my sister, your mistress, as if

God had given us both one father and one mother.' She knew she had lost some of her bargaining power and so hoped her personal appeal to Elizabeth as 'my dear sister, so tender a cousin and friend as she is to me',[70] might touch her heart a little.

In Mary's use of the word 'destitute' to describe her state of mind on the death of the Duc de Guise she implied the sense of being forsaken. It was quite possible that this loss of the man who had been of such central importance in her life as father figure, mentor, protector and guide, made Mary subconsciously begin to search for someone to fill the void he had left in her imagination and heart. To begin with, her own half-brother, Lord James Stewart, seemed a possible candidate. Blood family mattered to Mary and she had accepted him as a natural ally from the moment she returned to Scotland, despite his strong adherence to the Protestant cause and admiration for John Knox. Lord James, however, was a pragmatic politician rather than an inspirational leader. His interest in Mary was political and self-serving rather than personally affectionate and loyal. She was to learn quite quickly that, far from being a substitute for her heroic uncle, Lord James was not someone whom she could trust with her interests, let alone her life.

The Earl of Arran, a Hamilton and the main legitimate claimant after Mary of the Scottish throne, once mooted as a prospective husband for either Elizabeth or Mary herself, had a reckless energy and fanatic decisiveness which on short acquaintance appeared masterful. But this young man was already suffering from a periodic mania which resulted in him being declared insane when he was twenty-five.* His incipient madness focused on a number of madcap schemes to kidnap the queen with the intention of marrying her. The one in spring 1562 involved his longtime enemy, the Earl of Bothwell. Nothing came of it and there was much doubt as to the verity of Arran's statements, but the resulting furore and scandal was an unwelcome tempest in Bothwell's already stormy life. It also further blackened his reputation.

*   *   *

* He was incarcerated for most of his long life, and died in 1609 aged seventy-two.

Mary had already shown an interest in the Earl of Bothwell. First her mother and then Mary herself had bestowed on him various honours in recognition of his loyalty and youthful prowess as a guerilla commander in the borderlands he patrolled. When he had escaped from prison after being implicated by the unstable Arran, Mary seemed to have more sympathy for him than Randolph or Lord James, now Earl of Moray, deemed appropriate. Although a passionate and forceful fighting man, he had spent much time in the French court acquiring intellectual and cultural refinements that belied his powerful frame and turbulent nature. He had all the qualities necessary to become either a hero or a villain and was to rouse passionate contradictory emotions all his life.

Bothwell was a Protestant but stalwartly anti-English and pro-Scottish. In a daring raid in 1559 he had ambushed an emissary galloping through his own lands en route north, carrying clandestinely six hundred English crowns. Through loyalty to Mary's mother Mary of Guise, and self-interest too no doubt, he had stolen the money sent seditiously by Elizabeth to help finance the rebel Protestant lords. This made him bitter enemies within the Lords of the Congregation and the embarrassed English council. Randolph, the usually stolid English agent, writing to Cecil three years later could not contain his loathing of the man: 'I knowe hym as mortall an ennemie to our whole nation as anye man alyve, dyspytefull owte of measure, falce and untrewe as a divle; yf hys power had byne to the wyll he hath, nether the Quenes Majestie [Elizabeth] had stonde in so good termes of amytie with thys Quene [Mary] as she dothe [violently malicious beyond measure, treacherous and dishonest as the devil; if his power had been equal to his will, her majesty Queen Elizabeth would not stand on such good terms of friendship with this queen [Mary] as she does] . . . [he is] one that the godlye of thys whole nation hathe a cawse to curce for ever.'[71]

Despite Bothwell's apparent later involvement with the treasonous plot to kidnap her, Mary refused to think ill of him. Randolph reported a conversation with Moray, Argyll and Lethington where they felt that their queen 'was more favourable to him than there was good cause' believing as she did that the disapproval her main advisers bore Bothwell 'is rather for hate of hys person . . . then that he hathe deserved'. Although Mary had requested the return of Bothwell from England, where he had fled, these same lords agreed that they were to instruct Cecil otherwise, in the rather sinister phrase: 'in no way should he return but be disposed of as her Majesty [Elizabeth] pleases'.[72] Of course he did return, and from that fateful moment the unravelling of Mary's reign ensued.

Now in her early twenties, Mary's sexual attraction was beginning to disturb a number of young men. The Earl of Arran had already lost his sanity, with her as the focus of his obsession. Lord John Gordon had lost his head as a result of his intractable threat to her authority and chastity. Much of her charm was her power as queen, but there was a personal magnetism too which seemed to encourage men to behave recklessly towards her.

In a peculiar incident which shocked Randolph so much he was embarrassed to relate it to Cecil, a soldier, identified as Captain Hepburn, (it was perhaps just a coincidence that he shared Bothwell's family name) handed a note to Mary as she walked in the garden at Holyrood House in Edinburgh. Passed to Moray to open for her, there was found a poem, 'as shamfull – and saving your honour, as ribbalde verses as anye dyvleshe wytte [devilish wit] could invent',[73] followed by an obscene drawing of a man and woman's sexual organs in the process of copulation. This had happened in front of Sir Henry Sidney and another English visitor, and Mary was particularly distressed that the boldness of the man could be misconstrued to reflect badly on her own reputation. He had fled to England and she had asked Randolph to request that he be detained by the governor of Berwick.

The courtier poet Chastelard was another casualty of Mary's charm and the laxity of her court. He had travelled with Mary to Scotland in 1561 and then, within days of the rout of the Gordons and the beheading of Lord John, he had returned from France to her court at Edinburgh, bringing with him a book of his poems. It was November 1562 and the queen was pleased to see this bright and attentive young Frenchman with news of what she still considered home. Ever suspicious of envoys from France, Randolph reported, 'he is well entertained and has great conference with the Queen, riding upon the "soore [sorrel] gelding" that my Lord Robert [Dudley] gave her grace'.[74] He joined in the merriment at court, apparently writing courtly poetry to the beauty of his mistress, much to the amusement of the women. One of the Four Maries, Mary Beaton, was said to be enamoured of him. Knox, already stiff with disapproval at the fun and games encouraged at court, claimed that Queen Mary would 'sometimes privily steal a kiss from his neck'.[75]

Even if this had happened it was highly unlikely that anyone attached any importance to it at the time, apart from the lovelorn Chastelard himself. It had already been noted that the Queen of Scots' warmth and impetuousity of feeling was open to misinterpretation. On this occasion it fuelled an already volatile infatuation. The following February the twenty-one-year-old poet was found hidden under Mary's bed as she was about to retire for the night. This was outrageous enough and when Mary was told the following morning, rather than 'disquieting of her that night', she ordered him from court. However, the mad hothead followed her to Dunfermline and a few days later was found again hidden in her bedroom, ostensibly to protest his innocence of evil intent the first time.

An especially fast messenger had set off from Edinburgh to spread the news to Elizabeth's court. There was some suggestion Chastelard was a Huguenot intent on besmirching Mary's honour but Lady Throckmorton, writing to her husband (whom as French ambassador she called 'good froge'), put a woman's gloss on the Queen of Scots' discomfiture. She saw it as a misguided passion and probably got the measure of the case: '[Chastelard] did privily convey himself behind the hangings in the Queen's chamber, and in the night would have lain with her, whereat she, making an outcry, the Lord James [Earl of Moray] came, whom she prayed either to kill the gentleman, or that she might kill him with her own hands.'[76] Moray refused to do the deed then and there, but the importunate Chastelard was beheaded within the week in St Andrews market place on market day. Knox had the last words on his lips to be, 'O cruelle dame!' The contemporary French historian, Brantôme, who was not there, preferred to render them, 'Adieu, most beautiful and cruel princess!'[77]

Contemplating her marriage possibilities, Mary was beginning to see that the grandest of all, to Don Carlos, was increasingly unlikely, that the Archduke Charles was not really a possibility, and that she was running out of suitable foreign alliances. Still in the prime of her beauty and animal spirits, she was ready for love. Enforced celibacy – virginity even – for a young queen surrounded by lovesick youths and ambitious men, and gratifyingly aware of her own power over them, grew wearisome. Mary was a healthy young woman with strong appetites – for food, for hunting, dancing and even running skirmishes against rebel forces. One of her Protestant lairds was frank about the desirability of marrying their queen off quickly to a sympathizer of the Reformed religion: 'Remember', he said, 'howe earnestye she is soughte otherwyse. You know her yeares; you see the lustyness of her boddie, you know what these thynges requere . . .'[78]

Always wilful and impetuous, once Mary discovered sexual desire she became reckless of her own safety and unheeding of the security of her kingdom and her future as queen. Mary needed to be married again, to a real husband, someone to relieve her of her virginity and provide her with an heir. She wanted a prince to share her onerous kingdom and a fellow adventurer who, above all, would help bring her Elizabeth's throne – by fair means or foul. The stage was set for the laying out of the dynastic and physical attractions of Henry Stuart, Lord Darnley, the tallest young man a tall young queen could hope to meet. When introduced to him as a prospective husband Mary said 'that he was the lustiest and best proportioned long man that she had seen; for he was of a high stature, long and small [finely-built], even and erect . . .'[79]

There were those who thought Elizabeth, despite her protests, had planned it all. If she wanted to wreck the prospects of her rival she could not have planned it better. Certainly the choice of Lord Darnley was to be the first disastrous decision of Mary's life. It propelled her into a vortex from which there seemed no escape, until shipwreck tossed her out, deprived of everything but her increasingly imaginative claim on the throne of England.

CHAPTER SEVEN

Raison de Coeur: Raison d'État

De Foix, the French ambassador:
'This game [chess] is an image of the words and deeds
of men. If, for example, we lose a pawn,
it seems but a small matter; nevertheless, the loss often
draws after it that of the whole game.'
Elizabeth looked up long enough to reply:
'I understand you; Darnley is but a pawn;
but he may well checkmate me if he be promoted.'

*Elizabeth in discussion with de Foix, of Mary's intention
to marry Lord Darnley, 1565*

IN UNSTABLE TIMES, with no clear successor to the throne, royal
blood was a doubtful blessing. More often it was an inheritance
filled with suspense, that suddenly could prove fatal. Suspicion,
imprisonment, banishment, death, all were common companions
for those with a share in the royal bloodline. Attempts at manipulation through marriage alliances and implication in the conspiracies of others were the occupational hazards that attended
them. Even for the chief claimant to the throne, with rewards as
overwhelming as the dangers, there was still no safety in blood. In
her tortuous journey to the crown, Elizabeth had suffered from all
these adversities. Even as she sat upon her throne she was never
secure and was to inflict on a number of other blood relations the
same constraints and threats that she herself had endured with
dread.

Mary's unquestionable legitimacy outweighed the disadvantages of her sex, but her illegitimate and ambitious half-brother Lord James, Earl of Moray, was an always influential presence on the left hand of her throne. Barred from inheriting the crown, regency and the administration of power was the best for which he could hope. Meanwhile the Hamiltons, the Duke of Châtelherault and his son the Earl of Arran, loomed as alternative princes of the blood, their claim inherited from the daughter of James II of Scotland. On the death of James V, only Mary herself, his fragile infant daughter, kept a Hamilton from becoming king.

Where the father had failed to grasp the highest honour, his hopes were transferred to his son. Had the young Earl of Arran not been confounded by insanity he would have been an obvious suitor for the queen, or proved a rallying point for disaffected opinion both at home and abroad. Certainly the Hamiltons' pre-eminence among the Scottish lords intensified the opposition ranged against them. Scottish politics was distorted by the deep-dyed rivalries of the nobility which lived on through the generations, one of the most inveterate feuds being between the Hamiltons and the Lennoxes, the bloodline which produced Lord Darnley.

In the same deadly grip of family ambition, Darnley was related to both the English and Scottish dynasties, and was from birth expected by his mother to inherit both crowns. His mother, the Countess of Lennox, was already a formidable woman with a strong sense of her own place in the Tudor line as granddaughter of Henry VII and cousin to Elizabeth. Her first son died at less than a year old. Having conceived again almost immediately following his birth, her second pregnancy was well advanced and a soothsayer consoled her with a vision of the dazzling future awaiting her unborn child. The momentous idea put into Lady Margaret's head by 'her pro-phecyers at the death of her first son' was that this second child 'should by King both of England and Scotland'.[1] With this thought her aspiration was given wings.

From the start, Darnley was groomed by his parents for greatness. Like Mary Queen of Scots, he was a grandchild of Margaret Tudor, Henry VIII's eldest sister. On his Scottish side he was descended from James II through his daughter Mary, who married James Hamilton, Earl of Arran. He was encouraged in the kingly pursuits of hunting, hawking and jousting. His manners as a courtier were practised. He could play the lute, sing, compose passable poetry and dance extremely well. Physically he was a commanding presence, if only by virtue of his height which at well over six foot in his late teens was a good head taller than his contemporaries. He never lost his open-faced, smooth good looks, and his body was long-limbed, elegant and athletic.

For the first eleven years of his childhood, Lord Darnley was the only surviving child of six born to his parents. With each infant death his own life became more precious to them and the vision of his destiny more pronounced. He was eventually joined in the hothouse of Lennox ambition by another brother, Charles, whose life was as short if not quite so eminent, although the family's dynastic ambitions were then vested in his daughter Arbella Stuart. Like Mary too, Darnley's upbringing was focused more on the advancement of his sense of unique supremacy and certainty than on developing his character through any trial or adversity. He was a gilded youth and high rewards were his due.

Although his own religious affinities were mutable and open to debate, his mother was considered a staunch Catholic and it was this which made him first a focus for Catholic sentiment in England. As early as the spring of 1560, when Darnley was fourteen years old and Elizabeth had been on the throne for just over a year, Bishop Quadra, the Spanish ambassador, wrote optimistically to his king: 'many Catholic lords would proclaim [Darnley] king. In any case they will not have any more women to rule them as they are so afraid of foreign influence. He has the best right of any of the claimants, and is the best in every way.'[2] But the Countess of Lennox had long planned that Mary would be Darnley's route to kingship and, on news of François II's death in December 1560, her son and heir, aged fifteen, was dispatched to France to offer his condolences to the new young widow, herself just eighteen years old. (Mary and Darnley's birthdays were within a day of each other's, 8 and 9 December respectively, three years apart.) Quadra's prescient mind was already working: 'Lady Margaret Lennox is trying to marry her son Lord Darnley to the Queen of Scotland, and I understand she is not without hope of succeeding.'[3]

It took a few months more for such speculation to be common in Edinburgh, and by November 1561 Elizabeth herself could not ignore it. Court chatter suggested that even if Mary should be denied the succession because she was born out of the country, and was therefore deemed 'a foreigner', she could by marrying Darnley 'nevertheless reign over the kingdom by right of this youth, the son of Lady Margaret ... as he is an Englishman and beyond doubt the nearest heir to the throne after her'. Elizabeth summoned Lady Lennox, Lord Darnley and his younger brother Charles. The lady was under no illusions about Elizabeth's touchiness on the subject of the succession, and her decided power to act. Quadra noticed the effect even on someone with a far from nervous disposition: 'Lady Margaret much distressed, as she thinks she will be thrown into the Tower, and that her son's life is in danger'.[4] In fact it was her husband who was thrown in the Tower three months later while Darnley made a discreet exit to France.

The rough treatment and exile endured by the Lennox family was suddenly reversed in early 1563 when Elizabeth released them from confinement, allowing them to resume their lives. More than that, the apparently capricious queen decided to embrace them wholeheartedly. By summer both parents and son were seen in high favour about court. The Spanish ambassador, writing to his king, found Darnley's improved fortunes significant. He believed that Elizabeth was using him as a stalking horse in her attempts to get Mary to marry someone of whom she approved, and not pursue her dynastic ambitions abroad. 'If the Queen of Scotland does marry a person unacceptable to this Queen, the latter will declare as her successor the son of Lady Margaret, whom she now keeps in the palace and shows such favour to as to make this appear probable.'[5]

Certainly Elizabeth's sense of the proximity of death during her attack of smallpox in October the previous year had left her less confident of her robust health, yet strengthened in her will to overcome anything. In one of the many prayers she wrote she referred to this time of fear and admonished God for his lapse of concentration in letting her and her people suffer so. 'Thou has affected me in this body with a most dangerous and nearly mortal illness. But Thou hast gravely pierced my soul with many torments; and besides, all the English people, whose peace and safety is grounded in my sound condition as Thy handmaid nearest after Thee, Thou hast strongly disregarded in my danger, and left the people stunned.'[6]

The following summer when plague broke out she was un-characteristically fearful of falling ill herself, and was careful on her progresses not to travel to areas considered unhealthy. Her sense of her own mortality might well have been intensified by the prophecies that were being vigorously circulated at the time of her imminent death. 'Everyone is talking of them.'[7] In this super-stitious society, it was a grim foreboding which assailed her on all sides.

Elizabeth had realized how alarmed people were at the prospect of her death leaving no clear successor, how terrified of any possibil-ity of civil war. In the aftermath of her restoration to health, how-ever, she had been disturbed to find her councillors favouring the Grey sisters in the event of her untimely death. Despite her genuine sympathy for these concerns, all her deep reservations about naming a successor remained. Elizabeth sought, however, to disconcert those most obviously in line for her throne. Central to her concerns always were the political manoeuvrings of her cousin Mary, whose tenacious ambition for a marriage alliance with Don Carlos and Spain still posed for her the greatest threat.

For that reason it made diplomatic sense for Mary to keep this possibility alive. She may not have been as adept as Elizabeth at political fencing, in which to feint and parry were the English queen's favoured tactics, but Mary was well aware of the necessity of retaining power, or the threat of power, to add muscle to her negotiations. Her nature was much more impulsive and straightfor-ward than Elizabeth's, more fiery and immediate in her way of interacting with the world. Being forced to deal at Elizabeth's negoti-ating pace, embroiled in her style of procrastination, evasion and denial, was almost unbearably frustrating. Attempts to unravel the real motives behind her cousin's words and actions disheartened much more patient, insightful and experienced diplomats than Mary.

Elizabeth's apparently contradictory actions towards Darnley and his family were a case in point. Elizabeth may have felt that by cultivating the young lord she had at her disposal a range of ways to disconcert Mary's plans. She could implicitly threaten her with a rival whose claim on the English throne was as compelling as Mary's own, and to the men around Elizabeth probably preferable, for Darnley had one inestimable quality: he was male. Even the devoted (though exasperated) Cecil had been heard to mutter he could not countenance another female monarch. Alternatively, offered as a prospective bridegroom, Darnley's own connections and personal attractiveness might distract Mary from her single-minded pursuit of the Spanish alliance and procure for the English queen more time in which to work out an alternative strategy. Then again, there were those who attributed to Elizabeth even greater prescience and Machiavellian intent. Perhaps she meant the marriage to proceed, anticipating the wreckage of a match in which Lord Darnley was to prove disastrous as both husband and king.

When it came to Elizabeth's dealings with Mary nothing was quite as it seemed. As the French ambassador de Foix's chess analogy shows, Elizabeth could not be certain that her strategies would not rebound on herself. Whatever the reasoning, if indeed it was yet clear even to Elizabeth, in June 1563 she petitioned Mary on Lennox's behalf to restore the family's hereditary lands. (Lennox's loyalties to Henry VIII in the 1540s had resulted in his Scottish property being forfeit and he and his family living the next two decades largely in England.) Relations between the two queens were officially still amenable, even affectionate. When Randolph delivered Elizabeth's letter Mary received him while in bed, recovering from a day's illness, and kept him closeted with her for a full hour. This informality caused her own councillors and courtiers some amusement and surprise as they gathered outside her chamber door. Mary's spontaneity extended to her reception of Elizabeth's letter which she kissed, saying 'I wyll kysse yt also . . . for her sake yt commethe from.'[8]

A ring sent by Elizabeth a few months later, as a token of goodwill, was similarly made much of, as Randolph reported back to Cecil: 'the "juell" was marvellously esteemed, often looked upon and many times kissed . . . "Well" said [Mary], "two jouels I have that muste die with me, and willinglie shall never owte of my sighte," and showed me [the other] ring which was the King her husband's'.[9] Part of this effusion of feeling was natural to an impetuous, passionate nature but there was also the realization that she was relaying her thanks and appreciation through Randolph to Elizabeth herself. This was the cousin who held the key to her greatest ambition, and with whom she could only communicate by letters and through third parties. Mary was still straining every nerve to keep Elizabeth friendly and sympathetic to her claim as her heir, while maintaining whatever small bargaining power she might feel she had in this protracted duel of wits. But it was an emotionally draining business dealing with the English queen. Her position seemed so changeable, impenetrable and indeed perverse that attempting any negotiations with her was more akin to grasping at quicksilver. Mary's attempts at discerning Elizabeth's true wishes, so that she might at least know how she was meant to comply, met vagueness and evasion. 'Let me knowe playnlye what your mestres mynde is', she asked Randolph, 'that I maye the better devise with my self, and confer with other, and so gyve you a more resolute answer, then by these generall wordes spoken by you I cane.'[10]

Some of the strain may have been beginning to tell on Mary. By the end of 1563, when finally she received the ring from Elizabeth which she esteemed so, she was suffering from a mysterious illness that had resulted in two months of 'melancholies'. This malady had manifested as fits of weeping 'when there is little apparent occasion'. Randolph found her confined to her bed again in mid-December with a pain in her right side, 'judged to be melancholy'.[11] Much dosed on various medicines and subjected to blood-lettings, the patient endured the doctors' attempts at cure which more often than not exacerbated the disease, or at the least undermined the body's natural vitality, delaying recovery.

It was this detail of a persistent pain in her side together with bouts of vomiting that has stimulated more recent speculation that Mary suffered from porphyria, an inherited enzyme deficiency which, although mostly symptomless, can cause intermittent acute attacks of abdominal pain, gastrointestinal disturbances, muscular weakness and psychiatric complaints, like depression, hysteria, hallucinations – even a full-blown psychosis, such as the madness suffered by one of her descendants, King George III.[12] These are wide-ranging symptoms that individually can be due to a number of physical and psychological conditions. Inevitably, there has also been a suggestion that Mary was an anorexic, even a bulimic.[13]

In the absence of a body, retrogressive diagnosis can only be suggestive. The one distinctive symptom of an acute attack of porphyria is the passing of urine the colour of port wine. As an unmistakable aberration and in a queen so watched and monitored for signs of illness, pregnancy or poison, such a striking excretion would not have passed without notice. In Mary's case there was no intimation in any of the copious letters and reports that surrounded her activities of any symptom as untoward as this. The intermittent pain, weakness and emotional collapses which she suffered, in an otherwise physically vigorous and robust life, could be explained just as plausibly by other less extreme conditions.

However, for a healthy young woman, these two months spent largely in bed would appear to mark a serious episode of illness, so much so that for a few days her life was thought to be in danger. The opinions of those who attended her as to the causes have some authority. The question of her marriage had been weighing on Mary heavily during the previous three years and at about this time she had accepted finally that her long-desired alliance with Don Carlos and Spain was unlikely to happen. 'Some think the Queen's sickness is caused by her utterly despairing of the marriage of any of those she looked for, they abroad neither being "verie hastie," nor her subjects here "verie wyllinge" or bent those ways.'[14]

Throughout her life Mary had exhibited both poles of a passionate and impetuous nature, the 'melancholies' alternating with periods of extreme energy and inflated mood. Certainly the emotional collapse and depression she appeared to be suffering from at this time concurred with her previous reactions to loss, disappointment and thwarted will. Mary was used to having her own way and was energetic in the pursuit of her interests and desires. Now every route she had tried in the pursuit of a dynastic marriage seemed to be blocked by obstacles largely thrown up by the two most powerful women in Europe. Catherine de Medici was doing her best to thwart any Guise pretensions to marry Mary to a French prince. Neither did she care for the Spanish connection. Having married her own daughter Elizabeth to Philip II, she naturally feared Mary gaining any ascendancy by marrying Don Carlos, Philip's heir. And Elizabeth, in seeking to safeguard England's and her own security by controlling her cousin's marital choices, had used the weapons she knew best, confusion, frustration and delay. Unlike the two queens ranged against her, Mary did not bear frustration and delay with patience.

Her ambition to marry a prince of equal status to her first husband now seemed to be melting into the distance like a mirage. To make matters worse, there appeared no real alternative on the horizon. With typical archness and her supreme ability to confound, Elizabeth threw her own diversion into the ring. Having already held out the promise that if the Scottish queen should marry someone of whom the English queen approved then the succession would be hers, why not, Elizabeth suggested, marry the man she herself would have chosen, if she had had a mind to marry? The most desirable man by her lights was offered – who knows how seriously? – to Mary Queen of Scots. In conversation with the wily Maitland of Lethington, the fencing English queen appeared to have met her match. The gist of this verbal duel was reported by Bishop Quadra to his king Philip II at the end of March 1563:

ELIZABETH: 'If his mistress would take her advice and wished to marry safely and happily she would give her a husband who would ensure both, and this was Lord Robert [Dudley] in whom nature has implanted so many graces that if she wished to marry she would prefer him to all the princes in the world . . .'

LETHINGTON: 'This was a great proof of the love she bore to his Queen, as she was willing to give her a thing so dearly prized by herself, and he thought the Queen his mistress [Mary], even if she loved Lord Robert as dearly as she [Elizabeth] did, would not marry him and so deprive her of all the joy and solace she received from his companionship.'

ELIZABETH: 'She wished to God the Earl of Warwick his brother had the grace and good looks of Lord Robert in which each [queen] could have one ... [yet] the Earl of Warwick was not ugly either, and was not ungraceful, but his manner was rather rough and he was not so gentle as Lord Robert. For the rest, however, he was so brave, so liberal and magnanimous that truly he was worthy of being the husband of any great princess.'

LETHINGTON (upset that Elizabeth should demean Mary in offering Lord Robert's brother and wishing to bring this embarrassing conversation to a close): 'The Queen his mistress was very young yet, and what this Queen [Elizabeth] might do for her was to marry Lord Robert herself first and have children by him, which was so important for the welfare of the country, and then when it should please God to call her to himself she could leave the Queen of Scots heiress both to her kingdom and her husband. In this way it would be impossible for Lord Robert to fail to have children by one or other of them who would in time become Kings of these two countries.'[15]

Touché, Lethington may have felt as Elizabeth fell silent.

Mary of course had much grander designs than Elizabeth's hand-me-on lover. But she still longed to meet the English queen, still badly desired the recognition of her succession, and feared alienating her. Desultory negotiations continued for quite a while but no one really thought Robert Dudley was a serious candidate for the Queen of Scots, not least he himself whose own high aspirations still centred on marriage to Elizabeth. He admitted to Melville, the envoy Mary sent to deal with Elizabeth in the summer of 1564, that the whole scheme had been thought up by 'his secret enemy' Cecil, '"for if I", says [Dudley], "should have appeared desirous of that marriage, I should have lost the favour of both the queens"'.[16] Elizabeth had offered to Melville a further explanation for the surprising offer of her favourite. As she had determined to remain a virgin it was only sensible that 'the Queen her sister' should have him and then she could declare Mary her successor, secure in the knowledge that 'being matched with [Dudley], it would best remove out of her mind all fear and suspicion, to be offended by usurpation before her death; being assured that he was so loving and trusty that he would never give his consent nor suffer such thing to be attempted during her time'.[17]

In fact nothing would be more certain to put Mary off. Elizabeth was stating as clearly as possible that Dudley's allegiance, love and loyalty would remain centred on herself, that even marriage to Mary and all the honours that would bring could not win for the Scottish queen his primary loyalty. It was all the more indication that Elizabeth never meant to share her favourite with Mary, and Mary had not the slightest intent to try. Apart from this confusing sham offer, the Scottish queen had been given only vague encouragement to 'marie [with]in England', which caused much merriment when she related it to the Earl of Argyll and he enquired – 'how so then? Is the Quene of Englande become a man?'[18] Along with these unspecific prescriptions from Elizabeth were threats of loss of favour, even enmity, if Mary should disobey and marry out of the kingdom, choosing instead some forbidden European prince. Uncertainty and frustration and constant, if covert, demands for her submission to Elizabeth's will certainly added their emotional toll.

Randolph also felt that a tragedy that befell two popular members of the Scottish court contributed to Mary's mood of depression and despair. One of her French maids-in-waiting became pregnant by the queen's apothecary who, in a panic, turned to abortifacient potions in an attempt 'to cover his fawlte with medicines, the childe was slayne in the mothers bellie'. The young woman had been highly favoured by Mary who was 'so offended, it is thought they [the lovers] shall die'. Randolph's mention of the closeness of this young woman to the queen, together with Mary's extreme reaction, implied that she was not only concerned with the crime but was careful that the immorality did not taint her own maidenly reputation too. Both the apothecary and lady-in-waiting were friends to many in what was a very small and intimate court and when they were duly hanged, within a fortnight of their confession, their tragic deaths upset everyone. The pragmatic Moray was keen to stress to Cecil (and therefore Elizabeth) how much moral probity mattered in this new Protestant government helped into being by English support. He related how even a man as mighty as the Lord Treasurer of Scotland, having made a woman pregnant outside marriage, had to subject himself to a public confession in church on Sunday, and then endure one of Knox's blistering, self-righteous sermons. This Moray hoped would prove '"oure great severitie" to offenders'.[19]

A more interesting suggestion perhaps was that Mary's illness that winter was partly diplomatic. She was practising some of the negotiating tactics of her cousin. Randolph commented on how well she looked, even while she kept to her bed, and certainly being indisposed gave her the best excuse for procrastination and evasion, two of Elizabeth's most effective tools in her diplomatic armoury, at a time when the English queen herself was pressing for some kind of decision. Randolph explained that Mary would as readily change her mind, her words 'so drawne backe agayne from me as thoughe theie had not byne spoken'. Also, he recognized in Mary a habit he claimed as common to all women, when she denied most vehemently her liking for the very person she liked most. On this occasion she was almost as successful at sowing confusion as her cousin. Mary exasperated Randolph, who awaited some kind of answer, being willing to discuss her marriage one day, then capriciously denying any interest the next, professing rather 'the weddows lyf is beste, honorable, quiet etc'. Such contrariness had strong echoes of Elizabeth as Mary claimed, 'Sometimes she may marry where she will, sometimes she is sought of nobody.'[20] In desperation, Randolph urged her to take pity on her Four Maries, contemporaries and friends since childhood, who apparently had all vowed celibacy until the queen had made her choice, and by marrying herself release them from this unnatural state.

In fact Mary was learning fast other lessons her cousin had perfected. Her conversations with Elizabeth's ambassadors showed an increasingly sharp intelligence and sure-footedness in the quick-fire debate of realpolitik. To Randolph, she enquired whether Elizabeth's professed care for her as a sister or daughter was best expressed by requiring she marry a subject like Lord Robert. Was it not better to marry her where some helpful foreign alliance would ensue? When Randolph pointed out that the chief alliance sought by Elizabeth was to live in amity with Scotland, something Mary's own people desired, she was quick to fire back: 'Are you', said she, 'so assured of my subjectes myndes, that you dare assure that?' And when Randolph described Scotland as 'wonte to be verie troblesome, full of contention, I wyll not say commotions agaynste the authoritie', and therefore influenced for the better by proximity with England and thereby 'shall for ever live in obedience with so friendly a neighbour as England', Mary retorted, 'You myghte . . . have saide the same of your owne countrie.' To which Randolph partly had to agree.[21]

Despite her apparent eagerness to please Elizabeth, despite the professions of love and admiration for her cousin and desire for nothing more than friendship and support, as long as Mary managed to keep her emotions in check she was an increasingly intelligent, crafty and competent politician. Her ambition, her attractive manner and the high sense of herself had an immutable force that persuaded others she was someone to be reckoned with. Sir James Melville, meeting her again when she was twenty-one, described the effect. 'She was so affable, so gracious and discreet, that she won great estimation and the hearts of many both in England and Scotland, and mine among the rest.' So much so, that he decided to give up his own foreign connections and ambitions to settle for Scotland and Mary, as someone 'more worthy to be served for little profit than any other prince in Europe for great advantage'.[22] Despite Mary's increasing stature as a monarch, she was up against a consummate politician in Elizabeth, someone who seldom allowed her emotions sway. In fact, exhibiting an instinctive brilliance, Elizabeth harnessed emotion, her own and her people's, to add force and poetic resonance to the workings of her will.

It was when the wills of these two queens clashed that the hidden rivalries and animosities fractured their professions of love. The rivalry was, however, a natural one. Two queens governing adjacent countries in one small island would naturally harbour an intense interest in each other, as well as rampant competitiveness. The fact that both claimed the same crown just fuelled the flame. Each's obstinate refusal of what the other requested – Mary to ratify the Treaty of Edinburgh whereby she relinquished her claim on Elizabeth's throne while she lived, and that of Elizabeth to recognize Mary as her successor when she died – had been complicated by the whole issue of whom Mary should marry. There was also an underlying power struggle in which Elizabeth assumed she was the senior partner in their relationship, and had rights to dictate terms. Mary, however, was unused and unwilling to accept dictation from anyone. One of Mary's lairds, discussing with Randolph how best to get his queen and Elizabeth to collaborate, astutely understood the clash of wills: 'I wolde that bothe the Quenes wolde laye aparte these worldlye opinions and termes of greatnes and suche lyke, and in thys poynte I wolde that theie lacked some what of their willes; for whear all is in will, reason ys not the guide.'[23]

With the spring of 1564 came renewed health and vigour, and despite any diplomatic protestations to the contrary, Mary was ready to marry again. Having accepted the probable end of her hopes for a dynastic alliance she turned her eager gaze closer to home. She seemed to have been as aware of Lord Darnley's possibilities as anyone. By the middle of the year relations between the two queens had so cooled that the weekly flow of letters between them had all but stopped, as Mary's agent James Melville explained, 'for in their hearts from that time forth there was nothing but jealousies and suspicions'.[24] The immediate cause was a brusque letter from Mary to Elizabeth objecting to Elizabeth's ambivalence and accusing her of double-dealing over the return to Scotland of Darnley's father, the Earl of Lennox. Elizabeth admitted in a private note to Cecil that she was confounded by how best to deal with the troublesome question of Mary's marriage. Her own stratagems threatened to get the better of her. As she said to de Foix, the French ambassador,

'Darnley is but a pawn; but he may well checkmate me if he be promoted.' Much as she needed to feel in control of everything, there were so many imponderables in every situation; she could never be sure of the outcome. She was confounded too by Mary's own character, a nature so unlike her own: 'In such a manner of labyrinth am I placed by the answer that I am to give to the Queen of Scotland that I do not know in what way I will be able to satisfy her, since I will not have given her any answer for all this time, nor do I know what I now should say,' she wrote despairingly to her chief minister, asking that he suggest something appropriate for her brief to Randolph.[25]

That summer of 1564 had provided a small triumph for Elizabeth, away from the diplomatic wrangles and frustration over her intractable cousin. She had visited the university at Cambridge and been greeted by a half-hour speech in Latin by the official orator. Every virtue he praised in her elicited a self-deprecating response such as shaking her head, biting her lip or her fingers and even occasionally calling out with passion, *'Non est veritas, et utinam* [It is not true; would that it were]'. However, when he praised her for her virginity Elizabeth did not deny that particular virtue but gracefully concurred, 'God's blessing of thine heart' and bade him continue.[26] When the speech had come to an end she was urged by all the dignitaries present, including Lord Robert, Cecil and most of her lords, to respond likewise, if only in a few words.

With apparent reluctance and maiden shyness, afraid, she said, of making a fool of herself with her inferior grasp of the language, Elizabeth then launched into an extempore speech, in her excellent Latin, in which she promised to 'leave an exceptional work after my death, by which not only may my memory be renowned in the future, but others may be inspired by my example'.[27] This was greeted with an eruption of gratitude and approval. Such progresses into her kingdom invariably increased her popularity and renewed her confidence in the love her people bore her, the one insurance Elizabeth had against rival claims to her throne, plots on her life, the loneliness of her state and the random blows of fate. She returned to London, prepared to enter the diplomatic fray once more.

Mary appeared to be more concerned than Elizabeth over the recent estrangement between them. Characteristically, she was impatient and more inclined to act. In late September she dispatched Melville south, ostensibly to smooth matters over with Elizabeth, but also to meet with the Spanish ambassador and other select sympathizers, as well as secretly to deliver a message to Darnley's mother, Lady Margaret, 'to procure liberty for [Darnley] to go to Scotland'.[28]

Melville's record of the series of meetings he had with the thirty-one-year-old Queen of England in September 1564 is celebrated. Yet, it offers such a fresh and powerful evocation of the character, cunning and wit of this great queen in the making, and also throws into relief the human curiosity and rivalry at the heart of the relationship between Elizabeth and Mary, that its reiteration here is apt. Melville himself was twenty-eight and had been in France for most of the last fourteen years. His experiences had given him an urbane and wide-ranging viewpoint that was stimulating to someone as intellectually demanding as Elizabeth. Now, as envoy on this historic visit, his own perceptions were acute and free from prejudice, although his memoir was composed when his career was over, and with some of the benefit of hindsight.

The queen was at Westminster and early in the morning Melville was escorted there on a horse provided by Lord Robert. Shown into the garden, he came upon Elizabeth walking in a narrow alley between high hedges. She offered her hand to him to kiss and he greeted her in French, apologizing for not yet regaining an easy fluency in his own language. Elizabeth was well prepared for his embassy and produced from her pocket not only the offending letter from Mary, so 'full of despiteful language that she believed all friendship and familiarity to have been given up', but her own angry response which she had only refrained from sending, she said, because she thought it was too gentle and she should write another 'more vehement'.

Melville, shown both letters, confessed himself confused as to how Elizabeth could have so misconstrued Mary's 'loving and frank' missive to her, suggesting that although 'Her Majesty could speak as good French as any who had not been out of the country, that yet she lacked the use of the French court language, which was frank and short', and liable to more than one interpretation. Good friends and familiars could be counted on always to choose the best of possible meanings, he added. Elizabeth seemed to take this slur on her linguistic sophistication in good part. In what appeared to be more an episode of diplomatic shadow-boxing than a sincere expression of outrage appeased, she theatrically tore up both the letters in front of Melville, promising to interpret for the best all future dealings with 'her good sister'.

Melville stayed at court for nine days, in audience with the queen sometimes as many as three times a day. Elizabeth had told him that 'seeing she could not meet with the Queen her good sister to confer with her familiarly, she should open a good part of her inward mind to me, that I might show it again unto the Queen'. Professing great affection for Mary and a 'great desire to see her', a great desire also that she would accept her proposal of Dudley for a husband, Elizabeth took Melville into her bedchamber and out of her desk produced a collection of miniatures wrapped in paper and named in her own handwriting. The first had 'My Lord's picture' written upon its paper wrapping. Holding a candle, Melville leaned forward to look. Elizabeth feigned reluctance, turning it away from him, but he managed to ascertain that it was indeed Lord Robert's picture. When Melville asked that he might have it to carry back to Mary, Elizabeth refused, saying it was the only one she had. Looking across to Lord Robert in conversation with Sir William Cecil at the far side of the room, Melville pointed out that Elizabeth already had the original. 'Then she took out [my] queen's picture, and kissed it; and I kissed her hand, for the great love I saw she bore my mistress. She showed me also a fair ruby, as great as a tennis-ball.' When Melville asked that she send either the picture of Lord Robert or the ruby as a token of goodwill to Mary, Elizabeth answered 'if the Queen would follow her counsel, that she would in process of time get them both, and all she had'.

The following day Elizabeth cross-examined him about his European travels; for a woman steeped in European culture, she would never manage to travel outside the boundaries of her own small country and she liked to converse with educated foreigners and adventurous Englishmen. Elizabeth also asked Melville about the fashions abroad and what kinds of dress best became a gentlewoman. The queen herself paraded the best of her wardrobe, wearing something different every day, representing the styles of France, Italy and England. When he was asked to choose which suited her best she was flattered when he said her Italian outfit, 'for she delighted to show her golden coloured hair, wearing a caul and bonnet as they do in Italy. Her hair was more reddish than yellow, curled in appearance naturally.' There followed the most pointed questioning of how the two queens compared in beauty and accomplishments, judicious answers to which Melville was hard pressed to find: 'Then she entered to discern what colour of hair was reputed best; and whether my Queen's hair or hers was best; and which of them two was fairest . . . I said she was the fairest Queen in England and ours the fairest Queen in Scotland.' Elizabeth, however, was not happy with these discreet evasions and pressed the poor man further. His ingenious reply, 'they were both the fairest ladies of their courts and that Her Majesty was whiter, but our queen was very lovely', seemed to satisfy her.

Then she turned to their respective heights; which was the taller she asked. Melville thought this would not prove problematic and answered truthfully: Mary was. Elizabeth mischievously turned this to her own account: 'Then, saith she, she is too high and that herself was neither too high nor too low.' The comparisons then ranged over the queens' sporting interests and accomplishments. Melville mentioned that as he left the Scottish court to come south Mary had just returned from a hunting expedition in the Highlands, then added, 'when she had leisure from the affairs of her country she read upon good books, the histories of diverse countries, and sometimes would play upon the lute and virginals'. Elizabeth asked if Mary played well: Melville replied, 'reasonably for a Queen'.

This was a gauntlet that could not be allowed to lie. That evening after dinner Melville was taken up to a gallery by one of Elizabeth's nobles, ostensibly to hear some music on the virginals played by an anonymous musician. After listening for a while, he pulled back the tapestry that hung over the door of the chamber to find what he had expected. The queen's back was towards him and he stood watching for a while 'and heard her play excellently well'. The moment Elizabeth caught sight of him she stopped playing and pretended to strike him playfully with her hand, 'alleging that she used not to play before men, but when she was solitary, to shun melancholy'. Then, sitting on a cushion on the floor with Melville kneeling beside her (she insisted he take a cushion for greater comfort which rather touched him), she proceeded to ask whether Mary or she played the virginals better. Melville was relieved to be able to say that Elizabeth was the more accomplished. He was keen to get back to Scotland but she pressed him to stay a further two days, long enough to see her dance. Elizabeth was praised generally for her high-stepping style and the tireless energy she brought to everything she did: when Melville was cross-examined on the dancing abilities of both queens he had become more skilled in his own footwork, 'I answered that [my] Queen danced not so high and disposedly [with measured steps] as she did'.[29]

During this time at Elizabeth's court, Melville had been present when Lord Robert Dudley was ennobled at last as the Earl of Leicester. Elizabeth claimed this was to elevate him to a status more acceptable as a consort for the Queen of Scots, but it was just as likely to be the long-promised reward for the love and support of the man she 'esteemed ... as her brother and best friend'.[30] This was an occasion of historic pageantry, symbolism and solemnity. Melville noticed that as Dudley knelt before the queen, 'keeping a great gravity and discreet behaviour', she helped put on his ceremonial garb and then 'could not refrain from putting her hand in his neck to tickle him smilingly'.

Was this a gesture that showed she was unable to resist him, or was it more to show that, whatever might happen, he belonged to her and as his monarch she could do with him as she wished? Either way it was a remarkably intimate gesture on such an august occasion, and one which surprised Melville, performed as it was in clear sight of himself and the French ambassador. Thinking of her cousin and the current debate over her marriage, Elizabeth then turned to Mary's envoy and asked him how he liked the new earl. Melville was carefully noncommital in his reply and Elizabeth, artful as ever and probably aware of the covert communications between Mary and the Countess of Lennox, pointed to the languid youth who was holding the ceremonial sword before her: 'Yet', she said, 'you like better of yonder long lad.'[31] Lord Darnley, as nearest prince of the blood, favoured with ceremonial duties such as this, was prominent at court at the time while his parents and Mary were making overtures to obtain his passport to Scotland. Melville's answer to Elizabeth was possibly coloured by discretion, if not by hindsight: 'no woman of spirit would make choice of such a man, that was more like a woman than a man; for he was very lusty [pleasing], beardless and lady-faced'.[32]

On his return to Scotland, Melville was questioned just as penetratingly by his own queen on the condition of Elizabeth's heart towards her. Mary professed herself delighted that the two queens' friendship was restored, not just for sentimental reasons but because an easy dialogue between both countries allowed her 'access to get intelligence from a great number of noblemen and others her friends and factioners in England'. This implied that Mary even at this early stage in her relationship with Elizabeth was hopeful, if not active, in attempting to build a clandestine faction of support for her interests, under the English queen's nose. When she asked of Melville whether Elizabeth's inner feelings for her matched her fine words of affection, he replied: 'in my judgement there was neither plain dealing nor upright meaning, but great dissimulation, emulation, and fear that [Mary's] princely qualities should over soon chase her out and displace her from the kingdom'.[33]

By August 1564, the Earl of Lennox finally had his licence to travel to Scotland, twenty years after he had left. At first, however, Elizabeth would not allow his family to follow. Her acceptance of the Lennoxes' return to Scottish affairs appeared to embody on her part both political manoeuvring and inducement, with young Darnley as bait. Cecil and Robert Dudley, Earl of Leicester, were more unequivocal. In fact it was likely that Cecil authorized financing the cost of Lennox's re-establishment. But it was a risky move, for an alliance with Darnley offered to Mary a further strengthening of her own substantial claim on the English throne. Melville believed that Elizabeth had suddenly become concerned that Mary was considering her proposal of Leicester more seriously, and as she never intended to relinquish her favourite she hoped that reinstating Lord Darnley's family fortunes and introducing him as a more attractive suitor might temporarily deflect the Queen of Scots. Perhaps the English intent was to destabilize the political alliances north of the border. Certainly there were many who were made uneasy at the re-emergence of Lennox power, not least the Duke of Châtelherault, head of the Hamiltons, ancestral foes of the Lennoxes, who feared 'the overthrow of hys house, if the Lord Darlie marrye the Quene'.[34] Many of the other Protestant lords feared such a major shift in tribal power and strengthening of the Catholic party. Whatever the spur, as was often Elizabeth's way, almost as soon as she had given permission she regretted her move.

The most extreme and outspoken among the opposition was John Knox, always canny and unconciliatory in his approach. 'It is whispered to me', he had written to Randolph in May, 'that licence [for the Lady (Lennox) and the young Erle] is allready procured for thare hitther-cuming. Goddis providence is inscrutable to man . . . But to be plaine with you, that jorney and progress I lyke not.'[35] Moray had at first mooted the marriage between Lord Darnley and Mary as early as February 1564 and later actively lobbied for Lennox's return, but very soon political acumen and self-interest had him rue the day that father and son set foot on Scottish soil.

Events seemed to move forward with an inexorable force. By November the new Spanish ambassador to Elizabeth's court, Guzman de Silva (sent to replace Bishop Quadra who had died, possibly of the plague), reported to Philip II that the Lennox estates in Scotland had been restored and the earl wished his son, Lord Darnley, might be allowed to join him to be introduced at last to his inheritance. Elizabeth issued a licence, this time for Darnley, but again immediately revoked it, with the excuse that Lady Margaret had been less than straightforward in her dealings. She was persuaded to reinstate it but the passport was still not forthcoming. 'This is the way with everything – absolutely no certainty',[36] the new ambassador commented on what he was learning to be the leitmotif of Elizabeth's negotiating tactics; procrastination, disguise, equivocation, then sudden disconcerting audacity. If Elizabeth was more a Greek, then Cecil was a Roman and the same ambassador was thankful for the relief of Cecil's straight road: '[He is] truthful, lucid, modest and just, and, although he is zealous in serving his Queen, which is one of his best traits, yet he is amenable to reason ... With regard to his religion I say nothing except that I wish he were a Catholic, but to his credit must be placed the fact that he is straightforward in affairs.'[37]

Elizabeth had insisted that only if Mary chose an approved suitor from the nobility of England or her own country would she remain friends and name her as her successor. Mary and her advisers, however, had been exasperated for months by Elizabeth's evasiveness about an acceptable consort. Only Lord Robert, now Earl of Leicester, had been formally suggested and no alternatives had been openly admitted. In fact, in a list of negotiating instructions for the Earl of Bedford and Randolph, written in Cecil's hand, there was the startling suggestion that Elizabeth was willing to have Mary and Leicester come and live with her, and to shoulder the household expenses, should Mary accept Leicester as a husband: 'if the Queen her sister pleased to be "conversant with" and live with her "in household" she will gladly bear the charges of the "famyly" both of the Earl of Leicester "and hir, as shall be mete for on sister to doo for another" '.[38] With Mary so completely in her control, this suggested that Elizabeth would have dominion implicitly over both kingdoms. But Mary was a spirited and proud woman and such a scheme, even if it was seriously mooted by Elizabeth and Cecil, even if it assured her the inheritance of the English throne, was a lost cause. If the suggestion showed anything, apart from the English queen's mischievous sense of humour, it revealed how loath Elizabeth was to lose Leicester, her 'Robin', from her side.

In the deep cold of December, Elizabeth acceded to Mary's

requests for some action on the matters of her marriage and the English succession. She sent the Earl of Bedford on the long ride north to Berwick to meet Randolph, together with Mary's half-brother Moray and her chief minister Maitland of Lethington, with the express purpose of discussing the English queen's wishes on the Scottish queen's marriage. It is likely that in his pocket were these instructions, neatly written out in Cecil's orderly hand.

The central proposal made by Elizabeth to Mary was 'that she should choose between the following three Englishmen: the Earl of Leicester, the Duke of Norfolk and the son of Lady Margaret Lennox, and in the event of her marrying *either* of them [an interesting slip] she will declare her heiress to the crown'. Mary apparently was willing 'to marry an Englishman if the succession was declared, but not the Earl of Leicester although she said nothing of the other two'.[39] Perhaps she had already turned her mind to Darnley. According to the Spanish ambassador, Mary had written recently to Elizabeth asking the English queen's permission for him to travel to Scotland.

Christmas and the new year of 1565 were marked by unnaturally bitter winter weather. The Thames in London was frozen fast 'and people walk upon it as they do the streets',[40] and in Scotland a 'great storm of snow and wind, as the like many years has not been seen',[41] had sent Mary to her bed, not through sickness but to ward off the worst of the cold. In fact, everyone at her court was ill at some time during that severe winter but Mary alone escaped and remained in the best of health and spirits, 'never merrier nor lustiar!'[42] On the contrary, Elizabeth herself was unwell, suffering from catarrh and extreme headaches. Cecil was seized once more with worry: an ill queen, no clear succession; it was a grim season indeed. The doctors pronounced her constitution weak, which the Spanish ambassador was pleased to relate to Philip II, adding that, with the widespread predictions of her short life, she was not expected to live much longer.

This news had reached Mary in her snowy fastness. Her true feelings were not so well dissembled beneath the fulsome declarations: 'I wysshe [her full recovery] for . . . she is everie daye more dere to me than other, and I am assured that her lyf, and that compagnie that I truste to have with her, shalbe more worthe to me, then her whole kingedome with her deathe, yf she were dysposed to leave yt me.'[43] Not surprisingly Elizabeth discerned through the blandishments something more sinister: she declared that Mary 'doth looke for her death, and that all thys kyndenes is pretended onely to hunt a kyngdome!'[44]

The deep freeze then turned to sudden thaw and the southern part of the country was in flood. In the midst of this extreme weather Lord Darnley began his precipitate ride north to rejoin his father. There was a sense of expectation. His father had been spending money lavishly, refurbishing the ancestral pile, entertaining influential lords and giving expensive gifts to Mary, Lethington and each of the Four Maries, amongst others, 'thus to win all their hearts'.[45] Randolph estimated that in just a month Lennox already had run through most of the £700 he had brought with him. The longer he stayed, the more he bragged (he was heard to say to the Lord of the Session, in hearing of the Earl of Atholl, that his son would marry the queen), the more anxious certain factions grew.

Randolph, who had favoured Leicester's suit and did not believe Darnley would prevail, told Cecil in mid-December 'more was thought of Darnley before his father's coming than at present. The father is now here well known; the mother more feared than beloved of any that know her.'[46] The talk went that Darnley's mother might gain as influential a hold on the Scottish queen as she had on Mary I and '[send] home as greate a plague [of Catholicism] unto this countrie'.[47] Randolph wrote to Cecil that there was general unrest and some foreboding with stories of unruly bands of armed men on the loose in Edinburgh at night, 'fighting one with the other. The strokes they say are heard, the clamours of men great . . .'[48]

Into this rumour mill, this court of intrigues, shifting rivalries and brazen ambition, Henry Stuart, Lord Darnley, arrived in the middle of February, travel-weary and nursing a cold. At first his graceful manners and good looks meant he was well received. Although some were doubtful as to his true nature and others concerned by the possible outcome of his coming, they generally considered him 'a fayer yollye yonge man'.[49] Everyone trod carefully: this presentable youth might be just another noble scion, or alternatively he might become their king whom those with aspirations needed to placate. Darnley had ridden north at such speed he had turned up sooner than expected and remained in Edinburgh for three days, introducing himself to his fellow lords and awaiting advice from his father. The queen's court had removed from Edinburgh across the Firth of Forth to Fife. Lennox sent word to his son advising him to visit Mary first and only then come on to see him at Glasgow. Darnley's horses had yet to arrive and so he borrowed two from Randolph before setting off for Wemyss Castle.

The first meeting on Scottish soil of Mary and Lord Darnley was watched from all quarters with beady eyes. It was Saturday, 17 February 1565, and the ambassadors were agog, their dispatches winging their way between Edinburgh and London, and out to the courts of Spain and France where the news that Darnley had reached Scotland 'had wonderfully awakened' the French court and inspired the general belief that 'the Scottish Queen shall marry him'.[50] Randolph reported back to Cecil and Elizabeth, 'The young lord was "welcomed and honourably used ... [and] lodged in the same house where [Mary] was"'.[51] Darnley returned from his father's in time to accompany the queen on her return over the Queen's Ferry to Edinburgh. In an attempt to calm Protestant disquiet the following Monday he attended Knox's sermon in the company of the Earl of Moray. In the evening he danced a galliard with Mary who surprised Randolph with how radiantly healthy she appeared, although she had just endured a journey through atrocious cold and blizzards: 'come home lustiar then she wente fourthe'.[52]

Mary's renewed energy and ebullience continued and a few days later when she heard that Moray had organized a great dinner with Darnley, his father, Lennox, Randolph and 'most of the noblemen in town and the ladies of the court', she sent her messenger to say she wished to be present too and was sorry not to be invited. This impulsive informality from the queen caused much delighted surprise: 'It was merrily answered, the house was her own, she might come undesired; others said they were merriest when the table was fullest, but princes ever used to dine alone.' They all ended up in robust discourse with the Queen of Scots, asking her to defend her position on the Mass, and cross-examining her about her marriage plans. She was in the best of moods and full of goodwill towards 'her good systar' Elizabeth, commending her government, her judicial mercy towards offenders and her refusal to follow her forbears 'in shedding blood'.[53] Mary had enjoyed herself so much she summoned them all to another banquet the following Sunday.

Randolph who had long promoted the match with Lord Robert, now Earl of Leicester, found it hard to accept that there was any immediate attraction between the Queen of Scots and this handsome youth who had arrived in their midst. He was not a subtle man and was confused by his own government's motives and how he was meant to act. He knew that Lennox was being funded by Cecil, and in fact had written to point out to his government that at the earl's current rate of expenditure, 'he must shortly be supported with more money, or shall find lack in what he has to do'.[54]

Soon after Darnley's arrival there were mutterings among the lords expressing already their anxiety and disapproval of how affairs between him and the Queen of Scots were progressing. The Earl of Argyll was plain spoken – he disliked this youth's homecoming and feared for the future, but after all, he pointed out, women's affections were notoriously fickle. Almost to reassure himself Randolph wrote to Cecil: 'For myself, I see no great goodwill borne to [Darnley]. Of her grace's good usage and often talk with him, her countenance and good visage, I think it proceeds rather of her own courteous nature, than anything is meant which some here fear may insue.'[55]

Melville, however, recalled that Mary from that first meeting at Wemyss had liked what she saw, being particularly struck by Darnley's remarkable height and fine physique. She was twenty-two and in the prime of life, her prodigious energies and appetites restored to her. Her patience with the dilatory and confusing directives on her marriage, issued over the preceding years by ·Elizabeth, had been stretched to the limit. Absent princes and distant promises could not compete with the real presence of a young man of flesh, blood and ambition. The young Scottish queen was lonely, in need of companionship, adventure, and ready for love. She also believed that a suitable marriage would strengthen her position at home and abroad. Mary was not a queen prepared to remain ruling alone.

Although Elizabeth could not have known that the dramatis personae were being assembled for the enactment of a tragedy, from her ambassadors' reports she monitored the growing unease surrounding Mary. News travelled so fast between the two courts that, as Randolph related, 'We lack no news, for what is most secret among you, is sooner at this Queen's ears, that some would think it should be out of the privy chamber door where you are!'[56] To Cecil he likened the posts and packets that flew back and forth almost daily as being like fowls in the air. He disapproved of the resultant gossip. While Mary waited increasingly impatiently for her cousin's response to her marriage plans, news of Elizabeth and Leicester's latest indiscretions entertained the Scottish and European courts.

One such incident had the new earl and the much longer established Duke of Norfolk playing tennis in front of Elizabeth. Leicester, 'beinge verie hotte and swetinge, tooke the quenes napken owte of her hande and wyped hys face'. This was an action which implied great intimacy between Elizabeth and her favourite; it was also highly disrespectful. The Duke of Norfolk, who had never liked Leicester, called him saucy and threatened to hit him across the face with his racquet. Such brawling in front of the queen was contrary to all the laws of etiquette, but instead of admonishing both, Elizabeth took Leicester's part and was 'offended sore with the Duke'.[57] Such stories, keenly embellished in rival courts, kept alive the years of speculation that Leicester was Elizabeth's true love. They made her offer of him in marriage to Mary seem all the emptier, and his evident lack of interest in the Scottish queen all the more insulting.

Elizabeth's prevarication in negotiations was difficult enough for anyone wishing to expedite matters, but for an impatient, impulsive woman like Mary, whose temperament was fiery, headstrong and unused to any check, the frustration was insupportable. Through her consuming desire to be recognized as the heir to the English throne, Mary had enslaved herself to Elizabeth's power, pulled one way and then the other, rocked by whatever policy or whim her cousin might advise. Temperamentally, Mary was ill-equipped to cope with inactivity and stasis. As long as she had freedom and will, then action – however wrongheaded – became inevitable. In her early twenties, with power in her own hands at last, the emotional polarities in her nature were beginning to be more marked. The episodes of illness and 'melancholies' to which she was subject speedily transformed into a state of high energy and remarkable physical strength, expressed with robust courage and recklessness. At times it seemed that action and madness were closely allied in Mary's experience: denied action she was susceptible to depression, but in her wildest, most wilful periods the action she embarked on too often appeared close to madness.

Nowhere was this more evident than in her precipitate relationship with Darnley. Propelled by Elizabeth's licence to travel, he had arrived in Scotland to a guarded welcome from his fellow nobles. Within weeks whatever goodwill had been extended to him was fast leaking away. According to Randolph, his father had done him few favours with his swaggering manner and aggrandizing claims of his son's chances with the Queen of Scots. Darnley's own behaviour, however, quickly alienated whatever support remained. He was young, spoilt and 'not well acquainted with the nature of this nation'.[58] Unable to hold his drink and not very bright, this boy who was barely out of his teens surprised even the combative Scottish nobles with his loutish ways and ill-judged comments. Shown the extent of the Earl of Moray's lands on a map, he told Moray's brother that he thought they were 'too much', implying he would do some judicious pruning once he was king. His uncontrolled temper earned him an ugly reputation: while ill in bed he threatened the august Duke of Châtelherault that he would 'knock his pate';[59]

he hit people who could not return his blows and gained a reputation for being quick to pull a knife on anyone who displeased
him.

As her nobles turned away from Darnley, Mary appeared all the
more set on favouring him. Elizabeth was alarmed at how events
north of the border were fast slipping from her control. Mary's
abandonment of diplomacy was a direct result of the English
queen's blocking of all her marriage choices. The last straw had
been the message via Randolph on 15 March. In this Elizabeth had
declared that even if Mary chose to marry Leicester, still England's
preferred candidate, she would not commit herself to naming a
successor until she herself had decided to marry – or not. And
this she was still deliberating. Mary's anger and frustration at her
powerlessness to effect anything when dealing with the shifting
sands of Elizabeth's diplomacy found its characteristic outlet in a
paroxysm of tears.

In fact, Elizabeth had allowed her own marriage negotiations to
be reopened with the envoys of the Archduke Charles, son of the
Emperor Ferdinand. The Earl of Sussex had suggested that Mary's
imminent marriage plans would put Elizabeth under renewed pressure to marry and produce an heir. Elizabeth once more entered
the diplomatic dance, professing to be ready to marry for duty. She
could not hide her personal antipathy, however, explaining that if
ever she were to be induced to marry it would be as Queen of
England not as Elizabeth. When one of the imperial ambassadors
referred to marriage as a desirable evil, she had laughingly enquired
'Desirable?'[60] To the same ambassador she had declared: 'If I am
to disclose to you what I would prefer if I follow the inclination
of my nature, I will tell you. It is this: Beggarwoman and single,
far rather than Queen and married.'[61] The whole marriage debate
was continually rehearsed in her mind, and in conversations with
her own councillors and every foreign dignitary who paid their
respects to her at court, none of whom ever let the matter rest. To
the new Spanish ambassador, Guzman de Silva, Elizabeth elaborated
on her thoughts and revealed a radicalism more at home in feminist
thought four centuries later:

[Marriage] is a thing for which I have never had any inclination. My subjects, however, press me so that I cannot help myself, but must marry or take the other course, which is a very difficult one. There is a strong idea in the world that a woman cannot live unless she is married, or at all events that if she refrains from marriage she does so for some bad reason, as they said of me that I did not marry because I was fond of the Earl of Leicester, and that I would not marry him because he had a wife already. Although he has no wife alive now, I still do not marry him ... We cannot cover everybody's mouth, but must content ourselves with doing our duty and trust in God, for the truth will at last be made manifest. He knows my heart, which is very different from what people think, as you will see some day.[62]

Elizabeth continued to choose the much more difficult path, which meant she was pressured all her life to fulfil her destiny as a woman and her duty as a queen. However, in a conversation with Adam Zwetkovich, envoy of the Emperor Maximilian, concerning the projected marriage between herself and the Archduke Charles, a chink of light was cast on her insistence that there was nothing more to her lifelong celibacy than natural inclination. She had enquired about the rumour that the late emperor had loved his wife very much 'and therefore hoped that the same could be expected of his son [Charles]'. When Zwetkovich swore on his heart that the son had inherited all the virtues of his father and 'would hold his wedded consort dear all his life long', Elizabeth was apparently delighted and related a conversation with one of her ladies of the bedchamber who had assured her 'that even if her husband were not handsome, she, the Queen, should be content, if he but loved her and was kind to her'.[63]

In Elizabeth's closest family circle examples of conjugal happiness and a husband's loyalty were singularly lacking. She was the product of her father's grotesque fickleness of feeling and a bystander at his ruthless disposal of unloved queens. She had seen at close hand the pathos of her sister's passion for her consort Philip II, a love not only not reciprocated but publicly spurned. Then Elizabeth's fond

stepmother Catherine Parr had endured her husband Thomas Seymour's dangerous flirtation with Elizabeth herself with painful and
fatal consequences. Closer to home, her own beloved Leicester had
shown much greater care of her, his mistress, than of his poor,
neglected wife, who eventually, like the other wives of Elizabeth's
most intimate acquaintance, had died a lonely and premature death.
No wonder she laughed at the suggestion that marriage was an evil
which was 'desirable'.

Her discussion with Zwetkovich was also interesting in belying
the accepted view that dynastic marriages were always purely political with little expectation of personal attraction or affection. Elizabeth showed that emotion was very much a part of her reasoning
in the matter – even if only just another excuse to prevaricate. Mary
too brought emotion very much to the marriage choices she made
in her maturity: indeed it could be argued that she would have
made much better alliances, maintained her throne – and been
happier – if there had been more politics and less passion in her
preferences.

Elizabeth may not have desired a princely, or indeed any, suitor,
but she had an emphatic sense of her own majesty and a natural
competitiveness with Mary. In the preliminary marital negotiations
over the Archduke Charles she mentioned to his envoy how surprised she was to hear that Charles had made an offer previously
to Mary, 'this [Elizabeth] took to mean that if the Queen of Scotland
did not wish to have the Archduke, she, the Queen of England, was
to be the jester to the Queen of Scotland'.* When Zwetkovich
replied that he had heard the French ambassador praise Mary,
'saying that she was very beautiful, and the heir to the throne of
England and therefore worthy of such a Prince as the Archduke',
Elizabeth was quick to remind him, 'that she was superior to the

---

* In the same lengthy dispatch, Zwetkovich later cited Elizabeth's own jester's bold précis
of the alternative merits of her current suitors: 'She should not take the King of France,
for he was but a boy and babe; but she should take the Archduke Charles and then he
was sure she would have a baby-boy.' Elizabeth had translated this into Italian for
Zwetkovich, and when he had replied that babes and fools speak the truth the queen
just laughed. The name of Elizabeth's famous court fool was Robert Grene: there was
no evidence that this was he.

TOP James V of Scotland and Mary of Guise.

ABOVE Catherine de Medici, by François Clouet.

RIGHT François, 2nd Duc de Guise, nicknamed 'le Balafré' ('scarface'), uncle of Mary, by François Clouet.

OVERLEAF LEFT Mary, *c.* 1560–65. Artist unknown.

RIGHT Elizabeth, *c.* 1560. Artist unknown.

LEFT Elizabeth, the 'Sieve Portrait', *c.* 1570, by Quentin Massys the Younger.

RIGHT Mary, after the Nicholas Hilliard miniature of 1578.

LEFT Robert Dudley, Earl of Leicester, Elizabeth's lifelong favourite, c. 1560–65, attributed to Steven van der Meulen.

ABOVE William Cecil, Lord Burghley, c. 1560–70, by or after Arnold von Bronckorst.

RIGHT Sir Francis Walsingham, c. 1587, possibly after John de Critz the Elder.

ES BE THE SONES OF TH RIGHT HONERABLES TERLLE OF LENOX
LADY MARGARETZ GRACE COVNTYES OF LENOXE AD AN GW

1563

HARLLES STEWARDE
S BROTHER. ÆTATIS. 6.

HENRY STEWARDE LORD
LEY AND DOWGLAS, ÆTAT

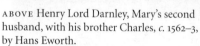

ABOVE Henry Lord Darnley, Mary's second
husband, with his brother Charles, c. 1562–3,
by Hans Eworth.

ABOVE RIGHT James I and VI, Mary and Darnley's
son as a child, c. 1580, by Arnold von Bronckorst.

CENTRE RIGHT James Hepburn, 4th Earl of
Bothwell, Mary's third husband. Artist unknown.

RIGHT David Riccio, Mary's secretary. Artist
unknown.

Queen of Scotland'.[64] She might demand impossible conditions of a suitor, she might reject him outright, but she did not want her inveterate reluctance to mean she was passed over in favour of her cousin, nor did she welcome any intimation that she was inferior to her as queen, woman or bride.

Mary herself had a wilful and irresistible nature but she was entirely conformable to her church and society in her attitudes to marriage. She had never seriously questioned the desirability of the state, even for a regnant queen whose power, ordained by God, resided in her hands alone. She had been traded in marriage when barely out of babyhood and been bred to consider it the pinnacle of her achievement. Unlike Elizabeth, Mary's own personal experiences from childhood had been more benign, her first husband expressed real devotion to her and her father-in-law, Henri II, the closest husband-figure in her formative years, had shown affection and respect to both Catherine and Diane de Poitiers. For Mary, celibacy held no practical or emotional appeal: marriage was a central ambition to help attain every other ambition in her life. It was her only option and she embraced it with fervour.

As summer approached, Lord Darnley was firmly in the Queen of Scots' sights. She had waited long enough for her first experience of a true marriage. Her blood was up and an attractive young suitor was at hand. Darnley's pedigree was suitable enough. He was tall and elegant, he looked the part of a prince, and for a time at least she found him sexually irresistible. A fortuitous bout of measles* gave Mary the opportunity of attending his sickbed and entertaining him in his recuperation. In the close intimacy of his chamber, where illness temporarily disarmed his braggardly nature, Mary found her initial attraction become a simulacrum of love. Randolph reported, '[The queen's] care has been marvellous great and tender over him. Such tales and bruits of her spread abroad, that it is wonder to hear the discontent of her people.'[65]

Stories of this unseemly familiarity between them flew around the courts of Europe. News of their marriage was expected at any

---

* Given Darnley's reputed sexual dissipation, there was a possibility that the rash was a symptom not of measles but of syphilis.

time, indeed most ambassadors reported that the marriage had already been solemnized secretly. To general consternation, the Earl of Moray had left the court, some said banished, others said wilfully and in disgust at the queen's marriage plans and her dereliction of responsibility and duty. He only returned on 1 May to make his presence felt at the trial of Bothwell for treason: the border lord failed to turn up. In the absence of Moray and the eclipse of Lethington, Mary's secretary, the Italian Riccio, became even more obviously influential as her adviser. He was Darnley's leading champion. Suddenly the fact that he, the queen and the Lennox family, if not Darnley himself, were all prominent Catholics took on sinister significance. Fear, suspicion and confusion fuelled rumours that Mary would be encouraged to attempt nothing less than the restoration of Catholicism. The Protestant lords in Scotland, and Elizabeth and the English court, were concerned at the thought that Spain was stirring again and could seek some alliance with Scotland. There was even talk that the English Catholics might be energized into rebellion.

Randolph was in despair at how much his hopes for friendship between Elizabeth and Mary, and their countries were thrown into disarray, how threatening the situation was likely to become: from Edinburgh he wrote to Cecil, 'Such discontent, large talk, and open speech I never heard in any nation, and for myself see not but it must burst out in great mischief – for [Mary] is suspected of many of her nobles, and her people discontented for her religion, this match a-making without advice, and other as evil things they suspect, besides her unprincely behaviour in many of her doings . . . The speech of this marriage to any of them, is so contrary to their minds, that they think their nation dishonoured, the Queen shamed, and country undone . . . She is now in utter contempt of her people, and so far in doubt of them herself, that without speedy redress, "worce is to be feared".'[66]

Not least of Randolph's worries was the angry talk amongst the disaffected nobles that Elizabeth had masterminded the whole sorry state of Scottish affairs by allowing Lennox and his son Darnley to return: 'I would that her majesty [Elizabeth] were void of the suspicion that is here spoken to my face, that the sending him home was done of purpose to match the Queen meanly and poorly, rather than live long in amity.'[67] In fact the picture he painted of the breakdown of the recent and fragile civilities north of the border went some way to explaining the volatile emotions which dominated Scottish political life in the ensuing years: '[The master of] Maxwell . . . wiser than many, laments the state of his country and is ashamed of it. The country is broken – daily slaughter between Scotts and Elliots* – stealing on all hands – justice no where . . . such pride, excess in vanities, proud looks and dispiteful words, and so poor a purse I never heard of . . . [Lennox's] men are bolder and saucier with the Queen's self and many noble men, than I ever thought could have been borne; divers resort to the mass, and glory in their doings.'[68]

The mob expressed their antagonism by capturing a priest who was saying Mass on Palm Sunday and tying him, still in his vestments, to the market cross in Edinburgh, there he was pelted with eggs 'and filth of the street' so ferociously that it was thought he was killed. Mary was so incensed that she precipitately called all the men 'of Fife, Lothian, Tividale, and Liddesdale, to rise to revenge his death' then finding he had survived countermanded her hasty directive and sent the men home.[69]

In the grip of the *coup de foudre* that had befallen her in the intimacy of the young lord's sickroom, Mary had determined to marry Darnley in the teeth of all opposition. She sent Lethington to Elizabeth to ask her approval. Predictably Elizabeth was furious. She called in the more wily and diplomatic Sir Nicholas Throckmorton to take over from a demoralized Randolph the urgent dealings aimed at steering Mary away from the match with Darnley. Lethington and he became frequent travellers on the weary road

---

* The Scotts and Elliots were two of the border clans, or 'border reivers [robbers]' as they were called, who conducted fierce and bloody feuds among themselves, cattle rustling, pillaging and burning homesteads and crops. At this time each of these clans was largely a law unto itself, contemptuous of the jurisdiction of the kingdoms on either side of them. In 1565 there was a particularly violent confrontation when Scot of Buccleuch executed four Elliots for cattle rustling – barely a crime in those parts, more a way of life. Vengeance was swift and bloody.

between Edinburgh and London. On 11 May they met at Berwick, Lethington disobeying Mary's orders to return to Elizabeth with the defiant message that 'she minded . . . to use her own choice in marriage; she would no longer be fed with yea and nay, and to depend upon uncertain dealings'. The careful, judicious Lethington who, with Moray, supported the English alliance, was incandescent with rage at Mary's foolhardiness. This was so out of character that Throckmorton wrote to Leicester and Cecil that he 'would have little believed that for any matter [Lethington] could have been so moved'.[70]

Lethington's anger was not the most remarkable transformation that summer. The ambassadors' reports from the Scottish court were striking in their puzzlement and concern at the change wrought in Mary's character and behaviour. Even her looks seemed altered. Randolph had got to know Mary well and, although Elizabeth's agent, he admired the Scottish queen, being more than a little touched by her person and caring for her wellbeing. What he saw of this match filled him with doom: 'this Queen in her love is so transported, and Darnley grown so proud, that to all honest men he is intolerable, and almost forgetful of his duty to her already who had adventured so much for his sake'.[71] He had been shocked to see Darnley use his dagger to threaten Mary's justice clerk who brought him the unwelcome news that one of the honours promised him by the queen would be delayed.

By early June, Randolph was filled with a genuine pity for Mary's plight, a plight to which she seemed oblivious: 'In this Queen's mind', he wrote sorrowfully to Leicester, 'can no alteration be perceived, but as great tokens of love as ever before, which in her has wrought such strange effects that shame is laid aside, and all regard of that which chiefly pertains to princely honour removed out of sight.' Perhaps Mary's besotted behaviour towards Darnley shared a similarity with Elizabeth's own amorousness with Lord Robert, Earl of Leicester, which had caused so much embarrassment and outrage at the time. However, Randolph went on to describe a transformation more extreme and ill-favoured than anything of which Elizabeth was ever accused: 'This Queen is so much altered from what she was that who beholds does not think her the same. Her majesty is laid aside; her wits not what they were; her beauty another than it was; her cheer and countenance changed into he wots not what. A woman more to be pitied than any other that he ever saw. Such one now as neither her own regards, nor she takes count of any that are virtuous or good.' He stressed how much it pained him to write this of a queen he had come to esteem so highly, but he assured Leicester there were many witnesses to the sad facts he was relating.

Where modern interpretations might identify some kind of breakdown or mental illness in Mary, in an age where the supernatural coexisted with the everyday, and witches and spirits were interwoven with reality, Randolph thought only an occult reason could explain the dramatic alteration in the behaviour of the Queen of Scots: 'The saying is that she is bewitched, the parties named to be the doers; the tokens, the rings, the bracelets, are found and daily worn that contain the sacred mysteries.'[72] The parties named would probably have included the Lord Ruthven who was reputed to use witchcraft; Riccio, as a papist and an Italian, was also suspected in these matters.

Bewitched, in the grip of sexual desire, or suffering the manic stage of mental illness, Mary was certainly hell-bent on marrying Darnley, and the sooner the better. In this state she appeared to her contemporaries peculiarly immune to any kind of objectivity, or the apprehension even of reason. She ignored the dismay of her Guise relations. She did not falter in the face of heavyweight threats from her cousin Elizabeth, and dismissing the opposition of her nobles, she sought no permission from her own Estates. She did not even wait for dispensation from the pope. On 15 May 1565 Darnley rose from his sickbed. Mary made him Lord of Ardmanoch and then Earl of Ross. He was later to be awarded the dukedom of Albany, an honour exclusively retained for the Scottish royal family. Permitted to create fourteen new knights, Darnley with Mary attempted to secure a loyal party around themselves, many of the queen's old supporters having melted away.

In delivering Elizabeth's sharp message of rebuke, Throckmorton recognized that Mary was so committed to her marriage to Darnley that she was impervious to 'perswacion or reasonable meanes'. Much as Randolph also had intimated in his despairing dispatches, he reported back to Elizabeth that the only remedy that remained was 'vyolence': whether this was invasion, war, abduction or assassination of the prospective bridegroom was not committed to paper. He determined to discuss the possibilities when he returned. Mary nevertheless made one concession to her cousin by promising not to finalize her marriage for a minimum of three months (to the middle of August). Throckmorton, so admiring of the young Queen of Scots when he had been ambassador to France was bemused and sorrowful at the change in her. He warned Elizabeth: 'Yet I find her so captyved eyther by love or connying (or rather to saye truelie by bostinge or follie) that she is not hable to keape promesse with her self, and therfore not most hable to keape promess with your majestie in theis matters [Yet I find her so captive either by love or cunning (or more truthfully boasting or folly) that she is not able to keep a promise with herself let alone with your majesty in these matters].'[73]

Cecil drew up one of his judicious memoranda itemizing the threats of the marriage to Elizabeth, and projected courses of action, as discussed by the Privy Council at the beginning of June. Darnley's claim to the English throne was seen to reinforce Mary's own, therefore it was suggested Lady Catherine Grey (recognized by Mary as her main rival) should be shown greater favour. The lords sought to neutralize the threat to the Protestant religion and encouragement of the Catholics both in Scotland and England with the rather forlorn hope of Elizabeth's speedy marriage, 'and thus confirm the hearts of her subjects'.[74] The Countess of Lennox too was to be isolated from communicating with Catholic sympathizers at home and abroad, and her son and husband recalled from Scotland on threat of their English estates being forfeit.

In the face of so much opposition, Mary looked with some urgency to Spain. For once, Philip II responded swiftly and decisively. To his ambassador Guzman he wrote, 'the marriage is one that is favourable to our interests and should be forwarded and supported to the full extent of our power'. He was keen that the Catholic party in England should be notified of his wholehearted approval and given every encouragement. 'You will make Lady Margaret [Lennox] understand', he added, 'that not only shall I be glad for her son to be king of Scotland and will help him thereto, but also to be king of England if this marriage is carried through.'[75] This unqualified support for her choice of Darnley as husband and the implicit threat against Elizabeth delighted Mary and gave her heart. She was to need it, for within days she received an icy blast from Elizabeth: 'For divers good causes we have expressly commanded the Earl of Lennox and his eldest son Henry Lord Darnley, as our subjects, to return hither without delay: and we require you to give them your safe conduct for their speedier coming.'[76]

Elizabeth was enraged and alarmed by the news she received daily as to the activities north of the border. Moray's alienation from Mary grew while her Protestant lords became more agitated at supposed threats to the newly established religion and their own lives and lands. Some 'factious lords', Moray and Châtelherault chief among them, appealed to Elizabeth for English intervention. There was wildfire talk of conspiracies and counterconspiracies: one between Darnley and his followers to assassinate Moray; another claiming that Moray and certain disaffected Protestant lords had intended to ambush the Queen of Scots and Darnley on a projected ride from Perth to Callender House near Falkirk, due for 1 July. Debate about the likelihood or not of this wild plan washed back and forth. As Melville understood it the objective of the assault was to bundle Darnley over the border into England and Elizabeth's custody, while Mary he thought 'was in danger either of keeping [being confined] or heart-breaking'.[77] Whatever the real truth, it was clear that feelings were so inflammable at the time that something made Mary and Darnley suddenly fear for their lives and set off on a panic-fuelled ride cross-country on that first day of July. They arrived safely, having failed to find any hostile lords on the way, but it was an odd incident which indicated the level of tension and fear which made everyone suspicious and probable rumour real.

Foreign ambassadors to Elizabeth's court recognized that she avoided speaking of Mary's marriage plans and that when the subject was forced on her they risked an irritable explosion of temper. She did not like to see her control on Scottish affairs slipping. She feared the shift of power between Protestant and Catholic interests within both realms and the increased influence this marriage gave the Catholic powers abroad. But there were those, like the French agent Mauvissière, who thought that Mary's marriage 'was not so evil taken [in England] by Her Majesty and her Council as [Throckmorton] has shown in his negotiations'.[78] Elizabeth's antagonism, he figured, was just another of her crafty political feints, for it had seemed that initially at least she had manoeuvred for the very action which now she deplored. If she had not actively stage-managed the Darnley marriage, then Melville laid covert responsibility for it at Elizabeth's door: '[the] courtly dealing, shifting and drifting, by staying the Queen so far as they might from marrying with any man, far or near, great or small, caused the Queen to haste forward her marriage with my Lord Darnley'.[79]

There was no doubt that Mary's marriage to Darnley heartened Catholic interests at home and abroad, but more significant advantage would have been gained – and greater dismay caused to Elizabeth and the Protestants – if instead Mary had allied herself to a prince of Spain, Austria or France. It was perhaps more likely that Elizabeth's disaffection was genuine, owing more to Mary having sidestepped the delaying tactics and proceeded with her marriage without deferring to her cousin's wishes. The Scottish queen had thereby upset the status quo between the queens, had abandoned her earlier subservience towards her cousin and asserted her greater autonomy. Most tellingly, perhaps, Mary's marriage combined with her youth and robustness made it likely that eventually a son and heir would complicate their rivalry.

Elizabeth was adept at using outraged innocence as a diplomatic skill, and she maintained her stance as the injured party. Darnley's mother, Lady Lennox, had already been notified at the beginning of June that she was to be imprisoned again in the Tower, although this was not to take effect until the 25th. Her crime was allowing her son to seek Mary's hand in marriage without first seeking

permission from their sovereign Elizabeth, but in effect her imprisonment was aimed at putting Darnley under pressure and warning
Elizabeth's subjects how any disloyalty would be treated. While the
English queen meted out punishment and blamed others, the Scottish queen continued to behave as if she was in absolute control of
her destiny. Declaring 'she would only marry a King',[80] she ignored
the opinion of her lords and declared Darnley 'King of this our
Kingdom'[81] on the evening before she married him. So bent was
she on taking Darnley as her husband, Mary was said to have
valued her love even above her faith: the Imperial ambassador
wrote, '[Mary] is reported to have said: *sic libentius volo missam
missam, quam sponsum missam facere* [so I would rather miss the
Mass than miss the bridegroom]'.[82]

The following morning, on 29 July 1565 just after dawn, Mary
awaited her bridegroom in the chapel at Holyrood Palace. She was
dressed in black with a white cap and veil, the mourning clothes
she had worn for her first husband. Although her period of mourning had long passed, this garb was symbolic of the continuity of
her wifely state. Despite her inherited status as a regnant queen,
the wearing of her widow's weeds to her second marriage underlined
her essential existence as a woman in relation to a man.

After the simple marriage ceremony, Mary retired to her chamber
followed by her ladies-in-waiting and the attendant lords. Again, it
was her clothing that was invested with significance. With some
pretended reluctance, the queen was expected to submit to the
symbolic casting off of the old husband and her previous life. Her
lords withdrew strategic pins from her costume and when she had
been divested of the outward forms of mourning they withdrew.
Her women continued to undress her and then clothe her anew in
one of her court dresses of silver or gold, in a celebration of renewed
life.

Mary's sense of renewal through marriage to Darnley was notoriously short-lived. Her honeymoon period barely lasted the summer.
At the public proclamation of Lord Darnley's elevation to the monarchy of Scotland, her lords had stood glumly and silently by. The
only voice raised in acclamation was the Earl of Lennox's, Darnley's

own father. The historian Buchanan, who in quieter times had read Latin with Mary and knew her well, in the following decade wrote with the philosophical advantage of hindsight:

> Some thought a widowed Queen ought not to be denied the freedom allowed to the common people. Others, on the other hand, asserted that the case was different for an heiress to a kingdom, who by the same act took a husband to herself and gave a King to the people. Many were of the opinion that it was more proper that the people should choose a husband for a girl, than that a girl should choose a King for a people.[83]

As Elizabeth's ambassador to France in the early 1560s, Throckmorton had been touched by the newly widowed Mary, describing her as a paragon of maidenly modesty and good sense. He had implied she was everything a young queen should be: she compared most favourably with his own. Elizabeth at the time was not only intractable and autocratic, she was embarrassingly amorous in her relations with Lord Robert. Now, visiting Mary in her Scottish court, Throckmorton was shocked by her transformation. Perhaps it was at this point that he appreciated for the first time the self-discipline and sacrifice of Elizabeth. For a while, before the death of Lord Robert's wife, her passions were as actively engaged as Mary's were with Darnley. But whereas Elizabeth might have chosen her favourite for a husband she quickly realized she could not make him king and retain her own position and her people's trust. Her security on the throne and peace in her kingdom depended on the solidarity of her people and their support for her reign.

Mary's unshaken belief in her status as monarch meant she had never learned the lesson that she owed her continued authority to her subjects and could not rule without their collaboration. Or she knew this but had not the self-control to act upon it. Elizabeth, on the other hand, having been the heretical wanton of Europe, now in comparison with Mary during the following chaotic years came instead to epitomize majestic restraint. Throckmorton, surveying the disarray in the Scottish court during that fateful summer of 1565, wrote to Leicester and Cecil: 'I perceive the poet [Ovid] faylyd not that sayd *Non bene conveniunt nec in una sede morantur, majestas et amor* [Majesty and love do not sit well together, nor remain on one throne].'*[84] Elizabeth read the *Metamorphoses* as a girl and she would have seen the tragic disappointments of her family in the truth of Ovid's words. And it had made her wary in her own life. Mary was about to learn something of the same lesson, but later and with much more catastrophic consequences.

* Ovid, *Metamorphoses* II, 846–7.

CHAPTER EIGHT

Seeking a Future King

The Queen of Scots is lighter of a fair son and I am but
of barren stock.

Elizabeth to her ladies, on hearing of the birth of a son to Mary,
June 1566

MARY'S MARRIAGE TO DARNLEY fundamentally changed the
relationship between the cousins for ever. Until this point the world
of ambassadors, diplomats, philosophers, nobility, clergy and councillors, a world entirely peopled by men, had considered Mary to
be the wiser, more amenable, more tractable monarch. Apart from
a certain impetuosity and excess of feeling, she was praised for her
statesmanlike conduct and willingness to defer to her elders and
betters. Elizabeth, on the other hand, they agreed was undoubtedly
clever but, still in the first decade of her reign, considered capricious
and unreasonable, resistant to the advice of more experienced men
who counselled her and was the despair of any foreign negotiators.
Her reluctance to marry was seen as wilful negligence in a monarch
and unnatural perversity in a woman.

Those ambassadors who knew both queens displayed in their
dispatches a more personal and sympathetic response to Mary than
they ever felt for Elizabeth, however loyal to and admiring of her
they may have been. Mary had a gift of intimacy and spontaneous
feeling which touched everyone with whom she came into contact,
especially men. The prelude to her marriage to Darnley, however,

and the unbridled behaviour that followed left even the most sympathetic of these bemused and disapproving. Suddenly it seemed she had become a woman of wilful misjudgement, intent on the headstrong pursuit of her own desires with little regard for her kingdom.

To have two queens of the same generation, reigning as neighbours in one island, was a rare and significant anomaly in the history of kings. In a world of overwhelming masculine tradition, it was inevitable that each should find the other fascinating, the conduct of her life as a woman and a monarch of personal as well as political interest. In Elizabeth there was consciousness, too, of a wider responsibility to disprove the conviction that a woman was incapable of successful rule and that such a flouting of the natural order of things spelled disaster. Even the Queen of Scots' half-brother Moray, ostensibly loyal to her and a petitioner of Elizabeth for support of the Protestant lords, displayed his conventional prejudices: 'amongst his Friends lament[ing], that the warlike Nation of the Scots, as well as that of the English, were subjected to the Command of a Woman'.[1]

Elizabeth's own sister Mary Tudor had fulfilled the worst expectations of a woman wielding ultimate power. Her needy dependence on her husband Philip II, the compromise of her own country to support his Spanish interests, and fanatic re-establishment of her religion, had left her people wounded and wary. Always sensitive to the inveterate bias against her sex, Elizabeth was careful to parade her learning and, boasting of her masculine qualities of mind, denied her feelings, even as they continued to erupt through her well-practised patterns of disguise and control. Their rarity as regnant queens made Elizabeth of England and Mary Queen of Scots natural rivals, their failure to meet inflating the menace and the mystery of the other.

Elizabeth was the elder, her kingdom larger and wealthier, and life's hard lessons had left her better prepared for the artfulness required in diplomacy and the lonely responsibilities of the job. Mary's lifelong security as a cradle queen, and the lack of any character-defining trials in her youth, had given her an inflated confidence, great personal charm and a zest for adventure. Just at the point when wilfulness, impetuosity and passion propelled Mary into marriage and a suicidal flight from reason, she had recognized that she needed a new adviser and a loyal fighter by her side. James Hepburn, Earl of Bothwell, was one of the Queen of Scots' earliest loyal lieutenants. He came from a line of robust courters of dowager queens. His father Patrick had wooed Mary's widowed mother, the dowager queen and then regent of Scotland, Mary of Guise. With a telling symmetry his fiercest competitor for her hand was the Earl of Lennox, Lord Darnley's father. Both had been rejected by a woman wiser than her daughter would prove to be. Both young Bothwell and young Arran were the next generation of rivals with their sights set on the next Queen of Scots. Neither son would ignore his ancestral calling.

Bothwell, the son, had taken over the earldom and the position of Lieutenant of the Border on his father's death in 1556, when he was twenty-one. He had served Mary's mother loyally during the subsequent revolt of the Protestant lords. On Mary's own widowhood, he joined the party of noblemen who travelled to France to bring her home to Scotland. From the start of her active rule, Bothwell had commended himself to the Queen of Scots. Personally he had qualities which Mary recognized as familiar and attractive in a man. For her the seductive ideal of the heroic male had been modelled on her uncle, the celebrated military commander and head of the family, the Duc de Guise. Bothwell was an adventurer, a turbulent man of war whose anti-English belligerence, rough and ready domination of the Borders and manly courage had early commanded Mary's attention. The premature death of her Guise uncle in 1563 had left her with a sense of being bereft of family protection and support. Her other prominent uncle, the Cardinal of Lorraine, had upset her more recently with his apparent lack of concern for her welfare in the promotion of his own, during the whole protracted business of her marriage negotiations: 'Trewlye I am beholdinge to my uncle: so that yt be well with hym', Mary told Randolph in the spring of 1565, 'he carethe not what becommethe of me.'[2]

Mary's sense of isolation and friendlessness grew as she realized increasingly that her half-brother, the Earl of Moray, so warmly embraced by her at first, so well rewarded, did not fully reciprocate her warmth and loyalty. Personal ambition was always to be his motivating force. Her affection for him had turned to violent antipathy over his refusal to welcome Darnley as her husband and his king. He had thought better of his initial enthusiasm for Darnley's suit, fearing the strengthening of the Catholic party and the loss of personal influence.

During the previous four years, Mary had learnt better the difficulties of ruling a country where there was no proper legal system, no organized taxation and the necessity of relying on her lords to safeguard her person and enforce her government. The Scottish lords were notoriously factional, unruly and self-interested, their loyalties first to their clans and their fiercest antipathies focused on each other. Loneliness and the lack of a decisive man of action on her side meant Mary looked to Bothwell as her warrior hero. Although he had spent much of her active reign in exile and in nominal disgrace for his apparent involvement in the Earl of Arran's deranged scheme to kidnap her, and despite his escape from prison and possible charge of treason, Mary had shown herself sympathetic to his petitions for pardon and freedom. It was even rumoured that the Queen of Scots had turned a blind eye, if not actually offered assistance, when in April 1563 he fled across the border to Berwick, escaping her brother Moray and the Protestant lords.[3]

Mary had written to Elizabeth requesting she allow Bothwell licence to leave England, ostensibly for France, and by February 1564 Randolph's suspicions about her intentions towards this reprobate were confirmed: 'Such as have written (and I amongst the rest) in the favour of my Lord Bothwell (saving the Queen and Mary Fleming) repent their haste. It is found out that this way it is purposed to bring him home.'[4] He certainly caused consternation among the Scottish lords. After a panicky warning went out to Moray and his servants that Bothwell had somehow re-entered Scotland and 'come secretly [to Dunbar] to speak with the Queen, with many horses',[5] Moray's life was thought to be in danger. As it turned out, this was only a rumour but it showed Bothwell's ability to strike fear into rival hearts and disconcert the plans of those who wanted to maintain the status quo.

By the early summer one of those uneasy Protestant lords had written to Randolph: 'Among ourselves things are presently quiet, but I fear not for long: "for thyngis begynes to grow to a rypnes and thair is great practesoris, quho ar lyk to set all thyngis a loft" [for things begin to grow to a ripeness and there is great scheming, which are like to set all things aloft] . . . I wish, as you know I have always done, "that the Erll Botheill wer keipet [restrained] still: for our quene thynkis to have hym at all tymes redye to schaik out of hir pushet agaynst us protestantis" [for our queen [Mary] thinks to have him at all times ready to shake out of her pocket against us protestants].'[6]

In fact Elizabeth delayed attending to the licence and only by the beginning of November 1564 did Bothwell finally get to France, carrying letters of introduction from Mary to her brother-in-law the king, and her Guise uncle the Cardinal of Lorraine. But within four months the unruly earl, uninvited, was back in Scotland for mysterious reasons and in some peril of his freedom, if not his life. Certainly, by the beginning of March, when he appeared unexpectedly in Edinburgh, Bothwell would have heard all the rumours of Mary's imminent marriage to the son of his father's old rival. Perhaps this projected marriage stirred his own ancestral ambitions and his desire to participate in the inevitable shifts in power such a marriage would bring.

Bothwell's arrival was heralded by a dust cloud of rumour: that he had threatened to kill Moray and Lethington the moment he set foot again in Scotland; that while in France he had called Mary the 'Cardinals hoore'[7] and had abused both Elizabeth and Mary by declaring 'both the queens could not make one honest woman' between them.* His disobedience in returning to Scotland without

---

* The death threats are plausible, as is Bothwell's swaggering irritation with both queens. However, the description of Mary as the whore of her uncle the Cardinal of Lorraine, Bothwell's own patron, does not ring true. If in fact Bothwell had ever used those words it would be much more likely a reference to Mary's mother Mary of Guise who had rejected Bothwell's father's suit and of whom it was scurrilously rumoured that she had been involved sexually with her Catholic Cardinal Beaton.

licence had irritated Mary, the stories of his rudeness incensed her. The Earl of Bothwell was told in no uncertain terms by the Sergeant at Arms to submit himself to the law by 2 May (giving him a leisurely two months' grace) or be pronounced a rebel. There was still a suspicion, however, that Mary remained sympathetic and faithful: the Earl of Bedford wrote from Berwick: 'The length of time and the easiness of his bond [£200 Scottish] maketh me to think that the Queen there doth secretly favour him. If he get fair weather on his back, he may chance to wax wanton and work them some trouble before they catch him.'[8] He had already seen the effect Bothwell's arrival had on the Borders, 'to whom resort all the outlaws, thieves, and rovers [robbers] of these marches'.[9] As this notorious adventurer had based himself in the forbidding Hermitage Castle, well supported by his loyal Liddesdale men, Bedford had good reason to talk about fortifying border strongholds against any trouble to come.

The Earl of Bothwell's reputation as a cunning and fearless fighter, together with his commanding presence, evoked fear and loyalty in equal measure. His position as a border lord with wide-ranging influence and ambition, and an inflammable following in that most lawless of territories, made him powerful enemies. Amongst them were Mary's half-brother Moray and his fellow pro-English lords, as well as the majority of the English executive, although Elizabeth seemed to have recognized his capacity to fuel dissension and disarray wherever he turned up, and this appealed to her covert style of diplomacy. The day of Bothwell's trial approached amid continuing rumours of his perfidy and a growing anxiety that his freewheeling presence in the realm would make trouble for the recent peace and amity between the two kingdoms. He was known for a certain sexual incontinence (Randolph had joked to Cecil that when Bothwell was detained in England it should be far from Dover, where his sister lived with many nubile daughters) but much more lurid stories were related, possibly to incriminate him further.

The Earl of Bedford was governor of the frontier town of Berwick and, feeling vulnerable to a raid from Bothwell's borderers, requested extra provisions and reinforcements. He wrote to Cecil citing the opinion of the Warden of the Middle Marches as to Bothwell's proximity and the danger he posed, as well as pointing out the depravity of his character and implication of the Queen of Scots: 'He is as naughty a man as liveth, and much given to that vile and detestable vice of sodomy; and whatsoever countenance of justice that Queen pretendeth outwardly, yet is she thought to favour him much.'[10] Accusations of sodomy were commonplace in religious arguments of the time, although used more often as a slight against those who practised the Catholic religion than against the more puritanical Protestants. Bothwell was that rare beast at the time, a Scottish nobleman who was constant in his main allegiances; a Protestant but pro-Mary and fiercely anti-English. The slur of sodomy may well have been part of an underlying accusation that this manly warrior and Scottish patriot was in fact a closet papist and not at all what he seemed.

It became increasingly clear to Bothwell that his prosecution was just as likely to be military as judicial: Moray was marshalling a considerable force against him; all the Protestant lords were expected at the trial, together with various armed retainers (as many as 6000 men in all were mentioned). Rather than risk appearing in person Bothwell jumped bail and headed back to France. To the surprise of many, and as confirmation of their suspicions of Mary's continued support of him, he was mildly dealt with and not proclaimed a rebel in his absence. Even more surprising perhaps, barely three months had passed before he received the call from the Queen of Scots to return from exile to her side. This was a positive act on Mary's part and in that exercise of will she had assembled everyone who would enact the tragic undoing of her life.

As Elizabeth's main diplomatic concern at the time had been the temperature of Scottish opinion and control of the choice of a husband for Mary, the dispatches from that court to the English queen had grown increasingly anxious. Frustrated beyond endurance by Elizabeth's attempt at control, impatient and increasingly suspicious of her own pro-English ministers, Moray and Lethington,

Mary had begun already to look to other more maverick advisers. Having been full of the activities of Darnley and, to a lesser extent, Bothwell, towards the end of 1564 and into 1565 the name of another more intimate denizen of Mary's close circle began to occur more frequently in dispatches. He was variously styled as Riccio, Richio or Rizzio, and then latterly as just David, and the circumstances of his death were to propel the tragedy of Mary's destruction and bring him a notorious immortality.

Bothwell, the epitome of a hard-living and unruly Scot, an ambitious adventurer, was one kind of growing influence; David Riccio, Italian musician and secretary to Mary, was the other. He was everything Bothwell was not. Physically small and unaggressive, unashamedly Catholic, he provided a sympathetic ear and an insinuating presence in Mary's inner court. Riccio became increasingly indispensable to the queen as an adviser and confidant. Most probably on the recommendation of Mary's uncle, the Cardinal, he had entered Mary's employ in December 1561, initially as someone whose good bass voice could supply the missing part in a quartet of male voices who sang for Mary at Mass, and at court.

Mary had grown up in a cosmopolitan French court full of Italians, an itinerant race of courtiers drawn by the presence of the queen, Catherine de Medici. Riccio exhibited all the Continental qualities of mind and manner that were familiar and attractive to Mary. Isolated in Scotland from the family and friends of her youth, she had been subjected to the brusqueness of her own nobility and the downright rudeness of reformist clergy like Knox. In this austere and robust atmosphere, gallant, light-hearted frivolity and shared memories of warmer, more luxurious times, held a certain charm. When her French secretary was dismissed in 1564 (it was rumoured for being too friendly with Elizabeth's agent Randolph), Mary appointed Riccio to that post, even though his written French was inferior to her own. In fact, Melville suggested that the rivalry between Elizabeth and Mary was exacerbated by Riccio's ill-expressed French in their subsequent correspondence.

This new position in the household involved him increasingly in Mary's affairs. Her solitariness meant she sought his company and confided more in this foreigner who, by his exotic looks, his manner and Catholic sympathies, appeared to her Scottish court as sinisterly alien, intent on promoting foreign interests over legitimate Scottish concerns. Mary's nobles were proud Scots. They were naturally xenophobic and ambitious for their own advancement, jealous of the influences of others. On those occasions when they sought out the queen for advice or preferment, their resentment grew as they found her often in close conference with her odd little secretary. The apparent intimacy between Mary and her inscrutable servant was galling. Too often, Riccio was the main conduit to the queen and, increasingly, those who wished their business attended to approached him first and, it was rumoured, speeded the process with bribes. David Riccio became more hated as he gained in wealth and influence. Inevitably rumours became more garish as they elaborated on Riccio's improper intimacy with the queen, even on his being an agent of the pope.

Mary, however, seemed unwilling to alleviate or even to recognize the combustible situation. Melville recalled a conversation he had with Riccio who was frightened by the malevolence of the lords towards him, some of whom 'would shoulder and shoot him by, when they entered the Queen's chamber and found him always speaking with her'. Melville, the practised courtier, advised him to be less obvious in his dealings with the queen, not to sit with her at every opportunity and to withdraw discreetly when others drew near. Riccio reported that when he suggested this modification to Mary, 'the Queen would not suffer him, but would needs have him to use himself in the old manner'. Melville went to remonstrate with Mary directly, and rather boldly reminded her of two painful episodes when her affectionate manner was misconstrued by others, with tragic consequences: 'I remembered Her Majesty what displeasure she had taken of before for the rash misbehaviour of a French gentleman called Châtelard, transported by her affability; and likewise the Earl of Arran for the same cause; not doubting but Her Majesty's grave and comely behaviour towards such strangers . . .'[11]

Mary's dismissal of these warnings shared a similar recklessness with Elizabeth herself, whose initial resistance to modifying her own scandalous behaviour with Lord Robert had caused her ambassadors and ministers so much grief at home and embarrassment abroad. Elizabeth, however, was cautious and wise enough to pull back from the brink. Her favourites were never allowed to gain too much power. She quickly slapped them down if they exhibited too great an arrogance towards others, reminding them always who was monarch of them all. In reprimanding Leicester for insulting a fellow lord, Elizabeth had no compunction in reminding him, 'that if by her favour he had become insolent he should soon reform, and that she would lower him just as she had at first raised him'.[12]

Such natural authority and self-awareness was alien to Mary's nature. Instead, impulsiveness, impatience, lack of judgement and uncontrolled animal spirits meant she was cavalier with her own power, relinquishing it to her Guise uncles, her half-brother Moray, to Elizabeth, in her desperation to gain her crown, to Darnley through sexual desire, and then eventually to Bothwell. Elizabeth valued and conserved the sacred power which was vested in her as queen while Mary disregarded her proud responsibility as a monarch of Scotland and delegated the authority awarded her to unworthy and self-seeking relations.

Randolph wrote to Leicester in saddened disbelief as to how Darnley's recent elevation had gone to his head, and how Mary's besotted love for him had debased her legitimate authority:

> [Darnley's] words to all men against whom he conceiveth any displeasure, how unjust soever it be, are so proud and spiteful, that rather he seemeth a monarch of the world than he not long since we have seen and known as Lord Darnley ... No man pleaseth [Mary] that contenteth not him, and what may I say more. She hath given over unto him her whole will, to be ruled and guided as himself best liketh.[13]

As she grew increasingly impervious to cautionary counsel and obstinate in pursuing her own desires, the Queen of Scots became more headstrong, intent on impulsive unilateral action instead of diplomacy, preferring the sudden plunge rather than the long plan.

To the dismay of those who had striven for a closer relationship with England, Mary acted fast to punish one of the main architects of Scottish foreign policy, her once favoured half-brother. Moray had been adamantly opposed to Mary's marriage to Darnley and alarmed at what appeared to be her closer relations with France and Spain. He had been mustering support from other disaffected earls, amongst them Châtelherault and Argyll. On 6 August he was 'put to the horn',* outlawed, his lands confiscated. Other rebellious noblemen of his party were ordered to confine themselves to the north, although few obeyed, but they retreated to their castles and strongholds uncertain as to what lay in store. A majority of Mary's noblemen, however, including many of her leading Protestant lords, remained at this point still loyal. Despite her avowed intent to the pope and other Catholic powers that she intended to restore the true religion, Mary continued to reaffirm her tolerance towards her Protestant subjects and her acceptance of the new reformed religion as the religion of Scotland.

Elizabeth, however, was disconcerted both personally and politically by the turn of the tide in Scotland. She dispatched John Tamworth, a member of her Privy Council, with a strongly worded admonition for Mary about 'her proceedings of late very strange, not only towards us but also her own subjects'.[14] But Tamworth and his mistress Elizabeth were unprepared for the newly emboldened Mary. She was no longer willing to be, or feign to be, subservient to Elizabeth. In their conversations, in which Elizabeth had authorized veiled threats to be used should Mary not reconcile herself with Moray and assure the safety of the Protestant religion, Tamworth was taken aback by her vehemence: 'I have had by the way, "some sharpe wordes that bytethe the quicke,"' he wrote, 'I find her marvellous "stowte" [unyielding] and such one as I could not have believed.'[15]

He was certain that Mary disliked Moray and his fellow rebellious Protestant lords so fervently that there was little chance of an amicable outcome; this animosity, he believed, was extended to Elizabeth herself: 'so far as I can perceive, [Mary] "as mortally hatethe the Quenes

---

* An ancient Scottish legal practice whereby a person was declared an outlaw by three blasts of the horn at the market cross at Edinburgh.

majestie as she dothe them [her rebel lords]"'.[16] Certainly Mary's reply to Elizabeth's disapproving letter struck a completely new tone in its assertiveness and defiance. She asked that her 'gud suster' should not meddle in her affairs, just as she had refrained from meddling in Elizabeth's, even though there was every reason to do so, as she tartly pointed out, with the continued imprisonment in England of her mother-in-law, Margaret, Countess of Lennox.

Once more distressed Scottish Protestants were looking to Elizabeth for armed support to safeguard their religious and personal interests against Mary: 'they fear the overthrow of religion, the breach of amity with the Queen's Majesty [Elizabeth], destruction of as many of the nobility as [Mary] hath misliking of, or that [Darnley] pick a quarrel unto'. Randolph was in despair, urging Elizabeth to act; a small force he believed would mean 'she may shortly do with this Queen and country as she will'. In a blatant attempt to rouse Elizabeth through sisterly rivalry, he wrote that in a similar situation, the Queen of Scots 'wolde leave nothynge unattemptede'.[17]

In fact this was to prove an accurate assessment of Mary's mood at the time. In the height of her excitement, and what can only be described as infatuation for Darnley, she expressed herself in bold, decisive action. No attempt at conciliation, diplomacy and consideration of the longer view reined her spirit in. Mary determined to deal ruthlessly with her rebel half-brother and his followers. She had been heard to declare, with what Randolph considered 'owtragieus wordes', that she would rather lose her crown than fail to seek revenge on Moray.[18] Ever the emollient diplomat, Melville urged reconciliation: 'your subjects, and also a good number in England who favour them and their religion . . . would admire such princely virtues, as to see Your Majesty to master your own passions and affections, and thereby think you most worthy to reign over kingdoms'. The use of kingdoms in the plural was held out as a carrot suggesting England and Ireland as well.

Mastering her passion and deferring action in favour of the long view was not Mary's style: 'Her Majesty entered into choler, saying, "I defy them; what can they do, and what dare they do?"'.[19] Summoning a large band of well-armed supporters, Mary engaged in a number of hard-riding pursuits of her brother's considerably smaller rebel force, during August to early October of 1565. This period of vigorous, and potentially bloodthirsty, hide-and-seek became known as the Chaseabout Raid. Although no battle was entered, Mary appeared to be in her element, impressing all with her energy and bravado. She rode many score miles at full tilt, a steel helmet on her head and a heavy pistol in her saddle which she was more than ready to use. Darnley rode at her side, wearing a gilded breastplate as much for show as safety, but her ladies were unable to come near to keeping pace with the Queen of Scots, apart from one who was described as 'stronger' than the rest. Largely unattended by her women, Mary, for a few weeks, lived the life of an itinerant soldier, with the kind of rough freedom she had said she dreamed of when she first set out to avenge the Huntly Rebellion, three years before.

Her campaign of revenge received a fillip when Bothwell arrived in the middle of September. He had been set upon at sea by pirates in the pay of Bedford, Elizabeth's commander at Berwick, determined as the English were to try and stay his return. Bothwell's enemies were in awe of his fearsome reputation. Randolph, already in despair at the anarchy that had overtaken Scotland, where 'no honest man is sure of his life or goods', felt the arrival of this prince of darkness marked the end of all common security: '[Bothwell's] power is to do more myscheif, than ever he was mynded to do good in all his lyf, a feete man to be made a minister to any shamfull acte, be yt ether agaynste God or man.'[20] As far as Mary was concerned, however, he was just the person she needed to energize her campaign. In a later letter to the Bishop of Dunblane, she credited Bothwell with the ultimate rout of Moray and his followers: 'being callit hame, and immediatlie restorit to his former charge of Lietenent-generall, oure authoritie prospered sa weill in his handis, yat suddanlie oure haill* rebellis [that suddenly all our rebels] wer constranit to depart the realme, and remane in Ingland'.[21]

Elizabeth had been loath to give any encouragement, other than

---

* A Scottish version of *hale* meaning 'whole of' or 'all'.

minimal (and clandestine) financial support, to subjects in rebellion against their lawful sovereign. This would invite too many dangerous parallels and precedents to rebound against her. Without outside help, Moray and his followers eventually admitted defeat, and in the first week of October sought refuge in England. Mary, armed and ready for action, had ridden with a ragbag army of between six and twelve thousand men from Edinburgh to Dumfries, her unruly troops laying the country waste as they passed. At Dumfries, Bothwell was left in charge of a sizeable force while she returned to Edinburgh, still spoiling for a fight. Her aggressive note to Elizabeth on the day she rode out at the head of her army was animated with the warning that she could rely on Spanish or French support against her neighbour, if need be. She began peremptorily, '*Madame ma soeur*', and then barely bothered to veil the threat, 'If it pleases you to make your cause that of our traitors, which I cannot believe, we shall be compelled not to conceal it from our princely allies.'[22]

This was a dramatic change in her attitude towards the English queen. In the dynamic between them, she had seized the initiative. Although she had always been proud of her status as queen and careful to maintain her place in the hierarchy of European monarchs, Mary had been unsure how to assert her own political will. Prior to the moment when she decided to marry Darnley against the wishes of Elizabeth and most of her own nobility, she had assumed the attitude of a junior partner who desired to please, a supplicant in search of favour, someone whose power was conditional on the charity of others. The once diplomatically docile and temporizing Queen of Scots was now in the grip of an irrepressible confidence, whether born of the potency of newly discovered sexual love, or the relief of acquiring a husband to share her kingly burdens, or indeed as an expression of the reckless energy of a manic-depressive mania.

This latter explanation has some plausibility given the extremes of Mary's behaviour on previous and subsequent occasions. Even at the height of her triumph in asserting her authority over her lords, her tireless energy imploded into episodes of weeping and a two-day retirement to her chamber, in the old pattern she had already exhibited of elation and extraordinary strength followed by despair. So quickly too would Mary's overwhelming passion for Darnley turn to loathing in such a rapid and extreme volte-face that it gave some pause for thought, even to her contemporaries.

Randolph, once so fond and admiring of the Queen of Scots, admitted to Leicester it seemed strange to write of her in such derogatory terms but to his amazement and dismay she had 'so myche chaynged in her nateur, that she bearethe onlye the shape of that woman she was before'. He characterized both Mary and Darnley as having grown impossibly arrogant: 'a wylfuller woman, and one more wedded unto her owne opinion, withowte order, reason, or dyscretion, I never dyd knowe or hearde of. Her howsbonde in all these conditions, and maynie worce, farre [sur]passethe herself.'[23]

Alarmed by the Catholic league contracted by Catherine de Medici between France and Spain 'to maintain papistry', Elizabeth had reason to believe that Mary was a covert supporter of this 'band'.*[24] Two years previously the pope's council at Rome had issued a resolution inviting the faithful to assassinate Elizabeth and be rewarded on earth with 'a perpetual annuity', and in heaven: 'A pardon to be granted to any that would assault the Queen, or to any cook, brewer, baker, vinter, physician, grocer, chirurgeon, or of any other calling whatsoever that would make her away.'[25] The Catholics in Scotland were growing more confident and militant, encouraged as they were by their newly emboldened queen and her husband's ambitious Catholic family. In early 1566, Mary was showing signs of some determination to restore Catholicism to Scotland. She put pressure on her lords to attend Mass (the newly reinstated Huntly and Bothwell were amongst those who refused) and impressed the newly consecrated Pope Pius V with her intention to fulfil the promise made to his predecessor: to 'make all our subjects obey [the Holy Church] if God by his Grace can reduce and annihilate the heresies as I hope'.[26]

---

* Scottish term for 'confederacy'.

This keen new pope sent Mary fulsome but premature congratulations for 'the brilliant proof of your zeal by restoring the due worship of God throughout your whole realm'.[27] All of this over-confidence had repercussions on Elizabeth and the balance of influences in her kingdom. Any undermining of Protestantism in Scotland gave heart to the sizeable Catholic constituency in England and raised again the spectre of her own illegitimacy. Elizabeth was mindful of the need to maintain her diplomatic advantage through equivocation and uncertainty and resorted once more to her well-tried act of smoke and mirrors.

Careful not to antagonize the powerful forces of Spain and France, she was embarrassed that the rebel Scottish lords fled to her side, claiming she had offered them moral and practical support. Having attempted to stay them at the border, Elizabeth summoned Moray to appear before her council in the presence of the two French ambassadors, de Foix and Mauvissière. With Moray on one knee and speaking in Scotch, translated by Elizabeth into French for the benefit of their audience, the English queen launched into an imperious admonishment of the rebel lord. Humiliating as this was meant to appear, it was generally suspected to be a charade to impress her Catholic neighbours with her best intentions towards Mary Queen of Scots, 'whom she had hitherto regarded as a sister and hoped to be able to do for the future, although the Queen had given her reasons to think to the contrary'.[28] (Guzman de Silva, the Spanish ambassador, related to his king how Elizabeth and Cecil had been in conference with Moray the previous night, rehearsing the following day's proceedings.)

In her messages to Mary, Elizabeth continued to patronize her as if she was an unruly subject in need of disciplining and control. But in fact, in her new incarnation, Mary seemed to have become a much more wily opponent. There was even the possibility that she had followed her cousin's unscrupulous example by covert encouragement of rebels in a neighbouring sovereignty, which Elizabeth herself had done to such devastating effect when the Scottish Lords of the Congregation rose against Mary's own mother to dethrone her as regent of Scotland, and expel her French allies.

Mary's possible interference was in Ireland. She admitted later, 'I had power at that time, of which [Elizabeth] was much afraid.'[29]

The fact of Mary's marriage reflected badly on Elizabeth. Even though '"Jarres" had already risen between her and her husband'[30] no one yet knew what a disaster the Darnley match would prove to be. Instead Mary's acceptance of what was regarded as the chief duty of a queen had made Elizabeth's determination to remain unmarried look all the more careless of her responsibility to her people. Through studied ambivalence and the courtship dance of flirtation and repulse, Elizabeth had turned the conundrum of her marriage into her greatest diplomatic tool. Her prevarication, however, had made the major European ambassadors all come to believe, with some exasperation, that she would never marry. If by chance she did decide to take a husband, they all assumed that the only possible candidate was Leicester, the man she so obviously favoured above all others. This weariness of the whole fruitless business had meant that the French and Spanish ambassadors had abandoned proposals of serious candidates. Consequently Elizabeth's foreign policy risked losing its element of equivocal threat and surprise.

Perhaps in a determination to re-energize her marriage prospects with foreign princes, specifically the Archduke Charles, Elizabeth attempted to appear to distance herself from Leicester with a couple of half-hearted flirtations. These resulted in Leicester's sulky withdrawal from court followed by passionate, even tearful, reunions with the queen. In the immediate aftermath of news of Mary's precipitate marriage, Elizabeth began her flirtation with Sir Thomas Heneage, a good-looking and trusted courtier, and member of her Privy Chamber. Leicester retaliated by turning his attentions to one of the court beauties, Lettice Knollys, Viscountess Hereford, later Countess of Essex. She eventually persuaded an ageing Leicester to make her his countess. She was also a cousin of the queen.

Elizabeth's flirtation with Heneage had been contrived. As Cecil explained to the Spanish ambassador, the whole thing 'was baseless nonsense. The Queen made a show of it for purposes of her own.'[31] However, so emotionally insecure and reliant on Leicester's presence and evident devotion was she, his withdrawal from her and attentions instead to the beautiful Lettice caused her anguish. Elizabeth put pen to paper, and in the last leaf of her French psalter wrote the following heartfelt poem:

> No crooked leg, no blearèd eye,
> No part deform'd out of kind,
> Nor yet so ugly half can be
> As is the inward, suspicious mind.
> Your loving mistress, *Elizabeth R**[32]

Attempts to separate Elizabeth and Leicester were doomed to failure. Her love, lifelong loyalty and emotional reliance on him, his affection for her and vaulting ambition for himself, were such that they were more wedded than any married couple. Her lack of family meant he was family. She had known him since they were barely out of childhood and she called him her brother. They shared a long history together, the most painful experience of their lives being imprisonment in the Tower under threat of death, endured separately but binding them in fellowship for ever. They were together in the bad times and the good, and although they argued bitterly on occasion it was never for long. Elizabeth's aversion to marriage, and the danger for her of consummation of sexual passion outside marriage meant Leicester was the focus too of her amorous nature. She made huge demands on him and she rewarded him with titles and significant riches. But Leicester's pre-eminence in Elizabeth's life was seen by Cecil to be a major obstacle to one of his most urgent duties of state: to persuade his obstinate queen to marry and secure the succession.

Cecil's antipathy to Leicester was long-standing and well known.

---

* The editors of *Elizabeth I: Collected Works*, date this poem to this time of the Heneage/Lettice flirtation by a reference by Cecil of the queen writing an 'obscure sentence . . . in a book at Windsor' when she was 'much offended with the Earl of Leicester' in August 1565. The psalter is now owned by Elizabeth II whose archivists put forward an alternative suggestion that the poem was a rebuke by Elizabeth to Robert Cecil, Burghley's son, for his jealousy of either Leicester or his stepson Essex. (*Sunday Times, 5/1/2003*)

He deplored his influence on the queen and was disconcerted at talk of their marriage. Elizabeth's loyalty extended as steadfastly to her devoted Secretary of State, and in 1560 she had promised Cecil she would never marry Lord Robert. In his judicious way, however, Cecil made a list of the reasons why marriage to Leicester would be undesirable. Apart from the obvious, 'Nothing is increased by Marriadg of hym either in Riches, Estimation, Power', he was concerned that by finally marrying her favourite, Elizabeth would give credence to all the 'slanderooss Speches'[33] about her immoral behaviour with him that had circulated ever since she had first come to the throne. For years these salacious rumours had been common currency around the courts; this time, at the beginning of 1566, the French ambassador swore to the Spanish ambassador that he had been reliably informed that Leicester 'had slept with the Queen on New Year's night', but then added that the French were promoting the Leicester marriage in opposition to the Spanish and their backing of the archduke and so there was some vested interest in the claim.[34]

As news of Mary's pregnancy reached the English court – it was formally announced on New Year's Day when she was in her third month – Cecil, Elizabeth's council and her people were all the more desperate for Elizabeth to marry. Just twenty-three years old, Mary seemed well on the way to proving she was a queen who could secure the succession: the contrast with Elizabeth could not have been more marked; she was already thirty-two and there was not a suitable husband in sight. More disturbing was the possible effect of this pregnancy on Elizabeth's throne. If Mary was to have a son, her claim on Elizabeth's crown gained psychological and political force. There was nothing more consoling to a people than to have a fertile monarch and a healthy male heir waiting in the wings. Randolph wrote gloomily to Leicester, 'The Queen of Scots' faction increass greatly in England.' But she appeared to undermine her advantage by her reckless indulgence of an unpopular favourite. Randolph added a doom-laden – and scurrilous – prediction, 'Woe is me for you when David [Riccio] sone shalbe a kynge of England.'[35]

This comment from Randolph revealed the extent to which Riccio was seen to be in closest collaboration with Mary. She spent so much time with him and blatantly enjoyed his company more than that of her drunken, boorish husband, that a nervous whispering had begun that Riccio, not Darnley, was the father of her unborn child. Elizabeth too was well aware of the mistakes her cousin was making in not separating her personal feelings from political expediency. She told the French ambassador, de Foix, that the reason for Mary's implacable hatred of her half-brother Moray was his antagonism to Riccio. Moray had wanted to hang Riccio, 'whom [Mary] loved and favoured, giving him greater influence than was good either for her interest or her honour'.[36]

Elizabeth cannot have failed to see the significance of Mary's pregnancy. At the very least it increased the pressure on her to make some kind of decision. In conversation with the Spanish ambassador in January 1566, having heard Mary's news, she explored the fantasy of marrying Leicester. Always ready to compare herself with Mary, she then laughingly told de Silva that if she went ahead with such a marriage 'two neighbouring Queens would be wedded in the same way [marrying a subject and out of personal choice]' but she ended the speculation by saying that her 'inclination tended higher [the Archduke]'. Guzman de Silva wrote to Philip II in amazement and no little exasperation: 'She is so nimble in her dealing and threads in and out of this business in such a way that her most intimate favourites fail to understand her, and her intentions are therefore variously interpreted.'[37]

The two people who came closest to understanding the sensitivities and subtleties of Elizabeth's complex nature were the men who loved her best. Cecil and Leicester were inveterate enemies, rivals for the queen's ear, and yet lifelong colleagues in council and at court. They were Elizabeth's most influential ministers and later, with Walsingham, became the triumvirate who helped her transform a demoralized country into a largely peaceful and prosperous realm. But Cecil was ever wary of Leicester. He showed his care of the queen as well as his mistrust of her favourite in his final entry in the list of reasons to oppose Elizabeth's marriage to him: 'he is lyke to prove unkynd, or gelooss [jealous] of the Quene's Majesty'.[38]

Leicester knew that he was blamed by everyone for the fact that Elizabeth remained a spinster. Proud as he was to be her favourite, he had recognized by this time that the ultimate prize could not be his. He accepted the Duke of Norfolk's threatening analysis that, while he promoted his own interests over the needs of the country, 'so great would be the hatred aroused against him that evil could not fail to befall him'.[39] To mitigate this tide of malignity Leicester agreed to absent himself from court, and give the archduke's suit with the queen a fighting chance.

However pleased Cecil and the other lords might be that a crestfallen Leicester had accepted rustication, no one had considered Elizabeth's feelings. On his way to his Warwickshire estates at Kenilworth on a cold February day in 1566, Leicester stayed the night at the Earl of Pembroke's house. Having just said farewell to him, Elizabeth travelled from Greenwich in disguise to join him for dinner that first night. The queen returned to Greenwich and Leicester continued on his way, expecting to be absent for at least ten days. Elizabeth, however, missed him too much and 'sent immediately for him to come back'.[40]

Her fundamental solitariness and need of familial company had been made more poignant by the death in July 1565 of Catherine Ashley, her old governess and the woman who had come closest to showing Elizabeth maternal concern and unconditional love. Mrs Ashley had shared with her every vicissitude of her youth: the excitement and then danger of Seymour's courtship; her more deadly imprisonment when she was still Princess Elizabeth and her interrogation in the aftermath of the Wyatt Rebellion, the scandal of her flirtation with Leicester and the sinister implications of the death of his wife. She had been the one person who could admonish Elizabeth without fear of her flaring temper, and was never shy of reminding her imperious monarch of the times she had fed her, cleaned her up and dandled her on her knee. She had been one of the keenest advocates for the marriage of her mistress, pointing out it was her duty to save her country from civil war by securing the succession with a son. Never one to be afraid of speaking her mind, Catherine Ashley had been rewarded with loyal affection and care from Elizabeth throughout her life. As she lay dying, the queen visited her and grieved so much at her death that she postponed her official business for some days.

At the beginning of 1566 the old certainties seemed to be slipping from Elizabeth's grasp. She was harried with increased urgency to expedite her marriage, preferably to the Archduke Charles, but there was talk again of Charles IX of France who, at fifteen, was less than half her age and, she demurred, made her feel in comparison an absurd old woman. Although Leicester had been summoned back to her side, she was less intimate with him than she had been before the upset of their mutual infidelities. In a facetious party game of questions and answers, Heneage had demanded a reluctant Leicester to ask a predetermined question of Elizabeth in front of her court-iers: it being a game, the earl could not refuse. The question, 'which was the most difficult to erase from the mind, an evil opinion created by a wicked informer, or jealousy?', was pondered seriously by the queen. Her courteous reply was that neither was easy to overcome 'but that, in her opinion, it was much more difficult to remove jealousy'.[41] This sentiment embarrassed Leicester but it echoed the genuine feeling of the poem Elizabeth had written expressing her own struggle with that emotion.

If her private life was beleaguered, there were worries of greater import abroad. Ireland, whose warring chieftains were endlessly troublesome, offered a particular threat to English security and supremacy in the unyielding form of Shane O'Neill, self-styled 'King of Ulster'. Cecil had sourly commented that he hoped his head would be separated from his body before it had a chance to wear that crown. This wish was to be unexpectedly fulfilled when he was hacked to pieces by a rival clan in 1567, and his head was sent to Elizabeth's governor, Sir Henry Sidney, who stuck it on a pole over Dublin Castle. A succession of English governors had become obsessed with the turbulent Irishman who was wild, cruel and cunning and, as they were to find to their cost, completely ungovernable. Sidney wrote to Leicester, 'I believe Lucifer was never puft up with more pryde nor ambytyon than that Onele ys.' For a while he was supported by Mary Queen of Scots, and it was rumoured even that he had offered Ireland to Scotland, seeking alliance with France to drive the English out. Cecil and Elizabeth were alarmed by the connection: 'We have cause to feare that O'Neyle's boldness is fedd out of Scotland,'[42] Cecil confided to a friend.

Elizabeth herself wrote the most enigmatic letter of advice to Sir Henry Sidney, her new Lord Deputy of Ireland, which she asked him to consign immediately to 'Vulcan's base keeping [the flames]'. In it she urged action, even if based on imperfect information, 'if we still advise we shall never do; thus we are ever knitting a knot, never tied' and called on the enduring myth of Prometheus to urge herself from habitual caution: 'Prometheus let me be, Epimetheus hath been mine too long.'* In a vivid image of a predatory she-wolf prowling Ireland in sheep's clothing, 'her woolly garment upon her wolfy back',[43] Elizabeth could have been referring to either Catherine de Medici or Mary Queen of Scots, both being courted by Shane O'Neill for their support. With or without the worrying of Mary's wolfish teeth, Ireland continued to be a wound on England's back that would not heal.

Mary's continued encouragement of Catholic hopes under Elizabeth's nose too was detailed in an incriminating conversation, reported to Cecil and Elizabeth by one of their assiduous spies, which had more than a little of the daydream about it:

> [The Queen of Scots] sitting down on a little coffer without a cushion, and I kneeling beside, she began to talk of her Father Lascelles, and how she was much beholden to him, for he had travailed to get her a true pedigree of her title to the crown of England; and how she trusted to find many friends in England, whensoever time did serve, and did name [Sir Thomas] Stanley, Herbert, and Darcy, from whom she had received letters; and by means she did make account to win friendship of many of the nobility, as the Duke of Norfolk, the Earls of Derby, Shrewsbury, Northumberland, Westmorland, Cumberland: she had the better hope of these, because she thought them all to be of the

---

* Where Prometheus meant 'forethought' and the Greeks gave him a brother Epimetheus, to epitomize the opposite quality of 'afterthought'.

old religion, which she meant to restore again with all expedition, and thereby win the hearts of the common people ... after she had befriended herself in every shire in England with some of the worshipful, or of the best countenance of the country, she meant to cause war to be stirred in Ireland, whereby England might be kept occupied. Then she would have an army in readiness, and herself with her army to enter England; and the day that she would enter her title would be read, and she proclaimed Queen ... For the better furniture of this purpose she had before travailed with Spain, with France, and with the Pope for aid, and had received fair promises with some money from the Pope, and more looked for.[44]

Mary, however, could not countenance the same subversive support for her dissident lords from Elizabeth and banished Elizabeth's ambassador Randolph from Scotland, in angry protest at the dispatch of £3000 over the border to aid her rebellious subjects. Elizabeth responded coldly that 'the like dealing has not been heard of in Christendom between princes', and threatened tit-for-tat retaliation.

While struggling with renewed pressure to marry, unease at growing Catholic confidence, the continual demand from her council that she settle the succession, with Mary's insistence that it should be on her, and anxiety at Irish insurgency, Elizabeth succumbed to some disease that left her so thin 'her bones may be counted'.[45] Her doctors muttered about kidney stones and, more seriously, the consumption that had prematurely robbed the country of her brother Edward VI. Rumours and prognostications that the queen was not long for this world were quick to resurface. Mary, meanwhile, was enjoying a period of excessive self-confidence. Her pregnancy was well established. Reputedly she had already felt her child move and her women of the bedchamber had reported that even as early as the new year, 'she hathe milke in her brestes'.[46] There was a sense of triumph for the Queen of Scots and new hope. But there was corruption at the heart of her new order.

Her passion for her husband had receded as fast as it had come and already the court was well aware that the king and queen were barely speaking, let alone conducting a conjugal relationship. Darnley's violent and boorish treatment of Mary and his fellow nobles, his drunkenness and utter unreliability, had finally dispelled the infatuation that had sprung from her sexual and political need of him. Having at first been so eager to please, lavishing him with titles and privilege, Mary's first act of defiance was to refuse to grant Darnley the crown matrimonial. This would have increased his power dramatically, awarding him the rights of a king independent of his relationship to her as queen. If she was to die before him and without living heirs, for instance, it would be his line that would continue as kings of Scotland. This refusal was humiliating enough for someone as full of pride as the youthful Darnley; just as humiliating and hard for him to bear was Mary's emotional and sexual withdrawal. Darnley accused her of neglecting her wifely duties: 'am I failed in any sort in my body? Or what disdain have you of me? Or what offences have I done you that you should coy [scorn] me at all times alike, seeing I am willing to do all things that becometh a good husband?'[47]

Mary recognized none of the danger signals. She continued to pursue her own interests with some verve, but increasingly isolated she turned more blatantly for company and advice to David Riccio. This was the very person who had become the focus of the growing resentment against her inconsistent and unconciliatory government. Mary's greatest mistake was her reckless disregard for the support of her nobles, who were not a naturally cohesive or submissive group of men. She alienated them at her peril, and her insistence on openly preferring the counsel of a despised, and papist, foreigner over her council made for lethal resentments.

Perhaps thinking of Elizabeth, while despairing at the wrongheadedness of Mary's rule, Randolph wrote that a monarch cannot rule if suspicious of her people and at war with her nobility. Neither can she succeed through favouritism and factionalism: 'To be ruled by the advice of two or three strangers, neglecting that of her chief councillors, I do not know how it can stand.'[48] Ignoring all sage warnings and any previous example set by either her mother or her cousin, Mary appeared to flaunt her favour of the unpopular and indiscreet Riccio, and promote him further. The resentment and aggression against him, and through association towards Mary too, was palpable. It was obvious to every courtier, to each foreign ambassador. Court gossip was full of it. Riccio was suspected by her Protestant nobles of being a papal spy, by anyone at court of being an opportunist on the make through extortion and bribery, and by her husband of being a rival for his wife's affections, if not her sexual favours. Her wilful flying in the face of this wave of dangerous sentiment against her favourite bordered on madness.

The Queen of Scots' inflated confidence, encouraged it was believed by Riccio's counsel, led her to a further show of strength against her intractable lords. Parliament was called for 12 March 1566 to confirm the forfeiture of the banished lords, Moray and his fellow rebels. This sustained confrontation between the queen and her nobility was neither wise nor popular. It made for uneasiness and insecurity, and a further loss of confidence in her government. It also increased anger at her preference for foreign favourites as advisers over the nobles of her council. Her ambassador Sir James Melville urged forgiveness, pointing out that Moray and the banished lords were popular in England, as was their religion. To pardon and reinstate them, he argued, would promote best her own dearest ambition of inheriting Elizabeth's crown: '[the English sympathizers] would admire such princely virtues, as to see Your Majesty to master your own passions and affections, and thereby think you most worthy to reign over kingdoms; finding you ready to forgive, and loath to use vengeance ... for extremity frequently brings on desperate enterprises'.[49] Sadly, mastery of her passions and affections was not one of Mary's princely virtues.

Mary's return to Scotland a mere four and a half years previously had been welcomed with enthusiasm by the vast majority of her people. Her policies of religious tolerance within her newly Prot-estant kingdom and friendship towards England were thought judicious and far-sighted, and her lords largely rallied to her side. Although her choice of Darnley for her husband was cautiously accepted by most at first, too soon both his behaviour and increasingly hers alienated much of her immediate support. Alarm and dismay spread rapidly through the ranks of Mary's nobles. This sprang partly from self-interest, with the inevitable clan rivalry and determination not to cede power or position to a new order. More unsettling, however, was the intimation of a shift in Mary's policy to a more pro-Catholic bias, with an ever-present threat of interference from Spain or France. There were real fears that Mary's wilfulness and disregard for her council meant the Protestant religion would be undermined and Scotland's new-found amity with England squandered. Certainly Melville believed that interference from Mary's uncle, the Cardinal of Lorraine, who urged her to remain steadfast against the rebel lords, stiffened her resolve.

Conservative Catholic opinion was hardening against Elizabeth too, since she was considered to be actively promoting the Scottish rebels, and the solution was surprisingly bloodthirsty. The new pope Pius V was militant in his wish that a league of the Catholic powers should prosecute war against the English queen or 'at least prohibit commerce with her kingdom, which would be its total ruin'.[50] For good measure the Papal Nuncio suggested Mary execute the six leading rebels (including Moray, Morton, Argyll) but this was less enthusiastically embraced by the Queen of Scots.

Encouraged by the hardline Catholic Riccio, Mary was loath to alienate the pope, her Guise family and the new confederation of Catholic princes. Her Protestant nobles felt increasingly marginalized and fearful of these foreign influences. The Scots were proud and even more chauvinistic than the English, while Mary was much more at ease with the great European Catholic traditions and interests with which she had grown up. The rift between her and her nobility widened as suspicion grew at her obstinate insistence on governing through favourites (a characteristic she was to pass on to both her son, James VI and I of England, and her grandson, Charles I).

By 4 September 1565, just over a month after Mary and Darnley's marriage, Randolph had written to inform Cecil and Elizabeth of a plot against the new king's life: 'One hundred gentlemen are determined to set upon him in battle wheresoever the Queen's husband be, and either to slay him or tarry behind lifeless amongst them [or be left for dead in the attempt].'[51] The assassination of Darnley, now King of Scotland, was not in fact carried through at this point, although there were a number of alarms and excursions during the first months of Mary's marriage when both suspected some sinister plot of kidnap or murder. However, as distrust and fear of Riccio's increasing power grew, a plan to rid Mary's government of both his and Darnley's unwelcome influence began to take form. Information flowed freely between the disaffected lords and Randolph, who passed it immediately to Elizabeth's ministers at Berwick and London. Elizabeth herself knew long before Mary that Riccio's murder was plotted and Darnley's situation was far from secure.

By the middle of February, Randolph was writing to Leicester, who was in constant contact with Elizabeth: 'I know for certain that this Queen [Mary] repenteth her marriage – that she hateth him [Darnley] and all his kin ... I know that there are practices in hand, contrived between the father and the son, to come by the [matrimonial] crown against her will. I know that if that take effect which is intended, David [Riccio], with the consent of the King, shall have his throat cut within these ten days.'[52] This was a sensational piece of reporting, but there was no reaction from Elizabeth or her ministers, just a policy of wait and see. In the sixteenth century, political assassination was acceptable as a necessary evil. Murder of a king, however, was treason.

Morton, Argyll and Ruthven were the main protagonists, with Moray and his supporters closely implicated, poised to return from exile once the deed was done. Darnley was propelled to the centre of the conspiracy, his callowness, arrogance and sexual jealousy the means by which the lords harnessed his destructive energy. So great was his hurt and anger at being cold-shouldered by his wife, frozen from her bed and eased out of government, it was an easy matter to convince the young king that the cause of his fall from grace was 'that villain David', who had 'done hym the moste dishonour that cane be to anye man'. A deed of association was entered into to kill the usurper. Darnley determined to be there 'at the apprehension and execution of hym'.[53] A bond was signed between Darnley and the lords whereby they promised to support his claim to the matrimonial crown, even against the queen's wishes. Morton had played on Darnley's inflated ambition and the universal prejudice against female power, urging him 'to free himself from the Command of a Woman, seeing it was for Women to obey, and for Men to rule'.[54] In exchange for promoting his kingly rights over his wife, the lords extracted the promise of pardon for the rebels and the restoration of their lands.

Spurred by the fact that Parliament was summoned for 12 March 1566 at which the rebel lords were due to face confirmation of their forfeiture, the conspirators decided that Saturday 9 March would become the day of execution. It was early evening and Mary was entertaining Riccio and some friends* to supper in a small cabinet room adjacent to her bedchamber when Darnley arrived by his own private staircase, followed closely by Ruthven and his followers. The story of what followed is well known but none the less sensational for that: the confusion of armed men, the frightened shouts, the flash of weapons; the upending of the table and everything upon it in front of Mary and her guests; the rough hands on Riccio, cowering in terror behind Mary's skirts; the disrespectful manhandling of the queen as she tried in vain to protect him; the violent expulsion by a group of large, vengeful men of the pathetic Italian, screaming for mercy; the frenzied butchery of him with fifty-six dagger wounds, and the victim's cries, echoing through the stone rooms of the palace.

There were other details that added to the horror for Mary. In part explanation of the deadly act, Ruthven apparently rounded on her and furiously denounced her tyranny and misgovernment, and the immorality of her relationship with Riccio. Although she was weeping with anger and the undoubted shock, she remained uncowed and defiant. In a subsequent report on the murder from Bedford and Randolph to Elizabeth and the Council of England, relating an

---

* Amongst those present were the Countess of Argyll and Lord Robert Stuart, both half-siblings to Mary, illegitimate children of her father James V.

argument between Mary, Darnley and Lord Ruthven, Mary is shown as exhibiting an unwavering resistance to their attempt to put some responsibility for the situation on her own failings:

> She blamed greatlye her husbande, that was the author of so fowle an acte. It is sayde that he dyd answer, that David had more companie of her body than he, for the space of two moneths, and therefore, for her honor and his owne contentement he gave his consent that he shold be taken awaye. 'It is not', sayth she, 'the woman's parte to seeke the husbande, and therefore in that the faulte was his owne.' He said, that when he came, she eithere wolde not, or made herselfe sicke. 'Well,' sayth she, 'you have taken your laste of me and your farewell.' 'That were pittie,' sayth the Lord Ruthven, 'he is your Majestie's husbande, and you must yelde duetie to eache other.' 'Why may not I', sayth she, 'leave hym as well as your wife did her husbande? Other have done the like.'
>
> The Lord Ruthven saide that [his wife] was lawfullie divorced from her husbande, and for no suche cause as the King [Darnley] found hymselfe greeved. Besides, this man [Riccio] was meane, base, enemie to the nobilitie, shame to her, and destruction to her Grace's country. 'Well,' sayth she, 'it shall be deare blude to some of you, if hys be spylte.' 'God forbid,' sayth the Lord Ruthven, 'for the more your Grace showe yourself offended, the worlde will judge the worse.'[55]

If this exchange was accurately reported, Mary was in remarkable control of the situation, unfazed by the lords' slanderous accusations and strong in her outrage and appetite for revenge. She was convinced that harm was also meant towards her and her unborn child, claiming that in the desperate melée one of the murderers had threatened her with a dagger, and another had pressed a cocked pistol to her pregnant belly. Certainly, as she wrote in her account to Catherine de Medici and the French king, 'we remained not only wonder stricken and astounded, but had great cause to fear for our own life'.[56]

Although not placed in any further physical danger, the psychological aggression continued. More than a hundred armed men guarded the entrances to the palace where she now was kept prisoner. The Earls of Bothwell and Huntly, both close supporters of Mary and enemies of Moray, also feared for their lives and escaped out of a window into the night. When news of the commotion had reached Edinburgh the Provost ordered the bells to be rung and a group of armed townspeople rushed to the palace to enquire after the queen's safety. The conspirators threatened Mary that if she attempted to speak to them they would cut her into 'collops' (pieces of meat) and throw her over the wall. Fear and the scent of blood made ordinary men brittle and unpredictable, but it made men used to violence treacherous and brutal.

After the initial shock and sense of outrage, Mary showed a calm presence of mind and considerable courage. Despite believing her life hung in the balance, she confronted the murderers. She defended herself stoutly against the accusations from Darnley and Ruthven of being an unsatisfactory monarch and a cold wife. On hearing that Riccio was dead she dried her eyes and, with proper sixteenth-century implacability, declared, 'No more tears; I will think upon revenge.'[57] She showed a certain ruthlessness too. Just as with the earlier deaths of Huntly's impassioned son, Sir John Gordon, and the foolish young French courtier Chastelard, here another man lay bleeding, killed for his presumptuous intimacy with the Queen of Scots. In this state of clarity she ordered one of her servants to reclaim a coffer from Riccio's room which contained her private writing and her ciphers. Mary was going to have to think fast to salvage what she could from this disastrous day.

Although Elizabeth and her ministers had been forewarned of the murder of Riccio they did not appear to give much credence to the charge, of which Darnley made much, of Riccio's adultery with the Queen of Scots. Their chief concerns had been his malign political and religious influence on Mary. The fact that he was an Italian and of moderate social status probably contributed to the general lack of concern in the English court at his murder. However, the harrowing circumstances of his death in Mary's presence, her being nearly six months pregnant at the time, seemed to have genuinely shocked Elizabeth and roused her sympathies for her unfortunate cousin.

Riccio could have been set upon and killed at any point in his daily round, but the fact that Darnley and the lords chose to burst into Mary's private rooms at Holyrood Palace to do their bloody deed in front of her, revealed a purposeful malevolence aimed at the Queen herself. The Spanish ambassador, Guzman de Silva, wrote of Elizabeth's 'great sorrow' and her 'desire to assist the Queen of Scotland'.[58] Quite what assistance Elizabeth meant was unclear, although she did express her anger at this new band of rebel lords and swear they would not find refuge in her kingdom. But this was more diplomatic persiflage than actual threat. Elizabeth might have been less benignly disposed to Mary if the Earl of Bedford had related to her, rather than to Throckmorton, an incident a month previously which revealed Mary's still-active ambition and reckless confidence. In a conversation in a merchant's house in Edinburgh where the likeness of a portrait of Elizabeth was under discussion, Mary reputedly replied: 'Nay . . . it is not like her, for I am Queen of England.'[59]

Elizabeth's professed hostility to Mary's enemies was quickly unmasked. Just as Moray and the banished lords of the Chaseabout Raid left Newcastle to return to Scotland, so this latest band of the dispossessed, the lords implicated in the Riccio murder, were to travel in the opposite direction a week later to take up reluctant and temporary residence in England, 'where . . . they might find the other lords' nests yet warm'.[60] Although Elizabeth had failed to persuade Mary to reinstate Moray and his followers in order to avert such a crisis, this latest and perilous loss of confidence, and Darnley's own betrayal, had forced the Queen of Scots to offer them quickly an expedient pardon.

Where Mary lacked the foresight and diplomacy to prevent disaster, she was heroic in her capacity for action and thrived in a crisis when actually gazing into the abyss. She truly believed, as she explained in a letter to the Archbishop of Glasgow, that the full extent of the plan was to keep her prisoner until her child was born, and then either kill her or continue to confine her. In this way Darnley, awarded the crown matrimonial, would rule in her place with his fellow conspirators taking responsibility for the

administration of his reign. Unaware of her half-brother's involvement in the whole murderous business, on his return to Edinburgh
two days later, Mary fell into Moray's arms declaring, 'That if he
had been at home he would not have suffered her to have been so
uncourteously handled',[61] a sentiment which reputedly brought
tears to Moray's eyes. Mary, brought up to believe that to know
her was to love her, interpreted this as evidence of true fraternal
affection when hindsight suggests it was more likely to have been
guilt or remorse.

Her calculated decisiveness at a time of real confusion and danger,
however, managed to transform her situation, temporarily at least,
from desperation into near triumph. In the immediate aftermath
of Riccio's murder, Mary decided her best chance lay in separating
her husband from Ruthven, Morton and their fellow lords. In a
state of high anxiety and fear, he was relieved to have his wife so
strong and determined, and apparently on his side. He had denied
all knowledge of the agreement to dispose of Riccio. Although Mary
most probably knew otherwise, she overcame her own revulsion
and allied herself to him to defuse the situation and effect her
immediate escape. Having spent one night in captivity, fearing for
her life and alone, the following night she agreed to let her husband
into her bed to seal their alliance. The emotional exhaustion of the
previous days took its toll, however, and sleep overcame him. But
Mary's masterful plan was complete and now she was able to turn
the tables on the rebellious lords.

Elizabeth meanwhile was outraged on Mary's behalf at the contempt with which Darnley had treated his wife and queen: she asked
the Spanish ambassador: 'Do you think the Queen of Scotland has
been well treated to have armed men entering her chamber, as if
it were that of a public woman, for the purpose of killing a man
without reason?'[62] At an earlier meeting she had indignantly
expressed her own uncompromising reaction, 'if [Darnley] had
treated her the same as he had treated the Queen of Scotland, she
would never see him again or enter his chamber'.[63]

Darnley's abandonment of the lords, however, earned the contempt of his friends while fulfilling the worst expectations of his

foes. As Elizabeth was informed, 'The King hath utterlie forsaken them, and protested before the counsell that he was not consenting to the death of David, and that it is sore agaynst his wyll: he wyll neither mayntayne them nor defende them.'[64] A public declaration to this effect was made on 20 March at the market cross in Edinburgh. With this act of perfidy he set in train the writing of his own death warrant.

By the night of the 12th, Mary had persuaded the rebel lords to withdraw some of her closest guards by promising to sign a bond of pacification the following morning, pardoning them. This was all a feint for at midnight she and Darnley and one of her women stole out of the palace and, spurred by fear for their lives, rode full tilt in the depth of the night across more than twenty-five miles of rough terrain towards a place of safety.

By dawn they arrived at mighty Dunbar Castle where Bothwell and Huntly and other loyal lords awaited them. Here an exhausted Mary carefully composed the letter to the woman she most sought to impress, her usually disapproving cousin Elizabeth. Again it was her blood connection and their shared status which Mary played upon: 'Praying you therefore to remember your honour and our nearness of blood, and "the Word of God quhilk commandis that all princes sould favour and defend the just actiouns of uther princes als well as their awin [as well as their own]"'. She was desperate for support, but despite the uncertainty and danger of her position, Mary's blood was up and her tone was masterful rather than supplicatory. She had meant to write by her own hand, she said, to add import and intimacy to her missive, but she explained the toll these exertions had taken on her health, now she was six months pregnant and in fear of her life: 'bot of trewtht we ar so tyrit and ewill at eass, quhat throw rydding twenty millis in v houris of the nycht as with the frequent seiknessis and ewill disposition, be th'occasioun of our chyld [In truth I am so tired and ill at ease through riding twenty miles in five hours at night, with the frequent sickness and discomfort occasioned by my pregnancy]'.[65]

In less than a week, Mary had restored her energy, reclaimed her authority and turned flight into fight. She summoned her faithful subjects and, heavily pregnant*, rode out at the head of between three and seven thousand armed men. She returned in triumph to Edinburgh. The latest band of rebel lords slunk away 'with dollorous hartis'.[66] Again physical courage and precipitate action had won for Mary a princely though temporary triumph. Elizabeth, closely informed of all these sensational and fast-changing events north of her border, can only have been disconcerted. She told the Spanish ambassador 'so many things had happened that it would take her three hours to tell'.[67] With so much unrest, with exiled Scottish lords constantly shuttling between England and Edinburgh, with open conflict between the queen and king, how soon before Mary looked to the mighty Catholic powers for more decisive support?

Elizabeth might have deplored Mary's rashness and lack of foresight as a queen but she cannot but have admired her boldness as a woman in leading her troops while so big with child. Being Elizabeth, however, she had to have the last say. To Guzman de Silva, the Spanish ambassador, she declared that if she had been Mary, faced with the assault on Riccio and insult to herself, '[she] would have taken her husband's dagger and stabbed him with it'.[68] She added mischievously that on the other hand she, herself, would not want Philip II to think that if her current suitor, the Archduke Charles, were to become her husband she would be as ready to stab him! Despite her facetiousness, however, this comment revealed Elizabeth's idea of herself as a figure of authority and justice, free of the usual female constraints of passivity and mercy.

While the merry talk of her possible marriage to the archduke continued at diplomatic levels, Elizabeth's heart was as needy as ever of Leicester. His attempt to retire from court for a few days, no doubt to deal with some affairs of his own estate, was immediately scotched by Elizabeth's demand that he return in haste, deaf to his

---

* Interestingly, according to Randolph (*State Papers, Scottish*, II, 69), Mary considered her pregnancy to be six weeks more advanced than it was. On 21 March 1566, she thought she only had six weeks more to go; in fact her son was not born for another twelve weeks (19 June). Her dating of her pregnancy would have meant she thought she had conceived immediately after her marriage to Darnley. It seemed that her passion for Darnley in the early months of their relationship was sheer sexual infatuation: the fact that she dated her pregnancy from that short-lived post-marital bliss may be significant of that fact.

pleadings to the contrary. Leicester's position as the queen's unofficial consort was an exhausting and time-consuming one. It also claimed his life and soul, demanding all of the duties and responsibilities of marriage but offering few of the rewards. Elizabeth's generosity to him, however, was expressed in substantial gifts of land and money. The fifth son of a disgraced and dispossessed Duke of Northumberland, he was a handsome and ambitious but impoverished young man when Elizabeth in 1558 raised him to power as her favourite and Master of the Queen's Horse. By his creation as Earl of Leicester in 1564, she had bestowed on him the estate of Kenilworth which he enlarged and aggrandized to make it a seat for a prince. It was estimated that he spent £60,000 (roughly equivalent to £11.5 million)* on its castle, manors, parks and chase which, when he had finished, extended to twenty miles. And this was just one of his many estates. When Leicester died he was heavily in debt; to be Elizabeth's favourite was as ruinously expensive as it was transformative of his place in history.

Elizabeth had taken to wearing a miniature of Mary, hanging ostentatiously on a gold chain from her waist, and telling everyone who was interested that she was full of sympathy for her cousin and had offered her help. She had promised not to shelter the rebels, but the leaders were quickly settled in Newcastle with no prospect of official harassment. Mary's notorious lack of regard for popular feeling found her once more failing to capitalize on the natural sympathy that her own people had extended to her during the whole debacle. Flying in the face of common sense and political reality, in the emotionally charged aftermath of the murder, she appointed to the controversial post of secretary Riccio's brother Joseph. Not only did it imply an obstinate refusal to accept any responsibility for the breakdown in relations between herself and her lords, it was an act of overt defiance and continued confrontation which could only rebound on her.

It seemed Mary had gained nothing in wisdom as she secluded herself at Edinburgh Castle to await her confinement. Her grip

* See John J. McCusker, 'Comparing the Purchasing Power of Money in Great Britain from 1264 to Any Other Year Including the Present', *Economic History Services*, 2001.

on an already slippery situation was weakening. Darnley seesawed between his wife and the rebels 'in a boyish and unstable manner'. Guzman de Silva, the Spanish ambassador to Elizabeth's court, relayed how 'when [the king] is with the Queen he is controlled by her; when with her enemies he follows their advice'. Mary was increasingly isolated with 'few upon whom she can depend'.[69]

Knowing that childbirth was a danger that she might not survive, Mary made her will, careful to include present and former friends, being particularly generous to her French family who retained her deepest affections. Seven months pregnant she wrote to Elizabeth, apologizing for her handwriting for she did not feel well and being so '*grosse*' made it difficult to sit to write. 'To make firmer our friendship, I pray you, whatever God may send me, to agree to this alliance by acting as godmother.'[70] Mary went on, hopefully, to suggest that by July, when she would once more have regained her strength, Elizabeth might consider meeting her at a prearranged location in the north of England, as they had attempted before. Sidestepping this last request, Elizabeth answered Mary by wishing her a speedy and happy delivery, as free of pain as possible, and mentioning that she herself was '*grosse du desir*'[71] for good news of the birth of her child.

She was as aware as anyone of the ordeal that awaited Mary, and of the risk to her life, and her letter offered a sincere sympathy. Elizabeth, however, was just as sensitive to the political significance of her closest rival to the English throne producing an heir. Her own health was giving cause for alarm; she was in the grip of a fever at this time that an edgy council 'believed [that] any other but death to be the end of it'.[72] According to Mary's ambassador, Sir James Melville, there were powerful factions both in England and Scotland who were preparing, in the event of Elizabeth's demise, precipitately to set the English crown upon Mary's head.

When the news finally came that on 19 June 1566 Mary had given birth to the prayed-for son and had survived, it was delivered to the English court by Sir James Melville after a breakneck ride south.

Elizabeth's famous reaction was momentarily not delight but despair. She was at Greenwich, recently risen from her sickbed, and enthusiastically engaged in the merrymaking and dancing that succeeded supper. Cecil whispered the news into her ear. The music and dancing suddenly stopped as Elizabeth sank into her chair with her hand to her face. She burst out to her attendant ladies who crowded round, 'the Queen of Scots was lighter of a fair son, while she was but of barren stock'.[73] The entertainment was over for the evening.

This spontaneous outburst was revealing of a deeper Tudor fear, possibly absorbed from her own father's terror of sterility and desperate longing for a son. He had managed to produce only three children from six traumatically contracted marriages, and wondered if this was a judgement from God on his dynasty, or on himself for some fundamental sin. His daughter Elizabeth had seen at close quarters the anguish of childlessness destroy her sister Mary. Whatever visceral fear there may have been of her own part in the unfruitfulness of her royal line, Elizabeth was practised at quickly regaining her composure and control. When Melville went to see her the following morning he was greeted by a transformed queen. Dressed in one of her most gorgeous outfits, she greeted him with a smiling face and gracious words: 'that the joyful news of the Queen her sister's delivery of a fair son ... had recovered her out of a heavy sickness which had holden her for fifteen days'. Melville mentioned how surprised he was that Elizabeth launched into this bravura without waiting for the formality of his letters of introduction, but it showed how much Mary's situation was in the forefront of her mind, as indeed was her own.

Melville then imparted the distressing detail of Mary's long and difficult childbirth: 'dear bought with the peril of her life, for I said that she was so sore handled that she wished she had never been married'.[74] This, he admitted, was a ploy to put Elizabeth off the idea of marriage for herself, as the Archduke Charles was still being mooted whenever the matter of Mary as Elizabeth's successor was raised. As everyone recognized, the birth of a son strengthened Mary's cause immeasurably.

It also added fervour to the long-running debate of the succession. On 5 November 1566 a joint delegation of Lords and Commons, emboldened by Elizabeth's dire need of extra funds, suggested that the money would not be forthcoming unless she settled the succession. The queen was incandescent with rage and her self-righteous rhetoric took their breath away: 'Was I not born in this realm? Were my parents born in any foreign country? Is there any cause I should alienate myself from being careful over this country? Is not my kingdom here? Whom have I oppressed? Whom have I enriched to others' harm? What turmoil have I made in this commonwealth, that I should be suspected to have no regard to the same? How have I governed since my reign? I will be tried by envy itself. I need not to use many words, for my deeds do try me.'[75] She got her subsidies without any further settlement of the succession.

Mary, however, hearing of the delegation's frustration with Elizabeth, wrote to the English Council direct, promoting her own case with an insinuating feline intelligence: 'We believe ye have always been good Ministers to move your Sovereign to show her own reasonable favour to our advancement in that which is right, and firmly believe ye shall continue. We take ourself (as we doubt not ye know) to be the Queen your Sovereign's next cousin, and, next herself and the lawful issue of her body, to have the greatest interest of all other to that which has been (as is reported) lately moved in the Parliament House.'[76]

In all her formal communications with the English, she was always careful not to stress her supremacy over Elizabeth but rather after her, as her most rightful successor. The temperature was raised even further by the publication of a book by a Scot called Patrick Adamson who claimed Mary's baby was the rightful heir to the English throne. Elizabeth acted fast and wrote to Bedford sending him a copy of the title page and describing it as 'a small tryfflinge boke in Latin verse'. She must have thought better of using such a dismissive adjective because 'tryfflinge' was crossed out. She requested that Bedford inform the Queen of Scots of this 'audacious rashe attempt', and suggest that she punish the author accordingly and destroy his book. What rankled most was the declaration that Mary's son was 'Prince of Scotlande, Englande, and Irlande'[77] with Scotland first! So exercised was Elizabeth that she followed this directive up a month later with a letter in French to Mary herself. She declared herself sorrowful at seeing a book '*si scandaleux pour vous, si injurieux a moy, si fol en soy* [so scandalous to you, so injurious to me, so foolish in itself]' and sharply reminded Mary, 'You know, Madame, nothing can touch my honour more, than there should be another Queen of England than myself. For as Alexander said, Carthage cannot endure two kings.'[78]

Despite the triumph of delivering a son, Mary's pregnancy and labour had been fraught with emotional extremes of fear and danger. Even in the immediate aftermath of delivery she still could not rest. She was aware of the scurrilous rumours that had circulated about her and her murdered secretary, she knew that people whispered her baby was not the king's, and so when Darnley entered her chamber she greeted him with the defiant words, 'My Lord, ... God has given you and me a son, begotten by none but you!' She was desperate to convince Darnley of her child's parentage and establish his legitimacy. Of course, if Darnley refused to acknowledge the baby as his child not only would that deprive Mary of a legitimate heir but it would also ruin her reputation. According to Lord Herries' memoirs Mary took her newborn into her arms and, uncovering his face in front of Darnley and her women of the bedchamber and other lords there assembled, declared:

> My Lord, here I protest to God, and as I shall answer to Him at the great day of judgement, this is your son, and no other man's son! And I am desirous that all here, both ladies and others, bear witness; for he is so much your own son that I fear it will be the worse for him hereafter!

In fact Darnley appeared perfectly willing to accept the baby as his own but the slanderous rumours were never quite erased. Riccio had been considered an ugly, unprepossessing figure; the baby who was soon to become James VI, and eventually James I of England too, grew into the unhandsome son of handsome parents: speculation and gossip followed inevitably, even into adulthood. Mary, her son still in her arms, then turned to Sir William Stanley: ' "This" says she, "is the son whom, I hope, shall first unite the two kingdoms of Scotland and England!" '

In the conversation which followed, Mary alluded to the breach with her husband. When chided by Darnley, 'Sweet Madam, is this your promise that you made to forgive and forget all?' she answered, 'I have forgiven all, but will never forget.'[79] She was over-optimistic in her analysis. Just as she would never forget so too was she obdurately unforgiving. Mary had pledged revenge in the cold aftershock of Riccio's murder. Darnley's shifty witlessness, arrogant nature and betrayal of every principle and person had alienated her completely. He had introduced her to the power and pleasure of sexuality and had provided her with a son and heir. The fever of desire had turned cold and now she could barely endure his presence. He had become less than useless to her. Patience, forbearance and self-sacrifice were never Mary's forte; being constrained by circumstance made her restless for freedom. Trapped in her personal unhappiness, she was ready to take desperate measures to effect her escape.

CHAPTER NINE

Outrageous Fortune

Madame: My ears have been so deafened and my
understanding so grieved and my heart so affrighted to
hear the dreadful news of the abominable murder of your
mad husband and my killed cousin that I scarcely have
the wits to write about it . . . I cannot dissemble that I
am more sorrowful for you than for him.
O madame, I would not do the office of faithful cousin
or affectionate friend if I studied rather to please your
ears than employed myself in preserving your honour.
However, I will not at all dissemble what most people are
talking about: which is that you will look through your
fingers at [ignore] the revenging of this deed . . .
However I exhort you, I counsel you, and I beseech you
to take this thing so much to heart that you will not fear
to touch even him whom you have nearest to you if the
thing touches him, and that no persuasion will prevent
you from making an example out of this to the world:
that you are both a noble princess and a loyal wife.

*Letter from Elizabeth to Mary, on hearing the news of Darnley's
murder and Bothwell's involvement: 24 February 1567*

FOR MORE THAN FOUR HUNDRED YEARS, Henry Stuart, Lord
Darnley, King of the Scots, has been vilified as amoral, pernicious
and stupid. It is worth remembering, however, that he was just
twenty when he was thrust under Mary's nose by his ambitious
parents. He had lived a pampered and prodigal youth, brought up to
expect great things with little recognition of the responsibilities that

337

came with greatness. There was barely much chance to learn, for Darnley was murdered when he was just twenty-one. More sympathetic and insightful contemporaries painted a pathetic picture of an ostracized young man in the latter part of 1566 and early '67, cast off by his wife, the queen, friendless and alone, trying to curry favour with Mary or the lords who had once courted him. Sir James Melville recognized him as a 'good young prince ... who failed rather for want of good counsel and experience than of evil will'.[1] Guzman de Silva, the astute Spanish ambassador to Elizabeth's court, pointed out that the continued imprisonment of the Countess of Lennox, Darnley's forceful mother, had contributed to the waywardness of her son: 'if she had been in Scotland ... her son would not have been led astray ... as she is prudent and brave, and the son respects her more than he does his father'.[2]

Melville was more psychologically subtle in his insights than many of his contemporaries who passed judgement on the Icarian destruction of the ill-fated youth. Although loyal and sympathetic to Mary, he nevertheless pointed out that she had some responsibility for the way her feelings for Darnley had inverted from overwhelming desire to implacable hatred, and all in a month or so of marriage. He counselled tolerance and understanding, 'praying Her Majesty, for many necessary considerations, to remove out of her mind all causes of ill-feeling against him, seeing that she had chosen him herself against the opinion of many, and promised him favour again of new'.[3]

This was not what Mary wanted to hear. Passionate as a lover she was equally passionate in her hatreds. Not only did she spurn Darnley, she demanded no one else show any friendship or favour to her outcast spouse. Bedford, writing to Cecil, related an incident involving Mary and Melville: 'an Englishe merchaunt there, having a water spanyell that was verie good gave him to James Melvyn [Melville], who, afterward for the pleasure that he sawe that the King had in suche kind of dogges, gave him to the King. The Quene thereupon fell mervelously out with Melvyn, and called him dissembler and flatterer, and sayed she could not trust him who wold gyve any thing to such one as she loved not.'[4]

The vengefulness of his wife and the abandonment by his peers frightened and depressed Darnley, and he talked of escaping abroad. When a herd animal is cast out by its group, death is the usual outcome, although seldom brought about by its own kind. Darnley became a rogue male, in danger and dangerous. His dreams of grandeur veered away from seizing the Scottish crown matrimonial and encompassed instead pretensions to Elizabeth's own crown. He boasted that he was better loved in England than Scotland and had at least forty English gentlemen who would support his claim; his fantasy invasion starting in the north and centring on Scarborough and including Irish rebel Shane O'Neill. All this crazy talk was reported to Cecil by a spy in Darnley's company.

Elizabeth was adamant in refusing to recognize Darnley as King of the Scots but she had no trouble in accepting his son as legitimate and embraced her position as chief godparent with princely generosity. A dazzling solid gold font,* encrusted with jewels and 'of exquisite workmanship',[5] was ordered as soon as Elizabeth heard the news. She feared, however, that perhaps her generosity had been slightly stretched and that the font would be too small for full immersion by the time of the baptism six months later. She was careful to send a message via the Earl of Bedford, whom she instructed to 'say pleasantly ... it may be better used for the next child, provided it be christened before it outgrow the font'.[6] In fact, this impressive gift which, as the aesthetically sensitive Venetian ambassador pointed out, 'combined elegance with value', did not last long enough to baptize another baby. After Darnley's death Mary sent it off to the mint to have its ornamental 330 ounces of gold reduced to useful bullion and coin.†

Although it may not have been reciprocated, Elizabeth appeared to extend a certain female solidarity and sympathy to Mary at this time. Certainly she did not choose to believe, or make any kind of

---

* Estimated to have cost Elizabeth £1000 (£230,000 by today's currency).

† According to Kirkcaldy of Grange, Mary used 5000 crowns of this to part-finance 500 foot soldiers and 200 horsemen to defend herself and Bothwell against the confederate lords (*State Papers, Scottish*, II, 328). After Mary's surrender at Carberry Hill, the lords searching the Royal Mint found only 6lbs of gold from the font remaining.

capital from, the rumours which abounded of Mary's immorality with Riccio, precipitate sexual relations with Darnley prior to marriage, or indeed the wild accusations that she and her half-brother Moray had been closer than siblings ought to be. Loath to join the band of gossips and defamers, she was to urge Mary in the crises to come to protect her reputation and princely authority at all costs, advice her cousin was to treat with as scant regard as that shown to her gift of the font of solid gold.

Mary's relationship with her husband could only deteriorate further as Bothwell rose to be the lord upon whom she most relied. By nature he was neither popular nor naturally conciliatory, but his new prominence in the queen's affections and her own fatal lack of discretion meant that her obvious favour of him fuelled even greater resentments. Bedford did not mince his words to Cecil: 'Bothwell carries all credit in the Court', he wrote, adding that he had become 'the most hated man among the noblemen in Scotland.'[7] Bothwell was a renowned fighter, a man of action and ambition with large appetites and a direct manner. Above all he was unwaveringly loyal to his queen and country. As an uncompromising patriot, he was a Scottish nobleman who had never accepted tainted English money – having only ever stolen it. Consequently he was just as hated and distrusted by the English as he was by most of the Scottish nobility, although the English animus against him was less personal.

Bothwell's ascendancy in Mary's affections gained some momentum in early October when he was seriously injured in an attack by one of the notorious border rievers, Elliot of the Park. The queen set out within the week to ride from Jedburgh to Bothwell's fortress, the Hermitage, a forbidding fourteenth-century castle with dark associations of past cruelties, murder and devil worship. This was a round trip of more than sixty miles through country as rough and unforgiving as the borderers themselves who rustled, thieved and brawled for a living. Although accompanied by Moray and a small party of noblemen, it was an expedition fraught with danger and a gruelling ride for a woman who only three months previously had been through a long and difficult childbirth. But Mary was an accomplished horsewoman who thrived on physical exertion, and welcomed risk and adventure. She was also propelled by a desire to see the man on whom she had come to rely, a man who according to first reports had died from his injuries. Just as Mary's passions had been suddenly engaged during her vigil by Darnley's sickbed, so now the sight of Bothwell, brought low by sword blows to his head, torso and hand, may have touched her volatile heart.

A week after the exertion of the ride and understandably weakened with the emotional stresses of the last few months, Mary fell grievously ill herself. News reached Elizabeth not just of Bothwell's demise '[the Queen of Scots] has lost a man she could trust, of whom she had but few'[8], but of Mary's imminent death too. Elizabeth was in the middle of being battered by the militants in her Parliament who were determined to wring a promise from her to settle the succession or marry. One of the main candidates to succeed to her throne lay mortally ill, even her baby son and heir, it was rumoured, was ill.

The unpredictability of life was never so pointed. Elizabeth ranted and stamped her feet, ducking and weaving as speech after speech exhorted her to have a care for the state of her country if she should die without issue. At least Mary had produced a son and heir. Mary had fulfilled her central duty as queen while Elizabeth was treated by her presumptuous Commons as a recalcitrant who was neglectful of her people. She felt beleaguered also by her Lords: 'saying that they had abandoned her, and were all against her'. In her hurt and fury she attacked the Duke of Norfolk, calling him 'traitor or conspirator, or other words of similar flavour', and felt particularly betrayed by Leicester, declaring 'she had thought if all the world abandoned her he would not have done so'. When he answered that he would die at her feet, she irritably retorted, 'that had nothing to do with the matter'! She was outraged – and almost outmanoeuvred. Elizabeth thought the best way to head off the opposition was to say she would marry, 'And I hope to have children; otherwise I would never marry.'[9] With that she left her escape route open.

In early November 1566, while Elizabeth promised, with fingers crossed, to do her duty as a woman, Mary lay close to death with what the Spanish ambassador reported as 'a female complaint, which is called "*mal de madre*"'.[10] She had collapsed with a pain in her side, convulsed with continuous vomiting, some of it of blood. After days of virtual coma, Mary seemed so cold and rigid that her distraught household had given her up for dead. Her ladies of the bedchamber already had flung open the windows so that her soul might escape to heaven while her half-brother Moray, more temporal minded, had begun helping himself to her jewellery and other pocketable valuables. At this point of extremity the queen's spirit in fact returned.

Contemporaries initially blamed her life-threatening symptoms on poison, the universal assassin. Quickly this theory was replaced by the supposition that grief and strain had taken their toll, the cause being Darnley who 'recompensed her with such ingratitude, and misuses himself so far towards her'. Maitland wrote to Mary's ambassador in Paris 'that it is heartbreaking for her to think that he should be her husband, and how to be free of him she sees no outgait [escape]'.[11]

More modern interpretations have acknowledged the extent of the emotional stress to Mary during the eight months since seeing her favourite murdered, powerless to save him: of the betrayal of those closest to her; the threat to her own life and that of her unborn child; the loss of love for Darnley transformed within weeks of her marriage into revulsion. With this emotional legacy she then endured on 19 June a childbirth so difficult she was brought close to death. Postpartum exhaustion and despair followed. Subsequent rumours of Bothwell's own death and abandonment of her exacerbated her sense of being friendless and trapped by circumstances. Mary had been raised as a pampered princess and queen. Life had not turned out as she deserved and had left her desperate to wreak revenge for wrongs done to her. Few individuals could bear this catalogue of fraught emotion and lack of insight without cracking.

Purely physiologically, however, the collapse, the pain, the vomiting of blood could be explained by a bleeding gastric ulcer, exacerbated no doubt by stress. Or in fact she could have been suffering some gynaecological problem as suggested by the ambassador's reported diagnosis of *mal de madre*. A retained placenta from the birth would have resulted in rapid descent into toxic shock. Alternatively Mary could have been suffering from an acute attack of endometriosis which then evolved into its chronic stage with occasional flare-ups of pain and collapse.* Whatever the possible diagnosis, the significant factor was that her lords at the time blamed her pathetic state on her distress over Darnley. These were pragmatic, unsqueamish Scotsmen, willing to employ desperate measures and ambitious for themselves. Without any room for psychology, morality or sentiment, they recognized that a cull of one of their number had become necessary.

Mary recovered slowly, possibly profoundly anaemic as a result of blood loss at the birth of her child exacerbated by the further bleeding of her later illness. Bothwell came from his border fastness to visit her. Not yet healed enough to ride himself he was carried in a horse-litter. Her husband arrived a few days later but, given short shrift, stayed only a day before returning to his father's estate at Glasgow. After a desultory progress through her border region, Mary arrived on 20 November at Craigmillar Castle near Edinburgh where her malaise continued. Certainly depressed in spirits and low in energy the queen was reputed to have told Moray, Huntly and Lethington she was so 'tormentand' by her situation that unless 'she war quyt of the King be ane meane or uther, she culd nevir have a gude day in hir lyff [unless she were quit of the king by one means or another, she could never have a good day for the rest of her life]',[12] she then threatened that suicide was preferable to continuing in her current condition.

This highly charged statement has a number of interpretations: modern medicine would suggest Mary was suffering a clinical depression, probably postnatal but possibly part of a larger pattern

---

* This condition can mimic symptoms of pregnancy and there was a rumour relayed by the Spanish ambassador to Philip II of Spain on 12 October that Mary was pregnant again. On the other hand she might have been pregnant and suffered a miscarriage after the gruelling sixty-mile ride, but that possibility would have occurred to her contemporaries and there was no mention of it at the time.

of manic depression. Psychoanalysis might suggest an immature character reluctant to take responsibility and resorting instead to threats of self-harm as an escape from responsibility and as a form of revenge. Elizabeth and her contemporaries were more practical and robust. She had written a letter of kindly and judicious marriage guidance to one of her privy councillors, the Earl of Derby, some six years previously. He had suddenly turned against his third wife and the queen had written of her sorrow at his 'alteration' in feeling, reminding him how recently he had held this wife in such esteem (as she herself did), and exhorting him to 'receive her to such favour as heretofore you did bear her'.[13] It was a policy of necessity which Elizabeth, not prone to self-pity, applied to both the demands of the heart and the exigencies of state.

Sir James Melville had tried this Elizabethan approach, reminding Mary 'to give place unto necessity and reason, to rule over the beastly passions of the mind. Wherefore are princes called divine persons? No prince can pretend to this title, but ... [by] being slow to punish and ready to forgive.' But Mary had not been brought up to this idea of responsibility and self-sacrifice; her nurture in France had placed her at the centre of the universe, pampered, loved, admired. Whatever she had desired was hers. Now as Queen of Scotland, a long way from those verdant châteaux on the Loire, the demands of her life were radically different but the person living that life was much the same. Beneath the depression of spirits she was still fundamentally an adventurer who defied restraint. She wanted some escape route and she looked to her lords to help provide it.

In the dramatic events that followed every small detail, motive and possibility has been subject to more than four hundred years of passionate, mostly partisan, debate. There is little that is undisputed fact. Melville, who had no time for Bothwell and was writing with hindsight, maintained this ambitious man was the malevolent motivating force: 'The Earl of Bothwell, who had a mark of his own that he shot at ... had already in his mind to perform the foul murder of the King, which he afterwards put in execution, that he might marry the Queen.'[14] Mary's later detractors claimed that the queen was already embarked on an adulterous affair with Bothwell, and through sexual blandishments and wicked feminine wiles manipulated him and his fellow lords into carrying through the murderous deed. By bloodily freeing herself from an abhorrent marriage they thought she could be certain then of claiming Bothwell and satisfying her shameful desires. Contemporary accounts, however, only mentioned Mary's partiality for her Border lord. In a time of wildfire rumour and little reticence there was nothing at this point linking her name inappropriately with his.*

In fact Bothwell had only recently married at the end of February 1566. His wife was the beautiful Jean Gordon, sister of the executed Sir John and of his elder brother, now the new and reinstated Earl of Huntly, and one of Mary's leading Catholic supporters. Bothwell also had a less exalted mistress. Neither of these facts was considered impediments to the rumour-mill. After all, the Earl of Bothwell was not a man to let mere love, or conventional morality, stand in the way of ambition.

It was clear that a discussion had taken place at Craigmillar involving the queen and her lords, Bothwell, Moray, Huntly, Argyll and Lethington. Divorce was mooted, an uncommon and difficult manoeuvre but possible for Mary if the papal dispensation was set aside. This, however, would bastardize her son, disqualifying him from the line of succession of both the Scottish throne and also the more coveted crown of England: Mary vowed she could consider nothing that would impair her son's inheritance or impeach her honour. It seemed likely that she was not actually soliciting the murder of her husband but was prepared to turn a blind eye, to 'look through her fingers', at whatever solution might be forthcoming.

In Darnley's isolation and distress, his means of revenge was not murder but defamation. He wrote to the pope and the kings of Spain and France, including Mary's uncle the Cardinal of Lorraine, accusing his wife of being 'dubious in the faith'.[15] This manifestly upset and alarmed Mary who hurriedly dispatched letters and messengers to the various Catholic powers to disabuse them of the slur.

---

* This compares revealingly with the universal rumours about Elizabeth's lack of chastity at a time when she was almost certainly innocent of anything other than flirtation.

Mary always saw herself in relation to the rest of the European world. It was important to her to have a place upon the wider stage and she was jealous of her status there. She did not see herself foremost as a Scot. It was alleged that during the discussions at Craigmillar about her possible divorce, Mary had suggested returning to France, the country of her childhood, where she had been most happy. Although there was no real place or welcome there for her now that Catherine de Medici was the effective ruler, Mary's willingness to contemplate such a move showed a diminished commitment to the land of which she was queen.

Elizabeth, so different, was proudly chauvinistic, her gaze ever focused on her island. Never to travel outside England during her sixty-nine years, her undiluted English blood and her unwavering love for her English people (this love did not seem to extend across the Irish sea) were characteristics of which she often boasted and to which she continually returned. She was fond of familial metaphors: she was the Virgin Queen married to her people; she was the childless woman whose love for them had all the protective and autocratic passion of a mother. This loyalty was largely reciprocated not just by her common subjects but by her closest ministers who found her exasperating, intractable and unpredictable, but ultimately open to reason and fundamentally theirs. This family feeling she engendered made her more secure at home, but weak abroad and without alliance, except when engaged in her long-running sagas of marital negotiation.

The Spanish ambassador was puzzled by the English character, a character epitomized by Elizabeth herself. As Scottish nobles plotted murder against their king and kind; as the Spanish prosecuted their religion with the effective terror of the Inquisition; as the French fell upon their own people in gruesome religious wars, Guzman de Silva noted how few English disputes ended in bloodshed, due to the 'very cool headed ... temper of the people'.[16] This coolness extended to their religion too: 'These people are so curious that they think the question of religion is of the least importance,'[17] he marvelled. Guzman, who was an educated and urbane man, nevertheless admired Elizabeth despite all these failings, despite even that she was a heretic in his eyes, and she liked and seemed to confide in him. He commented indulgently on the kind of idiosyncracies which used to drive his predecessors apoplectic: 'she is a great chatterer, and the people, even the aristocracy are offended at her manner of going on [at this time, simultaneously flirting with the Earls of Ormond and Leicester] but everything is put up with'.[18]

In relation to the Spanish, the English temperament was certainly cool and lacking in fanaticism. Religion, however, was of supreme importance in English political concerns and preoccupations at the time, for instance the drive to assure the succession was largely in order to safeguard the newly established state religion and maintain a fragile status quo. Powerful emotions animated the dissident wings in English life of Puritanism and Catholicism but at the centre was Elizabeth, uninterested in enforcing uniformity of belief while demanding a show, at least, of uniformity in worship. It was fear of civil disobedience rather than spiritual dissension that motivated her punishment of her Catholic subjects and their priests. In a much longer reign she executed more Catholics than her sister Mary I burned heretics, the number of deaths increasing in direct proportion to the perceived danger to national security. But throughout, Elizabeth maintained a pragmatism and willingness to compromise which fitted comfortably with her people's own innate conservatism.

Philip II of Spain was deeply devout, procrastinating, dour and aloof. The English queen amazed the ambassador with her ability to combine emotional accessibility and a sure common touch with the imperiousness of majesty. Her identification with her subjects was expressed in part through her disconcerting sense of humour, a difficult quality for her courtiers and ambassadors to gauge, necessary as it was to laugh with the queen but never at her. She was arch, shrewd, earthy and ironic, and these qualities, shared with her people, perhaps also explained the lack of fanaticism and serious high-mindedness which saved the English generally from the extremes of religious persecution and popular insurgency. There were many instances of her mischievous turn of mind, the most famous perhaps being on the return to court of the Earl of Oxford after seven years self-imposed exile, having embarrassed himself in front of the queen: Elizabeth's merry words of greeting were, 'My Lord, I had forgot the fart!'[19]

Mary Queen of Scots was not known for her sense of humour; romantics and those given to self-dramatization seldom are. She differed from her cousin also in considering religion to be of the greatest importance, and she assured the Catholic powers and the pope that 'in the religion in which she was born and bred she will remain for ever, even though it may entail the loss of her crown and life'.[20] To Elizabeth nothing mattered more than her life and her crown; religion to her was more a case of personal conscience and she accommodated her official stance to the forces of expedience. Mary's keenness to reaffirm her place in Catholic Europe meant she baptized her baby on 17 December 1566 in the full ceremonial of the Holy Roman Church, while most of her Protestant nobles and Bedford, the representative of the English queen, withdrew, to kick their heels outside. Her sensitivity to her role on the European stage meant she insisted the celebrations be as magnificent and hospitable as possible,* thereby claiming her son's rightful place in the hierarchy of princes. Even before the Scottish heir was three months old there was talk of his betrothal to the daughter of Philip II of Spain, recently born to Mary's playmate of her youth, Elizabeth de Valois.

The watchful English noted how Bothwell's ascendancy with Mary seemed assured. 'Bothwell is appointed to receive the ambassadors, and all things for the christening is at his appointment, and the same scarcely liked with the rest of the nobility'[21] was one of the messages sent back to Cecil and Elizabeth. The news would not have improved the excruciating gout suffered by Cecil at the time. (Elizabeth had consoled him with the words, 'My lord, we make use of you, not for your bad legs, but for your good head.'[22]) Even more painful to him was the letter that followed at the end of the year: on Christmas Eve 1566, Mary had pardoned the nobles

---

* She had raised taxation of £12,000 to pay for the baptism, rich clothes for herself and her nobles, and presents for the ambassadors (a rope of diamonds to the Earl of Bedford).

involved in the killing of Riccio, the deed which she had sworn to avenge. Darnley recognized at once what this meant to him. He was equally implicated but had betrayed his fellow conspirators, Morton, Ruthven (who had subsequently died and been succeeded by his son) and Lindsay: now they were free to return from exile and prosecute their own interests. His wife, so implacably set against him, had unloosed a pack of hounds and the frightened quarry left Stirling Castle immediately to hasten back to his father at Glasgow. From that point his life hung by a thread.

When the news of Darnley's murder reached Elizabeth and her court there was shock and dismay. No one knew what to think. The facts were confusing enough. On the night of the 9/10 February 1567 the town of Edinburgh was woken by an enormous explosion. An explosion of such power was novel and alarming enough, but this was probably the first assassination attempt on a king using gunpowder alone. The house in Kirk o' Field where Darnley had been sleeping was razed to the ground. In Mary's own amazed words it had been 'blown into the air . . . with such a vehemency that of the whole lodging, walls and other, there is nothing remaining, no, not a stone above another, but all carried away or dashed in dross to the very ground stone'.[23]

Even more amazing was the discovery of the body of the king, not in the ruins of this house but about sixty paces away in the orchard. He lay lifeless in his nightshirt without a mark upon him. His favourite manservant Taylor was just as mysteriously dead beside him. It was soon ascertained that both had been strangled. It was thought that, disturbed by the final preparations of the gunpowder plotters, they had escaped by a window and been apprehended fleeing across the garden in their nightclothes. There, unknown assassins had strangled and suffocated Darnley. The young King of Scots, just two months after his twenty-first birthday, had been tossed lifeless and half-naked to the ground. His servant was reported to have exclaimed before succumbing to the same fate: 'The King is dead. Oh. Luckless night!'[24]

Mary was shocked rather than grief-stricken. She claimed that if it had not been for an act of God she too would have been killed that night. In a letter she wrote immediately to her ambassador in France she promised to take 'a vigorous vengeance of that mischievous deed, which ere it should remain unpunished we had rather lose life and all'.[25] This was to prove tragically prophetic. Given that her people generally held the Queen of Scots in affectionate esteem, especially warm since the birth of the prince, it was remarkable that dangerous rumours of her complicity in the king's murder began to rise almost immediately the dust of the explosion had settled. But those further from the drama found it harder to believe that Mary could have had anything at all to do with the outrage.

Elizabeth showed genuine sorrow at Darnley's death, explaining that as he was her cousin and a royal personage she took his murder very seriously, even though she had been displeased by his marrying in the first place against her wishes. She took to wearing a black veil in mourning. The Spanish ambassador reported that Elizabeth had said the whole business was incredible, adding: '[I] cannot believe the Queen of Scotland can be to blame for so dreadful a thing notwithstanding the murmurs of the people.'[26]

Less charitable was Margaret, Countess of Lennox, Darnley's mother, who was still languishing in the Tower. Elizabeth knew her as passionately maternal and sent Cecil's wife Mildred* and Lady Howard to break the news of the death of her much-loved son. Lady Margaret was so beside herself with grief that the queen's own physician was summoned. She was released immediately from the Tower and her last remaining son brought to her side. The grieving mother had little compunction at blaming Mary for her elder son's death: 'Lady Margaret used words against his queen, [Mary]' Guzman de Silva, the Spanish ambassador, reported to Philip II. Naturally sympathetic to Mary, he continued with a worry-

---

* Mildred Cooke was Cecil's second wife, one of the five impressively intelligent and well-educated daughters of the evangelical politician Sir Anthony Cooke, and mother of Robert Cecil. Another daughter, Anne, married Sir Nicholas Bacon. She was a translator and mother of Francis Bacon.

ing report, '[Lady Margaret] is not the only person that suspects the Queen to have had some hand in the business, and they think they see it as revenge for her Italian Secretary, and the long estrangement which this caused between her and her husband.'[27] Even six weeks later, Darnley's mother, whom the Spanish ambassador considered a 'sensible' woman although 'impassioned, as is natural in her position',[28] was still maintaining the queen's complicity in the murder.

This was the popular verdict too. It had been common knowledge for months that Mary and her husband were estranged, it was thought irreconcilably so. The queen made no secret of the fact that she could hardly bear to spend a couple of hours in Darnley's company. There had been many rumours, some of a plot to kill the king, one reaching the ears of the Cardinal of Lorraine who sent a letter to Mary at about the time of the murder urging her 'to take heed whom she trusted with her secrets', warning her 'that her husband would shortly be slain'.[29] Her ambassador in Paris, Archbishop Beaton, had also written at the end of January of a similar but vague threat of 'some surprise to be trafficked in your country'.[30] Although in her reply to Beaton's letter on the day following the murder Mary expressed her fear that she too had been the target of the assassins, popular opinion did not share her interpretation of events. Already it was bruited that Bothwell was the main perpetrator of this murder. It was even suggested that he would similarly rid himself of his own inconvenient spouse so that he could pursue his main purpose, his marriage with the queen. Local anger was beginning to build and Mary's nobles were eddying around the drama, collecting into rival factions and building their defences.

Apart from the much publicized antipathy Mary bore her husband, there was one act of hers so seemingly incriminating it added pathos to the king's position and apparent malice aforethought to the queen's. As Darnley had hurried away from Stirling Castle to return to his father's stronghold in Glasgow he had immediately fallen ill. It was thought initially he was poisoned but then pustules erupted on his skin and smallpox was diagnosed (although there was a possibility it was secondary syphilis). During his convalescence, Mary came to visit him, bringing with her a horse-litter with which to return him to the environs of Edinburgh, she said the better to nurse him back to health.

The sudden and remarkable change in the queen's demeanour towards her loathed husband was hard enough to explain without suggesting some ulterior motive on her part. Perhaps Mary feared a plot by Darnley against her – and there had been rumours of this in the general mill of speculation – and so felt safer if she had her husband in sight and under her influence. Then again, there were even more insistent rumours of a plot against the king: the plotters would have required that he be removed from his Lennox power base before they could act against him. Least likely was the possibility that Mary had suddenly experienced a Pauline conversion on the road to Glasgow and decided to save her marriage. Therefore, to extract Darnley from the relative safety of his own family demesne and carry him back to the bosom of his enemies, for whatever reason, required a certain inducement. Mary used her considerable charms, and the naivety and concupiscence of her young husband as her means of persuasion. There was little doubt that she promised Darnley they would resume sexual relations if he agreed to accompany her back to Edinburgh.

Mary may not have known that the plot to kill her husband was about to be enacted. She may have known that something was in the wind but have chosen not to enquire too closely what it might be. It is hard to believe, though, that Mary, at the centre of a small and gossipy court, should have been entirely ignorant of something known to all Europe, that the King of Scots was about to be murdered. Certainly she had bewailed in public and in private her anguish at being married to the man and had expressed in spirit at least Henry II's notorious rant against the thorn of Thomas Becket, 'Will no one rid me of this turbulent priest?'

Whatever Mary in anger and despair might have wished, when faced with the actual fact there was little doubt that she was shocked by the deed. Bothwell reported that he found Mary 'sorrowful and quiet',[31] a natural reaction to such an extraordinary and violent event and yet also entirely in keeping with any foreknowledge that some murderous plot was in train.

This situation psychologically mirrored Elizabeth's shock and grief when she finally gave permission for the long-expected execution of Mary herself. The momentous act of regicide always caused a seismic shock, with ramifications much deeper and wider than the purely personal tragedy. As her cousin would be required to do two decades later, Mary now had to face her responsibilities and placate her conscience over a similarly unnatural act: a king was dead and, directly or indirectly, by her will. The rebellion of her subjects and loss of her crown were not inevitable, but to reverse the vortex that had swept her up she would have to prove her wit as a politician and her self-discipline as a prince.

Elizabeth, liking always to be in control, found the rapid and anarchic procession of events in Scotland alarming. She was made uneasy by the unnatural act of insurgency against any monarch, even though she had given her share of support to Mary's rebels in the past. She was never so secure that she did not seek promptly to disarm rebel activity in her own realm. Still unwilling to believe that Mary had any part in the violence against her husband, Elizabeth feared that it might have been due to a general lawlessness that could infect her own nobility. She increased the guard on her palace and ordered that all the doors leading to her private rooms were to be locked, save one, and the keys put in safe keeping.

Despite the shock and rumours rife in Scotland and throughout Europe, there was a general belief that Mary's reputation could still be salvaged. Her crown was still safe, as long as she acted prudently and acted fast. What she did next was of critical importance. Lord Herries, one of Mary's supporting nobles, arrived promptly in Edinburgh with fifty mounted men, as protection against Bothwell, for what he had come to say concerned the rumours that Mary was to marry the murderer of her husband. Herries fell on his knees before her and begged her not to marry the earl but 'to remember her honour and dignity and the safety of the prince, which all would be in danger of loss' if she was to proceed on this calamitous path.[32]

Guzman de Silva, sympathetic to Mary and a confidant of Elizabeth, wrote to Philip II, 'every day it becomes clearer that the Queen of Scotland must take steps to prove that she had no hand in the death of her husband, if she is to prosper in her claims to the succession here'.[33] The advice, however, expected to carry most weight came from the one woman Mary had always sought to impress with her credentials to be named first in line for the English throne. Elizabeth was jealous of her reputation as a prince and expected Mary to show the same scrupulous care of what she believed to be a role given to her by God. Cool in matters of religion the English queen may have been, but for her the burden of monarchy was a sacred calling that involved personal sacrifice and solitary duty.

Elizabeth had learnt much from the scandal of the death of Amy Robsart, Lord Robert's wife, six and a half years before. She knew then how important it had been for her own probity to distance herself immediately from her favourite, and make sure that an enquiry was initiated and justice seen to be done. Although it might have been expected that Elizabeth would now be pleased to see her rival so undone, her reaction to Mary's parlous situation was much more human and magnanimous. Her letter to her cousin sent on 24 February was one of the most vivid she wrote, urgent in its concern and sincere in its emotional force. She wrote in French, to ally herself with Mary and to imbue her words with a visceral immediacy: 'Madame', she addressed her without embellishment, before launching straight into one of the best opening sentences in Elizabethan prose:

> My ears have been so deafened and my understanding so grieved and my heart so affrighted to hear the dreadful news of the abominable murder of your mad husband and my killed cousin that I scarcely have the wits to write about it.

She then expressed her particular concern for Mary's reputation and welfare, surrounded as she was by so much ugly rumour. Aware that the Queen of Scots was singularly lacking in good advice, with 'no wiser counselors than myself', Elizabeth excused her frankness on the grounds that she was a 'faithful cousin' and 'affectionate friend' determined to preserve Mary's honour. With this in mind she offered the nub of her advice in the most ringing of tones: 'I exhort you, I counsel you, and I beseech you to take this thing so much to heart that you will not fear to touch even him whom you have nearest to you [Bothwell] if the thing touches him, and that no persuasion will prevent you from making an example out of this to the world: that you are both a noble princess and a loyal wife.'[34]

With this letter Elizabeth showed how important she thought it that the supreme status of monarchy should not be besmirched by the human failings of those called to rule. It revealed too how she needed Mary's solidarity in 'making an example to the world' that queens could exercise their power with all the courage and rational decisiveness of kings, defusing some of the oppressive weight of prejudice against them both.

Sadly, Mary, from this point on, was not only bound to fail to impress anyone as to her ability as a monarch, she failed so spectacularly that she only reinforced every sixteenth-century stereotype of women as weak-willed, intellectually challenged and emotionally corrupt. Even in the confused aftermath of Darnley's death she seemed to be increasingly in Bothwell's thrall. He was a strong man with a sense of mission when she was feeling at her most bereft and in need of guidance, but he was also the main suspect in the conspiracy against her husband. He was popularly denounced as the murderer of the king. Her blindness to this moral impediment to her continued relationship with him could most easily be explained by her being in the grip of some great sexual passion, as contemporary rumour was not slow to assert once the king was dead.

However there may have been more subtle imperatives at work. Bothwell was known and feared as a man with personal qualities of great ruthlessness and ambition. A naturally forceful leader, he was quick to assert his power and, with at least 500 armed men at his immediate command, he scared the opposition. Mary had spent the whole twenty-five years of her life having abdicated her own authority as queen to a series of men. Hoping for the childhood ideal of her uncle, the heroic Duc de Guise, she ended up more often with weak or self-serving specimens like her half-brother Moray, Riccio and Darnley.

Bothwell at least seemed to have the character and courage for the job, but was so universally disliked and latterly feared, his name indelibly contaminated by the murder of the king, that there was little likelihood of his reinstatement as a nobleman of virtue. Undoubtedly, Mary found him attractive on more than one level; he was militarily effective, politically authoritative and sexually dynamic. There was plenty of evidence, however, that she was suffering one of her intermittent depressions, and had been since the birth of her child. In her debilitated state she may not have had the will to oppose him, and certainly not the strength to bring the most powerful man in the country to account. By the end of March 1567, Elizabeth recognized that Mary was pretty much in thrall to Bothwell's power and unlikely to proceed against him.[35]

Mary's half-brother Moray, who could have offered advice and support to her, was himself implicated in the murder and so was busier protecting his own back. Absence had always been his best defence and passivity his best form of attack. He quickly organized his flight abroad, to bide his time until he could take advantage of the power vacuum created by the actions of others. When he arrived in London he explained that he 'thought it was unworthy of his position to remain in a country where so strange and extraordinary a crime went unpunished'.[36] However he did not think it unworthy of his position to flee, leaving his queen and half-sister without support. Mary wept as she said goodbye to Moray, telling him how she wished he was not so committed to his Protestantism. This parting comment expressed a personal rather than a political regret, that Mary in need of greater intimacy and solidarity felt she could not find in her half-brother the familial closeness she so desired.

Despite the calls from the streets for justice (there were posters characterizing Bothwell as a murderer and Mary, in the form of a mermaid, as a whore), the queen continued to procrastinate, still favouring Bothwell with new grants of land and influence, among them the captaincy of Dunbar Castle. Whether in the grip of malaise, madness or passion, she still refused to act despite the disapproval, threats even, from her French connections whose good opinion and support had mattered so much in the past. Catherine de Medici had written 'very severely to the Queen [of Scots] affirming that if she performed not her promise to have the death of the King revenged to clear herself, they would not only think her dishonoured, but would be her enemies'.[37] Crafty political animal that she was, Catherine could not have been more frank or uncompromising in her threat to withdraw the powerful friendship of France. Even Mary's old friend, Archbishop Beaton, in Paris as her ambassador, was brutal in his disapproval, suggesting with all the authority of his office that as God had preserved her to 'take a rigorous vengeance' on the assassins of the king, should she fail to do so it would have been preferable if she too had died alongside him.[38]

As a former Queen of France, Mary might have expected kinder treatment from her traditional allies but in fact it was Elizabeth who emerged at this time as the most sympathetic voice, showing more concern for Mary's plight than outrage at what the world was whispering. Prior to Mary's marriage to Bothwell, Elizabeth was more than ready to treat her as if she was innocent. Even in her first reaction to the news of the murder of Darnley, Elizabeth had written to his widow, 'I cannot dissemble that I am more sorrowful for you than for him', a remarkable statement of sympathy and solidarity, borne out by her subsequent heartfelt advice to look to her honour and distance herself from the scandal.[39]

Elizabeth explained the source of the authority of her plainspoken advice: 'You see, Madame, I treat you as my daughter, and assure you that if I had one, I could wish for her nothing better than I desire for you ... the one for whom one wishes the greatest good that may be possible in this world.'[40] Mary appeared to respond to her concern and self-appointed position as chief adviser and mother substitute. She wrote a letter to Elizabeth which the Spanish ambassador in London reported 'contained a lamentation for the troubles she had suffered in her life and a request that the Queen should pity her, especially in her present grief at the wicked death of her husband, which was greatly increased by the desire of wicked people to throw the blame of such a bad act upon her. She therefore asked the Queen to help her in her troubles as she could turn to no one else.'[41]

This very lack of trustworthy advisers within her closest circle was perhaps the greatest part of Mary's ill fortune. Elizabeth might rail against Cecil, and sometimes make him ill with despair, but she never failed to appreciate just how loyal, astute and tireless he was in prosecuting her interests and her country's security. Leicester too, although more obviously self-interested, and nurturing still a lingering hope of claiming Elizabeth as his wife and becoming king, was kept by the queen all his life as a loyal friend and confidant for whom she maintained the warmest affection. Sir Francis Walsingham was yet to take his prominent place in Elizabeth's government, although as a more austere individual he was never to come so close to her heart as Cecil. But he exhausted himself with the diligence of his intelligence gathering and foreign diplomacy which effectively protected Elizabeth and her realm.

It was a sign of Elizabeth's good judgement and luck that she managed to surround herself with men of the highest calibre who devoted their lives to her and her government. She maintained a continuity of familiarity and excellence when her old friends handed on their responsibilities, in Cecil's case to his brilliant son Robert, and in Leicester's to his stepson, the showy Earl of Essex. She united them all in a great enterprise bonded by a sense of family feeling. Unmarried, childless, her parents and siblings long dead before her, these men and their heirs became the closest Elizabeth had to family.

The paucity of good advisers in Mary's own reign may have been partly due to her semi-detached attitude to the country of her birth, which undermined the mutual bands of loyalty. Certainly it did not help that her avowed Catholicism was opposed to the newly adopted and hard won religion of her country. Mary's religion had incurred constant vilification, to her face, not only from preachers like Knox, but also from members of her nobility. Her Protestant lords petitioned her in April 1567 praying for 'the abolishment of the contrare religioun (or rather supersticion) quihilk [which] is papistrie'[42], and this was in an official document. The Scottish Protestants were passionately engaged in their religion and Mary's insistence on practising what they considered a depraved, idolatrous, subversive form was inevitably alienating. The fact too that she appeared to be more French than Scottish, and had a propensity to put her country's affairs in the hands of a series of favourites, also undermined the natural allegiances her nobles felt for her. They ended the same petition with their demand 'that the cruel murder of the late King "be so dilligently triet and circumspectlie handlit, as the lawe of God in Deuteronome* requiris", and also the law of man, so that the wicked committers thereof may be punished as they deserve'.

Recognizing the clamour for justice would not fade away spontaneously, the council, with Bothwell at its head, called for a hearing of the accusations against the murder suspects, the main one being the earl himself. The date was set for 12 April. Edinburgh was packed with armed Bothwell supporters: the Earl of Lennox, Darnley's father, had to present his case against Bothwell in person, but was limited to no more than six retainers. Not unreasonably, he feared for his life and wrote to Elizabeth requesting that she intervene with Mary on his behalf, asking for the hearing to be postponed for forty days to allow him to gather his proof. Elizabeth sat down to write to the Queen of Scots, making a point of dispensing with the services of a secretary and writing herself to stress the importance of what she had to say, and dispatched her letter with a messenger post haste.

A letter from Elizabeth in her own handwriting always carried

---

* They were probably referring to Deuteronomy 19:18–21: 'And the judges shall make diligent inquisition: and, behold, *if* the witness *be* a false witness, *and* hath testified falsely against his brother; Then shall ye do unto him, as he had thought to have done unto his brother: so shalt thou put the evil away from you. And those which remain shall hear, and fear, and shall henceforth commit no more any such evil among you. And thine eye shall not pity; *but* life *shall* be for life, eye for eye, tooth for tooth, hand for hand, foot for foot.'

an extra freight of significance and intimacy. In the early years after Mary's return to Scotland, when she still nursed hopes of a close emotional relationship with her sister queen, she used to plead plaintively for Elizabeth to write to her in her own hand. The following exhortation, written to Mary in French, her mother tongue, in Elizabeth's distinguished and speedy hand, could not have been more affecting: 'For the love of God, Madame, use such sincerity and prudence in this matter, which touches you so nearly, that all the world may feel justified in believing you innocent of so enormous a crime, which, if you were not, would be good cause for degrading you from the rank of princess, and bringing upon you the scorn of the vulgar.'[43] Nor could it have been more prophetic. Elizabeth's messenger arrived early on the morning of the show trial but Bothwell's henchmen would not let him deliver the letter to Mary until the proceedings were over. When told of this Elizabeth was irate at having her will so slighted and her messenger so 'violently used, deluded'.[44] There was not much doubt, however, that even such impassioned intervention from Elizabeth would have had little effect on the rapid procession of astounding events that followed. An irresistible momentum was building, driven by Bothwell's will and with Mary, strangely complicit, at his side.

As expected, the earl was cleared for lack of evidence and had posters distributed around Edinburgh declaring the 'not guilty' verdict, adding belligerently, 'any person who said he had been concerned in the King's death would have to meet him in combat, and be taught the truth'.[45] What had seemed unthinkable, now seemed to be inevitable. On 19 April, Bothwell summoned his fellow lords to Ainslie's tavern for supper and there got them to sign a piece of paper consenting to his marriage to the queen. Kirkcaldy of Grange, a man admired for his courage and largely sympathetic to Mary, thought there was little doubt that she would accept this presumptuous offer. Elizabeth would have been made aware of Kirkcaldy's assessment of Mary's headlong feelings: 'She has said that she cares not to lose France, England, and her own country for him, and will go with him to the world's end in a white peticoat ere she leave him.' Such passionate abandonment of duty was bad enough, but he seemed more shocked by Mary's willingness to abuse the law to protect an obviously guilty man: 'She is so past all shame that she has caused make an Act of Parliament against all them that shall set up any writing that shall speak anything of [Bothwell]. Whatever is unhonest reigns presently in the Court.'[46]

Mary's apparent relinquishing of her princely authority to Bothwell resulted in general unrest, random violence and eruptions of lawlessness, all of which disturbed Elizabeth. She was wary always of the infectious nature of these things and minded very much that monarchy was brought into disrepute by behaviour such as Mary's. How could she appear to reward the suspected murderers of the king, she wondered, while 'the father and other of the King's friends who should orderly seek for revenge are forced to retire from the Court, and some of them deprived from their offices'.[47] A man who paraded through Edinburgh at night 'with the cry of vengeance for the murder' was summarily incarcerated in a prison called the 'foul thief's pit' because of the 'loathsomeness of the place'.[48] Others, it was rumoured, whose consciences pricked them to talk of their complicity, were secretly disposed of. The unruly borderers, traditionally Bothwell's people, were emboldened, intent on aggravated mayhem, burning buildings, rustling livestock and killing anyone who opposed them. And even the soldiers guarding the queen 'began to mutiny, demanding their pay',[49] while in the presence of the queen herself. Not even Bothwell's threat of violence against the ringleader subdued them; they rushed him, emerging victorious on one of the few occasions when the combative earl was bested by anyone. Confirming that might was the only right, the queen immediately offered them 400 crowns pay. It was a time when no one felt safe and security came armed with sword, dag and harquebus.

To the astonishing stream of news flowing south to the English court, of regicide, lawlessness, general violence and disrespect was added a sensational tale of sex and bondage. The fact that it involved the highest person in the land, a young and beautiful queen, the widow of a murdered king and mother of the prince, and her swaggering, homicidal favourite, made it all the more sensational.

This latest scandal spread like wildfire through the European courts. Everyone had his or her own opinion about how co-operative Mary had been in the whole shameful business. Was the Queen of Scots kidnapped or complicit? Was it rape or a put-up job? Was she a wronged madonna or a murderous, lustful Jezebel? These were the questions avidly discussed and even those closest to her could not be sure of anything, their opposing sympathies and antipathies rehearsed passionately at every turn.

Astounded as she was, Elizabeth still maintained a more sympathetic stance towards Mary than most of the other commentators at the time. She shared her Tudor blood, she was a woman and a fellow queen. Elizabeth's letters during this tumultuous time reiterated these relationships, her main concern that Mary salvage her reputation and uphold her status as monarch. Loyalty was one of Elizabeth's great qualities and she was not yet ready to think the worst of Mary. She relayed the kidnap story as she understood it to Guzman de Silva, the amicable Spanish ambassador. Mary had ridden to Stirling Castle and arrived on 21 April 1567 specifically to see her son who was kept in careful custody there by the Earl of Mar. He refused to let her remove her baby to Edinburgh, and into the environs of the man generally believed to have been his father's killer, telling Mary, 'he had in his keeping the treasure of the kingdom and would not risk losing it'.[50]

Mary then set out to return to Edinburgh, accompanied by Maitland of Lethington, James Melville, the Earl of Huntly and a small armed escort. Elizabeth then continued her view of the series of fateful events which followed:

> on arriving six miles from Edinburgh Bothwell met [Mary] with 400 horsemen. As they arrived near the Queen with their swords drawn they showed an intention of taking her with them, whereupon some of those who were with her were about to defend her, but the Queen stopped them saying she was ready to go with the earl of Bothwell wherever he wished rather than bloodshed and death should result. She was taken to Dunbar, where she arrived at midnight and still remains [some 3 or 4 days later]. Some say she will marry him and they are so informed

direct by some of the highest men in the country who follow Bothwell. They are convinced of this both because of the favour the Queen has shown him and because he has the national forces in his hands. Although the Queen sent secretly to the governor of the town of Dunbar to sally out with his troops and release her it is believed that the whole thing has been arranged so that if anything comes of the marriage the Queen may make out that she was forced into it.[51]

Elizabeth did not spell out to de Silva what everyone was talking about. The nub of the mystery was what precisely had happened at Dunbar between the queen and Bothwell. There was little doubt that the earl's marriage proposal was accompanied by at least one incident of sexual intercourse, whether as a means of encouragement or intimidation no one would know. Melville, who was with the queen when she was apprehended by Bothwell, wrote in his memoirs 'the Queen could not but marry him, seeing he had ravished her and lain with her against her will'. He, however, was sympathetic to Mary and emphatically antagonistic to Bothwell. He did mention, however, that when he was being escorted by Captain Blackater to Dunbar during the notorious 'kidnap' of Mary, the captain had told Melville, 'it was with the Queen's own consent'.[52]

Although, as de Silva said, 'This [English] Queen is greatly scandalised at the business'[53], Elizabeth was amongst the most charitable in her interpretation of Mary's behaviour. Kirkcaldy of Grange was not a natural enemy of the Queen of Scots but his judgement of her behaviour was harsher. He had some prior intelligence that this pretended abduction was planned and the queen was fully cognisant of events as they unfolded. To Bedford, Elizabeth's governor at Berwick, he wrote with some anger: 'This [Scottish]Queen will never cease until such time as she have wrecked all the honest men of this realm. She was minded to cause Bothwell to ravish her, to the end that she may the sooner end [conclude] the marriage which she promised before she caused murder her husband.'[54]

This sounds rather too close to the prejudice of woman as Eve, temptress, manipulator and *femme fatale*, the perpetrator of the Fall. There was little evidence to suggest that Bothwell was shy of either ravishing women or killing men, and it was unlikely that Mary had to persuade him much to do either. Kirkcaldy, however, was considered one of the more steady witnesses, a man described by Melville as 'very merciful, and naturally liberal, an enemy to greediness and ambition and a friend to all men in adversity',[55] and his belief that Mary was entirely complicit in the whole abduction was the generally held opinion of the time. He certainly recognized that Elizabeth herself was likely to be strongly on the side of the reigning monarch in any dispute Mary might have with her subjects, for he added, 'There are many who would revenge the murder, but they fear the Queen of England.'[56]

By this point Bothwell's divorce and his marriage with Mary had been so long predicted with vigorous and widespread rumours that the actual fact caused hardly any more outrage. Mary's hasty elevation of her earl to Duke of Orkney and their precipitate marriage with Protestant ceremony on 15 May 1567 appeared to stun the opposition. It took place at four in the morning with hardly anyone in attendance, the most propitious time determined, it was believed, by consultation with 'witches and sorcerers'.[57] Bothwell had been cast as the devil and only those convinced they had God on their side had the courage to speak out in public. Mr Craig, a fearless preacher and friend of Knox, having been forced to publish the banns, railed against the marriage, calling it 'odious and slanderous befor the world'. Not surprisingly Bothwell threatened to 'provide him a cord'[58] with which to hang him.

Mary was quick to write to the heads of state with her own story before the scandal ran away with itself. Her version of the controversial abduction was slipped into the middle of a painstakingly detailed explanation to the French king and Catherine de Medici of the good qualities of Bothwell, and the progress of their relationship that had led to such a surprising and hasty marriage. In alluding to the 'kidnap' she wrote 'Albeit we fand his doingis rude, yit wer his answer and wordis bot gentill, that he wald honour and serve ws, and nawayis offend ws [Albeit we found his actions discourteous, yet were his response and words but gentlemanly, that he would honour and serve us, and in no way offend us].'[59]

She wrote a very similar apologia to Elizabeth, anxious to deflect her displeasure at her increasingly wayward cousin whose latest marriage had occurred without any prior discussion whatsoever. Surprisingly, Mary appeared to think this discourtesy might be Elizabeth's main concern, when the looming issue of Bothwell's supposed guilt of regicide still remained unresolved.

To Elizabeth Mary wrote her defensive explanation:

Destitute of ane husband, oure realme not trouchlie purgit of the factiounis and conspiraceis that of lang tyme hes continewit thairin, quhilk occurring sa frequentlie, had alreddie in a maner sa weryit and brokin ws, that be oure self we were not abill of any lang continewance to sustene the pynis and travell in oure awin persoun, quhilkis wer requisite for repressing of the insolence aand seditioun of oure rebellious subjectis, being, as is knawin, a peopill als factious amangis thameselfis, and als fassious for the governour as any uther natioun in Europe; and that for thair satisfaction, quhilk could not suffer we lang to continew in the stait of widoheid, mowit be thair prayeris and requeist, it behuvit ws to zield unto ane marriage or uther.

[Destitute of a husband, our realm not truly purged of the factions and conspiracies that for a long time has continued therein, which occurring so frequently, had already in a manner so wearied and broken us, that by our self we were not able for any long continuance to sustain the pains and travail in our own person, which were required for repressing of the insolence and sedition of our rebellious subjects, being, as is known, a people as factious among themselves, and as troublesome for the governor as any other nation in Europe; and that for their satisfaction, which could not suffer us long to continue in the state of widowhood, moved by their prayers and requests, it behoves us to yield unto one marriage or other.][60]

She was really admitting to Elizabeth that she could not rule alone; she had neither the authority nor the determination to impose her will unaided. Mary went on to explain her haste as a pragmatic response to the danger of the times. News had reached Elizabeth and the English court that the reason offered for the urgency of the marriage was that the Scottish queen was already pregnant with Bothwell's child.

The true nature of this extraordinary series of events will probably never be fully known. The only certainty was that they led to the wreck of all Mary's immediate hopes and the destruction of her reign. Certainly the extent of her culpability and her state of mind were a much more complicated story than any of the simplistic characterizations that have shadowed her from this moment to the present. And central to the whole tragedy was her relationship with the omnipotent figure of Bothwell. Mary was still only twenty-four years old. She was without any real political support or disinterested advice, she had been ill, and was certainly under great duress. Emotional, instinctive and sensation-driven, she did not have a naturally cautious or thoughtful nature but was kind-hearted. The murders of Riccio and then Darnley would have left her with feelings of loss and uncertainty, possibly troubled by guilt, even remorse. The Catholic de Silva, naturally an ally of Mary's and aware of her simple devotion to the tenets of their religion, reckoned the emotional extremes she suffered with Bothwell were part of the wages of sin: 'an evil conscience can know no peace'.[61]

Mary had an undeniable emotional and sexual connection with Bothwell, and there was evidence of their mutual passion and jealousy. Bothwell watched the queen closely and hated her natural sociability and flirtatious ways. Maitland of Lethington had told the French ambassador that, 'Bothwell would not allow her to look at or be looked on by anybody, for he knew very well that she loved her pleasure and passed her time like any other devoted to the world.'[62] 'He is held the most jealous man that lives', Drury, the Marshal of Berwick, related to Cecil with some hyperbole. But Mary too appeared to be equally possessive, seen to 'hang upon his arm' when walking in public, and their tempestuous arguments and her weeping were just as publicly paraded. Bothwell's reputation for 'unsatiateness towards women' was well known and Mary cried bitterly that he continued regular conjugal visits to his newly divorced wife: 'The Lady Bothwell remaining at Crighton* is much misliked of the Queen.'[63]

Messengers galloped south with the steady stream of sensational news and speculation about the latest indiscretions of the Queen of Scots and her unruly subjects. While all around her, even the Catholic contingent, expressed their disappointment and dismay, Elizabeth remained largely sympathetic to Mary. She told de Silva how surprised she was by the marriage but 'deplores [recent events] very much as touching the honour of that Queen'. When the Spanish ambassador replied he thought the King of France, despite Bothwell's evident guilt, would honour him with the chivalric order of St Michael,† Elizabeth was acerbic: 'She said she quite believed that, as he held the order so light as to give it to his grooms.'[64]

Elizabeth was much more sensitive, however, than Mary to the struggle to maintain authority against the inveterate prejudices concerning women in power. She had been pushing hard for the restitution of Calais – the Treaty of Cateau-Cambresis had allowed for French possession for eight years only and this time was now up. But the categorical and disrespectful rejection of their rights by the French negotiators had taken the English aback, and Elizabeth knew that these failures too easily were blamed on her being a monarch of the wrong sex. 'These Frenchmen know we have a woman for our head and therefore esteem us so little,'[65] was the reaction of her dejected ambassadors. In a world where political power was overwhelmingly masculine, Elizabeth had a natural solidarity with Mary and was loath to vilify 'one not different in sex, of like estate, and my near kin'.[66] Nor was she quick to cast the first stone: she was a woman too with natural appetites for affection, admiration and the fulfilment of desire. She knew what it was to love recklessly

---

* Crichton Castle, a Bothwell stronghold some twelve miles to the southeast of Edinburgh.

† *L'Ordre de St-Michel* was a chivalric order of knighthood established by Louis XI in 1469 (abolished in 1830) presented with great ceremony to Elizabeth's father in 1527 by François I.

and too well, but she recognized also when the woman in her had to be sacrificed for the queen she wished to be.

As Mary entered into her third marriage with all the worst omens in the world, Elizabeth was once more pretending to entertain the proposition of her own marriage to the Archduke Charles. Mary's star appeared to be on a trajectory of self-destruction, while Elizabeth half-heartedly rehearsed the actions of a dutiful monarch by pursuing the marriage alliance her ministers required. Her public face was difficult enough to read, especially by her prospective suitors. The Austrian Emperor Maximilian wrote to his younger brother Charles thoroughly puzzled by the English queen: 'This answer is most obscure, ambiguous, involved and of such a nature that we cannot learn from it whether the Queen is serious and sincere or whether she wishes to befool us.'[67] In fact befooling the Hapsburgs was entirely within Elizabeth's capacity. They were tentative, procrastinating and not the brightest of men. Austria's most famous poet, Franz Grillparzer, characterized them thus:

> This is the curse of our most noble house:
> But half-equipped, to try to do half-deeds;
> And half-way up, to falter and to stop.

Charles's courtship of Elizabeth was to be protracted over nine long years before petering out as another Hapsburg project fallen by the way.

Although Elizabeth, for political reasons, allowed the courtship to be resuscitated, her private opinions remained as uncompromising as ever. Having to endure performed before her at court a comedy, dealing pointedly with the subject of marriage, and keeping her up until one in the morning, she dismissed this unwelcome piece of propaganda, and told de Silva how much she disliked the woman's part. The Spanish ambassador wrote to Philip II, 'The hatred that this Queen has of marriage is most strange':[68] an antipathy perhaps less strange given the catalogue of marital disasters paraded by her cousin over the border.

The next concern over the fast-changing political landscape in Scotland was the safety of the small Prince James. Rumour had it that the French were desperately trying to get their hands on him, as they had succeeded twenty years before with his mother. As the heir to Scotland and probably to England and Ireland too, this possibility caused alarm in the Spanish and English courts, not least as there was talk of hefty bribes being dangled in front of Scottish noses. Elizabeth was urged to offer an alternative security to the future hopes of Protestant Scotland by taking the child into English protection, under the auspices of his grandmother the Countess of Lennox. This was a faint echo of Henry VIII's battles to ensure that Mary, as a baby, was brought up under his control. Elizabeth, however, was far from keen. She had told Guzman that having the baby in her care would make her anxious 'as any little illness it might have would distress her'. She was also afraid of inciting French aggression against her own country. The Scottish lords anyway were adamant that the baby stayed in Scotland. Bothwell too was using every form of coercive encouragement to get the doughty Earl of Mar to relinquish the baby to his safekeeping and that of his mother Mary in Edinburgh. But these manoeuvres were quickly superseded by the threat of civil war.

Nothing alarmed Elizabeth more than the threat of rebellion. She had seen first hand in her sister's reign the divisiveness and terror of a country split by internal strife. She had learnt to abhor the loss of trust and sympathy between monarch and people. Although not many people personally mourned Darnley, the blatant lack of justice, shame at the loss of prestige abroad and the people's anger at home, stirred the Scottish lords from an uneasy inertia. A confederacy formed on 1 May 1567 was re-energized two weeks later with the intent, 'that the Queen's majesty may be delivered from thraldom, the prince preserved, and the cruell murder of the King his father "tryit", whereby our native country may be relieved of the shameful slander it has incurred among all nations'.[69]

There may at this point have been some who hoped to deliver Mary also from her crown and proclaim the baby James king in her place. A child monarch and long regency was a well-established pattern of Scottish rule, one she herself had been part of from her first week of life. The main earls ranged against Bothwell were Morton, Mar and Argyll. Moray, Arran (the Duke of Châtelherault) and Lennox, all obviously anti-Bothwell, were absent from Scotland in various states of self-imposed exile. By the end of the month the confederate lords rode with accompanying nobles, lairds and three thousand men to Edinburgh. Their banner was an affecting representation of the half-naked Darnley, lying dead under a tree, with the infant prince kneeling beside the body of his father. The scroll at the top purported to be his childish prayer, 'Judge and revenge my caus O Lord'.[70]

Bothwell and Mary decided to decamp to the more easily defensible Borthwick Castle on the edge of the Borders, Bothwell's home ground. But by 10 June he had set off to ride to the impregnable Dunbar Castle, the better to defend his and Mary's position. Whenever courageous action was required of her, Mary's heroic qualities came triumphantly to the fore. Transformed from a weeping, jealous woman, for a few days she became once more a remarkable warrior queen. Booted and spurred and dressed in men's clothes she rode to meet Bothwell. The Duc de Guise had celebrated this quality in his niece, reputedly once saying to her: 'there is one trait in which, above all others, I recognise my own blood in you – you are as brave as my bravest men-at-arms. If women went into battle now, as they did in ancient times, I think you would know how to die well.' Loyal and protective of her husband, Mary was determined not to relinquish Bothwell and was ready instead to lead her troops into battle. An English messenger who followed her on that fateful day of 15 June reported that she was let down by her troops, and that she was among the most resolute, 'so willing by battle to have it tried',[71] even though she was already noticeably advanced in her latest pregnancy.

Her forces were ranged at Carberry Hill, just outside Edinburgh, against the forces of the confederate lords. There was little appetite for civil war. Instead a great deal of difficult negotiation ensued. The lords promised if Mary would abandon Bothwell then she would be reinstated as queen, declaring to the French ambassador du Croc, who was a reluctant go-between, that 'they would rather all be buried alive than that the truth as to the death of the late King should not be known'. At first the queen refused outright. Du Croc was impressed, against his will, by Bothwell's mastery of the situation; he appeared unconcerned at the danger he was in, declaring 'Fortune ... was to be won by anyone who chose' and that this malice against him was mere envy from men with less desire for greatness. Bothwell did express some anxiety, however, at the trouble all this was causing Mary, 'whose suffering was extreme'.[72] To save her and avoid any bloodshed, it was suggested, possibly by Bothwell, that the issue should be determined by one-to-one combat, for which ordeal Lord Lindsay offered himself. But as the hot day wore on, most of Mary's foot soldiers melted away, either to the ranks of the confederate lords or back to their homes and their fields. Recognizing the hopelessness of her position, she finally agreed to surrender herself to Kirkcaldy of Grange, but only after a delay to allow Bothwell a good head start on his headlong ride back to Dunbar.

Dressed now in an ill-fitting, borrowed dress with a red petticoat showing, Mary was led down the hill on horseback. The assembled ragbag of soldiers and peasant volunteers saw for the first time the heavily pregnant body of the queen. Here, 'with as great a stomach as ever',[73] was the unmistakable reminder of Mary's sexuality and, just one month after her marriage to Bothwell, damning evidence it seemed of her lascivious behaviour with him. The size of her belly suggested even an adulterous relationship during her estrangement from Darnley prior to the king's murder. Although unbeknownst to them, Mary was unlikely to be as advanced in her pregnancy as she seemed for she was carrying not one baby but twins. To be so noticeably pregnant, however, meant she must have conceived prior to the abduction on 21 April, only two months before.

Here too, in the clothes of an ordinary Edinburgh townswoman, dishevelled in defeat, Mary appeared fallible and female, not the awesome figure of a queen ordained by God and set above other women. Elizabeth always took special care to look the part of an unassailable monarch. When she became queen, the plain princess had assumed the necessary carapace of glittering fabric and priceless jewels. She transformed herself into the glamorous, suprahuman vision of royalty. Even though she might treat her common people with familiar affection and engage in their repartee and jokes, they never doubted who was queen nor how that transmuted her into something semi-divine. Her lords, ministers and courtiers too, if ever they stepped too far out of line, were sharply reminded of her supremacy and her ability to cut them down as determinedly as she had raised them up.

Mary's manners as a charming, cultured French princess, her warmth and high spirits, had meant people were attracted to her but did not fear her. Her initial authority, when she had ruled judiciously a curious and grateful populace who made allowances for their newly returned queen, had long been frittered away. In her grubby dress, heat-stained and straining over her pregnant form, Mary appeared merely a degraded and dangerous woman. In Edinburgh a new flowering of popular ballads cast her variously as Delilah, Jezebel and Clytemnestra:* insulated from her people by her own troubles and desires she had not realized how her heedlessness of the larger world and its expectations of her as queen had damaged her reputation. The spontaneous raw anger of the soldiers as she passed among them took her by surprise and brought shocked tears to her eyes. 'Burn the whore!' they shouted with one voice, as the lords leading Mary away drew their swords to try and quell their oaths.

Still maintaining her allegiance and love for Bothwell, and concern for his safety, the Queen of Scots was smuggled out of Edinburgh at night, ostensibly to protect her from the mob hurling stones and baying for her blood: 'Burn her, burn her, she is not worthy to live, kill her, drown her.' Drury quoted these terrible

---

* Three proverbially devilish women: Delilah, beautiful but treacherous mistress, who betrayed to his enemies the ancient Hebrew hero Samson; Jezebel, infamous wife of Ahab, King of Israel, whose name came to mean any immoral woman; Clytemnestra, in Greek legend an adulterer and husband slayer, who with her lover killed Agamemnon, King of Mycenae, on his return from the Trojan wars.

words to Cecil, pointing out 'The people cry for punishment with-out respect of persons.'[74] It was possible also that the confederate lords feared an insurrection from supporters of the pitiful queen if they had removed her from Holyrood Palace by day. She was taken twenty miles north to Loch Leven and rowed across to the island fortress that was to become her home for almost a year.

Elizabeth quickly heard of the surrender of Mary at Carberry Hill. Her outrage at the whole sorry episode centred on the fact that a sovereign queen was treated with such disrespect, particularly by her lords who should have known better. The aristocracy itself depended on the sacred hierarchy that placed a monarch at the apex of society, answerable only to God. It was not only dangerous and presumptuous to invert that pattern, it was positively unnatural. The disruption of world order in this fundamental way threatened collapse, anarchy, disaster. Elizabeth wrote to Mary, 'we assure you that whatsoever we can imagine meet for your honour and safety that shall lie in our power, we will perform the same that it shall well appear you have a good neighbour, a dear sister, and a faithful friend ... you [shall not] lack our friendship and power for the preservation of your honour in quietness.' She signed it with a meaningful adieu, 'And so we recommend ourselves to you, good sister, in as affectuous [ardent] a manner as heretofore we were accustomed.'[75]

Elizabeth immediately dispatched the experienced and sympath-etic Sir Nicholas Throckmorton to offer Mary her commiserations, pointing out that she would treat her with all the care and concern as she would 'her natural sister or daughter'. Mary's imprisonment had been the final impertinence and Throckmorton was told to promise her that Elizabeth 'would not suffer hir, being by Goddes ordonnance the prince and soverayne, to be in subjection to them that by nature and lawe are subjected to hir'.[76]

To the confederate lords, who looked to her for support, she was stern. Throckmorton's brief was 'to declare that as a sister Sovereign their Queen cannot be detained prisoner or deprived of her princely state. To show them how incredibly her majesty [Elizabeth] took it at first, that persons of such honour as they be (the principal nobility of that realm), could offer such violence to their sovereign as to commit her to any manner of prison.' She wanted it made clear that this did not mean she was unconcerned by the 'faults imputed by report to their Sovereign' but that 'it does not appertain to subjects so to reform their prince, but to deal by advice and counsel, and failing thereof, "to recommend the rest to Almyghty God"'.[77]

Elizabeth at this time was alone among her fellow monarchs in offering human sympathy and moral support for Mary. The French majesties, Charles IX and his mother Catherine de Medici, although natural allies to Mary and important family members of her youth, were chilly and distant. Throckmorton spoke from long years as French ambassador to Elizabeth: 'The French do in theyr negoti-ations as they do in theyr drynke, put water to theyr wyne. As I am able to see into theyr doings, they take it not greatlye to the heart, how the Quene [Mary] spede; whether she lyve or dye, whether she be at lyberty or in prison.'[78] His experienced opinion was that, given Catherine de Medici's antipathy for Mary, there was no obligation of family feeling: all that mattered was maintaining their old alliance with Scotland in order to confound the English. Whether that alli-ance was negotiated with the regent, on behalf of the baby king, or with the lords, little mattered. As far as the French majesties were concerned, Mary's fate now was largely an irrelevance.

In fact, in her uncompromising defence of Mary's sovereignty and her stance against the illegality of the lords' action against her, Elizabeth stood alone even amongst her own advisers. The more pragmatic Throckmorton, weighing the dangers upon the ground in Edinburgh, was seriously concerned that if they were to carry through Elizabeth's orders that the lords' first duty was to restore their monarch, then England would lose Scotland to French influ-ence. In an attempt to persuade Elizabeth, he wrote to Leicester: 'If the Queen's majesty still persist in her former opinion to the Queen [Mary] (to whom she can do no good) then I see these lords and their complices will become as good French as that King could wish.' The French were already lobbying hard to get their hands on the little prince and were courting Moray, and any other useful lords they could attract, with offers of cash advances, generous pensions and the bestowal by Charles IX of the chivalric order of St Michael (Elizabeth was right about its commonplace value in the hands of this king).

Throckmorton was an experienced diplomat and he was worried enough to lean on both Leicester and Cecil, with the hope that they could persuade Elizabeth to be more accommodating to the lords and less scrupulous about the sovereign rights of their Scottish queen: 'What an instrument the young prince will prove to "unquyet" England! I report me to your lordships' wisdoms: and trust you will bethink you in time ("for yt is hye tyme") how to advise her majesty to leave nothing undone to get the Prince in [Elizabeth's] possession or at least at her devotion.' Having discussed the matter with Maitland of Lethington he pointed out the English would have no chance of succeeding unless the baby James was named as Elizabeth's successor. Otherwise it would seem 'that the Scottyshemen have put theyre prynce to be kepte in salfetye as thoose which commyt the sheepe to be kept by the wolves!'[79]

As it was, Throckmorton was not allowed to deliver Elizabeth's stirring words of support to Mary. The confederate lords prevented him from seeing her because, as they explained, such comfort from the Queen of England might stiffen her resolve in resisting their proposals. Mary continued to insist that nothing would induce her to renounce Bothwell. The lords were taken aback at her vehemence and her threat to avenge any move made against him. Throckmorton wrote to Elizabeth, '[she] avows constantly she will live and die with him, and say that if it were put to her choice she would leave her kingdom and dignity to live as a simple damoisel with him, and that she will never consent that he shall fare worse or have more harm than herself'.[80] Admirable as this declaration of passion before duty might seem to a modern romantic sensibility, to Elizabeth such sentiments from a fellow queen could only have been deplorable. To trade one's kingdom for love was to fly in the face of divine law, denying every accepted tenet of princely responsibility and good government.

The lords explained to Throckmorton that they could not release

Mary as long as she refused to divorce Bothwell, for if she was free and once more in power they would have no redress against him. A month after her imprisonment Mary sent word to Throckmorton of a further reason why she would 'rather die' than consent to divorce: 'by renouncing Bothwell she should acknowledge herself to be with child of a bastard, and to have forfeited her honour, which she will not do to die for it'.[81] He was quick to relay this to Elizabeth, together with his fatherly advice to Mary that for the sake of her own health and safety, and that of her child, she should take the easiest option. A further kindness he attempted to do her was to counsel Knox, who had just returned to Edinburgh fired up with self-righteousness, to use less vitriol and violence in his preaching against the queen. Whether he reined in his rhetoric or not, this extraordinarily powerful preacher still threatened the whole of Scotland with 'the great plague of God' if Mary was allowed somehow to escape her 'condign punishment'.[82]

In fact no one came to save Mary. She was kept 'very straightly' in her lake-bound prison, limited in the servants, clothes and furnishings she was allowed. Only a select few were given permission to see her. Her personal magnetism was considered a further security risk. Already young Lord Ruthven had been moved from guard duty for becoming besotted and passing on sensitive information. (Mary later related to her secretary Claude Nau that he had offered to procure her freedom if she would sleep with him.) Mary remained faithful to Bothwell who had attempted to raise an army and come for her but failed and, it was rumoured, set off to join the pirates in the North Sea. A band of loyal lords, amongst them Hamilton, Argyll and Huntly, talked much and milled around but to little effect.

Elizabeth's good intentions were modified by her ministers' considerations of realpolitik. Cecil, Leicester and Throckmorton all felt it much wiser to support the Protestant lords. They were reasonable men, keen to stay on good terms with England and to maintain Scotland free of French influence; above all they were of the right religious persuasion. They provided a far better prospect for English security in Europe than the unpredictable and troublesome Mary

Queen of Scots. Elizabeth's pragmatic ministers would have been happy if Mary was erased for ever from the political landscape. Catherine de Medici also washed her hands of her ex-daughter-in-law. She dismissed talk of armed intervention, for the French, she said, 'had irons enow [enough] in the fyre'.[83] Even a month after her defeat at Carberry, Mary still seemed to be unforgiven by the people of Edinburgh, whose anger threatened to spill out on anyone: 'The women be most furious and impudent against her, and yet the men be mad enough, so as a stranger over busy may soon be made a sacrifice amongst them.'[84] Throckmorton wrote to Elizabeth that he seriously feared for Mary's life.

The confederate lords finally got their way. While the queen lay sick, recovering it was presumed from the miscarriage of twins, Lord Lindsay and Robert Melville crossed Loch Leven on 24 July, carrying the papers of abdication. They were empowered to extract Mary's signature through persuasion, threats, or, as a last resort, 'violence and force, as well for the coronation of the Prince, as for the overthrow of the Queen'. If she still proved obdurate then it appeared that they would charge the queen herself with the murder of her husband, having 'proof against her as may be, as well by the testimony of her own handwriting, which they have recovered'.[85] This news of how the final curtain was wrenched down on Mary's reign was reported direct to Elizabeth by the vigilant Throckmorton.

The evidence mentioned, written in her own hand, which was deemed to prove Mary a murderess, was possibly a reference to the notorious 'casket letters' – love letters, purporting to be from Mary to Bothwell, stowed away in a silver casket in his keeping and taken from Bothwell's servant on 20 June, after the rout at Carberry Hill.

Whatever blackmail or force had been brought to bear on Mary as she languished, powerless to resist, she did sign the abdication documents, with many tears, and vowing to overturn them once she was free. On 24 July her reign formally came to an end and her year-old son became James VI. He was crowned five days later on the 29th, with the Earl of Moray, hurrying back from France, installed as regent.

Mary subsequently related that Lindsay had intimidated her with threats, variously to throw her in the lake, secretly incarcerate her for life on an uninhabited island at sea, or slit her throat. She believed herself to be in real danger of her life, a fear which did not abate as she was moved into the castle's tower and watched ever more closely. Her charm once more had brought her this latest grief, for her jailers, the women as much as the men, had grown fond of their captive queen and become talkative and too lenient in their care.

Throckmorton and Drury believed that so great was the hostility towards Mary, from the confederate lords down to the common townspeople, that the Scottish queen at this time was very close to being killed. Elizabeth's doughty disapproval of the lords' unconstitutional behaviour ('a precedent most perilous for any Prince',[86] she feared) and insistence on Mary's reinstatement caused her ministers grave concern. 'Nothing will sooner hasten [Mary's] death, as the doubt these Lords may conceive of her redemption to liberty and authority by the Queen [Elizabeth]'s aid,'[87] Throckmorton lamented to Leicester. But Elizabeth was not cowed and for once was unimpressed by the call for equivocal diplomacy. Leicester answered Throckmorton, explaining that Elizabeth's combative spirit was up: 'She is most earnestly affected towards the Queen of Scots ... There is no persuading the Queen to disguise or use polity, for she breaks out to all men in this matter, and says most constantly that she will become an utter enemy to that nation if that Queen perish.'[88]

Despite the concerted warnings of her advisers, Elizabeth insisted that word was got to Mary, in her watery isolation, of 'the Queen's great grief for her, and how much she takes care for her relief, and [Throckmorton] is to use all ways of best comfort to her in the Queen's name'.[89] The more Elizabeth thought about the presumption of the Scottish lords the more incensed she became. She ranted at Cecil and threatened war. Like all Elizabeth's close advisers, Cecil was pleased to have the threat of Mary neutralized by her imprisonment, and was keen to maintain good relations with the Protestant lords. But none of these considerations carried much weight for Elizabeth, fuelled with outrage that they could treat a sovereign queen with so little respect. Throckmorton was ordered by her to give the following message to the recalcitrant lords 'as roundly and sharply as he can':

> The more she considers these rigorous and unlawful proceedings of those lords against their sovereign lady, the more she is moved to consider how to relieve the Queen her sister . . . having cause to doubt, that as they have begun so audaciously, they will increase in cruelty against her, whom they have it seems violently forced to leave her crown to an infant, to make her appear but a subject, and themselves, by gaining the government, to become superiors to her whom God and nature did create to be their head! . . . For as she is a prince, if they continue to keep her in prison or touch her life or person, she will not fail to revenge it to the uttermost.[90]

There was no doubt that Elizabeth was sincere at the time, although her strength of feeling rose from a deep vein of doctrinal and pragmatic self-interest. If a bunch of mere subjects could get away with dealing so outrageously with their queen, how inevitably was her own position undermined. It was God's place alone to appoint and to punish a sovereign, but the Scottish lords had shown how easy it was to overthrow that sovereign and in effect usurp the kingdom for themselves. Elizabeth, more than anyone, recognized that for all the implication of the divine in her vocation as queen, it was the will of the people who maintained her reign: to continue that supremacy she needed to uphold their perception of her role as inviolable. The unwavering principle of the divine right of kings reiterated forcefully by their irascible neighbour unsettled the Scottish lords. It could have pushed them either way, and for a while Elizabeth's ambassadors argued it might in fact further threaten and not protect Mary's safety. The prospect of the English invading to reinstate the disgraced queen might appear to those with most to lose as a worse alternative than regicide. Throckmorton, however, believed that Elizabeth's implacable principle forcefully expressed actually stayed their hand. His presence as an ambassador empowered by the might and majesty of the English queen defused the lords' 'fear, fury or zeal',[91] and actually saved Mary's life.

Mary's ambassador Robert Melville agreed. His queen had also recognized the singular and unwavering support that was offered, for the first time, by her neighbour and cousin Elizabeth. In her weakened and beleaguered state it was little wonder that Mary thought Elizabeth was about to become the intimate and powerful friend she had initially hoped she would be. Melville reported to Elizabeth her fateful response: 'She would rather herself and the Prince were in your realm, than elsewhere in Christendom.'[92]

When Mary Queen of Scots finally escaped, and in haste and fear bade farewell to Scotland, she thought she was leaving ignominy and danger behind. It was England and Elizabeth which she sought. This seemed the most sympathetic refuge, the most effective means by which she could restore her crown. But hers was a heritage recklessly squandered through wilfulness, lack of political instinct and princely control. Her own crown was lost but her flight to England, she felt, would bring closer that other crown, long coveted and, in many ways, valued more.

CHAPTER TEN

Double Jeopardy

Sonnet to Queen Elizabeth by Mary Queen of Scots (*c.* 1568)

> One thought, that is my torment and delight,
> Ebbs and flows bittersweet within my heart
> And between doubt and hope rends me apart
> While peace and all tranquillity take flight.
> Therefore, dear sister, should this letter dwell
> Upon my weighty need of seeing you,
> It is that grief and pain shall be my due
> Unless my wait should end both swift and well.
> I've seen a ship's sails slackened by taut ropes
> On the high tide at the harbour bar
> And a clear sky suddenly fill with cloud;
> Likewise fear and distress fill all my hopes,
> Not because of you, but for the times there are
> When Fortune doubly strikes on sail and shroud.

The Doubt of Future Foes by Elizabeth I (*c.* 1568–71)

> The doubt of future foes
> Exiles my present joy
> And wit me warns to shun such snares
> As threatens mine annoy.
>
> For falsehood now doth flow
> And subjects' faith doth ebb,
> Which should not be if reason ruled
> Or wisdom ruled the web.
>
> The daughter of debate
> That discord aye doth sow
> Shall reap no gain where former rule
> Still peace hath taught to know,

No foreign banished wight
Shall anchor in this port:
Our realm brooks no seditious sects –
Let them elsewhere resort.

My rusty sword through rest
Shall first his edge employ
To poll their tops who seek such change
Or gape for future joy.
Vivat Regina

THERE WAS NO DOUBT that Mary became the bane of Elizabeth's life. For the first two decades of Elizabeth's reign, she was truly the 'daughter of debate/that discord aye doth sow': now with her exile from Scotland she brought that discord straight to Elizabeth's door. Her presence in England and the conduct of her life grieved Elizabeth on many counts. Everything Mary did had a direct or implied effect on her English cousin, struggling to maintain the delicate balance between her emergent Protestant country and the Catholic powers, her role as a great prince despite her perceived weakness as a woman, her determination to govern a united and peaceful kingdom while rebellions and wars raged abroad. Mary threatened all of this.

Yet Elizabeth, right to Mary's death, had sympathy with her plight. While at times filled with real fear for her own life and kingdom, and astonishment and anger at Mary's self-righteousness, arrogance and scheming, Elizabeth could not erase her deep uneasiness at having Mary imprisoned on her soil, by her will. She too had suffered imprisonment and had feared for her life, and the memories never fully faded. She held as sacred the role of queen and found it hard to countenance, let alone conspire with, those who would keep Mary from her rightful throne.

Mary chose Elizabeth and England as her refuge, rather than Catherine de Medici and France, because of the fundamental sympathy she recognized in her ambivalent cousin. Elizabeth was thirty-four years old and Mary was twenty-five. Mary had been brought up in the protective embrace of her powerful Guise family and the

Valois monarchy. She was not educated for government. Powerful and intelligent herself, she was not easy striking out alone, personally or politically. Mary was happier always in a collaborative relationship. In her desperation, she thought she might find in Elizabeth the kind of protection and support she had received in her defining years. Her letters to Elizabeth, plaintive, longing, often accusatory, stressed a maternal and filial relationship between them. Lonely on their solitary thrones, devoid of close family relations, perhaps for a short while both thought their loneliness could be breached, that their solidarity as regnant queens would overrule their rivalry and capacity to cause each other harm.

If such a thought had ever existed in Elizabeth's mind it can only have been short-lived for more sinister elements soon began to alter the balance of power between them. She had written to Catherine de Medici in outrage at Mary's imprisonment by her lords, 'These evils often resemble the noxious influence of some baleful planet, which, commencing in one place, without the good power, might well fall in another . . .'.[1] The evil she referred to was the insolence of the Scottish nobility in respect of the Queen of Scots, but Elizabeth's arresting image was as truly applicable to Mary herself on her catastrophic trajectory towards England.

Although she brought death and disruption to many in her path, although her political and diplomatic skills were intermittent and often misguided, Mary excelled on those occasions where physical resilience and courage in action was required. Like her cousin Elizabeth, she was a fine horsewoman and possessed of terrific energy and stamina, but as a ruler she was more bellicose and less afraid of consequences. Mary's temperament was more that of the independent adventurer, not that of a great tactician or general. She had shown soon after her return to Scotland how much she had enjoyed the roustabout skirmishes of the Huntly Rebellion. She appeared in her element in such situations, on horseback, riding hell for leather on some clandestine journey, or leading a body of armed men in pursuit of revenge or freedom.

She was to have one more chance for this kind of enterprise before her combative energy was frustrated for ever, to be expressed only through tortuous scheming, emblematically aggressive embroidery and physical ill-health. The means by which she effected her last escape from Loch Leven Castle combined her greatest strengths of an adventurous spirit and irresistible charm. The events that followed, however, embodied her greatest weaknesses – poor political judgement and wilful disregard for the interests of others.

Mary's physical beauty and pathetic circumstances had long before spun a web around the susceptible heart of the young George Douglas, brother of the Laird of Loch Leven, whose misfortune it was to confine her. After two failed attempts at escape and more than ten months of imprisonment, the Scottish queen once more was free. In the evening of 2 May 1568 she slipped out of the castle and was rowed across the lake by another young male devotee, Will Douglas, to be delivered to the waiting George, 'who was in fantasy of love with her'.[2] With him were ten horsemen and a friend of Bothwell's, the Laird of Riccarton. A further body of horsemen waited in the hills under the command of Lord Seton and they conveyed her by land and then sea to Seton's castle at Niddry, then on to Hamilton, from where she sent out messages to muster an army and an extensive and enthusiastic following began to convene. Nearly a year had elapsed since the outraged passions roused by Darnley's murder had threatened her life. Now their beautiful, mistreated and rightful queen had gained a certain lustre in memory.

News of her escape astounded her half-brother, the regent Moray. Immediately he issued an urgent proclamation demanding that all loyal men congregate with him in Glasgow, carrying fifteen days' provisions and ready to fight 'for the preservation of the King's [the infant James VI] person and authority and the establishing of quietness'.[3] Elizabeth was equally astonished at the news but, unlike the male advisers who surrounded her and the Protestant lords in Scotland, she was delighted to hear that Mary was free. Much against her ministers' pragmatic politics, and despite the English support of Moray and his regency, Elizabeth still hoped that Mary would now not only reclaim her throne but deal severely with her treasonous lords. In reasserting her sovereign authority and punishing her presumptuous nobility she would reinforce the rights of all princes in every realm.

Cecil had been suspicious of Mary's ability to cause trouble ever since she had first made concrete her claim to the English throne. A more radical Protestant than Elizabeth, he also recognized Mary's Catholicism as a perennial focus and encouragement for dissidents, and a dangerous point of natural alliance with the Catholic powers of France and Spain. He was unimpressed with Elizabeth's passionate belief in the sacred hierarchy – with God at the apex, then His prince and then the people – which no mere subjects could override.

From Hamilton, and under some influence from the Hamilton family of which the Duke of Châtelherault was head, Mary wrote the most coruscating document attacking all those who had betrayed or abandoned her. Moray was 'James, callit Erle Morray, quhome we of ane spurious bastard (althocht nameit our brother) promovit fra ane religious monk to Erle and Lord' [James, called Earl Moray, whom we from a spurious bastard (although named our brother) promoted from a religious monk* to Earl and Lord]. The other named rebels were variously described as 'hell houndis, bludy tyrantis . . . godles traitouris, commoun murtheraris and throt cutteris . . . and the rest of that pestiferous factioun, quhome fra mair indigence, schamefull slavery, and base estait, we promovit, and oft pardonit thair offences' [hell hounds, bloody tyrants . . . godless traitors, common murderers and cut-throats . . . and the rest of that pestilential faction, whom from mere indigence, shameful slavery, and base estate, we promoted, and often pardoned their offences].[4]

Although some of the document may well have been composed by one of the Hamilton family, the abuse heaped on the heads of the men whom Mary had personally elevated and then pardoned, specifically for the murder of Riccio, had the unmistakable mark of her own outrage and desire for revenge. These sentiments, in slightly more moderate language, were exactly those in her letter

---

* James Stewart had been Prior of St Andrews before giving up the ecclesiastical life.

to Elizabeth, announcing her arrival in England less than a week later. Although she was capable of using self-pity to dramatize her situation, and in rhetoric to get what she wanted, Mary was not a woman to remain a victim for long. Like her cousin she did not pass up an occasion for self-dramatization, but where Elizabeth relied on lofty hauteur and righteous indignation, Mary capitalized shamelessly on the seductive appeal of innocence betrayed.

Before she could wield sovereign power again, however, Mary had to work out the means by which she would once more resume her throne. She asked two of her lawyers 'how she might be restored again to honour and rule' and was given the answer 'by Parliament or by battle'. It was entirely in character that she should favour the quick and the combative over the measured and judicious. 'By battle let us try it',[5] was her impetuous response.

Such bellicose impulses ran counter to everything that was expected of women who were considered not only weak-minded but feeble of body too. At about the time Mary was plotting her escape from the middle of Loch Leven, the Venetian ambassador in Vienna reported home an incident in August 1567 which revealed the disadvantaged sex in a new and unsettling light. In a battle between the Kings of Sweden and Denmark, of the fifteen hundred Swedes dead on the battlefield, five hundred were found to be women. They had worn their hair 'knotted under their helmets', and their clothes and the arms they carried were exactly the same as the men's. To everyone's amazement, they had fought with as much valour and strength as any army of men. The ambassador thought these warrior women must be a phenomenon of modern womanhood. 'Such a thing was never perhaps heard of by our grandfathers or greatgrandfathers',[6] he wondered. But while Mary did not engage in hand-to-hand combat, nevertheless she had few qualms at leading her troops into battle against fellow Scotsmen, 'father . . . against son and brother against brother'.[7]

Eleven days after her surprise escape, the queen's troops were gathering at Langside, a village outside Glasgow, to face the regent Moray and what were called 'the King's men', the soldiers of her own two-year-old son James VI. On Mary's imprisonment and forced abdication the previous summer, Moray had returned hastily to Scotland. Mary's reckless behaviour had tossed into his lap the most glittering prize he could attain as a royal bastard. To help reinstate his half-sister to her throne was not part of his scheme, and in her disempowered state he no longer needed to maintain even the fiction of fraternal love. His interview with her at Loch Leven Castle was so full of reproach and disdain that he had 'cut the thread of love and credit betwixt the Queen and him for ever'.[8] Now he faced a queen unexpectedly sprung to freedom and intent on revenge. His hastily raised troops were outnumbered but not outclassed by the queen's. She had between five and six thousand, he barely four thousand.

Elizabeth received the news officially about a week later. Watched carefully for her reactions, the foreign ambassadors reported back that she appeared delighted and promised every help necessary to restore the Queen of Scots. Like the rest of the court she was eager to hear of Mary's latest escapades. It was reported that on 13 May 1568 battle was engaged for three-quarters of an hour, fiercely for about a third of that time, with Mary's followers suffering the worst of it. There was no great loss of life – contemporary estimates put the dead at under 150 – but the queen, watching on horseback from a vantage point on the hill, suddenly lost her nerve, turned her horse and rode off at speed. Melville noted how out of character this was, but Mary herself explained that suddenly she was confronted by the dread of prison again, or even of her own murder. She set off with a few of her followers, including the boy Will Douglas who had rowed her across Loch Leven to freedom, and galloped the ninety miles through Dumfries to Dundrennan, on the Solway Firth, in fear of her life.

Against all the advice of her followers, Mary determined to throw herself on Elizabeth's hospitality, calling in her promises of help and restitution. From Dundrennan she sent a first letter, explaining her predicament and enclosing the great diamond Elizabeth had previously given her, 'the jewel of her promised friendship and assistance'.[9] Only daring to travel at night, to avoid detection, and ignoring her followers' misgivings, Mary was set on getting to England as soon as she could. On 16 May her party crossed the Solway Firth in a fishing boat to arrive at Workington, on the coast of Cumbria. She had barely the clothes she stood up in. Dishevelled and exhausted she wrote a long letter of explanation and justification to Elizabeth the following day, ending with the plea: 'I entreat you to send to fetch me as soon as you possibly can, for I am in a pitiable condition, not only for a Queen, but for a gentlewoman'. She signed herself emotionally, '*Votre très fidelle et affectionnée bonne soeur et cousine et eschappée prisonière, Marie R*'.[10]

Once more Mary was utterly lacking in political judgement. With a little forethought she would have recognized in what an impossible position she placed herself and Elizabeth by seeking refuge in England. On impulse, and certain she would get to meet her cousin at last, she gambled everything on her personal charm, claims of consanguinity and affectionate blandishments winning her the necessary support to restore her to the Scottish throne. In the grip of her fantasy, it seemed her presence in England might also secure her coveted place as successor to the English crown. This inflated sense of her own power and lack of real understanding of the political realities would begin to exasperate Elizabeth who by the beginning of the new year was provoked into issuing a sharp warning: 'the fine weather of fair promises and the echoes of voices which seem to honour you above all the world should not envelop you in so thick a cloud that you may not see plain day. They are not so dedicated to adoring you as they make your ministers believe ... be not blind nor think me blind.'[11]

With a four-day journey time between the Scottish and English courts, letters and dispatches were always crossing halfway. Never was this time lag more inconvenient than in reporting Mary's activities for she was so precipitate in her actions, and those were too often incredible, that it was impossible to keep up with the news. In fact Elizabeth had written her cousin a letter on the same day as Mary's historic announcement of her arrival and the messengers passed each other somewhere in the English Midlands. Elizabeth did not yet know that Mary had crossed the border and was already in her own country when she wrote rather less effusively of the 'joyful news of your happy enlargement [release]'. She felt constrained, she went on, to offer Mary advice 'touching your estate and honour', for 'if you had as much regard thereto as to "*ung malheureuse meschant*" [Bothwell]* all the world would have condoled with you, as to speak "*sans faincte*" [without pretence], not many do'. She ended abruptly with the warning not to try and put pressure on her by threatening to involve the French: 'remember that those who have two strings to their bow may shoot stronger, but they rarely shoot straight'.[12]

Mary did not take kindly to advice and her next letter to Elizabeth pressed even more insistently for a meeting, and repeated her old blackmail: 'If for any reason I cannot come to you, seeing I have freely come to throw myself in your arms, you will I am sure permit me to ask assistance of my other allies – for thank God, I am not destitute of some.'[13] This raised the old spectre of a French–Scottish alliance which reminded Elizabeth of her vulnerability to invasion through her distant and difficult northern borders. She could not countenance Mary transferring her troublesome presence across the Channel. As she angrily exclaimed to the Venetian ambassador a while later, 'My prudence would weigh but lightly were I to permit the departure of her who lays claim to be mistress of this realm, and who of yore assumed its arms and title.'[14] But to return her to Scotland against the wishes of Moray and the majority of the Protestant nobles was fraught with difficulties too.

The problem of Mary in England was to draw Elizabeth increasingly into a labyrinth of cause and effect from which there would be no escape. Although ostensibly Elizabeth was in control, with power to affect Mary's fate, in reality the relationship between the guest-prisoner and the host-jailer was much more complex and finely balanced. In her letters to Mary, Elizabeth's tone was often imperious but would turn tentative with guilt and uncertainty about

---

* The Earl of Bothwell was already a prisoner in Denmark. After being held captive for ten years, he died 14 April 1578 in Dragsholm, a forbidding castle in the north of Zealand, apparently in pitiful circumstances, chained to a pillar in a dungeon, filthy and insane. He was forty-three years old.

how best to proceed. Mary's voice, playing on Elizabeth's sympathies and reliant on her own sovereign status, was often the more confident and threatening. She might lack temporal power but this gave her access to the emotional power of the innocent in chains. She knew the unassailable moral force of suffering and martyrdom. Against this theatrical high ground, Elizabeth could only appear diminished.

News that Mary Queen of Scots had arrived over the border spread locally like wildfire. There was much excitement among the nobility and some competition as to who would temporarily give her shelter. The north of England was notoriously unresponsive to government from London, and still largely Catholic in its sympathies. Mary's reputation was already lustrous with the glamour of sex, monarchy and scandal, and her person seldom failed to work its magic, even when she was dressed in borrowed clothes and lacking the trappings of royalty. In fact the loss of her jewellery, left behind in various flights from the enemy, was of real concern to her. Mary described Moray at this time 'as hyr grevous enemye and seller of hyr juells',[15] as if appropriating her throne and threatening her life was on a par with stealing the furnishings. Venice was known as Europe's great marketplace and it was expected that if Moray chose to sell her jewellery it would end up there. The Venetian ambassador had sent notice to his court to look out for any pieces of fine quality and high value passing through their dealers' hands. Later in the year, Mary asked Elizabeth to persuade Moray not to sell her jewels, which Elizabeth promptly did, receiving an immediate undertaking that nothing yet had been sold to enrich himself or his friends.

Mary was escorted with great courtesy as befitted her rank to Carlisle Castle and there her retinue of forty, among them Lords Herries and Fleming, were accommodated and efforts made to supply her with more clothes and other necessities. Until Elizabeth had assessed the situation Mary's status was unclear and her hosts discomfited as to whether she was an honoured queen, seeking temporary refuge, or a fugitive from justice in need of close restraint.

Sir Francis Knollys, vice-chamberlain, and Lord Scrope, governor of Carlisle, were dispatched to Mary with letters of sympathy from Elizabeth. Knollys, despite his Puritan sensibilities, was immediately impressed by his first audience with Mary. His subsequent letter to Elizabeth was bound to deepen her incipient unease: 'We found her to have an eloquent tongue and a discreet head, and it seemeth by her doings she hath stout courage and liberal heart adjoined thereunto.' Inviting the two men into her bedchamber for greater privacy, Mary 'fell into some passion with the water in her eyes' and complained at how disappointed she was not to have been taken immediately into Elizabeth's presence. She wanted her cousin either to 'aid her to subdue her enemies' or failing that then allow her to pass through England to Europe to enlist help from a prince from France or Spain.

Knollys explained that Elizabeth desired a meeting as much as Mary did herself but she 'could not do her that great honour ... by reason of this great slander of murder, whereof she was not yet purged'. He was sensitive to Elizabeth's dilemma as to how and where to keep the Queen of Scots: 'a body of [Mary's] agility and spirit may escape soon, being so near the Border. And surely to have her carried farther into the realm is the highway to a dangerous sedition'.[16]

He had also brought with him a collection of Elizabeth's clothes for Mary to use until hers arrived but these were not well received by the Queen of Scots. An embarrassed Knollys, pressed by Elizabeth for news of the reception of her gift, wrote that Mary's silence 'argues rather scornful than grateful acceptance'.[17] But then he had thought the dresses were rather mean himself and excused them as having been selected by one of Elizabeth's maids, he suggested, mistakenly for the use of a servant like herself. The quality and richness of costume and jewellery were intimately bound up with perceived status. Elizabeth's gift of her inferior gowns was more a reminder of their relative power than solely an expression of lack of sisterly generosity.

On 8 June, Elizabeth sent an envoy north with a letter for Mary and one for Moray, both holding exercises while she determined how best to resolve the growing conundrum. To Mary she promised a parent's care for her honour and safety, and insisting that once she was acquitted of this crime 'among all worldly pleasures [meeting you] will hold the first rank'.[18] She explained that she had already risked her own reputation in defending Mary while these accusations remained unanswered. To Moray she rehearsed Mary's accusations against him and the Protestant lords, and mildly requested that he 'forbear from all hostility and persecution' against those followers of the queen. These were diplomatic sentiments but given Elizabeth's reputation for opacity and sharp dealing such judiciousness was easily interpreted as double-dealing. The Spanish ambassador, Guzman de Silva, who liked and admired Elizabeth, found himself agreeing with the words of one of Mary's followers: 'the Queen of England uses towards his mistress fair words and foul deeds'.[19]

Mary's criticism of her cousin was in a different vein. She found Elizabeth's caution maddening and her even-handedness galling in the extreme. She told Knollys she was unimpressed by Elizabeth's message to Moray. Such 'coolde dealyng' Mary declared would not satisfy her own 'fyerye stomake'. The kindly vice-chamberlain shared his astute opinion of the situation with Cecil and Elizabeth: 'it is great vanity to think [the Queen of Scots] will be stayed by courtesy, or bridled by fear, from bringing the French to Scotland, or employing her money, men of war, and friendship to satisfy her "bluddye appetyte to shed the blude" of her enemies'.[20] Poor Knollys had already had the tempestuous and tearful Mary ranting at him about how set she was on revenge, so determined to ruin Moray that she would rather 'all her partie were hanged' than that they should accept the regent's rule. Her blood was so roused that she cared not for Elizabeth's mediation. She would rather be back again in Scotland, she declared, 'to abide all adventures'.[21] As Knollys recognized, for such a temperament as Mary's, 'all deedes are no deedes with her, unless her vyolent appetytes be satisfyed'. She had threatened her English cousin, 'I have made great warrs in Skotland, and I praye God I make no troubles in other realmes also', adding as a parting shot, which was relayed by Knollys, 'if we dyd detayne her as a prysoner, we should have much ado with her'.[22]

None of this was music to Elizabeth's overstrained ears. Not only did Mary appear intractable and defiant, with the rash courage of a fighting man, she dangerously combined this masculine bellicosity with the full panoply of female seductiveness and guile. Puritan and loyal Englishman that he was, Knollys could not help but be impressed by the force of Mary's character and the contrast of her attractive and charming female form. Her emotionalism also brought out his protective side. He immediately dropped any subjects that made her cry and consoled her whenever she burst into paroxysms of weeping – tears more often of frustration at the lack of action or anger at not getting her own way. After two weeks of daily contact with Mary, he wrote a character sketch of such insight that Elizabeth and Cecil, to whom it was addressed, can only have been chillingly forewarned what a formidable adversary they were up against, and what trouble this queen would prove to be:

> this ladie and pryncess is a notable woman. She seemeth to regard no ceremonious honor besyde the acknowledging of her estate regalle. She sheweth a disposition to speake much, to be bold, to be pleasant, and to be very famylyar. She sheweth a great desyre to be avenged of her enemyes; she sheweth a readines to expose herselfe to all perylls in hope of victorie; she delyteth much to hear of hardines and valiancye, commending by name all approved hardy men of her cuntry, altho they be her enemyes; and she commendeth no cowardnes even in her frendes. The thyng that most she thirsteth after is victory . . . for victorie's sake, payne and perrylls semeth pleasant unto her . . . Nowe what is to be done with such a ladie and a pryncess.[23]

This was Elizabeth's problem. Mary's presence in the north of England was fomenting excitement and rumour. The Catholic nobility's numbers were greatest there and yet had caused their monarch little trouble so far, but their hopes were being roused from a long slumber. When even Knollys fell under the legendary spell of the Queen of Scots, and the Spanish ambassador drily commented that she 'knows how to ingratiate herself with her keepers',[24] Elizabeth, in the absence of a meeting with Mary, could only imagine a rival larger than life and more dangerous than Circe. This was at the heart of the tragedy of the relationship between these queens. Because they never met, the self-interested reports of others, malicious gossip and their own fantasies, coloured by wishful thinking or fear, took the place of reality. It was inevitable that for each their rival should grow to monstrous scale and, deprived of humanity, become a cipher for predatory threat.

Mary bombarded Elizabeth with emotionally charged, fluently authoritative letters, aimed at reminding her cousin of their blood ties and the injustice of imprisonment without a chance of reply. These were hard enough to answer, too easily wrong-footing Elizabeth who, having escaped from injustice herself, did not like being cast as the oppressor. Mary's attitude veered between the extremes of warmongering and tearful hysteria. At the halfway mark was a charming, energetic, fun-loving and self-aware woman who attracted affection and admiration from all quarters. She had an unerring sense of how best to win friends and influence people. Her keeper Knollys, a loyal Elizabethan, was filled with admiration for the way Mary conducted herself, assuring her allies with 'hearty letters and messages', promising 'liberal rewards', making much of the Hamiltons, whose support she relied on in her determination to return to Scotland, and craftily enticing into her circle 'those she would fain have as friends' by making them believe 'they were her friends at heart, however drawn otherwise'.[25] Knollys was watching a consummate networker and practised charmer at her art, and he could not hide his respect.

Mary did not employ an overtly threatening tone in her messages to Elizabeth at this time, but rather insinuated an emotional pathos laced with hints of her power to challenge and disturb the fragile status quo. To sympathetic ambassadors, like Guzman de Silva, she sent messages of helpless femininity: 'If the Christian princes abandon her she says being a woman and alone she does not know what she can do',[26] and dispatched affecting messages to every possible ally in Europe.

To her Guise uncle, the Cardinal of Lorraine, she poured forth her angry eloquence: 'I have endured injuries, calumnies, imprisonment, famine, cold, heat, flight, not knowing whither, ninety-two miles across the country without stopping or alighting, and then I have had to sleep upon the ground, and drink sour milk, and eat oatmeal without bread, and have been three nights like the owls, without a female in this country, where, to crown all, I am little else than a prisoner.'[27] Her catalogue of woes was unquestionably extreme, a queen should not have to endure such fear, danger and indignity, but Mary never acknowledged any responsibility, even in part, for the disasters that overtook her.

Elizabeth's instinct was to return her cousin with all haste to Scotland. But this she could not do without alienating Moray and the ruling elite who were essential to the English policy of keeping Scotland close and the French out. She toyed momentarily with a compromise plan which she confided to the Spanish ambassador: 'I am thinking of returning her to her Kingdom with the title of Queen, but without any power to govern; and I think that her acquittal should be so arranged that it should be left in doubt; for if her complete innocence were to be declared it would be dangerous to this Kingdom, to my friends and to myself.'

Elizabeth, however, increasingly realized the unhappy reality that she would have to keep Mary in a kind of honourable imprisonment, in the medium term at least. The Scottish queen had already given cause for alarm. She had been allowed to ride out to join a hunt coursing for hares, and the speed and skill of her horse riding had so alarmed Knollys, from a security point of view, that he felt she would need to be moved deeper into England, away from the rebellious Borders and a direct escape route back to her kingdom or away by sea to France.

Unsurprisingly Mary was adamant that she would not consent to such a change of abode, unless it was to take her directly into Elizabeth's presence. Otherwise they would have to take her by force, she declared dramatically. Elizabeth was more than exasperated. Mary had lost everything through her own mismanagement and wilfulness, and was in no position to dictate conditions to her.

Yet she continued to behave with the imperiousness of Elizabeth herself. In French Elizabeth addressed her sharply, rather as a mother reprimanding her adolescent daughter: 'begging you to have some consideration of me, in place of always thinking of yourself'.[28] A few days' easy ride south of Carlisle was Bolton Castle which had been decided should be Mary's next place of safety. After various inducements and veiled threats, Mary was persuaded to abandon her protest, causing the long-suffering Knollys to exclaim, 'Surely yf I shold declare the difficulties that we have passed, before we cowld gett hyr to remove, instede of a letter I shold wryte a storye and that sumwhat tragicall!'[29]

Despite Mary's reluctant removal to Bolton, Elizabeth's sympathies were being strained to the limit. At odds with her councillors, she still maintained that Mary should somehow be restored to her legitimate throne but she recognized, nevertheless, that Moray's regency was established and could not be ignored. She decided that a hearing was necessary to ascertain the facts that led to this unconstitutional rejection of Mary by her subjects. Her sensitivities to Mary's status as a monarch meant she insisted Moray and not his queen stood as the accused.

York was designated as the theatre in which the charges against Moray and his countercharges against the Queen of Scots would be heard. The commissioners representing both antagonists gathered at the beginning of October 1568. Moray came himself and although Mary was not present she had Lord Herries and the Bishop of Ross amongst others to make her case. The Duke of Norfolk, Earl of Sussex and Sir Ralph Sadler were there to represent Elizabeth in her role of arbitrator, given express instructions by her that Mary's responsibility for murdering her husband had to be established beyond doubt otherwise she would be instrumental in returning her cousin to her rightful throne, 'having regard to the princely state wherein she was born'.[30]

Moray was not slow to produce what he considered to be his *coup de grâce*, the letters purportedly written in Mary's hand, found in the silver-gilt casket in the keeping of a servant of Bothwell after his defeat at Carberry Hill. He revealed privately to Norfolk and his fellow commissioners these eight letters and a series of sonnets, astonishingly torrid with sexual feeling and suggestively conspiratorial in the murder of Darnley.

If these 'casket letters' were in fact genuine, they were unambiguously incriminating both of Mary's complicity in, if not incitement of, the murder of her husband, the king, and in her illicit and overwhelming sexual passion for the man who was the chief suspect in his death. There was much circumstantial detail which was reinforced by other sources, and the central strand of emotion in them had a certain sincerity and truth. However, the originals disappeared soon after their exposure, some said destroyed by James VI in the 1580s to protect his mother's reputation. Relying only on copies in the absence of the originals, debate has raged for nearly four and a half centuries, and the truth can not now be known. Mary was never allowed to examine them and consistently denied their authenticity. Buchanan, knowing the queen personally, having been her Latin tutor and therefore also in close contact with her handwriting and phraseology, declared the letters and poems were genuine. By this time, however, he had become a hostile witness, basing much of his subsequent notorious attack* on Mary on the revelations of these letters. The likelihood is that they were partly, or even wholly, forgeries; genuine letters from Mary interpolated with incriminating words and phrases, genuine letters from another of Bothwell's lovers that had been made to appear from Mary, possibly amalgamations of more than one source, or out and out fabrications.

Norfolk was horrified by what he read. In his letter to Elizabeth on 11 October 1568, he could not disguise his shock: 'they shewed unto us one horrible and longe lettre of her owne hand, as they saye, contayninge foule matteir and abhominable, to be either thowght of, or to be written by a prince ... The said lettres and ballades do discover suche inordinate "and filthie" [scored out] love betwene her and Bothaill, her loothesomnes and abhorringe of her husband that was murdered ...' He concluded that the writings contained

---

* *Detectio Mariae Reginae Scotorum (A Detection of Mary Queen of Scots)*, George Buchanan, 1571.

so much circumstantial evidence 'unknowen to anie other then to herselfe and Bothaill [Bothwell]'³¹ that it would have been hard to counterfeit them: yet if they were genuine then a judgement as to Mary's guilt as an accomplice to the murder of her husband could not be avoided. He awaited Elizabeth's response as to how they should proceed.

Elizabeth seemed not overtly alarmed, and certainly not concerned to press to establish Mary's guilt. Even when she eventually saw the letters for herself a couple of months later, after the enquiry had reconvened in London, she told Knollys matter-of-factly that they 'conteyned manny matters very unmete *to come from a "quene"* [scored out] to be repeated before honest eares, and easely drawn to be apparent proves ageynst the Quene'.³² She did demand, however, that the enquiry move to Westminster better to assess the evidence, and it was convened on 25 November. To assuage Mary's suspicions, Norfolk was ordered to explain that this move was in order to save time, bypassing some of the delay in sending communications to and fro. Elizabeth was anxious that Mary and her commissioners should continue to think that there was little doubt that her cause would be successful, and that the enquiry was concerned primarily in the detail of her restoration and the safeguarding of her son's interests.

Norfolk's personal ambitions, however, appeared to overcome his disapproval of Mary's unqueenly behaviour as suggested by the casket letters. Soon he was confiding a contrary view to her commissioner, Maitland of Lethington. In his opinion Elizabeth's real purpose was to prolong Mary's confinement, thus allowing Moray to blacken her reputation as much as possible and so damage her popular following in England. In this way, he suggested, Elizabeth meant to undermine the powerful Catholic support that was building around the charismatic image of the unjustly imprisoned Mary.

The Duke of Norfolk was Elizabeth's premier nobleman. A vain, vacillating man, he had grown resentful that his princely status and vast wealth did not translate into greater influence at court. He aspired to something even grander. To be the consort of the Queen of Scotland, with the chance of becoming even, through her, the

King of England, suited the *amour-propre* of this thrice-widowed, thirty-two-year-old magnate. Knollys had been postulating an English marriage for Mary as the only way, in the event of releasing her, to neutralize the threat she posed of inviting French or Spanish interference into the land. He thought the safest way to rein her in was to marry her to a kinsman of Elizabeth's, specifically his own nephew George Carey who was a cousin of the queen's on her Boleyn side. But Norfolk, in need of a wife himself, could think of no better way to advance his own status. He began making moves to canvass support for his plan almost immediately. By the end of the year the gossip around court was full of his aspirations, but for a while Elizabeth was kept in the dark. This was a perilous act. It meant Norfolk was less than impartial in a murder enquiry where the suspect was the focus of his own high ambitions. The secrecy meant too that his negotiations looked suspiciously like a conspiracy in the making.

Inevitably the rumours reached the queen. When Elizabeth asked Norfolk frankly if his marriage plans involved the Queen of Scots he theatrically denied everything: 'What! . . . Should I seek to marry her, being so wicked a woman, such a notorious adulteress and murderer? I love to sleep upon a safe pillow.'[33] Elizabeth was not to forget this and Norfolk's words would return to haunt him.

The enquiry continued at Westminster to the end of the year. With a flourish Moray produced the pretty casket, engraved with the imperial monogram of François II and unmistakably once belonging to Mary. From it he extracted the treacherous letters now for everyone to see. Copies were duly made: everyone was pruriently riveted and aghast in equal measure. But Mary refused to answer her accusers except in person, and Elizabeth was not about to allow her sweet eloquence and personal charm any formal airing before the most notable councillors and nobility of her land. With consummate skill she sidestepped her request by pointing out that she could not allow Mary to demean herself by giving credence, through her presence, to charges based on this tawdry evidence.

Although Mary had not been shown the letters, she consistently and forcefully maintained that any such writings were undoubted forgeries.

Moray swore to their authenticity. The truth was probably somewhere between the two. The author of any deception, however, was another area for surmise and debate. The longest letter, known as the second letter, probably caused the most trouble. If true, it revealed a murderous duplicity and contempt by a queen and wife towards her ill and pathetic husband. Doubly damning was the fact that this callousness was united with a venal passion for the masterful lover, and her husband's would-be murderer. Purportedly written from Glasgow, where Mary had gone to bring back the sick Darnley to Edinburgh, having promised to resume conjugal relations with him as an inducement, the writer addressed Bothwell:

> God forgive me, and God knytt us togither for ever, for the most faythfull couple that ever he did knytt together. This is my fayth, I will dye in it. Excuse it, yf I write yll, you must gesse the one halfe, I can not doo with all, for I am yll at ease, and glad to write unto you when other folkes be asleepe, seeing that I cannot doo as they doo, according to my desyre, that is betwene your armes, my deere lyfe, whom I besech God to preserve from all yll . . . Cursed be this pocky fellow that troublith me thus muche, for I had a pleasanter matter to discourse with you, but for him. He is not muche the worse, but he is yll arayde. I thought I shuld have bene kylled with his breth, for it is worse than your uncles breth, and yet I was sett no neerer to him than in a chayre by his bolster, and he lyeth at the furder syd of the bed.

The letter continued with a great deal more conversational, rambling detail, and then ended 'Burne this lettre, for it is too dangerous . . . Now if to please you my deere lyfe, I spare nether honour, conscience, nor hazard, nor greatnes, take it in good parte . . . I pray you give no credit, against the most faythfull lover that ever you had or shall have. See not also her [his wife Jean?] whose faynid teares you ought not more to regarde than the true travails which

I endure to deserve her place, for obtayning of which against my own nature, I doo betraye those that could lett me. God forgive me, and give you my only friend and good luck and prosperitie that your humble and faythfull lover doth wisshe unto you; who hopith shortly to be an other thing unto you, for the reward of my paynes.'[34]

The female character that emerged from this letter was obdurately set against her young, frightened and ill husband who was begging for forgiveness and a restoration of his conjugal life with her. She was prepared to sacrifice his life together with her conscience and honour in order to satisfy her own and her lover's desire to be united. The Scottish and English commissioners and nobility who read these apparently most intimate confessions of the Queen of Scots were likely to have found them initially as repellent and frightening as did the Duke of Norfolk. There was however less evidence of contemporary public denunciation of Mary's character as a result, or declaration as to the authenticity of the documents, than occurred in the centuries of debate that followed. This was possibly due to Elizabeth's coolness on the matter and strong disapproval of their public dissemination.

Elizabeth possibly understood better than anyone how the attitudes and emotions unmasked in the 'casket letters' were not just a devastating destruction of Mary's reputation but were also an attack on every 'unnatural' woman in a position of authority. Her attempts at protecting Mary from public vilification went on throughout her reign with various proclamations against a variety of books and pamphlets. The soldier-poet and playwright George Whetstone,* looking back on this time, commented that Elizabeth 'forbad the bookes of [Mary's] faultes, to be conversant among her English subjects which almost in every other nation were made vulgar'.[35] Norfolk's view that this was Elizabeth's double-dealing in action, being seen publicly to do well by Mary while allowing the slander of murder and adultery to hang over her head indefinitely,

---

* George Whetstone (1550–87) is principally remembered for his play *Promos and Cassandra* written in 1578 in rhymed verse which provided the plot for Shakespeare's *Measure for Measure*.

might have been part of the reason for her carefulness with Mary's fame. It was just as likely, however, that highly sensitized as she was to her own reputation, Elizabeth wished to protect them both personally and as female monarchs from defamation. All the worst qualities of emotionalism, weak-mindedness and treachery were still believed to belong to the female and to gain frightening proportions with the promotion of women to power.

Mary's commissioners repudiated the enquiry and withdrew when permission for Mary to appear in front of Elizabeth was refused. Judgement was deferred and the enquiry dismantled with no movement in any direction. As Norfolk had predicted, through sleight of hand Elizabeth had managed to maintain her favourite diplomatic stance, self-righteous and Janus-faced as the guardian of her throne without actually having to take any decisive action at all.

Mary was left bereft of hope. Suddenly the tide was comprehensively against her, and without her being aware of the turn. Peremptorily, she was moved in early February 1569 from Bolton to the medieval castle of Tutbury, a windy, exposed and semi-derelict fortress in Staffordshire. Of all the places Mary was kept during her long English imprisonment, Tutbury was the one she loathed most. Ill-furnished and uncomfortable, freezing cold and plagued with damp, it was one of the properties belonging to the Earl of Shrewsbury, an austere but sympathetic and just man, who had been chosen to replace the overly susceptible Knollys as Mary's keeper.

In an impassioned letter to Elizabeth written later that year from the fastness of Tutbury, Mary's description of the rough treatment of herself and her servants, and the 'bodily fear' it occasioned in her, had uneasy echoes of the fear Elizabeth endured at the hands of her own sister while imprisoned during the investigation of the Wyatt Rebellion. Mary's plea, not to be left 'to waste away in tears and complaints . . . at least let me not be placed in the hands of any one suspicious to my friends and relations, for fear of false reports . . .', was the exact anxiety which had haunted Elizabeth. Her valediction was also affecting: 'I shall pray God to give you a happy and long life, and me a better share of your favour than to my sorrow I perceive that I have, whereto I shall commend myself affectionately to the end . . . Your very affectionate distressed sister and cousin.'[36]

Elizabeth was not happy with the role in which she was cast by Mary in her unhappy imprisonment. She did not see herself as an unjust oppressor, and certainly not as the persecutor of a fellow queen. She was bombarded by Mary with pathetic letters full of complaints and half-suppressed rage. Much of the time she did not answer them, for the answers could only be the same. But the weight of them and the guilt, frustration and self-righteousness they roused in Elizabeth were hard to bear. Running through the letters was the threnody of Mary's close kinship with Elizabeth (daughter, sister, cousin) and her longing to meet her. This she was continually denied, and the anguished impotence of her enforced isolation from the queen had Mary resorting to the language of unrequited love: if allowed into Elizabeth's presence at last, 'I shall discover to you the secrets of my heart . . . I shall devote myself more and more to love, honour, and obey you . . . and if you please so to favour me, I would beg of you first of all to command me when you please, where you please, in what company, to remain as secretly, as long or as short, without seeing or being seen but by you, with whom alone I have to do'.[37]

While equivocating and parrying her cousin's pleas for an audience, for fairer treatment, for restoration of her crown, for her place in the succession, Elizabeth still tried to console Mary with warm promises which by now had grown increasingly threadbare. She vowed that she would protect her reputation and keep private the false accusations against her, 'praying her to take patience in [Elizabeth's] gentle ward, where she was nearer at hand to get the crown of England set upon her head', and assuring her that she herself, 'who was but the eldest sister',[38] was likely to die before her.

Mary was not consoled. Her expectation of freedom at last was replaced with the depressed realization that Elizabeth might profess determination to restore her to her throne but the hard prescriptions of politics and the prerogatives of power made it very difficult for her to do so. On one occasion in April 1569, when she had hoped to keep the French sympathetic in her stand-off with the

Spanish over their captured payships, Elizabeth thought the political benefits of releasing Mary might be worth the risks. After procrastinating for months, however, Moray flatly refused to have her back, much to Elizabeth's fury. The problem of what to do with Mary was left explosively in her hands.

By the end of the summer of 1569, the possible restoration of Mary had become bound up in many of the English councillors' minds with the advantage of containing her appetite for trouble by marrying her off to Norfolk. What had begun as Norfolk's singular ambition now involved a motley band of men with mixed, even contradictory, interests in a controversial enterprise initially cooked up behind Elizabeth's back. The most unlikely alliance was between the long-sworn enemies Norfolk and Leicester. Leicester's disingenuous explanation of his careerist involvement was that, despite his high regard for the duke and his low regard for Mary, he was prepared to countenance such a match if it was best for the queen and her kingdom: 'there could be no better Remedie to provide for so dangerous a Woman . . . considering the present state of the World'.[39]

Mary's own attempts at release had been focused more on inveigling support, even armed intervention, from one or other of the Catholic powers. To Philip II of Spain she had sent the rash and over-optimistic message that if he 'help me, I shall be Queen of England in three months, and Mass shall be said all over the country'.[40] This inflated boast was intended to lure Philip from his usual passivity into some sign of solidarity. It revealed more tellingly, however, the unreality of an indulged woman who had relied always on her charm to effect everything. It led her to believe that now, in a neighbouring kingdom, she could translate her personal charisma into a national fervour powerful enough, with the help of Spanish gold, to dethrone Elizabeth herself.

Her English cousin, after a decade of rule, had established herself beyond doubt as a competent and popular monarch who inspired in her phalanx of advisers a fundamental loyalty. Despite the storms of temper she unleashed periodically at their heads, Elizabeth could be relied on to offer Cecil and her council a reciprocal loyalty and an openness to reason and compromise, an utterly serious acceptance of her obligations as queen. Compromise and obligation were alien concepts to a princess raised in the French court of Henri II, and they were unwelcome restraints on the character of a queen who had ruled through personal passions, impulse and defiance.

The Norfolk marriage plan had been put to Mary in May 1569 and she had jumped at the chance.* Rather crucially, however, it needed Elizabeth's blessing, and no one was keen to be the one to tell her. Norfolk himself had already denied to her face that her suspicions were well-founded. His subsequent evasions only suggested something sinister was afoot. In fact when Leicester eventually told Elizabeth of the plan in September 1569 she was incensed and unsettled. That Leicester, her greatest intimate, should have supported such a match through his own opportunism, ingratiating himself, it seemed, with someone he thought might be a future sovereign, hurt her feelings. But what threatened her life, Elizabeth felt, was the alliance of her premier nobleman with the greatest rival for her throne. The Catholicism of one and the near Catholicism of the other only added to the danger. She told a chastened Leicester that she believed she would have ended up once more in the dreaded Tower if those two had been allowed to marry. Although this was an outburst sprung in the heat of emotion, the very fact that she could think her position so precarious indicated the extent of Elizabeth's insecurity in the face of Mary's legitimate claim to her throne.

Mary posed much more than a political threat to Elizabeth. For a solitary, unmarried queen, a woman bereft of immediate family, the loyalty of her closest associates was of paramount importance. Leicester was her lifelong intimate: the fever of passion may have passed but a possessive and close affection remained. For him to

---

* Mary was still married to Bothwell and would remain so until his death on 14 April 1578. From 1570 onwards there were various requests from Mary and her envoys to the pope for nullification of the marriage by reason of it being bigamous, or Bothwell having taken Mary by force. If Mary had had a serious suitor there is little doubt that she would have received dispensation from the pope to marry a fourth husband.

dilute his loyalty to Elizabeth with his favour of Mary's interests was an emotional betrayal of a particularly poignant kind. Elizabeth was jealous of the effect her Scottish cousin seemed to have on all who encountered her. It was becoming tediously predictable that every male bent a little at the knees and went weak in the head with even short-term exposure to Mary's personal charm. Sir Nicholas Throckmorton, seasoned ambassador, gave some compelling reasons why the Scottish queen, 'a Woman so ill thowght of heretofore', should suddenly be surrounded by English friends: 'the first, hir misery; whereof all Men naturallie take Compassion: The second, hir Entertaynment of such as came to hir: And the third, Th'opinion that some had of hir Title in Succession'.[41]

One of Elizabeth's officials had spent a night at Tutbury in the foul winter of early 1569. One hour in Mary's company had so impressed him that he wrote to Cecil and his queen warning them, 'there shulde veray few Subjects in this Land have Accesse to, or Conferens with this Lady. For besyd, that she is a goodly personadge, (and yet in trouthe not comparable to our Souverain) she hathe withall an alluring Grace, a prety *Scottishe* speche, and a serching Witt, clowded with Myldnes [and a searching intelligence softened with sweetness of manner].'[42] The highly infectious and indiscriminate nature of Mary's 'alluring Grace' made her the most formidable rival, all the more so given that Elizabeth would never meet her and had to rely only on such reports from her half-smitten nobles and executives. In a time when the supernatural was a companion to daily life, this physical alienation from Mary's human reality meant her power inflated in imagination into something almost like sorcery.

Knollys, Lord Scrope, her own cousin George Carey, Norfolk, Throckmorton, the northern earls and eventually even solid Shrewsbury himself, who could she trust not to be entranced? For a while it seemed only Cecil, Elizabeth's cast-iron Secretary of State, was immune to the Queen of Scots, a fact of which Mary herself was acutely aware. Like all beautiful women who were used to getting what they wanted, she was galled by the rare individual who did not succumb to her charm. When she was not in one of her passions, vilifying him as 'hir Enemy', she credited Cecil with intelligence and a respect for the law, for being 'a faithefull Servaunt to his Mistress', while wanly wishing 'it might be hir Luck to gett the Friendshipp of so wise a Man'.[43]

While Mary hankered after an adviser of Cecil's calibre, Elizabeth had to deal with her manoeuvres for a fourth husband in the form of the less intellectually impressive, but more princely, Norfolk. The perfidious duke was immediately summoned to Elizabeth's presence. In fright he feigned illness. His sudden departure from court to return to his estates had caused all kinds of alarmist talk; his disobedience and continued absence set tongues wagging that Norfolk was mustering his forces in a show of treasonous rebellion. Even Elizabeth was worried and moved to the more defensible Windsor Castle. The ports were temporarily closed and extra guard put on the Queen of Scots. Elizabeth recognized that it was essential for her to maintain authority, particularly against the highest nobleman in the land. She could not leave unpunished his defiance of her peremptory order to attend her at court, even if it meant coming in an invalid's litter. Elizabeth knew that strong leadership meant the pack mentality of her nobles worked in her favour but that if she showed any weakness the rogue males could as easily turn on her and establish their own hierarchy of power. With Mary as a legitimate candidate for queen, they could gloss any treason with legality.

Norfolk might have had the desire for power but he lacked the nerve. He had been in urgent communication with the disaffected northern earls, his brother-in-law Westmoreland and Northumberland being the most bellicose. Having sworn he would not answer the queen's summons, he did set out finally from his estates in Norfolk in the company of forty of his men on the last day of September. Within three days he was under house arrest, and by 10 October imprisoned in the Tower of London ('to[o] great a Terror for a trew Man'[44] as he had exclaimed to Elizabeth just two weeks before). He was to remain there for ten months, unhappy, uncomfortable but with his ambitions towards the Queen of Scots undimmed.

Mary's captivity and the close constraint of her days meant her hopes were artificially inflated and liable to extreme collapse. She was naturally a woman of action not reflection, and to be prevented from riding or hunting, which happened periodically as the political situation in England deteriorated, was a great hardship to her. Her energies were channelled into writing pleading, affectionate letters to Elizabeth, angry and inflammatory ones to her family in France and other supporters, and devising plots for escape. Mary delighted in codes and ciphers and hidden messages and this fascination translated into the embroidery work she had enjoyed ever since she was a girl in France. When asked by an English visitor the previous January how she passed the time when the weather kept her indoors, Mary explained 'that all that Day she wrought with hir Nydill, and that the Diversitie of the Colors made the Worke seme lesse tedious, and contynued so long at it till veray Payn made hir to give over'.[45] The long hours waiting for deliverance were spent in devising motifs to embroider, choosing the colours and investing the images with layers of meaning. Often she worked alongside her jailer's wife.

The Countess of Shrewsbury, better known to posterity as Bess of Hardwick, was a redoubtable woman of exceptional will and ambition. A squire's daughter from Derbyshire, she married four successively wealthier husbands and, remarkably for the age, managed to hang on to all her accumulated wealth. The Earl of Shrewsbury was her last husband and their notoriously quarrelsome marriage took a far greater toll on him than on her. She was a dynamic builder of magnificent houses (Chatsworth and Hardwick Hall being just two of them), property speculator, moneylender, dynastic engineer and gale-force personality. She outlived every husband by decades and even outlived her queen, though she was six years her senior, dying at last in 1608 at the defiant age of eighty-one. Perhaps she was more a woman to admire from a distance than to live with in close intimacy. Although Bess and Mary used different powers to get what they wanted from the world, neither was capable of neutral relationships. Mary loved and hated with passion, often the same person and within the same week; Bess was more calculating and disciplined but unused to being denied or gainsaid. Their relationship was an interesting one. The Earl of Shrewsbury's custody of Mary lasted fifteen years, an imprisonment as much for him and his family as it was for his ward. It added enormous financial and emotional strains to his life, which no doubt affected his health (he was plagued with gout) and hastened his death.

To begin with, Bess and Mary were friends, although they would end as enemies, with Bess accusing her husband of committing adultery with their royal prisoner. Fifteen years the elder, the Countess of Shrewsbury was cast more as a mother figure to Mary who was still only twenty-five when they first met. Their main activity together in those early years of captivity was embroidery, during which time they mapped out their images, selected their silks and wools, and practised their needlework. Shrewsbury wrote to Cecil that every day Mary would seek out Bess and they would work on their projects together, only talking of trifling matters he was quick to reassure. In fact the women's talk was full of court gossip, some of it highly malicious, about Elizabeth and her love affairs, her vanity, speculations about her recoil from marriage, all of which Mary later was to recount in a rash defamatory letter to Elizabeth, when she had fallen out with Bess and wanted revenge on the two iron-willed women who had her in their power.

Not only was the gossip anti-Elizabeth: some of the devices that Mary embroidered expressed her simmering anger, resentment against the queen, and hope for renewed life and glory. The women would leaf through emblem books, popular in France and England during the sixteenth century, or Gesner's book, *Icones Animalium*, a catalogue of fine woodcuts of animals, birds and fishes published in 1560. These gave ideas for their work, some with added detail or Latin mottoes satisfyingly suggestive of hidden meaning. Mary embroidered one small panel of a tabby cat worked in orange wool with a crown on its head (Elizabeth was famously red-headed) and a little mouse, not in the original pattern, was added to the picture to emphasize the threatening nature of the ginger predator.

The most telling piece of embroidery was worked by Mary in about 1570 while Norfolk was still imprisoned but keeping their marriage hopes alive. It was a panel with a large vine at the centre, one half fruitful and laden with grapes, the other half almost leafless and barren of fruit. A large hand with a billhook was shown in the process of pruning the barren branch under the motto *Virescit Vulnere Virtus*, 'Virtue flourishes by wounding'. This was sent as a cushion to Norfolk. Under the guise of a pious homily about accepting the necessity of suffering, its message from his impatient future bride was something much more aggressive. It was recognized by the protagonists and their supporters as a veiled encouragement to get rid of Elizabeth, the barren Tudor scion, possibly even by killing her, so that the fertile, fruitful, branch representing Mary could flourish.

Although Elizabeth did not know yet of this lethal embroidered message she feared that she was at risk from her disaffected northern earls attempting precisely this excision. She ordered Mary to be moved from the more salubrious Shrewsbury house at Wingfield, where she had spent some of the summer, back to dreaded Tutbury Castle. Mary's household also was reduced to around thirty, the better to maintain security. Prior to this she had been much more leniently treated and servants, friends and hangers-on frequently swelled her retinue to twice that number, all to be supported by Shrewsbury's estate, inadequately reimbursed by Elizabeth.

Immediately on return to Tutbury, Mary's coffers were searched for any incriminating correspondence, and her visitors and letters, usually closely vetted, now were forbidden. Nothing suspicious was found although Shrewsbury wrote to Elizabeth that, before they left Wingfield, the queen 'consumed with Fier very many Writings'.[46] Mary hated returning to Tutbury and resented deeply the harsh constraints placed on her activities while the crisis lasted. She was particularly incensed by the rude way in which she and her servants were treated. In a letter to Elizabeth on the first day of October 1569, her outrage burnt through her usual tone of sweet woebegone reason: 'they have forbid me to go out, and have rifled my trunks, entering my chamber with pistols and arms, not without putting me in bodily fear, and accusing my people, rifle them, and place them under arrest'.[47]

Elizabeth's sharp treatment of Norfolk had certainly reasserted her authority but it also panicked Northumberland and Westmoreland who had been in communication not only with Norfolk but with Mary and her agents too. These northern earls had always been more a law unto themselves with their own Council of the North, distant geographically and philosophically from the monarch and court centred in the south. They, like the majority of their people, remained reactionary and wedded to the old religion. They were solely concerned with restoring Catholicism and their association with Norfolk and his plans to marry Mary was with this intent, with Mary sprung from jail as their Catholic queen. Nor were they squeamish at the idea of inviting foreign aid to help effect this. Norfolk's capitulation without a struggle, however, left them exposed and alarmed.

At the end of October, Elizabeth demanded that Sussex, Lord President of the North, summon the earls to London. Fearful that this meant their freedom, if not their lives, were already forfeit, the reluctant rebels accompanied by a body of armed retainers rode to Durham to raise their standard of rebellion. On 14 November they took possession of the cathedral, threw the book of Common Prayer on the ground, overturned the communion table and demanded that Mass be said. Their aims, however, were confused and their force divided and lacking in conviction or focus. Some wanted to ride south and release the Queen of Scots, but that bold scheme was abandoned when they heard of the prompt action which had confined her more straitly. Others wanted the succession clarified with the Duke of Norfolk's name among the leading contenders, still others thought the main aim was to re-establish the Catholic religion.

Elizabeth's forces were mobilized on all sides. There was general alarm and confusion, some of the nobility hesitantly joining the breakaway earls, more joining the government, patriotic allegiances crossing religious lines. With Durham occupied, Berwick, Newcastle and Carlisle remained loyal. Poorly organized, too hastily initiated, the rebellion was soon over without a shot being fired in anger. By Christmas 1569 the two renegade earls had fled over the border into

Scotland. 'The earls are old in blood but poor in force,'[48] Elizabeth is reputed to have said to her court as they galloped towards the border, leaving their supporters in disarray.

In retrospect it was easy to dismiss the whole thing as a damp squib, but at the time Elizabeth and her council had real fears that the whole of the north might rise in rebellion, the inflammable borderlands catch fire too and in the ensuing chaos France or Spain gain a foothold. Elizabeth's long letter at the end of November to the Earl of Sussex expressed both anger and fear:

> these Rebells have nothing so much to Hart, nor seeke any other Thing so gredely in this theyr trayterous Enterprise, as the subduing of this Realme under the Yoke of foraine Princis, to make it the Spoile of Strangers . . . and so brede the Destruc-tion of our faythfull and loving Subjects; and under Colour of Religion, to bring this and other theyr sedicious and lewde Intentions to passe, to the manifest Contempt of Almighty God, to the Troble and Danger of our Estate, and utter Desolation, Spoyle and Ruyne of our whole Realme.[49]

Every county was ordered to ready itself with men, weapons and ammunition, some of it to be stored in the Tower where the arma-ments were old and worn out, having been cleaned for too long with sand and 'become to a great extent honeycombed from one end to the other'. Londoners under obligation to provide horses for military service were ordered to furnish them in readiness, as were 'armourers to provide corselets; harquebus makers to provide harquebuses, and the merchants to provide arms, each one accord-ing to his ability'.[50] 'Confidential estimates' of the numbers of men ready to be called up, according to the French ambassador La Mothe Fenelon, came to six thousand harquebusiers, six thousand men in armour and a further twelve thousand, but with some doubt as to whether there was enough weaponry for all of them. Elizabeth was not taking this threat lightly.

It did not bode well for Mary either. She was moved south from Tutbury to the greater security of Coventry, travelling at night as far as possible to avoid 'fond gazing, and confluence of the people',[51]

RIGHT Mary, *c.* 1578, a miniature by Elizabeth's miniaturist, Nicholas Hilliard, thought to be from life, that formed the reference for many subsequent portraits.

BELOW Mary, electrotype after Jacopo Primavera, *c.* 1580.

BELOW RIGHT Elizabeth, Armada medallion, after a design by Nicholas Hilliard *c.* 1588.

OVERLEAF
LEFT Mary, *c.* 1558 miniature by a follower of François Clouet.

RIGHT Elizabeth, *c.* 1575. Artist unknown.

FURTHER PAGE
LEFT Mary. Artist unknown.

RIGHT Elizabeth, 'Rainbow Portrait', attributed to Isaac Oliver.

MARIE
REINE
DESCOS·
SE·

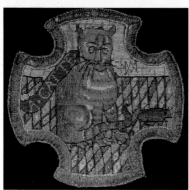

Embroidery designed and worked by Mary while imprisoned in England. The square panel with a grapevine, one branch fruitful with a pruning hook threatening the barren half under the motto *Virescit Vulnere Virtus* ('Virtue flourishes by wounding'). This is probably the work sent by Mary as encouragement to the Duke of Norfolk. The cruciform is of a ginger tabby cat with a mouse, said to represent Elizabeth and herself. The octagon is of Elizabeth and Mary monograms under a crown.

This sixteenth-century painting is traditionally believed to show Elizabeth dancing with Lord Robert Dudley. It could alternatively be of a French court scene.

Elizabeth on a royal progress, surrounded by her court, attributed to George Virtue.

Den VIII february werde onthalst Maria
Stuart Schots Coninginne's terwende Roomsch Catho-
lyck Hebbende gesocht veel onrust en te richten Haer schult
mee her te maecken van Engelant t'oneck Haer vanden stoel
ofte parlement Soleomelyck hoende vertoont, Anno 1587.
Metren XIII fol. XIII. en XIIII. b.

Execution of Mary at Fotheringhay Castle, 1587. Artist unknown.

Elizabeth, the 'Armada Portrait' *c.* 1588, attributed to George Gower.

as Shrewsbury wrote carefully to Cecil. There was real concern from Cecil, Elizabeth and those who guarded Mary that there should be no opportunity for the Scottish queen to be seen except by authorized persons, for fear that her affecting presence would become a focus for popular sympathy. Once the rebellion had faded, she was moved back, again discreetly through an unwitting populace, to inhospitable Tutbury. Here, in the bitter January of 1570, shortage of wood for fuel made the ancient castle even more evilly favoured.

As she had done in the case of Norfolk's disloyalty, Elizabeth needed to reassert her authority with the northern rebels too. To the Earl of Sussex, her Lord President of the Council of the North, she wrote: 'We do marvel that we have heard of no execution by martial law, as was appointed, of the meaner sort of rebels in the North. If the same be not already done, you are to proceed thereunto, for the terror of others, with expedition and to certify us of your doing therein. We understand that some in those parts, in this hour of service, have remained at home, or shown great slackness in our service, having brethren or children with the rebels; have an earnest regard to such, and spare no offenders in that case.'[52] Although only Northumberland forfeited his life, some six months later when he was returned from imprisonment in Lochleven Castle, it was the ordinary foot soldiers, poor country men on the whole who had joined the ill-starred earls in some confusion, who bore the brunt of her salutary revenge for treason. In the first few months of 1570, hundreds of them were summarily hanged, lands and livelihoods were forfeit. In the grim aftermath of rebellion, mercy was hard to come by.

Elizabeth had written a prayer in Greek, published in a 1569 collection of her prayers, which explained something of her belief that a monarch's duty was to employ just punishment as a cauterizing process and thus safeguard the health of the nation: 'Grant me to use mildness towards the virtuous, to encourage them still more to their duty and to chastise the wicked and lawless, so that I may turn them from evil and, truly in the manner of a physician, may bring this body of the realm from sickness to health and safety.'[53]

This concept of necessary justice was extended to her treatment of Mary too. When the French ambassador had the temerity to tell Elizabeth, soon after the northern earls' rebellion, that his monarch disapproved of the continued imprisonment of the Queen of Scots, she claimed that such treatment was nothing less than her duty as a monarch: '[Mary's] friends have given shelter to the English rebels, and with her aid and connivance they levied war on me with fire and sword. No sovereign in Europe will sit down under such provocation, and I would count myself unworthy of realm, crown and name of queen if I endured it.'[54]

Although the imprisonment of Norfolk and the disabling of the northern earls were all significant setbacks to Mary's plans, she was in one of her buoyant periods and was not cast down for long. Scheming and plotting her escape brought meaning and purpose to a monotony of uneventful days. If Mary could envisage a triumphant denouement that involved the utter disarray of her enemies and the award of the greatest prize of all, the scheming gained added piquancy. Marriage to Norfolk still offered her the clearest path to freedom and glory and by the end of January 1570 she was writing to him, still imprisoned in the Tower, with affectionate words and a bold, even foolhardy, plan for a double escape:

> Mine own lord, I wrote to you before, to know your pleasure
> if I should seek to make any enterprize; if it please you, I care
> not for my danger; but I would wish you would seek to do the
> like; for if you and I could escape both, we should find friends
> enough . . . If you think the danger great, do as you think best,
> and let me know what you please that I do; for I will ever be,
> for your sake, perpetual prisoner, or put my life in peril for
> your weal [welfare] and myne.

Although asking for his desires in the matter and promising blind obedience to his commands, Mary was the more adventurous and courageous of the two. She urged action where he seemed hesitant and was full of daring when he was in two minds. Although this alliance with Norfolk certainly suited her ambitions, Mary was also emotionally engaged by the idea. To a young woman in the prime of life, her imprisonment, inactivity, loneliness and long hours of wishful thinking added an inevitable aura of romance to a man she had not met, did not know, but hoped to marry and eventually love: she addressed herself to 'My Norfolk' and signed off 'Your own faithful to death, Queen of Scots'.[55]

With every year that passed, with each new scare, Mary's presence in England was becoming more clearly an incitement to plotters, religious fanatics, lovelorn noblemen, interventionist foreign powers, ambitious courtiers, to play the hero and rescue her from her pathetic state. There were some who were beginning to call for the death of the Queen of Scots as the only way to safeguard Elizabeth, the reformed religion and the peace of the nation. Knox, never one to pull his punches or choose a discreet word when a dozen rabble-rousing ones would do, wrote to Cecil in the new year of 1570 using the same horticultural analogy, but with different meaning, that Mary was busy embroidering on Norfolk's cushion. Mary's needlework depicting the need for excising a sterile vine threatened Elizabeth's life. Knox's gardening lore on the force of regeneration thundered out the threat to Mary's: 'Yf ye strik not att the roote, the branches that appear to be brocken will budd againe (and that mor quicklye then men can beleve).'[56]

In Cecil he had someone not altogether hostile to the idea, but Elizabeth was never to accept wholeheartedly the necessity of Mary's death. She was, however, often exasperated, rattled, intimidated even, by what was fast becoming a double bind, where she was as much imprisoned emotionally and politically by her relationship with Mary as Mary was physically constrained by her. She was reputed to have exclaimed to the French ambassador, 'I am just as anxious to see Mary Stuart out of England as she can be to go!'[57] For Mary the way out was continually blocked by decisions and events largely beyond her will, but the dream was kept alive in the letters and messages, the codes and confidences, which streamed from her various prisons. Increasingly, for Elizabeth, there seemed no way of ridding herself of her uninvited guest whose presence attracted such treachery.

The insecurity of life was once again brought home to everyone with news of the assassination of the Earl of Moray, natural brother to Mary and regent to her son. A Hamilton, kinsman of the Duke of Châtelherault, had ambushed Moray as he left Edinburgh on

21 January 1570. Despite the regent being in the company of one hundred and fifty armed horsemen his assassin managed to wound him fatally with a shot from a harquebus. Elizabeth was shocked by Moray's death. They were of similar age and had been mutually helpful colleagues during inchoate times when the new religion and new reigns were in the process of being established. On hearing of his death, she cried out, 'saying this would be the beginning of her ruin'.[58]

For Mary, hope rose again. It seemed that without being asked Hamilton had done her job for her. She had little impulse to pity or forgive the brother she had once professed to love and in fact by the summer of the following year she was promising a pension to be paid to his assassin. The queen's party gained enormous confidence and more noble recruits while the king's men (those supporting James VI and the regency) declined in support, reaching possibly their lowest point. Again the ancient feudal rivalry of Hamilton and Lennox remained the underlying scaffold for this deadly opposition. For six months Scotland was without a regent while the possibility that Mary might be restored seemed as close as it would ever come to reality. Elizabeth then gave her approval to the choice of Lennox, Darnley's father and the child-king's grandfather and a man inveterately opposed to Mary, as the next regent.

Leicester, possibly seeing the greatest threat coming from Spain not France, argued that France should be placated and made an ally. To best achieve that end, Mary needed to be returned to Scotland, albeit with drastically curbed powers. Elizabeth too seemed to be sensitive to the fact she could no longer justify holding her in custody. Writing to Sussex, her loyal Lieutenant of the North, she explained her thinking: 'if the Queen of Scots shall not refuse reasonable conditions – we do not see how with honour and reason we can continue her in restraint'.[59] Reluctantly, but willing to do anything to escape her debilitating situation, Mary did indeed agree to swingeing conditions. Her son would go to England to be brought up there; prominent members of the king's party, her enemies, would occupy the major administrative posts; and Scottish foreign policy would be bent to English will. In exchange Mary would be named as Elizabeth's successor. Desperate for freedom at any cost, and not one to plan ahead or put much value on foresight as a defensive tool, Mary chose to grab the opportunity while she could, and charm or storm her way through the consequences later.

A series of events however were to jeopardize Mary's chances of freedom and push Elizabeth further from the sympathetic solidarity she had felt when first her cousin had fled south. In the last days of February 1570, the aged Pius V acted finally to excommunicate Elizabeth, 'that servant of all iniquity ... pretended Queen of England'. The papal bull only reached England in mid-May when a foolhardy Catholic gentleman nailed it to the garden gate of the Bishop of London's palace. This pronouncement, purportedly from God, not only absolved all the faithful from any loyalty or obedience to Elizabeth or her laws, it threatened that anyone who remained loyal to the 'pretended queen' 'shall incur the same sentence of malediction'.[60]

This was a distinct threat to Elizabeth. In a time when the authority of the spiritual prince far outweighed the temporal, the pope in theory was commanding English Catholics to rebel on pain of similar anathema. In effect, most were happy to continue with the ideologically unsound practice of offering spiritual allegiance to Pius and his successors, and political allegiance to Elizabeth and hers. Elizabeth's policy of equivocation and tolerance towards the private matters of faith of her subjects, however, was forced increasingly during the new decade to become more wary and prescriptive.

Undoubtedly, Mary's presence and the Catholic ambitions that fomented around her, speeded this process of suspicion and division. There seemed to be numerous plots against Elizabeth's throne, even her life. With the benefit of hindsight most were amateurish, but all prior to discovery had the potential for harm. Norfolk's release from the Tower in the summer of 1570 provided a focus once more for the bolder schemes. He remained under a kind of house arrest at Howard House, his residence in London, and appeared to have gone cold temporarily on the plan to marry Mary. Possibly the ordeal of the Tower was still too fresh in his memory; possibly he did intend to keep the promise he had given Elizabeth which had persuaded her to release him at last: 'from the Bottome of my Harte [I] crave of your Majestie Forgivenes for that which is past ... with a full Intencion never to deale if that Cause of Mariage of the Quene of *Scottes*, nor in any other Cause belonginge to her, but as your Majestie shall commaund me'.

Begging that the omnipotent queen 'drawe me owt of the Dongeon of your Displeasure',[61] he was soon to show he had neither the wisdom nor the self-control to keep from a dungeon of far greater peril. Elizabeth had made a similar promise to Cecil that she would never marry Lord Robert, and had managed to keep it despite her passions being deeply engaged. Norfolk soon failed where ambition was the motive force, and Mary Queen of Scots its seductive charioteer. Too late he was to realize his mistake, and in an affectionate letter of concern and advice to his children written as he awaited execution for treason he warned: 'Beware of high degrees! To a vainglorious proud stomacke it seemeth at the first sweet ... in the end it bringes heapes of cares, toyles [snares] in the state, and most commonly in the end utter overthrowe.'[62]

The utter overthrow of the Duke of Norfolk caused Elizabeth great anguish, and brought Mary into deepest suspicion and closer to the risk of execution herself. This time, she had accepted Elizabeth's humiliating conditions for her release whereby she relinquished everything but her title as Queen of Scots and her claim to be a successor to the English throne. The procrastination of the Scottish king's party, concerned for their own power and security should she return, finally exhausted the negotiations. They would not countenance any reversal of the abdication document signed by Mary at Loch Leven, nor would they allow the king to be removed into England. By March 1571, Mary's expectation of a legal restitution to her throne was over. In fact that winter Mary was ill for a month or more, whether of her old complaints or of the strain of frustrated ambition no one could say. The deadly inertia while she waited, her hopes artificially elevated or plunged into despair, would have driven an impatient nature such as hers into chronic depression or mania. Instead she kept her hopes alive through elaborate schemes of escape and fantasies of derring-do, in the only serious activity left to her.

*   *   *

Roberto Ridolphi had already played a minor role in the conspiracies surrounding the earlier plan to marry Mary to the Duke of Norfolk, and the consequent rebellion of the northern earls in 1569. A Florentine banker and papal agent then living in London, he concocted a grandiose plan which became notorious as the Ridolphi Plot. Potentially dangerous to Elizabeth and the security of the realm, its effects in reality were to prove fatal to Norfolk and deeply damaging to Mary. Ridolphi had been busy distributing the papal bull excommunicating Elizabeth and denying her legitimacy on the English throne.

Spurred by this papal authority he aimed to enlist a Spanish army of invasion to support a rising of the English Catholics, under the leadership of Norfolk, and inspired by the prospect of placing a Catholic Queen Mary on the 'pretender's' throne. It was inevitable that Mary would put her name to this scheme. She was desperate to be free, and she thrived on the excitement and sense of hope that smuggled letters, encoded messages and clandestine meetings brought to her sorely constrained life. Even the intrigues of court life, the pleasures of dance and music, and the pursuit of love, were much diminished by captivity. All that was left to her was to plot her escape, however madcap and dangerous, and dream of revenge on her enemies by grasping Elizabeth's crown.

At the beginning of February 1571, Mary wrote to Norfolk using the Bishop of Ross as her envoy. She pointed out that Ridolphi intended telling Philip II that there were numbers of the English nobility together with thousands of their men ready to rise in support of her. All they needed was a sign of support from Spain. Norfolk was not immediately enthusiastic. He knew already the force of Elizabeth's displeasure; he had promised not to promote Mary's interests in any way and must have realized that to be exposed again as a central figure in such a conspiracy would be to forfeit his life. However, his pride and ambition to be elevated to the role of princely consort got the better of his caution. Reluctantly he agreed to join the enterprise.

The inception of this plot coincided exactly with Elizabeth's agreement that her ambassadors could open marriage negotiations with the Duc d'Anjou, Charles IX's younger brother. As Henri III, he was destined to inherit the French throne after Charles's death in 1574. He was not yet twenty years old and Elizabeth was in her thirty-eighth year, but by now she knew, and her closest advisers must have been wearily aware, that this was another proposal that would not develop beyond the fruitless discussion stage. This would prove, however, protracted and artificially sustained, and would secure for England the advantages of being in provisional alliance with a powerful European neighbour, saved for a time from the loneliness and vulnerability of being a renegade Protestant state in a continent of Catholic powers. It also cooled French concern for the fate of Mary, their erstwhile queen.

So far and deep had court gossip spread about Elizabeth's immoderate behaviour with Leicester that Anjou, renowned himself for his promiscuity and later for flamboyant transvestism and homosexuality, complained to his mother Catherine de Medici about Elizabeth's reputed immorality. He had to be assured she was the model of propriety before he would proceed. Such reservations as to her reputation only served to outrage Elizabeth when she was unfavourably compared to Mary. Upbraided by the French ambassador for not allowing Mary greater liberty, she was determined, she said, to point out to all European princes that her treatment of her cousin was of 'such rectitude' that she had no cause for shame or regret, unlike Mary herself. 'Would to God that the Queen of Scots had no more occasion to blush at that which can be known of her,'[63] was her sharp riposte.

Sir Francis Walsingham was propelled by this familiar charade into the political foreground, sent as ambassador to France to deal with the marriage negotiations. His talent for intelligence gathering was already well marked. He had been suspicious of Mary's potential as a focus, or even instigator, of rebellion from the moment she had set foot on English soil. From that point on he remained alert to her activities and watchful of those drawn to her flame. He joined the front rank of Elizabeth's ministers with her other great statesman, William Cecil, whom she created Baron Burghley at the end of February 1571: 'My stile is, Lord of Burghley, if you meane to know it', he wrote proudly to a colleague, adding the plaint, 'the poorest Lord in England.'[64] Leicester too, had grown in political stature and experience. From Elizabeth's favourite, willing to assume any stance that would promote his own position, he was showing himself to be a reliable and intelligent councillor and, despite Cecil's personal antipathy to him, took his place with Cecil and Walsingham as the third pillar of the powerful triumvirate that formed the solid base of Elizabeth's rule.

While Elizabeth and her ministers put a preliminary hand of friendship out to the French, Ridolphi set out for Europe in March determined on raising Spanish military aid in his scheme for Elizabeth's overthrow. Spurred by the explicit support of Mary and the covert agreement of Norfolk, his first stop was the Duke of Alva, Philip II's military commander in the Low Countries. Alva was engaged in ferociously suppressing the Protestants who were supported covertly by the English. Where Ridolphi was breezy and overoptimistic, Alva was tough-minded and not susceptible to dreams. He did not like the idea of forcibly deposing Elizabeth and thought Spain could only invade once the queen was dead or at least captive. Ridolphi passed on to Rome where the pope gave moral support for his schemes, but not much else. In Madrid, Ridolphi's enthusiastic view of the numbers of English Catholics on the verge of insurrection inflamed the chronically dour and cautious Philip. The Spanish king got carried away with the plan to order an armed incursion into England to get rid of Elizabeth, place Mary on the throne and re-establish Catholicism in that heretic isle.

In fact, nothing came of it. Messengers were apprehended, letters discovered, ciphers broken, confessions wrung out under torture.* Mary was immediately and incontrovertibly implicated. Her

---

* Elizabeth had to sign a warrant herself to allow, if necessary, two of Norfolk's servants to be tortured in the Tower. The usual procedure was to try the threat of the rack, and if that did not loosen the tongue of the prisoner then the full horror of the rack was to be used. She wrote: 'if they shall not seem to you to confess plainly their knowledge, then we warrant you to cause them both, or either of them, to be brought to the rack, and first to move them with fear thereof to deal plainly in their answers. And if that shall not move them, then you shall cause them to be put to the rack and to fe[el] the taste thereof until they deal more plainly, or until you shall think meet.' (*Collected Works*, 127)

ambassador, the Bishop of Ross, threatened with the rack, revealed Norfolk's part in the process. He also vilified the Queen of Scots far beyond the questions in hand as a serial husband-killer who, if she had married Norfolk, would have similarly brought his life to a premature end. The bishop's interrogator was stunned by the torrent of allegations; to Cecil he wrote, 'Lord, what a people are these! What a Queen, and what an ambassador.'[65]

It was not Mary as his future wife who ended Norfolk's life with violence, but Elizabeth. With Norfolk found guilty of treason, the English queen was put under enormous pressure from Parliament to sign his death warrant. She hesitated, she signed, she changed her mind four times in all, on one occasion she revoked the death sentence at two o'clock in the morning of the day projected for his execution. She could not bear to have the blood of such near kin on her hands.

Elizabeth was passionately exhorted by her Commons to arraign Mary for treason and thereby stop at source any more murderous plots. Tempers were frayed, voices raised and tears flowed, so strongly did they feel about the dangers Mary continued to pose. Realizing that she had to give some concession to her loyal Commons, Elizabeth agreed to Norfolk's execution as the lesser of two evils. He went to the block with dignity on 2 June 1572, admitting his transgressions and asking forgiveness from his queen. To Elizabeth he had written, 'The Lord knoweth that I myself know no more than I have been charged withall, nor much of that, although I humbly beseche God and your Majesty to forgive me, I knewe a greate deale too muche . . . For certayn it is, that these practyses of rebellions and invasions, were not brutes [rumours] without full intention. God, of his mercifull goodnesse, I hope, will disclose all things that may be dangerous to your excellent Majesty: and then I hope your highnes shall perceave that Norfolk was not such a traytor, as he hath, not without his own desertes, given great occasion of suspycion.' News of his death sent Mary 'into a passion of sickness',[66] and she took to her bed with grief.

Shrewsbury was charged by Elizabeth to tell the Queen of Scots of the discovery of the plot and her part in it. He had to explain too that he was ordered to reduce her attendants to sixteen and temporarily restrict her movements and communications with the outside world. Mary, confronted with evidence of her own incriminating letters, her own writing even, and the confessions of her ambassador and messenger, not only denied everything but was self-righteous in her defiance. 'I had of my own free will placed myself in the hands of the Queen his mistress,' she told Shrewsbury, 'relying upon her promises and friendship; that since she has detained me forcibly, if she suspects that I desire my liberty, I cannot help it. Nevertheless I am a free princess, and in that am not responsible to her or any other.'[67]

Mary was courageous and clever in her response. She knew that legitimacy mattered to Elizabeth, and that it was necessary to the English queen that actions were seen to be lawful. In a speech to her Commons some fourteen years later explaining why she would not comply with their urgent plea that she execute Mary, she elaborated on this principle: 'we Princes, I tell you, are set on stages in the sight and view of all the world duly observed. The eyes of many behold our actions; a spot is soon spied in our garments; a blemish quickly noted in our doings. It behooveth us therefore to be careful that our proceedings be just and honourable.'[68] Mary also knew that, much more than any of her ministers and much more than Mary herself, Elizabeth was an idealistic monarchist who considered herself to have a sacred authority which no mortal could put aside.

With the discovery of the Ridolphi Plot there was a heightening of tension in Elizabeth's government. It was significant that even cool-headed, rational Cecil, now Lord Burghley, considered his country to be in a perilous position in relation to its neighbours. Weak, ill-equipped and vulnerable as it still was, he knew England was incapable of withstanding an onslaught from an alliance of the Catholic states. That such a concerted action was expected brought fear to Elizabeth's supporters and some frisson of excitement to Mary's. Rumours of other plots, possible traitors and potential routes of invasion were everywhere. The ports were watched, guards around the queen increased and the militia placed in a state of alert.

Such nervous anxiety proved to be unmerited. Catherine de

Medici, queen mother of France, had given up long ago the pretence of warmth and concern for her onetime daughter-in-law. She and her son, Charles IX, required that a woman who once had been Queen of France should be shown all due respect, but they were not about to risk war in order to rescue her from captivity. The news of the Ridolphi Plot, however, and Mary's eagerness to ally herself with Spanish might, marked the end of even a pretence of anything more than mere verbal support for her from the French monarchy. Catherine de Medici had a revealing interview with Walsingham in the aftermath of the plot's discovery:

Catherine began, '[Mary] is alied to the King and to me, and brought up here ... [but] she seketh an other way to ruinate hir self, to hurt hir freends, to deserve no pitie nor favour, and sorie we must be for hir. And if she be so dangerous (as yt aperith) we can not nor dare not require liberty for hir, which is so perillous to the Queene my sister's [Elizabeth's] State.'[69] She continued that if, through Elizabeth's mercy, Mary's life should be spared then Catherine and the king would trouble the English queen no further.

On a personal level, the Ridolphi Plot marked the end of any sisterly solidarity that might have existed between the two queens. Elizabeth was forced to accept that Mary was prepared to have her assassinated in order to gain her own freedom and subsequently the English crown. She had long realized that here in the heart of her kingdom was a charismatic presence who seemed to have a fatal attraction for everyone who fell within her circle of influence. Mary, for her part, had recognized that Elizabeth may have longed to be rid of her but would not return her to Scotland where her Protestant lords were implacably set against her. Nor would she leave her free to go to France and there re-energize old alliances injurious to England.

Mary's next letter to Elizabeth, written from Sheffield Castle on 29 October 1571, acknowledged the irreparable deterioration in their relationship: 'Madam, the extreme severity with which by your orders I am used, so convinces me, to my great regret, of the misfortune which I have, with many others, not only of being in your disfavour, but, which is worse, esteemed by you as an enemy instead of a friend, as a stranger instead of a close relation – even the more detested that it does not permit the exercise of Christian charity between parties so nearly related by blood and propinquity.'[70] Her impervious self-righteousness made her very difficult to deal with. She emotively reminded Elizabeth in every letter of their close blood ties, the sanctity of their mutual queenship, the poignancy of her position as a lone woman, captive and away from friends, family and home. Her position was tragic, close to Elizabeth's own experiences, and affectingly expressed. But the implicit message was always self-justifying, sometimes pious and superior, yet fundamentally accusatory. Impossible as her situation was, Mary still operated on the principle she had demonstrated so strikingly during the Huntly Rebellion a decade earlier – attack was the best defence.

Elizabeth wrote far fewer letters in reply to her distressed cousin. As she explained, often there was no answer she could give that would placate her. However, writing on 1 February 1572, she was moved to remonstrate against Mary's previous letter which, she objected, was full of 'uncomely, passionate, and vindictive speeches'. Elizabeth warned her 'to qualify your passions, and to consider that it is not the manner to obtain good things with evil speeches, nor benefits with injurious challenges, nor to get good to yourself with doing evil to another'.[71] 'She then delegated all negotiations to the hapless Earl of Shrewsbury who still remained as Mary's host–jailer.

In that phrase *to get good to yourself with doing evil to another*, Elizabeth was more obviously thinking of the plots against her own life. However, it was a phrase that could be applied to Mary's career so far, and the devastating effect she had on the men who were drawn to marry or assist her. Elizabeth did not like losing family members. Her cousin Lord Darnley, fleetingly Mary's husband and King of the Scots, had been murdered in confused and unhappy circumstances. Norfolk's treason lay heavy on Elizabeth. When she wrote this letter he was still alive in the Tower, and she was under mounting pressure to have him executed. He was her leading nobleman, a suitor in the past for her hand and one of her inner circle.

it made her wonder at the powers of persuasion the promise of Mary had exerted over this vain and susceptible man. Elizabeth had every reason to believe that her own life had hung in the balance, and still would, while her cousin's presence inspired schemes of rescue, and dreams of religious restoration and personal ambition. But there were other lives too. How many more men, important and close to Elizabeth perhaps, would become caught and ruined in that web of ambition and desire?

At the same time as she wrote her exasperated letter to Mary, Elizabeth commented to the French ambassador, 'There seems to be something sublime in the words and bearing of the Queen of Scots that constrains even her enemies to speak well of her.'[72] On the face of it, Elizabeth had all the advantages in the relationship between the two queens. Yet she was as much captive to the situation as was Mary herself, imprisoned by the insecurities of her own past and her deep-rooted respect, both philosophical and self-serving, for the divine elevation of them both as queens.

Elizabeth, in her actions and her letters, seemed intimidated at times by the reputation of her rival. Perhaps Mary's unimpeachable pedigree, her unquestionable legitimacy, was part of her power over her cousin. In this way she challenged Elizabeth's deepest vulnerabilities. Perhaps, too, Elizabeth was daunted by the mystery of Mary's almost sorcerous power of attraction, even on the briefest acquaintance. She had been wary of her personal charm from the beginning, 'since her flying into our Realm',[73] as she vividly put it in a letter to her ambassador in France. Why, even that most reliable and adamantine of men, her own Burghley, had attributed irresistible qualities to the Queen of Scots and feared the effect she would have on anyone, including those naturally averse, who fell into her toils: 'she is able by hir great wytt, and hir sug[a]red eloquence, to wyn even such, as before they shall come to hir company, shall have a great mislykyng'.[74]

Mary knew that magical powers of bewitchment were supposed to be hers. When she had first blazed over the English horizon, uninvited, as potentially inflammatory as a smouldering meteor, she had tried to allay her cousin's suspicions, 'Alas! Do not as the serpent that stoppeth his heering, for I am no inchanter, but your suster and naturall cousyne . . . I am not of the nature of a basilisk, and lesse of the camelions, to turne you to my lykeness. And though I shuld be so dangerouse and curst as men: yow ar sufficiently armeyd with constance, and with justice.'[75] In the process, however, she just reinforced the uneasiness that here was a woman of super-natural power.

Elizabeth was armed with justice, but in her struggle with Mary this was to her disadvantage: how to act justly and yet safeguard herself and her country? Assailed by mysterious forces, by unknown plots and conspiracies against her life, Elizabeth recognized that her fate was inextricably linked with Mary's; that she too could not escape. 'I am not free, but a captive', she wrote in some despair[76] during a long constraint that both queens, in their different ways, shared till death.

CHAPTER ELEVEN

Singular Foes

I will appeal to the ever-living God, in whom onely I
acknowledge a Power and Dominion over us that are
Princes of equal Jurisdiction, Degree and Authority. And
upon him will I call, (with whom there will be no place
for Craft nor Fraud,) that in the Last day he will reward
us according to our Deserts one towards another.

Letter from Mary to Elizabeth 1582

She wishes by way of invocation that God should
'retribute' to us at the time of His last Judgement
according to our deserts and demerits one towards
another, putting us also in mind that all disguisements
and counterfeit policies of this world shall then not
prevail . . . if that severe censure should take place it
would go much more hardly with her than we . . . can in
Christian charity wish for her.
For howsoever she is bold with men, who can judge but
of things outwardly, she ought to beware how she dallies
with God.

Answering letter from Elizabeth to Mary 1583

THE POWER OF AN ISLAND PEOPLE, encircled by an unpredictable sea, is forged in independence, self-reliance and insularity from
continental influence. Inward looking, slower to change, an island
race has an enduring sense of identity and the confidence of knowing who they are, where they have come from and where they are
bound. Elizabeth's father, through desire for her mother and for

herself, the unborn heir who should have been a boy, had ensured for his country a spiritual and ideological isolation too. Elizabeth's sister, Mary I, had attempted to rebuild the bridge with Europe and Catholicism, with catastrophic results. Elizabeth was herself quintessentially English and insular, an island queen who, despite her long life, her wide learning, linguistic skills and intellectual curiosity, never travelled beyond her immediate frontiers.

Yet within those limitations she claimed great strengths. She knew her people intimately, and was quick to remind them that she was like them and had been a subject too. She was proud that she was born of a domestic union and not from a dynastic alliance with a foreign power. Her claim that her blood was unsullied by foreign taint reinforced the chauvinism, superiority and suspicion shown towards foreigners that was beginning to characterize her people. Confident of their love and with her familial images as wife and parent she promised them her care and loyalty to death, and was believed.

This comfortable fertile fortress, protected by an inhospitable sea, was safe even from incursion through her borders with Scotland now that the Protestant lords were well established there. The Scottish queen's precipitate flight, however, and her continued unwelcome presence in the heart of Elizabeth's kingdom had breached the walls and once more thrown a bridge to Catholic Europe through which interest, influence and outright aggression could be channelled. Mary's nature was far from insular. She was not immediately identifiable as truly belonging anywhere. She had spent only seven years in her kingdom, always an exotic presence for whom her subjects initially felt a greater patriotic feeling than she could return. French was her natural language of choice and she never lost her accent. Her connections of family and religion extended from France to Spain and to the pope himself, and her affections remained unwaveringly Francocentric, indelibly impressed with the charismatic family and the influences of a charmed youth.

As prisoner of the English queen, Mary may have been deprived of personal and political power, but she was the symbol of something more powerful and more elusive than any individual could aspire to be. A born queen kept in captivity; a mother separated from her son; a Catholic martyr abused by heretic subjects and harassed by a godless queen; a French princess and dowager queen living in conditions far beneath her dignity; a beautiful, noble and ill-used woman in need of heroic rescue: these personae were already being woven into a Marian mythology of the Queen of Scots as sainted victim. She had become a magnetic pole for any dissenting opinion in Elizabeth's England and a focus of guilty shame for those sympathetic to her plight. Above all, she was a signal of hope for the Catholic population who dreamed of a counter-reformation, and a cause for every messianic hothead in need of a holy war.

The opposing mythology of Mary, forged by fearful English Protestants, was of a queen who had forfeited every divine right of monarchy through her immoral behaviour. In their overheated rhetoric she was an adulteress and husband-slayer – worse, a regicide; a ruthless papist plotter intent on taking their own queen's life and subjecting their kingdom to a vengeful Catholicism. Through rumour, fear and alienation, Mary was easily transmuted into a mysterious, even diabolical, seductress whom men approached at their peril.

When the entrails of the Ridolphi Plot were displayed to Elizabeth's councillors in 1572, the threat of a Catholic league against England, based on the legitimacy of Mary's claim to the throne, seemed imminent. The whole enterprise was sanctified by the papal bull excommunicating Elizabeth and denying her legitimacy as queen.

The relative tolerance of religious difference that marked the first decade of Elizabeth's reign was fractured not just by plots against her but by the instability of events in neighbouring countries. There was a growing religious extremism that disconcerted Elizabeth's secular political instinct for the noncommittal and the inclusive. It was not just the conservative Catholic forces which were growing in confidence. The Puritan wing were also becoming more demanding, although posing less threat through their lack of powerful states as allies.

After the assassination of the Scottish regent Moray in 1570 by a Catholic Hamilton, the barely suppressed anarchy of Scottish politics once more gained the upper hand. Moray's eventual successor as regent, Darnley's father Lennox, was also killed by one of Mary's supporters in September 1571; as was the next regent, the anti-Mary Earl of Mar, just one year later, some said as a result of poison. The Spanish campaign against the Protestants in the Low Countries brought Huguenots streaming through the eastern ports of England seeking asylum, with tales of cruelty and suffering, and the threat of the imperial ambitions of this most implacably Catholic of states extending across the Channel too.

The religious wars in France had lasted almost a decade, periodically quiescent and then flaring into savage bloodletting and fanatical excess. A series of massacres of Protestants beginning on 24 August 1572, the feast of St Bartholomew, convulsed the Protestant states with horrified disbelief. In the afterglow of a royal wedding feast, Catherine de Medici had initially intended a political act of assassination against certain Huguenot leaders, specifically Admiral Coligny whose impressive character and powers of organization were gaining unprecedented influence for the Huguenot party. The still mighty and ultra-Catholic Guise family had long vowed revenge for what they believed to be Coligny's implication in the murder of François, Duc de Guise, almost ten years before. They too were in on the plot, as was the Duc d'Anjou, soon to become Henri III. It was a plot to assassinate Coligny, but when he was merely wounded Catherine and her followers thought it too dangerous to leave his followers alive. What appeared to be a plan to kill the governing body of the Huguenot party turned into a bloodbath. The Parisian mob were encouraged to go on the rampage where every Protestant, and then anyone who crossed their paths, was destroyed in an orgy of killing.

This bloodlust lasted for days, sweeping across France and settling its bloodied fangs into other towns and districts until tens of thousands lay butchered in the streets and the fields. The emblem of St Bartholomew was a knife, recalling his death by flaying: the massacre that was for ever to bear his name was made notorious through its similar barbarous inhumanity. It was the most shocking episode in the French religious wars and was greeted with celebration by the new pope Gregory XIII, who struck a commemorative medal, and Philip II of Spain, who congratulated the king and Catherine, his historic enemies, on a job well done. The militant faithful considered turning back the tide of European Protestantism as much an expression of God's will as Christianity's onslaught on the infidel Turk, and the sword therefore became a legitimate means of conservation and conversion. The papal medal on the reverse side depicted an angel with the cross in his left hand and a drawn sword in his right while before him lay the bodies of the slain, the inscription, *Ugonotorum Strages*, 'the Massacre of the Huguenots', quite unambivalent in its meaning.

The news reached Elizabeth while she was hunting. Immediately the day's sport was abandoned and the court went into mourning. The predominant response was one of shock, puzzlement and fear. Elizabeth had only recently allowed her ministers to respond with some encouragement to the French king's latest offer of his youngest brother, the Duc d'Alençon*, as a possible husband for her. What appeared to be a policy of systematic destruction of the French Protestants filled her with outrage and alarm. All anyone could talk about at court was these latest revelations of the perfidy of the French. Was this part of a greater Catholic plan which would spread to England's shores and sweep up the Queen of Scots as its heroine?

Mary's inheritance was both Stuart and Guise, and on all showings the courage, passion and charisma of her nature made her more her mother's daughter than her father's. It was wondered whether she would also prove herself as ruthlessly fanatic as her Guise uncles in the pursuit of her religion, in the willingness to destroy others. Certainly Mary was aware that her close blood ties and affective connection to this powerful family was considered suspicious. In a letter to the French ambassador she admitted, 'they say that I love the house of Guise too much'.[1] Elizabeth, however, was disinclined to use the horrors across the Channel as a way of

---

* Hercule became François, Duc d'Alençon, and then Duc d'Anjou, but is usually referred to as d'Alençon to differentiate him from his brother, the Duc d'Anjou who became Henri III in 1574. Monsieur was the more usual contemporary name for him, the name Elizabeth used when she didn't call him her nicknames of Frog, or Little Fingers.

reflecting more opprobrium on Mary. To the French ambassador who, soon after the massacre, asked her not to punish Mary further, she retorted: 'The Queen of Scots has enough sins of her own to answer for, without ascribing to her those of other people.'[2]

She was less understanding towards Mary's brother-in-law, Charles IX. Elizabeth wrote to him that even if this was punishment for rebels intent on relieving him of his life and his crown – an excuse frankly she doubted – it was 'a terrible and dangerous example' to set by not taking these nobles for trial before executing them. She turned her outrage next to the reported treatment of the common people, 'that women, children, maids, young infants and sucking babes, were at the same time murthered and cast into the river; and that liberty of execution was given to the vilest and basest sort of the popular [populace], without punishment or revenge of such cruelty done afterwards by law'.[3] To his ambassador who delivered the king's version of events to her at court, Elizabeth interrupted the excuses with a thunderous expression, 'even if everything had happened as the King said, and the conspirators had been rightly punished', she said sharply she would like to know 'what blame was attributable to the women and children who were murdered'.[4] The ambassador left soon afterwards.

Assassination had become a commonplace tool of policy among the European powers at this time. Yet it was striking how easy it was to gain close access to anyone in a position of power. The series of dead regents in Scotland was indication enough of how simple and unremarkable such a lawless act had become. Even in Elizabeth's court, full of rumours of individual plots against her, fearful of concerted actions by hostile states, access to her palaces and even her person seemed to be surprisingly relaxed. In one of the prayers composed while Mary was in captivity in her kingdom, Elizabeth expressed the ever-present awareness of uncertainty: 'I see all things in this life subject to mutability, nothing to continue still at one stay . . . I hear ofttimes untimely death doth carry away the mightiest and greatest personages.'[5]

Although Mary was at the mercy of Elizabeth and the English state, and vulnerable to some contrivance that appeared legal enough to justify her execution, closely confined as she was, she was much more protected from opportunist assassination than Elizabeth could ever be. The English queen pursued her life at court and on regular progresses round the country, with immediate access to her nobles, her visitors and the people. There are fascinating travelogues of visiting foreign nobility who detail how they walked into any of the queen's residences, inspected her living quarters, handled her plate and furnishings, gazed at portraits of her ancestors, turned up at church while she was at worship, joined the company around her and were presented to her, with very little barrier or protective protocol.

With so much turmoil abroad, with the pope's call to action, and the Queen of Scots at home attracting support from disparate and dangerous factions, it was not surprising that Elizabeth's ministers and Commons should fear for her life. The Bishop of London wrote urgently to Cecil, 'these evill tymes trouble all good men's heads, and make their heartes ake, fearing that this barbarous treacherie will not cease in Fraunce, but will reache over unto us ... Hasten her Majestie homewards, her safe returne to London [from a royal progress] will comfort many hearts oppressed with feare.'[6] During the Parliament of 1572, the members pleaded for the chance to try Mary for treason and thereby sentence her to death. Elizabeth, pressed by emotional speeches to safeguard herself and her country, would only agree reluctantly to the more modest suggestion that Mary be deprived of her right of succession. However, despite being passed by both houses, she unexpectedly backed away from ratifying the newly drafted bill.

Burghley was exasperated at her obduracy and apparent blindness to the danger: as long as Mary retained her claim on the English crown Elizabeth would not be safe from every kind of European or Catholic ambition against her. Anxieties grew to fever pitch when she fell ill with a pox that was immediately assumed to be a recurrence of the dreaded smallpox. No one was more fearful than Shrewsbury. If Elizabeth should die, Mary still remained the next in line to the throne. His position was perilous if in this sudden change of fortune his prisoner would become his sovereign, intent on revenge. After the execution of the Duke of Norfolk in early June 1572, Mary's bitterness against Elizabeth had been vitriolic. Shrewsbury had thought it wise to let Cecil know: 'She still continues great enmity, and gives no hope of other intent. It is too plain her heart is overhardened with deadly hate against the Queen's majesty – the more, therefore, her majesty's safety is to be thought upon.'[7]

What faithful and literal-minded old Shrewsbury could not fathom, however, was the volatility of Mary's emotions. Living in the moment, thriving on sensation, Mary's expression of feeling was fundamentally intense but mutable; exuberance quickly followed despair, depression metamorphosed into action. Although, in her desperation to be free, she was an eager participant in any passing plot she knew that her own life so easily could be forfeit in the chaotic process of a rescue attempt. Mary cannot have forgotten the pack frenzy of Riccio's murder and the danger to herself in the panicky aftermath.

Elizabeth too was capable of outbursts of uncontained emotion. The strain of living with Mary's presence, and the problems and dangers that she threatened sometimes got the better of her diplomatic cool. Introduced to Gondi, the French envoy, in the summer of 1578, 'she told him loudly in the audience chamber that she knew very well he had come to disturb her country and to act in the favour of the worst woman in the world, whose head should have been cut off years ago'. When Gondi reminded her that Mary was a sovereign queen and a kinswoman, Elizabeth angrily shot back at him, 'that [Mary] should never be free as long as she lived, even though it cost her [Elizabeth] her realm and her liberty'.[8]

After the Ridolphi enterprise it was more than a decade before there were again significant conspiracies to rescue Mary or murder Elizabeth. Various plots of varying incompetence continued to come to light, thanks to Walsingham's efficient intelligence gathering, but none of them, until Throckmorton's involvement in 1583, caused any great consternation. Mary continued in her stately imprisonment, her household once more allowed to increase to royal proportions, and treated with increasing laxity until rumoured plots or threatening conditions abroad meant her activities were temporarily constrained. Her negotiations with Elizabeth turned to requests for more opportunities for outdoor recreation and expeditions to improve her health.

Her indoor leisure activities were still embroidering fine bed hangings and smaller pieces, their motifs charged with meaning, often in the company of the Countess of Shrewsbury. The gossip that animated these long hours of stitching was much enlivened by details of Elizabeth's last significant courtship that unexpectedly became a love affair. More than a decade after her amorous activities with Leicester had set the scandalmongers of Europe alight, Elizabeth's reputation remained dubious, to her Catholic neighbours at least. Don John of Austria* had commented to his natural brother, Philip II, on the fleeting suggestion of a marriage between himself and the Queen of England: 'I blush while I write this to think of accepting advances from a woman whose life and example furnish so much food for gossip.'[9]

In fact, he was happier to consider marriage to Mary, admittedly a Catholic like himself, but a queen whose life gave more food for unfavourable talk than any queen living or dead. Elizabeth was vilified for being a heretic and, worse still, a woman and a monarch who had defied nature and God's law by refusing to marry. In choosing to rule alone, thriving in her heresy instead of being struck down for her sins, she challenged every principle, succeeding where all prejudice decreed she would fail. To the fanatical Catholic rulers of Europe, Elizabeth was an affront. Her unmarried state made her vulnerable to the judgements of others, but it also made her personally vulnerable to the promise of love.

The youngest French prince, François, Duc d'Alençon, finally began his courtship of Elizabeth in earnest in the beginning of 1579. This youthful, over-excitable young man was described as 'featherbrained' by Walsingham, who added dourly that this characteristic was true of most of the prince's countrymen. Monsieur, as

---

* Don John was a dashing young prince who had become the hero of Europe since commanding the Christian fleet at Lepanto in 1571 in a historic victory against the previously indomitable Turkish fleet.

he was universally called, had added his support to the Huguenot struggle against the Spanish in the Low Countries. With his army in disarray, starving and beginning to desert, he faced an ignominious return to France. Instead he decided to try his fortune with Elizabeth. There were those in England who muttered cynically that he, like Aeneas, was seeking merely the easier option, with Elizabeth as the Dido he would betray. Already he had sent a series of extraordinary, passionately effusive letters, lauding her beauty and personal attractions to the skies and promising undying love, promising to die himself if deprived of her.

Elizabeth had embarked on this courtship, as she had on every other, as a diplomatic ruse, this time with the intent to make some kind of holding alliance with the French. The lowering presence of the Spanish, marauding the Protestant rebels in the Low Countries and just too close for comfort, was Elizabeth's real concern. Marriage negotiations were always a good way of disturbing an unfavourable status quo, unsettling the established power balance and delaying proceedings that might be injurious to her country. There were some alarming reports that the Spanish were building ships and fitting them out in Italy in such numbers that could only be explained by an enterprise against the English. This spectre of Spanish aggression loomed increasingly during the coming decade. The possibility, however faint, of an alliance between France and England menaced the Spanish in a way that English power alone could never achieve.

A major factor in the success of the Duc d'Alençon's courtship of the wily queen was a highly sophisticated courtier, Monsieur's best friend, Jehan de Simier. He travelled with an entourage of French courtiers to England in January 1579, with the express purpose of softening Elizabeth up before his master arrived in person. A series of extravagant entertainments were organized 'with Tiltings performed at vast expense . . . to say nothing of other Courtly Sports and Pastimes, which are not so proper for an Historian to relate',[10] so Camden, Elizabeth's earliest historian, related. The marriage had first been proposed when Elizabeth was thirty-eight and Alençon barely sixteen. From the start Elizabeth found the age difference embarrassing, saying she considered herself an old woman compared with this 'beardless youth', a characteristic gleefully pointed out to her by the many detractors of the match. By early 1579, she was forty-five and Monsieur had become a man. Although Elizabeth would conduct other flirtations to flatter her vanity and beguile her loneliness, this would become her romantic swansong.

The impetus for this *coup de foudre* was Simier rather than his master. He was a man of forceful character with a capacity for Machiavellian ruthlessness.* Yet Simier was also a consummate courtier and practised in the ways of courtly love. He had an unexpectedly electrifying effect on the Virgin Queen. She was so taken with him that she insisted on seeing him daily, and simpered and posed and flirted so amorously that the whole court and the eagle-eyed ambassadors were agog. She also flagged her intimacy with him by awarding him a fond nickname, 'monkey' or 'ape', which punned in Latin on his name.

Simier seemed optimistic that his master's suit would be successful, 'but will wait to say more till the curtain is drawn, the candle out, and Monsieur in bed'. Whether he was sincere or merely diplomatic, he seemed almost as delighted with Elizabeth as she was with him. To Monsieur's commissioner in the Low Countries he wrote: 'I swear to you that [Elizabeth] is the most virtuous and honourable princess in the world; her wit is admirable, and there are so many other parts to remark in her that I should need much ink and paper to catalogue them. In conclusion I hold our master very fortunate if God will further this business.'[11] Hopes were running high. The usually sedate French ambassador wrote to Catherine de Medici, Elizabeth's prospective mother-in-law: 'This discourse rejuvenates the Queen; she has become more beautiful and bonny than she was fifteen years ago', adding optimistically, 'not a woman or a physician who knows her does not hold that there is no lady in the realm more fit for bearing children than she is.'

---

* Prior to his arrival in London, Simier had heard that while away, serving Alençon in his campaign in the Low Countries, his young wife had committed adultery with his younger brother. He sent his men ahead to kill this brother at the gate of his château, and his young wife died soon after, of poison, fear or grief, no one could say.

It was juicy gossip like this that Mary Queen of Scots and the Countess of Shrewsbury shared over the embroidery. The women suggested a more commonplace reason for Elizabeth's rejuvenation – sex. According to the letter Mary wrote, detailing the most scandalous aspects of these conversations, she and the countess had discussed Elizabeth's lascivious nature and how she had enjoyed sexual relations both with Simier and his master. It was not only the average Englishman however, who was alarmed at Elizabeth's evident relish for this suit. The Spanish were busy working on undermining, through rumour and bribery, any support there may have been at Elizabeth's court.

Mary's interest in Elizabeth's potential marriage into the French royal family was not just for its entertainment value. She believed that such a match would substantially change her situation, hopefully for the better, and might even effect her release. She wrote to her long-time ally and ambassador, James Beaton, Archbishop of Glasgow, asking him to make overtures on her behalf to her youngest brother-in-law. Alençon had been only six years old when she had last seen him as she embarked for Scotland from France. The rackety life he had led subsequently, much of it at odds with his mother Catherine de Medici and his brother, Henri III, meant Mary was uncertain of his religious or political allegiances, and concerned that he should be told of her own rights and complaints: 'take care that no wrong be done to me, during his government, in the succession of this kingdom, demonstrating to him the right which I have to it'. She then added the unrealistic gloss, 'in the maintenance of which [right] I hope that the greatest and best part of England will hazard their lives'.[12]

She was feeling hopeful again. To an optimist with an opportunistic nature, change was energizing and if Elizabeth was to marry at last that would prove the greatest catalyst for change. Mary felt things were going her way and she was impatient to help them along: 'in the state in which the affairs of this country are at present, and, as I again understand, those of Scotland are, it will be very easy to form great intrigues and factions', she wrote to the archbishop at this time, 'and, in my opinion, I never have had so much opportunity and convenience for looking to the restoration of my affairs as now.'[13] She followed the unpredictable romance of the English queen and the French prince, 'my very dear frog' as Elizabeth fondly called him, with intense interest.

The English courtiers were just as interested but distinctly hostile: always suspicious of foreign men and their Continental ways, they saw in Simier 'a most choyce Courtier, exquisitely skilled in love toyes, pleasant conceipts, and court-dalliances'.[14] He had so bewitched their usually rational queen, so their rumours ran, that only by the use of 'amorous potions and unlawfull arts' had he 'crept into the Queenes mind and intised her to the love of [Monsieur]'.[15]

Elizabeth's insecurity, her overweening vanity, her need for love, all were made more keen by the melancholy realization that she was growing old. Her spies in France had relayed the cruel gossip which was circulating there and which she repeated indignantly to the French ambassador: 'that Monsieur would do well to marry the old creature, who had for the last year an ulcer in her leg, which was not yet healed,* and could never be cured; and, under that pretext, they could send me a potion from France of such a nature that he would find himself a widower in the course of five or six months, and after that he could please himself by marrying the Queen of Scotland and remain the undisputed sovereign of united realms'.[16]

It was particularly galling that this revealed Mary as her rival even here, popularly considered the more desirable match because she was a younger woman. Elizabeth's letters during this time emphasized her awareness of the passing of the years. To Monsieur she wrote 'grant pardon to the poor old woman who honours you as much (I dare say) as any young wench whom you ever will find'.[17] And this from an autocratic and imperious queen? Elizabeth proved to be far from fireproof in the presence of Simier's skilful coquetry. His delicious flattery made her feel that she could defy time, that she still possessed youth and beauty, and that love and marriage might still be hers. His bold innuendo, the hints of

---

* Apparently it was an ulcer just above her ankle which did not heal for seven years.

Monsieur's persuasiveness between the sheets, reminded her of the longed-for consequences of desire.

The last time Elizabeth had allowed herself to imagine she could enjoy the pleasures of companionship, sexual fulfilment and marriage was in the fever of her love for Leicester. All the subsequent marriage negotiations had been business as usual for the queen, of barely passing interest to the woman. Now, during this late courtship, Elizabeth for a while forgot her hard-learned lessons of self-protection and control. For a while she believed she could be as other women, pursue her love, share sexual pleasure, even give birth to the heir which would secure her beloved father's dynasty. She railed against her council members who increasingly opposed the match. Her cousin, Sir Francis Knollys, was emotionally reprimanded for blocking her last chance to fulfil her destiny as a woman: 'It was a fine way', she said, 'to show his attachment to her, who might desire, like others, to have children.'[18]

The French were insisting on conditions that her council could not accept, that Alençon should be crowned immediately after marriage and have a large pension for life. They threatened to walk away from the marriage if these were not satisfied. Elizabeth's feelings were already deeply engaged. She had declared to her women of the bedchamber that she had determined to marry. She became 'so melancholy since' her council's verdict, and felt diminished by the thought that Alençon was only interested in her for what advantages could be wrung from her and the country. To the French she wrote the timeless feminine plaint that she wanted to be valued for herself alone: 'The mark that is shot at is our fortune and not our person,' she complained.

This was a surprisingly romantic view of marriage, particularly a dynastic marriage, but it was upheld by her people's stated concern that her suitor was so much younger he might not love her for herself, instead using the marriage to advance his own interests. Elizabeth continued, with some defensiveness, that she could better understand the mercenary behaviour of the French if they were negotiating marriage with a princess who lacked beauty or intelligence, 'But considering how otherwise, our fortune laid aside, it hath pleased God to bestow his gifts upon us in good measure, which we do ascribe to the giver, and not glory in as proceeding from ourselves (being no fit trumpet to set out our own praises) . . . we may in true course of modesty think ourself worthy of as great a prince as Monsieur.'[19]

By the time Monsieur finally arrived, early one August morning and incognito, everyone's blood was up. Contrary to the usual deflation attendant on reality, Monsieur in person was even more delightful to the queen than she had hoped. Elizabeth's fears about his ugliness and the scarring of his deeply poxed skin were erased by his exquisite gallantry, humour and the lively grace of his manner. To her cynical and disapproving courtiers, the queen, simpering, fawning and showing off outrageously, was very close to making a complete fool of herself over this ridiculous Frenchman. In fact, Elizabeth's sensitivity about the age difference was given cruel credence by a report from Catherine de Medici, admittedly a not impartial source, relayed in cipher by the Venetian ambassador in France to the signory just after this visit: 'that Monsieur was somewhat embarrassed, when as a young man devoted to pleasure, he called to mind the advanced age and repulsive physical nature of the Queen [*le brutta qualità del corpo della Regina*], she being, in addition to her other ailments, half consumptive; . . . the lust to reign will contend with the lust of the flesh, and we shall see which of these two passions possesses the greater force'.[20]

In the grip of unloosed feeling, Elizabeth's tautly strung self-control had unravelled in the skilful hands of the courtier-lover Simier. For a while she had forgotten her deep-rooted reservations, even her age, in the longing to be in love again. She wrote to Monsieur after his departure, exceeding the usual diplomatic utterance with rare abandon: 'I confess there is no prince in the world to whom I would more willingly yield to be his, than to yourself, nor to whom I think myself more obliged, nor with whom I would pass the years of my life, both for your rare virtues and sweet nature.'[21]

It would not be long, however, before reality asserted itself and duty called. Elizabeth's whole philosophy of monarchy was expressed by her in a letter to Simier: 'how near it touches me that our people do not perceive in their Prince a negligence or a luke-warmedness for their well-being and safety; we were not born only for ourselves'.[22] In fact the dour antagonism of her people for this match had worried her from the start. For a while her passions were so engaged that she managed to overlook this dark cloud threatening her hopes, but she was less able to ignore the disapproval and forebodings of her councillors. Her favourites were particularly put out. During the heat of the proxy courtship there were two attempts on Simier's life, with suggestions that at least one of them had been instigated by a murderously jealous Leicester. Elizabeth was outraged and mortified. This turned to white rage when Simier, in retaliation, revealed to Elizabeth something kept secret only from her, that Leicester had remarried the previous year, the widowed Countess of Essex, Francis Knollys's beautiful daughter, Lettice, a woman who had been her friend.

The resulting furore, the bitter accusations, the hang-dog Leicester, his rustication, Elizabeth's tears, all proved immense entertainment to Mary and Bess of Hardwick, plying their needles in Sheffield Castle. It proved another poignant reminder, however, to Elizabeth that *tempus fugit*, and even the companion of her youth, the love of her life, could betray her in love. A poem she wrote in the 1580s expressed eloquently the passing of youth and her melancholy acceptance of responsibility for what she had made of her life:

> When I was fair and young, and favour graced me,
> Of many I was sought their mistress for to be.
> But I did scorn them all, and answered them therefore,
> > 'Go, go, go seek some otherwhere,
> > Importune me no more.'
>
> How many weeping eyes I made to pine with woe;
> How many sighing hearts I have no skill to show.
> Yet I the prouder grew, and answered them therefore,
> > 'Go, go, go seek some otherwhere,
> > Importune me no more.'

Then spake fair Venus' son, that proud victorious boy,
And said: 'Fine dame, since that you be so coy,
I will so pluck your plumes that you shall say no more
    "Go, go, go seek some otherwhere,
    Importune me no more".'

When he had spake those words, such charge grew in my breast
That neither night nor day since that, I could take any rest.
Then lo, I did repent that I had said before,
    'Go, go, go seek some otherwhere,
    Importune me no more'.[23]

Elizabeth's frustrated love for Leicester may have been the inspiration for this poem. It may have been rather the regretful realization that she could not pursue late passion and marry Monsieur. Then again the poem may have been more generally symbolic of change and loss, and the painful gaining of wisdom. Leicester was her enduring love, and although she was quick to anger and easily hurt, Elizabeth was always open to reason in the end. He had been a widower for eighteen years and the queen was realistic. By then, both Leicester and she had accepted that their marriage could never be, not that this prevented Elizabeth from wanting him to be unconditionally hers, more devoted and loyal than any husband could ever be. Without much time in the wilderness, he was back in the centre of Elizabeth's emotional landscape, particularly as the passion for her 'dear frog' faded to affectionate, if increasingly exasperated, friendship.

The unfortunate young man who apparently had discharged a firearm towards Simier, as he travelled with the queen by barge up the river at Greenwich, protested his innocence of any evil intent and was released. Elizabeth had exercised a characteristic parental mercy, according to Camden, for, 'she was many times wont to say, *That she could believe nothing of her people, which Parents would not believe of their children*'.[24] She had certainly proved that she had the strengths and insecurities of a lone parent in her unwillingness to do anything that her children might veto.

Loyal as she was to her people, however, Elizabeth was capable of acts of savage retribution when threatened, for instance, by the power of print to disseminate dissension and revolt. The writer and distributor of a tract published in September 1579 entitled, 'The Discovery of a Gaping Gulph whereinto England is like to be swallowed by another French marriage . . .' were sentenced immediately to have their right hands hacked off. The offending work expressed in intemperate language what most of her populace believed to be the case – that the Valois princes were sly papists and worthless reprobates, that Elizabeth was too old for Alençon and he could not love her, that she anyway was past childbearing. In short, he was a rat who should not have been allowed even to look on their Queen.

Patriotic it may have been, but Elizabeth was still trying valiantly to reconcile her personal desires with her duties as monarch, and could not allow this powerful popular view the added force of widespread publication. By her brutal and precipitate action against the perpetrators, she acknowledged the growing power of print which brought rapid and effective communication direct to the people, supplementing the official message of state or church. Elizabeth's subjects attending the public mutilation of these good burghers greeted the sentence with sullen silence and shock.

The queen knew that her fantasy of love could not long survive. As she withdrew further from the courtship, she wrote to her French ambassador: 'My mortal [foe can] no ways wish me a greater loss than England's hate; neither should death be less welcome unto me than such mishap betide me . . . Shall it ever be found true that Queen Elizabeth hath solemnized the perpetual harm of England under the glorious title of marriage with Francis, heir of France? No, no, it shall never be.'[25]

Mary's growing realization that Elizabeth's French marriage, like all her previous proposals, would wither unripened on the bough, meant that she once more looked to Spain for her deliverance. Her thoughts were increasingly focused on her son, James VI, who in the summer of 1580 was fourteen and already exhibiting an independent intelligence and capacity to rule. Morton was still regent, although not for long, and Mary showed a continuing maternal solicitude for James as well as a political interest in what he might be able to do to effect her freedom, once he was free to rule himself. When she heard he was ill with some kind of digestive complaint her insistent letter to the Archbishop of Glasgow was eloquent of her 'excessive sorrow and uneasiness'. Having suffered from a similar complaint when she was young she recalled that wearing ivory close to her stomach had helped and urged that, in a ritual to safeguard his health, his weight in virgin wax be sent to the church of 'nostre Dame de Cléry'* and a novena to be said there. She asked also that a Mass be sung daily for a year at the same church, and thirteen *trezains* (a base metal coin) be distributed to the first thirteen poor people who arrived on each successive day.[26]

While Elizabeth made much of her relationship as mother to her people, Mary was a real mother with a real son. She had been separated from this boy from the time he was barely one, when her disastrous marriage to Bothwell ended with her subsequent flight from Scotland. She had attempted through letters and gifts to maintain some sort of motherly contact, to keep his memories and affection for her alive and to influence his religious ideas. She feared but did not know fully that he had been brought up with the belief that his mother was closer to a jezebel than a madonna, responsible for the murder of his father and obstinate in her adherence to popery, which to the extreme Calvinists who surrounded him was close to witchcraft in its reliance on symbols, ritual and mystery.

He cannot have been so thoroughly shielded, however, from the influence of his mother's sympathizers. Certainly James seemed particularly proud of his glamorous Guise inheritance, writing to

---

* The thirteenth-century church in the diocese of Orléans, a favourite place of worship and pilgrimage for the Valois kings. Orléans was an important city for Mary. It was here she had nursed her first husband François II to his death in 1560. It was also the setting for one of the great stories of French feminine heroism when, at the battle of Orléans in 1429, Joan of Arc saved France from England. There is no reason to doubt that Mary was affected herself by the stories of this singular woman's heroic martyrdom and her subsequent immortality in the sentimental history of her country.

the Duc de Guise, when he was seventeen, to declare he was greatly encouraged 'to imitate the virtues of our ancestors of the house of Lorraine, who have so borne themselves that their name shall be honoured to all eternity'. It is likely some of his adulatory information came as a result of the flatteries from such Francophile sophisticates as the first favourite of many in his reign, his cousin Esmé Stuart.* He and another attractive youth, the Master of Gray, had just made the young king's acquaintance. James ended his paean of praise by noting that his worthiest attributes came from this ancestry, 'from which I descend through my mother'.[27]

When James finally had the choice, however, he did not wish to share his governance of Scotland with his glamorous but discredited mother, preferring instead to make his alliance with Elizabeth, thereby safeguarding his prospects of succeeding to the English throne. The Master of Gray, originally Mary's friend, had been sent to negotiate with Elizabeth in what Mary believed was a tripartite alliance, involving both her son and herself. In fact the young Gray was keener to exclude Mary and court Elizabeth on behalf of James, in whom Scottish power now resided. He sent back a message to Elizabeth that James's affection was 'such to your Majesty as though he were your natural son'. To his own natural mother, James wrote without any of the filial love Mary had hoped would survive their separation: 'as she was held captive in a remote place, [he had no choice but that] of declining to associate her with himself in the sovereignty of Scotland, or to treat her otherwise than as Queen-Mother'.[28]

This complete loss of her son in every sense, physical, emotional and spiritual, was a devastating blow to Mary. She had to relinquish one of her dearest held illusions, that an instinctive filial love for her would survive everything. James lacked even a memory of his

---

* Esmé Stuart, Duke of Lennox (1542?–83), cousin of James VI and some thought successor to his throne should he die childless. Handsome, charming, an adroit and plausible schemer, on his arrival in Scotland in 1579 he was immediately irresistible to the young, fatherless king. Ambition made him convert to Protestantism. After the execution of the regent Morton in 1581, his influence over James was at its zenith and he was rewarded with his dukedom. In 1582 he clandestinely agreed to command an army, raised by Philip II, to invade England. Philip's procrastination meant this came to naught, but controversy over Lennox's true religious affiliation meant he was forced to leave Scotland and return to France, where he died.

mother and this, combined with an ambition as fierce as her own to inherit the throne of England, meant ultimately he would reject her for Elizabeth. Mary unleashed on Elizabeth a pitiful rant of misery and revenge against the son she claimed to love more than anyone in the world. 'Without him I am, and shall be of right, as long as I live, his Queen and Sovereign . . . but without me, he is too insignificant to think of soaring.' She refused to be a queen mother 'for I do not acknowledge one; failing our association, there is no King of Scotland, nor any Queen but me'.[29]

As James's real mother, she had given birth to him at risk of her own life, and produced a son and heir of her own blood and dynasty. Now she was to lose him to the pretended mother, his godmother Elizabeth, the woman she had sought as a mother, a sister, a close blood relation for herself. Mary had been denied every intimacy for which she had begged and bullied. Even her rightful place as Elizabeth's successor had never been acknowledged formally. Her precious son, however, in betraying her would gain the prizes she had desired always.

While captive, Mary's only means of affecting events was through letters, either official or coded, clandestine, contraband. Her letters to Elizabeth were in French, numerous, heartfelt and repetitive in their plaints. She was a clever and emotionally manipulative writer who managed very different tones of voice to different recipients. A typical letter to Elizabeth combined pathos and seduction with hidden menace, but never once was she close to accepting responsibility for any of the ill-fortune that had befallen her, or for the plots against Elizabeth in which she starred. In early May 1580 she wrote:

> Madam, my good sister, – I have written to you several times during the last year, to lay before your consideration the unworthy and rigorous treatment which I have received in this captivity, notwithstanding the evidence which I have made a point of giving you, on all occasions, of my entire and sincere affection for you . . . I am constrained to beg and entreat you, as I humbly do, by my liberation out of this prison, to relieve yourself from the charge which I am to you, and from the

continual suspicions, mistrusts, and prejudices with which [my
enemies surrounding you] daily trouble you against me ...
Think that you can have me, out of prison, more your own,
binding my heart to you by so signal a courtesy, than by confin-
ing my body within four walls.

Mary then added an insight into her own sense of inviolable
queenship and characteristic defiance, as candidly she explained,
'compulsion not being the usual mode of gaining much from those
of my rank and disposition, of which you may have some experience
from the past'. She reiterated her credentials as a sovereign queen,
nearest relative to Elizabeth and *'plus juste hérétière* [most lawful
heretrix]' and threatened she would soon die of her increasingly ill
health. She ended with a request to be allowed to go to the baths
at Buxton, which was granted, for three weeks at the end of July.[30]

Mary's imprisonment at this time was more of a house arrest
with horse-riding and periodic therapeutic visits to the Buxton spa.
Throughout she was treated with the full courtesy due to a queen,
dining under her canopy of state and waited upon by servants of her
own choosing. Although her mail had to pass through Shrewsbury's
hands, there was a limited welcome to courtiers and visitors who
requested access to the queen. However, Walsingham's nose for
traitorous activity had long been alert to the comings and goings
of friends and correspondence around the Queen of Scots. He
arrested one of Mary's go-betweens, Jailheur, but found nothing
incriminating.

Her relief was palpable in her letter to Archbishop Beaton, written
in code just a couple of weeks after her plaintive missive to Elizabeth.
The change in tone was instructive; here was a woman who was
decisive, businesslike and ready for any adventure. She informed
the archbishop she would find someone to replace the exposed
Jailheur to 'obtain service in my more important and secret matters'.
One of these more important and secret matters was her request for
help to Spain, the seriousness of which she wanted the archbishop to
underline by proposing 'the removal of my son to Flanders or
Spain, according as shall be agreeable to the King [Philip II]'. Mary
then went on to mention her letter to Elizabeth requesting her

freedom. Should that fail, though, she promised her ambassador she was ready for any available plot or enterprise, 'I shall expose myself to the risk of such other invention as may present itself'.[31]

The following year, Mary was writing to the archbishop in similarly decisive vein: 'I am earnestly exhorted to bring back my son to the faith, and to labour all at once for its restoration in this island, so as to engage in the cause all the Catholics in this country.' She continued in sanguine vein, 'Walsingham boasts of being acquainted with the plans of my cousin Monsieur de Guise for my deliverance, and also with the negotiations which have been entered into respecting it . . . offering likewise to prove that I have written to you in these very words, – "That I shall leave no stone unturned to escape from this imprisonment". Consider from what quarter he could receive such information, and beware of it, I entreat you.'[32]

Mary was in an impossible situation. Desperate to escape and reclaim her life and her crown, and even the crown of England too, she had to endure a long imprisonment from which hope of legitimate release had all but faded. Temperamentally she was not one to wait with patience for the tide, to resign herself to fate. She was a fighter who worked for freedom and paid whatever price. Secrecy, subversion and dreams of revenge gave her the necessary excitement and kept hope alive. Plotting was her lifeblood and games of risk saved her from insanity or chronic depression. Principal Secretary and arch spymaster Walsingham recognized the recklessness implicit in the nature of such an adventuress. He knew that it was just a matter of time before he had Mary implicated up to her neck in a cast-iron case of treason.

Only with overwhelming evidence did he, Cecil and the more radical Protestants of Elizabeth's council hope to be able to rid themselves of the troublesome presence of the Queen of Scots. While she lived, they believed she threatened the very core of Elizabeth's reign, the Protestant succession, the continuance of a peaceful Reformation, the safety of the realm. Religious wars had riven France and the Low Countries. Elizabeth's ministers feared civil war while Mary lived, but they knew well their own queen. Passionately attached to the concept of the inviolability of kings, she was repelled when it came to talk of their assassination. Desperate to keep faith with her people and not antagonize her Catholic neighbours, Elizabeth was determined that everything she did was seen to be legal. To destroy Mary, her ministers would need incontrovertible evidence.

Not only were Mary's hopes alive that some foreign power would come to spring her from jail into the welcoming, and militant, arms of the English Catholics, the English Catholics themselves were awakening to a new hope as their own faith enjoyed spiritual renewal. Although religious wars raged just across the Channel, Elizabeth had hoped initially that a policy of non-intrusive tolerance would ensure Catholicism conveniently withered in her realm through lack of nurture. In 1570 she had promised Catholics freedom from 'inquisition or examination of their consciences in causes of religion', as long as their religion was practised in private, and that outwardly they conformed and kept the law. Harried as she had been herself during her sister Mary's reign, this policy of freedom of conscience was close to her heart. She is reputed to have said to Philip II about his campaign against the Protestants in the Low Countries, 'What does it matter to your Majesty if they go to the devil in their own way?'[33]

Elizabeth herself had never been driven by religious conviction and was more conservative certainly than the strongly Protestant Cecil, Leicester and Walsingham. But freedom of thought mattered to her and she pursued, until cornered, an evasive policy of laissez faire. The compromise and veiled hypocrisy she demanded of English Catholics who wished to maintain their faith, along with their liberty and wealth, were merely reflections of Elizabeth's own diplomatic style. She did not see why a certain pragmatic pretence should be rejected in favour of an awkward truth.

The papal bull of 1570 was the first alarm bell: taken literally, a true Catholic was exhorted to rid England of the heretic pretender to the throne, with the promise of heavenly reward. Bills proposed by the Parliament of 1571 to make every subject take Protestant communion were vetoed by the queen, still insisting on freedom of conscience for all. However, a bill was passed which designated as high treason any attempt to convert an English subject into a subject of Rome, or even to be an English subject whose first allegiance was to Rome. It would take six years, however, before a priest was prosecuted and executed for treason under this new act. More than a hundred would follow by the end of Elizabeth's reign.

While the papal bull breathed fire, the arrival of missionary priests, trained at the recently established Douai seminary in the Low Countries, gave heart to the Catholic faithful in England. They entered the country clandestinely and were greeted with great enthusiasm as they carried new blood into the cells of the disheartened resistance across England. Many of the priests were English exiles, hastily trained and ill-prepared for their missions. According to Camden, Elizabeth thought 'these silly priests' were mostly innocent of 'plotting the Destruction of their Countrey'[34] and were much more the instruments of their superiors' treasonous will.

A far from silly priest was the English Jesuit Edmund Campion. A brilliant scholar at Oxford he had debated before the queen during her historic visit to the university in 1566. She had been particularly impressed during the Natural History Disputation with his contribution to the proposal that the tides were caused by the moon's motion. Both Cecil and Leicester, who were present, offered to become his patrons. He had been a deacon in the Church of England in his twenties before converting to Catholicism and fleeing to Europe to train at Douai and then Prague. He arrived back in England in 1580 and was arrested, accused of plotting against Elizabeth to place Catholic Mary on her throne.

Even under torture Campion denied his motives were anything other than spiritual. He had written an apologia before embarking on his mission in which he denied any political intent: 'I never had mind, and am strictly forbidden by our Father that sent me, to deal in any respect with matter of State of Police [policy] of this realm, as things which appertain not to my vocation, and from which I do gladly restrain and sequester my thoughts.' But the Pope's bull, disputing Elizabeth's legitimacy, had made the spiritual political. Any support from these priests for the English Catholics would implicitly involve them in the treason of offering greater obedience to the pope than to the queen.

Elizabeth was sensitive to accusations of religious persecution and cruelty towards the missionary priests. Her government was careful to make the sophistical point that they questioned their suspects on political allegiances and steered clear of any spiritual matters. There was uneasiness too at reports of excessive cruelty being used to extract confessions (the Spanish ambassador had reported to Philip II that Campion had been viciously racked, even subjected to nails driven into the quick beneath each fingernail) and a declaration was published that although Campion was put on the rack it was never so extreme that he was not 'presently able to walk, and subscribe his Confession'.[35] Under English law, torture was illegal but could be used by special dispensation and, during these years of conspiracy and intrigue, it was one of the tools used frequently in the search for evidence.

The increasing influence of rebel priests and the upsurge of Catholic support meant that the Parliament of 1581 passed an act aimed at restricting aberrant behaviour. It became a dangerous and expensive world for English Catholics. Converts were subject to the charge of treason, as were the priests who converted them. The recusants who refused to attend church and accept the Protestant sacrament were liable to be fined twenty pounds a month, a sum to beggar even the wealthiest of families. Elizabeth had long resisted the pressures of her ministers to deal more decisively with her Catholic subjects and had consistently been more lenient in her attitude towards the confinement and punishment of Mary. Uneasy when having to conduct her rule in broad strokes of black and white, Elizabeth was much happier when lines were blurry and detail open to a variety of interpretations.

Suffering ever more savage reprisals against the priests and the laity who shielded them, the English Catholics were harassed, but their faith was spiritually invigorated. The executions, particularly of self-evidently courageous and principled men like Campion, fuelled a lively martyrology. However draconian their Members of Parliament might wish to be in their measures against the Catholics, ordinary people were less willing to inform on or prosecute those neighbours who appeared to be otherwise peaceable, law-abiding citizens.

This revival of support energized Mary too. Temperamentally inclined to optimism and never short of confidence in her powers of attraction, she believed that there was a very significant body of dedicated English Catholics ready to take up arms for her cause. Mary sent the Spanish ambassador a remarkable message for Philip II: '[She] did not mean to leave where she is, except as Queen of England . . . her adherents and the Catholics were so numerous in the country that, if they rose, it would be easy even without assistance, but with the help of your Majesty it would soon be over, without any doubt.'[36] With that she hoped to encourage armed Spanish intervention in the fates of herself and of Elizabeth.

Such naivety and overconfidence meant she gave her blessing to any schemes and intrigues that came her way, and would in the end even put her name to incriminating letters of intent. Just as the rise of Catholic solidarity in England gave Mary cause for hope it also meant her position grew increasingly perilous. It would make it easier to implicate her legally in the treasonous activity of others. Also as factions became polarized and fear took a grip there would be some prepared to assassinate Mary rather than risk losing English autonomy and their Protestant monarch.

In the final decade of Mary's life there came a variety of plots based on this papal plan. The spiritual imperative to restore to England the true faith and the rightful heir was stamped with the pope's – and therefore, to the English Catholics, God's – imprimatur, while the force to effect this was expected to come with Philip II's army and the spontaneous uprising of Mary's newly invigorated supporters. Ever vigilant, Walsingham was full of foreboding but frustrated by the reluctance of his sovereign to act swiftly and harshly in protection of her self, her religion and her realm. It was to his advantage to prove the ubiquity and ruthlessness of the plotters, and persuade Elizabeth to stiffen her resolve against the Catholics and Mary herself, the focus of their hopes.

The discovery at the end of 1583 of what was to become known as the Throckmorton Plot was further proof to Walsingham, Cecil and Leicester that the status quo between Mary and Elizabeth was too dangerous to leave undisturbed. For a while Elizabeth had appeared willing to accommodate again a plan put forward by Mary two years before. In return for her freedom and recognition of joint sovereignty with her son James of Scotland, Mary declared herself ready to relinquish her claim on the English throne while Elizabeth lived, denounce the papal bull of excommunication, safeguard the Protestant religion in Scotland, and proclaim an amnesty for all those who had wronged her in Scotland and England. Mary's willingness to accept such terms exhibited either a sincere desire for freedom at any cost or, as Walsingham warned, a lax approach to promises and treaties which could be modified or even ignored as occasion demanded. In the end it was James himself who declined the power sharing, and temporarily broke his mother's heart at his betrayal of her maternal illusions.

Mary's insistence during the revived negotiations in the summer of 1583 that she was a practitioner of 'plain and upright dealing', desiring 'nothing so much as her majesty's good favour', and 'greatly wearied . . . of her long captivity. She is much decayed in health . . .',[37] sounded rather hollow when it was discovered that simultaneously she was keenly engaged in the workings of another plot. After six months' surveillance, Walsingham emerged with evidence of close involvement of the Duc de Guise, the Spanish king and the Queen of Scots, with Sir Francis Throckmorton, as go-between, in an ambitious plan of invasion, rescue and assassination, the dream being to place Mary on Elizabeth's throne through force, and return the heretic isle to Catholicism.

In November 1583, Throckmorton was arrested and confessed under torture. Mary denied everything. She had long ago decided that it was far more noble to be persecuted for her faith than for the tawdry machinations of treason. The combative Spanish ambassador, Bernadino de Mendoza, was summarily expelled from the English court the following January. 'Being a man of a violent and turbulent Spirit', he did not go quietly. He insulted Elizabeth by telling her ministers that as she was a woman he had expected nothing better than her rank ingratitude. He threatened that 'as I had apparently failed to please her as a minister of peace she would in future force me to try to satisfy her in war'.[38] So injured was his pride he wrote to Philip II that the only point of life now for him was to avenge the insolence of the English, 'even though I have to walk barefooted to the other side of the world to beg for [God's commission to do it]'.[39] From his vantage point in Paris, he laboured to promote the next great plot against Elizabeth but died just before the insolent English rout of the Spanish Armada.

Not only was Mary once more implicated in treason, her own personal behaviour again was under attack. The Countess of Shrewsbury, a friend no longer, had taken damaging allegations to court about the leniency of her husband's wardship of the Queen of Scots, due to the fact, she claimed, that he was in love and had enjoyed sexual relations with her. Mary was incensed and quick to write to the French ambassador begging him to acquaint Elizabeth, her council, the French king and Catherine de Medici, as well as all the Guises, with her innocence of 'anything in the world contrary or prejudicial to my honour'.[40] A second, but this time secret, letter was also intercepted and decoded by Walsingham's agents: in this Mary requested that the ambassador should pass on a veiled threat to Leicester, intimating that if nothing was done to clear Mary's name from 'this false and unhappy imposture'[41] then she would reveal certain information concerning his intimate behaviour with Elizabeth, as well as his personal ambitions. (He had a scheme to marry his son to Arbella Stuart, Mary's niece-in-law, the Countess of Shrewsbury's granddaughter, and a claimant to the English throne.)

None of these revelations consoled Elizabeth. The Throckmorton Plot brought together her two most powerful enemies, Spain and France – in the form of the Guises – in nightmare alliance. The fear of invasion by a superior force had haunted her reign. The Pope's support for a religious crusade against Protestantism had made the sacred political. In June 1584 the assassination by a Spanish agent of the Prince of Orange in the middle of his campaign in the Low Countries brought Elizabeth's own death closer. There were increasing rumours also of a great Spanish fleet in the making, with the fear that it meant some aggressive intent against England. In the heart of her kingdom too was the canker of a captive Catholic queen whose presence focused every form of dissent and wrung sympathy from even the most incorruptible of hearts.

Although officially Elizabeth did not give them much credence, the stories the Countess of Shrewsbury had to tell of Mary's seductive presence subverting one of the most solid and trusty of Englishmen merely reinforced the mythology of the Scottish queen's supernatural powers of attraction. All scurrilous rumour around Mary also undermined Elizabeth's struggle to maintain her own reputation and probity against the malicious talk that her status and sex always had attracted. Her answer to Mary's distress over these allegations expressed how closely Elizabeth identified with the need to maintain the honour of all queens: 'we can neither forget [Mary's] quality nor her proximity in blood. We have always had special care to suppress the licentiousness of this corrupt age in speaking evil of princes, whose credit and reputation ought to be held sacred.'[42] She feared the disrespect of the people and the condescension of her fellow monarchs who were keen to denigrate the feminine inadequacies of every queen. These many precarious elements hung heavily on Elizabeth. She was conscious of her own vulnerability, her country's poverty and weaknesses, and frightened always of war.

The confused details of another possible plot to assassinate the queen involving one of the Members of her own Parliament, William Parry, were revealed hard on the heels of the Throckmorton Plot. In an atmosphere where potential assassins lurked at every turn, Cecil produced a declaration in October 1584 aimed at protecting Elizabeth's life by removing the reward expected on her death – a Catholic queen on the English throne. The signatories to this document swore to defend the queen and to pursue to death anyone who attempted any violence against her. Its clauses were broadened to disallow the succession of any person involved in an attempt on Elizabeth's life. This became known as the Bond of Association, and by the end of the autumn was enthusiastically signed by tens of thousands of loyal subjects up and down the land. Elizabeth was touched by the evidence of her people's love and loyalty, and thanked her Parliament, promising as much care for her people in return: 'I am not unmindful of your Oath made in the Association manifesting your great goodwills and affections ... done (I protest to God) before I heard of it or ever thought of such a matter, until a great number of hands with many obligations were showed me at Hampton Court, signed and subscribed with the names and seals of the greatest of this land. Which I do acknowledge as a perfect argument of your true hearts and great zeal for my safety, so shall my bond be stronger tied to greater care for your good.'[43]

Although it did not name Mary, the Bond was aimed directly at anyone who might act against Elizabeth in order to place her rival or that rival's heirs on the throne. If it was made law, which Parliament attempted that November, in effect it would have become Mary's death warrant. Should any other plot to assassinate Elizabeth be uncovered with the objective of placing Mary on her throne, even if there was no evidence that she had any part in it, she could be found guilty by association and summarily executed. Elizabeth was unhappy with the extremity of the proposed act and insisted that guilt should be established first, by a minimum of twenty-four councillors and noblemen.

Careful also not to debar James, Elizabeth ensured the heirs of a guilty party were not prevented themselves from inheriting. Mary, writing to Cecil in January 1585 from Tutbury Castle, was so keen to impress him and Elizabeth with her trustworthiness she offered to put her signature to the Bond of Association to prove 'before God and on her honour' she was not 'one who would wish to attempt, support, or favour an act so wicked as an attempt against her person or her kingdom'.[44] Within eighteen months she was deep in the final conspiracy of her life in which the murder of Elizabeth and the invasion of England by Spain were integral parts.

During this Parliament an act against the Catholic missionary priests was introduced which ordered any priests ordained abroad to leave England within forty days or be executed for treason. Scores of priests, some already condemned and imprisoned as traitors, were deported to France, where the militant Spanish ambassador Mendoza noted with delight that these English attempts to stem the flow only served to increase the fervour of the 'seminarists [who] go over daily to England with glad hearts and wonderful firmness to win the crown of martyrdom'.[45]

This general alarm meant Mary was moved from Sheffield Castle and finally out of the care of the Earl and Countess of Shrewsbury. Shrewsbury had discharged his onerous duty over a period of fifteen years, during which time his health and his fortune had been significantly depleted. On taking leave of Elizabeth the following year he had kissed her hand and thanked her fervently for having 'freed him from two devils, namely, the Queen of Scotland and his wife',[46] the indomitable Bess of Hardwick.

Mary was moved, with great forward planning and in the company of a body of armed men, to Wingfield Manor, to be temporarily in the care of the kindly old diplomat Sir Ralph Sadler. Now in his late seventies, he had been Henry VIII's ambassador to Mary's mother, Mary of Guise, when she was regent of Scotland. At that time he had been impressed both by her, and by the beauty and vigour of her tiny baby, Mary herself. Nearly forty-two years ago she had been unwrapped and undressed in the middle of winter to prove to the King of England's envoy that the baby he coveted in marriage for his son Edward was both healthy and perfect, and likely to survive. If Sadler was touched by her then, inevitably he would be putty in the hands of the now grown-up and tragic woman, the deposed queen.

In January 1585, despite protestations and delaying tactics, Mary was transferred once more to the grim stronghold of Tutbury Castle. On the way Sadler, Mary and their party had unexpectedly to stay the night in a lowly house, kept by 'an ancient wydow, namid Mrs Beaumont'. Mary's charming manners and gift of empathy in her concern to put at ease this unimportant woman gave an insight into why her own female servants, particularly, remained so affectionate and loyal to her all their lives: 'So sone as [Mary] knew who was her hostesse, after she had made a beck [nod] to the rest of the wemen standing next to the doore, she went to her and kissed her, and none other, sayeng that she was comme thither to trouble her, and that she was also a wydow, and therefore trusted that they shulde agree well inough together, having no husbands to trouble them'.[47]

One of Sadler's favourite sports was hawking. Mary too was an enthusiast and long ago had surprised her French family when she first arrived in France, aged not yet six, by exhibiting precocious expertise as a falconer. When Sadler sent for his hawks and falconers to wile away what was an unhappy situation as jailer, he could not resist Mary's blandishments, even when it got him into trouble. On the arrival of his birds, she had 'ernestly intreated me that she might go abrode with me to see my hawkes flie, a passetyme indede which she hethe singular delite in'. Sadler could not deny her and allowed Mary to accompany him three or four times, even though it meant riding on horseback some miles down the valley from the castle. Elizabeth was far from happy when she heard of this breach of security in his keeping of the Queen of Scots, alarmed at a possible escape or rescue attempt. Sadler explained that he was an unwilling jailer and anyway had never had less than forty armed men on horseback with them. Weary of life, he said, he desired nothing more than to relinquish this unsought charge, to return home to prepare himself for death and 'the euerlasting quyetnes of the lif to com'.[48]

His wish was to be granted, for his duties as Mary's keeper were handed over in April 1585 to Sir Amyas Paulet, a scrupulous Puritan and the least susceptible of men. Sadler had mildly complained to Elizabeth that it was impossible to keep track of all the correspondence and conversation that eddied about the Queen of Scots, so large was her household and the numbers of Scottish, English and French servants and courtiers who came and went almost without check. Paulet immediately imposed his more austere will. He pared down her household and closed off the channels of her private mail, even for a while to the French ambassador. The casual expeditions were also stopped. There were no more summer visits to Buxton baths and certainly no more days hawking miles down-river from the castle gates. If Paulet was unimpressed by Mary, she was equally dismissive of him: 'he is one of the most gruff and rebarbative [*un des plus bizzares et farouches*] of persons whom I have ever known; and, in a word, fitter for a jail of criminals than for the custody of one of my rank and birth'.[49] She also felt that should Elizabeth die, Paulet would have little compunction in eliminating her, rather than countenance a Catholic successor to the English throne.

Mary fired off an indignant complaint to Elizabeth at these new restrictions. Even as she wrote, however, it occurred to her that her letters were barely read by the recipient as they were 'so long and customarily tedious, according to the subject that is daily provided to me for them'. Through the years the stream of letters from Mary to her cousin veered from professions of love to the pathos of the victimized, through queenly outrage to veiled menace and threats of foreign intervention. Elizabeth at first had been sympathetic, sometimes intimidated, even amazed, but after nearly two decades when neither the content nor context had much changed she had grown distant; as Mary perceptively feared 'you yourself will not always give yourself leisure to read my letters'. Mary was not a fool and as a natural charmer and entertainer she also regretted the paucity of her experiences now, the narrowed horizons so different from the glamour and promise of her youth. She ended the letter with her unique combination of apology, accusation and pathos: 'I regret that my letters convey to you only continual complaints and grievances; but still more the so pregnant cause which I have, to which I beseech my God to send a termination in some shape or other.'[50]

Elizabeth did not immediately read this letter, if in fact she ever did. Despite the heightened awareness of her vulnerability to assassination and the complete lack of protection from anyone wishing her ill, she was on one of her annual summer progresses greeted by crowds who pressed close with offerings, any one of whom could have killed her. Elizabeth had never forgotten that she owed her crown not only to God but to her people, and she recognized the power of her presence and the necessity of pageant and display.

Leopold von Wedel was a young German adventurer from Pomerania of independent means who arrived in England in the summer of 1585. In his informative diary, he not only admired the beauty of the fair-skinned English women but was surprised at their forwardness and the fact that they participated so wholeheartedly in public events: 'the womenfolk in England wish to be in at everything',[51] was his half-admiring aside. He also noted how accessible the queen was, despite the level of anxiety raised by the discovery of various plots and possible assassination attempts. He had already been shown around her palaces, with great informality, noting the wealth and luxury of the furnishings and jewel-studded objets d'art; the pearl-encrusted bed hangings of the queen's bed of state and the even larger pearls embroidered onto the pillows, being amongst the details which caught his eye.

Wedel was struck by Elizabeth's popular touch despite the overwhelming grandeur of the pageant of her public life. Having been to church at Hampton Court she walked between two rows of her 'common people', who as she approached fell upon their knees. 'The Queen's demeanour, however, was gracious and gentle and so was her speech, and from rich and poor she took petitions in a modest manner.'[52] Her surprising patience and affection seemed to be reciprocated by the populace many times over. Elizabeth managed to combine personal familiarity with semi-divine spectacle, with herself at the centre of the show. On her arrival in London in early November, ready for the annual festivities on the 17th, the twenty-seventh anniversary of the day she was proclaimed queen, the glamour of the procession on horseback was recorded vividly by Wedel:

> [Burghley and Walsingham] were followed by the Queen in a gold coach, open all round, but having above it a canopy embroidered with gold and pearls ... The Queen sat alone in the carriage. She was dressed in white and cried to the people: 'God save my people', to which the crowd responded with 'God save Your Grace'. This they repeated many times, falling on their knees. The Queen sitting all alone in her splendid coach appeared like a goddess such as painters are wont to depict. Behind the Queen's coach rode my Lord Lester, who is an Earl of princely blood.[53]

Remarkably, this procession, almost three decades after that first triumphant entry into London on her accession, was fundamentally unchanged. Her two closest advisers then, Cecil and Lord Robert, some thirty years later were her closest still. Despite the passage of eventful years, only Walsingham had been added to the intimate family circle around Elizabeth, and this continuity and enduring loyalty was one of the keys to the stability and success of her reign. Wedel appeared as caught up in the general emotion of fealty and gratitude to Elizabeth. A young man overwhelmed by the palaces he had visited, the pageants and jousting tournaments, the feasts and the balls, it was not surprising that he should declare the English as 'rich, wealthy, very ostentatious and pleasure-loving'.[54]

Just as this starry-eyed tourist was preparing to return to Germany, life in England was growing more difficult and dangerous for both Mary and Elizabeth. The Protestant rebels in the Low Countries were in disarray since the assassination of the Prince of Orange and were petitioning desperately for more help from Elizabeth than just the money and munitions she had supplied during the previous decade. Fear of Spanish aggression meant there were many in England who considered that Spain, having reasserted its authority over the Low Countries, would turn its warlike energies at last on England. Bowing to the passionate advocacy of an ageing Leicester, determined on his chance of military command in the Protestant cause for which he had long campaigned, Elizabeth reluctantly allowed her favourite to go to the Low Countries in command of her forces, with the title of the queen's Lieutenant General.

Accoutred with magnificence, and in the company of an impressive array of noblemen, the portly earl arrived in Flushing to an ecstatic welcome. He had a fleet of one hundred ships to transport his entourage and was in charge of thousands of foot soldiers and cavalry. Camden recorded how Elizabeth's decision to come to the Netherlanders' aid meant 'all the Princes of Christendom admired at such manly Fortitude in a Woman, which durst, as it were, declare War against so puissant [powerful] a Monarch: insomuch as the King of Sweden said, "That Queen Elizabeth had now taken the Diadem from her Head, and adventured it upon the doubtfull Chance of War" '.[55]

To distract the Spanish further, Elizabeth let loose again Sir Francis Drake and his band of venture capitalists to prey on the Spanish colonies, their treasure ships and trade routes. This overt piracy enraged the Spanish further as the looted treasures enriched not only Drake's own coffers and those of the grandees who lent their support to his expeditions, but Elizabeth herself. Mendoza, writing to Philip II, explained the outrageous deal: '[Drake] did not take precise orders from the Queen, except to plunder as much as he could, to enable her to sustain the war in Flanders.'[56] Her unashamed encouragement of her rapacious adventurers extended even to ennobling them. This insult combined with every other English outrage against his proud and powerful nation and drove the chronically cautious Philip II closer to waging outright war on English soil.

Elizabeth was the princess he had once saved from the bitter wrath of her sister, his wife Mary I. Now a presumptuous and ungrateful queen, a heretic who encouraged heretics within his own territories, she was about to face the consequences of his slow deliberations. The greatest Catholic power intended putting a brake on this renegade state. His duty as the military arm of the Catholic church, and with great commercial interests at stake, gave Philip every reason to act decisively at last.

Elizabeth was outwardly defiant, although anxious not to be seen as aggrandizing her own kingdom. To the Prince of Parma she wrote: 'Do not suppose that I am seeking what belongs to others. God forbid. I seek only that which is mine own. But be sure that I will take good heed of the sword which threatens me with destruction, nor think that I am so craven-spirited as to endure a wrong, or to place myself at the mercy of my enemy.'[57] She always found it hard, however, to be decisive and now, as the Swedish king remarked, venturing her diadem on the doubtful outcome of war, she struggled with the consequent danger and expense and the threat of worse to come. The drain on her resources was emotional too; she missed Leicester whose prominence in the war meant he was now in greater peril of losing his life. Even more alarmingly, he was pursuing his own grandiose plans. When he accepted, against his queen's express wishes, the title of Supreme Governor of the Low Countries, offered by the grateful rebels, Elizabeth's nervous tension exploded: 'How contemptuously we conceive ourself to have been used by you', she wrote to her old favourite. 'We could never have imagined . . . that a man raised up by ourself and extraordinarily favoured by us above any other subject in this land, would have in so contemptible a sort broken our commandment, in a cause that so greatly toucheth us in honour.'[58] Leicester's contrary ambitions made Elizabeth all the more desirous of extricating herself from this troublesome and ruinous enterprise.

Like all her furious rows with Leicester, this one was soon over and Elizabeth was friends with him again. After the storms of more than thirty years' closest companionship, her letter to him in the summer of 1586, while he was still in the Low Countries facing failure rather than the triumph he had expected, makes her ease and intimacy with him clearly apparent. She began without preamble, 'Rob, I am afraid you will suppose by my wandering writings that a midsummer moon hath taken large possession of my brains this month, but you must needs take things as they come into my head, though order be left behind me.' She then ended a letter largely concerned with administration with, 'Now will I end, that do imagine I talk still with you, and therefore loathly say farewell, Ô Ô,* though ever I pray God bless you from all harm, and save you from all foes with my million and legion of thanks for your pains and cares.' She signed it 'As you know, ever the same,† E.R.'[59]

The stresses on Elizabeth of expansion, as she engaged in her first foreign war, were mirrored by the stresses of containment endured by Mary under the stern Puritan regime instituted by Amyas Paulet. Neither queen was happy in these unaccustomed roles and both intended to escape them, Elizabeth through an initially secret treaty with Spain and Mary through another unrealistic but deadly conspiracy.

---

* The cipher used by Elizabeth in her letters for 'eyes', one of her pet names for Leicester.
† Elizabeth's motto, *semper eadem*, which had also been her mother's.

Mary's fascination with coded messages, secrets, plots and lies was in large part an expression of a risk-taker's need for excitement when confinement and constraint had closed off more conventional adventures. It was also a kind of revenge. As a clever and insightful spymaster, Walsingham recognized the Scottish queen's peculiarly reckless temperament and hunger for action. The day before Christmas 1585 she was moved from Tutbury to Chartley, a great moated manor in Staffordshire. When a limited channel of clandestine communication was again made available to her on Walsingham's orders, courtesy of the local brewer and a small wooden box, to conceal her letters, submerged in a keg of ale, he knew that Mary would be incapable of resisting any projected madcap scheme that came her way. Just one month later, having recovered after another collapse in her health, she was writing to the French ambassador, via the keg of ale, with enthusiastic plans for continuing her covert operations. Authoritatively suggesting he beware of spies and the bribery of his staff, Mary launched off into a discussion of methods of conveying secret messages, unaware that Walsingham and his agents were reading every word:

'The plan of writing in alum is very common, and may easily be suspected and discovered, and therefore do not make use of it except in a case of necessity; and if you should use it, write ... between the lines of such new books [sent in], writing always on the fourth, eighth, twelfth, and sixteenth leaf ... And cause green ribbons to be attached to all the books, which you have caused to be written on in this manner.' She also suggested writing on 'white taffeta, lawn, or suchlike delicate cloth', advising the ambassador to add an extra half yard to the bolt of cloth which had been inscribed so 'this word "a half" may inform me that within there is something secretly hidden'. Another ingenious hiding place occurred to her; letters in cipher could replace the cork inner sole of the high-heeled slippers which seemed to be delivered frequently to her women and herself.[60]

With the protective fervour of the Bond of Association now made law, the legal framework was in place by the beginning of 1585 to convict Mary in the event of her being implicated, even passively, in a plot to overthrow Elizabeth and place herself on the English throne. All Elizabeth's advisers knew that in order to get rid of Mary once and for all they would have to present Elizabeth with overwhelming evidence of her perfidy. Mary was never one to be passively part of anything dangerous or exciting when she could be wholeheartedly complicit and in the centre of things. So it was only a matter of management and time before Walsingham's crafty surveillance would have her in his web.

December 1585 was a busy month. If the relationship of Elizabeth and Mary was seen as a marathon chess match, this marked the beginning of the endgame. Just as Leicester sailed as a knight in splendour for the Low Countries, Mary took up her residence in Chartley and Walsingham apprehended at Dover a dubious priest and envoy to Mary, one Gilbert Gifford. He was persuaded to join the opposition, to become a double agent now, intent on opening communications with the Scottish queen. Walsingham's own queen was distracted by the movements of her unruly knight and not fully aware of the trap being set for Mary. With a motley crew of English refugees, religious fanatics, double agents and romantic young hot-heads, a plan to rescue Mary was merged with a simultaneous plot to take Elizabeth. It was a two-pronged move on Elizabeth's life and throne which would leave Mary vulnerable to a devastating checkmate, masterminded by Walsingham.

The catalyst was a priest, John Ballard, who sought out a young Catholic gentleman, Anthony Babington, a passionate supporter of Mary since he was a boy and had first had contact with her when she was held at Wingfield, near his family estates. Now, barely twenty-five and with the zealotry and arrogance of youth, he was determined to play the hero and rescue Mary. There was a new generation of idealistic and romantic Catholic youth who knew little of Mary's previous history yet found the poignancy of her situation, her adherence to her faith, her long captivity by a heretic sovereign, affecting and arousing. The papal bull had sanctified if not encouraged the murder of Elizabeth and for young men wishing to serve their God and earn their spurs, the death of the bad queen and salvation of the good seemed to be a thrilling and righteous enterprise. When Ballard suggested that Spanish and French forces were ready and willing to invade, the plan became more grandiose and concrete.

Mary was liberated by her new channel for sending and receiving contraband messages and wrote in May to Mendoza, Philip II's ambassador in Paris. She was in despair at her son's continued Protestantism and desire to make his political alliances with Elizabeth rather than with herself, his own mother. The last shreds of hope were abandoned with the news that James had made formal his alliance with Elizabeth by accepting a pension of £4,000* a year. Certainly wishing to elicit support from the Spanish, and possibly seeking revenge on her ungrateful son whose desire to succeed to the English throne was as great as her own, Mary made this extraordinary offer. 'I have resolved that, in case my son should not submit before my death to the Catholic religion . . . I will cede and make over, by will, to the King your master, my right to the succession to this [i.e. the English] crown, and beg him consequently to take me in future entirely under his protection, and also the affairs of this country . . . I again beg you most urgently that this should be kept secret, as if it becomes known it will cause the loss of my dowry in France, and bring about an entire breach with my son in Scotland, and my total ruin and destruction in England.'[61]

Mary was right. This action risked all those calamities and yet she seemed compelled to seek the most perilous path along which to career, unconcerned with the consequences. Her dealings with the conspiracy that was brewing around her showed a recklessness so extreme it could be thought suicidal. Contemporaries, even, recognized a certain self-destructiveness in her obsessive plotting and collaboration with any hare-brained conspiracy that raced past her door. The writer and her contemporary, George Whetstone, suggested that in her conspiracy letters 'there is nothing more manifest, than that her malice thirsteth to death of her own life'.[62]

Mary was highly conscious of her effect on others and aware that what she did had ramifications far beyond England's parochial

---

* Roughly equivalent to £750,000.

shores. She had a strong element of self-dramatization in her nature and a desire for transfiguration. She had already written to Elizabeth in 1585 that she would welcome the opportunity to sacrifice her life for her faith: 'I am perfectly ready, with the grace of God, to bow my neck beneath the axe, that my blood should be shed before all Christendom; and I should esteem it the greatest happiness to be the first to do so. I do not say this out of any vain glory, while the danger is remote.'[63] Although impatient and inexperienced in the chicanery of political life, she was astute enough in her directives to her ambassadors. To Beaton she wrote in code from Chartley that summer, 'Endeavour by all means which you can to discover for certain the design of the King of Spain for revenging himself against this queen, and especially if it is for an enterprise in this country, or only thereby to counteract the attempt of the Earl of Leicester in Flanders, and of Drake upon the Indies; because upon that depends entirely the resolution which I and all the Catholics here have to take for our part.'[64] If Philip's avenging armies were aimed at England's shores then she would take hope.

As what became known as the Babington Plot took root and grew, the assassination of Elizabeth became a central necessity. Babington's inflated plans involved six assassins and a group of a hundred gentlemen ready simultaneously to release Mary from captivity. In July he wrote to the woman he hoped to make his future queen, explaining that he and his co-conspirators were ready for the coming invasion of Catholic power. Quite unaware of how insecure his letters were he stated boldly in his letter to Mary his treasonous intent: 'For the despatch of the usurper [Elizabeth], from the obedience of whom we are by excommunication of her made free, there be six noble gentlemen, all my private friends, who for the zeal they bear to the Catholic cause and your Majesty's service will undertake the tragical execution.'[65]

This was a gift to the patient Walsingham. Now he had to wait and see if Mary would incriminate herself in her reply. Mary's eventual answer was everything they could have hoped. In a long letter and with a matter-of-fact tone she accepted all the details of Babington's scheme, but added her own logistical concerns about the need for foreign aid and for substantial quantities of armed men and money. She asked him to assure his aforementioned gentlemen friends 'of all that will be required from my part for the entire accomplishment of their good intentions'. Declaring that even should the plan to rescue her fail and she end up in the Tower, she would pray that Babington and his followers continue with their enterprise 'pour l'honneur de Dieu'; she would die happy 'when I shall know that you are delivered from the miserable servitude in which you [as English Catholics] are held captive'.[66] It was a letter inviting foreign invasion and the utter overthrow of Elizabeth and the Protestant religion. Walsingham had his queen.

He wished to delay just a little longer in the hopes of uncovering more of the conspirators but Elizabeth, who had just recently been acquainted with the conspiracy, was shocked 'that so dreadfull a Storm hung over her head, on the one side from her own Subjects at Home, and on the other side from Strangers abroad'.[67] She commanded Walsingham to act immediately to round up what plotters he could, 'lest [as she said herself] by not heeding and preventing the Danger while she might, she should seem rather to tempt God, than to trust in God'.[68] Babington's immediate fellowship of assassins were, like himself, very young, aged between twenty and twenty-five. On news of his apprehension on 14 August, the bells of London pealed out in triumph and celebratory bonfires lit his enforced journey back to the city.

While the conspirators were being arrested and interrogated, Mary was kept in ignorance of the dangerous turn in the tide of events. Her spirits were buoyant and when Paulet suggested a day's stag hunting she agreed with alacrity. She was in such an optimistic frame of mind that, when a body of strangers on horseback galloped up over the horizon, for a moment she believed these were her young gentlemen conspirators come to rescue her and carry her away. Unexpectedly and terrifyingly she was confronted instead by Elizabeth's commissioners with the brutal message that she was under arrest for treason.

Separated from her servants, Mary was conveyed to Tixall, a nearby manor. She was confused and distressed. She had been taken completely unawares and for a while was frightened that her life would be ended then and there. During her days of seclusion at Tixall it appears her thoughts became settled on her final plan. This was to be the last time that she was to express in public any fear or anxiety as to her fate. While she waited for news of how Elizabeth would proceed against her, Mary must have known that whatever happened next the tedium and stasis of her prolonged genteel captivity was at an end. Anything was preferable to a return to those leaden hours of inactivity and hopelessness.

In her absence from Chartley, Mary's belongings were searched and incriminating letters and a variety of coding alphabets were found, 'about 60 Indexes or Tables of private Cyphers and Characters'.[69] In the careful inventory of her possessions were mentioned miniature portraits of Elizabeth herself, Mary's son James and mother, Mary of Guise, her father James V and all the previous Scottish kings from whom she was descended, back to James II. Her dead Guise uncles who had had such a powerful influence on her life, the duke, and the Cardinal of Lorraine, were also represented, as was the present Duc de Guise, inheritor of that line of which Mary and her son were so proud.

Most distressing for Elizabeth amongst the discoveries were letters from some of her own noblemen swearing loyalty to her rival. Camden noted that Elizabeth bore these revelations in silence, disguising her true feelings, 'according to that Motto which she used, *Video & taceo*, that is, I see, but say nothing'.[70] The nobles themselves, however, in terror made great play as to their fealty to Elizabeth and abhorrence of Mary's deeds. Disloyalty upset and disturbed Elizabeth, unpopularity frightened her. Her suppressed emotion was discharged explosively at the French ambassador, whom she had summoned to her presence. 'Well, what do you think of your Queen of Scotland? With black ingratitude and treachery she tries to kill me who so often saved her life. Now I am certain of her evil intent, and it may be she will not have another opportunity to behave like this,'[71] she raged.

The country was in a state of alarm. Rumours such as '10,000 Frenchmen had landed and captured three villages' gathered potency with the telling; the sight of three ships near the Isle of Wight, and a haystack set alight by chance, meant all the warning beacons were torched to summon the country to arms. Lord Buckhurst, the local governor, found himself suddenly in charge of four to five thousand men, armed and ready to defend England from invasion. Mendoza reported to Philip with glee the extent of the country's fear and confusion; eyewitnesses, just arrived in Paris, 'are never tired of recounting it with infinite laughter'.[72]

Elizabeth's vengeance was first of all directed at the young conspirators. Torture had wrung full confessions from them and death was the only punishment, but Elizabeth was adamant that it should be as cruel a death as was judicially possible. The death of a traitor was terrible enough if enacted to the letter, when the victim would be half hanged and then disembowelled still alive and sentient. Most executioners waited until the prisoner was dead before proceeding with the savage sequel. On 20 September, Babington and six of his fellow conspirators were brought to the scaffold. With the immediacy of the eyewitness, Camden wrote that they were 'hanged, cut down, their Privities cut off, their Bowels taken out before their Faces while they were alive, and their Bodies quartered, not without some note and touch of cruelty'.[73] Elizabeth was reputedly taken aback at the cruelty, and sensitive to reports of the watching crowd's pity and sense of shock, she commuted the sentence for the next batch of prisoners. They were hanged until they were dead, 'by the Queen's express Command', and then cut down and quartered.

But what to do with Mary herself? By the confessions of these men and the freely given evidence of her two secretaries who had transcribed their mistress's incriminating letters, her complicity in the plot was clear enough to all. A trial for treason, invoking the newly ratified Act of Association, seemed the next logical step. There was uneasiness even then, however, among some councillors about the means used to entrap the Queen of Scots; others were wary of the presumption of subjects sitting in judgement on a divinely ordained monarch. But these were mere cavils. To the majority of Elizabeth's councillors this was not the time to quibble when such gross intentions had been revealed. They were not about to allow the queen to evade her duty to safeguard herself, her people and her realm, by pleading some metaphysical nicety be respected. They were determined that this time the Queen of Scots must die. All they needed now was for Elizabeth to agree.

Elizabeth had long recognized how equivocation and inde-cisiveness had been both her weakness and her strength; now she could procrastinate no longer. Years before she had told a French ambassador: 'I know that it is true I have the imperfection of being longer than necessary in coming to a conclusion in these deliberations – a fault that has caused me much injury in the past ... it is true the world was made in six days, but it was by God, to whose power the infirmity of men is not to be compared.'[74]

As Mary left Tixall to return fleetingly to Chartley, she was greeted by a crowd of beggars who knew of her reputation for largesse to the poor. Mary gave them a sad valediction, 'Alas, good people, I have now nothing to give you. For I am as much a beggar as you are yourselves.' She can have meant this only as a self-dramatizing metaphor, for she was still a queen with her jewels and her dowry to protect her from beggary. But the distribution of alms to the poor was an important part of her sense of herself as merciful and endearing. When Paulet had forbidden this activity, she wrote to the French ambassador that without this contact with the people she feared that in the locality she would be 'reputed and held as some savage and complete stranger'.[75] To connect with others and have an effect was the driving force of her life.

Soon after, Mary wrote a letter to the Duc de Guise outlining her plan for this the final act. She had always denied any implication in the treasonous plots that had sprung around her throughout her captivity. She had decided that she would stand on her unimpeach-able sovereignty and die freely now as a martyr for her faith. Mary appeared to wish to dignify her struggle with Elizabeth by making it a microcosm of the religious wars of Catholic against heretic which were raging over the Channel: 'I have declared to them that for my part I am resolute to die for mine [my religion] as she declared that she would do for the Protestant [religion]', she explained. Having determined on this course of public martyrdom Mary feared most the secret assassin, robbing her death of its power and meaning. She confided to her Guise cousin, 'I am expecting some poison or other such secret death', a thoroughly plausible fear at that time.

She continued her letter despite, she said, the pain she suffered from her swollen arm: 'the heart will not fail me in the hope that One who made me to be born what I am will do me the mercy of making me die for His cause'. Her abandonment of Scotland was complete with her request that her body be sent to Rheims to rest beside her mother and her heart be placed beside her first husband, François II. She ended the letter with an intimation that her death would be avenged by the Catholic princes. But even as Mary bade her cousin an affecting farewell she requested that he pass a message on to Mendoza, the Spanish ambassador in Paris, that meant her betrayal of Guise and French interests in favour of the Spanish. The message – that she would not abandon what she had promised to Mendoza's friends – could only refer to the promise she had made to will her rights to succession of the English throne to Philip II, should her son continue to refuse to convert to Catholicism. A draft of this document in her own handwriting was found in her papers after her death.

As Mary was moved to Fotheringhay Castle in Northamptonshire on 25 September 1586 the stage was set for the final act in the struggle between the two queens. They would deny the roles of cruel oppressor and villainess that each had written for the other and display instead the archetypal characters that each had chosen for herself, as heroic populist queen and Catholic martyr. Mary the bold adventurer and enchantress had her chance to draw on her inner reserves for a dramatic consummation of her life that would gain her immortality at least. Elizabeth, until then the great equivocator, now made up her mind at last and through action transcended royalty to become an iconic queen.

CHAPTER TWELVE

The Consequence of the Offence

Give me my robe, put on my crown; I have Immortal
longings in me.
Antony and Cleopatra, act 5, scene 2

ELIZABETH AND MARY SHARED a grand sense of the dramatic.
They were aware that their theatre was the world, everything they
did was noticed and interpreted by a constituency much wider
than their immediate kingdoms. They had the expectations of their
ancestors upon them and the hindsight of history would judge
them. Their public utterances rang with appreciation of their significance in the great drama of human affairs. Mary, addressing
the commissioners sent to Fotheringhay in October, was exhorting
Elizabeth. They were 'to look to their Consciences, and to remember
that the Theatre of the whole World is much wider than the Kingdom of England'.[1] In that warning was her recognition that she was
above all, a European prince and a Catholic queen. She could look
to her fellow Catholic princes to avenge her and to future generations to absolve her.

Elizabeth, addressing her Parliament in the following month,
expressed her own awareness of the situation: 'for we princes, I tell
you, are set on stages in the sight and view of all the world duly
observed. The eyes of many behold our actions.'[2] Not only was
personal privacy denied them, every public word and action was

relayed, embellished or interpreted, through the country and beyond to the capitals of European power.

Having protested with tears and anger at her impotence during the long years of her captivity, having complained volubly at every change of abode from castle to manor house and back again, Mary accepted the move to Fotheringhay without demur. With characteristic courage she had decided to embrace what she now recognized as the inevitability of death with the nobility of the righteous and the resolve of the martyr. In doing so she stage-managed her exit for maximum impact on history and the watchers of the world. Mary had shown already how well she rose to the most daunting physical challenges. Just as she had done when riding with her troops to battle, in taking control of her fate she became fearless herself, and awesome to others.

Elizabeth and Mary's last confrontation was a struggle for the moral high ground. Their reputations at stake, they sought now to justify their actions towards each other throughout their lives, with the eloquence of their own rhetoric and a canny use of propaganda. Both masters of their arts, they reduced to tears the Members of Parliament and trial commissioners who heard their emotive submissions. Elizabeth was determined that Mary should admit her wrongdoing and ask for forgiveness, and she still clung to the possibility of saving her life and saving herself the agony of that capital decision, 'a most grievous and irksome burden'.[3]

One of Elizabeth's most famous letters, much copied and distributed in her lifetime to show Elizabeth's magnanimity and Mary's guilt, was to Sir Amyas Paulet, in the month Mary was conveyed to Fotheringhay, recommending his safekeeping of his royal prisoner:

> Amyas, my most careful and faithful servant,
>
> God reward thee treblefold in the double for thy most troublesome charge so well discharged. If you knew, my Amyas, how kindly besides dutifully my careful heart accepts your double labours and faithful actions, your wise orders and safe regards performed in so dangerous and crafty a charge, it would ease your troubles' travail and rejoice your heart . . .
>
> But let your wicked mistress know how with hearty sorrow

her vile deserts compels these orders, and bid her from me ask God's forgiveness.[4]

In her communications on the discovery of the Babington Plot, Elizabeth intimated more than once that if only Mary would admit her guilt and show herself ready to make amends then she would be happy to pardon her. Mary herself knew this was the bargain. Even after being found guilty, she wrote to Mendoza, the Spanish ambassador, suggesting that if she would only admit her guilt and ask for forgiveness her life might be saved: 'I am threatened if I do not plead for pardon, but I reply that they have already condemned me to death.'[5] Mary's stance was uncompromising; she wanted martyr not traitor to be the judgement of history.

For her part, Elizabeth conveyed a wistfulness that she and Mary had never met and been able to conduct their relationship unencumbered by the weighty matters of politics, religion and the balance of European powers. To her Parliament that November she memorably explained:

> I assure you, if the case stood between her and myself only, if it had pleased God to have made us both milkmaids with pails on our arms, so that the matter should have rested between us two; and that I knew she did and would seek my destruction still, yet could I not consent to her death ... Yea, if I could perceive how I might be freed from the conspiracies and treasons of her favourers in this action – by your leaves she should not die.[6]

To Mary she sent a similar message via her councillors: 'if the consequence of the offence reached no further then to ourself as a private person, wee protest before God we coulde have bene verie well contented to have freely remitted and pardoned the same'.[7] If these sentiments were even half-sincere it was interesting to see that she considered how simple and less threatening their relationship would be if they had been merely private citizens. Elizabeth went on to explain that the fact that they were queens and represented opposing religions and alliances abroad complicated the situation and increased the danger. The danger Mary represented emanated more from those adherents and interests that attached themselves to her cause. The need to execute her only became a pressing debate because the security of the realm, not just Elizabeth's life, was at risk.

To break this cycle of plots and threats of invasion, Elizabeth's ministers desperately argued for Mary to be tried, found guilty and executed for treason. With this intent, the thirty-six commissioners assembled at Fotheringhay by 12 October 1586, ready to proceed. They hoped to persuade Mary to attend the trial in person as her recognition of the proceedings would add an extra dimension of legality. Although it was decided she should be tried under the newly minted Act of Association, there were some doubts as to whether their country's laws could be applied to a foreign queen, particularly one who had sought asylum and then been constrained against her will.

Mary knew that by the terms of this new Act she was clearly guilty by association, at the very least. Her own defence was to stand on her sovereign power and immunity from the laws of an alien state. 'It seemeth strange to me, that the Queen should command me as a Subject, to submit my self to a Trial. I am an absolute Queen, and will doe nothing which may be prejudicial either to Royal Majesty, or to other Princes of my place and rank, or my son. My Mind is not yet so far dejected, neither will I faint or sink under this my Calamity.' She also made an affecting plaint by stressing how bereft she was of friend or counsel, deprived even of her personal papers: 'The Laws and Statutes of England are to me altogether unknown, I am destitute of Counsellors, and who shall be my Peers I cannot tell. My Papers and Notes are taken from me, and no man dareth appear to be my Advocate.' She continued to deny everything and would admit only one thing, 'I have recommended my self and my condition unto foreign Princes.'[8]

Elizabeth had been exasperated throughout the nineteen years of Mary's captivity by her obdurate refusal to accept responsibility or guilt for any of her actions or enterprises. In this perilous situation where she was about to authorize a trial of a fellow sovereign and foreign queen, watched by the world, she needed Mary to submit to her authority in some small way. Her reputation as a just queen required that Mary relinguish her haughty stance of injured innocence, her insistence that she was persecuted purely for her faith alone.

This was precisely what Mary intended to maintain. It was now clear that she would never freely admit any guilt or any conscious complicity in treasonous acts against Elizabeth. She was absolutely sure that the way to escape notoriety and claim immortality was to prove herself a martyr for her faith. Mary had to deflect the gaze from the wreckage of her reign and the ruination of her reputation through an act of nobility and courage. A heroic death went a long way towards reconciling a less than heroic life.

Elizabeth was not sympathetic to Mary's bid for transfiguration. On hearing that she was refusing the right of the English commissioners to try her, Elizabeth dispatched an imperious broadside to Mary, post haste. This was in response to Mary's insistence that she be tried only by her peers, not by those inferior to her in status. Elizabeth was her only available peer but she insisted her councillors were there as her representatives. It was indicative of Elizabeth's ire that this letter carried no titles and no address, just a peremptory statement of fact and intent:

> You have in various ways and manners attempted to take my life and bring my kingdom to destruction by bloodshed. I have never proceeded harshly against you, but have, on the contrary, protected and maintained you like myself. These treasons will be proved to you and all made manifest. Yet it is my will, that you answer the nobles and peers of the kingdom as if I myself were present. I therefore require, charge, and command you make answer for all I have been well informed of your arrogance.

Yet even given the sharpness of the riposte, Elizabeth appeared still willing to pardon Mary if only she would bend her pride, submit to Elizabeth's authority and admit her guilt. Her valedictory sentence was peremptory: 'Act plainly without reserve, and you will sooner be able to obtain favour of me.'[9]

Mary continued to argue fluently and persuasively against the legality of the trial and, despite her protestations that she knew nothing of English law, she showed herself more than capable of debating legalistic points with the best of her interlocutors. When they threatened to proceed anyway against her, even in her absence, she gave a brave, defiant answer, 'that she was no Subject, and rather would she die a thousand Deaths than acknowledge herself a Subject'.[10] Her long years of enforced inactivity had given her endless opportunities for rehearsing the wrongs done to her; now at last with an attentive audience, Mary could not resist running through her catalogue of woes. The commissioners eventually stopped her in mid-flow and asked her to answer plainly if she would attend the trial, yes or no. Her grasp of the weak points of the prosecution against her was impressive. She declared:

> The Authority of their Commission was founded upon a late Law made to intrap her; That she could by no means away with the Queen's Laws, which she had good reason to suspect; That she still had a good Heart full of Courage, and would not derogate from her Progenitours the Kings of Scotland, by owning herself a Subject to the Crown of England; for this was nothing else but openly to confess them to have been Rebels and Traitours. Yet she refused not to answer, provided she were not reduced to the Rank of a Subject. But she had rather utterly perish than to answer as a criminal person.[11]

Mary was lame and her physical suffering added a distinct pathos to her appearance. This, together with her passionate self-righteousness, affected the more chivalrous and soft-hearted of the councillors. Sir Christopher Hatton, one of Elizabeth's privy councillors and prominent in uncovering the Babington Plot, was not so easily moved. He pointed out to the Scottish queen the way she should best proceed, 'appear to your Trial, and shew your Innocency; lest by avoiding Trial you draw upon yourself a Suspicion, and stain your Reputation with an eternal Blot of Aspersion'. He added that, should Mary clear herself, 'the Queen herself will be transported with joy, who affirmed unto me at my coming from her, that never any thing befell her that troubled her more, than that you should be charged with such Misdemeanours'.[12]

Mary did agree to appear at her trial, despite suspecting that it would have no effect on the verdict. Her dramatic temperament led her to prefer to be centre stage in any arena. Mary had spent nineteen years out of power, away from the glitter and attention of court life. Through these long years she had felt abandoned by all governments, been refused consistently any interview with Elizabeth, barely offered acknowledgement of her requests, let alone a hearing to defend herself. She still maintained a strong sense of her importance and her ability to affect events. Now thirty-six of the most powerful men in England had assembled and here Mary had a stage and an opportunity to present herself and her case in public for the first time. Every word would be relayed with urgency to Elizabeth, who had held herself increasingly superior and aloof from Mary's plaints. Now all of them would have to pay attention.

Fotheringhay was the theatre for her final act of revenge and salvation. The only way to redeem her reputation and make sense of her life was to control the manner of its ending. She saw her death in these histrionic terms; writing to Mendoza she referred to the scaffold as 'a stage whereupon I am to play the last act of the tragedy'.[13] Now that her death was inevitable, she no longer sought Elizabeth's approval or pardon. The only world that Mary hoped to impress now was a Catholic one, the redemption she sought was spiritual and the immortality she craved was as a martyr for her faith. If she could manage that then she would not only establish her rightful place in history and the hearts of her supporters, she also would store up posthumous trouble for Elizabeth and her counsellors too.

On the morning of 15 October, Mary was led into the great chamber for the commencement of her trial. Because she had been secluded from London and the centres of power in the country, many of the nobility there assembled had never seen the Scottish queen before. The lurid tales of her past history and her reputed supernatural charm had endowed her with a glamour and fascination. Even though now middle-aged, her height and demeanour meant she was still a compelling presence.

The stage was ready. Burghley had worked carefully on the symbolic detail of the setting. On a raised platform at the head of the room was placed the chair of state under a canopy of state. This was to represent the presence and authority of Elizabeth, Queen of England, and remained empty throughout. A smaller chair, placed further into the heart of the room, was designated for Mary Queen of Scots. The commissioners were seated on benches down either side of the long room. Mary objected to the inferior position of her chair: 'I am a queen by right of birth and my place should be there under the dais [canopy of state]'[14], she is reputed to have said, pointing to the empty throne intended for the absent Queen of England.

The charges were read out against her, 'that you have conspired the destruction of [the Person of the most Serene Queen Elizabeth] and the Realm of England, and the Subversion of Religion'. Mary defended herself eloquently and emphatically, and admitted not one scintilla of evidence that could prove her guilt. The Babington letters were read out; she absolutely repudiated any suggestion that she had known him, let alone knowingly written him letters or received any from him. She demanded that she be shown the originals with her signature upon them.* Babington's confession she tossed back at her inquisitors: 'If Babington or any other affirm it, I say plainly, They lie. Other mens Faults are not to be thrown upon me.' Her 'stout Courage' and forceful denials were punctuated with explosive bouts of weeping, one of which accompanied a statement of loyalty to Elizabeth: 'I would never make Shipwreck of my Soul by conspiring the Destruction of my dearest Sister,' she declared with feeling.[15]

The most damning evidence, however, was that given by her two secretaries Nau and Curle, whose confessions, recorded independently and not under torture, tallied with each other. They

---

* Her prosecutors only had the copies made by Walsingham's secretary, Phelippes. In order not to arouse the suspicions of the writers and recipients, the letters were intercepted, deciphered, copied, and then resealed and sent on.

confirmed that the letters Walsingham had intercepted, deciphered and copied had been written on Mary's dictation. She even parried this damning evidence with cool composure: 'As well the Majesty as the Safety of all Princes must fall to the Ground, if they depend upon the Writings and Testimonies of Secretaries ... If they have written anything prejudicial to the Queen my Sister, they have written it altogether without my Knowledge, and let them bear the Punishment of their inconsiderate Boldness.'[16]

In a letter the following month to the Spanish ambassador, Mendoza, who was complicit in the general detail of the Babington Plot and closely sympathetic to her, Mary wrote as if she accepted that her secretaries had spoken the truth: 'Nau has confessed everything, Curle a great deal, following his example, and all is on my shoulders.'[17]

In court she maintained her powerful, eloquent presence, insisting that her protestations be registered that she was a sovereign queen who did not recognize the authority of Elizabeth over her but came to the court voluntarily, 'to vindicate herself from the horrible imputation that had been laid to her charge'.[18] She continued to take the floor, undefended by anyone. Quite alone and having to act as her own counsel, she argued her case with passion. She was determined to promote the religious component of her arraignment which her prosecutors were equally adamant in denying: '[my religion] has been my sole consolation and hope under all my afflictions, and for its advancement I would cheerfully give my best blood, if so be I might, by my own death, procure relief for the suffering Catholics; but not even for their sakes would I purchase it at the price of the blood of others ... It is, in sooth, more in accordance with my nature to pray with Esther than to play the part of Judith.'*[19]

The trial was adjourned and the commissioners returned to London to meet again in the Star Chamber in Westminster on 25 October. Although they had not been asked to travel to Fotheringhay and give evidence before Mary, her secretaries here appeared

---

* Esther interceded with Xerxes, the Persian king, to save the Jews, whereas Judith cut off the head of the Babylonian general Holofernes in order to save her people.

in person to confirm their evidence about the letters. The commission, unanimously except for one vote,* pronounced Mary guilty of having 'compassed and imagined within this Realm of England divers Matters tending to the Hurt, Death and Destruction of the Royal Person of our Sovereign Lady the Queen'.[20]

When the councillors went to Elizabeth to give her the news the French ambassador reported that she sank to her knees and remained in prayer for at least fifteen minutes. She asked God to 'inspire her how to act for the greater glory of His name, the greater safety of her kingdom, the greater security of her person'. Elizabeth in this prayer reiterated the fear she had at 'putting to death a woman, a Sovereign Queen like herself, relation of all the great Princes of the world, and closely allied to herself by blood'. Aware perhaps of her audience, she also shared with her maker how hard she found the decision, given that she herself was a woman, 'and the most tender hearted on earth'.[21]

Elizabeth may have been a little disingenuous but she was not being melodramatic. Her fear was real on a personal, spiritual and political level. When the momentous news of the verdict reached the European courts there was talk of retaliation. Spain's long-planned revenge for England's heresy, for her own fleet's piratical depredations on Spanish treasure ships and foreign colonies, for Elizabeth's intransigence, was prodded into life by the projected execution of Mary. In December 1586 a dispatch from the Venetian ambassador in Spain reported in cipher, 'the King [Philip II] and his Ministers are extremely anxious to avenge themselves on the Queen of England, but two considerations of great weight present

---

* Lord Edward Zouche (?1556–1625) was only twenty when he bravely and uniquely set himself apart from his fellow peers and sovereign in this sensational trial. In youth he considered himself feckless and his passion for creating gardens had apparently helped lose his patrimony. In old age he seems to have attained more conventional honours, including in 1620 being one of the first members of the New England council in Virginia. He was buried in a vault connected to his wine cellar, a fact which inspired this from his friend Ben Jonson: 'Wherever I die, oh, here may I lie/Along by my good Lord Zouche/That when I am dry, to the tap I may hie/And so back again to my couch.'

themselves, the questions of how and when'.[22] The Guises too were busy stoking French antagonism to Elizabeth for her treatment of their kinswoman. The general feeling abroad was that the English queen would never be so rash as to allow the execution of the Queen of Scots to proceed: 'there is no reason in the world why England should commit an act which would rouse all Christendom in wrath against her'.[23]

With such threats from beyond her shores, Elizabeth's own anxiety and alarm were exacerbated by Mary's ecstatic embrace of her sentence: 'so far was she from being dismayed thereat, that with a settled and steadfast Countenance, lifting up her Eyes and Hands towards Heaven, she gave Thanks to God for it'. Even more disconcerting was Mary's sense of triumph when told by the commissioners that as long as she lived the reformed religion in England would never be secure. She greeted the news 'with a more than wonted Alacrity, giving God Thanks, and rejoicing in her Heart, that she was taken to be an Instrument for the re-establishing of Religion in this Island'.[24]

Greatly troubled as to what to do, Elizabeth faced a delegation from her Lords and Commons that November, most of whom were pleading that she execute Mary as soon as possible as the only way to re-establish security in the country. She wished to show her gratitude for their loyalty and her understanding of their fears. She explained that although infinitely grateful to God for every gift and mercy He had shown her, in keeping her safe from constant perils, the greatest miracle to her was her people's love: 'as I came to the crown with the willing hearts of my subjects, so do I now after twenty-eight years' reign perceive in you no diminution of goodwills, which if haply I should want, well might I breathe but never think I lived [without which I might as well be dead]'.

She then addressed the pressing problem of Mary: 'it is and has been my grievous thought that one not different in sex, of like estate, and my near kin, should fall into so great a crime ... I secretly wrote her a letter upon the discovery of sundry treasons, that if she would confess them and privately acknowledge them by her letter to myself, she never should need be called for them into so public question'. Acutely sensitive to Mary's charge that the Act under which she had been found guilty was made law expressly to entrap her, Elizabeth specifically denied this was the case. She declared it was more just to try Mary under this statute which allowed for judgement from a commission of the noblest in the land than to subject her to a common court of law and a jury of common men, which Elizabeth speciously claimed as 'a proper course forsooth, to deal in that manner with one of her estate!'.

Elizabeth was ever mindful of the need to prove herself as resolute as any king. She was aware of how Mary's transgressions fulfilled every expectation of female fallibility, reinforcing the suspicion that women could not rule. Well into the rhythm of her eloquence, Elizabeth explained how her experiences separated her from her cousin and made her worthy of her crown:

> I have had good experience and trial of this world: I know what it is to be a subject, what to be a sovereign; what to have good neighbours, and sometimes meet evil willers. I have found treason in trust, seen great benefits little regarded, and instead of gratefulness, courses of purpose to cross. These former remembrances, present feeling, and future expectation of evils, I say, have made me think an evil is much the better the less while it endureth, and so, them happiest that are soonest hence [in the face of evil the sooner one is dead the better] and taught me to bear with a better mind these treasons than is common to my sex – yea, with a better heart, perhaps, than is in some men.

Having proved her superiority, she ended her rhetorical flourish with the statement that brought the terrible possibility of her own death into the public mind, a mind now having to contemplate the execution of the Queen of Scots: 'I would be loath to die so bloody a death [as assassination] so doubt I not but God would have given me grace to be prepared for such an event.'[25]

The juxtaposition of her violent but innocent death with Mary's emphasized on many levels their interconnectedness. Increasingly it seemed that one had to die for the other to live, but Elizabeth was determined to show too that even in dying, Mary's queenly courage could be matched by Elizabeth's nobility of spirit. By talking with equanimity of the greatest terror that her councillors faced, the murder of their sovereign, she assumed the mantle of the monarch she wanted to be. These great speeches of Elizabeth's were quickly published and distributed and there was a sense that she was addressing a wider public than solely these Members of Parliament who had sought audience with her at Richmond Palace.

After the verdict Mary was divested of her canopy of state that had been symbolic of her status as queen throughout her captivity. In a letter to Beaton, she related how, since she had refused to admit her guilt and ask repentance of Elizabeth, the English queen had ordered this dishonour, 'to signify that I was a dead woman, deprived of the honours and dignity of a queen'.[26] The following day Paulet offered to reinstate her canopy, explaining it was not Elizabeth but one of her council who had demanded its removal, but Mary refused. She had already replaced it with a crucifix. Mary's enigmatic motto 'In my end is my beginning' had been embroidered on her cloth of state. Its removal symbolized the relinquishing of her temporal life as a queen in preparation for the eternal life as martyr and myth.

Mary explained to Mendoza her subsequent conversation with her jailers, who would be executioners, in which she argued for this new focus of her life:

> 'It was a fine thing', they said, 'for me to make myself out a saint and martyr; but I should be neither, as I was to die for plotting the murder and deposition of their Queen.' I replied that, 'I was not so presumptuous as to pretend to honours of saint and martyr; but although they had power over my body, by the divine permission, they had none over my soul, nor could they prevent me from hoping that, by the mercy of God who died for me, my blood and life would be accepted as offerings freely made by me for the maintenance of His church.'[27]

Mary was determined on securing her spiritual reputation and personal salvation and her apparently serene self-satisfaction did not fail to irritate and disconcert Elizabeth. Just as she made much of her willingness to die for her faith, so Elizabeth was fond of declaring she would sacrifice her life for her people. At this time of danger averted and new perils to come her rhetoric was particularly resonant, bringing tears to the eyes of her loyal audience of parliamentary Lords and Commoners: 'if by my death, other nations and kingdoms might truly say that this realm had attained an ever prosperous and flourishing estate, I would (I assure you) not desire to live, but gladly give my life to the end my death might procure you a better prince'.[28] While Mary aimed for spiritual glory Elizabeth, always pragmatic and parental, sought more material insurance for her people: 'I look beyond my lifetime to the welfare of my subjects and the security of my kingdom'[29] was her vision of a more practical immortality.

To condemn to death a fellow monarch and defenceless neighbouring queen made for all kinds of uneasiness and outrage both within her country and without. The ruling nobility in Scotland preferred their alliance with Elizabeth to any sentimental attachment for Mary. Although most were sanguine about the prospective execution of the Queen of Scots, the people were not. They had once called her a whore and threatened to burn her, but her transgressions had been lost to memory. Her suffering, her unjust treatment, her enforced exile from their land and long captivity in the inhospitable heart of Scotland's old enemy, was a source of raw emotion. She was born of the proud race descended from Robert the Bruce and had provided them with a good strong male heir to carry on that line. They were incensed at the idea that the English could claim a legal right to destroy her.

James VI, ambitious for himself, pragmatic and clever, was unmoved personally by his mother's plight. By this time he was twenty-one years old and had known her only through letters and by repute. The discovery of the Babington Plot, he felt, justified keeping her in closer captivity, claiming dismissively 'it was meet for her to meddle with nothing but prayer and serving of God'.[30] Her sentencing to death made him take account, however, of the outrage of his people.

James sent the duplicitous Master of Gray* to Elizabeth to plead for mercy, pointing out all the arguments that already exercised her greatly: the damage to her reputation for justice and clemency; the solidarity of sex, status and blood between the queens, and concern for himself, for 'what Straits and Hazzard of his Reputation among his own People he should be plunged, if any Violence be offered to his Mother'. The factor which most worried Elizabeth – that of the setting of dangerous precedent – was hammered home rather too heartily in James's submission: 'How strange and monstrous a thing it would be, to subject an absolute Prince to the Judgement of Subjects. How prodigious, if an absolute Prince should be made so dangerous a Precedent for the prophaning and vilifying her own and other Princes Diadems.'[31] But while this public entreaty was not entirely welcome, Gray reputedly 'buzzed into the Queen's ear that Saying, *Mortua non mordet*, that is, A dead Woman biteth not'.[32]

Elizabeth was besieged with advice and threats on all sides. She knew she had long ago lost her good relations with Philip II of Spain but this meant her amicable alliances with France and Scotland were crucial for the security of her realm. Her isolation, and the sense of loneliness in making this, the most momentous decision of her life, ran through her speeches and letters of the time. Reliant as she was on her trusty Burghley, and affectionate Leicester, they did not appreciate her profound emotional attachment to the idea of the sacredness of kingship, the sense that the relationship with God, his king and their people was a mysterious and hierarchical compact. To violate that divine order was to profane it. Elizabeth was horrified that the responsibility fell to her alone. In turmoil herself, she had

---

* Patrick, Master of Gray (d. 1612), became another of James VI (and I)'s favourites, apparently invulnerable despite a lifetime of double-dealing, intrigue and betrayals. He was part of Mary Queen of Scots' inner circle while she was in France and a close colleague of the Duc de Guise, who rewarded him handsomely. He returned to Scotland, probably with Esmé Stuart in 1579; both were agents of the Duc de Guise. Gray betrayed Mary's secrets to James and then to Elizabeth, who always saw through him, despite his being thought the handsomest man of his time, with exquisite French manners and a brilliant wit. After Mary's execution he was tried and found guilty of treason on a number of charges. James saved his life, welcoming him back to court after only two years' exile, where Gray continued to intrigue and betray. He still managed, however, to die in his bed.

to respond to another emotional petition from her Parliament at the end of November. Her answering speech to them was full of the anguish and uncertainties of her position.

'Neither hath my care been so much bent how to prolong [my life], as how to preserve both, which I am right sorry is made so hard – yea, so impossible. I am not so void of judgement as not to see my own peril; nor yet so ignorant as not to know it were in nature a foolish course to cherish a sword to cut my own throat ... But this I do consider: that many a man would put his life in danger for the safeguard of a king. I do not say that so will I, but I pray you think that I have thought upon it.'[33] This illustrated perfectly Elizabeth's powerful sense of the inviolability of monarchy, that she should think it preferable to risk her own life than break that taboo. Trespassing on God's territory in order to punish an anointed queen who, by definition, was above mere mortal intervention, filled her with dread.

From France, King Henri III sent his ambassador Bellièvre to plead for leniency. Elizabeth, pained, could only reply: 'It is impossible to save my own life if I preserve that of the Queen of Scots, but if you ambassadors can point out any means whereby I may do it, consistently with my own security, I shall be greatly obliged to you, never having shed so many tears at the death of my father, of my brother King Edward, or my sister Mary, as I have done for this unfortunate affair.'[34] Her official letter in January 1587 to Henri III, in response to his forceful arguments for clemency, revealed a more angry and imperious expression of her tension and fear: 'My God! How could you be so unreasonable as to reproach the injured party, and to compass the death of an innocent one by allowing her to become the prey of a murderess? ... that you should be angry at my saving my own life, seems to me the threat of an enemy, which I assure you, will never put me in fear, but is the shortest way to make me dispatch the cause of so much mischief.'[35]

Mary, herself, at the centre of the storm, seemed beatifically calm while all around her were fearful and grieving. She had always shown great care for her immediate servants and this concern was made more urgent as she contemplated her fate. She wrote both to Elizabeth and the King of France asking them to consider their safety and welfare. Her last weeks were busy with administration and communication, with speeding letters to the courts of Europe, desirous as she was to protect her posthumous reputation.

So eager were Elizabeth's ministers to have some sort of confession from the Queen of Scots before she died that Walsingham asked Sir Amyas Paulet to engage Mary in conversation as often as possible. The dour and disapproving Paulet admitted he had avoided any but the minimum of talk with his royal charge, but dutifully hung around and offered a willing ear. His self-sacrifice proved fruitless. Mary was in complete control of the situation and although more than willing to talk to anyone as she whiled away the long hours, and still clearly full of the injustices done to her, she was not about to tell Paulet, of all people, her guilty secrets. He reported somewhat irascibly to Walsingham: 'followinge your direction I have geven her full scope and tyme to say what she would, and yet at some tymes fyndinge no matter to come from her worthye of advertisement; I have departed from her as otherwyse she would never have left me; and I am deceaved yf my Lord of Buckhurst [who had just left] will not geve the same testimonye of her tediousness'.[36]

In her reply to Parliament's pleadings, Elizabeth expressed the kernel of her character and governing style when she asked them to be content for the present with 'this answer answerless . . . assuring yourselves that I am now and ever will be most careful to do that which will be best for your preservation. And be not too earnest to move me to do that which may tend to the loss of that which you are most desirous to keep.'[37] Here she was in the role she had most naturally assumed for the first twenty-eight years of her reign, like Janus, ambivalent between past and future, seeing both sides, judicious, measured, sometimes risking stasis in the quest for equilibrium. But she was about to be forced into a more active and decisive form of leadership, and the transition period was painful for her and those closest to her.

*   *   *

Under mounting pressure from her ministers to face up to her responsibilities, Elizabeth finally allowed Burghley to draw up the warrant for Mary's execution at the beginning of December. The proclamation was read out in public and bonfires lit all over London in celebration. William Davison, joint Secretary of State, however, was left with the task of obtaining Elizabeth's signature. They all remembered with foreboding the queen's painful indecision over the Duke of Norfolk's execution fourteen years before.

Close to Christmas and in the middle of this fevered anxiety, Mary's valedictory letter to Elizabeth arrived. Calm, magnanimous, wishing to make her peace with everyone, she mentioned the debacle over her canopy of state and said she 'praised God that such cruelty serving only to exercise malice and to afflict me after having condemned me to death has not come from you'. But like all her subtle letters to Elizabeth, the sweetness carried a hidden barb: Mary prayed that God would pardon all those responsible for her death, and 'I esteem myself happy that my death will precede the persecution which I foresee to threaten this Isle, where God is no longer truly feared and reverenced, but vanity and worldly policy rules and directs all'. She then delivered the *coup de grâce*: 'Do not accuse me of presumption if, on the eve of leaving this world and preparing myself for a better one, I remind you that one day you will have to answer for your charge, as well as those that are sent before, and that my blood and the misery of my country will be remembered.' She signed herself with royal assertion, 'Your sister and cousin, wrongfully a prisoner, *Marie, Royne*'.[38]

Anxiously her ministers watched Elizabeth's reactions. Tears sprang to her eyes, but otherwise she was calm. They feared anything that might soften her heart or encourage her natural equivocation. Leicester reported to Walsingham that the letter 'hath wrought tears, but I trust shall do no further harm'.[39] It was Mary who had the upper hand, her power gained through action and decision. Elizabeth struggled with contradictory advice and demands, and her innate fear of commitment. Although she 'sate many times melancholick and mute' muttering to herself '*Aut fer, aut feri* [bear with her, or smite her]' and '*Ne feriare, feri* [Strike, lest thou be stricken]',[40] she had not yet exhibited the same terrible indecision shown before Norfolk's execution.

The only way that Elizabeth could be induced to permit Mary's execution was if she feared that the country was in peril. At the beginning of the new year of 1587 a variety of sinister rumours began to gain credence as they inflamed an already anxious people. There was a general expectation that the Scottish nobility were preparing for war with England in the event of the execution of Mary; at the beginning of February, the Mayor of Exeter wrote to Cecil about a hue and cry that swept the West Country to 'make diligent search' for the Queen of Scots 'who is fledd'. Other broadcast cries told that the city of London 'by the enemyes is set on fyre'[41] and men were exhorted to assemble in armour and in haste and readiness to defend the kingdom. There was even another confused half-plot to murder the queen, said to involve the French ambassador, L'Aubespine. Independently, it seemed, he had started a rumour specifically to cause alarm, that 'the Queen of Scotland, disguised as a sailor, had fled from her palace' and had reached the sea, intent on reaching Brittany. All this made for a febrile atmosphere of threat and ever-present danger.

Elizabeth was not shielded from any of this hysterical alarm. Suddenly on the first day of February, she sent for the death warrant and signed it without fuss. Davison could hardly believe his good fortune. Then Elizabeth called him back. Frightened of taking sole responsibility for such a deed, she asked Davison to write to Paulet to ask him secretly to murder Mary and make it look as if she had died of natural causes. Although he could not salve her conscience and rescue her relationship with God, in this way he would protect his sovereign from the outside world. Elizabeth feared that personal defamation, loss of diplomatic alliances and even military aggression would follow any judicial execution. Davison was reluctant and, as he had surmised, Paulet was absolutely opposed. His principled rejection of the idea enraged Elizabeth. So much for the empty promises of the Bond of Association, she railed: in the absence of will and action, such bold declarations of loyalty from her subjects were useless hot air.

There was much anxious discussion amongst her closest ministers as to what exactly Elizabeth wished should be done with this now signed and sealed death warrant. She was utterly confused and confusing in her directives. Davison, inexperienced at dealing with his fearsome, exasperating queen, went to Hatton for advice and together they sought out Cecil. A council meeting was called for 3 February and they all agreed that they would proceed without further consultation, it being 'neither fit nor convenient to trouble her Majesty any further'.[42] With the precious document in hand, they dispatched Beale, the Clerk of the Council and a stalwart Protestant, to speed to Fotheringhay. With him went two executioners, their axe hidden in a trunk. The same day, 4 February, Elizabeth told a nervous Davison about a distressing dream she had had. She dreamt, she said, that Mary had been executed.

At Fotheringhay, Mary was told late on 7 February that she was to die the following morning. Shrewsbury was saddened by having to impart such news; he was her longest serving jailer and another who had not failed to warm to Mary's charms. Her servants protested at the brutal suddenness and lack of notice, but the lords had come with directives not to delay. Mary accepted her sentence with composure, 'I did not think that the Queen my Sister would have consented to my Death, who am not subject to your Law and Jurisdiction: but seeing her Pleasure is so, Death shall be to me most welcome: neither is that soul worthy of the high and everlasting Joys above, whose Body cannot endure one Stroak of the Executioner.' She took much satisfaction from the fact that the Earl of Kent burst out with, 'Your Life will be the Death of our Religion, as contrariwise your Death will be the Life thereof.'[43] This confirmed how significant they considered the threat of her faith and how important she was as a flame of that faith.

Back in London, it appeared that Elizabeth was still half hoping that Paulet could be induced to contrive some underhand way of getting rid of Mary. At Fotheringhay, Mary was in calm control of the situation. She spent her last hours in consoling her servants, dispensing her goods and any money left to her and remaking her will. She also wrote letters to Henri III and her almoner. To all the sorrowful faces around her she offered hope, by bidding them, 'leave Mourning, and rather rejoyce that she was now to depart out of a world of Miseries'.[44] The rest of the time she spent in prayer.

By eight o'clock on the morning of 8 February, the day designated for her execution, Mary had long been up. She had asked her women to dress her as if for a festival and, in response to the knock on the door, processed slowly in the company of her servants to the Great Hall where the scaffold had been erected. There would be many witnesses to the portentous events that followed, their accounts capturing vividly aspects of the gruesome drama. 'Forth she came with State, Countenance and Presence majestically composed', Elizabeth's chronicler Camden recorded. The Scottish queen was dressed in black with a floor-length veil of finest white linen falling from her hair. In her hands she carried her ivory crucifix, her rosary hung from her girdle.

At the entrance to the room she was prevented from bringing in her full retinue of servants. Sir James Melville, her long-time friend, was in tears before her. In the consolation she offered him she bade him take the news back to Scotland that she had died constant in her faith and 'firm in my Fidelity and affection towards Scotland and France'. She asked to be commended to her son, to have him reminded how greatly she had desired the unification of Scotland and England. Although her letters to Mendoza and the pope still stood, offering her rights to the English throne to Philip II, should her own son obstinately continue Protestant, she requested that Melville assure James VI 'that I have done nothing which may be prejudicial to the Kingdom of Scotland'.[45]

By calling on her consanguinity with Elizabeth, her status as an anointed queen and their shared sensibilities as women and sisters in a masculine world, Mary managed to get the presiding lords to agree she could be accompanied by six of her servants. She had been keen they were present not just for their support but also to bear witness and relate the detail of the extraordinary events of that morning to the foreign courts in which her reputation mattered most to her.

Mary was led to a low platform with a chair, a stool and the scaffold block, all draped with black velvet. A huge log fire was blazing in an attempt to keep some of the February chill from the room. Once Beale had read out the warrant, the Dean of Peterborough began an oration, urging her to repent and accept the true faith. Mary interrupted him, requesting he should not 'trouble himself, protesting that she was firmly fixed and resolved in the ancient Catholick Roman Religion, and for it was ready to shed her last Bloud'. When he attempted to pray for her sins, she and her servants recited their own prayers in Latin. She then prayed in English for her Church, her son and Queen Elizabeth, 'beseeching [God] to turn away his wrath from this Island'.

As was customary, Mary then forgave the executioners for what they were about to do. She seemed in a hurry to proceed and her women helped her out of her outer garments, in order to bare her neck for the axe. Her petticoat of deepest red suddenly showed startling against the sombreness of their surroundings: the colour heavy with symbolism as the liturgical colour of martyrdom. Binding her eyes with a linen cloth, she lay her neck upon the block, repeating continually *'In manus tuas, Domine* [Into thy hands, O Lord]'. The watching officials and Mary's servants recoiled to see the first blow of the axe miss her neck and slice into the side of her skull. The second blow severed her head. The emotion was palpable. A queen had been killed on the orders of a sister queen.

The Dean of Peterborough cried out 'So let Queen Elizabeth's Enemies perish' while the witnesses wept. All kinds of eyewitness reports replayed the ceremonial agony of the event and the rapt nobility of the queen. Rumours became entwined with fact, inevitably embellished in the telling of something more awesome and traumatic than anything they would ever see again. The Queen of Scots' head was held up for all to see, her lips still moving for a further fifteen minutes, it was said, in silent prayer; the lustrous auburn curls fell away in the executioner's hand to reveal the dead queen's own grey hair cropped close, transforming her from a beauty to an old woman in front of their eyes; one of her favourite pets, a Skye terrier, smuggled in under her skirts, emerged howling piteously and would not leave the severed head of his mistress: all these stories wracked the hearts of the Marian faithful and filled Elizabeth's supporters with an uneasy shame.

With faith and courage Mary had turned defeat and death into transcendent victory. The martyr was made. Amplified by the fraught publicity of her execution, the myth was born. The English councillors present on the day realized this too, for they insisted that every splash of blood was scrubbed away, every object and relic removed and destroyed. Her body, quickly wrapped in a cloth, was carried away and immediately embalmed. Her servants were kept confined in the castle and England's seaports were closed. The sense of threat that had inspired Mary's execution did not abate with her death.

As Mary's star shot heavenwards, Elizabeth's sank. Through personal insecurity and fear she failed to show the necessary princely virtue. Her behaviour following Mary's death was uncontrolled, dissembling and in certain aspects ignoble. The demons of her youth had returned to haunt her. But for Elizabeth too, Mary's death would mark a turning point in her life and reign.

Burghley was afraid at first to tell Elizabeth that the deed was done. When she learnt the truth she appeared little concerned. For Elizabeth, however, the night was always a time when fears seemed to multiply and loneliness went deep: it was at two o'clock in the morning that she had lost her nerve over the execution of the Duke of Norfolk and in a last-minute panic rescinded his death warrant. Now on the night of the momentous news of Mary's death a similar fear and panic gripped her. But this time it was too late. In the morning she sent for Sir Christopher Hatton and berated him for his part in what she saw as a shameful duplicity. She ranted and raved, she blamed everyone, and declared to the world that Mary's execution was something she had never intended. Someone had to pay for the grief and anxiety that engulfed her: peremptorily she sent Davison to the Tower. Despite her councillors' pleading on their knees for clemency, by the end of the month she was even threatening to have him summarily hanged.

Elizabeth's storms, frightening and destructive while they lasted, usually blew over pretty fast. This one did not. Her grief and anger seemed to grow with the days. Her now elderly and gout-wracked Burghley was banished from her presence. He remained out of favour for months, enduring from her the kind of defamation, by 'calling him traitor, false dissembler and wicked wretch', that such a loyal man found hard to bear. Aged sixty-six and in great pain, he was reduced to writing to Elizabeth pleading to be allowed even just to lie at her feet, in hope that 'some drops of your mercy [might] quench my sorrowful panting heart'.[46] For a while the queen was beyond reason, neither eating nor sleeping, distracted with woe.

Elizabeth was particularly careful of her fame abroad and fearful of what France and Scotland might do to avenge the Queen of Scots' death. Within four days and in the throes of her passion, she wrote to James VI denying she had authorized the execution of his mother:

> My dear Brother, I would you knew (though not felt) the extreme dolor that overwhelms my mind, for that miserable accident which (far contrary to my meaning) hath befallen . . . I beseech you that as God and many more know, how innocent I am in this case . . . I am not so base minded that fear of any living creature or Prince should make me afraid to do that were just; or done, to deny the same. I am not of so base a lineage, nor carry so vile a mind. Thus assuring yourself of me, that as I know this was deserved, yet if I had meant it I would never lay it on others' shoulders; no more will I not damnify myself that thought it not . . . for your part, think you have not in the world a more loving kinswoman, nor a more dear friend than myself; nor any that will watch more carefully to preserve you and your estate . . . Your most assured loving sister and cousin, Elizab. R.[47]

Breathtakingly hypocritical as it may appear on the surface, this letter nevertheless expressed the depth of her ambivalent anguish. Despite her miserable protestations, she 'had meant it' and had shamefully 'laid it on others' shoulders', but it was also true that she had not meant it and the guilt cut deeply into her heart. The extremity of Elizabeth's emotion and the fact that she remained overwrought for so long suggested there was something more troubling to her in the execution of Mary than the obvious tensions of safeguarding her reputation, balancing the Catholic powers, and squaring her conscience with God.

At first there were fears of Scottish revenge. The country was in uproar. Robert Carey was chosen by Elizabeth for the task, that no one else would perform, of delivering that letter to the King of Scots. Riding north he was stopped on the border and warned he would be murdered if he proceeded further. James suggested he go to Berwick instead, for the king admitted that 'given the fury [the people] were in ... no power of his could warrant my life at that time'.[48] Certainly on the streets of Edinburgh ferocious attacks on Elizabeth had spontaneously erupted. An example of the kind of libel being freely circulated was this simple and salty verse, attached with a hemp cord tied like a halter:

> To Jezebel, that English whore;
> Receive this Scottish chain
> As presages of her great malheur [misfortune]
> For murdering our queen.

Where the Edinburghers were louring and full of vengeance, the Londoners were in a merry mood, intent on the kind of noisy celebrations that exacerbated the outrage of the Scots and French. As Shrewsbury's son had ridden through the city with the news of Mary's death, 'instantly all the bells were rung, guns discharged, fires lighted in all the streets, and feasting and banquets and every sign of joy'.[49] This came from the report of the French ambassador who witnessed one of the street fires too close for comfort. When he refused some local revellers' request for wood for a bonfire, they retaliated by lighting a great bonfire against his own house door, which burned for two hours. But her own people's exuberance was not enough to lift Elizabeth's spirits.

The warlike rumours from Scotland, however, soon died down,

and James VI seemed willing to return to business as usual. To save his own face with his people he demanded a scapegoat, '*necesse est unum mori pro populo*'. That scapegoat was Davison, but he did not have to die: he was released from the Tower after the defeat of the Armada when Elizabeth had recovered her confidence and was no longer desperate to hang onto the allies she had.

Henri III of France also registered his protest forcefully and threatened the English ambassador with similar violence from the Paris mob should he venture from his house. He refused for some months to receive Walsingham as Elizabeth's envoy, come to explain the execution of the Queen of Scots. They put on an impressive show of mourning for their dowager queen, with her Guise family as prominent mourners, while angry crowds vowed vengeance on the 'Jezebel' across the water. But the French too did not have the stomach for war. Philip II, however, was being exhorted even by his confessor to attack England, 'to avenge the wrongs done to God and to the world by that woman, above all in the execution of the Queen of Scotland'.[50]

While Mary lived, Elizabeth's isolation as a regnant queen in a world of men was relieved; there was a sympathy between them and, until James's birth, they were among the closest blood relations that either had left in the world. Although temperamentally opposed and living their lives to different ideals, Mary had insisted on stressing this familial female relationship: mother, daughter, sister, cousin; in every one of her multitude of letters over the years she reminded Elizabeth of their blood connection. There was an attraction too in opposites, a fascination with those who lived out the unlived side of oneself. Mary had recklessly pursued her heart in a way Elizabeth would never contemplate and Elizabeth had assumed authority in government that had won the world's grudging respect. Elizabeth and Mary had offered to each other a different way of seeing, a point of identity and contrast. In their solitary queenship, the existence of the other, a cousin too, meant each was not entirely alone.

And yet Elizabeth, pressured by the male world, had sacrificed Mary, a member of her royal and human family. Perhaps it was not too fanciful to think that Mary, representing carnal femininity and motherhood, a queen who had produced a male heir, reminded Elizabeth of her own mother, bloodily put to death in the same way, by the will of men, for giving birth not to that precious son, but to Elizabeth herself, the undervalued girl.

These months after Mary's death were the emotional crisis of Elizabeth's life. For twenty-eight years she had reigned, proud of the peace of a kingdom kept by a queen averse to bloodshed, shy of commitment and prevaricating in her dealings. She had now been forced to draw her sword, and in the blood sacrifice of her close relation had been initiated into becoming a bolder sort of queen. In the struggle of these months she had to leave behind the woman of hesitation and equivocation, born of the insecurity and fear of her youth, and embrace a larger, more active vision of herself. Elizabeth faced the consequences of her actions.

The English Catholics had lost the focus for their hopes, their alternative queen. As the internal threats diminished, however, the long-feared shadow of Philip II stretched across the Channel. Within a year, all eyes would be turned outwards to a greater foe: for most of Mary's English supporters hatred of the Spanish was a more motivating force than antagonism to their Protestant queen. Mary's death had meant Elizabeth would have to remove her frugal coat and don the panoply of war.

Elizabeth and England stood alone. In the spring of 1588, she was fifty-four but still full of vitality. She had her great ministers around her, Burghley, Leicester and Walsingham, but they were ageing now, their health failing, although their prodigious work rate did not flag. To this great triumvirate was added Sir Christopher Hatton, her new Lord Chancellor. Her court had an injection of new blood too in the form of the next generation of favourites, Sir Walter Ralegh, Leicester's beautiful stepson the Earl of Essex, and Burghley's brilliant son Robert Cecil: all these helped maintain the sense of family connection and continuity around the increasingly solitary queen.

There had been rumours for the past four years or more of the amassing of a great Spanish Armada. Ships were being built in every allied port, food stockpiled, munitions and items of clothing ordered tens of thousands at a time, and men recruited across the empire. There was a sense of danger looming like a storm cloud over England. The exchequer was chronically short of money and Elizabeth was desperate to conclude some sort of peace in the Low Countries with the Duke of Parma. Her fear of all-out war with Spain had made her weak and vacillating but even while she sued for peace, she was forced into action by the news that the fearsome Armada had set sail at last.

It was May and England was thrown into a frenzy of activity, preparing to repel a full-scale invasion. Bad weather and good fortune played their part and by the time the English and Spanish fleets met it was 20 July. Camden's description of that first sighting of the Spanish fleet in the Channel was vivid with the eyewitness's excitement and awe. The galleons 'with lofty turrets like Castles' were spread out before them in a crescent, extending some seven miles, 'sailing very slowly, though with full Sails, the Winds being as it were tired with carrying them, and the Ocean groaning under the weight of them'. The Armada consisted of 130 ships, 'the best furnished . . . of any that ever the ocean saw, and called by the arrogant name of Invincible'.[51] During the following week there were various running battles up and down the Channel, with numerous acts of heroism and derring-do, a great deal of noise from the ordnance, and not much loss of men or ships on either side. Then on 28 July, the Spanish fleet were anchored just outside Calais, and the English selected eight of their least seaworthy vessels as fireships, 'besmeared with Wild-fire, Pitch and Rosin, and filled with Brimstone and other combustible matter', and sent them downwind at dead of night towards the unsuspecting Armada. The burning ships were reflected in the water, 'the whole Sea glittering and shining with the Flame thereof' and so panicked the Spanish that their fleet scattered, pursued by the lighter, faster English ships. A sudden storm caught the great Spanish galleons as they fled north to try and reach Spain around Ireland and Scotland's shores.

The fear of Spanish aggression that had accompanied the first thirty years of her reign was now confronted. In facing the spectre of invasion and defeat, Elizabeth rose magnificently to her new role as a warrior queen, no longer the ever-watchful, ambiguous Janus, but Athena, the goddess of wisdom and war. Cecil's son Robert was amazed at the reaction of this new Elizabeth to the news of the fleets' first engagement: 'how great magnanimity* her Majesty shows, who is not a whit dismayed'.[52]

Two major armies were assembled, one at St James's to protect the Queen and the other at Tilbury, at the mouth of the Thames, to repel the first invaders. Leicester was in charge of these 22,000 men and 1000 horse, and invited Elizabeth to visit the camp and show herself to the troops. She accepted with alacrity and on horseback rode among them with a staff in her hand. Some said she wore a breastplate of steel, others suggested it was gold – that was how she appeared invincible to her cheering, adoring troops.

The speech she gave to her army, in the full expectation that the Armada would reform and threaten her island once more, became as famous as any in English:

> My loving people, I have been persuaded by some that are careful of my safety to take heed how I committed myself to armed multitudes, for fear of treachery. But I tell you that I would not desire to live to distrust my faithful and loving people. Let tyrants fear: I have so behaved myself that under God I have placed my chieftest strength and safeguard in the loyal hearts and goodwill of my subjects. Wherefore I am come among you at this time but for my recreation and pleasure, being resolved in the midst and heat of battle to live and die amongst you all, to lay down for my God and for my kingdom and for my people mine honour and my blood even in the dust. I know I have the body but of a weak and feeble woman, but I have the heart and stomach of a king and a king of England too – and take foul scorn that Parma or any other prince of Europe should

---

* In early modern English magnanimity, literally greatness of spirit, meant above all a noble courage. The concept goes back to Aristotle, and was seen as one of the most important virtues, seldom applied to anyone other than men.

dare to invade the borders of my realm. To the which rather than any dishonour shall grow by me, I myself will venter [venture] my royal blood.[53]

This marked the apogee of her reign. Elizabeth, in embracing action and sharing danger with her people, inspired the popular imagination with the vision of a goddess of war. The Armada had been sent by Philip to visit God's punishment on her for her religion, her support of Spain's enemies and her execution of a Catholic queen. In repelling the greatest military power in Europe, she had proved herself as great as any king, perhaps even to herself. The pope, Sixtus V, on the eve of the Armada and hoping for victory, had renewed his bull of excommunication, yet even he could not hide his admiration: 'Just look how well she governs! She is only a woman, only mistress of half an island, and yet she makes herself feared by Spain, by France, by the Empire, by all.' Elizabeth was elated by her country's unexpected victory, exhilarated by her own success. That same month, she wrote to Mary's son: 'this tyrannical, proud and brainsick attempt ... hath procured my greatest glory that meant my sorest wrack [direst destruction]'.[54]

The relationship of Elizabeth and Mary continued even after Mary's death. In effect compassed by both of them, Mary's execution had allowed her to fulfil her spiritual aspirations. Courting the death sentence rather than begging for mercy, she ensured her transcendence into myth. For Elizabeth, the Armada, launched partly in Mary's name, provided the greatest challenge of her reign. Mary's death had demanded that Elizabeth rise to a greater authority and through that demonstrate her magnanimous power. In facing down Spain, she too was elevated to an idealized majesty.

But these moments of transformation marked the point when both queens became less recognizable in their individual characters, as they were overlaid increasingly with the projections of others: their natures distorted to support opposing narratives and adorn the romance of kings. But it is in their relationship with each other, as women, cousins and rivals, that their inward experiences were illuminated, in all their complex humanity. In their struggle as queens to overcome the expectation of failure in a male-dominated world, they chose quite different destinies. Their natural sympathy and solidarity evaporated as they became polarized in a lethal opposition where one of them had to die. Yet in death they achieved an extraordinary compromise that was impossible in life. Mary's ambition had been to inherit the throne of England and Elizabeth's to maintain independence, and the religion her father had established in order to legitimize her birth. Both wished for Scotland and England to be united under their rule. In Mary's son this ideal became reality. In the process both Mary's blood and Elizabeth's Church triumphed. Great Britain was born as a Protestant state under a Stuart king, James I.

NOTES

CHAPTER ONE *The Fateful Step*

1 *State Papers, Foreign*, I, 107
2 *Elizabeth I: Collected Works*, 95
3 *Italian Relations of England*, Sneyd, p. 20
4 *Annals*, Hayward, 1
5 *Carmen, Epithalamia tria Maria*, trans. Wrangham, 23
6 *Images of a Queen*, Phillips, 15
7 Ibid., 16
8 Burghley, *State Papers*, 71
9 *Lettres*, Labanoff I, 59
10 *The History*, Camden, 10
11 *Virgin Mother, Maiden Queen*, Hackett, 52
12 *Dissing Elizabeth*, ed. Walker, 30
13 *The Reign of Elizabeth*, Black, 15
14 *Queen Elizabeth*, Mumby, 280
15 *Fragmenta Regalia*, Naunton, 40
16 *Annals*, Hayward, 3
17 Ibid., 2
18 *Dictionary of National Biography*, 315
19 Ibid., 315
20 Genesis, 3:16
21 *The Peloponnesian War*, Thucydides, 2.45
22 *Elizabeth I: Collected Works*, 70
23 Ibid., 52
24 *State Papers, Venetian*, Vol. 7, p. 167 (24 March 1560)
25 *The History*, Camden, 39
26 *Annals*, Hayward, 6–7
27 *The History*, Camden, 53
28 *Annals*, Hayward, 10–11
29 *State Papers, Venetian*, VII, 6
30 *State Papers, Spanish*, I, 7
31 Ibid., 19
32 *Elizabeth I: Collected Works*, 58
33 *State Papers, Venetian*, VII, 3
34 Ibid., 11 (23 January 1559)
35 *The History*, Camden, 18
36 *The Queen's Conjurer*, Woolley, 60

37 *State Papers, Venetian*, VII, 3
38 Ibid., 12
39 Ibid., 17
40 *Annals*, Hayward, 16
41 *State Papers, Venetian*, 12
42 *Annals*, Hayward, 16
43 *Elizabeth I: Collected Works*, 53
44 *Annals*, Hayward, 6
45 Ibid., 7
46 *Actes and Monuments*, Foxe, 223
47 Ibid., 224
48 Ibid., 239
49 Ibid., 240
50 *Annals*, Hayward, 18
51 *State Papers, Spanish*, I, 51
52 *State Papers, Venetian*, VI, 17
53 For a close discussion of what exactly happened at Elizabeth's coronation see *The Coronation of Queen Elizabeth*, ed. Poole, *English Historical Review*, XXII, Longmans, Green and Co., 1907, pp. 650–673
54 *The Coronation of Queen Elizabeth*, ed. Poole, 670
55 *State Papers, Spanish*, I, 37
56 *State Papers, Spanish*, I, 25
57 *Lettres*, Labanoff, I, 59
58 Sadler, *State Papers*, I, 379
59 Ibid., 380
60 *State Papers, Venetian*, VII, 17
61 *State Papers, Spanish*, I, 17
62 *Elizabeth and Mary Stuart*, Mumby, 229
63 *Elizabeth I: Collected Works*, 59
64 Ibid., 51
65 *The History*, Camden, 39

CHAPTER TWO *The Disappointment of Kings*

1 *History and Chronicles of Scotland*, Lindsay of Pitscottie, I, 406
2 Leviticus, 20:21

3 *State Papers, Venetian*, IV, 873
4 *Anne Boleyn*, Sergeant, 52
5 *Ballads from Manuscripts*, ed. Furnivall, 374; quoted in *Anne Boleyn*, Warnicke, 126
6 *Anne Boleyn*, Warnicke, 166
7 *Camden Miscellany*, XXX, vol. 39, 1990, Lancelot de Carles, 1536, in Introduction to 'William Latymer's Chronickille of Anne Bulleyne' 37
8 *Girlhood of Queen Elizabeth*, Mumby, 3
9 Ibid., 4
10 *State Papers, Henry VIII*, XIII, XI, p. 132
11 *State Papers, Spanish*, IV, 40
12 *State Papers, Henry VIII*, IX, 187
13 *State Papers, Foreign*, I, 530
14 *State Papers, Venetian*, V, 27
15 *Nursing Mirror*, 27 December 1962, 'The Death of Queen Catherine of Aragon' MacNalty, 275; *Henry VIII*, Scarisbrick, 334 n. 3
16 *State Papers, Spanish*, V, 19
17 *Anne Boleyn*, Sergeant, 261
18 Ibid., 27
19 *State Papers, Spanish*, IV, 824
20 *Anne Boleyn*, Sergeant, 272
21 Ibid., 284
22 *State Papers, Foreign*, I, 529
23 *State Papers, Foreign*, I, 527
24 *Witchcraft in Tudor and Stuart England*, Macfarlane, 170
25 *Dictionary of National Biography*, I, 1061
26 *State Papers, Henry VIII*, XII, 339
27 *Hamilton Papers*, I, p. 358
28 *State Papers, Henry VIII*, XVII, 657
29 *State Papers, Spanish*, VI, 189
30 Sadler, *State Papers*, I, 88
31 *The Youth of Queen Elizabeth*, Wiesener, I, 14
32 Sadler, *State Papers*, I, 61
33 Ibid., 228
34 Ibid., 228
35 Ibid., 250
36 Ibid., 253
37 Ibid., 289
38 *State Papers, Henry VIII*, V, 355
39 *Histoire d'un Capitaine Bourbonnais as XVIe siècle*, Jacques de la Brosse, 1485–1562, ses Missions en Écosse, de

la Brosse 320–1, cited in *Mary of Guise*, Marshall, 139
40 *Hamilton Papers*, II, 325
41 *Elizabeth I: Collected Works*, 5
42 *Elizabeth I: The Word of a Prince*, 37
43 *Elizabeth I: Collected Works*, 9
44 Ibid., 97
45 Ibid., 10
46 Ibid., 15

CHAPTER THREE *The Education of Princes*

1 *Actes and Monuments*, Foxe, 116
2 *The History*, Camden, 10
3 *Annals*, Hayward, 46
4 *Childhood of Queen Elizabeth*, Mumby, 29
5 *The Six Wives of Henry VIII*, Fraser, 365
6 Burghley, *State Papers*, 96
7 Ibid., 95
8 Ibid., 102
9 Ibid., 96
10 Ibid., 99
11 Ibid., 99
12 Ibid., 96
13 Ibid., 96
14 *Elizabeth I: Collected Works*, 17–19
15 *Whole Works of Roger Ascham*, ed. Giles, I, 272–3
16 *Elizabeth I: Collected Works*, 21
17 Burghley, *State Papers*, 62
18 Ibid., 69
19 Ibid., 69
20 Ibid., 70
21 Ibid., 70
22 Ibid., 70
23 Ibid., 71
24 Ibid., 102
25 Ibid., 89
26 Ibid., 89
27 Ibid., 70
28 Ibid., 108
29 Ibid., 108
30 *Elizabeth I: Collected Works*, 32–4
31 Burghley, *State Papers*, 108
32 *Sayings of Queen Elizabeth*, Chamberlin, 3. This was taken from the often unreliable seventeenth-century biographer Leti
33 *Hamilton Papers*, II, 9 August 1548

34 *Balcarres Papers*, III, 132; *English Historical Review*, XXII, ed. Poole, 47

35 *Balcarres Papers*, III, 122; *English Historical Review*, XXII, 49

36 *Additions aux Mémoires de Castelnau*, I, Le Laborierière; *The Brood of False Lorraine*, Williams, I, 50

37 *Balcarres Papers*, III, 19; *English Historical Review*, XXII, ed. Poole, 44

38 *Lettres de Diane de Poitiers*, Guiffrey, 34–5; *English Historical Review*, XXII, ed. Poole, 49

39 *Mary Queen of Scots*, Fleming, 19

40 *Balcarres Papers*, II; *The Love Affairs of Mary Queen of Scots: A Political History*, Hume, 39

41 *English Historical Review*, XXII, ed. Poole, 48

42 *Balcarres Papers*, III, 130

43 *The Love Affairs of Mary Queen of Scots: A Political History*, Hume, 41

44 *La Première Jeunesse de Marie Stuart*, de Ruble, 181; quoted in *Mary Queen of Scots*, Fraser, 91

45 *Lettres*, Labanoff, VII, 277

46 *Queen in Three Kingdoms*, ed. Lynch, 39

47 *Lives of the Queens of Scotland*, Strickland, III, 31

48 *Lives of the Queens of Scotland*, Strickland, II, 136

49 *Lettres*, Labanoff, I, 9–10

50 *The Love Affairs of Mary Queen of Scots: A Political History*, Hume, 46 note

51 *Latin Themes of Mary Stuart, Queen of Scots*, ed. Montaiglon, 34

52 Ibid., 36

53 Ibid., 40

54 Ibid., xix

55 *Lettres*, Labanoff, I, 11

56 *Lettres*, Labanoff, I, 41

57 *Girlhood of Queen Elizabeth*, Mumby, 70

58 *Whole Works of Roger Ascham*, I, 86; *Roger Ascham*, 104

59 *Elizabeth I: Collected Works*, 327

60 *Girlhood of Queen Elizabeth*, Mumby, 70

61 *State Papers, Venetian*, VI, 13 May 1557

62 *Elizabeth I: Collected Works*, 66

63 *Parallel Lives: Life of Mark Antony*, Plutarch, 27

64 *Whole Works of Roger Ascham*, III, 143; quoted in *Roger Ascham*, Ryan, 224

65 *Elizabeth I: Collected Works*, 326

66 Ibid., 325n

67 *Elizabeth and Mary Stuart*, Mumby, 225

68 *Lettres*, Labanoff, I, 16

69 *Oeuvres complètes*, Brantôme, IX, 490

70 *Elizabeth I: Collected Works*, 169

71 *Vives and the Renascence Education of Women*, ed. Watson, 133

CHAPTER FOUR *Apprenticeship for a Queen*

1 *The First Blast of the Trumpet Against the Monstrous Regiment of Women*, Knox, 33v; *Virgin Mother, Maiden Queen*, Hackett, 39

2 *The Defence of Good Women*, Elyot; *Women in Early Modern England*, Mendelson and Crawford, 349

3 *Letters of John Calvin*, ed. Bonnet, 211–12; *Virgin Mother, Maiden Queen*, Hackett, 39

4 *Elizabeth I: Collected Works*, 51–2

5 *Lettres*, Labanoff, VI, 50

6 *Book of the City of Ladies*, Christine de Pizan, trans. Richards, 1.1.1. p. 3–4; 1.1.1–2, p. 5; *The Education of a Christian Woman*, Vives, xviii

7 *Elizabeth I: Collected Works*, 157

8 Ibid., 141

9 *Actes and Monuments*, Foxe, 164

10 *A Collection of Scarce and Valuable Tracts*, ed. Scott, I, p. 174

11 *Chronicle of Queen Jane*, ed. Nichols, 69

12 Ibid., 69

13 *Girlhood of Queen Elizabeth*, Mumby, 82

14 Ibid., 83

15 *Actes and Monuments*, Foxe, 119

16 Ibid., 119

17 *Girlhood of Queen Elizabeth*, Mumby, 108

18 Ibid., 109

19 *Chronicle of Queen Jane*, 59

20 *Actes and Monuments*, Foxe, 119

21 *Girlhood of Queen Elizabeth*, Mumby, 107
22 *Elizabeth I: Collected Works*, 42
23 *Girlhood of Queen Elizabeth*, Mumby, 227–8
24 Ibid., 230
25 *Elizabeth I: Collected Works*, 96
26 *Girlhood of Queen Elizabeth*, Mumby, 112
27 *Elizabeth I*, Somerset, 40
28 *Elizabeth I: Collected Works*, 41
29 Ibid., 41
30 Ibid., 42
31 *Actes and Monuments*, Foxe, 121
32 *Chronicle of Queen Jane*, 70–71
33 *Actes and Monuments*, Foxe, 123
34 Ibid., 123
35 Ibid., 124
36 Ibid., 124
37 *The Diary of Baron Waldstein*, 71
38 *Actes and Monuments*, Foxe, 124
39 *Chronicle of Queen Jane*, 71
40 *Actes and Monuments*, Foxe, 125
41 *Childhood of Queen Elizabeth*, Mumby, 228
42 *Actes and Monuments*, Foxe, 126
43 *Chronicle of Queen Jane*, 74
44 *Actes and Monuments*, Foxe, 130
45 Ibid., 131
46 *Queen Elizabeth and Some Foreigners*, ed. Klarwill, 76
47 *Actes and Monuments*, Foxe, 132
48 *State Papers, Spanish*, I, 4
49 *Elizabeth I: Collected Works*, 59
50 *Girlhood of Queen Elizabeth*, Mumby, 137n
51 Ibid., 154
52 *Elizabeth I: Collected Works*, 45–6
53 Ibid., 46
54 Ibid., 41
55 *Acts and Monuments*, Foxe, 140
56 *Childhood of Queen Elizabeth*, Mumby, 195
57 *Elizabeth I: Collected Works*, 44
58 Ibid., 141
59 *State Papers, Foreign*, I, 91
60 *State Papers, Foreign*, II, 3; quoted in *Elizabeth and Mary Stuart*, Mumby, 3
61 *Tracts*, ed. Scott, I, 163
62 *The History*, Camden, 25
63 *State Papers, Spanish*, VII, 251
64 *The History*, Camden, 13

65 *State Papers, Scottish*, I, 446
66 Sadler, *State Papers*, I, 379
67 Ibid., 377, 376
68 *State Papers, Scottish*, I, 317
69 *State Papers, Foreign*, I, 348
70 *State Papers, Foreign*, I, 370
71 *The History*, Camden, 39
72 *State Papers, Foreign*, II, 463
73 *Cathérine de Médicis*, Cloulas, 145
74 *State Papers, Foreign*, II, 462
75 *The Brood of False Lorraine*, Williams, I, 225
76 *State Papers, Venetian*, VII, 161
77 *Histoire de l'estat de France*, Regnier de la Planche quoted in *Cathérine de Médicis*, Cloulas, 146
78 *The History*, Camden, 39
79 *State Papers, Venetian*, VII, 172
80 *State Papers, Scottish*, I, 331
81 *State Papers, Foreign*, II, 464
82 *State Papers, Spanish*, I, 84
83 S. Haynes, 260; *Elizabeth I*, Somerset, 125
84 *State Papers, Foreign*, III, 72
85 *Elizabeth I: Collected Works*, 198

CHAPTER FIVE *Wilfulness and God's Will*

1 *Annals*, Hayward, 31
2 *State Papers, Venetian*, VII, 171
3 *State Papers, Spanish*, I, 551
4 Ibid., 7
5 *Tracts*, ed. Scott, I, 173
6 Ibid., 172
7 *Arcana seculi decimi sexti*, H. Languet, II, ep. xlvii, quoted in *Sayings of Queen Elizabeth*, Chamberlin, 198
8 *The History*, Camden, 53
9 Ibid., 52–3
10 *State Papers, Spanish*, I, 57
11 Ibid., 9
12 *State Papers, Venetian*, VII, 36–37
13 *State Papers, Spanish*, I, 73
14 Ibid., 67
15 Ibid., 67
16 Ibid., 7
17 Ibid., 75
18 Ibid., 74
19 Ibid., 72–4
20 Ibid., 75
21 *State Papers, Venetian*, VII, 81

22 *State Papers, Spanish*, I, 112
23 Ibid., 104
24 Burghley, *State Papers*, 212
25 *State Papers, Foreign*, III, 347
26 *Lettres*, Labanoff, VI, 50
27 *Tracts*, ed. Scott, I, 171
28 Sadler's *State Papers*, I, 380–1
29 *State Papers, Spanish*, I, 84
30 *State Papers, Scottish*, I, 227
31 *State Papers, Spanish*, I, 89
32 *Papiers d'État relatifs à l'histoire d'Écosse*, Teulet; quoted in *Elizabeth and Mary Stuart*, Mumby 50
33 Sadler's *State Papers*, II, 218
34 *Ibid.*, 219
35 *State Papers, Foreign*, I, 370
36 *Annals*, Hayward, 46
37 Ibid., 47
38 Sadler's *State Papers*, I, 376
39 Ibid., II, 248
40 *Queen Elizabeth and Her Times*, ed. Wright, I, 24
41 Burghley, *State Papers*, 253
42 *Forbes* I, 395; quoted in *Elizabeth I*, Seymour, 125
43 *State Papers, Foreign*, II, 594
44 *State Papers, Spanish*, I, 127
45 *State Papers, Venetian*, VII, 226
46 *Annals*, Hayward, 94
47 *State Papers, Foreign*, II, 581
48 Ibid., 597
49 *Lettres*, Labanoff, I, 71
50 *Elizabeth and Mary Stuart*, Mumby, 120
51 Burghley, *State Papers*, 311
52 Burghley, *State Papers*, 302
53 *Elizabeth and Leicester*, Jennings, 61
54 *State Papers, Venetian*, VII, 228
55 Ibid., 234
56 *State Papers, Foreign*, 3, 117
57 *State Papers, Spanish*, I, 159
58 Ibid., 166
59 Burghley, *State Papers*, 361
60 *Queen Elizabeth and Some Foreigners*, ed. Klarwill, 114
61 Ibid., 115
62 *Elizabeth and Mary Stuart*, Mumby, 128
63 *State Papers, Spanish*, I, 175
64 Burghley, *State Papers*, 362
65 *State Papers, Spanish*, I, 176
66 *Annals*, Hayward, 45

67 *State Papers, Spanish*, I, 188
68 *State Papers, Foreign*, III, 348
69 Ibid., 347
70 Ibid., 348
71 *BM Add. MSS* 35834–6, 35841, I, 121–3; quoted in *Robert Dudley*, Kendall, 37
72 *State Papers, Spanish*, I, 58
73 *Elizabeth and Mary Stuart*, Mumby, 147
74 *English Historical Review*, LXXI, 'The Death of Amy Robsart', I.A. Aird, 72
75 Burghley, *State Papers*, 361–2
76 *State Papers, Foreign*, III, 398
77 *State Papers, Foreign*, III, 394
78 *State Papers, Scottish*, I, 555
79 *State Papers, Venetian*, VII, 278
80 *State Papers, Foreign*, III, 421
81 Ibid., 421–2
82 *Corpus Reformatorum*, xvi, 270, quoted in *Mary Queen of Scots*, Fleming, 225
83 *Annals*, Hayward, 95
84 *Lettres*, Labanoff, I, 91
85 *State Papers, Foreign*, III, 566
86 *Bittersweet Within My Heart*, trans. and ed. Bell, 16
87 Ibid., 19
88 *Lettres*, Labanoff, I, 80
89 *Mary Queen of Scots*, Fleming, 229
90 *State Papers, Spanish*, I, 422
91 *Lettres*, Labanoff, I, 81
92 *State Papers, Foreign*, III, 472
93 Ibid., 423
94 Ibid., 573
95 *Elizabeth and Mary Stuart*, Mumby, 160
96 *State Papers, Venetian*, VII, 381

CHAPTER SIX *Complicity and Competition*

1 *Elizabeth I*, Somerset, 146; Knox II, 275–6
2 *State Papers, Foreign*, III, 472
3 Ibid., 475
4 Ibid., 473
5 Ibid., 472
6 *Mary Queen of Scots*, Fleming, 40
7 Ibid., 40
8 *State Papers, Spanish*, I, 210
9 *State Papers, Scottish*, I, 538
10 *Works*, Knox, II, 269

11 *State Papers, Scottish*, I, 547
12 Ibid., 551
13 Ibid., 565
14 *State Papers, Foreign*, IV, 152
15 *State Papers, Scottish*, I, 562
16 Ibid., 564
17 Ibid., 547
18 Ibid., 555
19 *Mary Queen of Scots*, Fleming, 253
20 *Annals*, Hayward, 75
21 *Mary Queen of Scots*, Fleming, 284
22 *State Papers, Scottish*, I, 562
23 Ibid., 559
24 *Collected Works*, 68
25 Ibid., 65
26 Ibid., 66
27 Ibid., 63
28 *Elizabeth and Mary Stuart*, Mumby, 188–9
29 *State Papers, Foreign*, IV, 322
30 *The History*, Camden, 39
31 *State Papers, Spanish*, I, 221
32 *State Papers, Foreign*, IV, 321
33 *State Papers, Spanish*, I, 308
34 Ibid., 309
35 *Elizabeth*, Somerset, 165
36 *State Papers, Foreign*, IV, 29
37 *State Papers, Spanish*, I, 240
38 *State Papers, Foreign*, 4, 580
39 Burghley, *State Papers*, 380
40 *State Papers, Scottish*, I, 608
41 Ibid., 592
42 Burghley, *State Papers*, 390
43 *State Papers, Scottish*, I, 632, 633
44 Ibid., 639
45 Ibid., 659
46 *State Papers, Foreign*, V, 232
47 Ibid., 304
48 Ibid., 303
49 *State Papers, Scottish*, I, 673
50 *Tyrannous Reign of Mary Stewart*, Buchanan, ed. Gatherer, 79
51 *State Papers, Scottish*, I, 658
52 *Tyrannous Reign of Mary Stewart*, Buchanan, ed. Gatherer, 78
53 *State Papers, Scottish*, I, 658
54 Ibid., 659
55 Ibid., 660
56 *Elizabeth I: Collected Works*, 71
57 *State Papers, Spanish*, I, 263
58 *State Papers, Scottish*, I, 666
59 *State Papers, Spanish*, I, 273

60 *Elizabeth and Mary Stuart*, Mumby, 263–4
61 *Elizabeth I: Collected Works*, 73
62 Ibid., 72
63 Ibid., 74–5
64 *State Papers, Spanish*, I, 296
65 *State Papers, Scottish*, I, 689
66 *State Papers, Spanish*, I, 315
67 *State Papers, Foreign*, VI, 157
68 Ibid., 260
69 *State Papers, Scottish*, I, 689
70 *State Papers, Foreign*, VI, 260–1
71 *State Papers, Scottish*, I, 679
72 Ibid., 678
73 Ibid., 646
74 Ibid., 669
75 *Elizabeth and Mary Stuart*, Mumby, 267
76 *State Papers, Foreign*, VI, 154
77 *Elizabeth and Mary Stuart*, Mumby, 268 note
78 *State Papers, Scottish*, II, 130
79 *Memoirs of Sir James Melville*, 45

CHAPTER SEVEN   *Raison de Coeur: Raison d'État*

1 *State Papers, Foreign*, 5, 13
2 *State Papers, Spanish*, I, 137
3 Ibid., 183
4 Ibid., 220
5 Ibid., 339
6 *Elizabeth I: Collected Works*, 140
7 *State Papers, Spanish*, I, 374
8 *State Papers, Scottish*, II, 13
9 Ibid., 28–9
10 Ibid., 32
11 Ibid., 29
12 *British Medical Journal*, 1966, 1: 65–71, 'The "Insanity" of George III: A Classic case of Porphyria', Macalpine, Hunter; *British Medical Journal* 1968, 1: 7–18 'Porphyria in the Royal Houses of Stuart, Hanover and Prussia: A Follow-up Study of George III's illness'
13 *Scottish Medical Journal* 1985; 30: 243–5, 'Was Mary, Queen of Scots, Anorexic?', J.A. McSherry
14 *State Papers, Scottish*, II, 30
15 *State Papers, Spanish*, I, 313
16 *Memoirs of Sir James Melville*, 40

17 Ibid., 35
18 *State Papers, Scottish*, II, 33
19 Ibid., 33
20 Ibid., 45
21 Ibid., 57
22 *Memoirs of Sir James Melville*, 22
23 *State Papers, Scottish*, II, 131
24 *Memoirs of Sir James Melville*, 22
25 *Elizabeth I: Collected Works*, 115
26 Ibid., 87 n. 1
27 Ibid., 89
28 *Memoirs of Sir James Melville*, 36
29 Ibid., 37–9
30 Ibid., 35
31 Ibid., 35
32 Ibid., 36
33 Ibid., 42
34 *Queen Elizabeth and Her Times*, ed. Wright, I, 194–5
35 *Knox*, Laing, vi, 541, quoted in *Mary Queen of Scots*, Fleming, 95
36 *State Papers, Spanish*, I, 391
37 Ibid., 401
38 *State Papers, Scottish*, II, 81
39 *State Papers, Spanish*, I, 399
40 Ibid., 401
41 *State Papers, Scottish*, II, 110
42 Ibid., 123
43 Ibid., 110
44 Ibid., 111
45 Ibid., 85
46 Ibid., 98
47 Ibid., 99
48 Ibid., 123
49 Ibid., 126
50 *State Papers, Foreign*, VII, 331
51 *State Papers, Scottish*, II, 125
52 Ibid., 128
53 Ibid., 133
54 Ibid., 116
55 Ibid., 136
56 Ibid., 140
57 Ibid., 140
58 *Memoirs of Sir James Melville*, 51
59 *State Papers, Scottish*, II, 154
60 *Queen Elizabeth and Some Foreigners*, ed. Klarwill, 185
61 Ibid., 193
62 *State Papers, Spanish*, I, 409–10
63 *Queen Elizabeth and Some Foreigners*, ed. Klarwill, 226–7
64 Ibid., 214–15

65 *State Papers, Scottish*, II, 147
66 Ibid., 152–3
67 Ibid., 143
68 Ibid., 154
69 Ibid., 145
70 *State Papers, Foreign*, VII, 361
71 Ibid., 372
72 Ibid., 381
73 *State Papers, Scottish*, II, 163
74 Ibid., 175
75 *State Papers, Spanish*, I, 434
76 *State Papers, Scottish*, II, 178
77 *Memoirs of Sir James Melville*, 47
78 *State Papers, Foreign*, VII, 371
79 *Memoirs of Sir James Melville*, 47
80 *State Papers, Spanish*, I, 463
81 *History of the Affairs of Church and State in Scotland*, Keith, II, 343
82 *Elizabeth and Some Foreigners*, ed. Klarwill, 245
83 *Rerum Scoticarum Historia*, book xvii; *The Tyrannous Reign of Mary Stewart*, Buchanan, ed. Gatherer, 85
84 *State Papers, Scottish*, II, 161

CHAPTER EIGHT *Seeking a Future King*

1 *The History*, Camden, 62
2 *State Papers, Scottish*, II, 94
3 *State Papers, Spanish*, I, 319
4 *State Papers, Foreign*, VII, 57
5 Ibid., 62
6 *State Papers, Scottish*, II, 61
7 Ibid., 140
8 *State Papers, Foreign*, VII, 320
9 Ibid., 319
10 Ibid., 327
11 *Memoirs of Sir James Melville*, 44–5
12 *State Papers, Venetian*, VII, 374
13 *Elizabeth and Mary Stuart*, Mumby, 387
14 *State Papers, Scottish*, II, 185
15 Ibid., 190
16 Ibid., 191
17 Ibid., 210
18 Ibid., 197–8
19 *Memoirs of Sir James Melville*, 49
20 *State Papers, Scottish*, II, 210
21 *Lettres*, Labanoff, II, 35
22 *State Papers, Scottish*, II, 221
23 Ibid., 225
24 Ibid., 254

25 *Elizabeth and Mary Stuart*, Mumby, 264, n. 2

26 *Lettres*, Labanoff, VII, 7

27 *Mary Queen of Scots*, Wormald, 160

28 *State Papers, Spanish*, I, 500

29 *Letters of Mary Stuart*, Turnbull, 149

30 *State Papers, Scottish*, II, 223

31 *State Papers, Spanish*, I, 505

32 *Elizabeth I: Collected Works*, 132

33 Burghley, *State Papers*, 444

34 *State Papers, Spanish*, I, 520

35 *State Papers, Foreign*, VIII, 13

36 *Papiers d'État*, Teulet, II, 93, quoted in *Elizabeth and Mary Stuart*, Mumby, 9

37 *State Papers, Spanish*, I, 514

38 Burghley, *State Papers*, 444

39 *State Papers, Spanish*, I, 518

40 Ibid., 527

41 *State Papers, Venetian*, VII, 374

42 *Queen Elizabeth and Her Times*, ed. Wright, I, 225

43 *Letters*, Harrison, 47

44 Burghley, *State Papers*, 446

45 *State Papers, Spanish*, I, 529

46 *Queen Elizabeth and Her Times*, ed. Wright, I, 217

47 Lord Ruthven's account quoted in n. 2 *Fall of Mary Stuart*, Mumby, 50

48 *State Papers, Scottish*, II, 213

49 *Memoirs of Sir James Melville*, 49

50 *Fall of Mary Stuart*, Mumby, 60, 62

51 *State Papers, Foreign*, VII, 448–9

52 *Church and State in Scotland*, Keith, II, 402, quoted in *Fall of Mary Stuart*, Mumby, 37

53 *State Papers, Scottish*, II, 260

54 *The History*, Camden, 64

55 *Queen Elizabeth and Her Times*, ed. Wright, I, 228–9

56 *State Papers, Venetian*, VII, 376

57 *Mary Queen of Scots*, Fleming, 127

58 *State Papers, Spanish*, I, 534

59 *Pepys Manuscripts*, quoted in *Fall of Mary Stuart*, Mumby, 59

60 *Memoirs of Sir James Melville*, 53

61 Ibid., 52

62 *State Papers, Spanish*, I, 553

63 Ibid., 545

64 *Queen Elizabeth and Her Times*, ed. Wright, I, 232

65 *State Papers, Scottish*, II, 268

66 *Diurnal of Occurrents*, 94, quoted in *Mary Queen of Scots*, Fleming, 57, 394

67 *State Papers, Spanish*, I, 537

68 Ibid., 540

69 Ibid., 547

70 *Lettres*, Labanoff, VII, 200

71 *State Papers, Scottish*, II, 284

72 *Memoirs of Sir James Melville*, 54

73 Ibid., 56

74 Ibid., 56

75 *Elizabeth I: Collected Works*, 95

76 *Fall of Mary Stuart*, Mumby, 137

77 *State Papers, Scottish*, II, 303

78 Ibid., 307–8

79 *Fall of Mary Stuart*, Mumby, 78

CHAPTER NINE *Outrageous Fortune*

1 *Memoirs of Sir James Melville*, 54

2 *State Papers, Spanish*, I, 550

3 *Memoirs of Sir James Melville*, 54

4 *Mary Queen of Scots*, Fleming, n. 45, 411

5 *State Papers, Venetian*, VII, 387

6 *Fall of Mary Stuart*, Mumby, 147

7 *State Papers, Foreign*, VIII, 110

8 *State Papers, Spanish*, I, 588

9 *Elizabeth I: Collected Works*, 95

10 *State Papers, Spanish*, I, 594

11 *Fall of Mary Stuart*, Mumby, 127

12 *Book of Articles*, quoted by Fleming, n. 422, 85

13 *Elizabeth I: Collected Works*, 111–12

14 *Memoirs of Sir James Melville*, 59

15 *State Papers, Spanish*, I, 597

16 Ibid., 549

17 Ibid., 551

18 Ibid., 565

19 *Oxford Dictionary of Quotations*, 274

20 *State Papers, Spanish*, I, 597

21 *State Papers, Foreign*, VIII, 155

22 *Sayings of Queen Elizabeth*, Chamberlin, 39

23 *Lettres*, Labanoff, II, 3

24 *State Papers, Venetian*, VII, 389

25 *Lettres*, Labanoff, II, 3;

26 *State Papers, Spanish*, I, 620

27 Ibid., 620

28 Ibid., 629

29 *State Papers, Foreign*, VIII, 176

Notes

30 *Fall of Mary Stuart*, Mumby, 156

31 *Memoirs of Sir James Melville*, 62

32 Ibid., 63

33 *State Papers, Spanish*, I, 623

34 *Elizabeth I: Collected Works*, 116

35 *State Papers, Spanish*, I, 628

36 Ibid., 635

37 *State Papers, Foreign*, VIII, 198

38 *Fall of Mary Stuart*, Mumby, 213

39 *Elizabeth I: Collected Works*, 116

40 *Fall of Mary Stuart*, Mumby, 219

41 *State Papers, Spanish*, I, 623

42 *State Papers, Scottish*, II, 323

43 *Fall of Mary Stuart*, Mumby, 219

44 *State Papers, Scottish*, II, 325

45 *State Papers, Spanish*, I, 636

46 *State Papers, Foreign*, VIII, 212

47 Ibid., 215

48 Ibid., 211

49 Ibid., 213

50 *State Papers, Spanish*, I, 638

51 Ibid., 638

52 *Memoirs of Sir James Melville*, 64

53 *State Papers, Spanish*, I, 638

54 *State Papers, Foreign*, VIII, 215

55 *Memoirs of Sir James Melville*, 101

56 *State Papers, Foreign*, VIII, 215

57 Ibid., 231

58 Ibid., 230

59 *Lettres*, Labanoff, II, 38

60 Ibid., 45–6

61 *State Papers, Spanish*, I, 648

62 *Mary Queen of Scots*, Fleming, 463

63 *State Papers, Foreign*, VIII, 229

64 *State Papers, Spanish*, I, 643

65 *State Papers, Venetian*, VII, 392

66 *Elizabeth I: Collected Works*, 192

67 *Elizabeth and Some Foreigners*, ed. Klarwill, 284

68 *State Papers, Spanish*, I, 633

69 *State Papers, Scottish*, II, 331

70 Ibid., 332

71 *Lives of the Queens of Scotland*, Strickland, III, 2

72 *State Papers, Foreign*, VIII, 255

73 *Fall of Mary Stuart*, Mumby, 257

74 *State Papers, Foreign*, VIII, 252

75 Ibid., 256

76 *Elizabeth I: Collected Works*, 119

77 *State Papers, Scottish*, II, 340

78 Ibid., 341

79 *Queen Elizabeth and Her Times*, ed. Wright, I, 264

80 *State Papers, Scottish*, II, 361

81 *State Papers, Foreign*, VIII, 283

82 *Fall of Mary Stuart*, Mumby, 276

83 *State Papers, Foreign*, VIII, 291

84 *Queen Elizabeth and Her Times*, ed. Wright, I, 260

85 *State Papers, Foreign*, VIII, II, 283

86 *Fall of Mary Stuart*, Mumby, 285

87 *State Papers, Foreign*, VIII, 311

88 Ibid., 305

89 Ibid., 311

90 *State Papers, Scottish*, II, 378

91 *State Papers, Foreign*, VIII, 305

92 *State Papers, Scottish*, II, 367–8

CHAPTER TEN *Double Jeopardy*

1 *Sayings of Queen Elizabeth*, Chamberlin, 216

2 *State Papers, Foreign*, VIII, 451

3 Ibid., 450

4 *Mary Queen of Scots*, Fleming, n. 116, 487–8

5 *State Papers, Foreign*, VIII, 469

6 *State Papers, Venetian*, VII, 402

7 *State Papers, Scottish*, II, 407

8 *Memoirs of Sir James Melville*, 74

9 *Fall of Mary Stuart*, Mumby, 330

10 *Lettres*, Labanoff, II, 76–7

11 *Scottish Papers*, II, 605

12 *State Papers, Scottish*, II, 407

13 Ibid., 415

14 *State Papers, Venetian*, VII, 418

15 *State Papers, Scottish*, II, 422

16 Ibid., 416–17

17 Ibid., 430

18 Ibid., 426

19 *State Papers, Scottish*, II, 57

20 *State Papers, Scottish*, II, 431

21 Ibid., 430

22 Ibid., 441

23 *Queen Elizabeth and Her Times*, ed. Wright, I, 280–1

24 *State Papers, Spanish*, II, 75

25 *State Papers, Scottish*, II, 480

26 *State Papers, Spanish*, II, 74

27 *Queen Elizabeth and Her Times*, ed. Wright, I, 163–4

28 *State Papers, Scottish*, II, 448

29 Ibid., 456

30 Ibid., 511
31 Ibid., 527
32 Ibid., 587
33 *Elizabeth I*, Somerset, 226
34 *State Papers, Scottish*, II, 723, 727
35 *The Censure of a Loyall Subjecte*, 1587, Whetstone; quoted in *Images of a Queen*, Phillips, 56
36 *Lettres*, Labanoff, II, 384–6
37 *Letters of Mary Stuart*, Turnbull, 178
38 *Memoirs of Sir James Melville*, 82
39 Burghley, *State Papers*, 542
40 *State Papers, Spanish*, II, 97
41 Burghley, *State Papers*, 548
42 Ibid., 511
43 Ibid., 511
44 Ibid., 528–9
45 Ibid., 510
46 Ibid., 537
47 *Letters of Mary Stuart*, Turnbull, 173
48 *Sayings of Queen Elizabeth*, Chamberlin, 301
49 Burghley, *State Papers*, 556
50 *State Papers, Venetian*, VII, 436
51 *Mary Queen of Scots in Captivity*, Leader 101
52 *Sayings of Queen Elizabeth*, Chamberlin, 24–5
53 *Elizabeth I: Collected Works*, 162
54 *Sayings of Queen Elizabeth*, 222
55 *Lettres*, Labanoff, III, 19–20
56 *State Papers, Scottish*, III, 40
57 *Sayings of Queen Elizabeth*, Chamberlin, 233
58 *State Papers, Spanish*, II, 232
59 *State Papers, Scottish*, III, 359
60 *State Papers, Venetian*, VII, 449, 450
61 Burghley, *State Papers*, 598
62 *Queen Elizabeth and Her Times*, ed. Wright, I, 404
63 *Sayings of Queen Elizabeth*, Chamberlin, 223
64 *Queen Elizabeth and Her Times*, ed. Wright, I, 391
65 *State Papers, 1571–96*, Murdin, 57
66 *State Papers, Scottish*, IV, 321
67 *Lettres*, Labanoff, III, 362
68 *Elizabeth I: Collected Works*, 194
69 *State Papers, Scottish*, IV, 209
70 *Lettres*, Labanoff, III, 388
71 *Elizabeth I: Collected Works*, 130
72 *Sayings of Queen Elizabeth*, Chamberlin, 235
73 *Letters of Queen Elizabeth*, Harrison, 71
74 *State Papers, Scottish*, II, 688
75 Ibid., 452–3
76 *Sayings of Queen Elizabeth*, Chamberlin, 246

CHAPTER ELEVEN   *Singular Foes*

1 *Lettres*, Labanoff, 4, 192
2 *Sayings of Queen Elizabeth*, Chamberlin, 229
3 *Letters of Queen Elizabeth*, Harrison, 116
4 *State Papers, Spanish*, II, 416
5 *Elizabeth I: Collected Works*, 320
6 *Queen Elizabeth and Her Times*, ed. Wright, I, 438
7 *State Papers, Scottish*, IV, 321
8 *State Papers, Spanish*, II, 581
9 *Correspondence of Philippe II*, Gachard; quoted in *The Courtships of Queen Elizabeth*, Hume, 185
10 *The History*, Camden, 131
11 *State Papers, Foreign*, XIII, 487
12 *Letters of Mary Stuart*, Turnbull, 280–1
13 Ibid., 281
14 *Annales*, Camden, 1578, 6
15 *Annales*, Camden, 1579, 2
16 *Recueil des Dépêches*, Cooper, vi, 85; quoted in *Sayings of Queen Elizabeth*, Chamberlin, 83
17 *Elizabeth I: Collected Works*, 251
18 *Elizabeth I*, Somerset, 315
19 Ibid., 309–10
20 *State Papers, Venetian*, VII, 628
21 *Elizabeth I: Collected Works*, 243
22 *Letters of Queen Elizabeth*, Harrison, 142
23 *Elizabeth I: Collected Works*, 304–5, see n. 1. p. 303 for discussion of attribution
24 *Annales*, Camden, 1579, 2
25 *Elizabeth I: Collected Works*, 248
26 *Lettres*, Labanoff, V, 135
27 *State Papers, Spanish*, III, 502
28 *Lives of the Queens of Scotland*, Strickland, VII, 367
29 *Lettres*, Labanoff, VI, 144
30 Ibid., 145–8
31 Ibid., 155–7

32 Ibid., 216
33 *Sayings of Queen Elizabeth*, Chamberlin, 135
34 *The History*, Camden, 138
35 Ibid., 172
36 *State Papers, Spanish*, III, 13
37 *State Papers, Scottish*, VI, 488
38 *State Papers, Spanish*, III, 514
39 *State Papers, Spanish*, III, 517
40 *Lettres*, Labanoff, V, 392
41 *Mary Queen of Scots in Captivity*, Leader, 549
42 Ibid., 563
43 *Elizabeth I: Collected Works*, 195
44 *Lettres*, Labanoff, VI, 89
45 *State Papers, Spanish*, III, 538
46 Ibid., 546
47 Ibid., 263
48 Ibid., 296–7
49 *Lettres*, Labanoff, VI, 369–70
50 *Letters of Mary Stuart*, Turnbull, 328
51 *Elizabeth and Some Foreigners*, ed. Klarwill 326
52 Ibid., 323
53 Ibid., 329
54 Ibid., 335
55 *The History*, Camden, 206
56 *State Papers, Spanish*, III, 583
57 *Sayings of Queen Elizabeth*, Chamberlin, 17
58 *Letters of Queen Elizabeth*, Harrison, 174
59 *Elizabeth I: Collected Works*, 282–3
60 *Lettres*, Labanoff, VI, 259
61 *State Papers, Spanish*, III, 581–2
62 *Mary Queen of Scots: Romance and Nation*, Lewis, 42
63 *Lettres*, Labanoff, VI, 158
64 Ibid., 295–6
65 *Mary Queen of Scots and the Babington Plot*, Pollen, 1–22; *Elizabeth I*, Somerset, 427
66 *Lettres*, Labanoff, VI, 391
67 *The History*, Camden, 233
68 Ibid., 234
69 Ibid., 235
70 Ibid., 236
71 *State Papers, Spanish*, III, 206
72 Ibid., 626
73 *The History*, Camden, 236
74 *Sayings of Queen Elizabeth*, Chamberlin, 305

75 *Lettres*, Labanoff, VI, 377, 439–40

CHAPTER TWELVE *The Consequence of the Offence*

1 *The History*, Camden, 243
2 *Elizabeth I: Collected Works*, 194
3 Ibid., 194
4 Ibid., 284
5 *State Papers, Spanish*, III, 663
6 *Elizabeth I: Collected Works*, 188
7 *Lettres*, Labanoff, VII, 216
8 *The History*, Camden, 242
9 *Letters of Queen Elizabeth*, 181
10 *The History*, Camden, 243
11 Ibid., 245
12 Ibid., 246
13 *State Papers, Spanish*, III, 663
14 *In My End Is My Beginning*, Mackay, 287
15 *The History*, Camden, 249–51
16 Ibid., 252
17 *State Papers, Spanish*, III, 663
18 *Lives of the Queens of Scotland*, Strickland, VII, 437
19 Ibid., 437
20 *The History*, Camden, 259
21 *State Papers, Venetian*, VIII, 226
22 Ibid., 223
23 Ibid., 227
24 *The History*, Camden, 266–7
25 *Elizabeth I: Collected Works*, 193
26 *Lettres*, Labanoff, VI, 469
27 Ibid., 468
28 *Elizabeth I: Collected Works*, 193
29 *Sayings of Queen Elizabeth*, Chamberlin, 267
30 *Elizabeth I*, Somerset, 434
31 *The History*, Camden, 273
32 Ibid., 281
33 *Elizabeth I: Collected Works*, 202
34 *Life of Elizabeth*, Strickland, 471
35 *Letters of Queen Elizabeth*, Harrison, 182
36 *Lettres*, Labanoff, VII, 221
37 *Elizabeth I: Collected Works*, 200
38 *Lettres*, Labanoff, VI, 475–80
39 *Elizabeth I*, Somerset, 434
40 *The History*, Camden, 283
41 *Queen Elizabeth and Her Times*, ed. Wright, II, 330
42 *State Papers, Scottish*, IX, 294

43 *The History*, Camden, 284

44 Ibid., 285

45 Ibid., 286

46 *Elizabeth I*, Somerset, 439

47 *Letters of Queen Elizabeth*, Harrison, 188

48 *Elizabeth I: Collected Works*, 297, n. 2

49 *State Papers, Venetian*, III, 258

50 *State Papers, Venetian*, III, 264

51 *The History*, Camden, 318

52 *Queen Elizabeth I*, Neale, 301

53 *Elizabeth I: Collected Works*, 326

54 *Letters of Queen Elizabeth*, Harrison, 194

SELECT BIBLIOGRAPHY

Unless otherwise specified, place of publication is London

Ascham, Roger, *The Whole Works of Roger Ascham*, ed. T.A. Giles, 1865

Ascham, Roger, *English Works*, ed. William Aldis Wright, Cambridge, 1904

Balcarres Papers, ed. Marguerite Wood, Scottish Historical Society, Edinburgh, 1923, 1925

Bell, Robin (trans. and ed.), *Bittersweet Within My Heart*, 1992

Bingham, Caroline, *Darnley: A Life of Henry Stuart, Lord Darnley, Consort of Mary Queen of Scots*, 1995

Black, J.B., *The Reign of Elizabeth*, Oxford, 1936

Brantôme, Pierre, *Oeuvres complètes*, Paris, 1823

Brigden, Susan, *New Worlds, Lost Worlds: The Rule of the Tudors 1485–1603*, 2000

Buchanan, George, *The Tyrannous Reign of Mary Stewart*, ed. W.A. Gatherer, Edinburgh, 1958

Burghley, Lord, *A collection of State Papers relating to affairs from the years 1542–1570 left by William Cecil Lord Burghley*, ed. Samuel Haynes, 1740

Calendar of Letters and State Papers relating to English Affairs, preserved principally in the Archives of Simancas, Elizabeth, ed. M.A.S. Hume et al., 1892–99

Calendar of State Papers, Domestic Series, ed. Robert Lemon and M.A.E. Green, 1856–72

Calendar of State Papers, Foreign Series, ed. Joseph Stevenson et al., 1863–1950

Calendar of State Papers and Manuscripts existing in the Archives and Collections of Venice, ed. Rawdon Brown et al., 1864–98

Calendar of State Papers Relating to Scotland and Mary Queen of Scots, ed. Joseph Bain et al., Edinburgh, 1898–1952

Camden, William, *Annales Rerum Anglicarum et Hibernicarum Regnante Elizabetha*, 1614

Camden, William, *History of the Most Renowned and Victorious Princess Elizabeth*, 1675; quotes from Wallace MacCaffry's edition, Chicago, 1970

Chamberlin, Frederick, ed. *The Sayings of Queen Elizabeth*, 1923

Chronicle of Queen Jane and two years of Queen Mary, ed. J.G. Nichols, Camden Society, XLVIII, 1850

Cloulas, Ivan, *Cathérine de Médicis*, Paris, 1979

Collected Works: Elizabeth I, ed. Leah S. Marcus, Janel Mueller, Mary Beth Rose, Chicago, 2000

Cowan, I.B., *The Enigma of Mary Stuart*, 1971

Dictionary of National Biography, compact edition, Oxford, 1975

Donaldson, G., *The Scottish Reformation*, Cambridge, 1960

Donaldson, G., *All the Queen's Men: Power and Politics in Mary Stewart's Scotland*, 1983

Fleming, David Hay, *Mary Queen of Scots: From Her Birth to Her Flight into England*, 1898

Foxe, John, *Actes and Monuments*, 4th edition, revised and corrected by the Rev. Josiah Pratt, 1877

Fraser, Antonia, *Mary Queen of Scots*, 1969

Gore-Browne, R, *Lord Bothwell*, 1935

Hackett, Helen, *Virgin Mother, Maiden Queen*, 1995

Haigh, C., ed., *The Reign of Elizabeth I*, 1984

Harington, John, *Nugae Antiquae*, ed. Henry Harington, 1804

Harrison, G.B., ed., *The Letters of Queen Elizabeth*, 1935

Hayward, Sir John, *Annals of the First Four Years of the Reign of Queen Elizabeth*, ed. John Bruce, Camden Society, VII, 1840

Holinshed, Raphael, *Chronicles of England, Scotland and Ireland*, 1807–8

Hume, Martin, *The Love Affairs of Mary Queen of Scots: A Political History*, 1903

Hume, Martin, *Courtships of Queen Elizabeth*

Ives, E.W., *Anne Boleyn*, Oxford, 1986

Jenkins, Elizabeth, *Elizabeth the Great*, 1958

Jenkins, Elizabeth, *Elizabeth and Leicester*, 1961

Johnson, Paul, *Elizabeth I: A Study in Power and Intellect*, 1974

Kendall, Alan, *Robert Dudley, Earl of Leicester*, 1980

Klarwill, Victor von, *Queen Elizabeth and Some Foreigners*, 1928

Knox, John, *Works*, ed. David Laing, Edinburgh, 1848

Labanoff, A., *Lettres, Instructions et Mémoires de Marie Stuart*, 1844

Latymer, William, *William Latymer's Chronickille of Anne Bulleyne*, ed.
  Maria Dowling, Camden Miscellany, XXX, 1990

Leader, J.R., *Mary Queen of Scots in Captivity*, 1880

Lewis, Jayne Elizabeth, *Mary Queen of Scots: Romance and Nation*,
  1998

Lindsay, Robert of Pitscottie, *History and Chronicles of Scotland*, ed.
  Mackay, 1911

Loades, D.M., *Mary Tudor*, Oxford, 1989

Lochhead, Liz, *Mary Queen of Scots Got Her Head Chopped Off*,
  1989

Lynch, Michael, ed., *Mary Queen of Scots: Romance and Nation*,
  Oxford, 1998

MacCaffrey, Wallace, *The Shaping of the Elizabethan Regime*, 1969

MacCaffrey, Wallace, *Elizabeth I*, 1993

MacCulloch, Diarmaid, *Tudor Church Militant: Edward VI and the
  Protestant Reformation*, 1999

Macfarlane, Alan, *Witchcraft in Tudor and Stuart England*, 1970

Mackay, James, *In My End Is My Beginning: A Life of Mary Queen of
  Scots*, Edinburgh, 1999

Marshall, Rosalind K., *Mary of Guise*, 1977

Melville, Sir James, *Memoirs of Sir James Melville of Halhill*, ed. A.
  Francis Steuart, 1929

Mendelson, Sara, Crawford, Patricia, *Women in Early Modern
  England*, Oxford, 1998

Montaiglon, Anatole de, *Latin Themes of Mary Stuart, Queen of Scots*,
  1855

Mumby, Frank A., *The Girlhood of Queen Elizabeth*, 1909

Mumby, Frank A., *Elizabeth and Mary Stuart*, 1914

Mumby, Frank A., *The Fall of Mary Stuart*, 1922

Naunton, Sir Robert, *Fragmenta Regalia*, ed. John S. Cerovski,
  Washington, 1985

Neale, J.E., *The Age of Catherine de Medici and Essays in Elizabethan
  History*, 1965

Neale, J.E., *Queen Elizabeth I*, 1934

Peck, Francis, *Desiderata Curiosa*, 1779

Perry, Maria, *The Word of a Prince: A Life of Elizabeth I*, 1990

Phillips, J.E., *Images of a Queen: Mary Stuart in Sixteenth-Century Literature*, Los Angeles, 1964

Plowden, Alison, *Two Queens in One Isle*, 1984

Rowse, A.L., *The England of Elizabeth*, 1981

Ruble, Alphonse de, *La première jeunesse de Marie Stuart*, 1891

Ryan, Lawrence V., *Roger Ascham*, 1963

Sadler, Sir Ralph, *State papers and letters of Sir Ralph Sadler*, ed. Arthur Clifford, Edinburgh, 1809

Scarisbrick, J.J., *Henry VIII*, 1997

Scott, Walter, ed., *A Collection of Scarce and Valuable Tracts*, 1809

Somerset, Anne, *Elizabeth I*, 1991

Smailes, Helen and Duncan Thomson, ed., *The Queen's Image*, [Edinburgh], [no date]

Starkey, David, *Elizabeth: Apprenticeship*, 2000

Strickland, Agnes, *Lives of the Queens of Scotland*, 1854

Strickland, Agnes, *Lives of the Queens of England*, 1866

Strong, Roy, *Portraits of Queen Elizabeth I*, Oxford, 1963

Strong, Roy, *The Cult of Elizabeth*, 1977

Strong, Roy, *Art and Power: Renaissance Festivals, 1450–1650*, Woodbridge, 1984

Strong, Roy and Julia Trevelyan Oman, *Elizabeth I*, 1971

Strong, Roy and Julia Trevelyan Oman, *Mary Queen of Scots*, 1972

Strype, John, *Annals of the Reformation*, Oxford, 1824

Vives, Juan Luis, *The Education of a Christian Gentlewoman: A Sixteenth Manual*, ed. and trans. Charles Fantazzi, 2000

Walker, Julia M., *Dissing Elizabeth*, 1998

Waldstein, Baron, *The Diary of Baron Waldstein: A Traveller in Elizabethan England*, ed. and trans. G.W. Groos, 1981

Warnicke, Retha M., *The Rise and Fall of Anne Boleyn*, Cambridge, 1989

Watkins, Susan, *Mary Queen of Scots*, 2001

Watson, Foster, ed., *Vives and the Renascence Education of Women*, 1912

Wedel, Leopold von, *Journey through England and Scotland*, ed.

Gottfried von Bülow in *Transactions of the Royal Historical Society*, *New Series*, IX, 1895

Weir, Alison, *Elizabeth the Queen*, 1998

Wiesener, Louis, *La jeunesse d'Elisabeth d'Angleterre*, Paris, 1878

Williams, H. Noel, *The Brood of False Lorraine: The History of the Ducs de Guise*, [no date]

Woolley, Benjamin, *The Queen's Conjuror*, 2001

Wormald, Jenny, *Mary Queen of Scots: A Study in Failure*, 1988

Wright, Thomas, ed., *Queen Elizabeth and Her Times*, 1838

INDEX

Aberdeen 238, 239, 241

Act of Association 478, 485

Adamson, Patrick 334

Alençon, François, Duc d'
(Monsieur) 432, 436–7, 439–42,
444–5

Alesius, Alexander 53, 55, 61, 62

Alva, Duke of 421

Amboise 164–8, 189, 191, 222, 246–7

Anjou, Duc d', see Henri III, King
of France

Anne Boleyn, Queen 53–6;
appearance 59; charges against 57,
59–61, 63, 76, 91, 93; coronation
48; disputed legality of marriage
7, 51, 56, 57, 62, 76; downfall
59–60; execution 62; family of 52;
as mother of Elizabeth xx, 49–50,
62, 76, 91; pregnancies 47–8, 55,
56–7; relationship with Catherine
of Aragon 54, 56; relationship
with Henry VIII 46–51, 53, 59;
religious views 43, 46, 54–5;
unpopularity 51, 53

Argyll, Countess of 324fn

Argyll, Earl of 250, 264, 279, 306,
322, 323, 345, 370, 376

Aristotle 22, 24, 127

Arran, James Hamilton, 2nd Earl of,
see Châtelherault, Duke of

Arran, James Hamilton, 3rd Earl of
192, 298, 304; claim to Scottish
throne 255; insanity 179, 249, 251;
plot to kidnap Mary 249, 299; as
prospective husband for Elizabeth
178–9, 194; in Protestant uprising
185

Arundel, Earl of 29, 143, 244–5

Ascham, Roger 81, 90, 117–20, 122,
123, 159

Ashley, Catherine 83, 86–9, 91, 93–6,
119, 195, 316

Ashridge 136, 143

Atholl, Earl of 277

Babington, Anthony 467, 470, 472

Babington Plot 467–70, 477, 480,
482–3, 488

Bacon, Francis 29

Baïf, Jean de 12

Ballard, John 467–8

Barton, Elizabeth 49

Beale (Clerk of the Council) 493,
495

Beaton, David, Archbishop of
Glasgow 69, 72, 300fn, 351, 357,
439, 446, 449, 469, 487

Beaton, Mary 98, 106–7, 219, 252

Bedford, Earl of 275, 276, 301–2,
308, 324, 327, 334–5, 338–40, 348,
364

Bedingfield, Sir Henry 145, 148

Bellièvre (French ambassador) 490

Berwick 301

Berwick, Treaty of 188

Black Saturday 77

Blackater, Capt. 363

Blount, Elizabeth 46

Boleyn family 52, 76

Bolton Castle 396

Bond of Association 457–8, 463,
466, 493

Border reivers 224, 287fn, 340

Borthwick Castle 370

Bothwell, James Hepburn, 4th Earl of : attacked and injured 340; background 298; confederate lords rebel against 370–1; death in Danish prison 389fn; first marriage and divorce 345, 364, 367; hostility towards 249, 251, 340, 349, 356, 362; involvement in Arran's kidnap plot 249, 250, 299; loyalty to Mary 308–9, 326, 329, 340; marriage to Mary 361, 363, 364–7; and Mary of Guise 250, 298; and murder of Darnley 337, 345, 351, 354, 356, 357; pretended abduction of Mary 362–5; Protestantism 250, 310; relationship with Mary 250–1, 298–302, 305, 340–1, 343, 348, 357, 361–2, 366–7, 371; and safekeeping of James VI 369; show trial 359–61; treason charges 286, 302

Bothwell, Patrick Hepburn, 3rd Earl of 219, 298

Boulogne 75, 76

Brantôme, Pierre de 208, 252

Breuner, Baron 170

Bryan, Lady Margaret 51

Buchanan, George 153–4, 241, 294, 397

Buckhurst, Lord 472, 491

Burghley, Lord, *see* Cecil, William

Buxton 449, 460

Calais 5–6, 8, 25, 39, 133, 156–7, 237, 242, 247, 367, 502

Calvin, John 127, 207

Calvinism 3, 21, 101

Cambridge University 268

Camden, William 437, 463, 472; *Annales Rerum Anglicarum et Hibernicarum*. . . 17fn; on Armada 501–2; on Dudley and Elizabeth 174–5; on Elizabeth 17, 82, 156, 444, 452, 471; on Henri II 154; on Mary Stuart 26, 163, 495; on rivalry between two queens 230

Campion, Edmund 452–3

Capello (Venetian ambassador) 113

Carberry Hill 339fn, 370, 373, 377

Carey, George 399, 406

Carey, Henry 76

Carey, Robert 498

Carlisle Castle 390

Carlos, Don, Prince of Spain 107, 232–4, 244, 247, 253, 258, 261, 262

Castlenau, Baron de 166

Cateau-Cambresis, Treaty of 157, 163, 367

Catherine de Medici, Queen of France 102, 303, 365, 383; on Elizabeth 442; and Mary's marriage 8; as mother 78, 104, 209; power of 99, 100, 109, 152, 160, 162, 164, 167, 186; as regent 206, 209–10, 232, 236, 237, 310, 318, 346; relations with husband 99–100; relations with Mary 104, 124, 160, 191, 208–10, 232, 262, 357, 374, 377, 423–4; role in wars of religion 21fn, 166, 431–2; superstitious nature 30, 162

Catherine Howard, Queen of England 67, 91

Catherine of Aragon, Queen of England 47; Anne Boleyn and 54; death of 55–6; disputed legality of marriage 24, 45; as mother of Mary I 44, 56, 118, 132; popularity of 47–8, 51

Catherine Parr, Queen of England 67, 75; death of 90–2; marriage to Seymour 15, 84–6, 88, 284; relations with Elizabeth 74, 83, 85, 87, 88–9, 109; religious views 86

Catholicism 292; in England 5, 7, 29, 132, 228, 347, 393, 411, 451–5, 458, 501; in France 13; in Scotland 286–7, 292, 310–11, 322

Cecil, Robert, 1st Earl of Salisbury 359, 501, 502

Cecil, William, 1st Baron Burghley 7,

168, 224, 462; created Baron
Burghley 420; desires Elizabeth's
marriage 41, 157, 173, 177, 179,
195–6, 228, 231, 244, 313–14;
'Discussion of the weighty Matter
of Scotland' 39, 182–3; on French
influence in Scotland 158; ill
health 349; and Leicester 176,
195–6, 201, 263, 313–16, 421; and
Lennox 273–4, 279; and Mary
Stuart 39, 158, 290, 378, 385, 406,
415, 426, 434, 450, 482, 491, 493,
497; 'Memorial' on Elizabeth's
accession 155–6; as politician 275;
relationship with Elizabeth 90,
142, 192, 358–9, 404, 497; and
Scottish rebels 184–5, 187–8, 194,
376; as Secretary of State 127, 155,
163; and succession question 457
Cellini, Benvenuto 102
Chaloner, Sir Thomas 180
Chapuys, Eustace 50, 57, 68
Charles, Archduke 177, 179–80,
282–4, 312, 315, 317, 330, 334, 368
Charles, Duc d'Angoulême 52
Charles V, Holy Roman Emperor
50, 144, 146
Charles I, King of England 44
Charles IX, King of France 205, 247,
284fn, 317, 367, 374, 423, 433
Chartley manor 466, 467, 469, 471,
473
Chaseabout Raid 308, 327
Chastelard (courtier poet) 219,
251–2, 304, 326
Châtelherault, James Hamilton,
Duke of 281, 385; anti-Bothwell
370; claim to Scottish throne 14fn,
255; disaffection of 291, 306;
dukedom bestowed on 110; and
Mary's marriage negotiations
69–71; military campaigns 77; as
regent 13; rivalry with Lennox
72–3, 274
Cheshunt 89

Cicero: *De Officiis* 120
Claude, Queen of France 45
Claude de Valois, Princess 31, 104,
108, 166
Clement VII, Pope 48
Coligny, Admiral 431
Condé, Prince of 163, 165
Congregation, Lords of the 184, 186,
250
Cooke, Mildred 350
Corrichie, Battle of 241
Courtenay, Edward, Earl of
Devonshire 134
Coventry 412
Craig, Mr (preacher) 364
Craigmillar Castle 343, 345, 346
Cranmer, Thomas, Archbishop of
Canterbury 46, 62, 84
Croft, Sir James 143
Cromwell, Thomas 1, 46, 54, 59, 60
Curel, Mademoiselle 105
Curle (Mary's secretary) 482–3

Darnley, Henry Stewart, Lord:
appearance 253, 256, 273, 279;
birth of son 335–6; character 288,
305, 310, 314, 319–20, 323, 336,
337–8; claim to English throne
155, 255, 257, 291, 339; conspiracy
against 291, 322–3; and crown
matrimonial 293, 305, 308, 320,
323, 324–5, 327, 339; at Elizabeth's
court 257, 273, 274, 291; honours
bestowed on 289; illness 352;
involvement with rebels 323–4,
332; marriage to Mary 293;
murder of 153fn, 337, 338, 345,
349–52, 377, 397–8, 425; and
murder of Riccio 323–9, 349; as
prospective husband for Mary
253, 254, 256–7, 259, 267–8, 274,
276; relationship with Mary
279–80, 282, 285–6, 319–20, 323,
336, 338, 340, 342, 344, 400–1;
religious views 256, 278; return to

Darnley, Henry Stewart, Lord – *cont.*
Scotland 274–5, 277–8, 281; as
rogue male 339; unpopularity
with Scottish nobles 279, 281–2;
visits Mary in France 234

Davison, William 491, 493, 497, 499

De Brézé (French commander) 99

Dee, Dr John 30–1

De Foix (French ambassador) 254,
259, 267, 311, 315

Demosthenes 119–20

Denny, Sir Anthony 89

Derby, Earl of 344

Diane de Poitiers 8, 99–100, 104–5,
109, 124, 152, 160, 162

'Discovery of a Gaping Gulph . . .'
(tract) 445

Donnington Castle 143

Douglas, George 384

Douglas, Will 384, 387

Drake, Sir Francis 464

Drury, Marshal of Berwick 367, 373,
378

Du Croc (French ambassador) 371

Dudley, Amy 182, 196–7, 200–1, 284,
354

Dudley, Lord Guildford 132

Dudley, John, Duke of
Northumberland and Earl of
Warwick 84, 112, 132

Dudley, Lord Robert, *see* Leicester,
Earl of

Dumbarton 78, 98

Dumfries 309

Dunbar 184, 329, 357, 370

Dunblane, Bishop of 308

Dundrennan 387

Durham 411

Dymoke, Sir Edward 42

Edinburgh, Treaty of 157, 192, 193,
203, 217, 218, 224, 267

Edward VI, King of England 1, 15,
18; accession 84; birth and
christening 67; coronation of 38;

death 4, 132, 319; marriage
contract 67, 69–71, 73, 77, 107;
place in accession 74, 83; relations
with Elizabeth 82; religious views
29, 132; Seymour and 92

Elizabeth I, Queen of England:
APPEARANCE 7, 34–5, 40, 85,
159, 271
BIOGRAPHY: ageing process 440,
443; as baby 51–2, 56, 62, 63; birth
7, 43, 44, 49–50; childhood 70, 79;
christening 50–1; death xvii, xxi;
girlhood 15, 18, 75; ill health 90,
135–6, 147, 242–4, 257–8, 276–7,
332, 434; imprisonment 139–51,
382, 402; isolation from court
81–2, 117, 123, 135, 153
CHARACTER XX, xxiii, 17, 35, 125,
126, 150, 347; chauvinism 346, 429;
common touch 27–8, 32–4,
39–40, 147, 347–8, 372, 461–2;
emotions 82–3, 266, 297, 435; and
female status xx, 23, 109, 127–31,
181, 198, 297, 367, 457, 485–6, 503;
indecisiveness 29, 464, 473, 489,
491–2, 500; insecurity 19, 41, 74,
123, 138, 217, 226, 244, 405, 426,
440, 497, 500; loneliness 316, 383,
489, 497; self-discipline 198, 294;
sense of humour 348; sexuality
91–2, 175; wisdom 82, 97
INTELLECT: diplomatic skills 18,
292, 297, 451; education 75, 79,
117–24, 127, 295; intelligence 23,
70, 236, 266; language skills 81,
159, 268; negotiating tactics 275,
281; poetry written by 148–9, 313,
317, 381–2, 443–4; prayers written
by 130–1, 150, 258, 413, 433, 484;
speeches 119–20, 122–3, 127, 128,
147, 150, 486, 503; tutors 90
MARRIAGE PROPOSALS AND
NEGOTIATIONS 171–4, 176–9,
195–6, 230–1; with Archduke
Charles 177, 179, 282–4, 312, 317,

368; with Arran 70, 194; with
Arundel 29; with Duke of Savoy
144, 146; with Philip II 24;
reluctance to marry xxi, 3, 18–19,
24, 29, 41, 91–2, 130–1, 146, 171,
177–8, 195, 202–3, 213, 225, 228–31,
283, 296, 312, 314, 368–9, 436; with
Valois princes 52–3, 419–20, 432,
436–45
AS MONARCH 294, 296, 372, 379,
461–2, 486; accession 3, 20, 26–8,
112, 154–6; advisers 358–9, 404,
462–3, 501; claim to throne 4,
6–8, 19, 23, 25, 56, 84; coronation
30–1, 32–8, 39, 42; court of 29–30;
disputed legitimacy 17, 19, 41,
62–3, 74, 129, 138, 154, 158, 311;
plots against 419, 421–3, 435,
454–8, 461, 467–72, 493; popular
appeal 7, 26–8, 32, 39–40, 139,
142, 145, 147, 197, 268, 462;
princely qualities 198–9, 202, 213,
305, 355, 375, 404, 413–14, 423,
442–3; progresses 258, 268, 434,
461; reluctance to go to war 169,
187–8, 457, 464, 501; rivals for
throne 155; succession xxi, 224–30,
235, 243–6, 257, 258, 262, 263–4,
267, 276, 282, 290, 334, 341, 375,
411, 416, 457; as Virgin Queen xviii,
50, 128, 129, 147, 171, 181, 202–3,
213; as warrior queen 502–3
RELATIONSHIP WITH MARY
STUART xviii–xxiii, 153–4, 168,
226, 232, 259, 264, 267, 269–70,
382, 383, 426, 500, 504; attitude
towards Mary's marriage plans
257, 259, 262–4, 274, 275–6, 282,
286–7, 290–2; coolness towards
casket letters 401; estrangement
267, 269, 424–5 godmother to
Mary's son 332, 339; kinship xix,
6, 394; prevarication over Mary's
death xvii, 353, 415, 423, 488–91,
493–4, 498, 500; proposes meeting

235–8, 392; protects reputation of
401–2; reaction to Mary's flight to
England 388–95, 403, 415;
reluctance to meet xix, 109, 237,
297, 394, 402, 406, 477; rivalry
xviii, xix, 41, 230, 266–7, 269–72,
284–5, 297, 383, 405–6, 440;
sympathy 207, 326–8, 331, 332,
339–40, 354–5, 358, 362, 367,
373–5, 378–80, 382, 384, 387, 390,
403; willingness to pardon 477,
479–80, 485
RELATIONSHIPS: with father
75–6, 83, 85, 109, 123; favourites
90, 109, 305, 438, 443, 501; with
Leicester 27, 174–6, 178, 194–202,
213, 216, 227–8, 229–30, 243,
262–4, 272–6, 280, 294, 312–14,
316–17, 330–1, 358, 405, 420,
443–4, 464–5; with Mary Tudor
138, 148–9; with mother xx, 76,
83, 109
RELIGIOUS VIEWS 33, 354,
451–3; coronation Mass 37–8;
equivocation in 29, 135, 172;
excommunication 417, 419, 430,
451, 455, 467, 503; expediency in
135; persecution of Catholics 347
REPUTATION xviii, xx, 216, 354,
392, 420, 457, 488; scandal and
slander xx, 15, 84–9, 92–7, 170,
179–82, 196–201, 203, 314, 345fn,
409, 420, 436, 439
Elizabeth de Valois, Princess 104,
107–8, 115, 160, 208, 232, 262, 348
Elliot of the Park 340
Elyot, Sir Thomas 127
Emmanuel Philibert, Duke of Savoy
144, 146, 160
Enfield 82
England 1–2, 4–5, 8; English
temperament 7, 346–8; fear and
alarm in 472, 493; and Ireland 318;
isolation of 428–9; plague 258;
Privy Council 84, 142, 243, 244,

England – *cont.*
250, 290, 334, 404; rebellion of
northern earls 410–13, 418;
relations with France 25, 154,
156–8, 168, 211, 237, 242, 416, 420,
424, 437; relations with Scotland
63–4, 65–6, 67–71, 73–4, 77–8, 97,
168, 178, 182–8, 212, 224, 231, 319,
429; relations with Spain 161,
463–4; religion in 347–8, 393, 411,
430, 450–3, 458, 501; supports
Scottish lords' rebellion 189,
192–3, 213; war with France 5–6,
7, 75; war with Spain 464, 501–3
Erasmus: *Colloquies* 115
Eric XIV, King of Sweden 29, 179,
231
Erskine, Lord 78, 98
Essex, Robert Devereux, 2nd Earl of
20fn, 90, 359, 501

Ferdinand, Archduke of Austria 177
Feria, Count de 36, 38, 147, 172, 175,
176–7, 188
Fisher, John, Bishop of Rochester 55
Fleming, Lady 98, 105, 106–7, 116,
124
Fleming, Lord 154, 390
Fleming, Mary 98, 106–7, 219
Fontainebleau 102
Forster, Anthony 200
Fotheringhay Castle 474, 475, 478,
481, 494
Fouquelin, Antoine 115
Foxe, John 82, 132fn, 145, 149; *Book
of Martyrs* 132
France: alliance with Scotland 3,
12–14, 24, 71, 73, 103, 112, 191–2,
374; alliance with Spain 310; court
99, 101–3, 111, 152–3, 180, 222, 303;
Guise power in 6, 8, 13; monarchy
9, 11, 28, 111, 160; rebellion in
163–8; relations with England 25,
30, 36, 156–8, 424; religious
dissent 101, 163–4, 167, 189–90;

St Bartholomew massacres 431–3;
war with England 5–6, 7–8, 12, 16,
75; wars of religion 190, 200, 236,
237, 242, 245, 247, 347, 431–2
François I, King of France 45, 47, 52,
67, 100, 101–2, 103
François II, Dauphin and King of
France 17, 25, 474; betrothal to
Mary 78, 82; childhood 103–4, 113;
illness and death 204–7; marriage
4, 8–12, 13; reign of 110, 152, 160,
162, 184, 204–5; relationship with
Mary 104, 106, 108, 109, 114, 204–5

Gardiner, Stephen, Bishop of
Winchester 135, 137, 139, 149
George III, King of England 261
Gifford, Gilbert 467
Gondi (French envoy) 435
Gordon, Jean, Lady Bothwell 345, 367
Gordon, Sir John 239–41, 251, 326
Gray, Patrick, Master of 447, 489
Greenwich Palace 49, 51, 62
Greenwich, Treaty of 71, 73
Gregory XIII, Pope 432
Grene, Robert 284fn
Grey, Lady Catherine 84fn, 155,
227–8, 229, 243, 245, 246, 290
Grey, Lady Jane 4, 84fn, 89, 130, 132,
137, 155, 227
Grey, Lady Mary 84fn, 155, 227, 229,
230
Grey, Lord 189
Grillparzer, Franz 368
Grindal (Elizabeth's tutor) 90
Guise, Antoinette, Duchess of 102–5,
108, 109
Guise, Charles de, Cardinal of
Lorraine 165, 194, 300, 395; and
Darnley 346, 351; death 190;
dynastic ambitions 110, 124;
establishes Mary in own
household 124–5; on Mary's
girlhood 81, 113, 116; and Mary's
marriage 6, 9, 206; Mary's

relationship with 298; power of
113, 152, 162–3, 189; and rebel
lords 322; and Riccio 303; wealth
of 152
Guise, Charles de, Duc de Lorraine
31
Guise, Claude de 103, 105
Guise, 3rd Duc de 446, 455, 473–4
Guise, François, 2nd Duc de 161,
236, 488fn; death of 190, 246–9,
431; dynastic ambitions 6, 31, 110;
marriage 108; on Mary's character
370fn; and Mary's marriage 6,
8–9, 206, 209, 210; Mary's
relationship with 247–9, 298; as
military leader 6, 242, 248; power
of 113, 152, 162–4, 206, 247;
religious fanaticism 248; in wars
of religion 163–7, 189–90, 237
Guzman de Silva 290, 311, 394; on
Darnley 274–5, 332, 338; on
Elizabeth's reaction to Riccio
murder 327, 330; on Elizabeth's
treatment of Mary 392; on
Elizabeth's views on marriage
282–3, 315, 368; on kidnap story
362–3; on Mary and Bothwell 366,
367; on murder of Darnley 351,
354; on religion in England 347

Haddington 97
Hamilton, Sir James 65
Hamilton, Patrick 53fn
Hamilton family 14fn, 385, 394,
415–16
Hampton Court 149, 462
Hardwick, Bess of, *see* Shrewsbury,
Countess of
Hatfield 4, 26, 51, 93, 117, 150
Hatton, Sir Christopher 480, 493,
497, 501
Hayward, Sir John 20, 82
Heneage, Sir Thomas 312, 317
Henri II, King of France 4, 9, 14, 16,
25, 36, 78, 285; death 100, 160–2,

184; imperial ambitions 112, 154;
and Mary 15, 103, 106, 108, 109,
158, 209; mistresses 100, 107, 152
Henri III, King of France 419–20,
431, 490, 494, 500
Henry III, King of England 37
Henry VII, King of England 6, 10,
38, 155, 234
Henry VIII, King of England 1, 6–7,
19, 24, 283, 369; and Anne Boleyn
46–9, 53–7, 59; death 79, 82–4;
and Elizabeth 50, 52, 63, 70, 75–6,
85; excommunication 48; ill
health 74; lack of male heir 43,
44–6, 51, 61, 333; and Mary of
Guise 64, 67–8; Reformation of
48, 55, 429; relations with Scots
63–4, 65, 67–71, 73–4, 77;
succession 83–4, 243; virility in
question 61
Hepburn, Capt. 251
Herries, Lord 335, 354, 390, 396
Hertford, Earl of, *see* Seymour,
Edward
Holyrood Palace 220, 251, 293, 327
Howard, Charles, Earl of
Nottingham 29fn
Howard, Lady 350
Howard, William 136
Huguenots 163, 236, 237, 247, 431, 437
Huntingdon, Henry Hastings, Earl
of 198, 243, 245
Huntly, Earl of 239–40, 241, 242,
310, 326, 329, 345, 363, 376
Huntly Rebellion 239–42, 248, 308,
383, 425

Inchmahome 78
Inverness Castle 240
Ireland 312, 317–18, 319
Isocrates 119

James II, King of Scotland 255, 256
James V, King of Scotland 43–4,
64–6, 67, 71, 109, 255

James VI of Scotland and I of England, King xxi, 44, 386–7, 397; accession 377, 504; alliance with Elizabeth 447–8, 458, 468; appearance 336; baptism 348–9; betrothal plans 348; birth 333–4; claim to English throne 334–5, 345; education 153fn; favourites 322, 447, 488fn; French designs on 369, 374–5; and Guise family 446–7; proposed removal to England 369, 375, 416, 418; Protestantism 468; reaction to mother's execution 499; relationship with mother 445–8, 468, 488, 498

Jane Seymour, Queen of England 57, 63, 67, 91

Jewel, John, Bishop of Salisbury 236

Joan of Arc 446fn

John of Austria, Don 436

Jones, Robert 201

Kenilworth 331

Kent, Earl of 494

Keyes, Thomas 229

Kircaldy of Grange 339fn, 361, 364, 371

Knollys, Sir Francis 391, 392–6, 398, 399, 406, 441

Knollys, Lettice, Countess of Essex 312–13, 443

Knox, John 3, 16, 21, 28, 184–6, 207, 249, 259, 278, 359; *The First Blast of the Trumpet Against the Monstrous Regiment of Women* 21, 24, 127; on James V 64–5; on Lennoxes 274; on Mary 79–80, 82, 219–20, 240, 252, 376, 415; relationship with Mary 221–2, 303

La Mothe Fenelon (French ambassador) 412

Langside 386

La Renaudie (French rebel) 164

L'Aubespine (French ambassador) 493

Leeds Castle 75

Le Havre 242

Leicester, Robert Dudley, Earl of 30, 90, 179, 212, 492; character 168, 193; chaste relations with Elizabeth 243; as councillor 224, 243, 245, 376, 420–1, 462; Elizabeth's generosity towards 331; Elizabeth's jealousy over 312–13, 317; Elizabeth's love for 174–5, 178, 194–6, 230, 313, 358, 444; ennoblement 201, 272, 331; exile from court 198, 201, 316, 330–1; friendship with young Elizabeth 174; intimacy with Elizabeth 272, 280, 465; and Mary 404, 405, 416, 456; jealousy 443; and Lennox 274; marital status 178, 182, 197, 199–200, 284, 443; as Master of the Horse 27, 33, 189, 193, 331; military commander 463–5, 502; prospective husband for Elizabeth 174, 175, 178, 197, 213, 216, 227–8, 230–1, 263, 312, 315–16; prospective husband for Mary 262–4, 270, 274, 275–6, 279; scandals and rumours involving 170, 175, 179–82, 196–201, 314; unpopularity of 27, 175–6, 179

Leith 186, 189, 192, 219

Lennox, Duke of, *see* Stuart, Esmé

Lennox, Margaret Douglas, Countess of 155, 269, 273, 274–5, 277, 290, 369; dynastic ambitions 234, 255, 256–7; imprisonment 234, 292–3, 307, 338, 351; marriage 73; reaction to murder of son 350–1

Lennox, Matthew Stewart, 4th Earl of 72, 294; ambitions for son 278, 281; claim to Scottish throne 14fn; death 431; enemy of Bothwell 370; funded by Cecil 279;

imprisonment 245, 257; marriage 73; and murder trial 360; property forfeited 259; prospective husband for Mary 73; recalled to England 291; as regent 416, 431; return to Scotland 267, 273–4, 277; suitor to Mary of Guise 298

Leonardo da Vinci 102

Lethington, William Maitland of 247, 342, 363; on Bothwell's jealousy 366–7; as chief minister 220, 224, 231, 275; as commissioner 397; conversations with Elizabeth 121, 225–8, 262–3; eclipse of 286; on Elizabeth's debating skills 235–6; hostility towards Bothwell 250, 300; on Knox 221; and Mary's marriage to Darnley 288, 342, 345; on safekeeping of James VI 375; as Scottish ambassador 121

Lever, Thomas 197

L'Hôpital, Michel 12

Lindsay, Lord 349, 371, 377, 378

Linlithgow Palace 64, 65, 71

Livingston, Mary 98, 106–7, 219

Livingston, Lord 98

Livy 122–3

Loch Leven Castle 373, 377, 384, 387, 413

London, Bishop of 434

Longueville, Duc de 66fn

Lorraine, Cardinal of, *see* Guise, Charles de

Machiavelli, Niccolò 122

Maitland, Sir Richard 12

Maitland, William, *see* Lethington

Mar, Earl of 239, 362, 369, 370, 431

Margaret Tudor, Queen of Scotland 10, 73, 84fn, 155, 235, 255

Marguerite, Queen of Navarre 101

Marguerite de Valois, Princess 161

Mary I, Tudor, Queen of England 1, 20, 28, 63, 130; accession 121, 131,

132; and Boleyns 52, 54; Catholicism 5, 132–3, 246, 297, 347, 429; childlessness 333; coronation 38; education 118; illness and death 4, 5, 19–20, 24; marriage 5, 132, 133–4, 135, 146, 148, 173, 283, 297; place in accession 19, 74, 84, 131; rebellions against 134–9, 150; reign of 5, 132–3; relationship with Elizabeth 138, 148, 149–50; relationship with mother 56, 131; repeals Act of Supremacy 6–7

Mary, Queen of Scots:
APPEARANCE 9–10, 72
BIBLIOGRAPHY: arrest and treason trial 470, 478–84, 486–7; as baby 69, 71–2; birth 43–4, 65–6, 68; childhood 77, 78–9, 81, 113–17; flight to England 380, 382, 385, 387–93, 429; French upbringing xxi, 3, 4, 7–8, 13–14, 16, 31–2, 79–80, 82, 97–117, 124, 152, 206, 222–3, 382–3, 429; ill health 191, 260–2, 265, 281, 341–4, 366, 377, 418, 449, 480; imprisonment xxi, 151, 325, 327–8, 373–9, 382, 384, 394–5, 402–3, 407–14, 422, 429–30, 434–6, 449–50, 458–60, 465, 474; pastimes 113–14, 152, 191, 223, 271, 407–9, 436; return to Scotland 210, 211, 214, 217, 219–22; widowhood 204–10, 217, 256, 293; will 332
CHARACTER 103, 116, 125, 215–18, 268, 393–4; arrogance and haughtiness 210, 307, 309, 310, 395, 479; courage xxiii, 78, 370fn; depressive nature 262, 281, 289, 309–10, 344, 356, 418; emotional nature xx, 205, 213, 238, 261–2, 366, 393, 394; impulsiveness 16, 191, 258, 262, 281, 298, 305, 386, 388; loneliness 299, 303, 332, 383;

Mary, Queen of Scots – *cont.*
  CHARACTER – *cont.*
  nervous sensibility 78; optimism
  439, 454, 470; passion xxiii, 191,
  298; self-destructiveness 468; self-
  dramatization 348, 469, 473, 481;
  self-righteousness 425, 480, 487;
  sense of humour lacking 348;
  spirit of adventure xxiii, 98,
  238–9, 281, 298, 383–4, 393, 414,
  419, 450, 466; volatility 435;
  wilfulness 116, 213, 298
  EDUCATION AND
  SCHOLARSHIP 106, 113–16, 153fn;
  poetry written by 207–8, 381
  EXECUTION xvii, xxi, 151, 488,
  491, 492, 494–6, 504; Catholic
  powers swear vengeance 484;
  Elizabeth's remorse 498; as
  martyrdom xxi, 151, 390, 430, 469,
  473, 474, 476–7, 479, 481, 485, 487,
  496; pressure for 415, 418, 434;
  signing of death warrant 493–4
  MARRIAGE PROPOSALS AND
  NEGOTIATIONS 211–13; with
  Charles IX 206, 209, 247; with
  Don Carlos 232–4, 247, 258,
  261–2; with Edward VI 66–7,
  68–71, 73, 77, 107; with Eric XIV
  231; with Leicester 262–6, 274–6;
  with Norfolk 276, 398–9, 404–7,
  409–10, 414–15, 417–18
  MARRIAGES 181–2, 240, 284–5;
  to Bothwell 364–7, 405fn; to
  Darnley 253, 259, 267–8, 287–94,
  300, 350–4, 391–2, 400–1; to
  dauphin 3, 6, 8–15, 17, 41, 78, 82,
  97, 153–4, 173, 203
  AS MONARCH 23, 162–3, 294,
  296, 305, 355, 383, 404–5;
  abdication 377, 418; alienation of
  nobles 286–7, 289, 291, 300–4,
  320–2, 331, 359, 369–74, 385; claim
  to English throne xix, 6–7, 24, 30,
  41, 84fn, 112, 154, 155, 163; 170–1,

  178, 224–6, 244, 247, 274, 314, 334,
  418–19, 455; coronation 72; court
  223; hostility towards 350, 357,
  372–3, 377, 378; influence in
  Ireland 317–18; lack of support
  and advice 358–9, 366; loses right
  to accession 434; military exploits
  240, 241, 248, 309, 330, 339fn, 370,
  383, 386–7; political judgement
  14–15, 16, 39, 152, 236, 265–6, 383,
  384, 388; progresses 223, 238, 343;
  public perception of 372–3, 488;
  as Queen of France 160, 162–4,
  166–7, 180, 184, 189, 203; as Queen
  of Scotland 130, 167, 222–4; wills
  accession to Philip II 468, 474,
  495
  MOTHERHOOD xxi, 314–15, 319,
  329, 330fn, 332–6, 343fn, 366, 371,
  376, 377; relationship with son
  446–8, 455, 468, 495
  PERSONAL CHARM 224, 235, 241,
  251–2, 266, 298, 372, 376, 384, 394,
  404–6, 424, 426; supernatural
  source of 215, 457, 482
  RELATIONSHIP WITH
  ELIZABETH xviii–xxiii, 153–4,
  168, 217–18, 226, 269, 281, 292,
  380, 383, 500, 504; affection 109,
  212, 214, 224, 235, 248, 259–60,
  277; animosity 306, 409, 435;
  desire for meeting xix, 224, 235–8,
  297, 332, 388, 391–2, 403;
  estrangement 267, 269; kinship
  xix, 6, 203, 212, 248–9, 329, 394,
  403, 500; lack of respect 39, 183,
  199–200, 204, 210; letters to
  448–9, 460–1; plots against 419,
  421–3, 435, 455–6, 467–70, 471;
  rivalry xviii, xix, 41, 230, 266–7,
  292, 297, 383; scandal letter to 129,
  180–1, 182, 409, 439
  RELATIONSHIPS: with Bothwell
  250–1, 298–302, 305, 340–1, 345,
  355–7, 361–3, 366–7, 371, 372,

375–7; casket letters 153fn, 377, 396–8, 399–401; with Darnley 279–82, 285–9, 305, 310, 314, 319–20, 323, 325, 328, 336, 338, 340, 342, 344–5, 346, 351; favourites 314, 322, 359; friendships 108–9; with mother xx, 98–9, 110–11, 194; with Riccio 314–15, 324–5
RELIGION: accused of being 'dubious in the faith' 346; aims to restore true religion 222, 306, 450; Catholicism 170, 322, 359, 385, 430, 495; importance attached to 348; tolerates Protestantism 115, 167, 220, 306
REPUTATION xxi, 216, 353, 355, 357, 362, 373, 390, 426, 479, 490, 495; and casket letters 401; mythology 430, 504; scandals xx, xxi, 180, 181, 199, 340, 345, 362–5, 391, 430

Mary of Guise 6, 168; children of 66; death 191–2, 193–4; as mother of Mary xx, 65–6, 68, 71–2, 77–8, 97, 98–9; as regent 3, 13, 21, 110–11, 112–13, 183–4, 185–6, 219, 250; suitors 64, 67–8, 298, 300fn

Matilda, Queen 130

Mauvissière (French ambassador) 292, 311

Maximilian, Holy Roman Emperor 283, 368

Melville, Sir James 332; advises restraint to Mary 307, 321, 322, 344; on Catherine de Medici 209–10; on Darnley 279, 291–2, 338; on Elizabeth and Leicester 271–4; and kidnap of Mary 363, 363–4; as Mary's ambassador 263; at Mary's execution 495; on Mary's personality 266, 387; meetings with Elizabeth 269–73, 333; on murder of Darnley 345; on relations between two queens 267, 303; on Riccio 304

Melville, Robert 377, 380

Mendoza, Bernadino de 455, 458, 464, 468, 472, 474, 477, 481, 483, 487

Michiel (Venetian ambassador) 138, 143

Montmorency, Anne, 1st Duc de, Constable of France 104, 159

Moray, James Stewart, Earl of 16, 252, 278, 341, 342, 375; accompanies Mary to France 98; assassination 415–16, 431; earldom 239; education 153fn; enemy of Bothwell 250, 286, 299, 300–2, 370; evidence to English commissioners 396, 399; on female rulers 297; flees to England 309, 311, 356–7; implicated in murders 323, 356; influence over Mary 220, 224, 231, 235, 255; and Mary's marriage to Darnley 274, 276, 299, 306, 345; outlawed following rebellion 306–8, 321, 322; pardoned and returns to Scotland 327; Protestant faith 220, 249, 265, 357; refuses Mary permission to return 404; as regent 377, 384, 386–7, 390, 391–2, 395, 396; relations with Mary 241–2, 249, 286, 291, 299, 306–8, 315, 328, 357, 385, 387, 392, 399, 416

More, Sir Thomas 46, 49, 55

Morton, James Douglas, 4th Earl of 322, 323, 324, 328, 349, 370, 445, 447fn

Nantes 164

Nau, Claude 376, 482–3

Navarre, King of 163

Neville, Margaret 83

Norfolk, Duke of 192, 316, 402; as commissioner 396–8, 401; on Elizabeth's intimacy with Leicester 280; execution for treason 418, 421–2, 425, 435, 497; imprisonment

Norfolk, Duke – *cont.*
and release 407, 414, 417; and
northern earls 407, 410–11; place
in accession 411; plots to place
Mary on Engish throne 419,
421–2; proposed marriage to
Mary 276, 398–9, 404–5, 407, 414,
417–18, 428; relations with
Elizabeth 341
Northampton, Marquis of 199
Northumberland, Duke of, *see*
Dudley, John
Northumberland, Earl of 407,
410–11, 413
Nostradamus 2, 30, 31

Oglethorpe, Bishop of Carlisle 37
Olivier, Chancellor 166
O'Neill, Shane, 'King of Ulster'.
317–18, 339
Orléans 204, 246, 446fn
Orange, Prince of 456, 463
Ormond, Earl of 347
Oxford, Earl of 348
Oxford University 120, 452

Paget, Sir William 188
Parliament: English 134, 147, 245–6,
334, 341, 422, 434, 451, 453, 457,
475, 477, 487, 489, 491; Scottish
321, 324
Parois, Madame de 116–17
Parry, Thomas 88–9, 93–6, 148
Parry, William 457
Paul IV, Pope 154
Paulet, Sir Amyas 460, 465, 470, 473,
476, 487, 490–1, 493, 494
Pembroke, Earl of 316
Percy, Lord Henry 62
Philip II, King of Spain 29, 36, 38,
40, 172, 207, 432, 453; character
347; court 180; and Don Carlos
234; marriage to Elizabeth de
Valois 107, 108, 160, 348; marriage
to Mary Tudor 5–6, 132, 133, 135,

146, 148, 173, 283, 297; Mary
appeals for help from 404, 419,
449, 454; and Mary's death 484,
500; Mary wills rights to accession
to 468, 474, 495; plan to invade
England 421, 447fn, 455–6, 464,
501; relationship with Elizabeth 19,
24, 150, 464, 489; supports Mary's
marriage to Darnley 290
Pickering, Sir William 29, 176
Pinkie Cleugh 77–8
Pisan, Christine de: *The Book of the
City of Ladies* 129
Pius V, Pope 310–11, 322, 346, 417,
421
Pléiade poets 12, 160
Plutarch: *Parallel Lives* 121–2
Pope, Sir Thomas 18
Protestantism xxi, 2, 13, 29, 167,
183–5, 206–7, 359; in Scotland 21,
71, 183–7, 211, 215, 220, 291, 306–7,
311, 322, 359, 455
Puritans 430

Quadra, Bishop 177, 179–80, 185,
196, 197–8, 233–4, 247, 256, 262,
263, 274

Ralegh, Sir Walter 501
Randolph (English ambassador in
Scotland) 224, 244, 267, 280, 303;
accompanies Mary on progress
238; attitude towards Guises 242,
247; banished from Scotland 319;
on Bothwell 250–1, 299, 301, 308;
on Darnley 277–9, 285, 290, 305,
322–3; on Knox 221; on Mary's
alienation of nobles 320; on
Mary's change of character 310;
on Mary's feelings towards
Elizabeth 214, 236–7, 248, 260; on
Mary's harsh justice 264–5; on
Mary's marriage plans 266, 275–7;
on Mary's military enterprises
240, 241; on Mary's pregnancy

330fn; on Mary's receipt of obscene letter 251–2; relationship with Mary 259, 289; on Riccio 314, 324; on unrest in Scotland 286–7, 300, 307, 308, 323

Reformation 3, 21, 66, 84, 170, 183

Regnier de la Planche, Louis 164, 165

Renaissance 102, 127

Renard (Spanish ambassador) 134–5, 137, 139, 144, 156

Riccarton, Laird of 384

Riccio, David: alleged immorality with Mary 314–15, 335–6, 340; influence over Mary 286, 289, 303–4, 322, 326; murder of 323–7, 336, 349, 351, 385, 435; relations with Mary 314–15, 324–5, 326; resented by court 320–1, 323

Riccio, Joseph 331

Richmond 145, 146

Ridolphi, Roberto 418–19, 421

Ridolphi Plot 418–24, 430

Robsart, Amy, *see* Dudley, Amy

Rochford, Lord George 52, 60, 61

Rochford, Lady 61

Ross, Bishop of 396, 419, 421

Ruthven, Lord 289, 323, 324–5, 328, 349, 376

Sadler, Sir Ralph 69, 71–2, 396, 459–60

St Germain-en-Laye 103

St James's Palace 75

Sander, Nicholas: *De origine et progressu schismatis Anglicani* 59

Schifanoya 27, 30

Schiller, Friedrich 107fn

Scotland 2–3, 222–3; alliance with France 12–14, 24, 71, 73, 97, 103, 112, 185, 193, 232, 374; anti-French feeling in 3, 13, 16, 183–4, 194; Catholics in 286–7, 292, 310–11, 322; claimants to throne 14fn; confederate lords 339fn, 369–74, 375–9; England supports rebellion 189, 192–3, 319, 322; nobles 64, 66, 68, 70, 72, 184, 215, 250, 255, 274, 286, 291, 294, 299, 304, 306, 311, 320–2, 370; Protestantism in 21, 71, 183–7, 211, 215, 220, 291, 306–7, 311, 322, 359, 455; reaction to Mary's execution in 498–9; relations with England 63–4, 68, 73–4, 77, 97, 184–8, 224, 322, 429, 488, 492–3; revolt of Lords of the Congregation 183–9, 219, 298, 311; unrest in 277, 286–7, 308–9, 361, 431; welcomes Mary's return 218, 220–1, 321

Scrope, Lord 391, 406

Seton, Lord 384

Seton, Mary 98, 106–7, 219

Seymour, Edward, Earl of Hertford and Duke of Somerset (Lord Protector) 15, 67, 74, 77, 84, 92–3, 94, 95, 139, 140

Seymour, Edward (husband of Catherine Grey) 227, 229

Seymour, Thomas, Lord Admiral 117; execution 96; imprisonment 92–3, 140; marriage to Catherine Parr 84–6; relationship with Elizabeth 15, 85–9, 92–6, 182, 284

Shakespeare, William 43, 45, 121

Sheffield Castle 424, 443, 458

Shelton, Lady Anne 52

Shrewsbury, Countess of (Bess of Hardwick) 181, 408–9, 436, 439, 443, 456, 458–9

Shrewsbury, Earl of 402, 406–10, 412, 422, 425, 434–5, 456, 458, 494

Sidney, Sir Henry 251, 317–18

Sidney, Lady Mary 244

Simier, Jehan de 437–8, 439, 440, 442–3, 444

Sixtus V, Pope 503

Smeaton, Mark 60

Smith, Sir Thomas 248

Solway Moss, Battle of 64, 65, 68

Somerset, Duke of, *see* Seymour, Edward

Spain 154, 449; alliance with France 161, 310; Armada 123, 456, 499, 501–3; campaign in Low Countries 421, 431, 456, 463, 501; Inquisition 347; invasion of England planned 437, 456, 458; involvement in plots 419; relations with England 24, 134, 161, 173; war with England 463–4, 484, 501

Stanley, Sir William 336

Stephano 190

Stewart, Lord James, *see* Moray, Earl of

Stirling Castle 71–2, 77, 78, 349, 352, 362

Stuart, Arbella 256, 456

Stuart, Charles 256, 257

Stuart, Esmé, Duke of Lennox 447, 488fn

Stuart, Lord John 98

Stuart, Lord Robert 98, 324fn

Stuart dynasty 44

Sturm, Johannes 81, 118, 120

Suleiman the Magnificent 128

Supremacy, Act of 6, 23

Sussex, Earl of 141, 142, 177, 282, 396, 411, 412, 413, 416

Tamworth, John 306

Throckmorton, Lady 252

Throckmorton, Sir Francis 435, 455

Throckmorton, Sir Nicholas 228; ambassador to France 162, 165, 168, 199, 203, 217, 294; dealings with Mary 287–90, 294–5, 373–6, 378–80; on Guises 162, 206; on Mary Stuart 186, 188–9, 191, 205, 211, 212, 215–16, 221, 295, 376–8, 406; role in rebellion 144fn; on Seymour 92; taken prisoner by Guises 242

Throckmorton Plot 435, 454–5, 456

Thucydides 22

Tilbury 122–3, 502–3

Tixall manor 471

Tower of London 139–45, 155

Tudor dynasty 44

Tutbury Castle 402, 406, 410, 412, 458, 459

Tyndale, William: *Obedience of a Christen Man* 55

Tyrwhit, Mrs 95, 97

Tyrwhit, Sir Robert 93–6

Verdi, Giuseppe 107fn

Vielleville (French ambassador) 159

Vives, Juan Luis: *De Institutione Feminae Christianae* 118, 125

Walsingham, Sir Francis 424, 490, 499; on d'Alençon 436; intelligence gathering 420, 435, 450, 456, 467, 469–70, 483; on Mary's character 455, 466; member of triumvirate 315, 421, 463; and plots against Elizabeth 454; relationship with Elizabeth 358

Warwick, Earl of, *see* Dudley, John

Wedel, Leopold von 461–2

Westmoreland, Earl of 407, 410–11

Weymyss Castle 278, 279

Whetstone, George 401, 468

Whitehall Palace 159

Windsor Castle 407

Wingfield manor 459, 467

witchcraft 57–9, 63, 289

Wolsey, Thomas 1

Woodstock 146, 148–9

Wriothsley, secretary 70

Wyatt, Sir Thomas 47, 60, 134

Wyatt, Sir Thomas, the younger 134, 136, 144

Wyatt Rebellion 134–8, 143, 144, 176

York 396

Zwetkovich, Adam 283–4

P.S.

Ideas,
interviews
& features
included
in a new
section…

About the author

2 Portrait

4 Snapshot

6 Life Drawing

8 A Random First Eleven Favourite Reads

About the book

9 Critical Eye

10 The Bigger Picture

Read on

13 Have You Read?

15 If you loved this, you'll like…

16 Find Out More

Portrait
Jane Dunn talks to Fanny Blake

JANE DUNN SUGGESTS her unconventional childhood is responsible for the recklessness and the romantic streak that has driven her through life. She was the oldest of eight children born to an English mother and a South African-Norwegian father in parched, colonial South Africa. When she was seven, the family moved to England where they initially lived in a wing of a decaying manor house near Yeovil. 'There was a real sense for me of coming home,' remembers Dunn. 'I was never comfortable in the African heat but the autumn dampness of the Devon lanes and the harvest being brought in made me think, 'This is where I belong.'

Although trained as a civil engineer, Dunn's father bought a large house in Wiltshire and took up farming. 'It was a magical house with mysterious gardens. We were brought up with old-fashioned values but with great physical and emotional freedom to explore, play elaborate games and dream. Our parents were busy and we were left to run free. A bell rang from the top of the house to call us in for meals. We had terrific privacy, something I think modern children don't have. We had enough space to be private but we also had the privacy of our thoughts without our parents continually asking us where we were going, what we were doing or traipsing us off to ballet lessons.'

The traditional country community considered them foreigners, so the family weren't expected to conform to the mores of English society. 'It was a strangely free but naïve and romantic sort of childhood. As a result, I entered adult life with an idealism about relationships and the world at large, accompanied by the terrific optimism that goes with it.'

She read Philosophy at University College, London before entering the Vogue Young Journalist competition that secured her a place on the staff. Married for the first time at 18, she became pregnant after a year at the magazine and turned to freelance journalism for Condé Nast. It was this background that made Christopher Falkus, MD of Weidenfeld & Nicolson, suggest at a dinner party that she should write a book. 'I didn't take him seriously,' Dunn recalls, 'Until I phoned a close friend who advised firmly, "Take him at his word." As I put the telephone down, Mary Shelley came into my head from nowhere. I knew nothing more about her than she'd been married to Percy and was the author of *Frankenstein*. However I joined the London Library, saw she was in dire need of a female hand and wrote a two-page proposal for Christopher. He commissioned me.'

The biography was written at night after her two children were in bed. It enjoyed a modest success and Dunn decided to tackle next the relationship between Virginia Woolf and Vanessa Bell. 'I have five sisters,' she explains. 'I think sisterly relationships are fascinating and not much lauded. There is no more brilliantly documented sisterly passion than Virginia's for Vanessa and Vanessa's for Virginia, though expressed more articulately in paint.' This was followed by her masterly biography of Antonia White ▶

SNAPSHOT

BORN
Durban, South Africa.

EDUCATION
Bentley Grammar School,
Calne, Wiltshire; Clifton
High School for Girls,
Bristol; University College,
London University to read
Philosophy.

CAREER
Journalist and writer.

BOOKS
*Moon in Eclipse: Life of
Mary Shelley*; *A Very Close
Conspiracy*, published
as *Virginia Woolf and
Vanessa Bell: A Very Close
Conspiracy*; *Antonia White*;
*Elizabeth and Mary:
Cousins, Rivals, Queens*.

Portrait *(continued)*

◄ whose much edited diaries had recently been published. 'Again, this was another family drama because the damage Antonia wrought continued long after her death.' The reviews were enthusiastic and lifted Dunn to the next stage of her writing life where again serendipity played its hand.

Asked to review a collection of Elizabeth I's writing, Dunn discovered the power of her rhetoric and language. 'She equals Shakespeare in eloquence. Her magnificent pungent personality comes bursting through, making me think of her more as a literary personage than as a queen. Mary, on the other hand, has always seemed more fallibly human.' For a non-historian, moving into one of the most well-trodden areas of history was a daunting prospect but Dunn's enthusiasm for her characters carried her on until it was too late to go back. 'In a way I came at them through sisterhood again. The book is a progression from my work on Virginia Woolf and Vanessa Bell in that it's another story of two women trying to make their mark in a pretty hostile world and the complexity and interdependence of the relationship between them.'

Rather than attempting an historian's global approach, Dunn deliberately chose a close biographical focus, using the letters, speeches and poems of the queens and their contemporaries, allowing them to explain themselves through their own words. Researching and writing the biography deepened her attitudes to the women. 'I certainly found Elizabeth a more tender, witty and insecure person that I had initially thought her to be whereas I found Mary was more tough-minded and ruthless, though prone to disastrous impetuosity and emotional collapse.'

Because of the power of her voice, it was hard not to let Elizabeth dominate the book, so, in an attempt to be as even-handed as possible, Dunn hung a portrait of Mary opposite her desk. 'I had to constantly remind myself that, like many physically charming people, Mary had a much more powerful effect on people who met her than the impression she leaves behind in her letters'. Though the portrait still hangs opposite her, Dunn's attention has moved on to a new double biography – the courtship and marriage between Dorothy Osborne and William Temple.

Her childhood has served Dunn well, giving her the freedom to pursue her adventures through the books she chooses to write. 'I think the sense of being an immigrant is interesting,' she says. 'You can never really be an insider, which gives you more freedom but also, I suppose, less security and one less layer of skin.' ∎

Life Drawing

What is your idea of perfect happiness?
Coming home on a blustery autumn day to
someone I love, reading by a roaring fire.

What is your greatest fear?
Drowning when failing to save someone else
from drowning.

Which living person do you most admire?
As I was born a South African, Mandela is my
immediate thought, but really any David who
outfaces a Goliath.

**What single thing would improve the
quality of your life?**
A waterfall.

**What is the most important lesson life has
taught you?**
The energy you offer to the world comes back
to you in unexpected ways.

What would be your desert island luxury?
A superking Siberian goosedown duvet.

**Which writer has had the greatest influence
on your work?**
Michael Holroyd and Richard Holmes
showed me how wide and deep and true
biography could be: but the writers who
made me want to write as a child were Enid
Blyton and her Famous Five, John Masefield,
C. S. Lewis and Georgette Heyer.

Do you have a favourite book?
The Oxford Dictionary of National Biography
– all of life and human character is there.

Where do you go for inspiration?
A luxurious bed.

Which book do you wish you had written?
Frankenstein by Mary Shelley – in a huge leap
of imagination it embodies a universal truth.

What are you writing at the moment?
*The Temples: Family Passions in Restoration
England*. Inspired by the brilliant letters of
Dorothy Osborne to Sir William Temple in
the middle of the 17th century, I want to
uncover the domestic pleasures and tragedies
of these two remarkable people at a pivotal
point in English history. ∎

A Random First Eleven
Favourite Reads

1. **The Diaries of Virginia Woolf**
   (Chatto)

2. **If This is a Man**
   Primo Levi (Abacus)

3. **First Love**
   Ivan Turgenev (Penguin)

4. **The Golden Gate**
   Vikram Seth (Faber)

5. **A Month in the Country**
   JL Carr (Penguin)

6. **Lytton Strachey**
   Michael Holroyd (Penguin)

7. **Bruno's Dream**
   Iris Murdoch (Vintage)

8. **The Getting of Wisdom**
   Henry Handel Richardson (Virago)

9. **The Gate of Angels**
   Penelope Fitzgerald (Flamingo)

10. **The White Goddess**
    Robert Graves (Faber)

11. **Evelina**
    Fanny Burney (Oxford)

Critical Eye

THE DYNAMIC BETWEEN Elizabeth and Mary, two regnant queens and cousins who never met, has exerted a compulsive fascination down the years. Reviewing *Elizabeth and Mary* in the **Daily Mail**, Roy Strong wrote, 'What is riveting for us today is that we are able not only to read what the rival queens wrote to each other but what they wrote and said about each other to everyone else. Jane Dunn has written a splendid piece of popular history with the ready pen of a highly skilled writer, endowed with a remarkable insight into the complex motives which drove these two powerful women.' In the **Daily Telegraph**, Margaret Drabble drew attention to the interdependence between the two women, '… decisions made by each altered the fate of the other … Why did one die in bed, the other on the block? This account suggests many plausible answers … This mythic story will never die.' The **Guardian**'s Katherine Hughes was intrigued by the book's concentration on the 'reverse symmetry' and resulting contrasts in the lives of the two women. 'Dunn works these contrasts hard, in the process creating a kind of psychological drama in which each woman becomes a fateful reverse image of the other.' For Lucy Hughes-Hallett in the **Observer**, the women, though opposites, were also equivalents. 'Dunn argues persuasively that Elizabeth cared passionately about Mary's failure, not for sentimental reasons of family or sister-hood … but because her own position as female monarch was so precarious that Mary's spectacular demonstration of a woman's unfitness to rule perilously undermined it.' ■

The Bigger Picture
Queens of Stage and Screen

IN HER OWN LIFETIME Elizabeth I, 'Gloriana', was the subject of fawning plays, such as Lyly's *Endymion* (1588) and Peele's *The Arraignment of Paris* (1589), while her cousin Mary Queen of Scots did not become a popular dramatic subject for another two hundred years. It was then that the romantic German poet Friedrich Schiller saw the possibilities of a drama built around the conflict between the two queens, and his highly successful play *Mary Stuart* (1800) was the first to include a fictitious confrontation between the two women. In modern times, and writing from a feminist stance, the Scot Liz Lochead has used the conflict to comment on the state of contemporary Scotland in her provocative play *Mary Queen of Scots Got Her Head Chopped Off* (1987).

Meanwhile the Elizabeth/Mary face-off had become a favourite theme for the movies. At the very end of the 19th century, Mary became the subject of one of the first films ever made, *The Execution of Mary Stuart* (1895). Another silent film was the celebrated *Loves of Queen Elizabeth* (1912) in which Sarah Bernhardt reprised one of her most popular stage roles in the story of Elizabeth and Essex, which was a hit on both sides of the Atlantic. Still in the silent era, there was *The Loves of Mary Queen of Scots* (1923 which starred Ellen Compton as Elizabeth and Fay Compton as Mary.

John Ford is more familiar as a director of westerns but his 1936 costume drama *Mary*

Queen of Scots was a favourable take on Mary, as played by Katherine Hepburn, opposite a scheming Elizabeth (Florence Estridge). In the same year the English actress, Flora Robson played a doughty Elizabeth in the British film *Fire Over England* (1936) and again in *The Sea Hawk* (1940). In the first the principal romantic interest lay in Laurence Olivier, playing Michael Ingolby. In the second, it was the swashbuckling Errol Flynn who stole the show. Another actress to play Queen Elizabeth twice on screen was Bette Davis. She did so first in *The Private Lives of Elizabeth and Essex* again with Errol Flynn donning the doublet and hose, and again in *The Virgin Queen* (1955), with Richard Rodd as Sir Walter Raleigh. After World War Two, a spirited interpretation of the teenage Elizabeth was given by Jean Simmons in *Young Bess* (1954), a film in which she is madly in love with Thomas Seymour (Stewart Grainger).

Perhaps the greatest of the screen Elizabeths has been Glenda Jackson, whose powerful portrayal of Elizabeth in the 1971 BBC serial *Elizabeth R* was later reprised in the film *Mary Queen of Scots* (1971), with Vanessa Redgrave in the part of Mary. The Oscar-winning comedy *Shakespeare in Love* (1998) had Judi Dench in a superb cameo role as an elderly, no-nonsense Elizabeth. The latest actress to shoulder the role of Elizabeth is Cate Blanchett in the highly cinematic (but historically not always accurate) ▶

The Bigger Picture *(continued)*

◄ *Elizabeth* (1998), which traces the young queen's struggle to be herself and rule in her own right. Meanwhile Quentin Crisp put in an amusing cross-dressing performance as a geriatric Elizabeth in Derek Jarman's *Orlando* (1992). ■

Have you read?

Moon in Eclipse: Life of Mary Shelley
Jane Dunn
'Jane Dunn has that sine qua non of the true
biographer, an eye for significant detail and
the power to fit it into a larger pattern'.
Richard Holmes, *The Times*

....

*Virginia Woolf and Vanessa Bell: A Very
Close Conspiracy*
Jane Dunn (Virago)
'Dunn plunges deep beneath the surface to
the complicated emotions and personalities
of these two women, illuminating them
with great clarity and understanding'
Observer

'Those who feel they've had enough of
Bloomsbury may find their interest revived
by this elegant double biography exploring
the relationship between its two formidable
sisters in whom sisterly love and sibling rivalry
were equally mixed. And if they think they
know only too much about Virginia, they will
certainly be intrigued by the more mysterious
and less famous Vanessa' *Sunday Telegraph*

'An outstanding work, and reading it is
a source of real pleasure ... one of the
best books on Virginia Woolf to date'
Literary Review

....

Antonia White: A Life
Jane Dunn
'Jane Dunn is one of our best biographers ...
She has the humanity, and the understanding
needed to unravel the story of a soul in
torment.' *Sunday Times* ▶

Have you read? *(continued)*

◄ 'A searing biography: Jane Dunn who writes with captivating elegance and piercing intelligence, is tender, scrupulous, ironic and wordly.' *Independent*

'Gifted, wounded and at times monstrous, White emerges as a woman who decided that suffering was the condition of living on the edge . . . an excellent biography'
Elizabeth Buchan, *Mail on Sunday*

If you loved this, you'll like...

Mary Queen of Scots
Antonia Fraser

Mary Queen of Scots and the Murder of Lord Darnley
Alison Weir

Elizabeth I
Anne Somerset (Flamingo)

Six Wives – Queens of Henry VIII
David Starkey (Chatto)

The Cradle King: A life of James VI and I
Alan Stewart (Chatto)

The History of Britain (boxset)
Simon Schama (BBC)

Henry VIII
David Starkey (Chatto)

The Elizabethan World Picture
EM Tillyard (Chatto)

The Cult of Elizabeth: Elizabethan Portraiture and Pageantry
Roy Strong (Pimlico)

London: A biography
Peter Ackroyd (Vintage)

Find Out More

www.marie-stuart.co.uk – the website of the Mary Stuart Society

www.royalstuartsociety.com – the website of the Royal Stuart Society

www.tudorhistory.org – an introduction to Tudor life

http://renaissance.dm.net – an introduction to many aspects of the Elizabeth world

www.elizabethi.org – information on the life and times of Elizabeth I

www.royal.gov.uk – the official website of the British monarchy

www.tudor-portraits.com – portraits and other works of art from the Tudor and Elizabethan eras

www.luminarium.org.renlit – section on Elizabeth I contains online poems, speeches and letters by her, essays and articles about her, an image, gallery and bibliography

Or Visit

Hampton Court Palace

The Tower of London

Linlithgow

Edinburgh Castle

Holyrood House

Stirling Castle

BOOKSHOP

Now you can buy any of these great paperbacks from HarperCollins at **10%** off recommended retail price. *FREE postage and packaging in the UK.*

Georgiana, Duchess of Devonshire
Amanda Foreman (ISBN: 0–00–655016–9)   £8.99

Daughters of Britannia
Katie Hickman (ISBN: 0–00–638780–2)   £7.99

Madame de Pompadour
Christine Pevitt Algrant (ISBN: 0–00–716609–5)   £8.99

The Queen: Elizabeth II and the Monarchy
Ben Pimlott (ISBN: 0–00–711436–2)   £9.99

A Scandalous Life: The Biography of Jane Digby
Mary S. Lovell (ISBN: 1–85702–469–9)   £8.99

The Queen's Conjuror
Benjamin Woolley (ISBN: 0–00–655202–1)   £7.99

The Lost King of France
Deborah Cadbury (ISBN: 1–84115–589–6)   £8.99

Redcoat
Richard Holmes (ISBN: 0–00–653152–0)   £8.99

Total cost   ....

10% discount   ....

Final total   ....

*To purchase by Visa/Mastercard/Switch simply call **08707 871724** or fax on **08707 871725***

To pay by cheque, send a copy of this form with a cheque made payable to 'HarperCollins Publishers' to: Mail Order Dept. (Ref: BOB4), HarperCollins Publishers, Westerhill Road, Bishopbriggs, G64 2QT, making sure to include your full name, postal address and phone number.

From time to time HarperCollins may wish to use your personal data to send you details of other HarperCollins publications and offers. If you wish to receive information on other HarperCollins publications and offers please tick this box ☐

Do not send cash or currency. Prices correct at time of press. Prices and availability are subject to change without notice. Delivery overseas and to Ireland incurs a £2 per book postage and packing charge.